Contemporary Political Studies 1994

by Patrick Dunleavy

British Democracy at the Crossroads
(Allen & Unwin), [with C.T.Husbands] 1985

Theories of the State
(Macmillan), [with B.O'Leary] 1987

Democracy, Bureaucracy and Public Choice
(Harvester-Wheatsheaf), 1991

Developments in British Politics 4
(Macmillan), [edited with A.Gamble, I.Holliday & G.Peele] 1993

by Jeffrey Stanyer

County Government in England and Wales
(Routledge & Kegan Paul), 1967

Understanding Local Government
(Fontana), 1976

Administering Britain
(Fontana), [with B.C.Smith] 1976

A History of Devon County Council, 1889-1989
(Devon Books) 1989

Centre and Periphery: Brittany and Cornwall & Devon Compared
(Exeter University Press) [edited with M.Havinden & J.Quéniart] 1991

CONTEMPORARY POLITICAL STUDIES 1994
Volumes I & II

Patrick Dunleavy

Professor of Government
London School of Economics

Jeffrey Stanyer

Senior Lecturer in Politics
University of Exeter

THE POLITICAL STUDIES ASSOCIATION
OF THE UNITED KINGDOM

CONTEMPORARY POLITICAL STUDIES 1994

Volume I

edited on behalf of
The Political Studies Association
of the United Kingdom

by

Patrick Dunleavy
&
Jeffrey Stanyer

Foreword
Patrick Dunleavy

Introduction
Jeffrey Stanyer

Political Studies Association
of the United Kingdom
1994

First published in Great Britain in 1994 by
THE POLITICAL STUDIES ASSOCIATION
OF THE UNITED KINGDOM
official address:
Department of Politics,
The Queens University,
Belfast BT7 1NN.

British Library Cataloguing in Publication Data

A catalogue record for this book is
available from the British Library

ISBN 0 9523150 0 9
ISBN 0 9523150 1 7

Typeset in LaTeX by Jeffrey Stanyer.

Printed and bound in Great Britain by Short Run Press Ltd, Exeter.

Cover Design by Delphine Jones, Graphic Design Unit, University of Exeter.

THE POLITICAL STUDIES ASSOCIATION OF THE UNITED KINGDOM

Contents

FOREWORD

by Patrick Dunleavy

For a professional community to develop and flourish, it must constantly change and adapt. The current era of professional 'deprivileging' has affected British political science in many ways. Along with other university professions we have suffered some serious damage from changes in public policies, such as increasingly burdensome bureaucracy imposed by a supposedly 'de-regulating' government. We have also experienced some positive benefits, such as overdue improvements in academic audit inside universities, and the ending of the absurd 'binary divide' between universities and polytechnics.

Yet these alterations in the external environment (whether positive or negative) should not be allowed to dominate our thinking. We need to carry on insisting that the mainsprings of professional advance lie with the discipline itself, that only autonomous developments can genuinely raise standards and promote new intellectual development. The Political Studies Association fulfils a key role here, in publishing two important journals, in running Specialist Groups, and in improving the flow of news and information within the profession.

But at the heart of the PSA's activity is undoubtedly the Annual Conference, which is regularly attended by nearly a third of the United Kingdom's political scientists. The Conference is a key means of creating and sustaining a political science 'community', and hence the way it operates resonates throughout the whole profession and the rest of the year, far beyond the three days when the Conference is actually in session. Over time the Conference format has changed a great deal, but many members of the profession have not been completely happy with how things are done.

The PSA Conference is an 'omnibus' conference which covers all aspects of the discipline. It has a superior academic format to the somewhat similar but much large American Political Science Association Conference. There all the action takes place in the bars, it is virtually impossible to track down papers, and many of the 2,000 paper givers (out of 5,000 people attending) have written 'meal ticket' papers simply to finance their air fares. None of these things is true of the PSA. On the other hand, the PSA rarely gives the extended opportunities for discussion and debate which are available at the ECPR's Workshops, for that is not its purpose.

This year the PSA Executive has decided to innovate by publishing as many of the Conference papers as possible in a form available to all attenders. The two underlying aims were to encourage the best possible standards of paper writing at PSA by offering the chance of immediate publication, and to provide for the dissemination of papers to libraries and the wider profession in an accessible and convenient way. Since we started a little late in the year, and the procedures involved were new to all concerned, we estimated that if we could get forty papers published in this way we should have made a good start. In fact nearly twice that number were submitted in time for our deadlines.

It may be helpful to stress that none of the papers printed here has been formally refereed in the manner of an academic journal. Of course, panel conveners sift and sort amongst the various proposals put to them, and the Academic Convener for the Conference exercises a small amount of background influence on who gets to give papers or organise panels. However, the PSA's recent Conference tradition has been one of openness to its members, and so all the papers here are still being worked up for full publication. Authors will no doubt respond to comments from the Conference sessions in preparing new versions of the papers to submit for formal publication in journals. I hope, nonetheless, that the opportunity to read these papers in 1994 (rather than late 1995 or 1996) will prove helpful to the wider profession.

The PSA Executive owes a special debt to Jeff Stanyer, who selflessly took on the task of marshalling all the disparate contributions into these volumes. Only his ideas and determination have made possible the realisation of project of this scale and importance. And only a person of exceptional resilience could have handled the whole sweep of logistical tasks involved so good-humouredly and effectively. My own personal gratitude to Jeff is very hard to phrase in terms commensurate with what is merited.

Finally, on behalf of the Executive I would like to thank all those members of the Association who have completed the papers included here. I hope that your efforts and commitment will enable us to carry forward the development of PSA into a new level of professionalism on the lines we collectively choose, rather than those imposed on us from outside.

PJD
21/2/94

INTRODUCTION

by Jeffrey Stanyer

A dream comes true! Since 1975, when the PSA changed from a narrowly-based, some said élitist, and quiescent organisation to an active, extended and complex association, successive Executives, Academic Convenors and Local Organisers have struggled with the 'the problem of the papers'.

For the first two decades of its existence the Annual Conference was an intimate gathering with a small number of alternative panels and papers at each session. Paper-givers were required to send 200 copies of their paper to the local organiser by mid-January and when in February or March a member registered to attend the Conference he or she received a package containing a copy of each. Papers, therefore, could receive a careful scrutiny in advance and a measured response from others. Giving a paper was a privilege and individuals tended to regard it as a big event in their year.

This system fell apart once the number of papers increased dramatically. Many papers were not available for circulation in advance and some of them were hastily prepared and badly presented. Figures from PSA's past, including Bob Dowse and David Steel, struggled to maintain the old system but eventually the Executive had to accept the 'papers room' as the only feasible method of dealing with the situation.

This device has never worked well for the paper-givers, the local organisers or the participants. The paper-givers reached a readership that was determined almost at random, the Conference staff were groggy with photocopying and those attending could easily spend £25.00 if they were interested in four or five of the panels – and still not get the paper they really wanted. My 'representative' or 'composite' memory of recent panel meetings is of being handed a paper of more than twenty pages, with half-a-dozen tables and a chart depicting the wiring of a power station – at 9.02am on the Thursday for a session starting at 9.05am. My own personal view was that this situation was the only serious weakness in the Conference system, but it was central to the Conference as an academic occasion.

Until 1993 the pessimists' view that PSA members would not respond to a deadline for papers in middle January dominated discussion of the problem. The Executive's decision to test this assumption by trying a different system has been endorsed by the paper-givers. They have voted with their word processors.

I have never before read all PSA Conference papers available in advance, certainly not each three times, twice character by character. My impression is that the new arrangements have succeeded in part in achieving one of the Executive's aims, that of raising the quality of the papers by giving them a more permanent and accessible form. What a paper-giver has written will now be easily available in New Zealand and Sri Lanka as well as Swansea. This has concentrated some minds and they have welcomed the opportunity to reach a wider audience.

The dream has not turned out to be a nightmare.

Panels & Papers

The papers listed here are those that were sent to the editors in time to be printed. Other papers will be brought to the Conference by the authors and will be available for purchase from the Papers Room. Sessions for which no advance papers were expected are listed but the panels which produced none are not.

A full and revised timetable will be given to participants as they register.

First Session   Tuesday, 2.00pm

Green Politics and the State (Neil Carter)

John Barry, (Glasgow), 'Discursive Sustainability: the state (and citizen) of green political theory' [1-12]

Derek Wall (West of England), 'Towards a Green Political Theory: in defence of the commons?' [13-28]

Roundtable
The End of the USSR
& the Collapse of Soviet Studies
convenor: Michael Cox

discussants
Stephen White (Glasgow), Richard Sakwa (Kent),
Terry McNeil (Hull) & Ron Hill (Dublin)

Michael Cox (Belfast), 'The End of the USSR & the Collapse of Soviet Studies' [29-44]

Hillel Tickin (Glasgow), 'The State of Soviet Studies in the Post-war Period: a view from the left' [45-58]

Policy Communities: Theoretical Issues (Mike Saward)

Keith Dowding (LSE), 'Policy Communities: don't stretch a good idea too far' [59-78]

Mike Mills (London Guildhall) & Mike Saward (Royal Holloway & Bedford), 'All Very Well in Practice but What about the Theory? a critique of the British idea of policy networks' [79-92]

First Session, Tuesday 2.00pm, continued

Politics of Health: Comparative Studies (Bruce Wood)

Melanie Latham (Lancaster), 'Policy Networks and Reproductive Rights in France and Britain' [93-105]

The European Union at the Crossroads (Juliet Lodge)

Ian Manners (Bristol), 'The Double Game: negotiating the association agreements between the EC and the Visegrad Countries of Eastern Europe' [106-118]

Liberal Political Theory (Matthew Festenstein & Noel O'Sullivan)

Sally Jenkinson (London), 'Bayle versus Locke on Toleration: reflecting on Horton and Mendus' [119-133]

Second Session   Tuesday, 4.00pm

Roundtable
American Government

convenor: Helen Margetts

discussants
Gillian Peele (LMH), Desmond King (St John's),
Christopher Hood (LSE) & Andrew Massey (Portsmouth)

Helen Margetts (LSE), 'The National Performance Review, the Clinton Presidency and the Future Shape of US Federal Government' [134-150]

The European Community and Policy Networks (John Peterson)

John Peterson (York), 'Policy Networks and Governance in the European Union: the case of research and development' [151-169]

Second Session, Tuesday 4.00pm, continued

The Politics of Small States in Europe: Case Studies in Domestic Politics (Clive Church)

David Arter (Leeds Business School), 'Estonian Politics Today' [299-313]

Liesbet Hooghe (Nuffield), 'The Dynamics of Constitutional Change in Belgium' [314-324]

Third Session   Tuesday, 8.00pm

Forum on Political Science and the PSA

convenor: Fred Nash

discussants

Mick Moran (Manchester), Jack Hayward (St Antony's), Andrew Taylor (Huddersfield), Gary Browning & Ben Rosamund (Oxford Brookes)

Fred Nash (Southampton), 'Editorial Gatekeeping in British Political Science' [325-338]

Specialist Group Meetings

Urban Politics Group
Rational Choice Group
(followed by)
Alternative Electoral Systems Group
Elections, Parties and Public Opinion Group
Post-Communist Politics
Liberal Political Theory
Hegel
Bentham
Information Technology in Political Science

> ## Fourth Session   Wednesday, 9.00am

The Core Executive: Analytic Approaches to Developments under Major (Oliver James)

Oliver James (Warwick), 'Explaining *The Next Steps* Reorganisation in British Central Government: applying the bureau-shaping model' [339-358]

Patrick Dunleavy (LSE), 'Estimating the Distribution of Influence in Cabinet Committees under Major' [359-382]

Hegel and Hegelianism (Howard Williams)

David Sullivan (Coleg Harlech), 'Fukuyama and the Idea of Progress' [383-394]

The Political Agenda in Eastern Europe and Russia (Karen Henderson)

Neil Robinson (York), '"Have Model, Will Travel": Russian and Western Reform Agendas' [395-406]

Karen Henderson (Leicester), 'Divisive Political Agendas: the case of Czeckoslovakia' 407-419]

Policy Communities and Urban Governance (Peter John)

Lawrence Pratchett (De Montfort), 'Policy Networks, Information Technologies and Local Government: defining a relationship' [420-432]

Women and Democratisation II (Haleh Afshar)

Rohini Hensman (Bombay), 'The Role of Women in Resistance to Authoritarianism in Latin America and South Asia' [433-440]

Delia Davin (Leeds), 'Women and Politics in China' [441-451]

Haleh Afshar (Bradford), 'Women and the Politics of Fundamentalism in Iran' [452-464]

Labour's Problems and the Changing Values of the United Kingdom Electorate (David Sanders)

Adrian Sackman (Manchester), 'The Political Marketing Organisation Model and the Modernisation of the Labour Party, 1983-1987' [465-479]

Fourth Session, Wednesday 9.00am, continued

Roundtable
Author and Critics: Hillel Steiner on Rights
convenor: Albert Weale (Essex)

discussants
Hillel Steiner (Manchester), Albert Weale (Essex)
Peter Jones (Newcastle)

Hillel Steiner (Manchester), '*An Essay on Rights*' [480-487]

Race and the Politics of Identity and Difference (Rosemary Gann)

Mike Rowe (Leicester), 'Race and the Politics of Identity and Difference' [488-499]

Rosemary Gann (Swansea), 'Apartheid Reconsidered: beyond the race/class debate' [500-508]

Rodney Barker (LSE), 'Four Dimensions of Political Identity: a theory of legitimacy' [509-518]

Fifth Session   Wednesday, 11.00am

Rational Choice: Collective Action and Group Theory (Keith Dowding)

Grant Jordan (Aberdeen), A.McLaughlin (Robert Gordon) & William Maloney (Aberdeen), 'Collective Action and the Public Interest Problem' [519-535]

Keith Dowding (LSE), 'Rational Mobilisation' [535-544]

Grant Jordan (Aberdeen), A.McLaughlin (Robert Gordon) & William Maloney (Aberdeen), 'A Marketing Perspective on Membership' [545-560]

Issues in Comparative Federalism (Murray Forsyth)

Nanette Neuwahl (Leicester), 'Limits to the Use of the Legal Concept of Subsidiarity in the European Union' [561-570]

John Pinder (ex-Federal Trust), 'Citizenship and Autonomous Union as the Basis for a Federal Constitution' [571-580]

Fifth Session, Wednesday 11.00am, continued

Comparative European Politics (John Caffney)

Alistair Cole (Keele), 'The French Socialists and the European Union' [581-595]

Feminist Political Theory (Ruth Kinna)

Diemut Bubeck (LSE), 'Form and Content in Gilligan's and Noddings' Ethic of Care and the Impartialism Debate' [596-609]

Jill Krause (Nottingham Trent), 'Political Theory, International Theory and the "Problem" of Gender' [610-621]

Democratic Consolidation in the Third World (Heather Deegan)

Heather Deegan (Middlesex), 'Democratisation in the Middle East' [622-635]

Alan Hooper (Hertfordshire), 'Democratic Consolidation or Democratic Crisis in Brazil: the Collor Presidency, 1990-92' [636-650]

The Holocaust (Norman Geras)

Norman Geras (Manchester), 'Richard Rorty and the Righteous' [651-662]

Harry Lesser (Manchester), 'The Holocaust: moral and political lessons' [663-671]

Sixth Session   Wednesday, 2.00pm

Rational Choice and Urban Politics (Peter John & Keith Dowding)

George Boyne (Glamorgan), 'Party Politics and Local Public Policies in Britain: ideological choice or rational choice?' [672-685]

Jim Chandler (Sheffield), 'Restructuring Local Government in Britain and the United States: different approaches to public choice' [686-699]

Stephen Cope (Portsmouth), 'Making Spending Cuts in Local Government: budget maximising or bureau-shaping?' [700-713]

Sixth Session, Wednesday 2.00pm, continued

Contemporary Political Theory (Ian McKenzie)

Norman Geras (Manchester), 'That Most Complex Being' [714-729]

Ian Mckenzie (Queen's, Belfast), 'Taylor and Ricoeur on Narrative Identity' [730-739]

Shane O'Neil (Queen's, Belfast), 'Tensions in Rawls' Liberal Holism' [740-750]

Political Corruption in Southern Europe: Iberian States (Paul Heywood)

José Magone (Hull), 'Democratic Consolidation and Political Corruption in the Southern European Periphery: the Portuguese case, 1974-93' [751-764]

German Federalism (Murray Forsyth)

Charlie Jeffrey (Leicester), 'Failing the Challenge of Unification: the länder and German federalism in the 1990s' [765-778]

Collingwood (David Boucher)

Peter Nicholson (York), 'Collingwood's "The New Leviathan": why Hobbes not Hegel?' [779-789]

Roundtable
The Whitehall Programme

convenor: Rod Rhodes (York)

discussants
Clive Ponting (Swansea), Peter Hennessy (Queen Mary Westfield)

Encounters with Marxism (Mark Cowling)

Russell Griffiths (University College), 'Marxism and the Environment' [790-802]

Sixth Session, Wednesday 2.00p.m. continued

Roundtable
The Politics of Thatcherism

convenor: David Marsh (Strathclyde)

chair: Mark Evans (Glasgow Caledonian)

discussants

Andrew Gamble (Sheffield), Vivien Lowndes (Birmingham,)
Colin Hay (Lancaster)

David Marsh (Strathclyde), 'Explaining Thatcherism: beyond unidimensional explanation' [803-827]

Seventh Session   Wednesday, 4.00am

PLENARY LECTURE

Professor Vitatis Lansbergis
Former President of Lithuania)

'The New Russian Expansionism:
Will the Molotov-Ribbentrop Pact be Repeated?'

followed by

PSA ANNUAL GENERAL MEETING

at the conclusion of the AGM
William Solesbury (ESRC)
will introduce a discussion of
'The Government's Science White Paper
and the Social Sciences'

Eighth Session   Thursday, 9.00am

The Politics of Small States in Europe: Case Studies in Domestic Politics (Clive Church)

Hugh Compston (Cardiff), 'Union Participation in Economic Policy-Making in Scandanavia: reflections on the politics of small nations' [828-841]

André Gillissen (IEIS, Luxembourg), 'Small States and the European Community – Influence without Power Revisited' [842-854]

Policy Communities and Economic Policy (Simon Lee)

Helen Thompson (Central Lancashire), 'Why is UK Economic Policy-Making Non-Strategic? the case of ERM membership' [855-865]

Roundtable
Problems of Causal Inference
in Empirical Social Research

• *convenor:* David Sanders (Essex)

discussants
Ian Maclean (Nuffield), David Denver (Lancaster),
Andrew Gamble (Sheffield), Anthony Heath (Nuffield)

Economic and Environmental Justice: The Contribution of Political Philosophy (David Merrill)

David Merrill (Southampton), 'The Public Enforcement of Economic Welfare' [866-876]

Joanna Pasek (Warsaw), 'International Justice and Environmental Policy' [877-890]

Postmodernism and Political Theory (Moya Lloyd)

Simon Thompson (West of England), 'Postmodernism, Foundationism and Contextualism' [891-905]

Index to Contributors

Convenors, Discussants & Paper-Givers

Page numbers 1-518 are in Volume 1.
Page numbers 519-1035 are in Volume 2.

Paper-Givers

Haleh Afshar	452	Jill Krause	610
David Arter	299	Melanie Latham	93
David Baker	278	Harry Lesser	663
Colin Barker	987	Steve Ludlam	278
Rodney Barker	509	Joanna McKay	973
John Barry	1	Vincent McKee	1002
John Bennington	943	Ian Mckenzie	730
George Boyne	672	Andrew McLaughlin	519, 545
Diemut Bubeck	596	José Magone	751
Jim Chandler	686	William Maloney	519, 545
Alistair Cole	581	Ian Manners	106
Hugh Compston	828	Helen Margetts	134
Stephen Cope	700	David Marsh	803
Michael Cox	29	Steve Martin	962
Philip Davies	181	Scott Meikle	923
Delia Davin	441	David Merrill	866
Heather Deegan	622	Mike Mills	79
Andrew Denham	270	Colin Mooers	987
Peter Doran	208	Fred Nash	325
Keith Dowding	59, 535	Nanette Neuwahl	561
Patrick Dunleavy	359	Peter Nicholson	779
Andrew Gamble	278	Shane O'Neil	740
Rosemary Gann	500	Joanna Pasek	877
Mark Garnett	270	Graham Pearce	962
Norman Geras	651, 714	Stephen Peckham	256
Peter Gill	170	John Peterson	151
André Gillissen	842	John Pinder	571
Dylan Griffiths	1023	Lawrence Pratchett	420
Russell Griffiths	790	Neil Robinson	395
Janet Harvey	943	Mike Rowe	488
Colin Hay	236	Adrian Sackman	465
Karen Henderson	407	Mike Saward	79
Rohini Hensman	433	Hillel Steiner	480
Liesbet Hooghe	314	David Sullivan	383
Alan Hooper	636	Helen Thompson	855
Oliver James	339	Simon Thompson	891
Charlie Jeffrey	765	Hillel Tickin	45
Sally Jenkinson	119	David Walker	934
Peter John	906	Derek Wall	13
Grant Jordan	519, 545	Georgina Waylen	198

Green Political Theory and the State

John Barry
Glasgow University

'Discursive Sustainability:
The State (and Citizen) of Green Political Theory'[1]

Introduction

The aim of this paper is to argue that the concept of the state and related issues are integral elements of green political theory, both in terms of its critique and positive proposals. The focus will be on the idea of sustainability and how its achievement depends on a positive commitment to the idea of a 'green state'. This idea goes against the anarchistic self-understanding that permeates green political literature. For many green theorists and commentators, that green political theory is basically a contemporary variant of anarchism is to a great extent self evident. Goodin offers a typical example in declaring that 'greens are basically libertarians-cum-anarchists' (1992: 152).

However, unless this affiliation with eco-anarchism is transcended the coherence of green theory cannot be guaranteed. Its theoretical consistency lies, I argue, in the articulation of a green theory of the state (and civil society) and citizenship. I use the idea of a green state as a way of both understanding recent developments in green theory, and, together with the idea of 'environmental citizenship', of indicating the direction of its future development.

Core Principles of Green Political Theory

Before I move on to develop these themes, it is necessary to indicate what and how I understand green political theory. For analytical purposes, I conceive of green politics as made up of three core principles or imperatives. In using the idea of 'core principles' to define green politics I do not wish to suggest that these principles offer an exhaustive account. These core elements I take to be:

(1) a theory of distributive (intergenerational) justice,
(2) a commitment to a process of democratization, and
(3) the achievement of ecological sustainability.

These are core in the sense that most conceptions of green politics embody these three imperatives to a greater or lesser extent.[2] They are useful as heuristic devices for deciding what is and what is not a conception of

---

[1] Not to be cited without author's permission.

[2] See Dobson (1990: 24-27, 39-41, 73-130), Eckersley (1992: 150), Goodin (1992: 62-73, 124-50), Wall (1990: 22-6), Porritt (1984: 126-30) for evidence that these three imperatives capture the essence of green political theory.

green theory. For example, we can understand survivalist green theory (or eco-authoritarianism) as the pursuit of sustainability at the expense of democracy and justice (Ophuls, 1977). What allows us to make sense of its rejection is if we see that green theory embodies democratic norms as well as a concern with sustainability. This is important to stress as some theorists have questioned the green commitment to democracy (Saward, 1993). Democratic practice and norms must be shown to be of intrinsic rather than instrumental value to green politics. However, there are also more instrumentalist arguments that can be used to supplement the former, which suggest that democratic practices such as decentralisation and devolution would, if applied to economic organisation, for example, have beneficial ecological effects (Dryzek, 1990, 1987).

These three aspects of green politics are not assumed to be automatically in harmony with each other. Incompatibility between values that greens espouse is rarely addressed, indeed the general assumption is that all elements are mutually consistent, guaranteeing the coherence of the theory. One reason for this may be that they argue that the unity of green politics is premissed on its particular conception of the good life (Dobson, 1990: 8, 88), a particular theory of value (Goodin, 1992: 14) or other some other substantive ethical basis such as Eckersley's claim that 'in terms of fundamental priorities, an ecocentric approach regards the proper place of humans in nature as logically prior to the question of what are the most appropriate social and political arrangments for human commnities' (1992: 29). Such conceptions of green politics leave green politics open to the charge that its political project is the realisation of a particular vision of the good, often 'read off' from nature. Any conception of the state premissed on this would see the state as the 'enforcer' of a particular way of life. The coercive aspects of the state are important for the realisation of sustainability, as I argue later on, but in a different (and more traditional) sense than that of either survivalist or 'moralistic' green theory.

These approaches make green theory unnecessarily contentious, and casts green politics as 'ecological morality' by other means. Although not denying the normative basis of green politics, because, like any other theory it has certain fundamental principles, the above approach makes these normative basis unduly substantive. A weaker, or less substantive ethical basis may serve the interests of green political theory better, *viz*, one that sees green theory as articulating a view of the state that establishes the necessary political framework needed to cope with ecological problems. Within this order people can live their lives as they themselves choose rather than others deciding what the content of their lives should be. In other words, the normative basis of green political programmes should be based on a 'thin' as opposed to a 'thick' theory of the good. Part of this 'thin' theory has to do with the duties of citizenship in instituting and maintaining the 'public good' of a healthy and life-enhancing environment.

Sustainability and Public Discourse

Sustainability is not simply a technical matter about implementing policies and practices that do not, from a human-prudential point of view, upset the ecological conditions of life and its flourishing. It is, I suggest, a moral concept because it explicitly refers to our relationship to future and present generations, and indirectly to our interaction with the nonhuman world.[3] 'Sustainability' itself must be discussed and interpreted, since by itself it is insufficiently precise to act as a social goal. That is, it is not self-grounding. There is a need for public deliberation where sustainability is concerned which, I argue, implies 'public spheres', and requires a notion of citizenship. In this way we can defend the concept of the green state from the charge that we are simply presenting a more acceptable argument for eco-authoritarianism. Although accepting the need for some degree of state regulation the argument here does not advocate the privileging of a survival principle which leads Ophuls for example, to claim that 'the golden age of individualism, liberty, and democracy is all over. In many important respects we shall be obliged to return to something resembling the pre-modern closed polity' (1977: 145). However, unlike the original 'limits to growth' argument, upon which his argument is based, there is nothing inherent in the idea of sustainable development that warrants such a conclusion. The issues of political and civil leadership, authority and regulation he alludes to are important for green politics, but not in way he suggests. The democratic and judical imperatives are together incompatible with the crude survivalist scenario. Authoritarian conceptions of green politics are rejected because the prioritisation of need-satisfaction may undermine the democratic or justice imperatives. The reason for this is quite simple: democracy is excess to the requirements of a objective/non-discursive conception of sustainability. A legitimate coercive body is a necessary, but not sufficient, condition for its realisation.

Sustainabilty must involve the preservation of democratic norms and institutions as much as it means the conservation of a life-sustaining environment. But equally, the means by which a conception of sustainability becomes a social principle integrating economy and environment, must itself be democratic. That is, discursively decided. And although democratic practices are to be sustained, there are good reasons for thinking that traditional economic practices (and preferences) may have to change to accommodate this.

The maintenance of an economy-environment exchange not only preserves the natural resources which sustain life, but should also be understood as preserving the social and natural resources necessary for a distinctly 'human' life.[4] In this sense it is ineliminably anthropocentric. Greens should not apologise for this. Indeed, it serves to show why a principled anthropocentrism is another necessary feature of green politics (Barry, 1993). The

---

[3] On consequentialist grounds there is good strategic reason for those concerned with caring for nonhuman nature to express it in terms of concern for future human generations.

[4] The 'environment' to be sustained has both human/social and natural/ecological dimensions.

paradox of sustainability is that although greens are often understood as setting a high premium upon its achievement, it turns out that by itself its value is indeterminate. By itself as a social principle it is meaningless since it does not specify what is to be sustained. The positive value greens impart to it is, in part, derived from the positive value attached to that which is to be sustained. What gives normative force to sustainability is as the context within which democratic practices, just institutions and a shared way of life or culture, are preserved and passed on to descendents.

The indeterminacy of this 'essentially discursive' concept is further evidenced in that that it is primarily moral and political, not scientific or metaphysical. It is not a given to be 'discovered' or 'read off' from nature, but a discursive, intersubjective creation, although the choice is limited by the nature of the world and ourselves. If with Barber we accept that 'Politics is what men do when metaphysics fails' (1984: 131), then sustainability is ineliminably a political issue. The need for the state is that such discursive 'will-formation' requires protected public spheres where such discussion can take place. As well as this input aspect, on the output side the state acts the agent of collective will. This traditional view of the state, as having the monopoly on legitimate coercion, and thus having the effective political power to enforce the collective will, is one greens can and must embrace. To deal with environmental public bads and goods, the state is necessary to assure obedience to the laws that sustainability will require. The other side of this is that people both consent, thus giving legitimacy to the state, and be willing to obey such ecological laws, for example, obligatory recycling. Along with the threat of negative sanction, greens also indicate the desirability of the state encouraging civic virtue in regard to citizens performing their duties and taking individual responsibility for the environment. This may indicate, as Weale notes, that:

> 'When the state affirms the importance of individual responsibility for the protection of environment, it can be argued that it is doing more than simply seeking efficient and effective means to previously chosen ends, it is instead choosing ends ... The object of policy must not simply be a good environment, but good citizens in relation to that environment.' (1992: 150).

As I argue in the next section, the focus for green politics should be on changing preferences the aggregative fulfilment of which results in collective bads, rather than seeking to change some allegedly environmentally-unfriendly form of consciousness (Barry, it op.cit, 45). Preference alteration can be faciliated *via* changing incentives facing individuals and, more importantly, through the interaction of people within discursive settings, which allows the possibility of normative persuasion in the light of argument and debate. Preferences and values are not, as some utilitarian-based theories hold, fixed and immutable. Greens would do well to explictly accept and work out the various implications of seeing that 'the central concern of politics should be the transformation of preferences rather than their aggregation' (Elster, 1983: 35).

There is not a sustainable society, but only frameworks and principles within which the instantiation of green regulative principles is possible.

Such framework-formation is a political task, one that cannot be effectively carried out without the state. But not any old state will do. What green political theory is concerned with is an 'enabling' or democratised state. The prime importance of democratisation in relation to the other imperatives is that abstract principles even when agreed upon, do not usually come with rules for their application. To apply abstract principles to concrete situations requires deliberation. And in this case of deciding an appropriate environment-economy exchange, that collective choice must be a democratic one, as I discuss below.[5] The importance attached to democratic decision making for greens has to do both with the possibility of preference transformation within discursive practices and also the normative content that democratic procedures express. This moral aspect is stated by Redcliff:

> 'Majority rule is the only legitimate form of decision-making (short of unanimity itself) in that it has a moral dimension. The decision reached by majority voting is binding not merely because it is an outcome we have all agreed to accept – for we could just as easily agree to accept the result from tossing fair coins – but because there is something special and unique about the sentiments of the majority. As members of a community (as opposed to atomistic egoists) we share certain bonds.' (1992: 40)

In a sense the green attachment to democratic decision-making motivated to show that what unites citizens is prior and (sometimes) more important than what divides them. Although democracy is commonly thought of purely as a procedure, it does have a substantive collective as well as individual ethical core.

Democracy can be understood as that process whereby a collective discusses and decides principles and procedures that are to govern its common life, such as sustainability, and also agree on policies, forms of collective action, and social practices that realise, or at least embody, such democratically deliberated aims. From the green perspective, it also involves democratising spheres of social activity often left out of purview of democracy as usually understood. Such areas are the world of reproduction and the family which feminists have highlighted as essential elements of any critical discussion of present social arrangements. Allied with this is the equally difficult question of the 'democratisation of welfare', the extent to which aspects of people's lives such as health-care, education, housing as well as work and leisure can be organised and regulated to enhance rather than diminish autonomy and choice (Keane, 1988: 25-7).[6] What either of these imply is an issue outside the scope of this paper.

---

[5] There is no necessary reason why this democratic will-formation be direct or participatory, although greens would probably opt for these as opposed to representative forms. It is worth remembebering that these are not mutually exclusive, but can be rendered compatible (Bobbio, 1987: 53).

[6] Increasing autonomy in welfare provision is also an aim of free market libertarians, although they see the market rather than a more 'enabling' and responsive state as the appropriate mechanism. See Gray (1993) for a typical example, in which he attempts, unsuccessfully, to argue that greens are 'really' misguided conservatives.

The democratic principle of allowing affected parties to have some say in decision-making that affects them, on the green interpretation, moves us in the direction of a wider understanding of political accountability.[7] If democratic norms are to catch up with actual practices, those affected often include citizens of other states. An obvious example is transnational pollution, which can be viewed either in legal or legislative terms. The former as it is currently practiced involves examination of claims for damages by one legal person against another. The role of the state here is as advocate for its affected citizens.[8] The most those affected can expect is compensation. The latter, democratic interpretation envisages the right of those likely to be affected to have some say in decision-making. In other words, an *ex ante*, pro-active, rather than *ex post* and reactive 'solution'. One deals with the effects, the other the cause.

Allowing another state to have a legitimate input, or right of consultation, in an ostensibly domestic matter represents an erosion of sovereignty, but is often less costly than the continuing misperception that there is a sharp divide between domestic and foreign policy.[9] For example, the effects of United Kingdom pollution affects both Ireland and Scandanavian countries, yet none are allowed any right of participation in the formulation of policy that may affect its citizens. In Dryzek's terms, abstracting from such non-localised effects represents a classic instance of problem displacement being mistaken for problem solution (1987: 10-11). From the point of view of the 'global commons', displacing ecological problems either across space or time is ecologically irrational. Ecosystems do not respect political boundaries, yet this is the territory to which effective and lasting policy solutions need to be adressed. The existence of such transnational environmental problems begins to erode the notion of sovereignty, partly as a result of the effective erosion of territorial integrity and autonomy. Not only the world economy, but also the global economy of nature undermines the autonomy of nation-states. Mutual vulnerability and interdependence are the twin faces of 'globalisation'.[10]

While full participation of all those affected can never be assured, retention of the state allows for mediated extensive participation, tht is, representation at the inter-state level.[11] There is thus a close link between justice, or more correctly justification, and democratic participation. The green argument rests, I would argue, on the extension of consultation, at least, beyond nationally defined borders, because the relevant community is not always co-extensive with the nationally-delimted 'demos'. We have no right, either as individuals or a collectivity, to 'force' (through our inaction) other people to pay or suffer for our particular lifestyles.

---

[7] An alternative interpretation is given by Held who claims that 'The result [of globalization] has been a vast growth of institutions, organizations and regimes which have laid a basis for global governance' (1991: 208).

[8] For a fuller discusssion of the state as advocate, see Goodin (1987).

[9] In other words, *ex ante* solutions are usually more pareto-optimal than *ex post* compensation.

[10] See Held (1991) for a discussion of other dimensions of 'globalisation'.

[11] Here we can imagine the state representing the corporate will, by implementing a previously agreed mandate from citizens, a 'sustainability charter' or plan. One could regard it as part of an 'ecological social contract' between citizens and the state.

Environmental Citizenship

In seeing environmental degradation as a collective problem with individual and group causes, green political theory can employ the idea of citizenship both as a desirable activity and a motivational basis for carrying out sustainability programmes. What the idea of the green state and citizenship attempt to articulate are the environmental as well as social economic and political conditions under which citizens take collective decisions binding on all. One of the obvious candidates for evoking a sense of interdependency and how individual actions have collective consequences are environmentally related issues. Community has an ecological as well as a political dimension, the former in some ways intensifies the latter, and sometimes expands the relevant community of affected interests.

The conviction of sustainability as a collective issue may be understood as meaning that the preservation of a healthy environment is a question of the 'common good'. In this way the state can be seen as provider of public goods, and a coordinator/enforcer for resolving public bads. Environmental dilemmas are such that the possibility of consensus is high, at least at the level of seeing them as problems for the collectivity. But to be effective this consensus must translate into effective and widespread consent. The uniqueness of environmental questions may be such that 'in debate and dispute over public policies it may be possible for participants of different posiitons to agree on action without agreeing upon the reasons for that action' (Dryzek, 1990: 96). The aim of green theory is to shift the legitimacy of the state to its success in 'managing the commons', rather than, or in conjunction with the traditional 'management of the economy'. This implies a degree of political leadership, and popular acceptance of civil authority.

A willingness on behalf of citizens not only to abide by laws, but to critically re-evaluate preferences will be necessary for green policies and social programmes to work. This is the central point of the discursive nature of sustainability. As Offe & Preuss note 'What are needed for effective implementation of policies, in addition to legal regulation, are enlightened, principled and refined preferences on behalf of citizens' (1991: 165). There must be an assumption of 'public reasonableness' to offset the idea that simply increasing the opportunities for participation will automatically enhance the ecological (or whatever) quality of collective decisions. A realistic starting point is that 'We cannot simply argue that the more democracy the better' (Tannjso, 1992: 2) Unreflective preferences and lifestyles do not automatically command respect, and are thus not beyond critical evaluation. The trick is for the state to create institutional structures to enable this to be discursively rather than authoritively implemented. It is the only body with the power, authority and legitimacy to enable or faciliate the democratisation of civil society. This implies the importance of civil society for educating preferences, *fora* for learning and debating. The general idea, then, is for the state to faciliate the move from self- to enlightened self-interest. One way of doing this is to submit preferences – not all, only those that directly impinge on others' enjoyment and access to environmental goods and services – to rational justification. Individuals are obliged to give good reasons for their action, behaviour etc.[12]

Citizens in a sense ought to be encouraged to both take part in the articulation of what sustainability means, as well as, for example, being obliged to pay taxes, needed for the fiscal and other measures involved in implementing it as specific policies. Here I think the green predilection for direct and participatory democracy needs to be critically examined. These forms of democracy as ways of voicing citizen preferences, assume either that all preferences are of equal value, which is doubtful, or in some Rousseauian manner can be thought to express the 'general will', which may have more merit, but cannot be discussed here. My main point is that representative forms of democracy have uses in filtering out unreasonable preferences. The discursive aspect of sustainability does not rule out different institutional structures of democratic discourse. The articulation of reasoned choices, as 'inputs', is not the exclusive preserve of direct democratic forms. One could also envisage a place for an ecological constitution, grounding citizens rights and obligations, as well as delimiting the scope of state action. The starting point for greens ought to be that 'The social and political world within which we live is much more complex than the attitudes and value-judgements that it still lets us get away with' (Offe & Preuss, *op.cit*, 169). Indeed, the ecological dimension makes it more complex, and citizens should take be encouraged to adjust their behaviour to that reality. Part of the goal of the state on this account is to change the incentives facing citizens to engender ecologically rational choices, and to show that this is a collective good, something shared with others, and this 'other-regarding' quality is an important aspect of being a good citizen from an environmental point of view.

Although some have criticised the ascription of blame for the environmental problems to an undifferentiated 'humanity' (Bookchin, 1991: 31) or 'anthropocentrism' (Hayward, 1992: 11), it is undoubtly the case that the interconnectedness of ecological problems implies that everyone, or a sufficiently large majority, must do their share to achieve a more harmonious ecology-economy interchange. To say that all must do their bit, is not the same as saying everyone must share the burden equally. Ecological problems have distributional causes, and their resolution will involve the distribution of benefits and especially burdens. In this sense an ecological conception of citizenship stresses the importance of duties and obligations as much as citizen rights. One of the greatest tasks facing the green position is to find compelling reasons for individuals, families, groups, associations to assume responsibility for both their immediate and the global environment. Act locally, think globally does have some resonance beyond a trite slogan, if we realise that the question is about overlapping 'environments' and the mutual vulnerability of citizens to each other's actions. The idea of 'environmental citizenship' is a way of reminding us that we are not just

---

[12] This seems to hark back to Mill's idea of the vote as a trust rather than a right, therefore something that demands public evaluation. However, this also led him to hold that 'Universal teaching must precede universal enfranchisement' (Acton (ed), 1972: 303), something only authoritarian greens would be prepared to endorse.

members of a particular society, but part of a wider ecologically defined human community.[13]

A practical example domestically would be 'environmental national service' or, more contentiously, adding environmental considerations to 'workfare' programmes. The dependency, apathy, and passivity of citizens in contemporary democracies are obstacles facing the resolution of environmental problems, made more imperative if we accept that neither government nor the market nor community can do everything that will be necessary. The environmental crisis offering a ready-made common purpose around which citizenship may be invigorated, and given practical as well as formal political expression. Citizenship is not just a purely 'political' activity, but manifests itself in having a particular attitude and living one's life according to that attitude. The place, therefore, of 'civic virtue' in green political theory needs to be more fully worked out so as to put more flesh on the concept of environmental citizenship. The motivation on behalf of citizens to do what is required cannot be taken for granted.[14]

The idea of giving every citizen a guaranteed basic income, despite its many problems, must be understood within the context of the importance attached to citizenship. Basic income attempts to give citizens the opportunity to drop out of the formal economy (but still obligated to do their bit for the environment), allowing them the time (if not the money) to become politically active. It gives some degree of material underpinning to equal citizenship, in a manner analogous to welfare state provisions. It is agnostic on the claim often assumed by participatory theorists that we are naturally political animals, that is, we realise ourselves as human beings in the active engagement and negotiation with fellow citizens. The citizenship idea is to allow people the opportunity to participate in the governance of the community, but more importantly, to allow the possibility of more reflective preferences emerging in the discursive understanding of sustainability.

One of the motives behind the green ideal of guaranteeing every citizen a 'social wage' not connected to work, is the conviction that each member of society ought to have a minimum level of economic security that gives some substance to formal equality. The justification for this scheme is also in terms of basic necessities required for political citizenship. Those with unfulfilled basic necessities are alienated, not quite part of society. The notion of basic income is a fiscal measure to integrate the marginal as members of society. As such, those who propose it assume the continuing existence of the state. The provision of such measures is part of what I undertand by an 'enabling state' (Keane, 1988). The danger, of course, is that there is no guarantee that citizens will conceive of their status in terms of a bal-

---

[13] Two radical extensions of this 'expanding community' logic would be the Marxist one of seeing the entire human species as my community, and the deep ecology idea of the global 'community of life' as the relevant collectivity (Fox, 1989).

[14] The danger in all of this is that authoritarian outcomes will spring from ostensibly democratic procedures, and that the state will 'force people to be ecological'. The other-regarding, public good aspect of this makes it qualitatively different from the problems of Rousseau's 'general will', but nevertheless greens need to be sensitive to the dangers. An example of this is given by Oldfield who claims, from a strong civic republican position, that 'The moral character which is appropriate for genuine citizenship does not generate itself: it has to be authoritively inculcated' (1990: 164).

ance between duties and rights. For example, they may come to value the means to citizenship as ends in themselves, thus securing their private preferences or interests, which does not guarantee their reasonableness. The difficulty for the ecologically sensitive state is protecting citizens' rights to certain environmental goods and services, but publicly demonstrating that as a corollary they share the burden in achieving and maintaining these. An enabling state, from a green point of view, is also an educative one.

Following Habermas (1992), green arguments for citizenship can be said to have a 'postnationalist' complexion, in two senses. The first has to do with the issue of rights to influence domestic legislation transcending the domestic electorate (example, the implementation of Agenda 21 from the Rio treaty by local authorities in the United Kingdom, or from the European Union). The second has to do with the idea of an 'ecological social contract' between citizens and the state (and suprastate bodies), where the allegiance of citizens is to constitutionally guaranteed rights as well as corresponding social obligations, rather than to the 'nation'. The legtimacy of the state on this account is in terms of 'environmental justice', a just distribution of benefits and burdens, rather than in expressing or embodying the national identity of the 'people'.[15] The traditional political dimension to citizenship lies in the state ensuring duties are performed, that is, that there is a bond of political obligation rooted in consent, between citizen and state. An example of this is the tax raising power of the state, which will be needed to finance such policies as basic income schemes.

Conclusion: The Politics of Sustainability

The politics of sustainability is in many ways antithetical to the current (economic/scientific) understanding of sustainability. Green economics as it stands is an attempt to apply classical and neo-classical models to ecological questions, as if the relationship between society and environment were a matter of matching quantities and inputs to outputs (Pearce et al, 1989). This has its place in the debate about sustainability, but is not enough. Seeing 'sustainability' as an indeterminate, essentially discursive concept implies that it requires political articulation. The politics of susatainbility and sustainable development is about the circulation of discourses within public space. As a way of conceptualising and institutionising this, the network of reciprocal relations between state and citizen, and between the latter are, as I indicate, indispensible for green political theory. The indeterminacy of the problem may be located in the fact that it is both a question of practical judgement, ethics and knowledge. All of which make the problematique of sustainability an irreducibly political concern. Each of these aspects makes different demands and requires different qualities from citizens, ranging from a willingness to refine preferences, adopt less ecologically harmful lifestyles, defer to accountable expertise in matters of knowledge rather than judgement, and adopt the other-regarding attitude indispensible for the lasting provision of the 'common good'.

---

[15] A third possibile argument rests on the claim that the connection between citizenship and birth has now been broken. At least in principle, citizenship is a matter of choice.

In accepting the finitude of the earth we must not blind ourselves to the finitude of human abilities. The task facing the politics of sustainability is to blend these two insights together in a way that does not jeopardise the emancipatory potential inherent within Hegel's dictum that 'Freedom is the recognition of necessity'.

References

Barber, B (1984), *Strong Democracy: Particpatory Politics for a New Age* (Berkeley: University of California Press).

Barry, J (1993), 'Deep ecology and the undermining of green politics', Holder, J et al (eds), *Perspectives on the Environment* (Aldershot: Avebury), 43-61.

Bobbio, N (1987), *The Future of Democracy* (Oxford: Basil Blackwell).

Bookchin, M (1991), 'Looking for Common Ground', in Chase, S (ed), *Defending the Earth* (Boston: South End Press), 27-41.

Dobson, A (1990), *Green Political Thought* (London: Unwin Hyman).

Dryzek, J (1987), *Rational Ecology: Environment and Political Economy* (Oxford: Basil Blackwell).

Dryzek, J (1990a), 'Green Reason: Communicative Ethics for the Biosphere', *Environmental Ethics*, 12:3, 195-210.

Dryzek, J (1990b), *Discursive Democracy: Politics, Policy and Political Science* (Cambridge: Cambridge University Press).

Eckersley, R (1992), *Environmentalism and Political Theory: Toward an Ecocentric Approach* (London: University of London Press).

Elster, J (1983), *Sour Grapes: Studies in the Subversion of Rationality* (Cambridge: Cambridge University Press).

Fox, W (1990), *Towards a Transpersonal Ecology: Developing New Foundations for Environmentalism* (Boston: Shambhala).

Goodin, R (1987), 'What's so special about our fellow countrymen?', *Ethics*, 98:4, 663-86.

Goodin, R (1992), *Green Political Theory* (London: Routledge).

Gray, J (1993), *Beyond the New Right: Markets, Government and the Common Environment* (London: Routledge).

Habermas, J (1992), 'Citizenship and national identity: Some reflections on the future of Europe', *Praxis International*, 12:1, 1-19.

Hayward, T (1992), 'Ecology and human emancipation', *Radical Philosophy*, 62, 3-14.

Held, D (1991), 'Democracy, the nation-state and the global system', in Held, D (ed), *Political Thought Today* (Cambridge: Polity), 197-235.

Keane, J (1988), *Democracy and Civil Society* (London: Verso).

Offe, C & Preuss (1991), 'Democratic institutions and moral resources', in Held, D (ed), *op.cit*, 143-71 .

Oldfield, A (1990), *Citizenship and Community: Civic Republicanism and the Modern World* (London: Routledge).

Ophuls, W (1977), *Ecology and the Politics of Scarcity* (San Francisco: W.H. Freeman).

Pearce, D et al. (1989), *Blueprint for a Green Economy* (London: Earthscan).

Porritt, J (1984), *Seeing Green: The Politics of Ecology Explained* (Cambridge: Basil Blackwell).

Radcliff, B (1992), 'The general will and social choice theory', *The Review of Politics*, 54:1, 34-49.

Tannjso, T (1992), *Populist Democracy: A Defence* (London: Routledge).

Wall, D (1990), *Getting There: Steps to a Green Society* (London: Earthscan).

Weale, A (1992), *The New Politics of Pollution* (Manchester: Manchester University Press).

Green Political Theory and the State

Derek Wall

The University of the West of England

'Towards a Green Political Theory – In Defence of the Commons?'

Introduction

The central argument of this paper is that green political theory, in contrast to green philosophy and political programme, is under theorised. Elsewhere I have criticised Greens for failure to develop a clear means of transition towards a sustainable society (Wall 1990) here I argue that with one exception (Goldsmith et al 1992) green theorists have failed to develop convincing accounts of the political workings of a green society. To develop an effective political theory, we must define green imperatives and the political metabolisms that will work to maintain them.

The evidence suggests that traditional conceptions of market and state fail to provide forms of metabolism that maintain these imperatives, and thus provides a considerable challenge to theorists. I argue that such metabolisms can only be gained (or in certain cases recreated) through the development of participatory and decentralised institutions. While anarchism, or to be more precise, opposition to the state may or may not be a core green value, green imperatives demand opposition to the traditional state and the construction of alternative forms of 'government'. The debate (to the extent that there has been a debate) over the governance of green societies has been a debate between eco-anarchists and eco-statists, while one party claims that the creation and maintenance of green imperatives demands centralised restraint the other argues that such imperatives are served by greater freedom, participation and self-government. This debate is illustrated by examining the concept of 'the commons' seen by some as the source of ecological destruction and by others as a political institution that overcomes the deficiencies of both state and anarchism in maintaining sustainability. The debate over the commons suggests that unless the state is redefined as a flexible micro-institution, green imperatives are best served by the development of a new institution that is neither market nor state. The metabolism between human and non-human nature demands the construction of a territory that may be developed with the aid of a number of maps most notably those provided by ecology, anthropological investigation and elements of Marx's social theory. Simple naturalism that describes the economy or government of nature as a simply reproducible model for a human polity is, of course, rejected.

A Poverty of Theory?

Analysing literature of green parties and green political movements it is obvious that 'greens are no single-issue movement. They take stands on a wide range of contemporary social and political problems.' (Goodin 1992: 202) Greens aim to 'restructure the whole of political, social and economic life' (Dobson 1990: 3). Porritt believes that 'the politics of radical ecology embraces every dimension of human experience and all life on Earth ...' (Porritt 1987: 216). When he is continuous stating 'it goes a great deal further in terms of political comprehensiveness than any other political persuasion or ideology has ever gone before,' we may condemn him for rhetorical exaggeration but may still agree with Goodin that green parties are concerned with political problems ignored by other ideologies (Goodin 1992: 182-4). Greens are particularly concerned to argue that their ideology is based upon 'holistic' philosophy, '... a new vision of reality; a fundamental change in our thoughts, perceptions, and values' (Capra 1984: 1984: xviii.).

While the green movement has policy and philosophy it lacks a theory that serves to show politically how a transition can be made from what 'is' to what, from a green perspective, 'ought' to be. Thus 'one reads very little about how to get there from here' (Frankel 1987: 277) and as Dobson observes 'it is noticeable how many conversations about green politics very soon dry up when the issue of change is broached' (Dobson 1990: 130). Dobson hints that green philosophical idealism blocks the development of a practical political theory (Dobson 1990: 70-71). In essence the belief that a change in consciousness will lead to a green society, allows greens to ignore the challenging questions of how to create and maintain a green society. Once a change in world view occurs, appropriate institutions will follow, naturally, from such a transition in perception. To the extent that greens practically intervene, for example, by contesting elections or taking part in direct action, it may be argued that they intervene educationally: direct action, electoral activity and lifestyle change can be see, perhaps, as strategies aimed primarily at changing 'consciousness'.

I have argued that greens must examine the problem of transition 'politically' as well as philosophically and have listed briefly some of the challenges in creating a theory of transition (Wall 1990). I equally believe that the problem of 'Getting There' is parallel by the challenge of 'Being There', thus green political theory needs to discuss the political instruments necessary to maintain a green society, once such a transition has been made. Prior to such a discussion we need to briefly discuss the imperative such green government would seek to maintain.

What do the Greens Want?

ecological sustainability

Examining the literature of green parties it is possible to determine three imperatives or sets of linked demands shared, to a large extent, with eco-anarchists and deep ecologists such as Earth First!

While we may agree that 'Traditionally conceived, political philosophy concerns itself with certain perennial problems involving the nature of justice, political obligations and, more generally, the good society' (Brown 1990: 58), we might note that the paramount demand of any political philosophy is the maintenance of society. In describing the 'good society', a precondition whether we follow Aristotle, Marx, Rawls or another theorist, is the maintenance of such a society. The modern green movement demands that conditions for the maintenance of society are discussed in any investigation of the nature of the 'good society'. Rightly or wrongly, they argue that such dangers as nuclear war or accident, increasing background radioactivity levels, severe chemical pollution, the disruption of vital global biochemical cycles etc, threaten our collective social existence. From an eco-socialist perspective, it is claimed 'Without overcoming the ecology crisis, which puts in question the very existence of human civilisation on this earth, the mere possibility of the socialist goal – the general emancipation of human beings, men and women – becomes an illusion' (Bahro 1982: 57). Equally it has been argued that more localised social process have led to the destruction of sustainable human-nature interactions and contributed to the collapse of particular societies (Hughes 1975). The ecological imperative, motivated by this wish to maintain human society, is obvious from the literature of green movements and parties (Green Party 1987). Any metabolism between humanity and non-human nature must be sustainable. What constitutes ecological sustainability is an extremely complex question with social and biological ramifications. Political ecologists, though, have long argued that a diversity of species and habitats is extremely important. Although some predictions have proved exaggerated and non-human nature may proved to be extremely robust, prior to maintaining any other demand the institutions of a green society must maintain a sustainable ecological relationship.

green humanism

Green parties have advocated ecological sustainability, while arguing that such sustainability is compatible with (and may depend upon) meeting a broad range of humanist demands including participatory democracy, social equality, community, pluralism and creative work. Bahro notes 'The Greens already have their sights on more than just the ecological aspect. It is clear from all the literature I've seen that they stand for the general emancipation of human beings, men and women, and that they want to overthrow all conditions in which people are debased and humiliated' (Bahro 1982: 14). It is clear from studying the literature of any green Party that ecological sustainability is to be achieved in a way that aims to promote human well being. For example, the first Ecologist candidate to contest the French Presidency stated in his 1974 manifesto 'It is one and the same system which organises the exploitation of the workers and the degradation of living and working conditions and puts the whole earth in danger' (Wall 1994: 247), implying a concern for sustainability and human welfare. Greens criticise the humanism of other contemporary ideologies for concentrating on 'the blind policy of economic growth, which is so extravagantly praised by all the political parties, (yet) takes no account either of human well-being or of the environment' (Wall 1994: 247). Such growth, as well as creating ecological implications, defines human welfare too narrowly, according to greens, leading to inequality and significant externalities. Liberal democracy, which according to greens, provides individuals with little say in the governance of their communities while being increasingly distorted by centralisation and the power of large corporations, is equally criticised. Green humanism includes demands, which even in the absence of ecological concern, might be used to define a green political programme . It is possible to apply green humanism to different policy areas and derive more detailed demands. For example, a green health policy would emphasis a low technology approach, greater patient participation, prevention before cure, seeking to solve problems holistically by placing illness in a social and environmental context (Porritt 1987: 82-4, 168-9). A green transport policy, while recognising the ecological imperative, would seek to strengthen local communities, emphasise access for those on low income rather than the necessity of economic expansion and encourage decentralisation of services.

To a surprising extent such a humanism is shared by many deep ecologists. Despite the much publicised misanthropy of some writers, supporters of Earth First! in Britain and North America argue that ecological sustainability must be maintained in a humanist context of social equality, economic democracy, pluralism and participatory democracy (Bookchin & Foreman 1991).

post-humanism

Greens would argue that the sustainable ecological society that meets human demands should do so with the least violence to other species. Policies for wildlife conservation may be derived from the first green imperative of ecological sustainability, equally practices that violate animals such as factory farming and vivisection may also violate aspects of the second green imperative. Although vivisection may give rise to inappropriate medical care or factory farming may contribute to the social degradation of rural communities, greens dislike practices that make other species suffer irrespective of anthropocentric concerns. It is argued that:

> 'The global Earth First! movement comes from a background
> of Deep Ecology that recognises the equality and inherent worth
> of every form of life. We consider our role as liberators of the for-
> est ecosystems together with all the life that inhabits it, whether
> they be Bears, Leopards, Plants or People, the survival of the
> Clouded Leopard is as important to me as the cultural survival
> of the Penan tribe of Sarawak.' (Burbridge 1992: 6)

Although less fundamentally held such post-humanism is an element of the discourse of green parties and many green anarchists. The United Kingdom Green Party, for example, has long advocated policies to promote vegetarianism. Porritt observes:

> 'For us, it is not enough to protect animals for practical,
> self-interested reasons alone; there is also a profoundly moral
> concern, rooted in our philosophy of respect for all that dwells
> on this planet ... vivisection would be abolished, all hunting and

coursing with hounds would be banned, battery farming would
be phased out, our reliance on animals to meet our need for food
would be reduced – and then we could start living in harmony
with the rest of creation!' (Porritt 1987: 184)

The debate over animal rights and a green politics that moves beyond anthropocentrism is complex and throws up a number of difficult conceptual
problems. Ecological sustainability and human welfare may demand, in
certain situations, the exploitation of animals (Einarsson 1993). Although
greens rarely define how much suffering is permissible to other life forms
in order to maintain other demands, post-humanism provides a third and
politically unique imperative for them. Where 'Traditional political theory
assumes a moral community consisting of all (rational) men ... green theory
expands this community to include animals, plants, and possibly even the
Earth itself' (Lucardie 1993: x).

Governing the Green Society

To be effective green political theory needs to describe the institutions and
practices best able to maintain imperatives of ecology, humanism and post-
humanism. It is possible to outline in broad terms, at least three forms of
potential green government:

1) Market mechanism;
2) State Regulation;
3) Non-state/Non-Market regulation.

the market

The market has been seen as a mechanism for maximising welfare and de-
centralising power. Equally as well promoting human benefit, environmental economists argue that the market, especially if adapted, can maintain
sustainability (Cairncross 1991) Pigou, who discussed the notion of 'inter-
nalising external costs', argued that pollution produced by a factory might
create costs for the local community. By making the firm pay for any
such costs it imposed upon the local community, it could be encouraged to
act in a more environmentally friendly manner. Such a process of turning
a social/environmental cost into an internal cost of production, might be
achieved through a pollution tax. Others have argued that resource taxes
might be levied to discourage the consumption of potentially scarce min-
erals and metals, while there has been much recent discussion of a carbon
tax to reduce CO_2 emissions. It has also been suggested that even without such fiscal adaptions, a market metabolism will maintain sustainability
(Elkington & Burke 1987). Green capitalism, it has been argued, will result
from firms cutting costs by reducing energy consumption and other forms of
unecological waste. Green consumerism, whereby individuals buy 'greener'
products will also encourage sustainability. The success of the Body Shop,

a cosmetics firm that has enjoyed consistent growth by supplying cruelty-free products, provides a example of how the market may maintain the post-humanist imperative.

There are problems associated with all of the elements of a green market metabolism outlined above. Rather than encouraging serious action on the part of industry, where demand is relatively inelastic, environmental taxes can be passed to the consumer without loss of company income. Environmental taxes like all indirect taxes tend to penalise poorer members of the community more than wealthier individuals, challenging the egalitarian demand within green humanism. Firms may prioritise a reduction in labour costs or an increase in sales before seeking environmental cost cutting that might generate only a small saving. Green consumerism is limited by the availability of information and products. There are more fundamental criticisms of a market approach than such doubts about the efficiency of its components. Where market advocates argue that the 'primary cause of environmental problems ... (is) the failure of markets and governments to price the environment appropriately', green opponents argue that there is a contradiction between the market and ecological sustainability (Goldsmith et al 1992: 175).

The market produces for profit and profit, generally, demands growth. Yet constant growth creates severe ecological problems according to many commentators (Trainer 1985, Wall 1994: 116-124). There are extreme difficulties in calculating and setting environmentally sustainable prices, 'Practically speaking, the sense of the phrase "ecologically correct prices" cannot come to anything more than "prices which enable the market economy to keep ticking over" while taking a bit more account than hitherto of the concerns of environmentalists, ecologists, business people with long views, and others with interests in "natural resources" ' (Goldsmith et al 1992: 176). Echoing criticism that 'Bourgeois society is ruled by equivalence. It makes the dissimilar comparable by reducing it to abstract quantities ... that which does not reduce to number, and ultimately to the one, becomes illusion.' (Adorno & Horkheimer 1966: 7), the notion that environment can be given a price is often rejected. 'Clean air should be protected, not traded and sold like a used car' (Goldsmith et al 1992: 178). Finally, it can be argued that the market rather than being 'free' is dominated, at present, by large corporations that distort its workings and are hostile to green imperatives.

state regulation or anarchy

It has been argued that without the restraining influence of the state's maintenance of green imperatives will prove impossible, neither the market nor decentralised institutions will tend to maintain green imperatives. Advocates of the eco-state argue that a state is necessary to create and maintain green imperatives.

For eco-statists the state is necessary to introduce measures that will create an ecological economy, may mediate between different interest groups in society, can act to coordinate decentralised units where necessary and has the means to enforce sanctions against those who break ecological rules

(Barry 1994, Frankel 1987, Goodin 1992). The state can act as a democratic institution, providing all affected when an ecological problem is discussed with representation. These are functions that cannot, it is often claimed, be fulfilled in the absence of the state, therefore, for a society to exist within environmental constraints it must evolve a sophisticated eco-state. Globalisation, means that ecological problems cannot, for the eco-statist, be solved on a purely local level by decentralised institutions).

Neither can anarchy maintain humanist values. It is argued that vital elements of green humanism including democracy, equality, justice and pluralism are unlikely to arise without the state. Despite green suspicions of the state and support for decentralisation, the essential plank of Green Party social policy, the basic income scheme, demands central organisation (Frankel 1987: 105). Eckersley notes 'The more we move away from the modern welfare state to local autonomy the less likely we can expect to find the same levels of wealth, welfare and social services among different local communities' (1992: 175). Equally while it is possible to find examples of anarchistic hunter-gatherer societies that have functioned effectively economically (producing enough to satisfy immediate needs, minimising labour time, preventing inequality and maintaining a sustainable metabolism with local ecosystems), it is more difficult to conceptualise how state-less societies would meet economic needs in a technological complex age. According to Frankel, writing in 1987, 'So far, no advocate of completely decentralised planning has been able to show how material redistribution, domestic and international trade etc, can be achieved without the existence of central state institutions' (Frankel 1987: 57).

It has been argued that stateless societies are undemocratic. Some advocates of anarchism argue that the evolution of strong reciprocal community bonds will allow government without formal institutions. Others believe that the creation of such an alleged form of *gemeinschaft* will, far from allowing full participation, end pluralism, politics and choice. Bahro, for example, 'appears to want a society where politics as an activity ceases – that is, a society of permanent harmony, reconciliation with nature and so forth. This is an anti-democracy, a social order of spontaneous or "natural" agreement – something which is foreign to human theory and practice.' (Frankel 1987: 230) Sale's organic society, based on natural bioregions, 'will tilt consensual communities towards conservatism ... but it will by the same token make them more stable, more predictable, and more "comfortable", and less prone to ill-considered decisions' (Sale 1980: 501). Hunt argues that hostility to 'others' is a functional necessity for the stateless society, 'If there is much social mixing between the groups, if people work outside the group, it will weaken the community bond ... xenophobia is the key to the community's success' (Hunt, n.d: 3). As Pepper notes, 'Hunt's "green anarchism" does not seem too people-friendly, unless those people are drawn from one's own bioregion or ecocommunity' (Pepper 1993: 168). Middleton examining the problem from the perspective of musical sociology asks 'How are diversity and solidarity to be reconciled, in the musical realm or any other? This, in a nutshell, is the problem of community – and nobody has

cracked it yet' (Eisenberg 1987: 69). It is a question that must be answered
if the stateless society is to serve the demands of pluralism, democracy,
equality and justice within the imperative of green humanism.

Finally, it might be argued that the post-humanist imperative, cannot be
achieved without state structures. One only has to examine anti-cruelty legislation already in existence and international agreement to protect wildlife
to see that the state may act to protect other species.

Against the State

Anti-Statists see the state as cause rather than cure for ecological and social ills. Examining the modern state in its various manifestations (liberal
democratic or authoritarian), at different tiers (globally, regionally, nationally, locally) and on different continents, examples of the maintenance of
green imperatives are rare. Writing this paper in December 1993, I hear of
the European Community, an example of a supra-state body 'sympathetic'
to environmental protection, urging the construction of a network of inter-
continental motorways. The United States Government in the 1950s, it is revealed, fed radioactive breakfast cereal to pregnant women and children with
learning difficulties. It might be added that its long publicised radiation experiments on other species breaks the third imperative, just as violently
as imperatives one and two. The nuclear waste of the former Soviet state,
dumped in the Arctic Seas, is a source of anxiety. In Britain THORP, the
processing plant that will create quantities of the most dangerous chemical
substance on this planet, is to open. The GATT agreement, an example of
global state agreement, will despite environmental counter-measures, cause
severe environmental problems, displace millions of peasants from the land
and strengthen agribusiness multinationals. In my city (Bristol) the Friends
of the Earth office was recently demolished to make way for a new trunk
road!

Such examples may seem like rhetorical exceptions to generalised state
attempts to serve civil society, situations where ignorance, secrecy or authoritarianism have distorted attempts to protect the environment. Yet despite a
long history of environmental legislation, a number of global agreements and
well publicised international conferences, followed by measures for alternative energy production, wildlife conservation and recycling, there is apparent
widespread opposition amongst modern states to sustainability. As commentators from Marx to Foucault have argued, even when themselves opposing 'humanism', the modern democratic state often stands against broad
humanistic values such as democracy, equality, justice and pluralism. This
is illustrated if we briefly note some of the attacks by democratic state institutions on radical environmentalists. The re-occupation of Bougainville by
Papua New Guinea in an 'Eco-War' that has killed many native Bougainvil-
lians, is the most significant and, perhaps least publicised example of this
antipathy occurring at the time of writing (*Economist*, 27.3.93). Even if we
reject Bougainville as a special case, we should remember that French special agents bombed the Greenpeace ship Rainbow Warrior (Day 1989: 251)
In 1985, authorities in Pennsylvania bombed a radical ecologist commune,

burning to death thirteen men, women and children (Harry 1987, Wall 1994, Walker 1988). We need to ask why these states or elements of a local state are (or were) so radically opposed to political ecologists? Equally we need to ask whether all state structures tend to oppose ecological sustainability? Why are some states more hostile to green imperatives than others? The challenge for any eco-statist is to construct a model that will, in contrast to contemporary examples of the state, maintains green imperatives.

Examining the state, we see an extreme hostility to ecological reforms that threaten accumulation. It has been argued that only where environmental measures allow continued economic growth are such reforms supported by the state, whether in a liberal or authoritarian mode, whether at a local, national, regional or global. Greens have long argued, rightly or wrongly, that the very process of continuous, accelerated accumulation threatens the first green imperative. Marxists have argued that the state far from being a servant capable of acting on behalf of the population is a product of a narrow class interest. As a servant of capitalism, the state must therefore promote economic expansion rather than ecological sustainability. Habermas stress the notion of legitimation in explaining the state's need for economic expansion; accumulation allows the maintenance of cross class support. To put the case crudely, when the economic cake is growing, question of distribution are eased, contradictions are less likely and less threatening. Anarchists would argue that rather than acting on behalf of a particular class, the state acts in its own (class?) interest, encouraging accumulation so as to strengthen it's own power.

For Carter:

> 'the state acts as a key element within an environmentally hazardous dynamic 'A centralised, pseudo-representative, quasi-democratic state stabilizes competitive, inegalitarian economic relations that develop "non-convivial", environmentally damaging "hard" technologies, whose productivity supports the (nationalist and militarist) coercive forces that empower the state. Technologies that facilitate centralised authoritarian control are preferred (such as nuclear power, which also provides plutonium for nuclear weapons). Such technologies serve the interests of state actors and those who benefit (the economically dominant class) from the economic relations the former choose to stabilize. Moreover, the competitive, inegalitarian economic relations that are stabilized maximise the surplus available to the state in order to finance its weapons research and to pay for its standing army and police (the coercive forces).' (Carter 1993: 45)

The earliest states in pre-capitalist societies worked within a similar dynamic, suggesting as Carter argues, that such state antipathy to the environment predates capitalism. In ancient Mesopotemia salinization degraded land, breaking the first green imperative and possibly led to the collapse of the state. Salinization was a product of over-irrigation used to create an economic surplus, utilized in turn to support centralised state structures and maintain an effective military machine (Hughes 1975: 30-5). Similar processes were apparent in Ancient Egypt, although here the fertility of the Nile allowed economic accumulation to continue for many centuries. The Roman Empire illustrates how legitimation processes may lead to the destruction of nature independently of Carter's postulated dynamic. The Roman state, especially in its later imperial form, used both bread (accumulation and redistribution as a product of military expansion) and circuses (mass entertainment in the Colosseum and thousands of amphitheatres) to retain political control. Over-farming may have accelerated desertification in the North African provinces and soil erosion in Italy. Mass spectacles of violence as a form of legitimating entertainment certainly contributed to the extinction of the elephant, rhinoceros and zebra in North Africa, lions in Asia Minor and tigers in Iran (Hughes 1975: 103-6).

Eco-statists need to challenge the view that any state demands ecologically destructive accumulation, the maintenance of repressive armed forces, development of centralised structures, economic inequality and destructive forms of legitimation.

The Commons: a Basis for Green Government?

There are significant reasons why we would expect the state to work against green imperatives and for anarchist alternatives to be inadequate in maintaining them. *The Ecologist* argues that the *Commons*, defined as either a particular kind of state or a form of stateless government, overcomes such objections providing a participatory, decentralised means of sustaining ecological conditions without doing violence to humanist demands for equality, justice and pluralism (Goldsmith et al 1992). Indeed it works to sustain ecological systems by virtue of its democratic nature, providing 'sustenance, security and independence, yet typically does not produce commodities' (Goldsmith et al 1992: 125).

The commons can take a number of different forms, a flexibility that does not fix its participants within a closed universal structure, thus 'the unlimited diversity of commons also makes the concept elusive'. As a form of organisation that regulates the metabolism between humanity and non-human nature, while regulating economic relations between members of its human community, it is marked by:

> 'local or group power, distinctions between members and non-members, rough parity among members, a concern with common safety rather than accumulation, and absence of the constraints that lead to economic scarcity'. [It provides a] 'structure of internal rules, rights, duties and beliefs which mediates and shapes the community's own relationship with its natural surroundings.' (Goldsmith et al 1992: 125)

The commons has been described as the source of, rather than the solution to ecological destruction. As a regime that rejects conventional private property, it cannot sustain the imperative of sustainability, argue critics. Hardin argues:

'The tragedy of the Commons develops in this way. Picture a pasture open to all. it is to be expected that each herdsman will try to keep as many cattle as possible on the Commons. Such an arrangement may work reasonably satisfactorily for centuries because tribal wars, poaching, and disease keep the numbers of both man and beast well below the carrying capacity of the land. Finally, however, comes the day of reckoning, that is, the day when the long-desired goal of social stability becomes a reality. At this point, the inherent logic of the Commons remorselessly generates tragedy.

As a rational being, each herdsman seeks to maximise his gain! ...

(and) concludes that the only sensible course for him to pursue is to add another animal to his herd. And another; and another ... Therein is the tragedy. Each man is locked into a system that compels him to increase his herd without limit – in a world that is limited. Ruin is the destination toward which all men rush, each pursuing his own best interest ... Freedom in a Commons brings ruin to all.' (Hardin 1977: 20)

For Hardin and more liberal eco-statists the commons, globally and locally must be enclosed by the state, if sustainability is to be maintained. Yet for advocates the commons, at least locally, does not represeent a territory without rules, but an institution that maximises local economic and ecological sustainabil.ty through popular negotiation. Advocates argue, for example that commons regimes in Britain worked for centuries, before being replaced by enclosure rather than devastated by environmental mismanagement. Between 1740 and 1840:

'common rights to arable land and pasture, fuel, fish and game were converted to private property by Act of Parliament or other legal processes ... such transfers of wealth and rights, with new extremes of hardship and inequality, required severe enforcement. At home the death penalty was extended to three times as many offences as formerly. Record numbers crowded the prison hulks and penal colonies.' (Stretton 1976: 37)

Prior to this process of enclosure, environmental over-exploitation was overcome by a system of locally agreed self-regulation that provided commoners with 'stints'. Although distorted by feudal control and ultimately, as we have seen abolished by the state, 'It seems fair to describe the stinting system, from the viewpoint of the commoners, as participatory and roughly democratic ... indeed, any change of system in the common fields – including the regulation of stinting – needed unanimous consent ... (Roberts 1979: 151) Unlike possible idealistic conceptions of anarchism, rules and politics are a feature of commons regimes but are agreed locally rather by a centralised state. *The Ecologist* argues that commons regimes continue to exist across the globe and despite constant pressure from the state and the market, provide both an agency of transition and an appropriate metabolism for the maintenance of a green society.

Liberal eco-statists borrow a concept from Malthus, when they argue that left to their own devices local communities will tend to break 'ecological rules'. Statists also argue that even if local decision making was sufficient at a local level, the global commons would require enclosure to preserve environmental integrity. For Goodin, it follows that environmental problems such as the depleted ozone layer or the potential greenhouse effect demand global solutions instituted by global bodies (1992: 157-8).

In contrast *The Ecologist* argues that ecological problems are unlikely to occur within the commons and any increase in state power will in diminishing the autonomy of the commons, stifling the growth of the most effective political mechanism of sustainability. The Earth Summit, an event working towards global solutions to environmental problems, held in Brazil in 1993 is condemned as a forum of, and for, the rich and powerful.

> 'For the major players, the Summit was a phenomenal success. The World Bank emerged in control of an expanded Global Environmental Facility ... The United States got the biodiversity convention it sought simply by not signing the convention on offer. The corporate sector, which throughout the UNCED process enjoyed special access to the secretariat, was confirmed as the key actor in the "battle to save the planet". Free-market environmentalism – the philosophy that transnational corporations brought to Rio ... has become the order of the day' (Goldsmith et al 1992, 122). Environmental solutions that maintain the current distribution of income and power will be promoted by global institutions. Thus "solutions" that make the poorest and least powerful sacrifice the most will be prioritised, explaining the concern with reducing population growth in the South rather than challenging high consumption (yet ecologically suspect) life in the North (Goldsmith et al 1992: 183).

The process of global management *will fail to maintain sustainability*, while eroding humanist welfare. Thus:

> 'an uncompromising drive toward a single global social structure fitted out with mechanisms for global surveillance and global resource conversion to feed unlimited material advance. "Sustaining" this process through damage control requires an equivalent level of surveillance and intervention [For global management to meet the demands of the market and state power] more of the world's people than ever before are now viewed by managers as "obstacles" to be removed or "social factors" to be cajoled into "collaboration" .' (Goldsmith et al 1992: 180)

Even global environmental management, motivated by green imperatives rather than the interests of the market and state, is suspect for those who argue that global environment ills are the product of varied local causes and can only effectively be cured by local management. The commons has to be ecologically sustainable to maintain the prosperity of its inhabitants who are likely to have the 'expertise' to do so. Any effective form of ecological restoration demands:

'an open-endedness, receptiveness and adaptability to the vagaries of local climate personalities, consciousness, crafts and materials ... In this and other respects, the concept of the commons flies in the face of the modern wisdom that each spot on the globe consists merely of coordinates on a global grid laid out by state and market: a uniform field which determines everyone's rights and roles "Commons" implies the right of local people to define their own grid, their own forms of community respect for watercourses, meadows or paths; to resolve conflicts their own way.' (Goldsmith et al 1992: 126)

For eco-statists local management increases the risk of ecologically unsustainable practice, for advocates of the commons greater centralisation ensures that those with the greatest interest in sustaining their environment and the greatest knowledge of how to do so will be marginalised. From the perspective of the first green imperative, there is a clear choice between extending state power or reducing it, between seeing 'localisation' as a solution or advocating 'globalisation', between accepting a Malthusian conception that human participation will destroy the environment or believing that local decision making is more likely to lead to sustainability. Examining such questions some conclude that 'local control, while not necessarily sufficient for environmental protection, is necessary, while under state control the environment necessarily suffers' (Khor cited in Goldsmith et al 1992: 128). *The Ecologist* marshals impressive empirical evidence to substantiate their claims for the commons. Their notion by introducing restraint but organising such restraint on a participatory basis, allows them to overcome criticism that the stateless society will be either ineffective or, by relying purely on a supposed *gemeinschaft*, attack broad humanist demands. For them the commons is not fixed but flexible and rather than seeking an unlikely abolition of politics, establishes mechanisms for dealing with conflict. They also argue that co-ordination between different communities is possible, 'system of common rights, in fact, far from evolving in isolation, often owe their very existence to interaction and struggle between communities ...' (Goldsmith et al 1992: 126). Equally they would reject the notion that inequality will result from a commons regime, for them, global inequality is a product of a global market that sucks resources from the poorest, greater local economic control is a prerequisite for reducing inequality and ending poverty.

Constructing New Political Landscapes

The Ecologist makes a remarkable contribution challenging the notions of both eco-anarchist and eco-statists. The commons contributes a distinctly green conception of government, providing a model that maintains nature without being based on a simplistic notion of the natural society. It is a rare example of a project in social ecology, successful or otherwise, informed by both an investigation of human society and ecological science. A number of serious criticisms remain, for example, while many global environmental problems are best tackled by promoting local solutions, perhaps the international energies demanded to clear the nuclear hazards created by dumped Soviet waste or sunken United States submarines, might justify supra-state action. That such problems exist is clearly a product of state action and as such can be used to justify the abolition of the state, yet in clearing up the grossest examples of state created danger, perhaps the state (or supra-state) is still needed? Equally we should ask whether the commons describe a number of contradictory institutions? Do some, or perhaps all, commons regimes tend to evolve towards the state or market? Are different interpretations of the empirical evidence for the existence and efficiency of the commons more plausible than the claims of *The Ecologist*? Are there any features of a commons regime that may be universalised to make the commons more effective?

To develop green government we need to build critically on the commons, while investigating other mechanisms that increase democratic participation so as to maintain sustainability. Whether we define such mechanisms as 'state' or 'anarchy' seems less important than understanding why traditional conceptions of both terms may be inadequate. Township meetings in New England (that inform Bookchin's municipal libertarianism) and the Songlines (that allowed hunter-gatherers to recognise a certain pluralism and communicate across the Australian continent) are obvious mechanisms that should be re-assessed. Such political anthropology would not seek 'the natural society' but instead analyse metabolisms between varied human communities and varied ecosystems that maintain(ed) green imperatives. In the construction of green government, while rejecting Marx's meta-narratives, we might borrow his concept of *praxis* and fear of prescriptive utopian models. It might, in conclusion, be fitting when we remember that Marx's first political works examined erosion of the commons, to speculate that contemporary advocates may have written a *Communist Manifesto* but have yet to present a *Capital* (Marx 1975: 224-263). *The Ecologist* has produced a document to which engaged greens may rally but have yet to fully satisfy critical attention.

Bibliography

Adorno, T. & Horkheimer, M. (1979), *The Dialectics of Enlightenment*, London: Verso.

Bahro, R. (1982), *Socialism and Survival*, London: Heretic.

Barry (1994)

Beckerman, W. (1975), *Pricing for Pollution*, Institute of Economic Affairs: London.

Bookchin, M. & Foreman, D. (1991), *Defending the Earth*, Black Rose: Montreal.

Brown, A. (1990), *Modern Political Philosophy*, Penguin: London.

Burbridge, J. (1992), 'Global action against rainforest destruction', *Green Revolution*, Spring 1992.

Cairncross, F. (1991), *Costing the Earth*, London: Economist.

Carter, A. (1993), 'Towards a Green Political Theory' in Dobson, A & Lucardie, P (eds), *The Politics of Nature*, London: Routledge.

Capra, F. (1984), *The Turning Point*, London: Flamingo.

Day, D. (1989), *The Eco Wars*, London: Harrap.

Dobson, A. (1990), *Green Political Theory*, London: Unwin Hyman.

Eckersley, R. (1992), *Environmentalism and Political Theory: Toward an Ecocentric Approach*, London: UCL Press.

Einarsson, N. (1993), 'All animals are equal but some are cetaceans', in Milton, K (ed), *Environmentalism*, London: Routledge.

Eisenberg, E. (1987), *The Recording Angel*, London: Picador.

Elkington, J. & Burke, T. (1987), *The Green Capitalists*, London: Victor Gollanz.

Frankel, B. (1987), *The Post Industrial Utopians*, Cambridge: Polity.

Goldsmith, E, Hildyard, N, Bunyard, P. & McCully, P. (1992), 'Whose Common Future?', *The Ecologist*, 22: 4.

Goodin, R. (1992), *Green Political Theory*, Cambridge: Polity.

Gould, P. (1988), *Early Green Politics*, Brighton: Harvester.

Green Party (1987), *General Election Manifesto*, London: Green Party.

Hardin, G. & Baden, J. (1977), *Managing the Commons*, San Francisco: W.H.Freeman.

Harry, M. (1987), 'Attention MOVE! this is America', *Race and Class*, 28, 4: 5-28.

Hughes, J.D. (19y75), *Ecology in Ancient Civilisations*, Albuquerque: University of New Mexico Press.

Hunt, R. (n.d.), *The Natural Society: a basis for Green Anarchism*, Oxford, EOA Books.

Lucardie, P. (1993), 'Introduction', in Dobson, A & Lucardie, P (eds), *The Politics of Nature*, London: Routledge.

Marx, K. (1975), 'On the law on thefts of wood', in Karl Marx & Friedrich Engels, *Collected Works*, 1, London: Lawrence & Wishart.

Pepper, D. (1993), *Eco-Socialism*, London: Routledge.

Porritt, J. (1984), *Seeing Green*, Oxford: Blackwell.

Roberts, A. (1979), *The Self-Managing Society*, London: Allison & Busby.

Sale, K. (1980), *Human Scale*, London: Secker & Warburgh.

Saward (1993), 'Towards a Green Political Theory', in Dobson, A & Lucardie, P (eds), *The Politics of Nature*, London: Routledge.

Trainer, F.E. (1985), *Abandon Affluence!*, London: Zed.

Wall, D. (1990), *Getting There*, London: Greenprint.

Wall, D. (1994), *Green History*, London, Routledge.

Walker, A. (1988), 'Nobody was supposed to survive', in *Living by the Word*, London, Womens Press.

The End of the USSR
& the Collapse of Soviet Studies

Michael Cox
The Queen's University of Belfast

'The End of the USSR
and the Collapse of Soviet Studies'

Acknowledgements

This paper began life as a series of conversations with colleagues. Here, I would like to acknowledge their help. First, Professor Michael Ellman of the Department of Economics at the University of Amsterdam. It was a long and interesting discussion with him on a plane somewhere between Phoenix and Charlotte in November 1992 that provoked me into putting my cluttered thoughts on the subject into some coherent order. These then received their initial public airing at a seminar given to the Faculty of Economics at the University of Amsterdam on April 5 1993. I would also like to thank Professor John Gaddis. It was another equally stimulating conversation with him in late April, this one held in an Oxford pub on the failure of historians to predict the end of the old world order, which impelled me to refine some of my original ideas. Finally, I must acknowledge the contributions of Professors Ron Hill of Trinity College, Dublin, and Geoffrey Hosking of the University of London. It was their invaluable comments on the end of Soviet Studies – made at the Annual Conference of the Irish Slavist's Association held at Queen's University, Belfast, in May – which in the end persuaded me to commit my iconoclastic thoughts to paper.

Introduction

Between 1989 and 1991 the Soviet Union collapsed in at least four senses: as an economy; as the actually existing alternative to capitalism; as a perceived or real threat to the western world; and finally as an empire. The consequences of this collapse have been and will no doubt continue to be profound. Of one thing we can be sure. The impact of a disintegrating Soviet Union upon the world will be enormous; every bit as significant, if not more so, as when an apparently stable Soviet Union stood outside of the international order. Clearly, there is no guarantee that the collapse of Soviet power will make the world a more stable place. In fact, the opposite seems to be happening. In Europe the collapse of the blocs and the demise of the Soviet 'threat' has made the continent a more, rather than a less volatile region. In the wider world system, allies once united against a common enemy are now more divided than at any time since the end of the Second World War. And in the United States there is confusion and division about America's role abroad. Certainly, the speed with which the US shelved President Bush's half-hearted plan to construct a 'new world order' would suggest that in the land of the last remaining superpower there is little confidence about the future.[1]

The impact of Soviet collapse upon intellectual life has of course been profound – throwing the socialist left into an even deeper ideological crisis than the one it was already in prior to the fall of stalinism, while giving yet another boost to the advocates of free market economics. At one level it has even compromised the very idea of 'progress'. But the one specific academic discourse that has been most affected by stalinist collapse has been Soviet Studies; until recently one of the most privileged of all academic disciplines. The results thus far have been calamitous: for some, personally traumatic as well. In effect, the subject has ceased to exist. As a result, journals have been forced to change their name. Those once trained to read between the lines of Soviet and East European newspapers now find they have no role. By the same token, those who once counted tanks, analysed Soviet foreign policy, or tried through various means to detect significant changes at the top of the Communist Party apparatus find themselves with nothing left to do. Symptomatically, the amount of money going into post-Soviet studies has declined dramatically for the simple reason that governments no longer need 'to know the enemy'. Why should they? The enemy no longer exists.[2]

Those who remain in what is left of Soviet Studies have a few options, though not many. They can, if they so wish, move into entirely new areas on the not unreasonable assumption that their skills are no longer required. They could return to the safer haven provided by history, quite a reasonable move now that there is more information issuing forth from Soviet archives. Or they could try and understand what is now going on in the former land mass once referred to as the Soviet empire; try in other words to analyse the highly contradictory processes now taking place in a disintegrating system – a system whose disintegration was neither expected nor foreseen. This brings me to the heart of the matter. In spite of its enormous output and the vast amounts of money invested into the subject over the years, few practising sovietologists actually foresaw the possibility of a specifically 'Soviet' history coming to an end. In this sense, the collapse of stalinism not only came as something of a shock to those who either supported, vilified or were neutral about the Soviet system. It came as one to those whose job was to analyse it as well.[3]

---

[1] For an official exposition of what the Bush administration meant by the term 'New World Order', see *The New World Order: An Analysis and Document Collection* (London, United States Information Service, July and 1991). The Foreign Secretary, Douglas Hurd, made clear what he thought of the idea in a lecture to Chatham House on 27 January 1993. 'Talk of a New World Order' he observed 'was not helpful'. Why? Because it 'promised more than we could perform'. The text of his speech can be found in *Arms Control and Disarmament Quarterly Review* (London, Arms Control and Disarmament Research Unit), Number 28, January 1993).

[2] As Professor Edward L.Keenan of Harvard observed: 'since the dangers are supposed to be less, the chance to tap the public purse for those activities is also less'. Cited in Felicity Barringer, 'Sovietology Loses Academic Glamour in Cold War Wake', *The International Herald Tribune*, April 1, 1993. Barringer noted that 'like the now-defunct empire it sought to understand, the field once known as 'sovietology' was 'undergoing a painful transition in the United States. Once heavily subsidized and often first among equals in the academic world, it is now a discipline in turmoil'.

[3] The inability of sovietologists to foresee the demise of the Soviet system was par-

The scale of the failure should not be underestimated. Most experts did not foresee the possibility of someone like Gorbachev coming to power in the first place. Many were then slow in recognizing the significance of his radically new agenda. A large number assumed – incorrectly – that he would soon be overthrown and the old order restored. Others believed, equally erroneously, that he would succeed in his endeavours and actually revitalize the USSR. Nobody expected the USSR to withdraw from Eastern Europe in 1989. Finally, few foretold of the coup; and following its collapse, only a handful predicted the rapid disintegration of 'probably the most powerful empire the world has ever known'.[4] Exceptions there were to this general rule. But in the main, those who had earlier suggested that the USSR may be historically doomed, or systemically unviable, were peripheral figures in the profession. The emigré, neo-conservative ideologue Richard Pipes, and Hillel Ticktin (editor of *Critique*) were hardly mainstream figures in Soviet Studies.[5]

What I intend to do in this essay therefore is try and understand what can best – and only – be described as the collective failure of a discipline: a failure to foresee the implosion of an entity whose structures, leaders and policies it had been studying in minute detail for over forty years. As I will show there is not one answer to this question but many. By the same measure, there is not just one ex-sovietologist with egg on his or her face but several. However, I want to begin my discusssion not with Soviet Studies as such, but with the position of the academic in the modern university. It is here that the cause of sovietology's present discomfort has to be sought.

The Academic Dilemma

Let us begin, then, with an observation about the structure of knowledge in the West. It can be argued (and I would certainly want to argue the point here) that academics teaching in highly specialized discipline areas in western universities are either discouraged, or not inclined to ask big questions. They are deterred from doing so in all sorts of ways: by a doctoral system which emphasizes the footnote over the idea; by the subdivision of knowledge which finds its organized expression in the departmental system; and finally by career opportunities. Those who stray outside of the narrow channel do so at some professional risk to themselves. Universities are, after all, like business organizations and reward its members for their ability to publish detailed monographs in increasingly specialized journals. Indeed,

alleled by an equally notable failure on the part of those in international relations to predict the end of the Cold War. This issue is explored very thoroughly by John Lewis Gaddis in 'International Relations Theory and the End of the Cold War', *International Security*, Winter 1992/93, Volume 17, Number 3, pp.5-58. Gaddis correctly observes that the inability of those in international relations to see the end of the Cold War coming, must raise big 'questions about the methods' it previously employed to understand world politics (p.6).

[4] Mary McAuley, *Soviet Politics: 1917-1991* (Oxford University Press, 1992), p.9.

[5] See Richard Pipes, *Survival Is Not Enough: Soviet Realities and America's Future* (New York, Simon & Schuster, 1984), and Hillel Ticktin, *Origins of The Crisis In The USSR: Essays On The Political Economy of A Disintegrating System* (New York, M.E.Sharpe, 1992).

there are few journals (except the less prestigious ones on the margins of academia) which actually publish material of a non-specialist nature.

Modern academics – including those within Soviet Studies – are thus caught (and have been for a long time) on the horns of a dilemma. To succeed he or she has to specialize and do 'useful' or 'practical' research recognized and rewarded by the university. However once involved in what is effectively a web of professional dependency, it becomes increasingly difficult to examine large issues. In fact, it looks decidedly odd if one does. In this way large-scale problems about the dynamics or contradictions of this or that social system (including, I would submit, the former USSR's) are simply pushed off the agenda. Far easier and almost certainly more rewarding to research very specific topics like interest groups, party structures, electoral systems and the like.

This leads to a second general observation; not about the structural constraints imposed upon the academic in the modern university, but the intellectual ones. To put it bluntly, the very nature of conventional social sciences would have made it extraordinarily difficult for the student of the USSR (or of any country for that matter) to have foreseen the country's decline and final break-up. The reason, quite simply, was because of the dominance of empiricism in the academy. The results of this were profound, but the most important consequence was that those so influenced simply avoided theorizing about systems. Indeed, they were literally urged not to by the 'greats' of social sciences – Weber and Durkheim in sociology, Marshall and Jevons in neo-classical economics, and above all Karl Popper in philosophy. The result of this persistent, and in the end, effective attack upon theory was to render most academics incapable of examining the large picture historically. In terms of their own training, the large picture was precisely what they were not supposed to look at. The proper object of study was the very specific and the highly detailed; parts of the whole but not the whole itself. Small-scale problems could be looked at. Large issues such as why systems – including the Soviet system – rise, mature and finally wither away – were ignored. These were best left to the speculator or the journalist. Or, it might be added, to the Toynbee or the Marx – neither of whom would have felt very much at home in an academic department in the postwar period.

The final dilemma was less methodological than institutional and professional. For over forty years careers had been made, journals produced, books written, budgets justified and international conferences organized on the assumption that something would continue to exist: that something of course was the Soviet Union. It would be no exaggeration to say that the USSR became a way of life for a very large number of people. And not just for academics in universities. Western intelligence services, military establishments, important industries, diplomatic missions and alliances abroad were all in a very obvious and direct sense dependent upon the Soviet Union. The object of their distrust, had, ironically, become the reason for their being. The idea that one day it may no longer be there was virtually inconceivable – as one academic discovered when he asked a group of leading American officials in 1985 whether or not we should be 'looking ahead to the possibility that the Cold War might someday end?' According to the academic in question, 'an embarrassed silence ensued'. This was finally broken by an observation from a highly-respected senior diplomat. 'Oh it hadn't occurred to any of us that it ever would end'.[6]

Soviet Studies and the Cold War

This brings us to Soviet Studies itself. Here we need to ask a simple but important questions: why was the Soviet Union a subject of western interest? For what purpose was it studied? And to what end? There is no one answer to these. Yet it would be somewhat disingenuous to abstract the discipline of Soviet Studies from its context. And that context was the Cold War. This, I would argue, profoundly influenced the assumptions of many sovietologists. To understand how we must briefly look at the development of the subject after the war.

The serious study of the USSR clearly pre-dated the Cold War. But its exponential growth as a subject was very much the result of the collapse of the war-time alliance and the West's need to understand the dynamics of Soviet policy. This, of necessity, required a reasonably objective understanding of the Soviet Union's capabilities and intentions. The problem was that as the Cold War unfolded this more or less balanced approach was substituted by one which increasingly emphasized the worst. The reasons for this happening were complex. In part it had to do with Soviet actions themselves which only seemed to confirm its threatening and monstrous character. But it also had a great deal to do with developments in the West itself: anti-communist hysteria in the United States, the Korean War, the requirements of military planning for the long term – but above all the need to mobilize domestic support for what was turning into a costly and lengthy struggle. Whether policy-makers believed their own propaganda is an open question. The fact remains, however, that in public at least they invariably emphasized Soviet power and understated its known weaknesses. Even talking about the latter was almost discouraged on the assumption this would undermine the consensus which supported and justified western policies towards the USSR.[7]

The tendency to exaggerate Soviet strengths and underestimate its flaws was at least one reason why many may have been surprised by the fall of the USSR in the late eighties. Another was the equally important Cold War assumption that the USSR was bound by its very nature to expand but not to retreat. The thesis was not an entirely unreasonable one of course. After all, before 1941 the Soviet Union had attacked a number of bordering countries and fomented revolution abroad. Then after 1945 (and until the late seventies at least) it tried, with varying degrees of success, to increase

---

[6] Quoted in John Lewis Gaddis, *The United States and The End of the Cold War: Implications, Reconsiderations, Provocations* (New York, Oxford University Press, 1992), p.vi.

[7] The importance of the United States creating – and the problems it faced when it lost – a 'consensus' on foreign policy is discussed at length in Richard A.Melanson, *Reconstructing Consensus: American Foreign Policy Since The Vietnam War* (New York, St Martin's Press, 1991).

its weight within the wider international system. The problem was that those who reasonably talked about Soviet 'expansion' seemed oblivious to other things: that Soviet influence was limited to the most backward parts of the world; that Moscow frequently exercised great caution, in fact on many occasions refused to take on new commitments; that it probably lost as much influence as it gained in the forty year period after the war; that it sometimes retreated voluntarily, as it did in Austria in 1954; and most importantly of all perhaps, that expansion for a system as inefficient and uncompetitive as the Soviet Union's was an extraordinary burden – and that this burden was likely to grow as the economy began to slow down. However, none of this seemed to lead commentators to the conclusion that the USSR might one day do what all other imperial powers have had to do: decolonize.[8]

The assumption that the USSR could never withdraw from entrenched positions also helps us explain why Soviet Studies failed to predict the most important strategic development of the post-war period: Soviet disengagement from Eastern Europe in 1989. In fact, on this particuar issue, all strands of sovietological opinion – from the most conservative to the most pro-Soviet – assumed the USSR would stay where it was. Even those who were reasonably sensitive to the impact of *perestroika* upon Soviet-East European relations felt the USSR could not withdraw from the region; and for apparently good reasons.[9]

First, according to the common view, the USSR would remain where it was because this both placed pressure on the West while reducing western pressure on itself. It also limited German ambitions by guaranteeing Germany's continued division. Indeed, if there were no other reason for the USSR remaining in Eastern Europe, the desire to keep Germany divided would have been enough. But there was more. The USSR needed Eastern Europe (or so we were informed) for economic purposes. It required it too for the conduct of its foreign policy, for without the support of its Warsaw Pact allies abroad it would not have been able to project its influence so effectively. And lastly, it could not withdraw from the region for the very important reason that to have done so would have threatened the integrity of the USSR itself. For all these reasons, the USSR could not possibly do what it finally did in 1989: disengage and return home to base.[10]

---

[8] Interestingly, one of the few serious commentators to suggest the USSR might be impelled to retreat from empire because of 'relative economic decline' was not a sovietologist, but an historian of comparative civilizations, Paul Kennedy. See his *The Rise and Fall of The Great Powers: Economic Change and Military Conflict From 1500 to 2000* (London, Fontana Press, 1989).

[9] Naturally most commentators assumed *perestroika* in the USSR would bring about what one called 'fundamental changes in the ways' East European societies were 'organized and run'. What they did not forsee – indeed almost precluded – was that the Soviet Union would finally disengage from the region. See David S. Mason, 'Glasnost, perestroika and Eastern Europe', *International Affairs*, Volume 64, Number 3, Summer 1988, pp.431-448.

[10] To give a few (typical) examples of the views expressed on Soviet-East European relations before Soviet disengagement in 1989. In early 1986, one noted writer believed that in Eastern Europe, Gorbachev 'recognized' there were 'limits that he himself cannot overstep'. See Vladimir V.Kusin, 'Gorbachev and Eastern Europe', *Problems of Communism*, Volume 35, Number 1, January -February 1986, p.53. The following summer

Finally, if we are considering the impact of the Cold War upon Soviet Studies we have to look at the dominant paradigm of the Cold War: totalitarianism. First used as a term to describe Fascist Italy in the 1920s and then by dissident socialists to understand the stalinist system of the thirties, after the war it became increasingly popular as a means of characterizing the USSR. The post-war popularity of the concept can be explained in several ways. Most obviously, it seemed to describe the peculiarities of the Soviet system rather well. It was simple. It was politically correct by the conservative standards of the time. And it provided a moral justification for western policy in the Cold War by equating the Soviet Union with Nazi Germany. In fact, precisely because it looked like an ideological device designed to legitimize (and perpetuate) the Cold War, the idea of totalitarianism soon came to be opposed by many within the Soviet Studies profession.[11]

Yet in spite of the backlash against the totalitarian thesis, it continued to to exert a tremendous influence on Soviet Studies. This had a number of consequences, but perhaps the most important was that those who supported the idea (and there were many) tended to assume the Soviet regime would persist; not because it was legitimate, but because it could deploy an enormous battery of controls to prevent latent discontent becoming overt. These controls, it was pointed out, had guaranteed the system after the Bolsheviks seized power in 1917. They had then been perfected under Stalin. And in spite of certain modifications after his death, still remained in being. The people might mutter, the intellectuals may moan; but given the power of the secret police and the atomized character of the population, there was no possibility of society's contradictions ever expressing themselves. In fact, according to emigré writer Alexander Zinoviev (whose work exercised a great deal of influence in the West following the publication of *The Yawning Heights* in 1976), 'Homo Sovieticus' was so traumatized, that he (and presumably she) preferred the order guaranteed by Soviet communism to the likely disorder that would follow its demise. The system therefore was secure. Not only was it strong in its own right, but by so shaping the in-

---

another commentator emphasized that 'no one can doubt that the region continues to provide a vital security guarantee that Moscow is unlikely to abandon'. See A. James McAdams, 'New Deal for Eastern Europe', *The Nation*, June 13 1987, p.800. In an important discussion of the Soviet bloc at about the same time, Charles Gati speculated that the most likely outcome of change in Eastern Europe would be to undermine *glasnost* in the USSR itself. See his 'Gorbachev and Eastern Europe', *Foreign Affairs*, Volume 67, Number 3, Summer 1987, pp.958-975. As late as June 1989, another expert could still write that the states of Eastern Europe would 'survive, albeit greatly changed'. See Valerie Bunce, 'Eastern Europe: Is the Party Over?', *Political Science & Politics*, June 1989, pp.238-239.

[11] One of the most influential early critiques of the totalitarian model was of course by H. Gordon Skilling, 'Interest Groups and Communist Politics', *World Politics*, Volume XVIII, Number 3, April 1966, pp.435-451. For a useful, and less critical discussion of the concept see Archie Brown, *Soviet Politics and Political Science* (London, Macmillan, 1974), especially pp.30-41. Rather oddly, once the applicability of the concept of totalitarianism to the post-Stalin period had been questioned, a number of writers began to challenge its relevance to understanding the thirties as well! This attempt to rethink stalinism (some would argue provide an apologia for it) was led by Arch Getty in his *Origins of the Great Purges: The Soviet Communist Party Reconsidered: 1933-1938*, (Cambridge University Press, 1985).

dividual actually implicated the ordinary Soviet citizen in his or her own subordination to this perfected form of the Leviathan state.[12]

The Social Sciences

The Cold War shaped the contours of Soviet Studies for nearly two decades. Yet it was not a self-contained subject, and in the sixties and seventies there was – what can only be described as – a serious and determined drive to both modernise the subect and integrate it more completely with the broader social sciences.[13] This drive proved very effective and by the early eighties the discipline had been changed beyond recognition by the grafting of modern scientific methods onto the original body of Kremlinology. But in spite of this methodological invasion of what had once been a rather isolated academic preserve inhabited by the emigré, the government official and the conservative, the new wave proved no more successful in predicting the upheavals of the late eighties than their more orthodox predecessors. Carrying neither the intellectual nor the political baggage of the 'totalitarians', the second generation of sovietologists nevertheless failed as completely as their less liberal opponents in anticipating the collapse of the Soviet system. The question is why?

One part of the answer, ironically, has to be sought in the new cohort's rejection of the original totalitarian model.[14] Supporters of the latter, we should recall, believed the USSR would remain in being, not because the system was popular or inherently stable, but because the Soviet state was extraordinarily repressive.[15] According to a number of social scientists who rose to intellectual prominence in the seventies and eighties, this view was profoundly misleading; not only because it overemphasized the role of force in maintaining the Soviet regime, but underestimated the reserves upon which the regime could draw to reproduce itself. The system may not been legitimate in the western sense. However, this did not mean it was without support. On the contrary, it had deep roots in the Soviet population. Some even spoke of a 'social contract' existing between rulers and the ruled in which the former fulfilled their part of the bargain by guaranteeing the latter full employment and minimal welfare. But this was not all. The Soviet people, it was argued, were proud of their country's achievements. They were very patriotic too. And they had far more educational opportunities than their parents or grandparents. Moreover, their children, crucially, had the chance of a better life than they.[16]

---

[12] See Alexander Zinoviev, *The Reality of Communism* (London, Paladin Books, 1984).

[13] 13. One writer saw the problems facing Soviet studies in the late sixties as stemming from its 'isolation ... from the best of systematic and comparative political science'. Because of this, it had 'grown up methodologically impoverished'. See Robert S. Sharlet, 'Concept Formation in Political Science and Communist Studies: Conceptualizing Political Participation', *Canadian Slavic Studies*, Volume 1, Number 4, Winter 1967, p.641.

[14] For a brief, but fairly scathing attack on the notion of totalitarianism by one of the new cohort of social science scholars see David Lane's highly influential *Politics and Society in the USSR* (London, Weidenfeld & Nicholson, 1970), pp.188-190.

[15] See Leonard Schapiro, *Totalitarianism* (London, Macmillan, 1972).

[16] Although as David Lane pointed out in the early seventies, as a result of 'greater economic maturity and political stability' in the USSR, 'one might expect the pattern of

But it was not merely social factors that challenged the totalitarian myth of a system without a base. Political developments in the post-Stalin period also suggested the regime had some support. The Communist Party clearly remained dominant in a single-party state. Nevertheless, the élite did pemit a degree of group involvement and popular participation in the political process. In fact, according to one leading American political scientist, the Soviet system was nearly as open (if not more so) than the liberal democracies of the West.[17] Moreover, while elections may have been a facade, it would be wrong to conclude the Soviets meant nothing. If nothing else they allowed yet one more access point for the ordinary citizen to be involved in, or at least bring pressure to bear upon the deliberations of government. Further proof, if prooof were needed, that the USSR was a long way away from the totalitarian nightmare portrayed in the popular literature by Orwell and in the academic field by such notables as Friedrich & Brzezinski.[18]

The consequence of all this new writing was twofold: it made the Soviet system look decidedly more pleasant than had previously been assumed; and, by implication, led those who analysed the USSR in this way to the not illogical conclusion that the system was relatively stable. Indeed how could such an order – which guaranteed jobs for life to an upwardly mobile, patriotic people who were not excluded from the political process – be on the verge of disintegration? It was just beyond the bounds of possibility. A mere fantasy entertained by extremists, but not supported by the facts.

This conclusion was endorsed (in part) by another innovation introduced by modern social scientists to understand the Soviet system: that of political culture. Once again trying to move beyond the limits of a totalitarian model whose residual influence probably had 'less to do with its scholarly merits than with its ideological attractions', a number of leading scholars – political scientists in particular – sought to use the concept as a way of 'allowing a greater degree of attention to be paid to the historical and national specificity of Soviet politics, as well as to the similarities it shares with other political systems'.[19] The results were not devoid of value or merit. Nevertheless, those who employed the notion of 'culture' generally tended to reinforce the view that the USSR was a good deal more stable than it was. That may not have been the intention. But that was the consequence of using an approach which stressed the deeply rooted historical character of many values, that emphasized the success of most (if not all) Soviet

social stratification to become more stable and the amount of upward mobility to decline'. See his *The End of Inequality? Stratification under State Socialism* (Harmondsworth, Penguin Books, 1971), p.119.

[17] This is certainly implied by Jerry Hough in his controversial rewrite of Merle Fainsod's classic, *How the Soviet Union is Governed* (Harvard University Press, 1979), p.276. It is also suggested in his *Soviet Leadership in Transition* (Washington, Brookings, 1980), p.15.

[18] For an early attempt to demonstrate how certain groups exploited their access to the policy-making process, see Joel J. Schwartz & William R.Keech, 'Group Influence and the Policy Process in the Soviet Union', *American Political Science Review*, Volume LXII, Number 3, September 1968, pp.840-851.

[19] Stephen White, *Political Culture and Soviet Politics* (London, Macmillan, 1979), pp.4, ix.

socialisation programmes in shaping beliefs and attitudes, and concluded that the regime might be regarded as legitimate because it did certain things (especially in the socio-economic sphere) which fulfilled popular needs and demands. As one noted sociologist pointed out in the late seventies, the study of Soviet political culture was especially useful, for not only did it reveal a previously unknown degree 'of congruity between the attitudes' of the political élite and the people, but showed that the political system itself was perceived positively because it was 'carrying out many desirable policies'. It was reasonable to conclude therefore that the élite (or more precisely 'political élites') had some level of 'support among the population' as a whole.[20]

The argument that the regime may have been more successful than the totalitarians assumed was implicit too in much (though not all) of the new writing on the national question.[21] Here, once again, traditional views came under attack from a group of social scientists who neither sympathized with nationalist aspirations, nor believed that nationalism was as potentially dangerous to the system as had hitherto been supposed. Implicitly, and in some cases explicitly attacking the thesis that the USSR was a 'prison house of nations', a modern generation of analysts arrived at some rather interesting conclusions about the ethnic question in the former USSR.

The first, and perhaps the least controversial, was that in spite of the great historical wrongs done to many nationalities, since Stalin's death the policy of the centre had been culturally tolerant, politically fair, and by and large, economically equitable too. Thus there was little reason to assume the so-called 'captive nations' were straining at the leash to escape from their now relatively benign captors. Nor did it follow that there was an inherent conflict between being a member of one of the various nations and a citizen of the wider Soviet republic. As one writer put it, ethnic consciousness 'did not necessarily signify a lack of loyalty to the Soviet regime'.[22] In fact, according to another analyst, it could be so channelled so as to make it 'integrative' rather than disintegrative of the state.[23] There was, in other words, no *prima facie case* to think that nationalism presented the system 'with an impossible or even a potentially disturbing future'.[24] Indeed, as one commentator noted in a popular and widely-used text-book published in the second half of the eighties, 'for the foreseeable future, most communist states, certainly the more legitimate ones' (like the Soviet Union) 'should

[20] David Lane, *The Socialist Industrial State: Towards a Political Sociology of State Socialism* (London, George Allen & Unwin, 1976), p.91.

[21] For a more 'traditional' (some believed at the time apocalyptic) treatment of the national question in the USSR, see Helene Carrere d'Encausse, *Decline of an Empire: The Soviet Socialist Republics in Revolt* (New York, Newsweek Books, 1979).

[22] Brian Silver, 'Social Mobilization and the Russification of Soviet Nationalities', *American Political Science Review*, Volume 68, 1974, p.66.

[23] Peter Rutland, 'Nationalism and the Soviet State: A Functionalist Account', Paper presented to the Annual Conference of the National Association of Soviet and East European Studies, Cambridge, March 1982, p.1.

[24] Mary McAuley, 'In Search of Nationalism in the USSR', Paper presented to the National Association of Soviet and East European Studies, Cambridge, March 1982, p.2.

be able to cope with', though 'not fully solve the problems of nationalism and ethnic conflict'.[25]

A final, and particularly important reason why social scientists might have assumed the USSR would persist was economic. While most accepted that the problems facing the country in the eighties were great (and growing), few felt they would actually lead to the collapse of the system.[26] The consensus, basically, was that the economy had enough reserves to get by. This was certainly the view of the CIA, which in a well-publicized report of 1984 concluded the leadership could muddle along almost indefinitely.[27] It was also the opinion of influential American economist Ed Hewitt. Hewitt, who later became adviser on Soviet affairs to the Bush White House, in fact warned the West in 1989 not to overestimate Soviet economic weakness. The Soviet economy he insisted was not 'teetering on the brink of collapse'.[28]

So why did so many western experts fail to detect the fact that the Soviet economy was in terminal decline? One reason was technical. Using Soviet figures – which most of them did – it was almost inevitable that economists would arrive at overly optimistic conclusions about the USSR's potential: partly because these figures hid the depth of the Soviet crisis, and partly because they seriously overestimated the actual size of the economy.[29] There was also a more specifically political reason why some underestimated the Soviet malaise. Opposed as they were to the Reagan policy of squeezing the USSR, many liberal (and not-so liberal) economists were inclined to

---

[25] Leslie Holmes, *Politics in the Communist World* (Oxford, Clarendon Press, 1986), p.353.

[26] Marshall I.Goldman expressed the dominant western view about the Soviet economy in 1987. Having surveyed the prospects for reform he concluded that 'short of some unexpected catastrophe, the Soviet economy is unlikely to come close to collapse ... In the end, Gorbachev, like his predecessors, will probably have to settle for an economy that has to rely more on its natural riches than on its creative potential'. See his *Gorbachev's Challenge: Economic Reform in the Age of High Technology* (New York, W.W.Norton, 1987), p.262.

[27] The CIA concluded in 1982 that although there had been a marked 'slowdown' in Soviet growth since the seventies, 'the Soviet economy' was 'not going to collapse'. Indeed, the Agency expected 'GNP to continue to grow, although slowly'. For the full text see Henry Rowen, 'Central Intelligence Briefing on the Soviet Economy' (1 December 1982). Reprinted in E.P.Hoffmann & R.F.Laird (eds), *The Soviet Polity in the Modern Era* (New York, Aldine Publishing, 1984), pp.417-446.

[28] Hewitt warned against overestimating Soviet weakness – 'something we have done in the past' – because there were still 'strengths and reserves' left in the system. These included 'a huge defense industry producing many world-class products; a formidable, hitherto underutilized scientific establishment; enormously rich natural reserves; a modest international debt, and a well-educated workforce'. See Ed A.Hewitt, 'An Idle U.S. Debate About Gorbachev', *The New York Times*, March 30, 1989.

[29] Conventional western analyses of the Soviet economy in the eighties were hardly glowing of course. However, even these seemingly unfavourable assessments were too optimistic; the true economic situation, on balance, being substantially worse than even these estimates suggested. According to officials from the ex-USSR, the 'real' Soviet economy was barely a third of the size of the American economy, and Soviet *per capita* output about a quarter. See Michael Wines, 'C.I.A. Accused of Overestimating Soviet Economy', *The New York Times*, 23 July 1990, and Colin Hughes, 'CIA is accused of crying wolf on Soviet economy', *The Independent*, 25 July 1990. For a defence of the CIA's record, see Richard J.Kerr (Acting Director of the CIA), 'C.I.A.'s Track Record Stands Up to Scrutiny', *The New York Times*, 24 October 1991.

find arguments with which to undercut the neo-conservatives in the White
House. The simplest, and most effective way of doing this was to pour cold
water on the argument that the USSR was in dire trouble and could be
forced on to what Reagan termed the 'ash-heap' of history.[30] In this way,
the fight over foreign policy within the United States led to some interesting
results when it came to estimating Soviet weaknesses and strengths in the
eighties.

Finally most economists were reformist at heart, and believed, for both
intellectual and political reasons, that there had to be a pragmatic and
moderate solution to Soviet economic problems. That there were profound
obstacles standing in the way of reform was obvious. On the other hand,
there was no reason in principle to conclude that improvements could not be
made; even possibly that some 'third way' might not be found between the
Scylla of the command system and the Charybdis of the free market. This
is where Gorbachev enters the picture. Assuming, or at least hoping that he
would directly address some of the difficulties facing the USSR, economists
helped reinforce the belief (very widespread before the Gorbachev strategy
began to implode) that the system would persist: not because the economy
was working particularly well – it obviously wasn't – but because it was
susceptible to improvement from above.[31]

The Gorbachev Factor

This leads us logically to Gorbachev himself. From the perspective of the
1990s Gorbachev looks like a transitional, quasi-tragic figure who failed in
nearly everything he attempted to do. In 1985 he set out to revitalize the
Soviet economy. In the end however he only managed to accelerate – some
would insist cause its collapse. He sought to turn the USSR into a more
dynamic and attractive superpower. By the time he was forced from office
in 1991 the country was no longer a major force in world politics. Finally,
he tried to construct a new relationship between the peoples of the Soviet
Union, but his ambiguous policies in this vital area only led to the empire's
fragmentation. History will not deal kindly with Gorbachev one suspects.

Yet at the time, this was not how things appeared. In fact, to most
professional students of the USSR, the early Gorbachev years were a golden
age dominated by an energetic reformist leader; the modern equivalent of
'Peter the Great and Stalin' according to one noted commentator.[32] Moreover, here was someone who actually courted the intelligentsia, who spoke
openly about the nations' problems, who liberated Eastern Europe and
wound down the Cold War. How could one not be impressed by the man –

---

[30] President Reagan's views on the 'crisis' of Soviet 'totalitarianism' were unambiguously expressed in a speech he gave to the British Parliament on June 8, 1982. See
'Promoting Democracy and Peace', in *Realism, Strength, Negotiation: Key Foreign Policy Statements of the Reagan Administration* (Washington, United States Department
of State, May 1984), pp.77-81.

[31] The best account of Gorbachev's economic reforms remains Anders Aslund, *Gorbachev's Struggle for Economic Reform* (London, Pinter, 1989).

[32] Quote from Philip Hanson, 'The Soviet Twelfth Five-Year Plan', *The Soviet Economy: A New Course?* (Brussels, NATO, 1-3 April 1987), p.10.

especially as he was providing Soviet Studies with the biggest boost it had received in over twenty years? Herein perhaps was the key to understanding the 'Gorbymania' which swept Soviet Studies for a short while. For the first time in nearly a generation, the world as a whole was actually interested in the Soviet Union. And who was on hand to provide instant, in-depth analysis about the latest developmemts in the Kremlin? None other the long-ignored experts from the sovietological profession. Many an academic career was given a sudden shot-in-the-arm by Mikhail Gorbachev!

That the vast majority of those in Soviet Studies were supportive of Gorbachev would be something of an understatement. Basically, until the end of 1989 at least, he assumed an almost heroic status in the eyes of most western experts. So much so that those who were less than enthusiastic about Gorbachev were either regarded as unreconstructed reactionaries who only wanted to return to the good old days of the Cold War, or ultra-left fanatics who were irrelevant anyway. Certainly for a period it was not *de rigeur* to be negative about the man or his policies.

Other than boosting the sales of textbooks on the USSR, this temporary cult of Gorbachev had a number of consequences for Soviet Studies. One was to make some well-known liberal scholars virtual cheerleaders for *perestroika* abroad. Another was to create the illusion that the end of the Cold War would deliver us all into a Kantian era of perpetual peace. But the most important, in my view, was to obscure from view what was actually taking place in the USSR. The common wisdom was that Gorbachev was recasting Soviet policies, which in the political and international spheres he was. At a deeper level however, the combination of changes taking place under his leadership was not merely changing the USSR, but accelerating its more rapid decline and fragmentation. Yet few seemed to appreciate the fact; certainly not many talked about it; and when they did, finally, it was too late. Momentarily buoyed up by the new man in the Kremlin, most seemed to feel – until it became clear in 1990 that the system was imploding – that Gorbachev was not only breathing new life into Soviet Studies, but into the Soviet Union as well. Consequently, they ignored or failed to see what was really occurring. That behind the facade of superpower summits and the new *entente cordiale* between East and West, the country, quite literally, was falling apart. It took the coup of August 1991 for many to find out just how far the process had gone.

Socialists and Stalinism

It would be easy to leave the discussion at this juncture; to point the finger (so-to-speak) only at those within the academy. However, this would be both intellectually one-sided and politically misleading. The fact remains that the so-called 'Russian question' has been as much a subject of controversy amongst socialists as it has been amongst those who are not socialist. It is also a fact that those on the left who have been preoccupied with the Soviet Union – and that means nearly all of them – seemed no more capable of understanding the dynamics of the system as their more mainstream colleagues. Consequently, they were as surprised as nearly everybody else when the country collapsed in the late eighties. The interesting question is why?.[33]

One reason, clearly, is that many on the left either identified with, were sympathetic to, or had residual hopes in the Soviet project. Accordingly they believed (or hoped) that the USSR would survive; prosper even. Their own understanding of the system led them to conclude it must. After all, the Soviet Union in their opinion still retained its socialist character. It therefore remained economically and socially superior to western capitalism. Naturally, it had its problems. But these had to be set against the USSR's many past achiements and its continuing deep reservoir of support amongst the Soviet people. Moreover, under Gorbachev's leadership there was every reason to believe its problems could be resolved; either through a process of economic adaptation or political reform, or a combination of the two. Anyway, the USSR had confronted hard times before and won through. It would do so again. Soviet socialism had been created against the odds in the thirties and forties. There was no reason to assume it could not be 'remade' in the eighties and nineties.[34]

Trotskyists, not surprisingly, took a somewhat more critical approach to the problem. The USSR, they accepted, was not a form of socialism, but rather a degenerated workers' state which could only be regenerated after the workers themselves regained political power. But even the most orthodox of Trotskyists did not believe the system would disintegrate. How could it? For according to their own theory, the USSR remained a planned economy with a superior mode of production to that found in the West. Thus in spite of its deformed nature, it would continue to function – albeit not very well as Ernest Mandel admitted.[35].

However, the idea that the USSR would continue was even upheld by those socialists who had no illusions in the system at all; namely the supporters of the politically virtuous but theoretically idiosyncratic view that the system was a species of state capitalism. The adherents to this particular school of thought travelled a different theoretical route to their rivals on the left. Yet in the end, they arrived at the same destination. The reason they did so was implicit in their original argument; for if, as they maintained, the Soviet Union was another form of capitalism, then it followed that it was no more – or less – likely to grind to a halt than the economies of the West. And as those economies were not on the verge of break down, it seemed reasonable to conclude that the Soviet system would not break down either. Indeed, one exponent of the state capitalist theory went to

---

[33] One of the few marxists (apart from Ticktin) who assumed the USSR tended towards absolute stagnation was Pavel Campeneau in his *The Syncretic Society* (New York, M.E.Sharpe, 1980). This was published under a pseudonym, 'Felipe Garcia Casals'.

[34] This was certainly the message conveyed in Jon Bloomfield (ed), *The Soviet Revolution: Perestroika and the Remaking of Socialism* (London, Lawrence and Wishart, 1989).

[35] For an orthodox Trotskyist assessment of the USSR under Gorbachev, see Ernest Mandel, *Beyond Perestroika: The Future of Gorbachev's USSR* (London, Verso, 1989). For a less orthodox Trotskyist perspective on the Soviet Union in the late eighties, see Tariq Ali, *Revolution From Above – Where is the Soviet Union Going?* (London, Hutchinson, 1988). One of the two people Tariq Ali dedicated his book to (the other being Boris Kagarlitsky) was Boris Yeltsin!

some length in 1987 to remonstrate with those who conjectured about Soviet collapse. The Soviet economy was extraordinarily wasteful he agreed. On the other hand, the level of waste – and by implication the degree of contradiction in the system – was no greater than existed in the West. It was all a question of degree, not fundamental difference.[36]

Crying Wolf – and beyond

Let us conclude this survey with a brief story about a wolf called 'Soviet collapse'. Since 1917 the end of the USSR has been proclaimed on several occasions: immediately after the revolution itself, under NEP, during the war, and finally in the high years of the Cold War by 'liberationists' on the American right. Even Trotsky at one stage suggested the USSR would not survive alone. But the pessimists were proved wrong. The revolution did survive. NEP did not lead to the restoration of capitalism. Hitler was defeated. And the USSR successfully recovered from the war. There was ample reason therefore to be sceptical of claims that the USSR was on its last legs. 'Wolf' had been cried before; many times in fact. But there had been no beast at the door then. So why assume it was there now in the eighties?

It is important to make this point, not by way of a defence of Soviet Studies, but to understand the context within which those in the discipline operated and continued to operate until the last years of Soviet power. Basically, the old hands had heard the bad news before. It had always turned out to be wrong. So why conclude it was not wrong again? Moreover by training and inclination, sovietologists (like all reasonable academics) were sceptics. As such, they had to be able to distinguish between fantasy and fact. And the fact of the matter was that it was just too fantastic to suppose that the USSR – with its vast apparatus of controls, huge arsenal of weapons, extensive welfare system, and economy that had transformed the country into an industrial giant – could simply fall apart. It might go to war with China; impose or reimpose its brutal control over one or more of the East European countries; even kill thousands of its own citizens. But collapse? That was just out of the question.

But why was it out of the question? Why did it have to survive? And why did those working in Soviet Studies think that it would? I have not sought to answer the first two questions. That would require another paper. What I have tried to do however is address the last issue; and to explain in as impersonal and I hope, fair-minded a way as possible, why sovietologists thought the USSR would endure in one form or another. As I have shown, they didn't assume this because they were foolish or ill-informed. Rather, it was because the intellectual tools at their disposal did not, perhaps could not incline them to the conclusion that the USSR had a finite life-span. But if nothing else, the fate of Soviet Studies should serve as a warning to us all: that we ignore the unlikely, the impossible, the absurd even at our peril. Yet we should not be too harsh. After all, the failure to foresee what

---

[36] See Mike Haynes, 'Understanding the Soviet Crisis', *International Socialism*, Number 34, pp.4-5.

later seemed inevitable has made fools of even wiser men and women than those who dissected the USSR before its unexpected disintegration in the last decade of the twentieth century.

The End of the USSR
& the Collapse of Soviet Studies

Hillel H.Ticktin
University of Glasgow

'The State of Soviet Studies in the Post-War Period
A View from the Left'

Introduction

Soviet Studies over the post war period has mirrored the course of the cold war but differently in different countries and at different times. This article is concerned with the different theoretical frameworks used to understand the USSR. The schools of thought concerned largely pertain to Britain and the United States.

It is possible to divide the different schools into 5 categories.

At one end of the spectrum have been those who have attempted to find ways of supporting Stalinism. In the first instance there were the Stalinist cold war veterans such as Andrew Rothstein who was at the head of the School of Slavonic and East European Studies, the University of London, in the immediate post-war period until his dismissal.[1] Other members of the Communist Party such as Maurice Dobb, of Cambridge University, who wrote an economic history of the USSR and various economic essays[2], and Jack Miller, the founder of *Soviet Studies*, produced more nuanced pro-soviet articles.[3] Jack Miller left the communist party in the early fifties and shifted his political stance to a more orthodox Soviet Studies position.[4] The early issues of Soviet Studies tended to be readable descriptions of the USSR, whose political orientation were nonetheless clear.[5] Later re-

---

[1] Andrew Rothstein, *Wreckers on Trial: A Record of the Industrial Party trial held in Moscow Nov-Dec 1930*, Modern Books, London 1931. Andrew Rothstein, *Soviet Foreign Policy during the Patriotic War: documents and materials* (2 volumes), Hutchison, London, 1946.

[2] See particularly: Maurice Dobb *Soviet Economic Development since 1917*, Routledge & Kegan Paul, London 1948, revised 1966.

[3] See Jack Miller in *Soviet Studies*, Volume 1, Number 1, June 1949, for an instance. Jack & Molly Miller, *Zhdanov's speech to the philosophers: an essay in interpretation*. The issue is discussed below in footnote 5.

[4] Jack Miller, *Life in Russia Today*, Batsford/Putnam, London/New York, 1969.

[5] The first issue (*Soviet Studies*, Volume 1, Number 1, June 1949, Basil Blackwell, Oxford) declared in its editorial that it would neither attack nor defend the USSR (p.2). The contributors were all well known for their past or present association with the Communist Party, with the exception of E.H.Carr. They were Rudolf Schlesinger, Jack and Molly Miller, and Maurice Dobb. The essay by E.H.Carr follows the line of the editorial on Soviet Foreign Policy and thereby produces a continuity between Lenin and Stalin as well as completely avoiding the real influence of the internal instability and upheavals of the USSR in the thirties. Four years later, the editorial is written by E.H.Carr on the death of Stalin. While it is a nuanced obituary, it is undoubtedly pro-Stalin. He concludes that 'it is perhaps in the role of Peter that history will best remember him. Paradoxically, posterity may yet learn to speak of Stalin as the great westernizer', p.7, *Soviet Studies*, July 1993.

incarnations of this tendency have been those who have tried to downplay the role of Stalin and the numbers involved in the purges.[6]

There are, secondly, the views of those associated with the interests of capitalism, who saw the USSR as an aberration, because anything non-capitalist was an aberration. They considered the various non-capitalist regimes as dictatorial non-market societies which were necessarily both oppressive and unstable. The advantages of this viewpoint were that they could see these regimes and particularly the USSR as in a process of change. They were, as a result, not caught out when the USSR did indeed begin to disintegrate. On the other hand, none of these scholars or writers understood the processes of change in these societies. At any rate if they did understand them, they never wrote or spoke about them. It was just taken for granted that a non-market society could not work. The CIA, Richard Pipes and others of the Reagan-Bush advisory team fall into this category.[7] In Britain, few subscribed to this doctrine.

In the third category there were those who saw the USSR as oppressive and non-market oriented but doomed to last for a long time. Of course, there is a long history to this attitude. It is implicit in Orwell and was explicitly enunciated by Solzhenitsyn.[8] It was the dominant school of Soviet Studies for many years. Much of the descriptive work on the USSR fell into this category, from the Harvard Project onwards. The work on *totalitarianism* by Carl Friederich & Z.Brzezinski falls into this category.[9] Indeed the whole post-war totalitarian school is in this grouping. Its strength was its ability to list features of the regime and describe a chilling reality which others hesitated to approach. Its enormous weakness was in its inability to describe the forces at work in the society. It remained at a superficial level of simply describing the existence of a controlling party with its tentacles infiltrating the whole society. The concept of totalitarianism is briefly discussed below. There is, in contrast with the first school, no dynamics at all. The political thought of these writers and scholars varied from liberal to social democratic, from supporters of capitalism to those who wanted a modern social-democratic regime.

The fourth grouping may be called those who wished to be fair to both sides. They emerged to prominence in the immediate post first cold war pe-

---

[6] See, for instance, J.Arch Getty, *Origins of the Great Purges: The Soviet Communist Party Reconsidered, 1933-1938*, Cambridge University Press, New York, 1985.

[7] This viewpoint is clearly expressed in the two essays by Richard Pipes, '1917 and the Revisionists' and Martin Malia, 'A Fatal Logic' in the *National Interest*, Number 31, Spring 1993, pp.68-79 & 80-90. The essays often point correctly to the mistakes and myths of the pro-Soviet or semi-Stalinoid writers whom they criticise but there is either a clear statement or an underlying assumption that an alternative to capitalism is utopian or necessarily totalitarian.

[8] 'If today they are crunching our bones, it is a certain pledge that tomorrow they will be crunching yours.' A.Solzhenitsyn, Letter of 27 May 1974, to Aftenposten, in *Mir i Nasilie, Possev*, Frankfurt 1974, p.48, quoted in John Dunlop, 'Solzhenitsyn in Exile', *Survey*, Volume 21, Number 3, Summer 1975, p.146. John Dunlop summarises his view with words 'Unceasing and needless concessions to the communists threaten the entire world with a totalitarian yoke', *Ibid*, p.153.

[9] Friedrich, Carl & Brzezinski, Zbigniew, *Totalitarian Dictatorship and Autocracy*, Praeger, London, New York, 1969.

riod, that is, during the Khrushchev period. Such writers as Alec Nove[10], and much later Stephen Cohen[11] came to typify this approach. They provided a much more detailed statistical and economic analysis of what was happening in the USSR. Joseph Berliner[12] gave a more realistic account of the real functional of the Soviet factory, Nove and Bergson[13] of the performance of the economic system. Economists developed a whole discipline of comparative economic systems, which often attempted to provide an account of advantages and disadvantages in the system. Textbooks on Soviet economics and books of readings were written as simple descriptions of a system in operation. While most writers were critical of the USSR, they bent over backwards to show that there were certain achievements or advantages to the system, even if capitalism might have done it better. The work of Bornstein & Fusfeld[14] and others fell into this category of post cold war descriptive work. Mary McAuley's book on Soviet politics was similar.[15] At one end of the political spectrum of this group lay the scholars who less unfavourable to aspects of the USSR. A number of scholars at Birmingham University, United Kingdom, were well known for this attitude.[16] Rather than showing the advantages of the USSR, they concentrated on building up a detailed nuts and bolts picture of the USSR, which tended to produce a picture which was more rather than less favourable to the system. Others concentrated on looking at the Soviet system in a more or less functionalist way, such that they could understand the static workings of the system. They were not necessarily at all favourable to the system but simply wanted to discover how it worked. The interest group approach was such a view. Professor Robert V.Daniels in a reply to Vladimir Shlapentokh has supported this method arguing that it came close to understanding the breakdown of the system.[17] He takes issue with the argument of many writers in the *National Interest*, Spring, 1993. This debate is discussed below.

The final category consists of those who took a strong anti-Stalinist viewpoint and looked at the USSR as a system which could never work. This viewpoint has been particularly associated with the journal *Critique*, Don Filtzer, Mick Cox, Dave Law, G.A.E.Smith, Bob Arnot and the present

---

[10] Alec Nove, *The Soviet Economy: An Introduction*, Allen & Unwin, 1962, and revised a number of times since. Alec Nove, *Was Stalin Really Necessary? Some Problems of Political Economy*, Allen & Unwin, 1964.

[11] Stephen F.Cohen, *Rethinking the Soviet Experience, Politics and history since 1917*, New York, Oxford University Press, 1984.

[12] Joseph Berliner, *Factory and Manager in the USSR*, Cambridge, Mass, 1957.

[13] Abram Bergson, *The Economics of Soviet Planning*, 1964.

[14] Morris Bornstein & Daniel.R.Fusfeld (eds), *The Soviet Economy: A book of Readings*, R.D.Irwin, Homewood, Illinois, 1962 and many revised editions.

[15] Mary McAuley, *Politics and the Soviet Union*, Penguin, London, 1977.

[16] R.W.Davies, who was director of the Birmingham University Centre for Russian and East European Studies, has written a considerable number of works on Soviet economic history beginning with *The Development of the Soviet Budgetary System*, Cambridge University Press, 1958. A classic statement from this school of thought comes from an article on 'Soviet Technological Performance' by Ron Amman, where he states clearly 'that we do not yet know why Soviet technology is on the whole backward', *Survey*, Volume 23, Number 2, Spring 1977-78, p.71. Clearly if the method is empiricist then it is difficult to find reasons. The adoption of empiricism is itself a statement.

[17] Robert V. Daniels, 'Letter under RSVP', in *Newsnet: The Newsletter of the AAASS*, p.13.

author among others are some of the names of authors in this school.[18] Although the *Critique* school became known for its work, it always existed as the outside left pole within the Soviet Studies profession. There were and are other scholars who were critical of Stalinism but they seldom provided a theoretical basis for the instability of the USSR. Antonio Carlo discussed the crisis in Eastern Europe and evolved a law of increasing waste but it was not very clear to what that was supposed to lead.[19]

The Sources of the Different Schools

In the United States and the United Kingdom the military and secret services played a crucial role in shaping viewpoints. It has to be said that it was the secret services of both sides. Clearly Maurice Dobb and Andrew Rothstein were not innocent of connections with institutions in the USSR. Indeed Dobb has been clearly linked through the Philby case. Nor does one have to assume that these were the only cases. On the other hand, the CIA and the US military has openly and covertly financed scholars to conduct research on the USSR. When the Harvard Project could openly pay tribute to the US Air force, it was clear that the US state had ensured that it would get what it was paying for.[20] This is not to denigrate the study itself except in so far as it had certain ideological limits. The US government financed studies of the USSR have often been the best available. Much of the research saw the light of day in the regular reports of the US Congress Joint Economic Committee.

Apart from Dobb and Rothstein there were other members and unreformed ex-members of the Communist Party who continued to exert influence in different ways. Whereas such Stalinists could be influential in academia in the United Kingdom that was less true of the United States. Nonetheless, the Communist Party and its various front organisations played an important role in providing a picture of the USSR which was far from accurate. Given the alienation of many intellectuals, as well as the many underprivileged, from the US establishment, many fell for the argument that the enemy's enemy is our friend. A notable casualty in this respect was Paul Robeson.

In contrast, the effect of Trotsky's writings and influence seemed to be considerably broader and more osmotic. Many who wrote on the USSR in other disciplines had developed their interest in large part because of their prior commitment to Trotskyist organisations. Alvin Gouldner, Seymour Martin Lipset and many others belonged or were close to US Trotskyist groups in their early life. James Burnham had an enormous effect with

---

[18] Hillel Ticktin, *The Origins of the Crisis in the USSR: the political economy of a disintegrating system*, Myron Sharpe, New York, 1992. Bob Arnot, *Controlling Soviet Labour*, Macmillan Press, London 1988. Michael Cox, 'The Cold War as a System', *Critique*, 17, 1986. The Journal *Critique* has been the location of much of the work involved.

[19] Carlo, A, 'The Crisis of Bureaucratic Collectivism, *Telos*, 43, Spring 1980.

[20] See the Acknowledgements to Raymond A Bauer, Alex Inkeles & Clyde Kluckhorn, *How the Soviet System Works*, Vintage, New York, 1956. Tribute is paid to the US Air Force and its personnel.

his book, it The Managerial Revolution[21], which derived directly from his intellectual faction fighting within the US SWP. Although Burnham ceased to be on the left, his thought clearly emerged from its Trotskyist embryo. George Orwell was another thinker who was unmistakably influenced by Trotsky, although he was never a Trotskyist.[22] The very word Totalitarian was employed by the left, notably Hilferding, Victor Serge and Leon Trotsky, long before it became fashionable, after the war.[23]

The only way that the pro-Stalinist writers and scholars could deal with the enormous intellectual influence of Trotsky was to denigrate all criticism of the USSR as inspired by the CIA. The 'two camps' line attempted to force intellectuals who supported neither the right in the United States nor Stalin and his successors to come to heel. It was largely successful until the late sixties in doing so. On the one side, words like 'totalitarian' and 'atomisation' were scoffed at as Cold War language. Stress was placed on whatever appeared successful in Western eyes, from so-called planning and growth rates to so- called technological achievements like Sputnik. On the other side, those who took a critical position on the USSR were lauded and given research contracts provided that they were not themselves Marxist. It was not the critical position of the marxists towards the USSR, that debarred them from jobs but their critical attitude to American or British society. Whereas the Communist Party functioned to place its members in jobs within academia, independent leftists were frozen out unless they moved into esoteric fields or ones which no longer had any social scientific relevance. Trotsky's secretary, Jean van Heijenoort, for instance, became a mathematical logician and so found a way of existing through the worst anti-left period.

While there were many individuals who insisted on the non-socialist nature of the USSR, few were able to resist the temptation to join the mainstream. While the Communist Party had been largely discredited particularly after 1956, many other intellectuals clung to the view that however bad it was, the USSR remained in some sense socialist. Such were Baran and Sweezy, who exerted an enormous influence on the US and British left over the years. Sweezy shifted over towards Maoism during the sixties and gradually became more and more critical of the USSR to the point where he finally declared that a new class had come to power.[24] Nonetheless, those who found their hopes fulfilled in this or that country, whether Cuba,

---

[21] James Burnham, *The Managerial Revolution*, Penguin, 1962.

[22] Orwell was most obviously influenced by Trotsky in three works: *Animal Farm*, *Homage to Catalonia* and *1984*. Whether he ever understood Trotsky is not clear but that he saw him as the authentic hero of the revolution is clear. Victor Serge, who was a left oppositionist to the end of his life, established a friendship with him.

[23] It is interesting to note that Leonard Shapiro fails to mention Trotsky and Hilferding as precursors of the Totalitarian School in his essay 'Totalitarianism in the doghouse', *Political Opposition in One Party States*, pp.268-269. He and others had written many articles and books on the subject but they still failed to discuss the left wing background to the term.

[24] See the 'Review of the Month: The Split in the Socialist World', *Monthly Review*, Volume 15, Number 1, May 1963, where the editors (Paul Sweezy and Leo Huberman) declare that 'The Chinese as its [Marxism-Leninism's] most faithful and powerful champions seem certain to become the spiritual leaders of all genuine revolutionary movements in the world.'

China, Nicaragua or Albania always seemed to regard the USSR as a mother socialist country which had unfortunately deviated. Even their fiercest denunciations implied a degree of support. After all it was *Monthly Review* which supported the building of the Berlin wall.[25]

Apart from intelligence organisations, there are also governmental institutions, such as the Foreign Office in the United Kingdom and State Department in the United States which have their own research organisations. That prominent Sovietologists such as Alec Nove, Leonard Shapiro and Hugh Seton-Watson gave advice when required is not in doubt. Alec Nove served in the Moscow Embassy in 1956. In the United States Brzezinski and Pipes practised what they preached in the Carter and Reagan administrations respectively. Private think tank, such as the Rand corporation, associated with UCLA, and various others, such as the Brookings Institute, expressed variations on the private enterprise theme. It is no accident that Ed Hewitt should have acted as an adviser to Yeltsin on privatisation. The School of Soviet and East European Studies of the University of London was once associated with the Foreign Office in that its director, Bolsover, was close to that institution.

Concepts

The fundamental issues around which discussion has proceeded were those of the surplus product, totalitarianism/atomisation, class, the purges, Stalinism itself, and the whole future of private enterprise, élite, intelligentsia, system.

Much of Soviet Studies has been permeated by the view that private enterprise and the market are eternal and 'normal'.[26]

Such is now the prevailing view among the intelligentsia in the USSR. Market clearing prices were therefore seen as the touchstone of a viable economy. The USSR was regarded as having a 'repressed inflation'. The effect of such verbiage and understanding was to damage any real comprehension irretrievably. The fact was that the USSR did not have money as understood either in a Marxist or non-Marxist sense. As a consequence prices, markets and inflation were terms inapplicable to the USSR. Naturally economists who had no other training could use no other concepts

---

[25] See 'Review of the Month: The Continuing Crisis', *Monthly Review*, Volume 13, Number 5, September 1961, where the editors justify Khrushchev's policy and support East Germany. In the next issue in the editorial Leo Huberman declared that 'On every major point of issue between the United States and the USSR, the Soviet Union has been right', *Monthly Review*, Volume 13, Number 6, p.242. The problem was that the left tended to require a homeland and therefore defend it.

[26] It is not, of course, difficult to show that most modern economists see the market in this light but the simplest proof consists in the terminology employed to understand the Soviet Union. The term suppressed inflation was extensively used, implying that the system actually had a money system which was politically controlled. Those not so biased could simply argue that money did not exist and hence there was no question of inflation unless you tried to introduce money. The actual system was based on a form of economic control. Hence Soviet and Russian economists were at pains to point out that money did not exist but had to be brought into being. The Western economists did not even notice that this undermined their own description of the USSR.

but it meant that they had no perception of the direction the USSR was heading. Their discussion was really little more than a moral one castigating the USSR for not applying 'bourgeois' or market economic concepts. Their discussion of economic events relied heavily on economic quantities, which were always dubious but became even more dubious when translated into orthodox thought. How does one discuss the standard of living of the population except in direct qualitative and quantitative terms for example, Flats are small and of poor quality, washing machines are not automatic, of poor quality, few people have cars but public transport is widely available even if stressful etc.

The term totalitarianism came to be extensively used, attacked and now again employed in Soviet Studies. In fact there were different definitions for the term. Although it may have arisen as a term from Italian and Mussolini, it was in fact the left which gave it a clear scientific meaning. As already mentioned, Hilferding, Trotsky and Victor Serge used it between the wars. Their understanding, however, was very different from the earlier and later incarnations. Effectively they saw it as a means of preventing the working class taking power. In contrast Shapiro argued that 'It is this mass democratic character of totalitarianism which distinguishes this form of rule from anything that has gone before'. The meaning of mass democratic character is made clear in the preceding sentences:

> 'the mass appeal of Bolshevism delves much deeper into the dark recesses of the mob mind. It draws response from the fear of freedom, the envy, the anti-intellectualism, the chauvinism – in short all the characteristic ambience of the mass man ... with his own mass morality, his crude egalitarian and levelling aspirations and his herd paranoia.'[27]

The contrast with Trotsky and the earlier left could not be greater. What it illustrates very clearly is the political animus lying behind a major viewpoint in Soviet studies. Not only did the practitioners of Soviet studies see capitalism as eternal but they were highly suspicious of the majority of the population. They somehow saw the masses as capable of extra-ordinary feats of evil through their demand for democracy, which could only be fulfilled by these evil Fascist and Stalinist parties. The truly undemocratic nature of totalitarian theory, therefore, appealed to the Soviet intelligentsia, with its hatred of the Soviet working class and to governments intent on preventing an extension of democracy. The paradox is that totalitarian theory probably helped prolong Stalinism by supporting the underlying tenet of Stalinism itself, which was the maintenance of rule by an élite in the name of enlightened few against the dark masses. The concept of the dark masses is once again a concept underpinning rule in Russia but this time it is in the name of the market and Boris Yeltsin.

The problem with the post-war totalitarian school, in short, was not their excoriation of Stalinism but their failure to understand it. Totalitarianism was little more than a moral term, expressing support for the forms of rule

---

[27] Leonard Shapiro, 'Totalitarianism in the doghouse', in Leonard Shapiro (ed), *Political Opposition in One Party States*, Macmillan, 1972, p.276.

prevalent in developed capitalist countries. It was the natural counterpart of the view that the market was eternal in that it regarded so-called Western democracy as the best possible and most natural political form. It was a static concept which entirely failed to understand the real instability of these regimes and consequently could not explain the real need for the atomisation of the population. It had no political economy and so provided no explanation at all for the system either lasting or disintegrating.

Social Groups In Soviet Society And The Orthodox Failure

The worst aspect of the failure of the economists, sociologists and political scientists was their inability to describe the social groups in Soviet society. Since they have been unable to do so in Western society that is not at all surprising. Western economists do not discuss class or social group at all, while sociologists tear such discussions from their economic context. Political scientists avoid discussing a ruling group or class. Yet when it comes to the USSR the absence of a political economy which embraces concepts of a ruling group, and other social groups makes all discussion unreal. For that reason, Western scholars who otherwise shunned words like 'ruling group' or 'ruling class' or 'governing (ruling) élite' for their own societies suddenly discovered them to apply to the USSR.[28] Schapiro discovered a working class.[29] Yet they became lifeless terms when used by scholars who had no theoretical context. Mervyn Matthews used terms like privilege and poverty and largely confined his understanding of the ruling group to a tiny number of people in the Communist Party hierarchy, thereby making the internal battles inside the Party unintelligible.[30]

the élite

While Soviet society was fundamentally atomised, the ruling group could not have lasted if it only consisted of the very top political functionaries. The heads of the enterprises, the economic planners, a large part of the KGB etc. were all part of this élite. It runs into at least 5 million people. Soviet statistics talked of 9 million 'leaders'.[31] This would make some from 3 to 7 per cent of the population in the ruling group. Yet many orthodox Western scholars could not admit that the Soviet élite consisted of such people because that would imply a similar analysis of their own societies. It would also imply that the USSR was a system of its own kind, though not one to be approved of. Nor would it be one which would necessarily last over

[28] See, for instance, the usage of 'governing élite' in S.M.Lipset & Richard B Dobson., 'Social Stratification and Sociology in the Soviet Union', *Survey*, Volume 19, Number 3, Summer 1973, p.118, where the authors discuss Trotsky. Classical sociological élite theory is not Marxist but it can be used in a Marxist context as in this case.

[29] See Leonard Shapiro, 'The End of an Illusion', in Leonard Shapiro & Joseph Godson (eds), *The Soviet Worker: Illusions and Realities*, Macmillan, 1981, 1982, pp.1-14.

[30] Mervyn Matthews: 'Top incomes in the USSR, Towards a definition of the Soviet élite', *Survey*, Volume 21, Number 3, Summer 1975, p.13.

[31] *Narodnoe Khoziaistvo za 70 Let*, Moscow, 1987 p.421.

time. As the *nomenclatura* included all these people, there was an uneasy compromise between descriptions of élite occupations, often produced by emigrés, and the orthodox scholars. It was an internal conflict which has never been resolved.

Any discussion of the Soviet élite has been fraught with problems. In the first place, there has been little or no discussion in the Soviet literature so that any description had to be based on oral evidence, emigré literature, and deduction from Soviet articles, statistics and books. In the second place, such a discussion required a clear theory as to their place in Soviet society, otherwise the result would be a woolly collection of data. Of course a simple statement that the USSR was ruled by a group of gangsters who ran the Communist Party would make description of the élite very easy. Although the word 'gangster' was not used in print, even if it was frequently employed in conversation, it accurately describes the work of scholars who discussed the Soviet élite. They refused to see the USSR as an alternative system and hence had to argue that the society had been hi-jacked by a few evil ideologically blinkered men. While there can be no question of the evil of Stalinism, the refusal to admit that it was a system actually underestimated the depth of human misery within the USSR and the extent to which Stalinism had thrown the whole world backwards towards a barbaric age.

The static nature of the analysis meant that the drives forcing the élite towards the dissolution of the old order were missed. Because the old élite was often regarded as evil people or ideologically motivated, the real interests of the élite were ignored. Interest group researchers were successful in describing different sub-groups within the élite. They were unable to describe the forces integrating and fragmenting the élite. It was inherently obvious that members of that élite would prefer to own property rather than remain in the élite on an uncertain bureaucratic basis. This view was never expressed because it would have implied that the ruling groups in East and West were fundamentally similar in that they both stood apart and above the majority of the population. Hence the majority of Soviet studies professionals never dreamed that the élite would actively move to the market. It was, however, blindingly obvious all throughout.

the intelligentsia

It took a long time for the Western literature actually to use the term *intelligentsia*. It was used in the Soviet Union to designate those with higher education of whatever kind. Again it created an ideological problem for those who saw themselves as defending capitalism. An intellectual was someone who dealt with ideas. Hence the intelligentsia as a category of people who received money or goods in return for dealing with ideas did not seem to fit into any hierarchical structure. 'Middle class' was the usual term for a social group to which they belonged. It made little sense in the former Soviet Union because the categories used were functional occupational groups as opposed to nebulous social groups divided according to income, and power. Most university professionals saw themselves mirrored in their Eastern counterparts and refused to see them as a social group playing a particular role. *Critique* early on criticised the Soviet intelligentsia for its élitism.[32]

Solzhenitsyn had berated the intelligentsia[33] but few took that seriously. The special role of the intelligentsia in supporting the élite against the working class was ignored. That many in the intelligentsia were racist, anti-Semitic and élitist was never described. The fact that they wanted to change the system was regarded as a positive feature of the society, but it was attributed to only a few dissidents.

Today it is not difficult to find members of the Russian intelligentsia who talk of the betrayal of the intelligentsia. Clearly it is not the same betrayal as that of which Solzhenitsyn spoke but it is related to it. The intelligentsia acted only in its immediate self interest said Solzhenitsyn and they used their families as an excuse. Today it is no different. The curious example of so-called intellectuals who regard the vast majority of the population as the dark masses, who are to be feared and if possible ignored naturally gives fuel to those who want to maintain a Pinochet style regime. It is amazing, however, that so few Western intellectuals have been prepared to attack and condemn the Soviet and post Soviet intelligentsia for these attitudes which in fact go hand in hand with anti-semitism. The rise of Zhironovsky is, in this respect, in no way surprising.

The reason why so few orthodox scholars have taken up the anti-semitism, élitism and chauvinism of the intelligentsia also lies in the fact that like Stupor quoted above they are themselves élitist.

The Soviet intelligentsia aspired to enter the élite but under market conditions if possible. The fact is that they have lost most through the shift to the market. The consequence of the transition period to this layer is still uncharted but orthodox Soviet studies does not even understand the problem.

the working class

Orthodox economics preferred to assume that there were no classes and non-Marxist sociologists tended to argue that the working class had vanished. It was, therefore, difficult to talk of the role and importance of the working class. As a result, it was only the evidently increasing power and activity of the workers which compelled a re-assessment. There were even those who found a positive role for the unions. There remains even now, however, a clear gap between the way in which the Russian élite describes its fear of the workers and the descriptions in the West. The official unions which now call themselves independent are more or less written off while the new unions, which often also call themselves independent, are regarded as independent, even though they more or less support the present Yeltsin regime. Sotsprof has become a more or less open propagandist for Yeltsin. A number of observers have reached the rather obvious conclusion that there are no independent unions. The real question is why there are no genuine

---

[32] See Cox, M, 'The Politics of the Dissenting Intellectual', *Critique*, 5; Ticktin, H.H, 'The Political Economy of the Soviet Intellectual', *Critique*, 2.

[33] See A. Solzhenitsyn, 'The Smatterers', in A.Solzhenitsyn (ed), *Under the Rubble*, Fontana, London, 1975, p.229ff.

unions and why the workers have not taken more militant action. The answer which often comes from Russia that the Russian soul is long suffering is unbelievable.

The reason for this failure is not far to seek. Most Sovietologists have never seen similar studies of their own societies. Hence they are unlikely to do it for the former Soviet Union.

On the one hand, there are those on the left, who belong to a Soviet studies nether world, who are looking for working class activity[34], while on the other there are the establishment liberals and others who find the workers only when mass action is visible. Both sides are limited. If there is a potential working class then its activities must exist in both *micro* and *macro* forms. In other words, its influence is crucial at all times but it requires theorisation in order to understand it. The social system itself is necessarily threatened by the potential of working class activity and hence all modern politics must be directed at minimising such action.

System & The Importance of Theory

The use of the word 'system', however, implies more than just a functioning social and economic order. A simple statement of that kind is of itself important but it must be placed in an historical context, or else it loses its meaning. To simply state that the USSR functioned in its own way does not explain how long it might do so. It does not tell us whether it was doing so with ease or difficulty, whether the population was contented or oppositional, subjectively and objectively, or whether it was more efficient or less efficient than capitalism or socialism.

These questions are not answered with opinion polls. Today there are enough opinion polls in Moscow to run through a supercomputer for coherence. In essence they tell us little that we did not know. Yeltsin has voting support but his policies are not backed by the population. It is clear that if policies are put forward against the interests of the majority of the population, a considerable number of the population will oppose those policies. If politicians claim that their policies require pain before they work, they may buy time, while no alternative presents itself. The nature of consciousness in the former USSR is a highly complex entity, and it requires to be unpacked by pointing to its determinants.

Such a theoretical discussion was seldom attempted in the orthodox journals. Alec Nove in 1975 did attempt a summary of views of the USSR, which was the first time that those theoretical statements had found their way into the orthodox journal, *Soviet Studies*.[35] The problem, however, was that Nove's own views were wholly static and non-theoretical. He saw the USSR in terms of an army hierarchy. While there are definite analogies, that does not explain the movement, changes or disintegration of the USSR,

---

[34] See for instance David Mandel, *Perestroika and the Soviet People*, Black Rose Books, Montreal, 1991.

[35] Alec Nove, 'Is there a ruling class in the USSR?, *Soviet Studies*, Volume 27, October 1975, pp.615-638. He argues that 'Indeed one could, without too much exaggeration, fit Soviet society into a "universal civil and military service" model' (p.616).

all of which were really strangers to him and indeed to the theories that he summarised.

When Bergson and others did try to tackle questions of efficiency, it was done within orthodox economics, which is itself fundamentally static. A system might be judged by its success in raising the standard of living of the whole population, or by its ability to do so while ensuring that no-one was much better off than anyone else, or by its ability to ensure that every individual in the population was able to develop his or her talents to the full. By these standards the Soviet Union was a singular failure. These criteria go beyond the existing system while orthodox economics is fundamentally functionalist. It can easily come to the conclusion that a society which for instance systematically ejected workers from employment and then killed a proportion of the employed to avoid political unrest was efficient. Today, for instance, Malawi, which has one of the lowest per capita incomes in the world is adjudged a success by the IMF and the World Bank, because it is fiscally and monetarily prudent. By the standards of a non orthodox economist this is inhuman and only in the interests of those who rule. The fact is that the tools of the economist were useless to understand the processes at work in the former USSR.

The Failure Of The Traditional Left

The problem with the theories of the USSR which existed on the left was their inability to discuss the USSR in their own terms. Marxists start from Marx's statement that he was trying to discover the laws of motion of modern capitalism. What then were the laws of motion of the USSR? If we look at the views of Burnham, Shachtman[36], the so-called bureaucratic collectivists, little is found other than a description of a ruling group, which is called a class, and a statement on the exploitation of the workers and peasants.[37] The state-capitalist variant automatically incorporates the laws of motion of capitalism, but fails entirely to explain why the system does not correspond to those laws and why in the end the system disintegrated as a system less efficient than capitalism.[38] The workers' state theory has a number of variants of its own. They vary from a semi-Stalinist apologetic defence of the USSR to a descriptive critique. They too had no theory of internal development of the USSR, other than a projection of growth into the future. By and large they posited the continued successful if contradictory growth of the USSR, not its disintegration in ignominious failure.[39] These theories were not so much wrong, that is now a question of

---

[36] Max Shachtman, *The Bureaucratic Revolution: the rise of the Stalinist State*, The Donald Press, New York, 1962; James Burnham, *The Managerial Revolution*, Penguin, 1962.

[37] Antonio Carlo was a notable exception in this regard. See Carlo, A, 'The Socioeconomic nature of the USSR', *Telos*, 21 (Fall 1974); Carlo, A, 'The Crisis of Bureaucratic Collectivism', *Telos*, 43, Spring 1980.

[38] Cliff, T, *Russia: A Marxist Analysis*, London Pluto Press, 1974.

[39] See in particular the work of Ernest Mandel in the following: Mandel, Ernest, 'Ten Theses on the Social and Economic Laws Governing the society transitional between capitalism and socialism', *Critique*, 3; 'Once again on the Trotskyist definition of the

history, as not theories at all. They did not provide an understanding of the laws of the system, its dynamics and the changing internal social group or class relations. Instead they were really political statements, with an added statement on contradictions in the system. As a result, right wing theorists could take little from them other than their descriptive analysis. For that reason they were not taken seriously. Left wing analysts, on the other hand, either ruled themselves out of court by utilising these frameworks or else copied the rest of Soviet studies and engaged in the thankless task of piecing together a particular part of Soviet history.

The Failure of Empiricism in Soviet Studies

It is, therefore, entirely understandable that Soviet studies ended up in the hands of practitioners who were sometimes little better than translators from the Russian. Translation is an honourable profession and it was made more honourable by those who went further and put the parts of the jig-saw together to produce a picture.

In Soviet studies it was very easy to make a career out of a few unknown articles plus a few good conversations with a few friendly Soviet officials. Of course it was essential to have a very good knowledge of Russian and important to know the field itself. 'Discoveries' were normally made in this way. The 'Tolkach' was discovered. 'Success indicators' were 'invented' by Alec Nove. The operation of the Soviet enterprise was thereby illuminated for the West. There can be no question but that these 'discoveries' assisted the understanding of the Soviet Union.

On the other hand, it was much like the so-called discovery of Africa. The natives had no need of the 'discovery', which was simply a question of bringing one aspect of Western ignorance to an end. The operation of the enterprise may have been illuminated but it was not explained. Its low productivity, the rejection of new technique and indeed the very refusal to obey the intentions of the planners, inherent in the necessary list of 'success indicators', all had to be explained and theorised. Such a question was not even raised. In so far as the question was raised it was simply assumed that planning could not work or that totalitarianism made for inefficiency. How was not at all clear.

In other words, much of Soviet studies really consisted of translation of Soviet material put into a coherent shape. The assembling of the material to the point where it could be said to be coherent could only be done in the West, as the Soviet system itself prevented any systematic thought about the USSR itself. While such work was essential, it was neither theoretical nor even scholarly. It could not be the latter since the material for traditional scholarly research was absent.

The problem here was that 'traditional scholarly research' has always been questionable. The dotting of the i's and crossing of the t's approach, has its uses but it is of necessity highly detailed and inevitably loses the wood for the trees. Detailed factual knowledge is obviously essential for good

social nature of the Soviet Union', *Critique*, 12; *Beyond Perestroika*, New Left Books, London, 1988.

understanding and theorisation. Knowledge itself, however, presupposes a developed theory which points to its own *lacunae*. Otherwise there is the danger of the development of enormous detail about trivial subjects. Such has been the stuff of many scholarly works, which, by being safe, have ensured the academic author a sound, successful and rewarding career.

At the November 1993 conference of the American Association for the Advancement of Slavic Studies, Ms Gail Warshovsky Lapidus made the point, from the Chair, that Soviet/Slavic studies could not be accused of making false predictions since it was not the job of social science to predict. They were not soothsayers. This is a highly controversial assertion cast in an apparently acceptable form. While politicians have to be able to understand the likely course of future developments in order to govern, it appears that Slavic studies can give no advice because social science can say nothing about the future. It is clear that many sovietologists did assist politicians around the globe. One has, therefore, to assume that their academic work was useless to them. In fact, of course, the work of the many scholars in Soviet studies had a considerable influence on governments.

More importantly, the fundamental assertion is false. Social science must explain events. Explanation itself must involve causation. Some will see driving causes and others only efficient causation. In reality, Soviet studies was full of statements about lack of democracy, totalitarianism, inefficiency, crises etc. They are all terms which attempt to provide an explanation of aspects of the society. Explanation and so causation has clear consequences. Thus, if human nature is pliable then the Soviet Union might have lasted forever. If not, then the so-called totalitarianism could not last.

The problem for the practitioners was that the USSR did not remain the unchanging totalitarian society that they had come to love to hate. In so doing it rendered them redundant and showed that they had failed to understand the society itself. While their works had enough fail-safe mechanisms not to be declared wrong, they had become useless in providing an understanding of the society.[40]

---

[40] See the article by Peter Reddaway, 'The Role of Popular Discontent', *The National Interest*, pp.57ff, where he points out that well known United States scholars had proclaimed that the USSR was not going to break up just two years before Gorbachev came to power. He then goes on to provide his own explanation in terms of the Gorbachev's accidental failures.

Roundtable
The Theory of Policy Communities and Policy Networks

Keith Dowding
London School of Economics & Political Science

'Policy Networks: Don't Stretch a Good Idea Too Far'

Acknowledgements

This article was written while the author was Hallsworth Fellow at Manchester University. I would like to thank the members of the Department of Government for providing such a congenial atmosphere in which to work. I would like to thank Anne Gelling, Grant Jordan, Peter John, Desmond King and Helen Margetts for their comments.

Introduction

Policy networks and policy communities were introduced into the language of British political science by Richardson & Jordan in their essentially undergraduate textbook *Governing under Pressure: The Policy Process in a Post-Parliamentary Democracy*. Explicitly applying an approach developed in the US this book attempted to shift the study of British politics away from the institutions of parliament, the cabinet, and 'the civil service' and into behavioural categories. They saw policy-making as a series of vertical components sealed off from other aspects of the policy process – other groups and departments, the public and parliament. Their argument fractured the standard evaluation of pressure group/government relations as a bilateral bargain, extending analysis into domains where the state/society distinction is not so hard-edged. They dissected the political world against the prevailing cleavages of British political science. They were successful in their aims, so much so that institutionalists have felt the need to fight back and argue that studying Parliament and other institutions is still important (Rush 1990, Judge 1993). The context of the early application of the concepts 'policy community' and 'policy network' should not be forgotten, though now political science hardly needs to be taught the Richardson & Jordan lesson.[1]

Richardson & Jordan initially used the concepts 'policy community' and 'policy network' interchangeably to refer to the close links to be found between civil servants and favoured interest group organizations. In 1979 they saw policy communities within broad policy areas such as 'education', 'transport' and 'local government'. More recently Jordan has argued that policy communities are best seen as commodity-based around sections or at

---

[1] We should note here, if just to save Gabriel Almond stoking his wordprocessor, that the Richardson & Jordan argument was not new. It was based upon the classic behaviouralist group theory texts from the 1950s and 60s (Bentley 1908, Truman 1951, Latham 1965). Theoretically institutionalism is enjoying a revival against behaviouralist domination though I am not convinced that they are necessarily rivals (Dowding 1994).

most divisions in government departments implying a more institutionally based conception (Jordan et al, 1992a, 1992b, 1993). This develops from the idea, contained in the earlier work, that communities are distinguished by commonality of interest. Neither Richardson nor Jordan has attempted to categorize policy networks, policy communities, issue networks or other similar terms into formal typologies. They have adopted a relaxed metaphorical usage based on certain characteristics they noted within policy-making arena.

The Richardson & Jordan approach to policy networks does not take itself too seriously. It is merely a set of metaphors aiding their task of creating a new structure for the study of British and European politics (Richardson 1982). Others have inflated this simple analogical idea into an explanatory model or 'theory' of the policy process creating numerous problems.[2] The idea has been stretched too far to bear the weight of a coherent model of explanation. A model, utilizing the sociological network tradition and rational choice bargaining models, may perhaps be constructed which encompasses the insights of the policy network approach. But the approach has signally failed to produce such a model, and is quickly submerging itself under a welter of petty classificatory squabbles. The work resembles that of a set of butterfly collectors who have classified (in rival classificatory *schema*) an impressive array of types of moths and butterflies but have yet to produce a theory which explains the diversity. Debates about the worth of the rival classificatory *schema* can only be based upon aesthetic grounds until an underlying explanatory theory is provided.

Four Confusions in Search of a Theory

There are four related confusions in the policy network literature. All of them, to some extent follow from the first.

1. a naturalistic fallacy

It is fallacious to believe that a useful way of categorizing the world denotes a natural category which requires defending as though the ontology of the world depends upon it.[3]

2. Spurious conflict

There is a debate over what 'level' policy network 'theory' should be located. Is it best suited to the *micro*, *meso* or *macro* level? This seems to be a completely vacuous debate for the same model may be heuristically useful at all levels of analysis.

---

[2] It seems to me that much of what counts as 'theory' in social science is nothing of the sort. I will often use scare quotations around this word when I am sceptical of its usage in context. Policy network 'theory' is about the policy process within states. I am not sure the word 'theory' is appropriate for this approach. Indeed it seems to me that the very idea of a 'theory' of the state, as opposed to a model of the state is a teleological hangover. Needless to say I do not desire a terminological dispute over the terms 'theory' and 'model' so leave this here as an acerbic assertion.

[3] I call this a naturalistic fallacy rather than the naturalistic fallacy to distinguish it from G.W. Moore's rather different account of the naturalistic fallacy in ethics.

Figure 1
The Marsh-Rhodes (and Jordan-Richardson) View

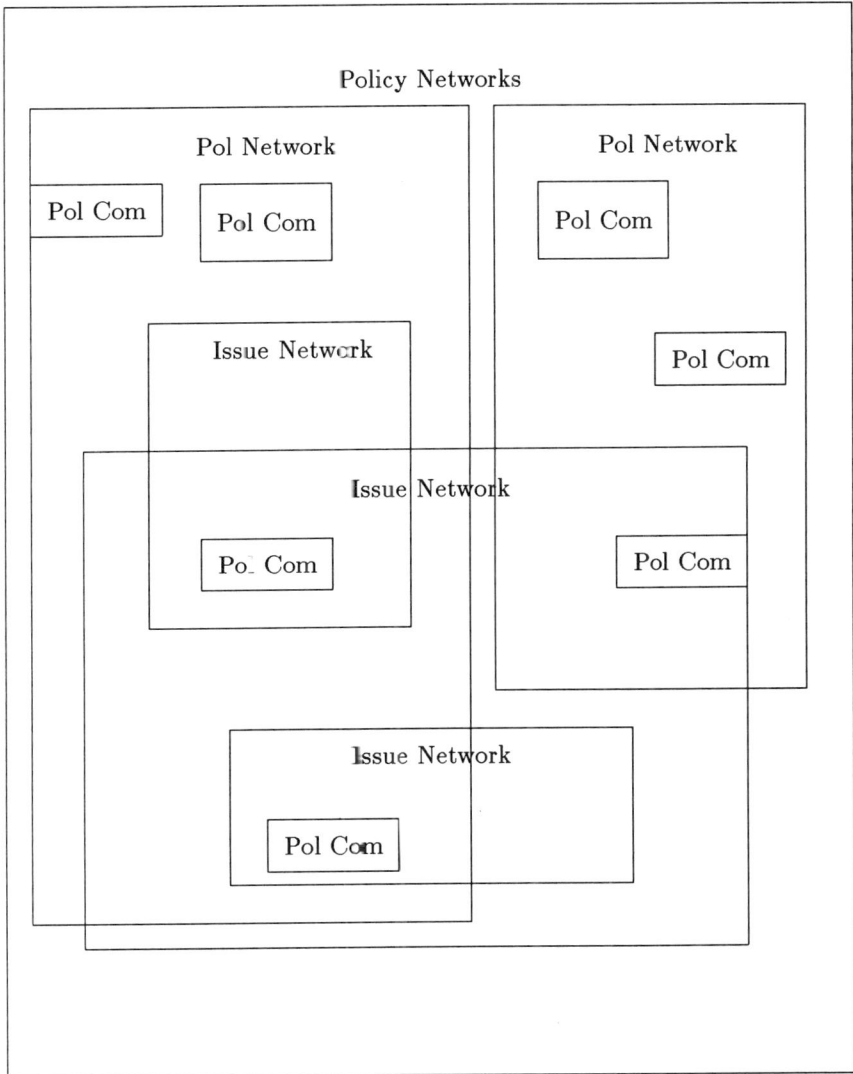

3. Theory and Evidence

The proponents have a strange conception of the relationship between theory and empirical research. Some empirical questions are answered by definitional assertion, whilst the same empirical evidence is marshalled to defend competing theories. Unless different implications (or predictions) are derived from rival theories we cannot test one against another (Popper 1972); indeed we cannot even demonstrate that they are rival theories.

4. Structure and Cause

The analysts confuse structure and cause leading them to offer identity statements as though they were causal explanations. The categorizations are largely a hodge-podge of characteristics, some of which are surely causes of others. In doing so they muddle *explanans* and *explanandum* (or independent and dependent variables). They do not seem to have a very clear conception of the relationship between typologies, models and theories. They seem to want to construct a theory on the basis of a typology, rather than seeing a typology as something in need of a theory to explain it.

A Naturalistic Fallacy

Figures 1 (p.61) and 2 (p.65) offer a schematic comparison between two rival ways of discussing policy networks. The debate between Rhodes & David Marsh on the one hand, and Wright & Wilks on the other is largely concerned with which version is preferable. Both sides claim that their version is better able to explain the policy process, but neither is capable of explanation. Each typology is just a different way of categorizing information about the world. Neither is descriptive of a natural category and empirical investigation cannot prove one typology superior to another. The explanatory claims made turn out, on inspection, to be completely spurious.

the Rhodes 'model'

The so-called Rhodes 'model' (Rhodes 1986, 1988, 1990) – which, as Rhodes seems to acknowledge (Marsh & Rhodes 1992, 25), is really a typology – categorizes policy networks along a continuum from policy communities at one end, through professional networks, inter-governmental networks and producer networks to issue networks at the other end (Figure 3).

Figure 3
The Rhodes Classification

Policy Networks

Pol Com —— Prof Net—— Intergov Net —— Prod Net —— Issue Net

An updated Marsh-Rhodes typology[4] offers formal definitions for demarcating the world into different types of network. The heuristic value of such definitional categorization depends upon the ability to construct a proper model which causally relates the characteristics to each other and different types of policy outcome. The problem for the original Rhodes typology in Figure 3 (besides the fact that there seems no reason to see the three intervening types as part of a continuum) is that it mixes up within

---

[4] See Appendix at the end of this Paper (Table 1).

a hodge-podge description both dependent and independent variables (see below). In order to go beyond typology and produce an explanatory model of the policy process these need to be more carefully demarcated. In the broad outline of Figure 1 Marsh-Rhodes suggest that 'policy network' is a generic category into which sub-categories such as 'policy community' and 'issue network' can be located. This is consistent with the Richardson & Jordan approach. Where they differ, perhaps, is over the precise details of what constitutes policy communities and issue networks, though that dispute, as far as it exists, is banal. The more general dispute between Jordan & Richardson and the followers of Rhodes (contained in Marsh & Rhodes 1992) is over the interpretation of the empirical evidence within broader 'theories' of the state (Dowding manuscript).

reinventing the wheel: Wilks & Wright

Maurice Wright and Stephen Wilks (Wilks & Wright 1987, Wilks 1989, Wright 1988) decided to branch out on their own (see Table 2). For them policy communities occur at both general policy sector level – 'chemicals', 'telecommunications' – and sub-sectorally – 'basic chemicals', 'pharmaceuticals'. A policy network is something which links these sub-sectoral policy communities over particular issues such as 'health and safety' 'company profits' and so on. Figure 2 is an attempt to make diagrammatic sense out of a discussion which is not always clear.

Wright (1988, 605) asserts that 'policy community' should not be seen as a subset of 'policy network'. His reason seems to be that the idea of 'community' requires a sense of unity, commonality of interests, identity, and so on which tend to develop in smaller groups. Why this should disqualify 'policy community' as a subset of policy networks is unclear. It is a strange method of analysis that answers empirical questions by definitional *fiat*. If policy communities are those subsets of policy networks which are small and harmonious then we need another name, say 'issue networks', to cover the relatively larger conflict-ridden subsets. Indeed small conflict-ridden subsets can also be called 'issue networks'. Whilst commonality of interest is surely more probable in smaller than larger groups, it might make sense to speak of 'an industrial policy community' in much the same way that it might make sense to suggest that during the second world war Britain developed a stronger sense of community.

Wright (1988, 606) suggests:

> 'Policy community identifies those actors and potential actors drawn from the policy universe who share a common identity or interest. Those actors will " transact" with each other, exchanging resources in order to balance and optimize their mutual relationships. Network is the linking process, the outcome of those exchanges, within a policy community or between a number of policy communities.'

The first sentence defines policy community in the way the rest of political science ordinarily defines 'group' (Bentley 1908, Truman 1951, Olson 1971,

Jordan & Richardson 1979, Moe 1980, Dowding 1991). It appears that eighty years of political science have been consigned to the dustbin. Wright then defines 'network' as both a 'linking process' and the 'outcome of those exchanges'. This seems to be simple confusion between structure, cause and effect.

Wilks & Wright (1988, 301) say that the distinctions they make between community and network 'enable us to identify those members of a policy community who are excluded from a policy network'. Are they seriously claiming that only if the political world is carved up in their way can we identify those groups excluded from policy-making? Nor do other 'advantages' they claim for their approach have any empirical benefits over rival classifications. No matter how the map of policy networks (seen as a generic term) is designed one should observe that some groups become excluded or ignored, and others work closely together. Categorical proliferation serves no useful purpose and stems from the attempt to force a disparate world into rigid natural categories which simply do not exist. There is no 'right way' of producing an exact definition of 'policy network' because the term is merely a means of bringing together certain elements of the world that contain similar characteristics.

Spurious Conflict

Debating the 'proper level' for network analysis demonstrates a lack of understanding of modelling techniques and tends to be a proxy dispute for deeper conflict. Controversy between pluralist and élitist accounts of the state is partly conducted through the 'levels of analysis debate' (Marsh 1992, Marsh & Rhodes 1992, Jordan et al 1992a, 1992b, Wilks & Wright 1987). Pluralists, often sceptical about the need for a theory of the state, tend to look at the micro-, or at most the meso-level for explanations. Their analyses concentrate upon the detail of legislation, case studies, and the particular personalities involved. Those desiring explanation of broader state structures, whilst also utilizing case studies, are prepared to formulate generalizations at a much higher plane of abstraction. Rhodes & Marsh (1992, 22) claim: 'To pursue micro-level analysis in order to explore personal networks will provide a wealth of detail but make it increasingly difficult to generalize about policy networks'. This is false. Can we not generalize that when a small personal group of individuals meet regularly they will form tighter bonds of common interest? Can we not generalize that if this group of people come from similar socio-economic backgrounds they will find it easier to form those bonds? Can we not hypothesize that the greater the power of such people the greater their personal interests (however these are formed) will affect policy outcomes? Surely these and many other generalizations can be assembled and investigated. There is no reason to restrict policy networks to the micro-level and there may be wider and more interesting generalizations to be found at the meso- or macro-levels. Let empirical research decide this rather than make definitional demands at the 'theory' stage. The concept of policy networks and their sub-types can be used at all levels. Models are just descriptions which denote the important structural features of social situations. The same model can be usefully applied at a micro-, meso- or macro-level to the extent that it denotes structural features at those levels. In one model, the actors may be real people, in another organizations, in a third social groups or classes. This is the social science method. The level of analysis' debate is simply otiose.

Figure 2
The Wilks & Wright Classification

Policy Universe

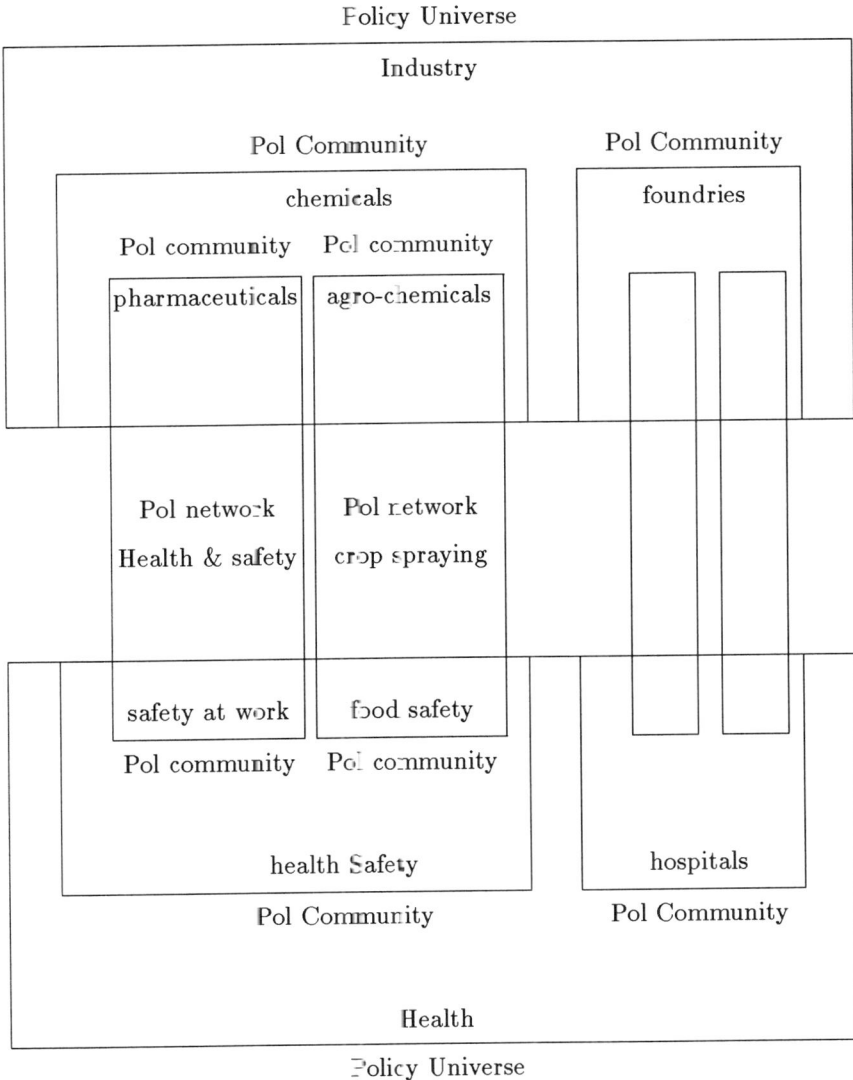

Policy Universe

Theory and Evidence

Should 'policy community' be restricted to small personalized groups (Wilks & Wright) or based around commodities (Jordan et al 1992b) or can it also refer to broader categories (Richardson & Jordan 1979, Rhodes 1990, Marsh & Rhodes 1992)? Surely this is an empirical not a definitional matter. All agree that 'community' implies a commonality of interest amongst the interacting groups, and that policy communities tend to have stable regularized contact.[5] Whether a community can be maintained at the meso level or only at the micro level is a question worth empirical investigation. The evidence suggests that communities can exist at the level of, say, 'agriculture' but are easier to maintain in the long run at micro levels. Wilks & Wright are surely correct when they argue that communities are fostered when the contacts are between individuals who know each other personally. Can we explain these empirical generalizations? I think so. It is well known that smaller groups find cooperation easier than larger groups (Olson 1971, Hardin 1982, Taylor 1982, 1987).[6] Trust develops where regularized contact occurs between agents with some common interests (Gambetta 1988). Norms of cooperation, so important to the Wilks-Wright vision, also develop through regularized contacts (Axelrod 1981, 1984) though they may require separate explanation (Elster 1989). Indeed an expanding institutional literature attempts norm-based explanation and provide meta-level explanation of those norms (see Grafstein 1992 for a critical review). These theories of social interaction can provide a structured but causal foundation for the empirical observations of the policy network approach. These theories separate what is to be explained (the *explanandum*) – greater cooperation and stability in smaller common interest networks – from the *explanans* – regular interaction helps develop trust, and givesthe opportunity to reward cooperation and punish defection. Thus two elements in Rhodes' classification of policy communities – stability and highly restricted membership – are shown to be causally related. Rational choice can also model disequilibrium suggesting why issue networks tend to be unstable or fail to form (Ordeshook & Shepsle 1982).

The network protagonists have tried to answer empirical questions by definitional dogma rather than constructing theories – which often already exist – to explain their empirical observations. Conversely they try to resolve theoretical disputes by reference to evidence compatible with both theories. Essentially the conflict between Jordan and the Rhodes-Marsh acolytes is over the nature of the state. Both sides use their versions of network theory to try to secure their position, but the empirical evidence they cite is exactly the same. Martin Smith (1993, 54) states:

> 'State autonomy is not a zero-sum. It is not something that
> belongs either to the group or to the state agency. By working
> together, a group and a state agency can increase each other's

---

[5] This is in keeping with most of the literature on the nature of communities more generally (Taylor 1982, Ostrom 1990 and references therein).

[6] Though see Marwell & Oliver (1993) for an argument that the nature of the production function and degree of group heterogeneity is more important than group size.

autonomy in relation to other parts of the state. Within a policy community the policy process can be sealed off from other state actors, pressure groups and networks. In pluralistic policy arena, it is difficult for the state to control the development of policy. Without a consensus, it is hard for a single state agency to control the final policy outcome, and, once policy is determined, implementation is harder to achieve because of the lack of assistance from groups. Therefore the degree of state autonomy available often depends on the type of policy network.'

Table 2
Policy Community and Policy Network

Policy Level		Policy Actors
Policy area	Industry, Education, Transport, Health etc	Policy universe
Policy sector	Chemicals, Telecommunications, Foundries etc }	Policy communities
Policy sub-sector (focus)	Basic Chemicals, Pharmaceuticals, Agri-chemicals, Paints, Soaps & Toiletries }	
Policy issue	e.g. Health & Safety, R&D, 'Over-capacity' e.g. Drug Licensing, Company Profits, 'Limited List'	Policy networks

Source:
From S.Wilks & M.Wright (eds), *Comparative Government-Industry Relations*, Oxford University Press, 1987.

I assume that the first two sentences (pp.66-67) are supposed to mean something like: 'The relationship between groups and the state is not a zero-sum game. By working together, a group and a state agency can increase the power of each against other elements of state and society.' State and group 'autonomy' in this account surely means power, and the extent to which groups and agencies within the state can extend their power 'depends on' the nature of the policy network.[7] First let us acknowledge that the Smith thesis here is exactly that which motivated Richardson & Jordan (1979) and most of their subsequent work. The only difference is that Smith insists on calling this 'state autonomy' whilst Jordan & Richardson (1987a, 1987b, Jordan 1990) contend it is 'pluralism'.[8] Secondly, note the problem of explanation generated by this paragraph. What is supposed to explain the greater power of state agencies and groups in some policies areas than others? It seems to be the nature of the policy network. Greater power in policy communities, less power in issue networks. But the type of policy network is defined by the nature of the relationship between groups and the department. Which groups are regularly consulted, which 'excluded', the degree of consensus, conflicts with other departments, and so on, define the type of policy network. How can the policy network then explain ('depends on' = cause?) the degree of state autonomy (power)? The type of network and amount of state power (degree of autonomy) are different descriptions of the same thing! Smith has used an identity statement in place of a causal explanation. We need to investigate the processes by which groups become excluded, the processes by which issue consensus often emerges, the processes by which network characteristics are transformed. In order to gauge the power of groups and state agencies we require a measure of their resources and an understanding of the institutions through which they utilize those resources. Policy network language does not explain these processes, rather it identifies characteristics in need of explanation.

Marsh & Rhodes (1992, 262), summing up the case studies in their collection, write:

> 'All the case studies suggest that networks affect policy outcomes. The existence of a policy network, or more particularly a policy community, constrains the policy agenda and shapes the policy outcomes. Policy communities, in particular, are associated with policy continuity.'

These statements have to be true. But in order to discover why policy communities are associated with policy continuity, or why, say, a professional network tends to produce policy outcomes distinct from an issue network we have to unpack their characteristics. It is the characteristics upon which we must build the theory; networks are merely the labels we attach. The Marsh-Rhodes typology begins to separate dependent from independent variables and separates the nature of the networks in terms of

---

[7] See Dowding (1991) for discussion of the confused use of 'autonomy' in state autonomy discussions.

[8] Christiansen & Dowding (1994) demonstrate that even in a comparatively simple case study it not easy to distinguish these two models of the state.

their professional membership, relationship to the productive process, and location within centre-periphery relations as separate dimensions. This can be developed much further. Generalization about structural properties requires a more formal approach to networks and the nature of the bargaining situations they represent. The extent to which professional networks operate differently from other networks depends upon the different resources professional groups enjoy. For example, the education professional network was disturbed by a sustained governmental assault upon the professional judgement of teachers and the educational establishment, thus undermining their legitimacy to speak for the best interests of pupils and as sources of authoritative information. Similarly trades unions, though never a part of professional networks once had much greater legitimacy than they now enjoy. Falling membership means that they can now less often claim to speak as the authoritative voice of workers, and they lost legitimacy in the eyes of the public at large through unpopular strike activity and an overwhelming propaganda effort by government to create new ideological circumstances. In the trade union case, of course, their major strike weapon was undermined by trade union reform throughout the 1980s. Both explanations look to the resources the groups had, and the way in which they use or can no longer use those resources. Labelling one network as 'relatively open' tells us that alliances are fluid, interests cross-cutting and the issue likely to be in the public eye. Another as 'relatively closed' suggests that alliances are formed, departmental policy entrenched and the issue out of the public eye. We can examine the bargaining process which led to such a closure, and we can examine the tactics by which other groups might try to break up the coalition of interests. Through such a modelling of the bargaining process we can go beyond the mere labelling or shorthand description contained in the policy network approach. The descriptive classificatory schema is not explanatory but requires a higher-level theory; a theory of power. The bargaining model of power can provide those deeper explanatory foundations which can elucidate the nature of the different policy networks (Dowding 1991). The theory can explain why distinct networks yield diverse policy types, and also explain network transformation. It can also illustrate why some groups need not enter the policy process where they enjoy systematic luck or advantage (Dowding 1991, Dowding *et al* 1993). This approach is structural, but allows for investigation of the different sorts of resources and therefore strategies that different organizations adopt. If political science wishes to go beyond the metaphorical usage of Jordan & Richardson it needs to borrow more from the sociological network tradition and from rational choice generalization. I shall make some suggestions for this direction.

The Logic of Network Analysis

Consider Figure 4. (p.71)

In 4(i) we have four dots on a page, each joined to each other by six lines forming the complete set of possible single-joinings. In 4(ii) and (iii) we have the dots joined in subsets of the ways in 4(i). All these figures can be called 'networks'. The first can be seen as the logically complete set of single line interactions between the four dots. The second two are subsets of the first. If the lines represent contacts at the political level then we can see exclusion in 4(ii) as one dot has no line to others. In 4(iii) we can see one dot is only linked to G and not the other dots. This might represent a group outside of the cosy 'policy community' represented by a, b, G. How influential c is, cannot be determined by the diagram; that requires empirical research. Now note, the differences between 4(i), 4(ii) and 4(iii) are contained in the fact they have different lines. The dots and their labelling are exactly the same. If the dots stand for actors (whether people, organizations, classes, or groups in the Bentley/Truman sense) they are invariate across the networks. What makes the networks different are the lines which represent the relationships between the dots. Networks are distinguished one from another by the relations between the actors. In other words, the networks denote different structures. Network analysis is, necessarily, structural. These linkages or different structural features of different networks can be examined by a number of mathematical techniques. Relational data on organizations drawn as a network can be represented in data matrices which can be transformed in various ways to reveal underlying structures (Galtung 1967, Knoke & Kuklinski 1982).

In the sorts of networks we are considering there is likely to be a focal point – a government agency, or rather a set of focal points. The social network literature has developed different measures of centrality to map important individuals within certain social networks (Freeman 1979, Bonancich 1972, 1987). Modifications of such measures, taking into account the greater exchange power of government agencies, could be developed to try to measure the closeness of community in certain networks. Graph theory has developed to try to measure the density (inclusiveness and number of connections between actors) of different networks (Christophides 1975, Marsden & Lin 1982). Such measures have been developed to quantify some of the insights that the less formal literature has noted. Network analysis produced by such techniques is still merely a map of the power structure within different policy networks. Nevertheless, as they are maps of the relations between actors they will enable a more comprehensive approach to structural generalizations across policy networks. I do not have great confidence that this type of formalized approach can, on its own, provide dramatic new insights into the policy process. It may well provide some counter-intuitive surprises and furnish objective generalizations to support the more subjective interpretations provided through structured interviewing. The important point to note, however, is that such analysis is the only way in which we can establish how the network structures help to determine outcomes. This is the manner in which the network approach may become explanatory in its own right. To understand more fully power relations in any given network however, we shall have to examine the resources of the actors in the bargaining game.

Figure 4 (i)

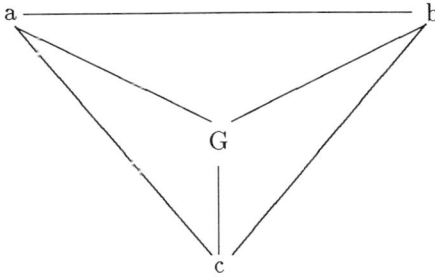

Figure 4 (ii)

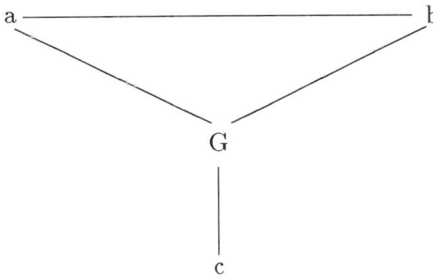

Figure 4 (iii)

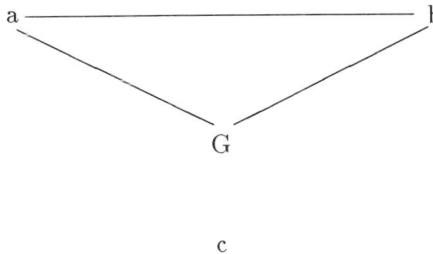

A Bargaining Model of the Policy Process

In Harsanyi's (1969a, 1969b) bargaining account of power, there are four general types of power resource: (1) knowledge or information, (2) legitimate authority, (3) unconditional incentives, and we must add a fifth resource which has proved vital in modern bargaining models: reputation (Roberts 1985, Kreps 1990, Rasmussen 1991, Ordeshook 1992). The first two and the fifth may have a fairly obvious meaning but a few words are

needed here to explain (3) and (4)[9]. An unconditional incentive is unconditional in the sense that if A provides such an incentive to B in order
to change B's preferences, interests, actions and so on, A bears the cost
whether or not the attempt succeeds. For example, if a millionaire gives a
contribution to a political party in the hope that at some future date his
lobbying efforts in some policy arena will be considered more favourably
by a government of that party, he pays the price whether or not such contributions are effective in this manner. Similarly if a government changes
the law to force trade unions to ballot membership over political levies in
order to reduce the income to some rival party, the government pays the
cost of that legislation (however small) even if the political payment to the
rival party is no lower. Conditional incentives occur when the costs to A
depend on B's compliance. For example, if a developer promises to build a
community centre, some low-cost housing and provide some local facilities
if it is allowed to develop commercial facilities on another site, the cost of
the promised non-commercial structures are only borne if the developer's
persuasion is successful.[10]

Differing outcomes in policy networks will depend upon the relative resources of the bargainers and the manner in which they use these resources.
The strength of governmental agencies largely revolves around their legitimacy and the greater opportunities they have to offer both conditional and
unconditional incentives. The formal powers of different agencies could be
compared to see how far this affects network relations. Government often
has greater facilities for information-gathering, though other groups have acknowledged powers here. Some organizations derive much of their strength
from their reputation for providing reliable information. To some extent
this is what distinguishes professional networks from others. They can provide technical information to counter that produced by other groups and
government, and because of the technical nature of the issues in such policy
networks, professional groups legitimate their claims by providing authoritative information. The tightly controlled professionalized policy network
surrounding Britain's sea defence is good example of the legitimacy accorded
to professional groups (Cunningham 1992).

These five resources of actors within bargaining games together with
other known characteristics of bargaining games[11] can provide a deeper and
more thorough explanation of the features of different varieties of policy networks identified by the informal empirical typologies. This approach also
enables us to overcome one of the major problems for policy network analysis (Dunleavy 1984), noted by many of its practioners (Rhodes & Marsh
1992), of explaining change rather than stability. Virtually all accounts of
change within network theory looks to exogenous variables such as changes
in the economic, ideological, or institutional environment, or look to technical change as the causal motivator. Despite Rhodes's disclaimer (Rhodes &
Marsh 1992, 20) his network approach does not explain change. It merely

---

[9] See Dowding 1991, chapter 4 for extensive discussion.

[10] Note one cannot unconditionally threaten.

[11] Such as the difference time constraints make on the arbitrariness of outcomes (Kreps
1990). This suggests that we should not expect to be able to fully determine policy
outcomes no matter how well developed our theories of the policy process.

provides a backdrop against which change can be assessed. Rather than viewing this as a problem for the network approach it should be seen as a limitation. Networks map structures. In most causal models, structures constitute the 'background conditions' around that which we ordinarily call a cause occurs (Mackie, 1974). Both the cause and the background conditions are *inus* (insufficient but non-redundant parts of unnecessary but sufficient) conditions, but what we ordinarily call causes are events. Policy change occurs through actors altering circumstances, perhaps in response to transformations outside of the network, perhaps to disturb the balance of power within it. At any given moment, the nature of the network, perhaps captured by the techniques mentioned above, explains the policy process therein. When the balance is upset, reference has to be made to the precipitating events. These may be exogenous though transformation may occur through relative resource-change of the actors. Where tight policy communities produce policies detrimental to excluded groups these may mobilize and try to alter the agenda, first from the outside, perhaps later from within. This cycle of group formation has been noted (Hirschman 1982) and mapped through time (Walker 1983). Thus events which seem to be exogenous to a network, may in fact be explained by that success of the network. Nevertheless, we can use one model in which the new groups are exogenous to explain change, and another model to explain how the new groups were able to mobilize. Such models are not rivals and thus may be utilized together.

Conclusion

Policy networks appeared to be a fruitful approach to the study of the policy process. The literature soon became bogged down as writers became embroiled in definitional squabbling, defensive posturing and an insular attitude which did not allow them to see relevant advances outside of their own empirical fields One response is to see policy networks much as Jordan & Richardson, merely as metaphors to aid the informal descriptive research for which British political science is renowned. There is nothing methodologically wrong with such an approach apart from the dimness of the light it sheds on the deeper questions that such empiricism shies away from asking (Jordan & Richardson, 1987b, 5). The metaphor is not capable of bearing the weight of deeper understandings however, unless it is supported by a general theory of the policy process: a theory of power. Without power there would be no politics, without a theory of power there can be no understanding of politics.

Bibliography

Axelrod, Robert (1981) 'The Emergence of Cooperation', *American Political Science Review*, 75, 306-18.

Axelrod, Robert (1984), *The Evolution of Cooperation* (New York: Basic Books).

Bentley, Arthur (1908), *The Process of Government*, edited by Odegard, Peter (1967), Cambridge, Mass: Belknap Press.

Bell, R, Edwards, D.V. & Wagner, R.H.(eds) (1969), *Political Power: A Reader* (London: Collier-Macmillan).

Bonacich, P. (1972), 'Technique for Analysing Overlapping Memberships', in Costner, H (ed), *Sociological Methodology, 1973* (San Francisco: Jossey Bass).

Bonacich, P. (1987), *'Power and Centrality: A Family of Measures'*, *American Sociological Review*, 52.

Christiansen, Lars & Dowding, Keith (1994), 'Pluralism or State Autonomy? The Case of Amnesty International (British Section): The Insider-Outsider Group', *Political Studies*, XLII, 15-24.

Christophides, N. (1975), *Graph Theory: An Algorithmic Approach* (New York: Academic Press)

Cunningham, Caroline (1992), 'Sea Defences: A Professionalized Network?', in Marsh & Rhodes (eds) (1992).

Dowding, Keith (1991), *Rational Choice and Political Power* (Aldershot: Edward Elgar).

Dowding, Keith (1994), 'The Compatibility of Behaviouralism, Rational Choice and "New Institutionalism" ', *Journal of Theoretical Politics*, 6, 105-117.

Dowding, Keith (), 'Institutional Pluralism', manuscript.

Dowding, Keith, Dunleavy, Patrick, King, Desmond & Margetts, Helen (1993), 'Rational Choice and Community Power Structures: A New Research Agenda', Paper to APSA conference Washington, September 3-5.

Dunleavy, Patrick (1974), 'The Limits of Local Government', in Boddy, Martin (ed), *Local Socialism?* (London: Macmillan).

Elster, Jon (1989), *The Cement of Society* (Cambridge: Cambridge University Press).

Freeman, L. C. (1979), 'Centrality in Social Networks: I – Conceptual Clarification', *Social Networks*, 1.

Gambetta, Diego (ed) (1988), *Trust: Making and Breaking Cooperative Relations* (Oxford: Basil Blackwell).

Grafstein, Robert (1992), *Institutional Realism* (New Haven: Yale University Press).

Hardin, Russell (1982), *Collective Action* (Baltimore: Johns Hopkins University Press).

Harsanyi, J.C. (1969a), 'Measurement of Social Power, Opportunity Costs, and the Theory of Two-person Bargaining Games', in Bell et al (eds) (1969), 226-38, and in Harsanyi (1976).

Harsanyi, J. C. (1969b), 'Measurement of Social Power in n-Person Reciprocal Power Situations' in Bell et al (eds) (1969), 239-48, and in Harsanyi (1976).

Harsanyi, J.C. (1976) *Essays on Ethics, Social Behaviour and Scientific Explanation* (Dordrecht: D.Reidel).

Hirschman, Albert O. (1982), *Shifting Involvements*,

Jordan, A.G. (1990), 'The Pluralism of Pluralism: An Anti-theory?', *Political Studies*, 38, 286-301.

Jordan, A.G & Richardson, J.J. (1987a), *Government and Pressure Groups in Britain* (Oxford: Clarendon Press).

Jordan, A.G & Richardson, J.J. (1987b), *British Politics and the Policy Process* (London: Unwin Hyman).

Jordan, A.G, Maloney, W.A & McLaughlin, A. (1992a), 'Assumptions abut the Role of Groups in the Policy Process: The British Policy Community Approach', British Interest Group Project Working Papers, 4, Aberdeen: Aberdeen University.

Jordan, A.G, Maloney, W.A. & McLaughlin, A. (1992b), 'Policy-Making in Agriculture: "Primary" Policy Community or Specialist Policy Communities?', British Interest Group Project Working Papers, 5, Aberdeen: Aberdeen University.

Jordan, A.G, Maloney, W.A & McLaughlin, A. (1993), 'Characterizing Agricultural Policy-Making', manuscript.

Judge, David (1993), *The Parliamentary State* (London: Sage).

Kreps, David (1992), *Game Theory and Economic Modelling* (Oxford: Clarendon Press).

Knoke, David & Kuklinski, James H. (1982), *Network Analysis*, Beverly Hills: Sage.

Mackie, John (1974), *The Cement of the Universe* (Oxford: Oxford University Press).

Marsden, P. V & Lin, N (eds) (1982), *Social Structure and Network Analysis* (Beverly Hills: Sage)

Marsh, David (1992), 'Beyond New Institutionalism: Meso-Level Analysis Is All Very Well But Let's Not Lose Sight of the Macro Questions', ECPR Joint Sessions of Workshops, Limerick.

Marsh, David & Rhodes, R.A.W. (1992), 'Policy Communities and Issue Networks: Beyond Typology' in Marsh & Rhodes (eds) (1992).

Marsh, David & Rhodes, R.A.W (eds) (1992), *Policy Networks in British Government* (Oxford: Clarendon Press).

Marwell, Gerald & Oliver, Pamela (1993), *The Critical Mass in Collective Action* (Cambridge: Cambridge University Press).

Moe, Terry M. (1980), *The Organization of Interests* (Chicago: University of Chicago Press).

Olson, Mancur (1965) (1971), *The Logic of Collective Action* (Cambridge, Mass: Harvard University Press).

Ordeshook, P.C. (), *A Political Theory Primer* (London: Routledge).

Ordeshook, P.C & Sheplse, K.A (eds) (1982), *Political Equilibrium* (Boston: Kluwer Nijhoff).

Ostrom, Elinor (1990), *Governing the Commons* (Cambridge: Cambridge University Press.

Popper, Karl (1972), *The Logic of Scientific Discovery* (London: Hutchinson), 5th edition.

Quine, W.V. (1981), *Theories and Things* (Cambridge, Mass: Harvard University Press).

Rasmusen, Eric (1991), *Games and Information* (Oxford: Blackwell).

Richardson, J. J (ed) (1982) *Policy Styles in Western Europe* (Hemel Hempstead: George Allen & Unwin).

Rhodes, R.A.W. (1986), *The National World of Local Government* (London: Allen and Unwin).

Rhodes, R.A.W. (1988), *Beyond Westminster and Whitehall* (London: Unwin Hyman).

Rhodes, R.A.W. (1990), 'Policy Networks: A British Perspective', *Jour- nal of Theoretical Politics*, 2, 293-317.

Rhodes, R.A.W. & Marsh, David (1992), 'Policy Networks in British Politics: A Critique of Existing Approaches' in Marsh & Rhodes (eds) (1992).

Richardson, J.J. (ed), *Policy Styles in Western Europe* (Hemel Hempstead: George Allen & Unwin).

Richardson, J.J & Jordan. A.G. (1979), *Governing Under Pressure* (Oxford: Martin Robertson).

Riker, William H. (1982), *Liberalism Against Populism* (San Francisco: W.H.Freeman & Co).

Roberts, R. (1985), 'Reputations in Games and Markets' in Roth, A.E. (ed), *Game-theoretic Models of Bargaining* (Cambridge: Cambridge University Press).

Rush, Michael (ed) (1990), *Parliament and Pressure Groups* (Oxford: Clarendon Press).

Smith, Martin (1991), 'From Policy Community to Issue Network: Salmonella in Eggs and the New Politics of Food', *Public Administration*, 69, 302-22.

Smith, Martin (1993), *Pressure, Power and Policy* (Hemel Hempstead: Harvester).

Taylor, Michael (1982), *Community, Anarchy and Liberty* (Cambridge: Cambridge University Press)

Taylor, Michael (1987), *The Possibility of Cooperation* (Cambridge: Cambridge University Press)

Truman, David (1951), *The Governmental Process* (New York: Alfred A. Knopf).

Walker, Jack (1983), 'The Origins and Maintenance of Interest Groups in America', *American Political Science Review*, 77, 390-406.

Wilks, Stephen & Wright, Maurice (1987), 'Conclusion: Comparing Government-Industry Relations: States, Sectors, and Networks' in Wilks & Wright (eds) (1987).

Wilks, Stephen & Wright, Maurice (eds) (1987), *Comparative Government-Industry Relations* (Oxford: Clarendon Press).

Wright, Maurice (1988), 'Policy Community, Policy Network and Comparative Industrial Policies', *Political Studies*, 36, 593-614.

Table 1
Types of Policy Networks:
characteristics of policy communities & issue networks

Dimension	*Policy community*	*Issue network*
	MEMBERSHIP	
Number of participants	Very limited number, some groups consciously excluded	Large
Type of Interest	Economic and/or professional interests dominate	Encompasses range of affected interests
	INTEGRATION	
Frequency of interaction	Frequent, high-quality, interaction of all groups on all matters related to policy issue	Contacts fluctuate in and frequency & intensity
Continuity	Membership, values, and outcomes persistent over time	Access fluctuates significantly
Consensus	All participants share basic values and accept the legitimacy of the outcome	Some agreement exists, but conflict is ever present
	RESOURCES	
Distribution of resources (in network)	All participants have resources; basic relationship is an exchange relationship	Some participants may have resources, but they are limited, basic relationship consultative
Internal Distribution	Hierarchical; leaders can deliver members	Varied, variable distribution & capacity to regulate members
Power	There is a balance of power among members. Although one group may dominate, it must be a positive-sum game if community is to persist	Unequal powers, reflecting unequal resources and unequal access – zero-sum game

* = Distribution of resources within participating organisations.
source: D.Marsh & R.A.W.Rhodes (eds), *Policy Networks in British Government*,
Oxford University Press, 1992.

Policy Communities: Theoretical Issues

Mike Mills
London Guildhall University
&
Michael Saward
Royal Holloway, University of London

'All Very Well in Practice, But What About the Theory?
a critique of the British idea of policy networks'

Summary

The concepts of policy networks and policy communities have become common currency in empirical political theory, despite the widespread disagreements on definitions and explanatory utility. Such disputes – and the ambiguities arising from them – can be positively useful in that they can open up the concepts for use by a wide range of authors with an equally wide array of concerns and purposes. However, they can be a weakness for similar reasons; an encompassing concept is often so only because it is underdeveloped. As the literature stands, the more specific and detailed studies of policy networks become the greater the difficulty of reaching agreement on their general character and importance. This paper explores some of the reasons which lie behind this problem. It offers linked arguments to the effect that the concept of the policy network, in the British literature at least, does not have a strong explanatory base, has problems with integrating levels of analysis, and tends to promote a proliferation of variables in ever-broader analyses rather than analysing fewer variables in greater depth.

Introduction

Perhaps the fundamental fact about modern politics is its highly complex nature.[1] This complexity – at once institutional, functional and technical –lends to the idea of policy networks an intuitive plausibility as a descriptive concept. At a general level, most people will have an intuitive idea of what a network is. Further, the literature on policy networks in various countries presents us with quite detailed descriptive typologies. Policy communities are widely defined as a highly integrated network of actors and organisations, exercising strong control over community membership and policy.[2] Issue networks, on the other hand, are far less integrated; the membership tends to change through time and it is easier for a plurality of interests to

---

[1] For definitional and descriptive accounts of complexity and its policy consequences, see Zolo (1992), Hogwood (1987), Hanf & O'Toole (1992), Luhmann (1990), Saward (1994) and Dryzek (1990).

[2] Smith (1990) argues that the relationship between the National Farmers Union (NFU) and the Ministry of Agriculture, Fisheries and Food (MAFF) is perhaps the classic British example of a policy community.

gain influence within the policy processes concerned (Marsh and Rhodes 1992; Heclo 1978).

Typologies are essential, but problems arise when we consider what analytical functions these typologies are meant to perform. As seen above, it is easy to jump from describing what a policy community looks like (a highly integrated network) to using the description to explain how policy is made (through strong control). There is a great deal of difference between using a concept to describe in shorthand what something looks like, and hypothesising from that description why it is like it is. Between description and explanation, the virtues of intuitive plausibility can begin to break down amid problems of ambiguity, confusion and inaccuracy.

The main problem surrounding explanation in policy networks theory is in accounting for the ways in which policy networks change (Atkinson & Coleman 1992; Smith 1993). However sophisticated and detailed one's networks typology may be, without it being allied to a full theory of explanation no adequate account of how networks change can be offered.[3] Explaining how networks change must involve putting networks e affected by links with other networks, for example, or locating them within broader structural variables such as prevailing national ideologies or cultures or economic interests. Although the two major strands of networks theory in Britain (Rhodes 1988 and 1990; Wilks & Wright 1988 and 1991) try to do this, our argument is that they go about it the wrong way.[4] Rather than adding depth to network analysis by employing a full theory of explanation, they follow the strategy of adding descriptive breadth by including yet more variables in their descriptions.

This problem is closely intertwined with that of levels of analysis. The concept of the policy networks operates at the 'meso' level, but it is at least questionable whether, in practice, explanations can be confined to this level. British and other authors have made some attempts to integrate micro, meso and macro levels of analysis (corresponding normally to individual actors and groups, policy sectors and national government respectively) (Atkinson & Coleman 1992; Rhodes 1988 and 1990; Smith 1993). Wilks & Wright (1988), for example, are strong on the relationship between micro and meso levels, and convey a well-developed sense of how agents relate to and change the networks of which they are a part. However, their framework finds it a little more difficult to demonstrate how broader macro variables affect those relationships. Rhodes (1988), on the other hand, is strong at the meso level, but tends to use macro-level variables merely to 'contextualise' before getting on with what he takes to be the more important business of analyzing relationships at the meso or sectoral level.

To take stock, then, it must be noted that the notion of levels of analysis can be interpreted in two basic ways. First, it can refer to the (attempt to)

---

[3] Explaining change has been the problem that has received most attention; however, explaining related problems such as why networks emerge at all, what policy impact they have, and what relations of power exist within networks, are equally important. All of these issues will be considered briefly later in this paper.

[4] Policy networks theory is alive well beyond Britain, of course. For a glimpse of the enormous range of related concepts employed by political scientists in Europe alone, see van Waarden (1992).

integrate national government trends and descriptions of sectoral politics. We call this broadening the analysis – adding more variables. Second, it can refer to the level of theoretical depth at which the analysis is carried out. For instance, description may be interesting and useful, but in analytical terms it will fail to add depth. Employing a full theory of explanation to try to account for, for example, change in policy networks, means deepening the analysis. British networks theorists have, for the most part, interpreted the problem of explaining policy networks in terms of adding breadth, in the sense described here. The results of these efforts, on their own terms, have been mixed, as we shall argue further below. They have been much more reluctant to add theoretical depth, and it is this aspect of the problem of levels of analysis which has provided the biggest challenge to the continuing utility of the concept of policy networks. Some distinctive ways in which explanatory depth might be added will be explored later in this paper.

Background to the Problems

Many of the problems of British networks theory can be traced back to the pluralist paradigm from which it emerged in the mid-1970s. This section will provide a brief critical overview of the theory's development. Its main aim is to identify the problems we have noted above in the use made of the concepts of policy networks and policy communities.

Heclo & Wildavsky's *Private Government of Public Money* 4) presents a useful starting point. Their analysis could be called 'anthropological' (Rhodes 1990), using terms like kinship, nuclear family, culture, communities and village life as metaphors for patterns of relationships in the life of the British Treasury. Applying such concepts enabled them to provide an understanding of the structural, institutional and cultural context within which Treasury decisions were made. They also drew attention to the dilemmas of dual loyalty faced by many civil servants – on the one hand, to their own communities, and on the other to their policy obligations. (1974: 365). Among other things, Heclo & Wildavsky demonstrated an acute, if under-theorised, awareness of the political context in which policy networks and policy communities operate.

Partly due to their desire to provide a means by which one could characterise micro politics by using meso labels (nuclear family, village, community), Heclo & Wildavsky were far less interested in macro theories and did not hold to a framework that would facilitate the integration macro and other levels of analysis. While their work was undoubtedly pathbreaking, it cannot be said that they made any real attempt to systematise or generalise the concepts of community and network or to integrate these concepts into a broader theoretical framework.

Much the same assessment can fairly be made of another key early work on Britain, Richardson & Jordan's *Governing Under Pressure* (1979). They saw that policy in a number of areas was being made primarily in sub-national settings between particular groups of politicians, organised interests and public officials, rather than at the level of parliament or cabinet. Accordingly, they wrote of such phenomena as 'personal networks', 'issue communities' and 'policy communities'. For example, they argued that there existed an education policy community consisting most importantly of the National Union of Teachers, the Associating of University Teachers and Metropolitan Authorities (1979: 44). However, their use of the term community was still largely metaphorical. So, when looking for explanations of the phenomena they described, they looked toward macro theory (in the sense of national government) in the form of 'pluralist corporatism', and supplemented this with meso level organising tools such as communities, networks and rules of the game. Here too, the concepts of community and network provide useful labels for observable patterns of political relationships, but explanations of these relationships are primarily historical and atheoretical, and explanation of their policy effects are found only through broadening to another level of analysis. As Smith (1988: 2) has argued, '... writings on policy communities have tended to be rather vague about policy communities, not specifying their internal workings'.

In short, Richardson & Jordan kept separate the characteristics of the policy process which they believed to be of explanatory importance (a negotiated order/environment, the accommodation of opinions, rules of the game) from the tools they used to organise their ideas. They were able to do this because they did not need the concept of networks to achieve explanations. Rather, they were simply using it as a label to help them to describe what happens when, as they put it, the centre 'disintegrates'.

At this point, all of the problems with policy communities and policy networks which we identified earlier remain. Their is no agreed definition of either concept, nor any systematic account of how micro, meso and macro levels of analysis might be integrated into network theory. Further, there has been little consideration of how different types of network might operate under different environmental conditions. In short, if network theory exists at all it is far from being explanatory.

Jordan (1981) takes a more systematic view of networks and their roles in policy-making. He has produced a table which distinguishes between different related models of the policy process: iron triangles, issue networks, cabinet government and corporatism (1981: 98). He argues that some amended version of the iron triangles and pluralist perspectives best characterises the nature of policy-making in Britain. This is a clear advance on the approaches canvassed above. Not only is there an overt attempt to integrate the levels of analysis by looking for the 'best fit' between options, but there is an attempt to systematise the difference between contending approaches. It is clear from Jordan's analysis that he expects more than mere descriptive utility from the model. Implicit in his work (1981, 1990) is the claim that once an accurate descriptive label has been found, it will be possible to explain policy outcomes better. However, Jordan does not use the concepts of networks or communities or iron triangles to help him to achieve such explanations – beyond demonstrating conceptual differences. The point is, as we noted earlier, that simply theorising about the different types of networks and communities does not leave one in a position to say much beyond the fact that different types of networks/communities exist. There still remains the crucial problem of discovering what difference, politically, the existence of these networks makes.

Grant, Paterson & Whitson (1988) provide another, somewhat better developed, example of the descriptive approach. They argue that to identify a policy community one must locate three elements: (1) differentiation (identifiable policy boundaries); (2) specialisation (particularly in terms of policy-making institutions); and (3) interaction (members of a policy community must interact with at least one other member) (1988: 56). They go on to disaggregate these categories in accordance with their findings from comparative research into relations between government and the chemical industry in Britain and Germany. In theoretical terms, there is little here that differs from the account of Richardson & Jordan. How the three defining characteristics would differ would depend in large part on the particular policy area under scrutiny. For example, Grant et.al. found that there were three sub-categories of 'differentiation' in their own case study; a researcher examining the motor industry, for example, might find several more.

The openness of the analytical framework in the hands of Grant et al is quite appropriate given their limited expectations for networks theory: 'We found the concept of a 'policy community' a useful conceptual tool for ordering the material obtained from our interviews and other research sources' (Grant, Paterson & Whitson 1988: 74). This is not to say that Grant et al were not concerned with matters such as the interests of the members of the policy communities or the bases of the relationships which existed within them; such variables were important in establishing who was in the community and who, if anyone, predominated.

The positive side of Grant et al's work is that they subsume their observations on the nature of policy-making (for example, policy identity, strategies, appreciative systems) under the framework of policy communities. In other words, they begin to attribute certain properties to policy communities which can be tested and which may make a difference to policy procedures and outcomes. However, Grant et al do not seek to account for their conclusions in theoretical terms. A proper theoretical explanation would require them to do more than just establish the fact that policy networks exist; they would also need to show that the fact of their existence means that things are importantly different from how they would otherwise have been. Having these elements implicit in the description of the policy community is insufficient because these concepts must be applied to the dependent variable in order to provide theoretical explanation. Furthermore, it is noticeable that there is no theoretical account of the context or conditions within which policy communities exist. Hence, if explanations are to be found we are left in the uncomfortable position of relying upon a characterisation of government-industry relations to explain government-industry relations.

Rhodes extends our understanding of policy communities and policy networks in a number of different ways. First, he recognises explicitly that there are different levels of analysis involved (1988: 46). Second, he offers an extensive typology of policy networks (policy or territorial communities, issue networks, professionalised or producer networks) and an account of how they vary from one another (in terms of constellations of interests, membership, vertical interdependence, horizontal interdependence and resource distribution, 1988: 77-8). Implicitly, for Rhodes policy networks can primarily be characterised according to whether they are tightly or loosely integrated (policy communities and issue networks are the extremes here), or according to which is the dominant interest (for example, professional networks) (Saward 1992).[5] Thirdly, his power-dependence model, focusing on mutual resource dependencies between a range of actors, suggests why actors belong to networks (if they do), what network boundaries are and the essential nature of political relations within the network.

How far does the Rhodes model take us in our quest for an explanatory theory of policy networks? The general answer is some way, but not far enough. Consider Rhodes' attempt to deal with the explanatory weaknesses of networks theory – 'it is rare for it to have any explanatory value' (1990:293) – by focusing on 'levels of analysis'. Rhodes interprets levels of analysis in terms of breadth:

The macro-level of analysis necessarily involves an account of the changing characteristics of British government during the postwar period. The meso-level of analysis focuses on the variety of linkages between the centre and the range of sub-central political and governmental organisations. The concept of policy networks is particularly appropriate at this level of analysis. The micro-level of analysis focuses on the behaviour of particular actors, be they individuals or organisations (1990: 304).

Even on this account, it is difficult to see how the levels are integrated. We know the general advantages that the centre holds over the periphery in terms of resources, but the theory provides only the idea of resource dependency to link these different levels; in fact, it is very difficult to know where resource dependencies begin and end (Stones 1990). When it comes to 'breadth' understandings of levels of analysis, in the effort to achieve a fully explanatory theory, Rhodes needs to go further in (a) developing a characterisation of the relationship between networks and their external environments (which after all must be a major source of dynamism) and (b) to explain why and how networks change through time.

Insofar as the lack of explanatory power of policy networks theory arises from the lack of depth of the theory, Rhodes' attention to the level of analysis question take us no further. Rhodes pays virtually no attention to theories of explanation that might add depth and explanatory value to networks theory. His efforts to contextualise policy networks are all conceived in terms of broadening the analysis – at best, only half of what is required.

Rhodes' efforts are directed at increasing the explanatory value of the idea of policy networks. In this, they are followed by the account of Wilks & Wright, which stresses the fact that 'The properties of the network are not reducible to those of individual actors ... the network is the outcome of their combined actions' (1988: 298). Like Rhodes, they stress 'transactions' between actors; unlike Rhodes, they emphasise that the network is the result of this process of exchange. In this way, Wilks & Wright give us the first version of networks which shows how they change over time. On Wilks &

---

[5] The Rhodes typology has since been revised, with policy communities and issue networks forming the sole extremes of the continuum along which particular networks can in principle be located. See Marsh & Rhodes (1992).

Wrights' account networks should be changing through time in much the
same way that Giddens argues that a feature of all structures is 'recursion'
(Giddens (1986). We also get an idea of how interactive processes affect the
network itself.[6]

What is particularly interesting about the work of Wilks & Wright is
the extent to which they both recognise the problems inherent in the use
of network theory on the one hand, and their own use of description on the
other. Of the problems we recognised with network theory, a number have
been acknowledged by Wilks & Wright: the concept of networks requires
more specification and elaboration in terms of influence within networks
and the generation, and reproduction of network relationships (1991:331).

To this extent then, while Wilks & Wright have a good understanding
of interactive processes and network changes, they too concede the need for
more theoretical work in this area. Similarly, they recognise that levels of
analysis is a crucial problem and suggest, although do not pursue, the possibility of integrating networks with an institutional form of analysis at the
macro level. Lastly, they note that when we assert a connectedness/political
relationship it may well be necessary to rely on qualitative, as opposed to
quantitative, judgements given that the problems involved in establishing
these relationships empirically are 'formidable'.

In each of these cases, then, Wilks & Wright recognise key problems of
network theory and indicate, in some instances, a broadening of the analysis
(for example, when considering what affects resource dependency 1991:333,
and when looking at certain aspects of the levels of analysis problem) and
hint at a deepening in others (for example, interaction and relationships).
Although they are 'pressing for more systematic and precise conceptualisations on which to base theories (1991:326)' we would, at this stage make
two points. The first is that although Wilks & Wright have, to their credit,
recognised problems with network theory, we have still to learn whether
some of the more formidable problems are, indeed surmountable. The second point is that Wilks and Wright suggest these problems can be approached in both an empirical, broad, case-specific way, or in a theoretical,
deeper, more general manner. Both may be necessary but only the latter
will enhance the cause of network theory in the longer term.

Description or Explanation?

There are many other problems in networks theory that would need to be
addressed if the theory were to have real explanatory power. One key problem can best be identified by noting that, despite Jordan's argument that
policy community approaches have become the 'new conventional wisdom',
within the literature itself there are two quite different approaches being

---

[6] It is worth noting one other key aspect of Wilks & Wright's work. They develop
as range of concepts such as policy universe (containing all those with an interest in
an area of policy), and policy focus (identifies common interests of network members).
These concepts are designed so as to allow for a highly disaggregated approach to policy
analysis, placing as much emphasis on the micro as the macro level. As such, their
approach helps in the effort to integrate different levels of analysis (in terms of analytical
breadth, at least).

used at the same time by different authors. On the one hand, there are those who appear happy to use the concept either to organise or clarify their empirical material (Grant et al, Jessop, Hayward, Richardson & Jordan). Generally speaking, this involves the accumulation of a substantial amount of empirical material which needs then to be ordered in some way – to be classified into sections or sub-sections so that a manageable picture of the policy area and the policy process emerges. In the more extreme cases, such as that of Jessop, only passing reference is paid to policy communities, and on these occasions it is clear that an appeal is being made to the 'intuitive understanding' mentioned in the Introduction to this paper. This approach is distinctive because, by and large, this classificatory role is the only one which is accredited to networks; once an adequate picture of the policy processes and relationships has been established the utility of the networks concept has been exhausted. If explanations are offered, then two further tendencies appear to apply. Either this is done empirically – for example, with reference to historical factors – or a theory (on a different, usually a macro, level) altogether is introduced, normally some variant of pluralism (Hayward, Richardson & Jordan, Jordan).

This primarily descriptive approach – attaching appropriate labels to visible patterns of political relationships – is, after a fashion, an explanatory approach. By distinguishing between one set of interests and another, we are 'explaining' that they are not the same, that they do not belong to the same policy community. Nevertheless, there is little about the processes within networks, or about their outputs, which can be explained only in terms of visible appearances.

On the other hand, there are writers who do use networks in a more explanatory sense. Rhodes, Wilks & Wright, and Laffin, for example, have, to varying degrees, wanted more from the concepts of policy network and policy community than simple descriptive labelling. They seek to offer explanations for certain patterned relationships by using the notion of networks within a broader perspective. They seek to broaden their analyses to say something about the contexts within which networks exist and operate, and by so doing provide explanations of (for instance) what difference networks make, or why networks exist at all. Wilks & Wright, for example, seem particularly interested in integrating meso-level concepts with micro-level concepts, but it is clear that they see the purpose of networks not only as a labelling device but also in the way they can be linked to micro 'transactions' to explain political changes. Rhodes, on the other hand, has placed more emphasis on linking the meso and macro levels. His explanations rely upon the fact that he can account, theoretically, for the basis of the intra- and inter-network relations (resource exchange and dependency), but he is also interested in accounting for such things as the 'hegemonic power of the centre'. Rhodes' efforts to give the model explanatory power by 'contextualising' networks in this way – broadening his analysis to include national level or macro phenomena to 'locate' particular networks and network types – fail, however, to provide the depth that explanation requires. He suggests no theory of explanation; without one, no amount of refining or enlarging the scope of descriptions can lead to adequate explanations.

To recap the argument, some efforts have been made to go beyond using the networks and communities labels as merely descriptive. Often, this has been taken to be a problem of 'levels of analysis'. Hence, Rhodes in particular has sought to locate meso-level networks within macro-level structures (national government environment). Our criticism is essentially this: the problem of explanation within the networks model of politics is a problem of levels of analysis; it is not, however, a problem that can be addressed adequately by merely broadening the range of empirical phenomena discussed. Rather, it requires deepening our analyses by using an explicit theory of explanation. To be sure, this does mean taking note of a different level of analysis; that level, though, must ultimately be one of theoretical depth rather than of empirical breadth.

The final section of the paper will briefly set out some of the main alternatives with respect to adding theoretical depth to the analysis of policy networks. We do not wish to recommend one alternative theory over another; that would take considerably more space than is available here. The main point of this paper is to show that the need for such a theory exists, and that networks theory will be importantly limited and limiting without it.

Theories of Explanation

We have argued that the policy networks literature has been too descriptive, and insufficiently explanatory. Where writers have recognised this problem, they have tried to address it by broadening their analyses to include more variables. However, this approach itself can only go so far; on the one hand, it merely involves providing a fuller description of networks and their contexts, while on the other it does not help us to integrate different levels of analysis. To address this problem, we need to distinguish what needs to be explained, and how analysts might go about it. There is insufficient space here to make more than some suggestive comments on possible ways forward; the main intention of this paper has been to point out and characterise certain problems in the policy networks literature, and not to offer hard-and-fast solutions to these problems.

We can distinguish four areas in which a more explanatory theory can play a part. First, we need the resources that can enable us to explain why policy networks come about. Secondly, we need to explain what impact networks have on policy. Thirdly, we need to explain who has power within networks. And finally, we need to explain how networks change.

There are two basic options to approaching the explanation of each of these things. One is to employ standard macro-theories in the study of politics. Here, for example, one could explore the place (whether the explicitly argued, the possible or the logical place) of (various types of) policy networks in stories told by Marxists, élite theorists, state-centred theorists and pluralists (see Smith 1993: 74). There are characteristic problems and characteristic outcomes of this type of work. The key problem is the great level of disagreement between would-be proponents of any of these macro-theories, which is inextricable from the problem of identifying the boundary assumptions of any one such macro-theory. They normal result achieved by such analyses (see especially Smith 1993) is that policy networks is a multi-theoretic field; no one macro-theory can provide encompassing explanations of the phenomenon in question, or of its variations, though each might provide insights that have value in providing part of the picture. This sort of conclusion is thoroughly in line with Merton's (1968) original line on middle-range theories – in principle, they can be compatible with, or can be incorporated within, a range of macro-theories.[7]

Is there a better approach? We believe that it may be more fruitful to focus upon meta-theory rather than macro-theory. Macro-theory is ambiguous as to whether using it deepens or broadens (see discussion above). Real explanatory depth, we would argue, can arise more clearly from employing meta-theories of explanation. The following brief comments are designed to show how useful hypotheses regarding policy networks can be derived from considering certain meta-theories.

Functionalism might suggest that networks come about in the first place because they – or something like them – are necessary to perform a stabilising function within the political system. All systems need to be manageable, and the existence of relatively stable sub-systems in the form of networks enhances the very 'systemness', and hence the very predictability and manageability, of the broader political sphere. Functionalists might subsequently suggest that networks must have a quite substantial policy impact, since more than merely symbolic rewards will be required for the maintenance of stable sub-systems and broader systems. Functionalists might have little to say that might help to predict power centres within networks, but they might hypothesise that a limited number of sub-systems – and a limited number of power centres within sub-systems (networks) – will be essential to the stable evolution of the overall system. On a functionalist perspective, network change might be seen to be due to (for example) technological and structural changes to which sub-systems must adapt if they are to survive.

A materialist approach – which I interpret largely as Marxist materialism – might point to shifts in the nature of productive technology and therefore of class relations, necessitating in turn changed structures of control of subordinate classes. Benson (1982) adopts a Marxist functionalist framework, concerned as he is with 'the necessity to maintain the accumulation process and to produce justifications for the order of things' (Benson 1982, 164). With new technology, maintaining the accumulation process may require new relationships between state agencies and professional and producer groups, sometimes formal and sometimes informal. Producing new justifications may involve expanding state structures and functions so as to demonstrate the universality of the state's role (cf. Poulantzas 1980). As Gramsci (1971) famously argued, the 'integral state' plays a crucial role in the reproduction of capitalist class relations; building on this argument, materialists might explore the complexity and extended (though relatively stable) functional definition of the state which the policy networks literature

---

[7]Macro-theoretical approaches have also tended to concentrate on the problem of explaining change in policy networks, and have consequently neglected, in relative terms, the related problems of explaining why networks come about, what their policy impact might be, and the power relations found within networks.

calls upon and develops as something which cements dominant class interests. In terms of explaining power relations within networks, materialists might point to the distinctly élitist, exclusive character of many policy networks, and seek to show how essentially unequal class relations contribute to this. As to the question of change, materialists could pinpoint changing technology, the necessary evolution of the efficient means of exploitation of subordinate classes, and subsequently to the role of the state in all this. In sum, policy networks, as state 'tentacles', at once add to the 'infrastructural power' (Mann 1986) of the state while playing a 'mystifying' function, blurring views of the nature and boundaries of central political authority.

From a game theory perspective, rational choice theorists might point to the need for trust-establishing knowledge of other agents with whom prisoner's dilemma-type games need to be conducted. Relatively stable networks might enhance the opportunities for repeated co-operative and non-zero-sum games between the agents within the network. As to policy impact, rational choice theorists would expect stable and substantial impacts, otherwise the game playing advantages for agents would be merely symbolic, and therefore networks would stand little chance of survival. In terms of power relations, rational choice theorists can point to the incentives facing bureaucrats, and the advantages in terms of information that network relationships afford them on this score (cf. Dunleavy 1991). To explain networks change, rational choice theorists would begin with the perceptions of individual actors aiming to maximise utility; if key actors in particular within a network cease to regard the network structure as being to their advantage, they might seek to alter its structure or revise it radically. Alternatively, as Dunleavy has shown, incentive structures differ according to the state agency involved, and the resulting incentives to (re)structure bureaus can only have a considerable impact on network structures attached to a given department or agency.

Finally, those working with structuration theory (see Giddens 1986).[8] would seek explanations which link agency and structure within and around networks. Structuration theory suggests the utility of an evolutionary approach whereby the actions of individual agents give rise over time to forms of organisation – and stable linkages between different organisations – which in turn provide constraints and opportunities for future agents. Networks would, on this view, arise through agents exercising opportunities within a structured context. This would help account for both the relative permanence – including the relatively constant policy impact – of policy networks, while offering the resources to analyse change. Entrenched power relationships within networks could be approached, at least in part, through structuration theory's view of rules as 'resources'. As formal and informal rules come to govern internal and external interactions of networks, so these rules come to be resources which better positioned agents within networks can exploit to their advantage.

Hopefully, these all-too-brief comments provide some indication of how depth can be added to breadth in explaining policy networks. It is no part of

---

[8] See Stones (1990) for one account of how this 'hermeneutic or interpretive' style of analysis can be applied to policy networks.

middle-range analysis that fully explanatory theories cannot be adopted and used. To realise its potential, networks theory needs to move in this direction in order to attempt to add explanatory depth to descriptive prescience.

Conclusion

The literature on networks has come a long way since the publication of *The Private Government of Public Money* – the typologies have become ever more sophisticated, the disaggregation of policy processes more detailed. We have argued that, while these developments are necessary, they are by no means sufficient if network theory is to achieve real explanatory value. In particular, we have argued that:

> – the tendency towards 'contextualising' the macro-level factors which affect networks has to be resisted and replaced by a proper integration of levels of analysis. Contextualisation at best simply by-passes the need to do this, and the theory of policy networks suffers as a consequence;
> – there needs to be some account of how networks change through time, and this in turn requires a well-developed characterisation of relationships within and between networks which can distinguish and anticipate the effects of structure and agency;
> – while the ability to describe political phenomena is undoubtedly a major virtue of networks given the complexity of modern decision-making this need not be an end in itself. We have attempted to show how the explanatory role of networks theory can be given greater priority without its descriptive qualities being diminished; and
> – in general terms, the search for increasingly accurate accounts of the policy process simply broaden the number of agents, organisations, sectors, and sub-sectors we incorporate into our models; we have contended that only parts of the models we have presented here have also achieved the analytical depth to achieve what their authors believe the models actually do achieve.

References

Atkinson, M.M & Coleman, W.D. (1992), 'Policy Networks, Policy Communities and the Problems of Governance', in *Governance*, 5.

Benson, J.K. (1982), 'A Framework for Policy Analysis', in D.L. Rogers & D.A.Whetten, *Interorganizational Coordination*, Ames: Iowa State University Press.

Dryzek, J. (1990), *Discursive Democracy*, Cambridge: Cambridge University Press.

Dunleavy, P. (1991), *Democracy, Bureaucracy and Public Choice*, Hemel Hempstead: Harvester Wheatsheaf.

Giddens, A. (1986), *The Constitution of Society*, Cambridge: Polity.

Gramsci, A. (1971), *Selections from Prison Notebooks*, London: Lawrence and Wishart.

Grant, W, Paterson, W. & Whitson, C. (1988), *Government and the Chemical Industry*, Oxford: Clarendon.

Hanf, K & O'Toole, L.J. Jr. (1992), 'Revisiting Old Friends: Networks, Implementation Structures and the Management of Inter-Organisational Relations', *European Journal of Political Research*, 21.

Hayward, J. (1986), *The State and the Market Economy: industrial patriotism and economic intervention*, Brighton: Wheatsheaf.

Heclo, H. (1978), 'Issue Networks and the Executive Establishment', in A.King (ed.), *The New American Political System*, Washington, D.C: American Enterprise Institute.

Heclo, H & Wildavsky, A. (1974), *The Private Government of Public Money*, London: Macmillan.

Hogwood, B. (1987) *From Crisis to Complacency*, Oxford: Oxford University Press.

Jessop, R. (1988), 'Conservative Regimes and the Transition to Post-Fordism: The Cases of Britain and West Germany', Essex Papers in Politics and Government, Number 47, Department of Government, University of Essex

Jordan, A.G. (1981), 'Iron Triangles, Woolly Corporatism and Elastic Nets', *Journal of Public Policy*, 1.

Jordan, A.G. (1990), 'Sub-Governments, Policy Communities and Networks', *Journal of Theoretical Politics*, 2.

Laffin, M. (1986), *Professionalism and Policy*, Gower: Aldershot.

Luhmann, N. (1990), *Political Theory in the Welfare State*, Berlin and New York: Walter de Gruyter.

Mann, M. (1986), 'The Autonomous Power of the State', in J.A.Hall (ed), *States in History*, Oxford: Basil Blackwell.

Marsh, D & Rhodes, R.A.W (eds), *Policy Networks in British Government*, Oxford: Clarendon.

Merton, R.K. (1986), 'On Sociological Theories of the Middle Range', in R.K.Merton (ed.), *Social Theory and Social Structure* (enlarged edition). New York and London: Free Press.

Poulantzas, N. (1930), *State, Power, Socialism*, London: Verso.

Rhodes, R.A.W. (1988), *Beyond Westminster and Whitehall*, London: Unwin Hyman.

Rhodes, R.A.W. (1990), 'Policy Networks: A British Perspective', *Journal of Theoretical Politics*, 2.

Richardson, J.J & Jordan, A.G. (1979), *Governing Under Pressure*, Oxford: Martin Robertson.

Saward, M. (1992), 'The Civil Nuclear Network in Britain', in D.Marsh & R.A.W.Rhodes (eds), *Policy Networks in British Government*, Oxford: Clarendon.

Saward, M. (1994), 'Legitimacy and the State in Europe', in J.Hesse, T.Toonen & R.A.W.Rhodes (eds), *The European Yearbook of Public Administration*, Oxford: Oxford University Press.

Smith, M.J. (1988), 'Consumers and Agricultural Policy', in Essex Papers in Politics and Government, Number 48, University of Essex.

Smith, M.J. (1990), *The Politics of Agricultural Support in Britain*, Aldershot: Dartmouth.

Smith, M.J. (1993), *Pressure, Power and Policy*, Hemel Hempstead: Harvester Wheatsheaf.

Stones, R. (1990), 'Government-Finance Relations in Britain, 1964-67', *Economy and Society*, 19.

Waarden, F. van (1992), 'Dimensions and Types of Policy Networks', *European Journal of Political Research*, 21.

Wilks, S & Wright, M. (1988), 'Conclusion', in S.Wilks & M.Wright (eds), *Comparative Government-Industry Relations*, Oxford: Clarendon.

Wilks, S & Wright, M. (1991), *The Promotion and Regulation of Industry in Japan*, Macmillan: London.

Zolo, D. (1992), *Democracy and Complexity*, Cambridge: Polity.

Politics of Health: Comparative Studies

Melanie Latham
Lancaster University

'Policy Networks and Reproductive Rights in France and Britain'

Introduction

The years since 1968 have seen the rise in Europe of New Social Movements such as the Green movement, the Peace movement and feminism. At the forefront of feminist concerns and campaigns in this period have been a set of issues that have come to be defined as collectively constituting women's reproductive rights. If motherhood 'is at the heart of women's "condition" (and therefore) central to feminist analysis',[1] feminist analysis in this period has come to centre on the claim that public policies should be reshaped in order to prioritise support for individual women's right to self-determination in respect of their child-bearing capacity. The concept of women's reproductive rights has thus centred on three distinct sets of issues, concerning respectively contraception, abortion and the new technologies of human reproduction.

It is therefore important to see how the three issues of contraception, abortion and the NRTs have been dealt with legally and culturally over a period of social change; to observe the power struggles that have gone on between those groups who have appeared to take a serious interest in reproductive rights: feminists (liberal, socialist and radical), moralists (Catholic and non-Catholic), pro-natalists and the medical professions. Interestingly these groups were the same in both countries. The policy under consideration was comprised essentially of laws passed in 1967 on contraception in both Britain and France; laws enacted, respectively, in 1967 and 1975 on abortion; and the law of 1990 on the NRTs in Britain. As yet no substantive statutory controls over the NRTs have been enacted in France.

In this paper, therefore, I want to give an introduction to my research on policy networks and reproductive rights in Britain and France, along with the essential conclusions of that research.

Policy Networks and Policy Communities

The policy community and policy networks literature has seemed to provide the most useful framework for this research. This literature is concerned with exploring and accounting for the variations that are found as between

---

[1] 'As a question that raises attitudes that defy logic and reason, it affects women on different levels and resists attempts to apply a simple political solution to its problems; as the first concerted campaign by feminists in France, the fight for voluntary maternity was a hugely successful but equally problem-laden mobilising issue, which highlights the different political positions and preoccupations of different feminist approaches, and shows the way in which the various groups, and the MLF as a whole, evolved over a decade.' C.Duchen, *Feminism in France*, (Routledge & Kegan Paul, 1986), p.49.

different policy sectors in any one state, as much as with exploring the differences, and also the similarities, that may be found cross-nationally in any one policy sector.[2] The typology of policy networks has varied. Marsh & Rhodes (1992) distinguish between that used by Rhodes (1981) and that used by Wilks & Wright (1987). For this case study I preferred to use the latter, whereby those in what I termed the 'policy network' were insiders closest to government policy makers, and those in what I termed the 'policy community' gravitated around this network as outsiders trying to get in. Outside both in each policy sector is the policy area. This is important as some groups, especially new social movements, choose not to attempt to take part in governmental policy making, preferring to use other methods to get their point across. In this study such a group were radical feminists. This terminology differs from that of Rhodes, and that of Marsh & Rhodes, as they term those closest to the government the 'policy community', and those gravitating around it as the 'issue network'. On Figure 1 the preferred typology has been expressed in diagramatical form, with differences between the two typologies pointed out.[3]

A number of authors have ascribed importance to policy communities and policy networks within the policy process. For example, Jordan & Richardson[4] argued that official consultative bodies on which group representatives sat, or which invited them to speak, were not in reality where policy was made.

> 'In practice, it is realistic to think of each policy sector as consisting of several, inter-related, policy communities – the sort of policy field covered by a civil-service assistant secretary or under secretary. Many linkages exist (for example, between branches of medicine, social services and social policy ...) and a system of overlapping memberships between policy communities develops.'

The network within the community or 'inner core' is created in order to reduce the number of actors and issues to 'a manageable polity'. These members are therefore chosen for cultural, psychological and practical reasons. There are also institutional and structural reasons for their existence.

---

[2] The status of the three issue areas of contraception, abortion and new reproductive technologies, in terms of their allocation to a specific policy sector is itself a contested issue. Of the established policy sectors with their own established policy communities and networks, these issue areas could not readily be assigned to the health sector. Here, however, given the entrenched position of the medical professions and their commitment to exercising clinical judgement, such issues are liable to be 'medicalised' at the expense of developing any clear definition of individual women's rights. Conversely, however, as feminists have argued, they may constitute a new policy sector in their own right.

[3] Maurice Wright, 'Policy Community, Policy Network and Comparative Industrial Policies', *Policy Studies* (1988), XXXVI (4), 593-612; Gerald Wistow, 'The Health Service Policy Community: Professionals Pre-Eminent or Under Challenge?', in David Marsh & R.A.W.Rhodes, *Policy Networks in British Government* (Clarendon Press, 1992), essentially distinguishes between policy communities, policy netorks and the professional network which obtains in relation to the medical professions and the National Health Service in Britain. However, in a comparative study of Britain and France it has been found more useful to use the term 'policy network' to describe the consultative relationship between the government and the medical professions during policy making.

[4] Wright, *op.cit*, p.605.

They bring in specialised knowledge and legitimise policy. In their view such networks took the form especially of the quangos, and of the standing and ad hoc advisory committees. Once established, communities rarely dissolve and membership is usually closed as 'members hang on to the benefits of mutual exchange which underpin the community.'[5]

The distinction developed by Wright, building on Rhodes' previous work[6] between policy communities and policy networks, is important since the former embraces all those affected by a particular sectoral issue area and which in the context of liberal democratic institutional arrangements and norms might potentially organise themselves to gain access to, and seek to influence, the making of policy. As Wright notes, 'this population of actors and potential actors ... is a large one'[7] In contrast, the policy network designates those actors and organisations which 'interact in a structure of dependent relationships'; they may be drawn from one or more 'policy communities'.

Network members exchange resources with each other in order to balance and optimize their mutual relationships, with government actors at the head of the network. These actors, according to Wright, are more concerned with relationship management than policy-making:

> 'It is at the level of the firm or group of firms ... that most issues or problems arise, are articulated and are brought to the attention of public policy-makers. It is here... that policy is carried out or evaded.'[8]

Because management of the relationships of the actors within the closed network within each community is paramount, the outcomes and behaviour of policy makers may become inconsistent with the general norms associated with them. It leads to a difference existing between what the government says policy is and why (government rhetoric or dual policy style) or what is expected of the government, and actual policy in practice as determined by the norms of the network and their 'rules of the game'. There is also much intersectoral conflict at all levels of the policy area in both Britain and France. The needs of the members of the network, according to function, strategy, resources, and objectives outweigh the general needs of the area (the Department) or government.

Membership of the network is controlled by the government agency. They are selected from the policy community involved in the subject area, such as Health and from others if the issue is a combination of subject areas. Exclusion of some members is often the condition of another's participation. Membership is determined by similar characteristics to membership of corporatist consultation and 'insider' status – a common identity or interest (size, politics, strategy, interest, members); stability; professionalisation. 'They possess resources of authority, money, information, expertise, and organisation.'[9] The members control the agenda, with the government keeping some issues off the agenda to placate certain members.

---

[5] *Op.cit*, p.175.
[6] 1987, see Wright Note 26.
[7] Wright, *op.cit*, p.605.
[8] *Ibid*, p.597.
[9] *Ibid*, p.605.

However, the members are limited by the accepted rules of the game. These have included in Britain mutuality, consultation and informality, acceptable mode and language, the avoidance of legal remedy by the government actor. These Wright inferred from the behaviour of members.

Mény, looking specifically at the French case, argues that the policy community concept 'has provided a stimulating analytical framework for research on the development and implementation of public policies.'[10] In France he argues, much more than in Britain, the strong, centralised state has created the organisation of members, by supporting them financially to create a manageable polity. Though how far the French state is obliged to work with entrenched professions, such as the medical professions, is unclear. Also in the French case the strength and legitimacy of the bureaucracy and technocrats ensures 'their unchallenged control of policy making.'[11] These points came out in the analysis of corporatism too. Ministers and civil servants 'are concerned to avoid being subjected to the rival claims of social pluralism or market competition between interest groups.' This creates a situation however where groups excluded from the network – 'insiders' – will try and force their way in. They are then incorporated by being included on a consultative committee (of which there are thousands), only to be ignored and thereby weakened.

> 'The most optimistic assumption is that these committees can provide information or exercise pressure on the administration. More frequently, they serve only as a forum for the ritual sword-play of adversaries ...'[12]

Reproductive rights' issues are an interesting example of policy making where outsiders such as feminists at first glance could presume to have been pitted against insiders (in this case the medical professions and moralist groups) in their efforts to persuade policy makers of their own aims and beliefs. The subject therefore makes a useful case study of what resources outsider groups need in order to influence policy and in order to be taken seriously moreover by policy makers. Additionally the study can be used to see if insiders really do have all the influence; whether policy networks were operating in this area of policy making; and how continuous their membership was over time.

What the study has shown is that outsiders may have an influence through alliance-building either with other outsiders to increase their lobbying power (here with the left-wing, for example), or with insiders in the policy network. Even groups on the outside of both the policy community and policy network can have an influence on the policy agenda. However in the reproductive rights sector the ultimate victory went to the medical professions, to the detriment of women and feminists. This will be borne out in this paper as we turn now to look in more detail at the three specific reproductive

---

[10] Yves Mény, 'The National and International Context of French Policy Communities', *Political Studies* (1989), XXXVII, 387-399, p.389. The terminology used by Mény differs from that used by Wright. The term 'policy network', in addition to 'policy community', used by Wright, to differentiate between community and network, is not used by Mény.

[11] *Ibid*, p.390.

[12] *Ibid*, p.394.

rights of contraception, abortion and new reproductive technologies.

Contraception

The contraceptive campaigns in both countries led to statutory provision in 1967. Campaigns therefore took place before the onset of the second wave of feminism. Thosse feminists involved were therefore liberal feminists rather than radical feminists whose tactics were to try and gain entry to the policy network using allies alongside them in the policy community such as individuals on the left-wing. Essentially, in both countries, the most influential groups in the policy community on contraception were the policy network members, namely the medical professions, moralists and, in France, 'natalistes', and not feminists, who were outsiders. Even though, as abortion was a conscience issue, much debate took place in Parliament, network members still managed to exert more influence than other groups represented there, thus reducing the potential of the support of allies for feminists.

The provision of contraception in both Britain and France was delayed by fears of low population growth. In France, however, this fear was not shortlived like that of the 1936-49 scares or those in the 1970s in Britain. Instead it lasted throughout the twentieth century and formed a basic tenet of health policy on all sides of the political spectrum. As for the comparative influence of demography on contraception provision, in Britain the issues of maternal mortality, women's health and initially immorality were more important to legislators than that of demography, due to the contrasting religious influence in both countries of the Protestants and Catholics, whereby Catholic interest in demography was only of any real influence in France. Indeed article 5 of the 1967 law in particular read, 'toute propagande antinataliste est interdite'. Moreover, it was for 'nataliste' reasons that the French government itself wanted to control access to contraception. The Social Affairs Minister spoke in favour of the law as it would place, 'entre les mains du gouvernement des moyens d'action dont il est actuellement dépourvu: on ne peut surveiller ou réglementer ce qui est interdit légalement mais que tout le monde tolère.'[13] It was for this reason that the French government attempted to frustrate the provision of contraception, and fundamental amendments were necessary in 1974.

Most importantly however it can be concluded that the medical aspects of birth control outweighed any demographic or moralist considerations by the 1960s. This was especially the case in Britain where, for example, contraceptive provision by general practitioners took precedence over clinic services until the 1970s to the detriment of women's rights. Medicalisation of the issue was exacerbated in both Britain and France by the necessary alliances with individual doctors by the family planners themselves.

Both contraception laws were inadequately implemented after 1967 and each was amended to provide free contraceptives and improved access by 1974. By this time in Britain liberal family planners were accepted in the

---

[13] Dhavernas, 'Droits des femmes, pouvoir des hommes', (Seuil, 1978), p. 152.

policy community and were fuelled by radical feminist demands, but concentrated on the more liberal actions of conducting surveys and lobbying and concentrated on the issue of overpopulation. In France by this time the influence of Catholics on the issue of contraception had waned and despite their opposition the law was further liberalised. Other policy community members now supported change and allied with second-wave liberal lobbying feminists, and this persuaded the government of the need for change. The significance of Parliament should be stressed too, as backbenchers played important parts. Their change of heart was an indirect result of feminist campaigns. There were also in the early 1970s radical campaigns by family planners and others on abortion, which at this time was still illegal, and this, perhaps even more than any radical feminist input into contraceptive campaigns, played an important part in persuading the French Establishment and opposition groups to further liberalise contraception.

Essentially then, in both countries, the lack of second-wave radical feminist input in contraceptive campaigns ensured that, even when contraception had been put onto the parliamentary agenda by liberal feminists, those groups who enjoyed the most representation in this policy sector, moralists, 'natalistes' and particularly the medical professions in later years, were able to shape the content of the laws of 1967 to the detriment of a clearer definition of women's rights.

Abortion

Abortion also saw the pre-eminence of policy network members in consultations on the preparation of statutes leading in Britain to the *Abortion Act 1967*, and in France to the abortion law of 1975.

Despite the fact that Britain is not a Catholic country, Catholics played an important part in the abortion debate there. Their initial failure was arguably due to the fact that they did not begin lobbying in earnest until after the law had been passed. It was the conflict of women's reproductive rights and embryo rights that led to abortion amendment in 1990 with the passing of legislation on new reproductive technologies. However Catholic and other moralists' strength was highlighted as they successfully lobbied the government to allow debate on the 1967 Act in 1975 and 1990, making use of British Parliamentary procedure to threaten abortion rights. Fortunately in 1990 this backfired somewhat as it led inadvertently to liberalisation, due to the lobbying of feminists and their medical and left-wing allies.

However, as with contraception, during the passage of his Bill, Steel pandered to the medical professions and altered the social clauses of the Bill to get the approval of those who would support a bill approved by these bodies[14]

As with contraception, due to their inherent moralism and 'natalisme', the French government did not liberalise abortion in order to increase the rights of women but to create a law that would be respected, to ensure respect for the State[15] Simone Veil emphasised, 'c'est le respect des citoyens

---

[14] Keown, 'Abortion, Doctors and the Law' (Cambridge University Press, 1988), p.109.
[15] Dhavernas, *op.cit*, p.169.

pour la loi, et donc pour l'autorité de l'Etat, qui est en cause.'[16] The MFPF complained that the main aims behind the law were not women's freedom, but medical security and demography.[17] Devreux & Ferrand-Picard[18] point out that the law was an instrument of control rather than liberation with an emphasis on prevention which facilitated Parliamentary consensus. Through it the government could control health by preventing backstreet abortion, and society and its morals by reducing the number of abortions. This could only be achieved with the cooperation of the medical profession, as in Britain, however, and this was gained through concessions to them. They would only accept therapeutic, not social, abortion as a medical act within their remit. Social aspects were thus rewritten to emphasise the therapeutic role of the doctor who alone would decide if the woman's situation was one of 'détresse' who could refuse in accordance with the conscience clause; must counsel the woman as to alternatives and prescribe contraceptives, thus controlling the numbers of abortions and all in all gaining moral and social control over reproduction. Moreover, doctors were further appeased by the fact that the woman herself had to make the initial request and take the moral responsibility for the abortion.

Nevertheless, in both countries, the legislation on abortion has been an undeniable gain for women. Abortion is now legal, available to all women of whatever social class, and completely free of charge.

Unfortunately for women and pro-choice members of ALRA, women in Britain do not have the right to choose an abortion, but must persuade two doctors of their case. In addition the NHS was not obliged to provide free abortions, which led to an average of 50% and in some areas 90% of women having to pay for theirs. Lovenduski concludes that, as in France, the Act was therefore merely 'posturing' on the part of the government[19] ALRA were hopeful that sympathetic doctors would take advantage of the vague wording of the Act and sanction abortion requests and to some extent these hopes were realised[20] Nevertheless, those groups which were available to ALRA as allies were only slightly useful.

By contrast in France, radical feminists had an agenda-setting role in that they radicalised the aims and methods of liberal feminist campaigners and their allies. Not only did the Government therefore invite feminists and their allies for consultation by the Commission of 1973, their arguments also contributed to the text of the 1975 law more than other extreme viewpoints for or against, as they wanted to safeguard the mother's health, have abortion on demand before 12 weeks amenorrhea, a social worker to offer advice, and contraception to be offered, (though minors need parental

[16] Anne Batiot, 'The Political Construction of Sexuality: The Contraception and Abortion issues in France, 1965-75', in P.Cerny (ed), *Social Movement and Protest in France* (Frances Pinter, 1982), p.127.

[17] Jenson, 'Struggling for Identity: The Women's Movement and the State in Western Europe', *West European Politics*, Volume 8, Number 4, October 1985, p.15.

[18] Isambert et al, 'Contraception et Avortement: dix ans de debat dans la presse, 1965-1974' (CNRS, 1979), p 100.

[19] Paul Byrne & Joni Lovenduski, 'Two new protest groups: the peace and women's movements', in Drucker, Dunleavy et al (eds), *Developments in British Politics* (Macmillan, 1984), p.53.

[20] Gardner, *Abortion: The Personal Dilemma* (Paternoster Press, 1972), p.68.

consent and doctors supervise and limit the remit of the woman's demand for termination).[21]

In France the government was forced into such legislation by the political uproar created by the French Feminist Movement (MLF) and its radical offshoots from 1970.[22]

Abortion was put onto the agenda and public opinion was shifted from the right to the centre. On this there is a consensus among commentators[23] This underlines the importance of radical feminism, as predicted by the feminist literature, despite the problems of disunity radicalism can cause.

As with contraception, though much more so, these radical campaigns therefore managed to initiate a public debate on sexuality, which in France was an important achievment in relation to women's rights generally and part of the radical ethos of the personal being political.[24] However it was not the only important factor, 'Given the plurality of motivations... the contemporary women's movement cannot be said to have dominated the universe of political discourse.'[25] 'Il répondait aussi à des nécessités économiques, politiques et idéologiques, qu'il faudrait analyser de près.'[26] Moreover, such changes in discourse are precarious – the State can revoke what is given; allies can move on, producing weakness and the old enemies remain ready to reassert themselves and their old familiar discourse on women that talks of patriotism and the family.[27]

---

[21] The change in the 1975 law from the emphasis in previous bills on therapeutic abortion to one on demand before 12 weeks, appears to have taken into account the safety of the Karman method as demonstrated by campaigners – the right of women could only be acknowledged on this basis.

[22] As to the involvement of the MLF, Lovenduski, *op.cit*, p.272, argues that, although Choisir played an agenda-setting role, no other MLF-affiliated groups played a part. Rather, it was the presence of feminists in governing élites and as professionals that led to the development of policies for women through policy networks. I would dispute this as do many other French commentators, such as Mossuz-Lavau, (Interview, Paris, 7 September, 1990), Dhavernas, and members of the MFPF and Choisir themselves. Jensen, *op.cit*, p.14, argues that the abortion campaign put the French State in a crisis situation. The law now appeared unenforceable and women were becoming involved in a volatile political situation which identified itself along class as well as feminist lines.

[23] There's no doubt that pressure from feminists and other groups plus women's courage in openly flounting the law and speaking out against the abortion law, were crucial to the eventual passing of the 'loi Veil' (Duchen, *op.cit*, p.58.). 'The abortion campaign was successful ... in expanding the parameters of political discourse in France ... By 1974, women's right to control their own bodies was one theme in the legislative debate surrounding the loi Veil, along with equity, fairness, and family planning ... L'interruption volontaire de la grossesse replaced l'avortement in official language.' (Jensen, *op.cit*, p.15.). '(F)eminist discourse on sexuality, reproduction, contraception, and abortion developed from women's specific experience of domination and resistance and radicalized the position in favour of abortion adopted by other political organizations. In this sense, it can be said that feminist discourse hegemonized the discursive terrain regarding abortion.' (Batiot, 'The Political Construction of Sexuality: the contraception and abortion issues in France, 1965-75', in P.Cerny ed., *Social Movement and Protest in France* (Frances Pinter, 1982), p.100.

[24] *Ibid.*

[25] Mouvement Francais de Planning Familial, *D'une revolte à une lutte: 25 ans d'histoire du planning familial* (Editions Tierce, 1983), p.235.

[26] *Ibid*, pp.383-396.

[27] This helped to ensure that half of all public hospitals did no abortions in 1976. (Ardagh, *The New France* (Penguin, 1977), p.397.) Feminists in both countries continue to campaign on the issue of abortion. Recently to ensure the continued provision of

When comparing the abortion campaigns in the two countries it would appear that second-wave feminism had a positive radicalising effect in France on the campaigns of liberal feminists and their allies. In turn, radical feminism in Britain intensified the aims and of abortion campaigners and their allies against the attempts at eradication of abortion rights of pro-life groups. However, more importantly, in France radical feminism managed to overcome the strength of the entrenched policy network members, such as the moralists and 'natalistes', and in comparison to Britain, particularly in respect of the medical professions, to ensure that after 1975, at least up to the tenth week of gestation, abortion was on the demand of the women herself and she had the 'right to choose'. This was especially surprising given the legal advances that had to be brought about by abortion campaigners in France.

New Reproductive Technologies

As with the previous two reproductive rights issues, policy on the new reproductive technologies made ostensibly since the beginning of the 1980s has seen the pre-eminence in consultations of policy network members. The main statutes passed in this time have been the *Surrogacy Arrangements Act, 1985*, and *the Human Fertilisation and Embryology Act, 1990*, in Britain, and a law on artificial insemination and donation in December 1991, with draft laws similar to the British 1990 Act published but not fully debated in France.

There appears to be a similar moral code underlying legislation in both countries. Established groups such as the medical profession and the churches have been invited to play a part in creating guidelines and the status of the embryo has been more important in debates involving the government and health policy network than women's rights. 'Natalistes' in France were more favourable to NRTs than on the former two issues as they encouraged couples to have children, they have therefore been successful in so far as NRTs have continued to be reimbursed. The Catholic Church in both countries has played an important part, ironically even to the point of preventing the passing of legislation in France. French Catholics have not had a far-reaching effect on infertility treatment however, nor on abortion rights, in contrast in the latter case to their British counterparts. This could be due to their political strength not being as great as in Britain, for example, those alongside the new right-wing Prime Minister Chirac in 1986 who attempted to repeal abortion reimbursement and met with such opposition that the idea had to be withdrawn. Alternatively the very public lobbying carried out by British moralists and Catholics could have been felt to be a necessity by moralists as they were excluded from the policy network on the issue.

As to the influence of the medical professions, as with other issues in the health policy sector, the French and British governments were disposed from the beginning of debates on NRTs towards the involvment of the most

the abortion pill, RU 486. The acceptance of feminist rights by the French State was emphasised when the Catholic Church pressurised the pharmaceutical company, Roussel, to withdraw RU 486.

important members of the network, the medical professions, who predetermined government preconceptions of the issues involved and were consulted much more than any other group. The bills that were presented to parliament by the government in both countries thus contained this partiality as it was the result of consultation organised by the government.

Moreover, British Parliamentarians were influenced by the lobbying of groups such as PROGRESS, who indeed found themselves, 'satisfied with the passage of those clauses relating to controlled research under licence on the human embryo', in the final Act.[28] Indeed there were doctors practising NRTs who would have liked more consultation. For example, Dr. Brian Liebermann, consultant at St. Mary's IVF clinic, argued that the Act produced social and practical implications for IVF centres and therefore for couples, arguing that many more procedures were more costly, more dangerous and involved third parties such as organ donation but it was only on IVF that Parliament saw fit to legislate. He was also amazed at the lack of support and respect the medical professions had received from the public and Parliament.[29] Moralists are, by contrast, not satisfied with the Act, even though moralist and medical lobbying groups were equally well-organised and funded. The British government were also impressed with the success of the structure of the Voluntary Licensing Authority (VLA). Indeed the fact that self- regulation was sanctioned by the government from the inception of the VLA made approval of its methods almost a foregone conclusion. Moreover, another useful resource for the VLA must have been that, unlike in France, no prominent doctor came out against NRTs whilst it was generally presumed that the VLA was set up by the State.

Similarly in France, the medical organisation, CECOS, escaped much criticism and indeed was warmly received by the government when they lobbied to base legislation on their own structure for artificial insemination treatment clinics. When, in 1988, they were excluded from a list of 79 licensed insemination centres, because of their 1901 status, the furore this created shows the extent of their influence[30] CECOS were also involved in consultations with the government. In July 1990, M. Jean Michaud, President of the NRT section of the 'commission nationale de médecine et de biologie de la reproduction' (CNMBR) reported to Jean- François Girard, director general of health, of a meeting between themselves and CECOS on the issue of testing sperm for the AIDS virus[31] It was also CECOS who complained to the government about sperm banks who were not operating legally[32] This led to the investigation of two private sperm banks. The rules were ostensibly laid down by CECOS and the banks were investigated at their instigation. Nor was CECOS the only medical organisation in France to be directly influential. The Braibant Report (1989) stated, 'Conformément à l'avis de différentes instances telle que le Conseil de l'ordre des médecins, la PMA fondée sur des dons de sperme ou d'ovocytes a donc été

---

[28] Personal correspondence with Anna Humphrey for PROGRESS, 4/3/92.

[29] Centre for Social Ethics and Policy conference, 'The Human Fertilisation and Embryology Bill', St. Mary's Hospital, Manchester, 9th May 1990.

[30] *Le Monde*, 19/5/90.

[31] *Le Monde*, 26/11/91 and 11/2/92.

[32] *Ibid.*

retenue.'[33]

British feminists did ally with the medical professions and campaigned for research, so that abortion rights would not be jeopardised. These campaigns were successful. This illustrates the usefulness of allying with a prominent member of the policy network as an outsider to that network. However there were aspects of the British Act that would also point to a certain amount of feminist influence *per se*. For example, in the *Code of Practice* doctors have got to obtain consents (Schedule 3) and there are guidelines for standards in laboratories and licensed centres. Also, more women than men were members of the original Human Fertilisation and Embryology Authority (HUFEA) However, during the passage of the Bill the only only real amendment was that on the welfare of the child and after the Act feminists were still worried that single, lesbian or virgin women would still be denied access to artificial insemination. What is worse the government introduced an abortion amendment despite the feminist-supported backbench Bill by Lord Houghton. Finally, feminists were dissatisfied that there was no formal structure for ensuring the representation of the interests of women or of any other group, such as infertile women.

In France, feminists have no Act to be dissatisfied with. Nor did they lobby and ally with the medical professions to the same extent as their British counterparts due to their more radical nature and the fact that abortion was not re-examined in France. However, the radical feminist cause may well have been assisted by the support of Jacques Testard and prominent sociologists such as Marcus Steiff. Feminists were invited to sit on the National Ethics Council (CCNE) in 1992 and the Parliamentary Committee for Science and Technology (OPECST) in 1992 interviewed, *inter alia*, Mme. André, Secrétaire d'Etat aux Droits des Femmes, the CNRS director M.Kourilsky, Jacques Testard, psychologists, psychoanalysts, lawyers, sociologists, and philosophers. Nonetheless, the parliamentarians responsible for the OPECST report were of the opinion that only the medical professions needed to be actually consulted, to allay ignorance and fears. Presumably feminist opinions would be dealt with during the public debate that would follow the report What appears to have been most important to the parliamentarians who authored the report therefore were the issues of embryo status, organ donation, access and filiation. In both countries the dangers and rights of women patients took a back seat to such issues.

Conclusion

In relation to all three issues membership of the policy sector included feminist campaigners, with radical feminists in the policy area, and that of the policy community included interested parliamentarians and liberal feminists, who relied on the former to increase their strength as outsiders. Those groups on the inside of the policy network who enjoyed the correct resources, who were invited to consult, and whose opinions appear to have had a direct influence on the content of the law, were essentially moral-

---

[33] 'Avant- projet de loi sur les sciences de la vie et les droits de l'homme', 1989, p.23.

ists, demographers, especially in France, and most importantly the medical professions.

It was these groups which therefore had an influence on the content of the contraceptive laws of 1967 in both countries, as well as the amendments of the early 1970s. These groups were also instrumental in influencing the implementation of the law at the level of the local policy community.

In relation to abortion moralists took a more active interest in the issue, perhaps due to the timing of debates as well as the more sensitive nature of the reproductive right being campaigned for. This is especially the case with British Catholic groups. The medical professions put forward 'nataliste' and moral as well as medical arguments, which were all respected in the format of the law. Again, these groups were also instrumental in influencing the implementation of the law at the local level.

In relation to NRTs debate took a philosophical turn but essentially the health policy network members were as influential on this reproductive rights issue as on the two previous issues. This time however 'natalistes' in France supported liberalisation of NRTs, and French doctors were less moralistic and 'nataliste' as they were no longer represented by the 'Conseil de l'Ordre'. Medical professions in both countries supported regulation, though they were split in France into AI and IVF doctors with the latter group promoting self-regulation. Both the British and French governments came down in favour of those doctors supporting regulation, with arguments favouring a statutory licensing authority being well-received by the British government and licensing being a major tenet of the 1990 Act, and the CECOS model for donor insemination being closely followed in the law of December 1991 in France. The close involvement in Britain of the medical professions when compared with France could also be attributed to the fact that it was in Britain that the first test-tube baby was born; that doctors are already more involved with the state due to the existence of the NHS; and that reimbursement of NRT treatments in France, due to the prevalent 'nataliste' ethos in that country, contributed to the setting up of private clinics outside of the public hospital system.

The reproductive rights study shows the negative effect of having policy networks' members solely in control of policy making in their sector.

What has emerged as being particularly significant in both countries has been firstly, the extent to which reproductive legal provision has been controlled by the medical professions, in addition by 'natalistes' in France, and to a lesser extent by moralist interest groups. This has been ensured as reproduction is important to governments and thus policy communities and networks exist on such issues. Such groups have secured membership of these policy networks by displaying the requisite resources, in contrast to feminists, whether or not this latter group can be the only ones deemed to represent the majority of health users on these issues. Control by these 'insiders' has therefore been condoned by the goverments in question both before and after modern statutory provision. This has been to the detriment of women's rights, and has meant that women have therefore been on the receiving end of reproductive laws that have been harsh, inadequate and sometimes non-existent, despite increasing feminism amongst reproductive rights campaigners.

Secondly, the content of laws and their subsequent effect on women's reproductive rights has been influenced to a large extent by the radicalism of contemporaneous feminism. Radicalism determined the issues and methods of feminists, and perhaps most importantly their unity or otherwise, as well as those of their allies, and policy network members such as government actors and medical professionals.

Liberal feminists have had an alliance-building capacity and the best ally appears to be the one most likely to be a policy network member. A left-wing ally is therefore less useful than a member of the medical professions. This has been borne out by the relative success for feminists in campaigns involving medical allies – that on abortion in France in the early 1970s, and that on NRTs in Britain in the late 1980s. Only liberal feminists have had a role further than the agenda-setting role, one of actually influencing the content of a law due to their alliance-building capacity and their methods.

Radicals by contrast have been shown to have a radicalising effect on the agenda of liberal feminists and their allies, as well as in some cases the agenda of the government. On the issue of NRTs there has been a fundamental difficulty in debates among feminists themselves as well as with potential allies – arguably it was only the linking of the abortion issue with NRTs in Britain which forced feminists into an alliance with the medical professions on the issue. Radicals have had opinions on NRTs but these have come at a time when feminists have been split by them, when liberals have drifted away because there are no issues to campaign on, and on an issue where medicalisation is even more intrinsic and likely. Liberal feminist demands were co-opted by the government and the medical professions. But liberal and radical desires are different. What radicals would see as co-option, liberals would see as success, because at least that is better than having no law at all, and it is always possible to modify and improve a law over time once it is on the Statute Book.

The ultimate conclusion of the thesis is therefore that, in both countries, the effective exclusion of feminists from the health policy networks meant that they had to ally with doctors and this exacerbated the medicalisation of reproductive rights already taking place. This leads to the question of whether, liberal or radical, feminists would have been ignored anyway on an issue that parliamentarians saw as medical above all, whether feminists and women did or not? This was not only unfortunate for feminists whose interest group aims remained unfulfilled; it was deplorable for the women they tried to represent who have to contend with the limited reproductive rights that were enacted as a result.

The European Union at the Crossroads

Ian Manners
University of Bristol

'The Double Game:
Negotiating the Association Agreements
Between the European Community and the Visegrad'

Introduction

The initial motivation was European support for democracy in Eastern Europe. In the wake of the end of the cold war the European Community agreed that the most effective support for the new democratic governments of Eastern Europe would be through the setting up of association agreements. The agreements were to provide a blueprint for democratic change and provide a positive incentive in the shape of eventual membership of the European Community. The second factor from Western Europe's point of view was fear of what might happen in the East. As Barry Buzan says, 'Political threats are felt by those whose domestic arrangements are either out of step with history, out of step with present trends, menaced by hostile neighbours, or unable to cope with the problems of government'.[1]

The political security of West European States was, and is still, threatened by the failure of political reforms in Eastern Europe. Just as during the cold war the continued existence of socialist states in Eastern Europe continued to threaten the political security of Western Europe, so could the failure of democratisation in the East. As Buzan states, 'political threats stem from the great diversity of ideas and traditions which is the key underlying justification for the international anarchy'.[2] If true, then a logical extension of this argument produces the conclusion that a loss of diversity and the acceptance of a common ideology, liberal democracy, will lead to a collapse for the basis of the international anarchy and the success of assumptions about global interdependence. The crucial assumption in this study is that focusing solely on political security, without reference to military defence or armed forces, is justified as a valid activity in European security cooperation. If the ventured costs and potential benefits were not great, then the choice of case and the issue of political threat would be valueless. The European Parliament acknowledged the importance of political security thus, 'Security policy as part of East-West relations depends increasingly less on the military dimension, than on a policy of global stability, which military means are powerless to achieve'.[3]

---

[1] Buzan, Barry, 1991, *People, States and Fear: An Agenda for International Security Studies in the Post-Cold War Era*, second edition (London: Harvester Wheatsheaf), p.369.

[2] *Ibid*, p.119.

[3] Langer, Alexander (Rapporteur), 1993. *Report by the Committee on Foreign Affairs and Security on developments in East-West relations in Europe and their impact on European security*, European Parliament Session Documents, 24 March 1993, A3-0108/93, p.12.

This work is based on my research method of applying different theories of international cooperation to the behaviour of the European Union member states. The study looks at how the negotiation of the Association Agreements between the European Community and the Visegrad Three was influenced by domestic constraints over the threat to particular economies, and by integration forces over the issue of widening. The implications of future enlargement affected the agreements and by studying their negotiation we might arrive at an idea of which road the European Union may take.

The first mention of a change in the relationship between East and West Europe came at the Council of Foreign Ministers in Esclimont from 14-15 October 1989. The agenda oversimplified the revolutionary change taking place in Europe when it noted that ministers agreed to study the basis for relations with Eastern Europe in the future.[4] The beginning of a revision of the basis for relations came on the 5 February 1990 when the Foreign Ministers met to agree a future strategy for relations with the Eastern European countries. The conclusions of the Council gave a programme of action for the Central and Eastern European Countries.[5] The Community then set about a simple programme of basic agreements, being mostly extensions of existing frameworks, with the fledgling democracies of Eastern Europe.

The delegations from Hungary, Czechoslovakia and Poland were strongly of the opinion that the association agreements were the first step towards full membership of the community.[6] The mutual benefit to be gained by these three countries was soon recognised as they were to admit:

> 'Cooperation among Poland, Czechoslovakia and Hungary is extremely important. Our countries have similar, coinciding and, on a number of issues, identical interests, and they are trying to develop new regional cooperation in this part of the European continent. This cooperation strengthens European cooperation and it serves our diverse interests.'[7]

This initial harmony of interest clearly led to the Polish, Hungarian and Czechoslovak representatives meeting in Visegrad, near Budapest, to coordinate their negotiations with the European Community.[8] The European Community can therefore be said to have been responsible for the signing on the 15 February 1993 Vaclav Havel, Lech Walesa and Jozsef Antall of the Visegrad Declaration.[9]

The European Commission renewed negotiations over the association agreements with Poland, Czechoslovakia and Hungary from the 18-26 March 1991.[10] The main aim was to finish the negotiations before the end of 1991 in order to begin the agreements in January 1992. However, it soon became apparent that the talks were not going as smoothly as might have been

---

[4] *European Access*, Number 6, December 1989, p.6.

[5] Press Release of Minutes of Foreign Ministers Council Meeting, 5 February 1990, p.6.

[6] *Agence Europe*, 29 December 1990, p.6.

[7] K.Skubiszewski quoted in *Pravda*, 25 January 1991, p.4, in *The Current Digest of Soviet Press*, Volume 43, Number 4, p.25.

[8] *Keesing's Record of World Events*, Volume 37, Number 9 (supplement), p.38508.

[9] *European Access*, April 1991, p.6.

[10] *Agence Europe*, 20 March 1991, p.8.

wished and negotiations to complete Association Agreements with Poland, Hungary and Czechoslovakia were said to be in great difficulty.[11] Both the European Community member states and the Visegrad states had reservations, in the first instance over trade in sensitive goods, and in the second instance over the likelihood of membership. The problems of trade were over the concern expressed by some states at the prospect of imports of textiles, steel, and certain agricultural products.[12] In contrast the East European countries wanted specific references to their future membership of the European Community to be included in the agreements.[13] The mandate given to the Commission to negotiate the association agreements was not broad enough to deal with the problems which were being encountered. The Commission was therefore forced, on 15 April 1991, to go back to the Council and ask whether and how to improve the Community's offer. The ministers were asked how to overcome four main sticking points. The first point was the specific request by the Visegrad countries to include an automatic path to membership, but the European Community could not undertake such a commitment.[14] The second point was the free access to all markets which had been offered in principle by the European Community, but was to be phased in over ten years.[15]

The real problem here was that the three products on which the European Community wanted to impose import controls – agricultural produce, textiles and steel – were actually the ones which the Visegrad countries wanted to export. The third point was the technicalities of origin and reference in the customs regime which had to fall in line with that of the European Community. The final point of contention referred to the status of East European workers already in Western Europe and the rules governing the flow of job seekers.[16] The General Affairs Council in Luxembourg on 15 April 1991 stated that it was 'ready to display the necessary flexibility for the continuation of the negotiations'.[17] The foreign ministers of the members states, presided over by Luxembourg's Jacques Poos, gave further guidelines for the Commission to continue with the negotiations. As part of these guidelines the Council reaffirmed that the European agreements were to reinforce democratic transition in two ways. The intention was firstly 'to accompany and facilitate their processes of reform' (referring to the Visegrad Three), and secondly 'to confirm these three countries' membership of a democratic Europe'.[18] However the western market access which the east really needed to facilitate reform was not referred to and membership of a democratic Europe did not necessarily refer to the European Community. Sources close to the Council alleged that there were 'additional concessions' to be made towards the Visegrad Three in an attempt to gain their agreement.[19] The

[11] *European Access*, June 1991, p.5.
[12] *Agence Europe*, 10 April 1991, p.11.
[13] *Ibid.*
[14] *Agence Europe*, 13 April 1991, p.8.
[15] *Ibid.*
[16] *Ibid.*
[17] Press release from the General Affairs Council meeting, 15 April 1991, 5690/91 (Presse 47-G), p.6.
[18] *Ibid.*
[19] *Agence Europe*, 17 April 1991, p.8.

concessions were reported to be on the issue of agriculture, with steel and coal carrying controls for five years and textiles carrying controls for ten years.[20]

An early morning coup on 19 August 1991 ousted Mikhail Gorbachev, President of the USSR, from power. Jacques Delors, who had been previously opposed to European Community enlargement at that stage, believed that disorder in the Soviet Union meant that the European Community had to be more open towards its Eastern neighbours.[21] On 20 August 1991 the European Community Foreign Ministers decided that it was necessary to speed up the Association Agreements with Poland, Hungary and Czechoslovakia.[22] By this time it was apparent that the European Community was split in two on its approach to the Eastern Europeans. The first group, led by France, was in favour of keeping the European Community small and 'deep'. They wanted the trade pacts to be called 'cooperation agreements'.[23] The second group, led by Britain, was in favour of widening the European Community through association agreements with eastern Europe. The compromise title used in 1991 was that of 'European Agreements'.

On 20 August 1991 the deputy foreign ministers and defence experts from the Visegrad Three met in Warsaw and and agreed to work even closer on the successful conclusion of the European agreements.[24] The collapse of the coup attempt led to increased calls in Western Europe for more aid for the Soviet Union and a speeding up of negotiations for associate membership for the Visegrad countries.[25] The events in Moscow had certainly changed the game, 'the regional cooperation among Hungary, Poland and Czechoslovakia ... has now been cemented by comment concern', admitted Vladimir Gerasimov in *Pravda*.[26]

The General Affairs Council meeting on 6 September 1991 attempted to achieve the 'adaptation of the negotiation directives' in light of the recent developments and the increased drive to conclude before the end of October 1991.[27] The member states of the Council held an examination of the Commission's package with the intention of giving it 'greater scope for negotiation'.[28] It soon became clear that the gathered foreign ministers had never been further away from agreement. The French foreign minister, Roland Dumas, was accused by the Danish foreign minister, Uwe Ellerman-Jensen, of 'living on another planet' as the French blocked all progress.[29] The French refused to accept 61% cuts in agricultural tariffs on the Visegrad

---

[20] *Ibid.*

[21] *The Times*, 22 August 1991, p.5.

[22] *Ibid*, p.15.

[23] *Ibid.*

[24] Perry, Duncan M, 1991, 'The Attempted Coup in the USSR: East European Reactions; Introduction', *Report on Eastern Europe*, Volume 2, Number 35, 30 August 1991, p.2.

[25] *The Times*, 23 August 1991, p.7.

[26] *Pravda*, 31 August 1991, p.5, in *The Current Digest of Soviet Press*, Volume 43, Number 35, p.43.

[27] Press release of Minutes of General Affairs Council Meeting, 6 September 1991, p.4.

[28] *Ibid.*

[29] *The Times*, 7 September 1991, p.1.

countries and to allow 500 tonnes of Polish beef to enter the community.[30] The Danes were joined by the Dutch and the British in their criticism of the French with the British Foreign Office minister, Douglas Hogg, commenting that he was 'very disappointed'.[31] The French were joined by Ireland and Belgium in vetoing the agreement on increasing meat imports from the Visegrad countries.[32] The counter-proposal was to give financial aid to the East European countries so that they might sell their surpluses in traditional markets such as the USSR.[33] The Italians also failed to support the Commission's proposals in the agricultural and textile sectors, suggesting that the Community should wait until after the conclusion of the Uruguay round of the GATT talks.[34] The Portuguese were similarly conservative over concessions on textiles, clearly attempting to block any agreement without benefits for themselves. The disagreements within the Council were such that a position could not be reached despite the Dutch presidency's stated intention to do so.[35] The Council concluded by announcing that it intended to continue its 'examination' of the problem at the next Council meeting on the 30 September 1991.

The argument over the association agreements reached their peak at a meeting between the British Prime Minister, John Major, and the French President, François Mitterrand on the 11 September. President Mitterrand led a pre-emptive strike at Prime Minister Major by denouncing his ideas on enlargement as an attempt to create a 'vague sort of free trade zone' at a televised press conference prior to the talks.[36] Mr Major counter-attacked by urging the President to drop the French veto on the agricultural aspects of the Association Agreements.[37] Despite this very visible public posturing the leaders were reported as having a very friendly meeting, lending the conclusion that the outbursts were for domestic rather than international consumption.[38] This interpretation is supported by Mitterrand's speech at his press conference:

> 'Let it be clearly said that we (the citizens of France) are not hostile to the draft agreements envisaged between the Community, Poland, Czechoslovakia, and Hungary. We are simply asking for guarantees. I believe that this problem will be settled this month, to everyone's satisfaction.'[39]

The Polish negotiators had reacted swiftly to the French intransigence by stating that 'continued negotiations are contingent upon enlargement of the mandate, which means that at this stage we cannot see the use for further

---

[30] *Ibid* and *The Times*, 9 September 1991, p.8.
[31] *The Times*, 7 September 1991, p.1.
[32] *Christian Science Monitor*, 11 September 1991, in Brada 1991: 28.
[33] *Agence Europe*, 7 September 1991, p.8.
[34] *Ibid*.
[35] Press release of Minutes of General Affairs Council Meeting, 6 September 1991, p.4.
[36] *The Times*, 12 September 1991, p.1.
[37] *Ibid*.
[38] Brada, Josef C, 1991, 'The European Community and Czechoslovakia, Hungary, and Poland', *Report on Eastern Europe*, Volume 49, Number 2, December 1991, p.28.
[39] *Agence Europe*, 12 September 1991, p.10.

rounds of discussions at plenary sessions'.[40] The Poles continued this line of argument by withdrawing from the European Community negotiations on the 19 September.[41] The compromise was struck when the Belgian Foreign Minister, Mark Eyskens, suggested that the 'triangular operation' with the USSR could continue for a transition period of one or two years. After that period the European Community would start to lower the barriers to meat imports from the Visegrad countries. Both the French and the Poles had indicated that they were interested in this compromise which would break the lock on the agreements.[42]

On 22 November 1991 the European Community reached an agreement with Hungary, Poland and Czechoslovakia for a new generation of Association Agreements in Brussels, the home of the Belgian compromise.[43] The agreements had first been proposed in September 1990 and had been under intense discussion from February 1990 onwards. They provided for free trade within 10 years, with import controls on certain goods. The final import control to be added was for Spain's steel industry to protect it against cheap exports from the Visegrad countries.[44]

Negotiating Strategies

My claim is that states will be more likely to cooperate if they use reciprocity in their negotiating strategy; 'governments may have incentives to practice reciprocity in a variety of situations that are characterised by mixtures of conflicting and complementary interests'.[45] The negotiating strategies factor describes the way in which the use of reciprocity, issue linkage and bargaining chips influenced cooperation. As Robert Axlerod argues, 'strategies of reciprocity have the effect of promoting cooperation by establishing a direct connection between an actor's present behaviour and anticipated future benefits'.[46] The strategies that differing states use can affect not only their potential gain from the situation, but also the overall outcome of the negotiations. There are two separate paths to the way in which negotiating strategy influenced the cooperation, the use of reciprocity and the use of multi-issue games. The first path which altered the outcome was the use of reciprocity, which is normally very difficult to distinguish from differences of opinion in negotiation analysis. However it becomes clear that at least two states realised that by breaking ranks and being awkward they could influence the other cooperators in the short term, even if in the long term it was against their own self interest. More importantly, these two states used this technique against their each other (as reciprocity) and against team solidarity (as a form of negative bargaining chip). The first instance

[40] *Agence Europe*, 9/10 September 1991, p.10.

[41] *Time*, 23 September 1991 in Brada 1991: 28.

[42] *Agence Europe*, 14 September 1991, p.10.

[43] *European Access*, February 1992, p.5.

[44] Keesing's *Record of World Events*, November 1991, p.38593.

[45] Axelrod, Robert & Robert O.Keohane, 1986, 'Achieving Cooperation Under Anarchy: Strategies and Solutions' in Kenneth Oye (ed), 1986, *Cooperation Under Anarchy* (Princeton: Princeton University Press), p.224.

[46] Axelrod in Oye (ed), *Cooperation Under Anarchy*, p.14.

of this is when France tries to defect on the issue of meat imports in an obvious attempt to gain an international bargaining chip as well as bene- fit from domestic support. In response Poland refuses to take part in the general negotiations, against the interests of the other Visegrad states, but also against the interest of the European Community's clearly stated wish to conclude the concurrent agreements with the Visegrad states. Denmark, Britain, and Germany attempt to punish the French defection by publicly deriding the international commitment and protectionism of the French. In response to this pressure Mitterrand and the French agree to cooperate on a compromise which brings a reciprocating response from Poland as they return to the talks. The European Community, including the French, agree to allow an increasing amount of meat in, and the European Community including the Visegrad Three reciprocate by agreeing to allow an increase in the control of illegal meat entering the Community.

The second path which altered the outcome was the use of multi-issue games. It is accepted that if an issue can be broken down into separate smaller bargains then it is decomposable. This decomposability of the issue allows the use of issue-linkage, bargaining chips, and reciprocity to log-roll an issue towards agreement. However in this study the issue was negatively decomposable as the dynamics of the agreements, the voting procedure in the Council, and the fact that the agreements had to be a single acceptance meant that agreement was harder to achieve. In practice only one or two states were vehemently opposed to any one particular part of the agree- ments. On the issue of agriculture it was France, Belgium, and Ireland; on the issue of textiles it was Italy and Portugal; on the issue of steel it was Spain and Greece. If the agreements had been dealt with by using majority voting within the Council on each of these issues then it would have been eas- ier to reach agreement (at the cost of sovereignty). The agreements tended to be discussed as a single issue which meant that opposition came from France, Italy, Spain, Greece, Belgium, Portugal, and Ireland jointly. The net influence on the outcome was to make cooperation particularly difficult to achieve, and with the exception of the Belgian meat compromise, always at the level of the lowest European Community common denominator.

Relative Payoffs

My claim is that states will be more likely to cooperate if the benefits outweigh the costs. The 'relative payoffs' factor describes the way in which the balance between benefits and costs influenced cooperation, 'The payoff structure that determines mutuality of interests is not based simply upon objective factors, but is grounded upon the actors' perception of their own interests'.[47] In the study of the Association Agreements the payoffs were made highly complex by the nature of the multi-issue games being played. At one level the payoffs were absolute for each state. This equation was simply how much each state had to gain from political stability and economic opportunities compared to its losses in terms of the cost of aid and market

---

[47] Axelrod & Keohane, 'Achieving Cooperation Under Anarchy', p.229.

share of its goods. At a second level the payoffs were relative for each state. This equation was how much political ground could be made from the agreements compared to the political ground made by other countries within the negotiations. The third level was the behaviour decisions which decided the cognitive payoffs. This equation was how much loss could be avoided in the short term compared with the profit to be made in the long term.

The problematic of the Association Agreements was two-fold, first the payoff structure was asymmetrical amongst the Western European states. In this sense the division was between those states who felt that the gains of cooperation outweighed the losses (primarily Germany and Britain), and those states who felt that the losses of cooperation outweighed the gains (primarily France, Spain and Portugal). Secondly the payoff structure was asymmetrical between the European Community states and the Visegrad states, the former wishing to avoid the loss of political security, whilst the latter were trying to gain the benefits of European Community membership.

The payoff structure influenced the cooperation in three ways; in absolute terms, in relative terms, and in cognitive terms. The absolute payoffs meant that all the European Community states felt they had something to gain from free access to the markets of the Visegrad Countries and that giving a form of affiliate membership to these countries in order to stabilise their political structures. However in absolute terms the European Community states with large primary sectors to their economies felt particularly vulnerable to the costs of free market access by the Visegrad countries. Included in this group to vary degrees and according to sector were Spain, Portugal, Greece, Ireland, Belgium, Italy and France. The Visegrad countries were willing to discount the current losses for the benefits of European Community membership in the future.

The relative payoffs meant that some states were in favour of the agreements because they had political profit to be made from widening the Community, such as Britain and Denmark. Similarly, some states with large secondary or tertiary economic sectors were in favour of the agreements because they had economic profit to be made from market access (the Netherlands for example). Germany was in favour of the agreements because its geographical position led it to fear instability to its east and because it would relinquish some of its donor burden. In contrast those states, including France, Italy, Belgium, Spain, Portugal and Greece, who were in favour of deepening the community were against the agreements because they would be losing political ground. Similarly, the poorer three states, Greece, Portugal and Spain, were still in a transitional phase themselves and feared the costs of losing cohesion funds and regional development support.

It is the cognitive behaviour which pulls the individual definitions of costs and benefits together to produce the resulting influence which the payoff structure had on the cooperation. The immediate absolute losses weighed heavier than the long term relative losses for France, Italy, Spain, Greece, Belgium, Portugal and Ireland. The long term relative benefits and the immediate absolute benefits coincided for Britain, Germany, and Denmark. The long term absolute benefit weighed heavier than the immediate absolute benefit for the Visegrad Three. In conclusion the importance of keeping import restrictions on agricultural produce, textiles, steel, and workers, combined with the value of widening the community and holding a carrot up to the East made the Agreements possible because eventually the Visegrad countries wanted to be given the hope of European Community membership with as little loss as possible.

Shadows of Interaction

My claim is that states will be more likely to cooperate when the shadows of interaction are positive: a positive shadow of the past and a long shadow of the future. The shadows of interaction factor describes the way in which the likelihood of future contact and historical experience of past contact influenced cooperation. The shadow of the future played an asymmetric role in influencing the outcome of the association agreements. According to Axlerod and Keohane, 'the more future payoffs are valued relative to current payoffs, the less the incentive to defect today – since the other side is likely to retaliate tomorrow'.[48] On the European Community side the likelihood that they would have to interact on general issues in the future was high. More importantly, the precedence that would be set on future applications for European Community membership also cast a long shadow. On the Visegrad side the likelihood of future cooperation with the other states was the driving factor and in reality overcame any temptations to defect. The shadows of the past were increasingly negative for the European Community as the approaching arguments over EMU and PU at Maastricht spilled over into the negotiations. The Eastern European shadow of the past was extremely short but the actual signing of the Visegrad Agreement had made it increasingly positive. The shadows of the past are just as important as those of the future as Buzan says, 'patterns of amity/enmity arise from a variety of issues that could not be predicted from a simple consideration of the distribution of power'.[49] As he explains, 'by amity I mean relationships ranging from genuine friendship to expectations of protection or support'.[50] The net influence on the outcome was to make the states very cautious about what they agreed to, but equally very aware that the agreement would have long term implications.

The Nature of Actors

My claim is that states will be more likely to cooperate if the number of actors involved is small enough to overcome sanctioning problems and yet large enough to make the cooperative action more effective than unilateral action. This claim is supported by Oye, 'as the number of players increases, transactions and information costs rise ... the likelihood of autonomous defection and of recognition and control problems increases ... the feasibility

---

[48] *Ibid*, p.232.
[49] Buzan, *People, States and Fear*, p.190.
[50] *Ibid*, 189.

of sanctioning defectors diminishes'.[51] The nature of actors factor describes the way in which the number and particular nature of states influenced cooperation. The twelve members of the European Community always make agreement on contentious issues very difficult because of the division of voting power within the council and the rules requiring a common position to be found. The opposite was true with the Visegrad states because to a certain degree the European Community was able to treat them as one actor, a specific aim of the Visegrad Agreement. The nature of the actors did have a major influence on the outcome as the European Community members divided into veto states (France), swing states, (Spain and Portugal), and lead states (Britain, Germany, and Denmark). These roles have been defined by Porter & Brown, 'a state whose cooperation is so essential to a successful agreement that it has an effective veto power over the agreement'.[52] The veto state appeared to be motivated primarily by domestic interest, while the swing states merely needed lubrication ('cohesion funds') to make them swing. The lead states all had vested interests in increasing the size of the European Community and securing its Eastern border. The net influence on the outcome was to slow down the cooperation procedure, but as the agreements will have set a precedence this will probably not be experienced again.

Presence of an Institution

My claim is that cooperation is more likely if an existing institution is present to influence the decision making of states. Evidence in support of this claim has already been seen as Martin points out, 'by means such as providing information about the actions of other states, setting standards by which to evaluate others' behaviour, or establishing penalties for non-compliance, institutions may allow states to overcome collective action problems'.[53] The presence of an institution factor describes the way in which an existing international institution, operating in a similar arena, influenced cooperation. Simply put, the only institution acting in the negotiation procedure was the European Community and as the agreement fell almost entirely within its policy machinery then the outcome merely reflects its bureaucratic process. It may be equally true to suggest that the study is one of an integrative community's membership procedure rather than one of true interstate cooperation. This oversimplifies the cooperation procedure of the European Communities and the influence which non-institutional factors have on this procedure. There were two institutions present in the negotiation of the Association Agreements and although one is legitimately the superior of the other they are worth considering in isolation. The Council of the European Communities consists of 19 interdependent councils, headed by the European Council of heads of state and government. The inter-

---

[51] Oye (ed), *Cooperation Under Anarchy*, p.19.

[52] Porter, Gareth & Janet Welsh Brown, 1991, *Global Environmental Politics* (Boulder, Westview Press), p.17.

[53] Martin, Lisa L, 1992, 'Institutions and Cooperation: Sanctions During the Falkland Islands Conflict', *International Security*, Spring 1992, Volume 16, Number 4, p.143.

governmental nature of the Council meant that this was the location for all the disagreements over the negotiations. The Commission of the European Communities worked as the civil service of the European Community, ultimately answerable to the Council and receiving all it negotiation directives from it. The Commission was mandated by the Council to conduct the negotiations with Hungary, Poland, and Czechoslovakia and was successful within the boundaries of its remit. The influence of the Commission on the outcome was positive but outweighed by the negative influence of the Council. It may be noted that it is this flawed relationship that the prospective members wish to become a part of.

Epistemological Community

My claim is that the role of an epistemic community will strongly influence cooperation through defining both state interests and the form of cooperative arrangements. The epistemological community factor describes the way in which an informed international community or organisation influenced cooperation. Haas defined this simply as 'epistemic communities are transnational networks of knowledge based communities that are both politically empowered through their claims to exercise authoritative knowledge and motivated by shared causal and principled beliefs'.[54] The fundamental weakness in this study was that no epistemic consensus was present to determine what sort of agreement should have been negotiated. The organisation which came closest was the Commission themselves but they were compromised by being given the responsibility for the negotiations without being given the power to set the agenda. Had the Commission been independent of the Council and not responsible for managing the negotiations (with the Council itself being given that responsibility) then cooperation might have been easier to achieve. A successful epistemic community is able to set the goals of cooperation, help determine national priorities and influence the negotiations themselves. In this study no group was able to influence the outcome to any positive degree.

Domestic Variables

My claim is that states will be more likely to cooperate if domestic conditions, in particular leadership and political mandate, are positive. The domestic variables factor describes the way in which national issues such as the strength of a pressure group, the electoral support for a particular issue, or a strong commitment to an issue by the leadership influenced cooperation. The importance of domestic issues in international agreements has been recognised by Robert Puttnam, as well as Axelrod & Keohane, 'analytic questions arise when considering connections between international relations and domestic politics. Negotiations involve not merely bargaining

---

[54] Haas, Peter M, 1990, 'Obtaining international environmental protection through epistemic consensus', *Millenium*, Winter 1990, Volume 19, Number 3, p.5.

between governments, but within societies as well'.[55] The domestic factor was strong in influencing the outcome of the negotiations by describing the agenda which must be seen to be addressed by each state's leadership. In this respect the Council can be a useful focus to negotiations because of its secrecy, but this may not help a leader explain to their electorate why they may have been forced to act in a particular manner. German domestic support demanded an end to instability in the east, most acutely felt through immigration pressures from asylum seekers. German business leaders were in favour of opening its markets to the east as they realised that they stood more to gain from reciprocal measures than the Visegrad Three. Germany has emerged as the largest trading partner with the Eastern Countries, particularly in the field of telecommunications. Domestic political opinion in Britain was felt more acutely by John Major as the widening of the European Community offered him a way to satisfy both Euro-sceptics and Euro-optimists within the Conservative Party. By widening the European Community he was lessening the likelihood of any further deepening from taking place, thus gaining favour with the Euro-sceptics. By taking a high profile position in the negotiations he was gaining favour with the Euro-optimists by demonstrating his commitment to European affairs. Similarly, supporting market access for Eastern Europe reinforced his anti-protectionist views in London and in Washington. It can also be said that Britain had a lot to gain from the East in terms of increased market access, especially in the banking and financial sectors. In symbolic terms the French, and President Mitterrand in particular, were in favour of a greater membership to the European Community, but not at the cost of deepening the Communities institutions. More than any other leader, President Mitterrand felt the anger of French pressure groups, the farmers in particular. In that respect the French President followed domestic interest in the negotiations, as his country produces nearly a quarter of the European Community's agricultural produce. Similarly, the French had been wholly unsuccessful in gaining a footing for their firms in the East European markets. The countries of southern Europe (Greece, Portugal, Spain, and Italy) all experienced widespread domestic opposition to the agreements as they would lose their status of preferential treatment. In the same way investment that use to go into these countries might be drawn into the East.

The Outcome of the Negotiations

The outcome of this study on the attempts to achieve cooperation on the European Community association agreements with Eastern Europe is that three distinct goals were achieved: cooperation *did* take place; an agreement *was* signed; and the Visegrad countries will *eventually* become members of the European Community. The loss of practically any market share of any worth by the East European countries did mean that the cooperation was a short term failure for a long term gain. More importantly it satisfied domestic pressure for membership which would have produced exactly the

---

[55] Axelrod & Keohane, 'Achieving Cooperation Under Anarchy', p.226.

wrong effect for the European Community if it had not been achieved. The defining variable in the influence which the seven factors had over the outcome was the asymmetry of the agreements. This meant that while the East Europeans largely dropped their barriers so the West Europeans institutionalised theirs. The unfair nature of this competition is reinforced by the observation that Eastern banks are far less able to compete with Western banks than Western farmers are able to compete with Eastern Farmers. Thus the payoff structure is the primary factor behind cooperation because it has been corrupted by the negotiating strategies motivated by domestic factors. In the end the Visegrad countries allowed this to happen because they were influenced by the shadow of the future motivated by domestic factors. The outcome of the association agreements produced neither immediate membership nor outright denial of market access. The compromise goal achieved satisfied the 'double game' being played in the European Community and the domestic support bases for governments of the Visegrad countries and the European Community member states.

Liberal Political Theory

Sally L. Jenkinson
University of North London

'Bayle *versus* Locke on Toleration
Some Reflections on Horton and Mendus'

Quotations

'All men know and acknowledge that God ought to be publicly worshipped.' (Locke, *Letter on Toleration*)[1] 1689.

'The sceptics did not deny that men ought to conform to the customs of their country and practise moral duties.' (Bayle, *Dictionnaire Historique*, article Pyrrhon,)[2] *(1696)*.

Locke, Bayle and the Moral Wrongness of Persecution

This paper considers certain recent interpretations of Locke's *Letter on Toleration* (1689) in the light of the critique of intolerance to be found in the *Commentaire philosophique* (1686) of Pierre Bayle. A comparison of the axioms underlying the work of each writer, it will be argued, can significantly illuminate some of the controversies of the present age about Locke, about the civil religion, about liberal theory and about the injustice of religious persecution. The controversies it refers to in particular are raised in the recent publication edited by Horton & Mendus, entitled *John Locke. 'A Letter Concerning Toleration' in focus.*[3] Within this compilation two mutually related issues are examined. The first broaches certain doubts cast upon the relevance to contemporary liberal concerns of Locke's understanding of toleration.[4] and implies that Locke's writings fail as liberal theory because of the supposedly 'christian' nature of the premises from which they proceed. A specific proposition which Susan Mendus considers, (though she does not endorse it one way or the other) is that given Locke's own belief in God' and 'the Christian belief of (his)

---

[1] Locke, John, *A Letter Concerning Toleration* in Gough, J.W. (ed), *The Second Treatise of Government and a Letter Concerning Toleration* (Basil Blackwell, Oxford, 1966), (hereinafter referred to as *Locke LT*), p.144.

[2] Bayle, Pierre, *Dictionnaire Historique et Critique*, 11th édition, Paris, 1820-1824, 16 volumes, Nouvelle Edition augmentée de notes extraites de Chaufepié. Joly, La Monnoie, Leclerc, Prosper Marchand etc, Slatkine Reprints, Genève, 1969, (hereinafter referred to as *Dictionnaire 1820-1824*), Article Pyrrhon XII pp.99-111, (B) p.101.

[3] Horton, John & Mendus, Susan, *John Locke*, 'A Letter Concerning Toleration' in *Focus* (Routledge, London and New York, 1991); (hereinafter referred to as Horton & Mendus (eds)). See in particular Waldren, Jeremy 'Locke: toleration and the rationality of persecution' in Horton & Mendus (eds), pp.98-12? (hereinafter referred to as Waldren); and Mendus, Susan 'Locke: toleration, rationality and persecution' in Horton & Mendus (eds), 147-162 (hereinafter referred to as Mendus).

[4] See John Dunn, 'What is living and what is dead in the political theory of John Locke' in Dunn, John, *Interpreting Political Responsibility* (Oxford University Press, Oxford, 1990) pp.18-19.

'audience ... Locke's case for religious toleration ... is well and truly dead and contains little if anything of lasting philosophic importance'.[5]

The second issue relates to the criticism by initiated in the article by Jeremy Waldren. He writes:

'What one misses above all in Locke's argument is the sense that there is anything morally wrong with intolerance, or a sense of any deep concern for the victims of persecution or the moral insult that is involved in the attempt to manipulate their faith.'[6]

Mendus will take up the point that Locke appears to associate no 'moral wrongness'[7] with persecution. Locke's position seems defective from a moral perspective, she agrees, because Locke seems to oppose merely certain kinds of reasons for religious persecution rather than its injustice.

This paper does not dispute the supposition that Locke's limited account of toleration is indicative of some deeper premise but it questions whether the deeper premise is about christianity rather than about power over what is taught to others; or whether it is without its parallels in the present age. Locke's real theoretical language, some critics suggest, is civic, republican, patriotic and erastian, carrying well understood ideological messages in its own time as well as atavistic resonances for later civic republicans such as Rousseau and Hegel.[8] What then is Locke's position, what arguments underpin it and, if it is morally defective, with what arguments should it be challenged?

One way of approaching these questions is to compare Locke's work with that of a contemporary who also wrote about toleration. Bayle, for example, a member of the recently 'tolerated' Huguenot community was becoming dissatisfied with the ancient institution of toleration in Europe just as Locke was making a case for extending it to English dissenters. While Locke, between 1686 and 1688, was revising a draft of his *Letter on Toleration*, Bayle, who had already published several works in the genre of humanist criticism, was putting through the press his *Commentaire philosophique* (1686).[9] The edition used here is that in Pierre Bayle, *Oeuvres Diverses* (4 volumes La Haye, 1727-31).[10], pp.375-444. Bayle's unique perspective on toleration and the duties of rulers arose out of neither jurisprudence nor theology but rather from his affiliation to the network of French philosophers who, like Descartes, were mathematicians and physicists, and who discussed for their own pleasure the pre-Socratic paradoxes of certainty, uncertainty

---

[5] Mendus p.147.

[6] Waldren p.120.

[7] Mendus p.148.

[8] See Mark Goldie 'The Civil religion of James Harrington' in Anthony Pagden (ed), *The Languages of Political Theory in Early Modern Europe* (Cambridge, Cambridge University Press, 1987) pp.197-224, p.199.

[9] Bayle, Pierre, *Commentaire philosophique sur les paroles de Jesus Christ 'Contrain-les d'entrer': Ou l'on prouve par plusieurs raisons demonstratives qu'il n'y a rien de plus abominable ques de faire des conversions par la contrainte et l'apologie que St.Augustine a faite des persécutions* (1686) (hereinafter referred to as *Com phil.*)

[10] Hereinafter referred to as *OD* I-IV.

and conjecture.[11] In the face of closure of the tolerated academy where he taught, Bayle would apply to the experience of persecution some searching questions usually raised only indirectly by philosophers of sceptical thought who operated in the penumbra of counter-reformation catholicism. Bayle supposed as did many others that the disposition to persecute in the name of religious unity could in no manner be motivated by a belief in goodness, still less by respect for the christianity of others.[12]

He would then turn to the political motives. When they examined the religion of the ancients, the scholars of the Renaissance, lay and ecclesiastical, were inclined to adopt a Florentine, Machiavellian or power-seeker's view.[13] They supposed religion to be man-made, politically useful and potentially dangerous in the hand of enthusiasts.[14] It followed that no one who governed the republic would be either wise or prudent to relinquish a controlling interest in the beliefs the populace.[15] The natural law philosophers of the Reformation and counter-Reformation – Bodin, Hobbes, Grotius and Spinoza, for example – would make this doctrine more morally serious by underpinning it with empirical and normative axioms drawn from natural law.[16] Civilian opinion in the wake of these theorists, whether Catholic or Protestant, did not contest that the religious impulse was universal and that, appropriately harnessed, it might be the source of all civility and piety. If the republic and its citizens controlled the priestly élite all would have a civic obligation to support the official religion.

If Locke insisted on excluding from public life specific sorts of thinking such as that associated with popery or atheism no clearer evidence is needed to conclude that he too adhered to the layman's erastian theory which entailed a unity of civic and religious obligation. Bayle, it will be shown, will contest the civil religion (without specificity as to doctrine) in its most fundamental empirical axiom. Without questioning the importance of piety, he will ask whether a person's doctrines – as opposed to moral sense – are as essential to the stability of the republic as natural law scholarship supposes.[17] By thus doubting the empirical truth of a crucial non-religious axiom Bayle will initiate the shift from the Hobbesian presumption of religious conformity to the Jeffersonian presumption of epistemological diversity. Thus the

---

[11] See for example, Pintard, Réné, *Le libertinage érudit dans la première moitié du XVIIè siécle*, 2 volumes (Paris, 1943); Keohane, Nanerl O, *Philosophy and the State in France: The Renaissance and the Enlightenment* (Princeton, Princeton University Press, New Jersey, 1980) especially Part II: 'Interest and Prudence: the State and the Sage', pp.119-229; Popkin, Richard H, *The History of Scepticism from Erasmus to Descartes* (Berkeley, L.A., London, 1979).

[12] Jenkinson, Sally L, 'Rationality, Pluralism and Reciprocal Tolerance: Pierre Bayle's Political Thought' in Hampsher Monk (ed), *Defending Politics: Essays in Honour of Bernard Crick* (London, British Academic Press, Imprint of I.B.Taurus, 1993) (hereinafter referred to as Jenkinson, '... Bayle's Political Thought') pp.22-45.

[13] See Machiavelli, *The Discourses* (Middlesex England, Penguin Books Ltd., 1970) (Books 11-15), pp.139-150, where is considered to what use it was put by the Romans.

[14] See Bayle, *Dictionnaire 1820-1824*, Article Savonarola Vol XIII pp.117-152.

[15] Cf Pocock J.G.A, *The Machiavellian Moment: Florentine Political Thought and the Atlantic Tradition* (Princeton, Princeton University Press, 1975) pp.104-113.

[16] Cf J.B.Schneewind, 'Kant and Natural Law Ethics', *Ethics*, 104 (October, 1993): pp.53-74.

[17] See Jenkinson, 'Bayle's Political Thought', pp.34-40.

historically concealed tension between the imperative of republican unity and the imperative of republican freedom is openly exposed. Locke, through Popple's introduction to his *Letter*,[18] will nod with a seeming benignity in the direction of 'absolute liberty' which was in vogue among dissenters. But his text, like his life, especially as it appears in Ashcraft's study[19], reveals a more ruthless disposition and a more revolutionary mission. The nod was enough, however, since, so it is argued here, regardless of Locke's goals, it was out of the confrontation between the two imperatives that posterity would construct a liberal theory of pluralism.

It follows from the foregoing that one purpose of this paper is to argue that the moral limitations lurking beneath Locke's account of toleration are inappropriately analysed in terms of Dunn's distinction between a christian age and a secular age.[20] Thus Horton & Mendus et al have, so I argue, illustrated the problem without identifying the causes. A second thesis of this paper is to propose with some textual illustrations, that Bayle did in fact explicate and criticise the conformist civic framework. Bayle would seek to show that no harm would befall the republic if the ruler's supposed obligation to promote the right religion were to be replaced with a new commitment to protect metaphysical diversity. It will follow that with the replacement the definition of toleration will change too – from exemption from the obligation to conform (that is, Locke's traditionalist republican version), to being a retrieval and a celebration of the pre-Socratic liberty to teach what was believed to be right (that is, Bayle's version). The ensuing intellectual revolution would not, in any case, affect the parallel ethical usage of the word 'tolerance'. Throughout the ages tolerance as an ethical virtue would of course continue to denote the perennially praiseworthy qualities of patience, non-violence and civility to strangers.

Structure of the Paper

As a preliminary to showing that Bayle contested the position presumed to have been supported by Locke, the first section will say something of the seventeenth century institution of the 'civil religion', and of its justification in natural law. It will discuss, in the context of the civil religion, the ancient intitution of 'toleration' understood as a legal exemption from the otherwise general obligation to conform; and it will contrast the views about both institutions held by Bayle and by Locke.

The second section of the paper will consider, comparatively, certain texts from Bayle's *Commentaire philosophique*, 1686 and Locke's *Letter on Toleration*, 1689. It will show that, unlike Locke, Bayle opposes the ideal of ideological unity as such, and not just certain ways of bringing it about. It will show that Bayle proposes 'true liberty' as an alternative objective, and that he argues that societies which depart from it, however slightly, are always likely to corrupt the republic and do harm to the innocent.

---

[18] *Locke LT*, 'To the reader' p.124.

[19] Richard Ashcraft, *Revolutionary Politics and Locke's Two Treatises of Government* (Princeton University Press, Princeton, 1986)

[20] Dunn cited *supra*, p.19.

The third section will summarise two models of the civic republic – one committed to the goal of unity the other to the goal of diversity – which are on the European agenda following the political turmoil of the 1680s. It will conclude that most of the dilemmas for commentators who interpret Locke's *Letter*, evaporate if his account of toleration is read in the context of a the first model. It observes finally that the confrontation between the single-faith aspiration and the plural alternative are not without their equivalents in the present age and that Locke and Bayle offer persuasive arguments for toleration in either context.

Natural Law and the Civil Religion

When Locke asserted that 'All men know and acknowledge that God ought to be publicly worshipped'[21], many would suppose him to be affirming a Christian belief. Others would recognise that he was stating the axiom on which the natural law thinkers of the age based their support for the civil religion. Undoubtedly the language of the civil religion which presupposes dualities of this sort has been neglected and misinterpreted by the political science of recent times. The neglect may well be due, as Goldie[22] has inferred, to a false modern dichotomy to which political science is prone, between the supposedly secular and the supposedly religious. Yet historians of ideas have always acknowledged that Hobbes's *Leviathan*, Spinoza's *Tractatus Theologico politicus*, Bossuet's *politique tirée de l'écriture sainte*, and Locke's *Letter*, are properly interpreted with reference to multiple understandings of certain concepts.

Among international statesmen, in particular, the civil order was presumed to be the creation of laymen rather than of theologians, and that presumption is reflected in all historically subsequent codes of international rights. They would summarise the position through the formula of *cuius regio eius religio*, intended to affirm the agreement among diplomats that, following the wars of religion, the states of Europe would henceforward agree to respect each other's religious affairs. Had the 'bons devots' of 'one or other communion' been responsible for the peace negotiations, Bayle commented, referring the Treaty of Westphalia of 1648 'the war' might 'have lasted until the end of time'.[23] Thus it was agreed that it was the duty of civil governments to keep the peace internationally and to maintain public order within. The prince should determine the official mode of worship within his frontiers and thus he – or she – must decide which sects might safely be tolerated and which refused toleration. Underneath the doctrine lay a premise which Locke would accept, but which Bayle would doubt, which presumed that without a firm religious association the civil association was necessarily diminished.

---

[21] *Locke LT* p.144.

[22] Goldie 'The Civil Religion of James Harrington', in Pagden (ed), *op.cit*, p.197.

[23] Bayle, Pierre, *Nouvelles de la république des lettres Oeuvres Diverses* (4 volumes, La Haye, 1727-31) (hereinafter referred to as OD.I-IV) Volume I, pp.245-6. Cf James Tully, 'Locke', *The Cambridge History of Political Thought*, edited by J.H.Burns (Cambridge, Cambridge University Press, 1991) pp.616-652) p.643, where it is noted that Locke had been interested in exploring the religious causes of war as early as the *Two Tracts*.

The point being made here is that after the Reformation it was supposed that a new civil society, forged through a set of common beliefs, inculcated by a suitably compliant clergy purged of ancient superstitions, would be defended with reference not to the external authority of a Roman Curia, but rather to the spiritual and political power of the republic. As late as the mid-eighteenth century, Rousseau in his account of the civil religion thought Bayle wrong to suppose that 'no religion' was 'useful to the body politic'.[24] Hobbes's *Leviathan*, on the other hand, he would praise for having reunited the 'two heads of the eagle'.[25] By this, Rousseau meant that modern society, through reformulating its religious mythology, might re-create the commonwealth to which it aspired. Locke's pamphlet, therefore, pre-supposes that the language of the civil religion connotes various layers of meaning. At the civic level there were axioms deduced from God or nature, and at the ecclesiastical level there were contributory arguments which, admittedly, might rely on agreed interpretations of appropriate scriptures. It follows that Locke, fluent in more than one 'language', opponent of Popery and suspicious of priestly claims, may be supposed to have proceeded, in the manner of the natural law theorists, from initial premises which were far from ecclesiastical but which were rather republican, naturalistic, and contractarian.

Inasfar as the empirical and moral content of particular axioms went un-contested much of the seemingly contradictory ecclesiastical policy of the age, and the fine detail of the pamphlet rhetoric – the debate between Locke and Proast.[26] for example – would fall into place. 'Toleration' in partic-ular was understood by leaders of communities as a legal 'privilege', to be bargained for by minorities or revoked by majorities.[27] Thus in pursuit of their presumed obligation under the doctrine of *cuius regio eius religio*, statesmen such as Richelieu, and Locke's patron, Shaftesbury, would de-ploy an armoury of strategies of which negotiation with leaders was merely one.[28] As a first priority, they would seek to reform and simplify the doc-trines of the established religion and ensure that they were taught. Failing to attain their aims through decree, rulers might attempt a re-unification of sects through irenical negotiations. Or, they might support a policy of civil toleration for a given sect, simultaneously attempting to convert non-conformists through inducement and persuasion. Or sometimes, as in the Gallican France after 1660, the regime might, as a step towards the

---

[24] Rousseau, *The Social Contract*, translated and introduced by Maurice Cranston (Har-mondworth, Middlesex, England, Penguin Books, 1971) p.180.

[25] Rousseau, *ibid*, p.180. Cited also in Goldie, 'The Civil religion of James Harrington', *op.cit*, p.202.

[26] See Peter Nicholson, 'Locke's Later Letters on Toleration' in Horton & Mendus (eds), pp.163-183.

[27] See Richard Tuck, 'Scepticism and Toleration in the Seventeenth Century', in Men-dus, Susan (ed), *Justifying Toleration: Conceptual and Historical Perspectives* (Cam-bridge, Cambridge University Press 1988), pp.21-36.

[28] See Ashcraft, *Revolutionary Politics*, for discussion of the pamphlet believed to have come from Locke's pen in 1675, at the instigation of Shaftesbury: 'A letter from a person of quality to his friend in the country'; later published in Desmaizeaux (ed), *A collection of several pieces by Mr.Locke, 1720*. It argued in a *politique* manner that if toleration were an established law protestantism even under a popish Prince 'would still be kept up among the cities towns and trading places'. (Cited Ashcraft, p.119).

Augustinian goal of re-unification, withdraw a former civil toleration.[29] A strategy, believed rational by Shaftesbury after 1660, and which Locke may be presumed to have supported for the rest of his life, was to consolidate political opposition to Popery in court or church, through cultivating 'among the cities, towns and trading places'[30] a diffused network of protestant sects.

If Locke, as a layman, supposed that the clergy should defer to his remonstrances, or that catholicism was incompatible with public office, or that the doctrines of the Restoration Anglican Church should be more latitudinarian or comprehensive, or that its clerics should be more tolerant, or that agnostics should conform outwardly, or that certain dissenting sects should be accorded a 'privileged toleration', his views would be wholly in accordance with the general deontology of his position. Lay politicians had a duty to control the republic's religion but through negotiation with religion's representatives.[31] This would explain why Locke can simultaneously support a general duty of conformity and a 'privileged toleration' for dissenters.[32] The hypothesis put forward here is that the strategies may have changed, but not the premises or the goals.

Bayle, as has been said, would regard 'privileged toleration' as second best and indicative of a deeper theoretical malaise. It was one of those 'ambulatory doctrines' which were 'dependent on time and place', resembling 'transitory birds which are in one country in summer and another in winter'.[33] As during the wars of religion 'the maxims of each party' had been 'reciprocally metamorphosed into their contraries'.[34] He meant that competent pamphlet writers throughout the age of the Reformation, including those of his own party, did not always write in good faith. Some pamphleteers made a compelling general case for toleration when they were in a minority, but that did mean that their party wished to see tolerance accorded to all sects. Furthermore the civil *convertisseurs* knew also how to find convincing arguments for imposing their religion on the rest when they were in a position of strength. This to Bayle was a reprehensible example of 'Machiavellian' power-seekers manipulating religious feeling in the service of their worldly goals.

Bayle's response to the moral malaise of religion abused, would be to contest the axioms on which the natural law supporters of the civil religion based their case. It had not been supposed before Augustine, he would point out, that all men were obliged to worship publicly. On the contrary, the academics and sceptics of the first three centuries supposed that men

---

[29] Labrousse, Elisabeth, *La Révocation de l'Edit de Nantes* (Paris, Editions Payot, 1990) Chapter V, 'Les fondaments ideologiques de l'intolerance actives', pp.81-96.

[30] See *supra*, n.26.

[31] See Richard Ashcraft, *Revolutionary Politics and Locke's Two Treatises of Government* (Princeton University Press, Princeton, 1986) pp.475-476); see also Goldie, Mark, 'John Locke and Anglican Royalism', *Political Studies*, Number 31, 1983, pp.86-102; Gough, J.H, 'The Development of Locke's Belief in Toleration' (1973), in Mendus & Horton (eds), pp.57-77.

[32] Cf James Tully, 'Locke', *The Cambridge History of Political Thought*, edited by J.H.Burns (Cambridge, Cambridge University Press, 1991) pp.616-652) p.644, where it is supposed that Locke must have changed his views.

[33] *Dictionnaire 1820-24*, VIII, Article Hotman (I) Rem. H. p.280.

[34] *Loc cit.*

'ought to conform to the customs of their country and practise (their) moral duties'.[35] Augustine and those who believed likewise must be mistaken in their axioms. The republic, he will say, would be more likely to prosper if, like the academics of antiquity, it undertook to keep the peace, protect the expression of critical thought and create the conditions for moral action. Such was Bayle's theoretical alternative to the compulsory civil religion and to the institution of 'privileged toleration'. His polemical aim, which he did not attain during his life, but which would clearly pass into the Kantian project, and into American and French constitutionalism, would be to persuade the philosophic and academic community that they should, in justice and in pursuit of the public good, support a different sort of republic.

Bayle names the theory which he associates with the institution of the civil religion, as a theory of 'non-tolerance', and he names the doctrine with which he will replace it, as a theory of 'true liberty'. In response to the Revocation of the Edict of Nantes, Bayle would conclude that the privilege of toleration formerly accorded to his party could, and should, be replaced with liberty for all. Unlike Locke, Bayle has no particular constitutuency such as Whigs or dissenters. He directs his argument therefore towards those who support the republic of letters. Catholics, protestants or *esprits forts*, laymen or theologiansshould prepare for, rather than fear, the consequences of diversity.

True Liberty: a Response to the Civil Religion

The *Commentaire philosophique* in structure is a formal treatise which shows with nine arguments why Augustine in the fourth century had been mistaken to insist that the state might oblige heretical subjects to conform to the official religion. Bayle tells his readers that he will draw on arguments from logic and natural morality, and that he will subject his axioms to the scrutiny which Descartes had called 'lumiere naturelle'.[36] In confronting Augustine and seeming to enlist Descartes in his support Bayle would have been casting a philosophic gauntlet before the civic and intellectual establishment of both protestant and catholic Europe. Locke, by contrast, as an associate of an English aristocrat, connected with the Court of Queen Mary of Orange and as member of an episcopalian church, would have appeared as an liberal establishment figure of the sort he might hope to influence.

The following textual excerpts illustrate the way in which Bayle, considers three issues fundamental to the notion of *cuius regio eius religio*. Firstly, he is concerned with refuting the arguments from natural law for a compulsory civil religion and with making a case for the alternative of plural diversity. Secondly he shows concern, as do Waldren and Mendus, with the moral wrong involved in persecution and the harm it does to whole communities and individuals. Thirdly he raises an issue which modern lib-

---

[35] *Dictionnaire 1820-24*, Volume XII, Article Pyrrhon (B) p.101.
[36] *Com phil* p.367.

erals might well consider, namely: how to assess the relative moral worth of societies which depart in different degrees from the ideal of absolute liberty.

republican pluralism: a feasible alternative to republican unity

It was taken for granted that a civil religion was a pre-requisite of law abiding behaviour and the maintenance of public order. Bayle's source for an overt statement of this politique position would not be Hobbes but the sceptical and humanist writer Justus Lipsius. In his *De una religione*[37], Lipsius had asserted, Bayle wrote, 'that one should suffer only one religion in the state nor use any clemency towards those that troubled religion'.[38] Intertwined with the believer's case for unity, there also lay the civil case. It was used by Gallicans, the Huguenot *nouveaux convertis* and latitudinarians to justify political compromise in religious matters. Bayle is especially interested in refuting it.

His 'adversaries' claimed, he began, that there could be no 'more dangerous pestilance in the state than a multiplicity of religions'; for it put 'neighbours in dissention with neighbours, fathers with children, husbands with wives, princes with subjects'.[39] But Bayle would reply that if that was so then the very fact would be a strong argument for 'tolerance'. For if 'each (society) has the tolerance I support, there would be the same harmony in a state divided into ten religions as in a town where the several sorts of artisans gave mutual support one to another'.[40] But he draws more than one picture of what he envisaged for a new golden age. The tolerant society might be like the 'vast empire' made up of various 'nations which differ in their laws and languages',[41] but where 'each would honour their master according to the usage and taste of his country'.[42] If that was too grandiose, then it might be seen as the small town in which the diversity of 'beliefs, temples and cults' would be no more a sign of disorder than 'the diversity of stalls at a fair lq where each honest merchant sells what he has without damaging the sale of another'.[43] Or to use a metaphor from baroque music, 'Tolerance would make a ... harmony of many voices and instruments, or different tones and notes, (which would be) at least as agreeable as the uniformity of a single voice'.[44]

Yet tolerance cannot be sustained through a weak prince who 'from wickedness or want of illumination'[45] capitulates to clerical accounts of his proper duties. Bayle is perhaps thinking of the Great Elector of Brandenburg (1640-88) who, in contrast to Louis XIV, considered his own religion as a private matter, and whose regime used its power to protect Lutherans, Calvinists and Catholics. In his defence of power rightly used, Bayle would

[37] Cited *Com phil* p.404.
[38] *Com phil* p.404.
[39] *Com phil* p.415.
[40] *Com phil* p.415.
[41] *Com phil* p.418.
[42] *Com phil* p.418.
[43] *Com phil* p.418.
[44] *Com phil* p.415.
[45] *Com phil* p.419.

say 'Our adversaries fail to distinguish between' the sovereign's rightful use of 'the sword' against 'subjects who use violence against their neighbour', and his wrongful use of it against the subject's 'conscience'.[46] But 'we', by contrast:

> 'do not confuse these two things ... I support strongly, [he continues] (the view) that it is the indispensable duty of princes where sects attempt to insult ministers of the dominant religion,[47] ... (or which) attempt to use the least violence against those who wish to persevere in their traditional confession ... to punish those sectarians by all due and reasonable means; [since] they would, frankly be persecuters, (who) through de(eds) would undermine the law.'[48]

The prince has, in such circumstances, an obligation to use juridical sanctions both to keep the peace, and to ensure the punishment of unruly elements who in the name of religion 'maltreat their neighbour, whether in his body, in his goods, or in his honour'.[49]

irrationality and injustice in persecution

Waldren criticises Locke for being insufficiently concerned with the morally harmful consequences of persecution. Bayle will demonstrate a similar perspective. He will of course show that doctrines are inappropriately combatted with 'any arms other than truth'.[50] But were it otherwise, this falsity of 'doctrine' would not give rulers rights to 'maltreat their subjects'.[51] He will conclude that persecution is not only inappropriate; it is also damaging and unjust.

For example a persecuting regime will commit the massive crime of corrupting the whole community of those who persecute, and Louis XIV's advisors ought to be aware that persecution damages persecutors as well as victims. It would be be 'curious', he observes, 'to know how a confessor behaves when a member of the dragoons confesses that he has beaten up his Huguenot host'.[52] For 'if he does not regard that as a sin' he must fall into some confusion since 'an action which would be a crime ceases to be one when it is committed against a heretic'.[53] This paradox shows that there are limitations to the power of rulers which cannot be exceeded without offence to natural justice. To be just, and not tyrannical, a law had to be 'possible in nature'.[54]

It was of course asserted by those who flattered royalty, that 'the king, being the master of his kingdom and the executor of his laws, could punish, as it seems fit to him, those who infringed the laws he has promulgated',

---

[46] *Com phil* p.416.
[47] *Com phil* p.416.
[48] *Com phil* p.416.
[49] *Com phil* p.416-7.
[50] *Com phil* p.412.
[51] *Com phil* p.412.
[52] *Com phil* p.381.
[53] *Com phil* p.381.
[54] *Com phil* p.383.

such as the law 'that one must conform to his (that is, the king's) religion'.[55]
But were they to consult St Thomas as published by the Jansenists they
would read that:

> 'a law that is not just is not law; and that only to the extent
> that it partakes in justice does it partake in the force of law ...
> [to be just, a law] should be possible in nature, it should be nec-
> essary, useful, pertain to the public good (utilité publique), and
> not to a particular interest.[56] ... the Edicts which (sovereigns)
> publish to that end, are of no validity and (are) a pure usurpa-
> tion ... (and) the penalties that they inflict on those who infringe
> them, are unjust.'[57]

Locke writes by contrast:

> 'For laws are of no force at all without penalties, and penal-
> ties in this case are absolutely impertinent, because they are not
> proper to convince the mind.'[58]

Thus where Bayle uses the word 'unjust' Locke uses the word 'impertinent',
and this difference does indeed imply that they are working from different
theories of the proper duties of rulers.

true liberty: assessing degrees of distance from it

It was common for the apologists of tolerated sects to suppose that other
sectarians were less entitled than themselves to the privilege of toleration.
Bayle who would refer to apologists in this category as 'M'Sieurs les Demi-
tolerans'[59], would tell his fellow exiles that non-tolerance in the Protestant
society was as unacceptable as non-tolerance in the Catholic society. All
who sought to suppress sects on the grounds of 'the falsity they believe to
be contained in the dogmas of other religions', he insisted, were 'wrong'.[60]
    There should, he said, be an ideal against which the policy of all republics
in matters of liberty might be judged. Thus there is a 'fixed point' where
'true liberty of conscience resides'[61] which, as it will be seen, lies less in the
freedom to worship than in the freedom of critical (as opposed to dogmatic)
modes of teaching. Once a 'fixed point' of liberty has been established,
degrees of 'non-tolerance' can be identified: societies can thus be graded
according to a scale. And, to 'the extent to which they distance themselves
more or less from this 'fixed point', they distance themselves more or less
from tolerance'.[62] The proper imperative for the good ruler is as follows:

> 'that (he) should should work with all his strength to instruct
> with strong and good reasons those who err, but if (he) has not

[55] *Com phil* p.383.
[56] *Com phil* p.383.
[57] *Com phil* pp.384-5.
[58] *Locke LT*, p.130.
[59] *Com phil* p.419.
[60] Com Phil p.411.
[61] *Com phil* p.414.
[62] *Com phil* p.414.

the fortune to undeceive them, (he should) leave them the liberty
to declare that they will persevere in their beliefs, and serve God
according to their sentiments; as for anthing further, (he) has a
duty not to propose any temporal penalty or reward in order to
win them.'[63]

However there are degrees of distance from the 'fixed point' and though
none are defensible, the critic can at least give moderate praise to the society
which departs least from the ideal arrangement. Thus:

1. The first degree of distance from the fixed point would
be 'If all the inhabitants of a country making profession of a
religion' were to establish the following fundamental law: 'not
to let enter into their country any person of a different religion
to live there or to preach their beliefs'.[64] This, though the least
severe departure from the principle would inter alia be flawed
because such a law would exclude the 'teachers of truth' as well
as the 'teachers of lies'. It follows that 'full liberty of conscience
is incompatible with these laws'.[65]

2. The second degree of distance would be where, in addition
to the prohibitions of the first case, 'no inhabitant of the country'
were permitted to 'make any innovation in matters of religion'
without being liable 'to be sent into exile'.[66] This would entail
further harm both to society, and to the moral consciences of
individuals. Society's capacity to benefit from 'the progress of
human or divine knowledge' would be prejudiced in unknown
ways since such a law would encourage hypocrisy among those
who, for fear of the penalties or enjoyment of their privileges,
would keep silent.[67] Bayle would return to the silence of the
catholic sceptics of the civil religion in other works including the
Dictionary, Pensées diverses ... (1681), and *Continuation des
Pensées diverses ...* (1704). A citizen, honestly convinced that
'he should teach certain things' or that he should 'reform this or
that abuse'[68], could not speak freely for fear of exile. He would
be made distressed and anxious because his conscience would be
'be torn between love of ... country and love of truth'.[69]

The general conclusion, Bayle says, is that 'violence' is done to potential
public good by any law which impedes the teaching of what may add to
new ideas or to 'progress in human or divine knowledge'.[70]

3. The third, furthest and most damaging degree of distance from the
'fixed point' is where a law is instituted which forces

---

[63] *Com phil* p.414; cf *Locke LT*, pp.129-30.
[64] *Com phil* p.414.
[65] *Com phil* p.414.
[66] *Com phil* p.414.
[67] *Com phil* p.414.
[68] *Com phil* p.414.
[69] *Com phil* p.414.
[70] *Com phil* p.414.

> 'any person, whether a stranger or a native, who teaches any-
> thing against the dominant religion to retract it, and to declare
> publicly that he believes as does his compatriots, under pain
> of physical penalties, burning, the wheel, hard labour (or) foul
> imprisonment.'[71]

All the previous consequences and objections apply. But the third degree
of distance from liberty is the most harmful of all because it is humiliating,
psychologically damaging, entails cruel punishments, and the brutalisation
of all concerned.

By means of his sliding scale of non-tolerance, Bayle could demonstrate
that the non-tolerance of some sects by some protestant nations, such as the
Netherlands, though not to be commended, was of a relatively low degree.
By contrast, the regime of Louis XIV, in 1660 in the first category, had
moved by stages into the third. Judged acording to the same standard,
the protestant city of Geneva had in the recent past erred shockingly in
subjecting Servetus and others to torture and death[72] and should be utterly
condemned. Such acts, he asserted, were 'a hideous stain upon on the
early times of our reformation' and they show 'that (protestants) can push
persecution as far as the Papists'.[73]

By thus identifying degrees of distance from the ideal of true liberty,
Bayle could judge – as a sort of one-man amnesty international – that to
accord dissidents such as the Huguenot party a 'privileged toleration', was
more defensible than to persecute them. Yet regardless of exemptions, a
policy of promoting an official 'truth', even with rewards rather than punishments, would bring about, morally unacceptable consequences for all
concerned. His alternative proposal implies (with a certain caution) that
there should be an absolute liberty to profess in public any faith or no faith
at all, and above all the liberty to teach to others what one believed to be
right. There are various consequences of such a theory, but the immediate
implication is that there shall be no religious test of citizenship. Subsequent thinkers such as Kant, Jefferson and Mill would associate liberty of
conscience with contractual democracy and constitutionally enshrined imperatives. Bayle would associate it with the emerging institution of the
strong sovereign presiding over the enlightened society.

Conclusion

These excerpts from Bayle's work have been selected to show that several of
the objections made, in the study by Horton & Mendus, to Locke's account
of toleration were identified also by Bayle when he considered the moral
failings of societies which departed from his 'fixed point' of 'true liberty'.
Locke's *Letter* testifies that by 1689, there was an *avant-garde* among dissenting intellectuals which was using the new expression 'absolute liberty'
to express its aspirations. Bayle's writing shows that, in his case, support

---

[71] *Com phil* p.414.
[72] *Com phil* p.415.
[73] *Com phil* p.415.

for liberty turned on criteria that went beyond mere freedom of worship for sects. It relied on criticising some commonly believed theoretical axioms and making some substitutions. For example, he would replace a pedagogy in the dogmatic mode with a pedagogy in the academic mode; an epistemology based on reason alone with an epistemology based on conjecture and refutation; an anthropology of religious learning with an anthropology of developmental learning; and a deontology of civic conformity with a deontology of civic diversity. If 'atheists' and 'pagans' were innately endowed with the moral resources to 'repress wickedness and preserve societies'[74] why would any ruler have a moral duty to enforce a civil religion? But the reference to 'absolute liberty' in the introduction to Locke's *Letter* could be read as a warning as well as a recommendation; it was an idea 'much talked of' but not 'much understood'.[75] Rousseau would show that he grasped something of Bayle's meaning because he saw it as a threat to the strength of the republic. Perhaps Locke judged it in that way also.

The two understandings can therefore be seen as two competing ideals of public life which would dominate the moral and epistemological sub-text of the constitutional debate for two centuries. In an earlier article they are referred to as two 'paradigms'. Here they are referred to as 'ideals: 'the civic/dogmatic ideal' on the one hand and the 'the civic/ academic ideal' on the other; and something will be said about each in turn. Thus:

> 1 *The civic/dogmatic ideal* was postulated on the natural law axiom that religion emerges from an innate human desire to recognise a creator and to worship him collectively. The prince who must be a Godly prince has thus a duty to promote the public good and to maintain the public peace by harnessing this impulse making sure that it works to the good of the republic rather than to its harm. Toleration, in this context would denote 'privileged toleration' an exemption, properly motivated by reason and charity, from the obligation to conform to the republic's collectively agreed norms binding on the others. The civic/religious republic was thus a controlled intellectual universe, teaching axiomatically certain agreed doctrines as moral 'truths', outside of which other civic debate might take place, but always within certain safe limits.

> 2 *The civic/academic* ideal was postulated on the principle (in generalcontested by theologians, supported by philosophers) that human nature had yet to be understood; there but that was no necessary connection between religious conformity and moral behaviour, that the disposition to strive after virtue was innate and could be pursued through many paths. It followed that the prince had a duty to maintain order and promote the public good but he – or she – had no duty to require citizens to conform to a civil religion. The prince must, in the public interest, resist legislation based on dogma and enact laws that

---

[74] Bayle, *Continuation des Pensées Diverses*, OD.III pp.198-415, p.438.
[75] *Locke LT* p.124.

conform to principles of simple morality and natural justice; and he must ensure, through appointing impartial judicial officials, that those who seek to criticise error, teach new ideas, or defend what they believe to be right, are not impeded from so doing. Toleration, in this context takes on its new liberal meaning: it becomes not an exemption from the obligation to conform (since there is no obligation fom which to be exempted), but a constitutional imperative to promote the open society. Thus rulers must protect critical thought, and ensure that all citizens peacefully and reciprocally give a respectful hearing to each others ideas. The libertarian republic provides the framework in which public debate, including criticism of its own institutions, will be unbounded but orderly.

Locke's notion of toleration, it is concluded, is puzzling only if it is read in the context of the second rather than the first paradigm. The proper framework for Locke's view is that of the ideal of civic republicanism – a radical tradition supported by Hobbes and which would be continued and transformed by Rousseau. Bayle's 'First degree of distance' thus represents the more praiseworthy sort of contractarian republic which designs and controls its own religious establishment and instructs its present and future citizens in what is right. It presumes a duty of conformity to what is taught so that tolerance is always understood as a privilege and not as a right. It follows that it is inappropriate for modern liberals (mistakenly assuming 'toleration' to have always denoted the republic's presumed duty to protect religious diversity) to attempt to read back into Locke's *Letter* a libertarian plea for guarantees of critical freedom. As it is pointed out in Horton & Mendus, Locke seems to display more interest in reminding the clerics and magistrates, as 'tolerators', of the detail of their duties, than it does in considering the rights of the 'tolerated'. In such a context the tolerated have no rights, only privileges, and – which is more important – they would not accord rights to others were positions reversed. Bayle, this paper suggests (with an apology for the seeming anachronism) thus completes the theoretical task, which Waldren and Mendus begin, by addressing the moral inadequacies of such a bleak if heroic theory in its premises and not just in its conclusions.

This is not to imply that the case for 'privileged tolerance' is without power to contest intolerance in the present age. Both writers were celebrated by later generations for having condemned state violence, and each would be interpreted as having written against the seductive attractions of the single-faith society. Nevertheless, some violent, dogmatic regimes in the present age – no less than in the seventeenth century – oppress with greater cruelty than others. Those who confront contemporary instances of unjust persecution will sometimes need, in the style of Locke, to make a case for limited tolerance within the given framework of ideological conformity. On other occasions they may be impelled, in the manner of Bayle, to challenge the framework itself.

Round Table
American Government

Helen Margetts
London School of Economics & Political Science

'The National Performance Review, the Clinton Presidency
and the Future Shape of American Government'

Acknowledgement

The author worked from 1992-1993 on the US Federal Budget
project in the Department of Government at the London School of
Economics funded by the ESRC. This project was supervised by
Patrick Dunleavy and Desmond King (St Johns College, Oxford) and
the author acknowledges and thanks them for any of the insights
or information contained in this paper that were gained during the
course of the project.

Introduction

The National Performance Review is Clinton's plan for creating a government that works better and costs less. Based on an intensive six month study of the federal bureaucracy, it is predicted to save $108 billion and reduce the federal workforce by 152,000 over the next five years. This is to be achieved by reorganisation of agencies, reform of the budgeting and procurement processes, decentralisation of personnel policy and the reduction of internal regulations by 50 per cent over the next three years.

These are brave plans, but the troubled history of administrative reform by incoming US presidents contains inauspicious precedents. The next section outlines the reform efforts of Clinton's most recent predecessors, the second section looks at the recommendations of the National Performance Review and the third evaluates their chances of success. The fourth section suggests that the National Performance Review is an example of the 'second wave' of the New Public Management, whereby governments use a mixture of old and new techniques to manage both the formal bureaucracy and a new zone of contract government.

Presidential Politics and Federal Administrative Reform

In Washington the announcement of intended civil service reforms is almost as frequent as new presidents. These reform plans have a common feature; they have been largely unsuccessful. Fewer of their recommendations have been implemented than have lain on the table to be incorporated in the reform plans of later presidents.

Plans for administrative reform have had many other features in common. All previous reform plans were economy and efficiency based. There has been no equivalent of reform on the depth or scale of the United Kingdom Next Steps, but many presidents have used managerial strategies. Eisenhower, Kennedy, Johnson, Nixon, Carter and Reagan all brought investigative teams into the government seeking to transplant private sector techniques. Their aims were most usually founded in a distrust of bureaucracy in general and the Washington establishment in particular.

Carter especially hated the Washington establishment, describing it as a 'horrible bureaucratic mess' (Massey, 1992). On coming to power he immediately set up a Reorganisation Committee. The committee consisted initially of a small permanent staff within the Office of Management and Budget (OMB) but quickly grew to around 300 voluntary outsiders and agency representatives. They concluded that the federal service was 'unnecessarily complex, unrepresentative of society, inefficient and unaccountable, unable to reward merit and excellent performance' (Massey, 1992). In response to their findings Carter proposed the *Civil Service Reform Act* which contained a clear commitment – albeit never fully funded – to performance pay and merit bonuses, and created the Office of Personnel Management (later used by Reagan for implementation of his own reforms) to oversee personnel policy. He also reorganised audit and investigation units within agencies and departments into single-headed 'Offices of Inspector General' under the *Inspector General Act* of 1978. The Inspector Generals were given broad and considerable powers to review legislation and regulation and to promote the economy and efficiency of their departments.

Carter also made an attempt at zero-based budgeting (ZBB) which in its purest form would mean agencies recreating their budgets from zero every year rather than working from last year's expenditure levels. Carter's modified form of ZBB, which he had used while governor of Georgia, meant that agencies were required to prepare alternative budgets for each program based on different levels of effort in comparison with the previous year. But, as in Georgia, it was never really implemented. Agencies tended to continue to start from their current budgets, working backwards and forwards to general alternatives. ZBB did influence the bureaucracy to some extent with more sophisticated justifying of increases but there was no evidence of substantial spending reductions or significant funding reallocations across departments. Moe (1992) summarised:

> 'Reorganisation, first viewed by Carter and his associates as the route towards both efficiency and governmental virtue, by the second year had degenerated to the status of a tool for gaining interest group support for the Administration generally.'

While Carter 'delighted in the minutiae of policy management' (Massey, 1992), Reagan had little interest in the intricacies of bureaucracy. His reforming zeal was based around the view that the less government the better and his first act was a federal hiring freeze. He created a commission of corporate executives, chaired by an industrialist J.Peter Grace to increase government efficiency. The Commission consisted of 36 task forces composed of entirely private sector personnel, staffed by 2,000 people generally on loan from their corporations. It cost the equivalent of £70 million. Its legal status was questionable (Moe, 1992). The Grace Commission's reports contained 2,478 recommendations with a potential saving of more than $424 billion, designed 'to get government off the backs of the American people' (Grace quoted in *Dow Jones*, 8.9.93).

Like the Carter Reorganisation Committee, the Grace Commission rejected the idea that any general principles of organizational management were unique to the public sector or the Federal government. Government should be organized like a large corporation with a structure permitting top down control. Decisions were to be brought to the top into a large new office of Federal Management. Privatisation through contracting out was seen as the most effective way of saving money. Blanket targets were introduced, whereby agencies were commanded to privatise three per cent of their operations. Some ($195 billion) of the savings were to come from a 'full-scale war on waste, fraud and abuse' (Light, 1993) and Reagan fired all the Inspector Generals created under Carter and recruited largely new personnel to fill their posts. These new Inspector Generals reached a pinnacle of power during his presidency but their focus on short term statistical results resulted in enhanced reporting on waste rather than recommendations for management improvement.

The Grace Commission report was criticised by both the General Accounting Office (GAO) and the Office of Management and Budget (OMB). A large proportion of the Commission's detailed recommendations had already been made by career civil servants or in GAO reports. Seventy per cent of the recommendations required legislative approval and Grace drastically underestimated the chance of their success. In fact very few of those requiring Congressional support were implemented, unsurprising due to the virulent criticisms of Congress contained in the report. Staff cuts were implemented with a 'meat-axe' approach (interview) and 11,000 employees were laid off during the first year. Reagan's political head of the Office of Personnel Management declared 'war on the bureaucracy' and politicisation of this organisation contributed to 'fear, paralysis and sagging morale' (Gormley, 1989). There was no no attempt at deep seated structural reform.

Reagan considered the budget the key to his overall objective. His plan, implemented by his budget director David Stockman, was to bring budgeting decisions to the top and reduce the part played by agencies, especially at the lower level, in the budget making process. In fact however, the executive budget process, remained largely intact. As one official interviewed put it:

> 'in the first years of the Reagan administration the emphasis began to shift much more to central budgeting and with less emphasis on agency requests although that process has never stopped, to this point they have continued the traditional bottom up process, it has never gone away.'

The only notable change was a far greater amount of 'Congress watching' by agencies as they tried to avoid the worst effects of the cuts. Budget offices and departmental secretaries became reliant on methods such as 'dead-on-arrival' budgets, whereby they were content to include zero appropriations for White-House targeted programs, confident that Congress would restore them and thereby help push their department's budgets back over target. Budgeting strategies based on the belief that no-one (especially government officials) could be trusted, resulted in a ratcheting upwards of caveats and control apparatus reminiscent of Downs' 'law of counter-control' (Downs, 1967).

It has now become evident that none of Reagan's strategies were successful at reducing public expenditure. Cogan & Muris (1990) characterise the period as one year of deep budget cuts in 1982, followed by seven years of rapid budget growth which restored the aggregate domestic discretionary spending to its 1981 constant dollar level.

The administration changed little during the Bush period. Bush provides one exception to the reforming zeal that characterises the first eighteen months of most presidencies. Administrative policy was a small and unimportant part of the neglected domestic policy arena. The most notable change that took place was due more to his budget director, Derek Darman, head of the Office of Management and Budget. Under his control the top-down budgeting that characterised the Reagan years reached its pinnacle. In the agencies and departments resentment and frustration built up over how their budgets were developed, while in the White House itself, OMB became the only policy making organisation within the White house that could influence the budget process, causing discontent amongst other White House staff.

In short, Clinton's inheritance included a burgeoning deficit, increased internal regulation and controls and a largely frustrated federal civil service. Not surprisingly Clinton was plagued by difficulties in the early days of his administrative take-over most famously for his slow and controversial political appointments. The first two nominees for Attorney General had to withdraw their names from consideration for reasons related to the hiring of illegal immigrants and the Commerce Secretary Ron Brown was investigated for accepting payoffs from the Vietnamese government. After six months, Clinton had nominated 30 per cent fewer people than Reagan and 44 per cent fewer than Carter at the same stage in their presidencies. After seven months the government was still printing dollar bills with Republican signatures on them because no new Treasurer had been named.

However, any incoming president has close to 3,500 political appointments to make and no president finds this easy. As Kennedy said directly after his election 'I must make the appointments now. A year hence, I will know who I really want to appoint' (*Washington Post*, 2.02.94). Filling government positions has become an increasingly time-consuming process since Kennedy's time, with tightened ethical standards leading to more paperwork and more investigation by the White House and FBI. Clinton made many of the sub-cabinet choices himself, with a far greater drive for ethnic and gender diversity than previous presidents have attempted. One year into his administration with more than three quarters of appointments filled, it seems that his caution has paid off, in respect to gender and ethnic minority representation at least. About three quarters of the appointments are filled by non-Hispanic whites, who make up 75 per cent of the population. Fourteen percent are African American compared to 12 per cent of the population, six per cent are Hispanic, compared to 9.5 per cent of the population. And three per cent are Asian American, the same as in the population. The gender split is not far from half and half: 54 per cent of appointees are men and 46 per cent are women. The appointees 'look like America' (Washington Post 23.01.94). With the benefit of a longer time perspective and the reminder that Americans falsely remember most Cabinets in history as smoothly working machineries with stable memberships, Clinton's team after his first year looks reasonably strong. As Thomas Mann from the Brookings Institution summarised after Clinton's first year,

> 'When you start to put the budget, NAFTA, health-care, and other reform efforts together, the President gains credibility. The public sees an activist Presidency coping with difficult problems'. (*Washington Post*)

The National Performance Review

Clinton put administrative reform on the agenda even before he was elected. He based his administrative proposals during the election campaign on the now internationally known book, *Reinventing Government* by David Osborne & Ted Gaebler. The authors envision a new form of 'entrepeneurial government' with increased competition in service delivery, devolved budgets allocated on the basis of outcomes and community oriented service provision. Their visions is based on the idea that in many cases policy decisions can be effectively separated from service delivery: 'separating steering from rowing', whereby state government becomes a 'catalyst', empowering communities to solve their own problems. The book is based on experiences from US state and local government and provides useful, pragmatic solutions to the type of problems faced by the Governor of Arkensaw. It is easy to see why Clinton was attracted by it and why it was useful to him in this role. It does not however tackle the scale or scope of problems found with administrative control of the US Federal Government.

It is perhaps this realisation that led Clinton to initiate the National Performance review, an intensive six-month study of the federal bureaucracy carried out by 250 government employees. He placed vice president Al Gore in charge, viewed widely as a commendable decision. Gore was both popular and in need of a distinctive role. He had a long term interest in administration especially relating to information technology. While Carter's micromanagement of his reorganisation project distracted him from the political realities of Washington, Clinton must have realised that the political problems of his first year, including introducing NAFTA and health care reform to a Democratic but still sceptical Congress, would prohibit him from day to day involvement with the review. Gore was widely praised by government employees for the time and tireless dedication he devoted to the review and the promotion of its findings. As one official who worked on the review put it in an interview:

> 'You have the vice president's personal involvement – unfor-

> tunately vice presidents have been kind of invisible people in the
> past and I think the president gave vice president Gore one job
> – go improve government and I think he has a fire in his belly
> to do that.'

The National Performance Review staff were divided into 22 teams, half
of which looked at the major agencies while the other half focussed on
'systems': organizational and management structures, budgeting, personnel, information technology, financial management, procurement, regulatory
systems and program design. The Agency Reinvention Teams consisted of
staff drawn from agencies other than the one their team was scrutinising, to
prevent problems when they returned to their normal jobs. Internal reinvention teams within all departments and agencies were also created, to
scrutinise agency-specific processes in detail.

David Osborne, co-author of *Reinventing Government*, probably wrote
the report of their findings; his racy style and gung-ho approach is evident
in the paperback version of the NPR report. This book is decidedly easier
to read than the output of the Grace Commission, (whose output ran to
47 volumes spread over 1,300 pages) or the Carter Reorganization project
(whose the reports can only be found buried deep in the Library of Congress
or agency archives). But as pointed out earlier *Reinventing Government* is
based on state and local government rather than federal government experience and it only skates along the surface of the problems of federal reform.

Consequently, although the NPR 'main' report takes up and reiterates
the Osborne & Gaebler themes, including much of their vocabulary, the
status of the 'main' report text remains unclear. All the key recommendations at the end of the report are the direct result of the work of the
reinvention teams and they do not relate directly to the snappily titled
and evangelically written sections: 'Cutting Red Tape'; 'Putting Customers
First'; 'Empowering Employees to get Results'; 'Cutting Back to Basics'.
This section focuses on these recommendations combined with interview evidence gathered directly after the NPR report came out and assesses their
future significance and chances of implementation.

budgeting

Reagan's administration was characterised by his avowed intention to enforce top-down budgeting. But in reality the executive budget process
changed little under Reagan, with the original bottom up process remaining
largely intact. At all levels of most departments, budget proposals continue
to be prepared by agencies and bureaus and negotiated with the level above
(for a fuller explanation of the executive budgeting process see Dunleavy,
King & Margetts, 1992). One consequence of this, as the NPR team observed, is that agencies spend a huge amount of time throughout the year
on the budgeting process.

One of the aims therefore will be to encourage the agencies to spend
less time on budgeting. The executive budget resolution formulated by the
President will take the form of agency by agency totals which have come
from studying the functional totals with sub-function ceilings and targets

for agencies in presidential priority areas. This resolution will be made known to the agencies earlier than at present and the time when agencies start budgeting will be later, so that agencies are not 'budgeting blindfold' as happens at present.

Agencies will be encouraged to shed budget staff, but will be given the discretion to choose at what level this happens. In some agencies it will be one layer taken out of the process. In HHS, the Public Health Service is an example of how layer upon layer of budget making processes create an overall protracted and extremely time-consuming process. The 22 institutes within the National Institutes of Health (NIH) all develop budgets, which go to the NIH for scrutiny, then to the assistant secretary for PHS, then to the head of Health and Human Services and then to OMB and Congress. The NPR team hope that by restricting the time agencies have to budget and by making the totals more definite at the beginning of the process, agencies will be forced to look at processes like this and remove layers or parts of layers like PHS. Agencies will be given discretion to decide what they do to reduce the amount of time spent on budgeting.

Concurrently, there will be a decentralisation of the budget making process within agencies, in the sense that agencies will have more discretion to create their own budgets within the set limits. The aim is to encourage the agencies to 'own' the targets more than they did under Reagan or Bush. In effect, officials suggested that this heralds a move towards portfolio budgeting, where departmental heads are given discretion to budget among the 'portfolio' of agencies and bureaus under their control. The budgeting team held extensive talks with government officials from Australia, New Zealand and Canada where portfolio budgeting has already been implemented.

The changes outlined above will mean a change of role for the Office of Management and Budget, created under Nixon and used extensively by Reagan as an agent of top-down budgeting. There will be more collegiality between OMB and the agency heads and more involvement of the agencies at the highest levels. Some of the policy decisions will shift to other organisations within the White House, the Domestic Policy Council and the National Economic council who will be more involved in the budget process than before. The role of the OMB budget examiners, which has traditionally been to scrutinise agency budgets in intricate detail, will change with less emphasis on line items of budgets. They will be expected to focus on performance measurement, through the already implemented *Government Performance and Results Act.*

One of the recommendations proposes a move towards biannual budgeting. This is viewed with suspicion by critics of NPR who watched the Department of Defence try the same move with only partially successful results. The proposal was consistently rejected by Congress, anxious that two year budgeting would reduce their opportunities between elections to appease constituents with appropriations that benefit their own constituencies. But as one official pointed out, even if this does not receive legislative approval it is possible for the executive to move to two year budgets, as happened in DOD. Another recommendation requiring legislation is that agencies will be permitted to roll over 50 per cent of their unobligated year-end balances in annual operating costs to the next year. If passed this might the current 'year-end spending sprees' by agencies, to avoid having to return the excess from line items in their budgets. The NPR team received more examples of this source of waste – in letters, in calls and at town meetings - than any other.

procurement

The prominence given to procurement and contracting in the NPR report relates to the considerable growth in time and money spent on buying goods and services. The government now employs 142,000 workers dedicated to procurement, recording about 20 million contract actions each year. They spend about $200 billion every year, $800 per American. Of all the 'system' reinvention teams, the procurement team made the greatest number with 20 recommendations.

The attention that procurement received is also related to the realisation that in many agencies the procurement process is completely rule bound:

'So many and severe are federal procurement rules that they are often observed in the breach ... It should surprise no one that the rules sometimes get folded, bent or mutilated. Nevertheless, violations are not to be undertaken casually since every step of the contracting process must be documented. The documentation requirements generate elaborate paper trails. Although violation of procedures rarely lead to prosecution, the paper trails can be made to yield evidence of wrongdoing.' (Garvey, 1992)

The burgeoning set of rules that must be rigorously applied means that the procurement process is extremely lengthy. The average time taken to complete a major buy is four years. This is an especial problem for buying information technology based products as technology is changing rapidly with an average product life-cycle of around 18 months. There are many examples in the report of idiosyncrasies produced by the procurement rules. For example, nine pages of specifications and drawings for the precise dimensions, colour and shape of any ashtrays bought by the government. The procedure for buying a personal computer includes obtaining 23 signatures and takes over a year.

One official we spoke to observed how procurement staff are judged purely on whether the process has been followed; evaluating the resultant product takes a low priority. While contract divisions concentrating on procurement have proliferated in agencies, few staff are given the task of evaluation.

Every procurement over $25,000 has to be made under the 1,600 page *Federal Acquisition Regulation* (FAR). One of the NPR recommendations proposes that this be converted from a set of rigid rules to a set of guiding principles. The FAR was compared with the Australian equivalent which is twelve easy to read handbooks. Small purchases are to be simplified by raising the threshold for the use of simplified acquisition procedures from $25,000 to $100,000. Penalties are to be allowed for frivolous protests and contract negotiation is to be allowed to continue up to the point of a contract award, both contributing factors to the strangulation of many large projects. There is a proposal to pilot an electronic marketplace, whereby vendors will be able to access the details of other vendors' prices and the details of all government purchases and adjust their prices accordingly. This would replace the current process whereby the General Services Administration negotiates deals for, say, bulk purchase of personal computers which quickly become greater rather than higher than the market price, a phenomenon now familiar to most federal employees as 'buying a 286 at a 386 price'. There is a commitment to recognize other factors besides price, to define 'best value' and provide regulatory guidance to buy on this basis rather than solely on price.

privatisation

Under Reagan's administration, the assistant secretary of HUD (quoted in Massey) outlined four distinct pressures for privatisation:

1. Pragmatic – More cost effective civil service;
2. Ideological – liberal economics;
3. Commercial – more business for the private sector;
4. Populist – choice in public services.

In the NPR report we can see evidence of the first and the last but not the second or third. Under Reagan and especially in the recommendations of the Grace commission it was ideological and commercial pressures that were paramount. Blanket reviews of in-house jobs and contracted out work took place, with agencies instructed to privatize at least three per cent of their operations every year. Although these efforts were largely unsuccessful in their intent to reduce operating costs, the effect was to impose controls that institutionally forced agencies to contract out work even where it was not cost effective. Ceilings were placed on full time equivalent staff, while contracting costs fell under programme costs and were not restricted in the same way as employing government personnel.

One recommendation made by the NPR budgeting team is to remove FTE ceilings on budget line items and replacing them with limits on operating costs, the definition of which will be changed to include contracting expenses that currently are included in operating costs. This will allow managers more freedom to judge whether work should be contracted out or carried out in-house.

This new pragmatic approach to privatisation is prevalent throughout the recommendations. As one interviewee put it:

> 'There is still some interest in privatization ... but I think it has lost its ideological thrust, there was a huge ideological thrust particularly during the Reagan administration, less so during the Bush administration and virtually none in the Clinton administration ... it would have to be on the basis of a pretty strong cost-benefit allocation – that is, it's no longer the issue the government should not be doing this regardless of whether

it is worth it or not, now it is much more on the basis of cost-benefit. The change means that it does get less attention than it did during the Reagan administration.'

deregulation

Many previous Presidents have used an endless variety of strategies to reduce the paperwork burden on the public and on the private sector, including the ironically named *Paperwork Reduction Act*. However, Carter, Reagan, their Offices of Management and Budget and Congress have all been willing to impose an ever increasing set of controls on executive agencies. For perhaps the first time, the NPR focuses on internal deregulation. The aim is to reduce internal regulations by 50 per cent over the next three years, by directing agencies to scrutinise all their internal regulations and develop ways to reduce them. The department of Veterans Affairs have already done this at five of their regional benefits offices, doing away with 895 of 1,969 regulations and saving staff more than 3,000 hours.

Many of the deregulation recommendations relate to procurement, but there are also attempts to tackle the 'army of overseers' (OTA, 1987) that many agencies now face when they undertake operations. These consist of central executive agencies such as the OMB and GSA, Congressional overseers such as the Office of Technology Assessment (OTA) and GAO and also internal agency auditors such as the Inspectors General. The NPR proposes that the focus of the Inspectors General should change from compliance auditing to evaluating management control systems. The Inspector General's method of operation is to be more collaborative and less adversarial. They have been much criticised for their tendency for 'scandal-hunting after the fact' (*Washington Post*, 16.9.93) and this recommendation has been praised.

personnel

It is noticeable throughout the NPR report that there is a departure from previous president's assumptions that no-one, but especially government employees can be trusted. Agencies will be authorised to design their own performance management programs and develop their own incentive award and bonus systems. Agencies will be encouraged to establish productivity gainsharing programs. Performance agreements with agency heads will be used to identify progress towards agreed upon downsizing goals, not across the board cuts or ceilings on employment. There is a commitment to create a more flexible and responsive hiring system and the 10,000 page Federal Personnel Manual is to be abolished.

One characteristic of Carter and Reagan's administrative reform was the extent to which they relied on bringing people in from outside and denigrated any role that government employees might play in the reform process. The NPR differs from past studies and reorganisation efforts in two ways. Firstly, because it was carried out by government employees. Gore concluded from a review of 500 previous studies that purported to be comprehensive reviews of what needed to be changed in the federal government that 'we didn't find a single one that was based on the ideas of federal employees themselves'. This is the first time that reform has been carried out by reformers who like government, as Osborne pointed out at the press launch. This means that the personnel reductions and reforms are more likely to achieve acceptance from government employees than previous efforts.

Secondly, the National Performance review plans the establishment of labor-management partnership councils, intended to give unions a say in how the agencies cut their work force and realigns some of their missions. GSA have already formed their council in October 1993, with a council which will meet twice-monthly and ensures that the two largest GSA unions (about 60 per cent of the workforce) will 'be afforded the opportunity for involvement at the pre-decision stage in all reinvention initiatives' (*Washington Post*, 20.10.94). Whether or not the signing of this agreement signifies 'a significant milestone in federal labor-management history' (president of the National Federation of Federal Employees, *ibid*), it has meant that the agencies have supported the NPR plan. Clinton's executive order that establishes a national partnership council to overhaul the government's recruitment policy directs agency heads to treat 'employees and their union representatives as full partners'.

Assessment

The National Performance Review has received reasonably favourable reviews in the *Washington Post* and in Washington generally. The General Accounting Office objected to only one of the plan's 350 recommendations, noting that the NPR 'emphasized many of the basic themes we have stressed for years'. This section looks at the main points of controversy that the NPR has provoked. Firstly, whether it is really intended to reinvent government or rather to improve processes through 'reengineering'. Secondly, whether the claimed savings, which have been criticised as implausible, are the main objective of the exercise. Thirdly, the doubts that have been expressed over implementation; will the 'follow-up match the fanfare?' (*Economist*, 15.1.94). The last section looks at the NPR as an example of the 'second wave' of the New Public Management.

reorganising, reinventing or reengineering?

Some of the recommendations simply represent reorganisation of institutions that have, over the years, become overgrown and unnecessarily complex. One example is the Agriculture Department, which operates 14,000 offices worldwide with more than 112,000 employees and 11,000 field offices. It is proposed that the headquarters operations should be reduced from 43 agencies and staff offices to 30. The headquarters staff, 11,886, will be reduced by seven per cent. As well as removing agencies, the reorganization will create new ones, including a Farm Service Agency, Rural Community Development Service and a Food and Consumer Service, which amalgamates and simplifies the existing arrangements.

It is noticeable that in spite of the famous clout of the agriculture lobby, there is little resistance to this proposal. Almost all the Senate Appropriations Committee that examined the proposals felt that this reorganisation was long overdue and the systems dating from the 1930s needed streamlining. Previous attempts to do this have been unsuccessful: the office director of the Agricultural Stabilization and Conservation Service office in West Virginia has been quoted in the *Washington Post* as saying his outpost had been told four times previously it would be closed (*Washington Post*, 30.9.93) but this time according to Mike Espy, the Agriculture Secretary 'we really mean to do it'.

Media attention focused on the *Reinventing Government* book by Osborne & Gaebler. But the NPR's detailed study of budget, personnel and procurement processes and internal regulation is based on the reengineering principal. This is a technique designed by Michael Hammer in a book called *Reengineering the Corporation* and widely used in the private sector. Formally defined by Hammer as the fundamental rethinking and radical redesign of business processes to achieve dramatic improvements in critical contemporary measures of performance, such as cost, quality, service and speed', it concentrates on processes rather than structures. It recognises that it is possible to change organisations via redesigning processes without destroying and recreating new institutions:

'Companies that earnestly set out to 'bust' bureaucracies are holding the wrong end of the stick. Bureaucracy is not the problem ... The underlying problem, wherever bureaucracy has been and remains a solution, is that of fragmented processes. The way to eliminate bureaucracy and flatten the organisation is by reengineering the processes so that they are no longer fragmented.'

The NPR were criticised for 'missing the boat on reengineering' (*Washington Post*, 14.9.93), but the criticism turned out to come from a rival reengineering consultancy. In fact, the organisational structures and leadership management systems team did look extensively at the concepts contained in the book and Michael Hammer was involved in the review, conducting seminars. The findings of the NPR report contains many examples of processes that may have originally made sense but are now causing increased transaction costs and employee frustration.

For example, the current rulemaking process involves a long succession of hearings and reviews which can generate costly litigation. Because the Department of Health and Human Services, for example, has been so slowed down by this process in the issuing of regulations, states have had to introduce their own regulations without the benefit of federal guidance. Some of these state regulations were later overturned after federal regulations were eventually issued, leaving states financially liable. The reengineering section of the NPR report proposes that agencies make greater use of 'Negotiated rulemaking', whereby representatives of the agencies and affected groups are brought together with a mediator before draft regulations are issued and before all sides have formally declared opposition. This allows informal give-and-take that can never happen in court or in a public hearing. When the parties do reach consensus, regulations are issued faster and costly litigation is avoided. The Environmental Protection Agency have already applied these techniques to the issue of emission standards for wood burning stoves; standards were put into effect two years faster and with better factual input than it could have been previously.

savings

According to the summary report, the NPR recommendations if enacted will produce savings of $108 billion over five years. The savings from the overhaul of the procurement system are expected to save $22.5 billion over five years. An executive order entitled *Streamlining the Bureaucracy* has already proposed the reduction of 100,000 full-time equivalent personnel and the NPR called for an additional 152,000, both over the next five years. As with budgeting reform, there has been no administration edict to cut personnel offices in every agency and 'every department is making the reduction in its own way' (spokesman for OMB in Washington Post 11.01.94). A recent report by the Congressional Budget Office argues that this is unrealistic and recalculated the net savings at $305 million from 1994 to 1998. OMB remains firm that their original estimates were valid.

Criticism of the proposed savings and personnel cuts have come from all sides and range from 'too little' to 'too great'. Some critics suggest that the removing of FTE ceilings will cause an increase in federal personnel and that the proposed decreases are quite impossible. Government employees expressed concern that they were too high. One official who worked in the NPR suggested that confusion had been caused by lack of information and fears of redundancy and that in fact these cuts can be made largely through attrition and early retirements:

> 'people are focusing on the downsizing of federal personnel, everyone thinks "thats me!" ... when I went back to my agency they all thought it was them and I said "none of you are managers, this is directed at managers". The downsizing is not really that great, it includes the 100,000 that was already published last year in executive order ... it is a 7 year period through from '93 which is less than 2 per cent per year, we nearly get there by attrition.'

What is clear is that the agencies will be able to make the decisions themselves, in contrast to the blanket reviews of federal jobs carried out during the Reagan reforms.

The conflict over what exactly the savings will be seem unlikely to be resolved. Even with the benefit of time, the disputes over calculation techniques and trade-offs between decreases and increases will be disputed by CBO and OMB. OMB have pointed out that the savings in most cases are not necessarily the primary reason for the proposed reforms: 'perhaps the larger point is that these reforms ought to occur regardless of the scoring' (spokesman for OMB). Gore (in an interview in Business Week 13.09.1993) put it this way:

'We will have significant savings. If you reinvent in the right way, you're going to save significant sums. If cutting spending is all you're interested in, you are going to make mistakes, and you won't get a transformed system of government. If you take a meat axe, all you will do is create tremendous anguish.'

implementation

The NPR team's work has been rightly criticised for the lack of attention paid to implementation. One official explained this as follows:

'the review process was a roller coaster ride of direction and mis-direction and go that way and wait a minute go back that way and every day it was a new direction. We were more focused on getting the recommendations down and then letting other people later on think about implementation.'

The question is whether there will be enough personnel to think about implementation. The NPR office was reduced from 250 to 25 personnel within a week of the summary report being launched and before the detailed reports came out. One official was back in her agency three hours before being asked to return to the NPR office for six months. It will be hard to deploy staff to implement the report when, given the staff reductions proposed in the report and the heavily scrutinised, press-sensitive world of Washington politics, any increase in personnel in regulatory units in central agencies would be politically embarrassing. The chief institutional lever will be a new President's Management Council, chaired by the Deputy Director for Management of OMB. This will include officials from 18 major agencies and the heads of GSA and OPM. It will launch quality management 'basic training' for all employees, starting with top officials and cascading through the entire executive branch. But it is unlikely that the President's Management Council will be permitted a significant increase in staff. The implementation plans are based on principles of osmosis rather than any institutionalised driving force.

However, many of the recommendations can be implemented by executive order, although what percentage it is difficult to establish. In some cases the internal regulations have been imposed on the agencies by themselves. One NPR official observed that:

'What we have found many times is that even though there's legislation that's kind of the original culprit then you see that all the way down the line the agencies have added layer and layer of bureaucracy. The 23 signatures to buy a PC had nothing to do with Congress.'

Thus many of the recommendations relating to procurement can be implemented relatively easily, provided that the process of information dissemination about the recommendations penetrates deeply and widely enough into the bureaucracy.

The proposals that require approval from Congress face a more turbulent future. Both Carter, who was more interested in administration than politics and Reagan, whose Grace Commission report was rampant with criticism of Congress, misjudged the extent to which Congress would block their proposals. The NPR teams have tried to establish levels of Congressional support for recommendations, for example the recommendation for biannual budgeting is based on research done by the Joint Committee on the Organisation of Congress which found that 70 per cent of Congress members favoured biannual budgeting.

Furthermore there are signs that the relationship between the Clinton administration and the appropriations committees is improving. Relations were strained during the passing of the 1994 budget, when the full House approved only $8.8 billion, 53 per cent of Clinton's investment spending for infrastructure, expanded eduction and jobs programs. But in October 1993 the proposal to eliminate mandated personnel levels in many departments of agencies which have previously ensured that congress can block personnel reductions was passed by both the House and the Senate.

The NPR will benefit from the pragmatic nature of US politics. It is difficult for substantial criticism of the report to be based on political ideology as Presidents of both parties have made similar proposals before. Republican senators released their own plan for government reform in December 1993, promising to cut spending by $50.7 billion over five years (*Washington Post*, 9.12.93). Called the *Government Downsizing, Performance and Accountability Act* of 1993, the plan contains almost nothing new, consisting of proposals that are already being implemented or have been voted down or are part of previous reform efforts. Many form part of the NPR itself.

The main argument currently taking place in Washington rests on (a) whether the savings are realistic and (b) whether the report should be judged on its savings potential at all:

> 'There was a big fight in the White House over whether to address reinventing government in deficit-reduction garb or suit it up in good-government clothing. The decision was made that politically it would not fly unless it were wearing deficit-reduction finery.' (Congressman in *Washington Post*, 13 11 93).

The NPR document points out that private-sector companies usually need six to eight years to transform their operations and says that the report should be viewed as a 'down payment' on reinventing the bureaucracy. The pragmatic nature of the recommendations means that some can be implemented, while others remain on the table. As one NPR team member said, 'I would like to have all of it but if we just got 10 per cent I would be happy with what I had achieved'. Ten per cent would also be a higher success rate than the Grace Commission or the Carter Reorganisation project.

managing conventional administration and the contract state

Comtemporary public administrative systems are bifurcating into a small core of conventional public administration and a zone of contract government (for example, see Garvey, 1992). This zone does not just consist of low level routine contracting but also high-level development work. Garvey (1992) designates these two areas of government the rigid 'formal' bureaucracy and the 'shadow' bureaucracy. What Garvey terms 'beltway bandit' firms have proliferated, supplying high-skill services that federal career officials have often not developed the competence to provide themselves. For example, Federal Systems Inc, a subsidiary of IBM exclusively working on federal information systems with some 14,000 employees, exists purely to provide services to government. Every employee in the formal classified service has at least one match in one member of the shadow bureaucracy, that is a private sector worker whose full-time job depends directly on governmental grants or contracts.

On this view we can look at the central government bureaucracy of the future in two parts. There will be a core of the traditional public administration state, formed because the transaction costs of market trading are too high to warrant conducting some government roles on a purely case by case basis. In addition, there will be a contract state consisting of the interface between the bureaucracy and outside corporations or consultants. Heads of administrations will have to learn how to administer both the traditional bureaucracy and the contract state and the techniques for the two tasks will necessarily be different.

Administrative change through the 1980s and early 1990s has seen a growth of the contract state. Both market testing in the United Kingdom and outsourcing in the US are based on the premise that when transaction costs are low, work previously done by government employees should be carried out by private sector agencies and competed in the free market. In the US, federal procurement officers take more than 21 million separate contract actions that affect some $200 billion of federal spending. This amounts to at least one fifth of the entire federal budget (Garvey, 1992, p.39). Reagan's administration, while setting privatisation targets and introducing numerous controls to enforce competition gave no guidance to agencies with respect to the management of this new area of government. Consequently, as the National Performance Review findings illustrated, the procurement process is rule-bound yet inadequate. The realisation that the process of contract management and procurement need specific techniques and processes puts the Clinton administration ahead of the architects of Next Steps in the United Kingdom, who appear sanguine about the effect of the increase in regulation that will probably result from contracting out.

Unlike the United Kingdom civil service reforms and unlike previous administrative initiatives in the US, the National Performance Review attempts to lay down guidelines for the management of the contract state, while retaining the traditional values of a core of public administration. Rather than 'using theories such as agency capture and iron triangles as the ultimate rationale for bureau bashing, thus casting suspicion on the institution of public service itself' (Garvey, 1992), it takes pains to salute the efforts of public employees. Based on trust rather than mistrust, it uses the skills and talents within the bureaucracy by giving agencies the tools to redesign their processes.

The understanding of bureaucracy

> 'begins with the recognition that resistance to change is the
> one real constant in an old-line agency ... The leader who would
> sustain a project of directed change in these unforgiving circum-
> stances needs a full satchel of management techniques and the
> staying power that may give him or her enough time to employ
> them.' (Garvey, 1992).

Reengineering, one of the more congenial of the myriad of private sector
techniques introduced into the public sector by an incoming president, may
provide managers with such a tool. It refocuses attention on processes that
the private sector now realise cannot be successfully left to incremental
change, which the 'new public management' has tended to ignore in its
stress on performance measurement.

If implementation is even in part successful, the National Performance
Review will corroborate existing evidence (for example Zifcak, 1989) that
governments of the left may have more success in cutting public expenditure. Graham Mather has observed the success of the Labour government's
redesign of the machinery of government in New Zealand during the 1980s
and commends the National Performance Review for following the same
track (*Financial Times*, 5.10.93). Case related and pluralistic, it goes with
the grain of what is feasible.

Bibliography

Downs, A, 1967, *Inside Bureaucracy*, Boston: Little Brown.

Dunleavy, King & Margetts, 1992, *Executive Budgeting in the United States: Parts I and II*.

Garvey, G, 1992, *Facing the Bureaucracy: living and dying in a public agency*, San Francisco: Jossey Bass.

Gormley, W, 1989, *Taming the Bureaucracy: muscles, prayers, and other strategies*, Princeton: Princeton University Press.

Hammer, M & Champy, J, 1993, *Reengineering the Corporation*, Australia: Allen & Unwin.

Light, P, 1993, *Monitoring Government: Inspectors General and the search for accountability*, Washington: Brookings.

Massey, A, 1993, *Managing the Public Sector: a comparative analysis of the United Kingdom and the United States*, Aldershot: Edward Elgar.

Moe, R, 1992, *Reorganizing the Executive Branch in the Twentieth Century: Landmark Commissions*, Washington: Congressional Research Service, Library of Congress.

National Performance Review (NPR), 1993, *From Red Tape to Results: Creating a Government that works better and costs less Report of the National Performance Review*, Washington: GPO.

Osborne, D & Gaebler, T, 1992, *Reinventing Government*, USA: Addison-Wesley

The European Community and Policy Networks

John Peterson

University of York

'Policy Networks and Governance in the European Union:
The Case of Research & Development Policy'

Acknowledgements

The author is grateful to the Secretariat-General of the European Commission, the Joseph Rowntree Foundation, and the University of York for grant funding to support the project of which this research forms a part. Special thanks are due to Peter Ludlow and the staff at the Centre for European Policy Studies (Brussels) for offering logistical support in 1994.

This is a draft paper: please do not cite without the permission of the author.

Introduction

Recent debates about the future of the European Union have acted to concentrate the minds of policy analysts on the nature of the European Union as a system of governance. On one hand, it has become tempting to conclude that the European Union now has most of the trappings of a 'state', as traditionally defined (see Dunleavy & O'Leary, 1987, p.2). On the other, the European Union does not command popular loyalties, hold a monopoly on legitimate coercive power, or retain any truly independent means to generate revenue (Shackleton, 1993) in the style of modern nation-states. The European Union is a system of governance in its own right, with substantial power to authoritatively allocate values, but we lack an agreed set of theoretical tools to understand its policy process.

Traditionally, theories of international relations – such as neorealism and neofunctionalism – have dominated European Union studies (see Cameron, 1992; George, 1991, Chapter 14). Usually, the Community (as previously known) has been approached as a sort of 'marriage of convenience' between sovereign nation-states, with strictly limited spheres of competence subject to tenuous intergovernmental bargains. But things have changed: recent literature reflects an emerging consensus on the value of understanding the European Union by resort to the analytical tools of comparative politics (see Sbragia, 1992; Greenwood *et al*, 1992; Bulmer & Armstrong, 1994; Peterson, 1994). Even those who reject the idea that the European Union can be understood as a 'state' can appreciate the argument that:

'The development of the European Community (EC) in the run up to 1992 can be regarded as a process of state formation, an unusual opportunity for social scientists to observe an experiment taking place in front of them.' (Grant, 1993, p.27).

An important element in this process has been the creation of new arenas for the mediation of the interests of governments, interest groups and European Union institutions as member states allocate new policy responsibilities to the European Union. Policy networks are a tool of comparative analysis for describing and analysing how policy outcomes emerge from such arenas. The existing literature on policy networks is mostly concerned with explaining policy outcomes which emerge out of interactions between central and local governments (Rhodes, 1988) and government and industry (Wilks & Wright, 1987).

The policy networks typology is an apt one for understanding the European Union's policy process for two essential reasons. First, European Union policies are products of bargaining between a diverse array of national and supranational, public and private and political and administrative actors. The term 'network' highlights the 'interconnectedness' and mutual dependency of European Union actors with responsibilities in specific policy sectors. Second, actors which seek to influence the European Union's policy process are usually most effective when they wield influence during the relatively early stages of the process, or when proposals are initially formulated and shaped (see Mazey & Richardson, 1993). Political control over these stages of European Union policy-making are tenuous. The policy networks literature emphasises that 'the legitimacy of networks is not political, but resides in the claims to superior expertise and/or increased effectiveness in service provision' (Marsh & Rhodes, 1992, p.265).

This paper deploys the policy networks typology to help explain outcomes of European Union policy-making in the research and development (R&D) sector.[1] Its general argument is that a policy networks model can generate powerful explanations for outcomes at the early, crucial stages of the European Union policy process when policies for particular sectors are initially formulated and shaped. It also helps us understand how European Union policies are managed or implemented after they have been set at a political level. Yet, different but compatible theoretical tools are needed to explain the European Union policy process at different levels of analysis, which are characterised by diverse dynamics, types of rationality and dominant actors.

Section 1 sets out a general theoretical framework for understanding European Union governance. The growth of European Union competence in the R&D sector is briefly sketched in section 2. Section 3 focuses on the role of different European Union institutions in governance of the R&D sector. The policy networks typology is used to explain recent developments in European Union R&D policy in section 4.

---

[1] The paper's conclusions are preliminary and tentative. They predate comprehensive empirical testing of the paper's theoretical framework across a range of European Union policy sectors in 1994. Full results will be presented in Peterson & Bomberg, 1995.

Table 1

Levels of Analysis in

European Community Decision-Making

Level	*Type of Decision*	*Dominant Actors*	*Rationality*
super-systemic	'history-making'	European Council; ECJ	political, legalistic
systemic	policy-setting	Council of Ministers; COREPER	political, administrative
meso-level	policy-formulating, formulating, shaping and implementing	Commission; Council Secretariat; committees; private actors	technocratic, consensual, administrative

Towards a Theoretical Framework for Understanding European Union Governance[2]

The European Union's policy process is highly complex and involves a dizzying array of actors and institutions. Any policy which emerges from this process may be disaggregated into a series of discrete but connected decisions taken to pursue a given course of action. Public policies are the products of decisions about what to do, how to do it, and how to decide what to do. European Union policies may be viewed as the outcomes of accumulated, discrete decisions taken by different sets of actors at successive stages in the Union's policy process.

The policy networks typology provides its most powerful explanations of decisions taken at relatively early and late stages in this process, when policies are formulated and shaped in pre-legislative bargaining between (mostly) administrative and private élites, and then ultimately implemented by many of the same actors. But different theoretical models are needed to explain outcomes at middle stages in the process, when political actors have more control over decision-making.

The framework offered here assumes that decision-making by the European Union occurs at three distinct but connected levels of analysis (see table 1). First, *history-making* decisions are taken at a 'super-systemic' level, or one that transcends the EC's ordinary policy process. History-making decisions alter the Union's legislative procedures, rebalance the relative powers of European Union institutions, or change the Union's remit. Usually, history-making decisions are taken at European Union summits by the European Council. Most reflect distinctly political rationality: the need for national governments to remain in power or the desire of European Union

---

[2] The theoretical framework sketched in this section is developed in more detail in Peterson, 1994.

institutions for increased powers. Occasionally, they may reflect legalistic rationality applied by the European Court of Justice (ECJ) to questions about the proper scope of the Union's Treaty powers.

History-making decisions have powerful effects on the operation of the European Union as a system of governance, particularly when policies are chosen or 'set' at a political level. *Policy-setting* decisions are taken, in terms of time, at the end of the European Union's formal policy-making process, and in terms of 'space', at a 'systemic' level. In most cases, the dominant actor is the Council of Ministers, owing to its preponderant legislative power. However, the Committee of Permanent Representatives (COREPER), which groups together member state ambassadors to the European Union, sets many less controversial policies.

When policies are set, administrative rationality often intrudes. Most Community policies are implemented by national authorities. COREPER is the primary forum for squaring political will to pursue a given policy with national administrative capacities. However, political rationality is usually the primary determinant of choices at the policy-setting level. Very few important policy-setting decisions are taken without the agreement of all 12 governments and a majority of members of the European Parliament (EP) to a Commission proposal, which often must be altered significantly to achieve consensus (see Scharpf, 1988).

A third and final level of analysis is where much European Union governance actually occurs. The 'meso-level' (or 'sub-systemic' level) of individual policy sectors is where *policy-formulating, shaping* or *implementing* decisions are routinely taken. The key actors are formally 'non-political': the Commission, the Council Secretariat, national officials, and private actors who often participate through committees or working groups. Most meso-level decisions are 'second-order' decisions which address the question: how do we do it? But 'what do we do' questions are also answered at the meso-level. The Commission's formal monopoly on policy formulation means that it can often decisively shape the policy choices presented to political representatives on the Council, even if it cannot dictate them.

Technocratic rationality, based on specialised or technical knowledge, tends to dominate at the meso-level, particularly when R&D policies are formulated. Private actors – especially firms involved in 'cutting edge' R&D into new technologies – provide expertise that is otherwise unavailable to the Commission, which is a remarkably small and under-resourced administration. Administrative rationality is often crucial, as the Commission must develop its proposals with a view to ensuring that the administrative power exists at the national level to implement its proposals. The need to forge consensus between actors at this level, in order to legitimize the choices offered to political decision-makers, is a powerful motivator.

Three key features of the European Union both set it apart from other systems of governance and invite analysis using the policy networks model. First, meso-level decisions often are not scrutinised by political actors in any systematic way. One Commission insider argues that although 'outcomes of many Council working groups of national officials go unreported ... it is precisely at this level that most European legislation is made, where most lobbying takes place and where most of the "national interest" is defined and decided' (Spence, 1993, p.50). An important feature of this type of transnational decision-making is that it often takes place at a level where collective political authority is weak and fragmented (see Peterson, 1993, pp.204-14). Helen Wallace (1983, p.77) argues that member states may seek to keep a tight rein on meso-level decision-making through a variety of 'gatekeeping mechanisms, [but] transnational networks of policy-making élites have emerged and become increasingly significant'.

A second and related feature of European Union decision-making is that it is more complex than in national systems because it implicates so many different types of actors with varying agendas. The European Parliament's committees and national legislative watchdogs, such as the House of Lords European Union committee, scrutinise European Union legislation thoroughly. But their ability to control bargaining at 'pre-legislative' stages of policy formulation is inherently limited because they have authority over only a few out of a multiplicity of effective actors.

A third feature of European Union meso-level decision-making is that it is more a important determinant of eventual policy outcomes than is meso-level decision-making in most other systems of governance. Put simply, 'in the policy process of the European Union the dominant actors are members of élite networks working in and through bureaucracies, to an even greater extent than in most national policy processes' (Wallace, 1983, p.56).

No one theoretical model can be expected to generate satisfactory explanations of decisional outcomes at all of these levels of analysis. The actors and types of rationality which dominate decision-making vary too much between different levels. A logical alternative to a single 'theory' of European Union decision-making is the application of different, but compatible theoretical tools to explain outcomes at different levels of analysis (see Table 2).

Table 2
Models for Understanding
Multi-Tiered Community Decision-Making

Level	*Decisive Variable*	*'Best' Model(s)*
super-systemic	change in wider political/economic environment	macro-theories
systemic	institutional change	new institutionalism
meso-level	resource dependencies	policy networks

Macro-theories' such as neofunctionalism or neorealism conceptualise the European Union as an alliance of sovereign nation-states. They are well-equipped to explain how broad trends in the wider global environment may lead to change at a 'super-systemic' level of analysis in European Union politics. For example, neorealism assumes that all states are 'unitary-rational actors' who pursue their own self-interests irrespective of their commitments to international organizations. The French 'walk-out' in the 1960s is perhaps best explained by resort to neorealism (Peterson, 1993b, p.56).

By contrast, neofunctionalism teaches that political integration between sovereign states can proceed in stages. Common policies cause 'spillover', or pressures to develop common policies in related sectors. Neofunctionalism can help explain the emergence of political momentum behind the SEA (Taylor, 1989, pp.23-4) or the empowerment of the ECJ through the gradual process of legal integration (Burley & Mattli, 1993).

At a systemic level where European Union policies are 'set', macrotheories lose their explanatory power because the preferences of national political actors are profoundly constrained by the structure of European Union institutions. Here, the literature on the 'new institutionalism' (March & Olsen, 1989; Weaver & Rockman, 1993) provides novel insights. Its central assumption is that institutions matter: 'actors in a political system, whether individuals or groups, are bound within these structures, which limit, even determine, their conceptions of their own interest and their political resources' (Krasner, 1984, p.225).

Political competition is mediated by institutional structures which 'define individual, group and societal identities' and 'the framework within which politics takes place' (March & Olsen, 1989, pp.17-8). Institutions can impose a 'path dependency' on policy-making: they usually change more slowly than do the preferences of policy-makers and often inhibit policy change.

The new institutionalism offers a set of assumptions about modern governance, as opposed to a coherent theoretical model. But it reminds us that the effect of history-making decisions 'only sketch the broad "rules of the game" and then delegate the authority to apply and adapt these rules' to institutions (Garrett, 1992, p.557). Institutions shape patterns of behaviour in European Union politics in decisive ways.

Within the European Union more than in other systems of governance, policy formulation and shaping often occurs outside of accepted institutions. Policy implementation involves far more actors than in national systems of governance and often necessitates close links between the Commission and multiple national administrations. More generally, the EC is a relatively 'young' system of governance. Its institutions – or significant practices, relationships or organizations – are often not well- established, particularly at the meso-level.

Policy networks have been developed primarily as meso-level concepts. Rhodes (1990) conceptualizes different types of networks based on three key variables: the relative stability of relationships between actors, the relative insularity of networks, and patterns of resource dependency between different actors. A continuum thus emerges (see figure 1). At one end are tightly integrated *policy communities* in which membership is constant, external pressures have minimal impact and actors are highly dependent on each other for resources. At the other are loosely integrated *issue networks*, in which membership is fluid, the network is easily permeated by external influences, and resource dependencies are either weak or changeable.

Figure 1
Conceptualizing Policy Networks

Policy Communities   Issue Networks

──►

stable membership	fluid membership
highly insular	highly permeable
strong dependencies	weak dependencies

Clearly, the ways in which different actors exchange information, develop strategies and (especially) depend on each other for resources in European Union meso-level decision-making are often decisive determinants of policy outcomes. For example, many distributional decisions about European Union policy for R&D into information technology (IT) are made within by a policy community which includes Europe's few large, globally competitive electronics firms and a relatively small group of Commission officials (Peterson, 1991, 1993b). Actors are strongly dependent on each other for the resources needed to make very expensive projects funded through the European Strategic Programme for Information Technology (ESPRIT) show results.

By contrast, decision-making on industrial R&D takes place within a much looser issue network. Far more actors compete for less funding from the Basic Research for Industrial Technologies in Europe (BRITE) programme than is the case with ESPRIT. Resource dependencies within BRITE are generally weak and alliances between actors are ad hoc and fleeting.

More generally, the policy networks model helps us come to grips with three essential characteristics of EC decision-making at the meso-level: the participation of a diverse variety of actors in policy formulation, shaping and implementation; different degrees of élite autonomy in different policy sectors; and the different resource dependencies which fundamentally shape relationships between actors. Policy networks are essentially descriptive, as opposed to predictive, theoretical tools. But they can help us to anticipate and explain European Union policy outcomes by providing insights into how and why decisions are formulated, shaped and implemented at a meso-level of analysis.

The Growth of European Union Competence in R&D Policy

Since its origins in the mid-1980s, the Framework programme has grown in size to the point where R&D now represents the single largest item of

European Union expenditure after agriculture (see table 3). Its launch and subsequent growth has been encouraged by a coalition of large European multinationals which has strongly supported European Union schemes for funding collaborative R&D (see Green Cowles, 1993). In the early 1980s, industry Commissioner Etienne Davignon brought leading executives from the (then) 12 major European electronics firms under Commission auspices to form the 'Big 12 Roundtable'. The Commission-Big 12 alliance persuaded national governments to fund the Commission's proposal for ESPRIT's pilot phase in 1982, which was an important precursor to more ambitious proposals which followed. The first Framework programme for 1984-7, with a price tag of 3.8 BECU, signified a massive increase in EC R&D actions.

Table 3
European Community Spending
on R&D 1987-93 (mecu)

	1987	1988	1989	1990	1991	1992*	1993
Total	939	1135	1412	1706	1749	2790	2556

* Includes budget + carryovers
Source: CEC, 1992

The Commission's proposal for Framework II (1987-91) was unveiled at virtually the same time as the Reagan administration sought European partners for research into the American Strategic Defense Initiative (SDI) and the French President, Francois Mitterrand, proposed the creation of the Eureka (European Research Co-ordinating Agency) programme. Eureka was offered as an alternative to the politically loathsome idea of French participation in SDI research. It also allowed European Union governments to endorse support a regrouping of European technological capabilities and public support for collaborative, cross-border R&D projects without either large increases in European Union funds for R&D or expanded Commission powers in R&D policy. After initial teething problems, Eureka grew to rival in size the EC's Framework programme by the early 1990s. The Commission had to learn to live with it (Peterson, 1993a).

Still, the Commission managed to link the freeing of the internal market with a significantly expanded Framework II budget of 5.6 BECU. Moreover, the *Single European Act* (SEA) amended the Treaty of Rome to provide a much stronger legal basis for an EC R&D policy after 1987. The overall budget for multiannual Framework programmes still required unanimous agreement on the Council, but the Community now had a legal mandate to 'strengthen the scientific and technological base of European industry and to encourage it to become more competitive at an international level'.

However, negotiations on multiannual Framework programme budgets remained acrimonious. As net contributors to the EC's general budget, Germany and the United Kingdom remained the most frequent critics of the Commission's proposed price tags. Smaller member states, which lacked large, integrated 'national champions' in technology-intensive industries, argued that European Union programmes were biased in favour of large multinationals from large Member States.

Moreover, the Maastricht Treaty made the Framework budgetary negotiations subject to the new 'co-decision' procedure. It provided the European Parliament with effective veto powers over Council actions, and thus threatened to further complicate the adoption of a EC R&D budget. Negotiations in 1993 on the Framework IV programme (1994-98) were no less combative than those previous. The Commission proposed a very large increase in Framework's budget to 13.1 BECU and ran into resistance from Germany, France and the United Kingdom. After Research Ministers failed to agree on an overall budget, a common Council position on Framework IV had to be referred upwards to the European Council at the Brussels summit of December 1993. European Union leaders finally agreed on an overall budget of 'not less than 12 BECU, to which might be added a reserve of 1 BECU ... at a later date' pending review of the proposal by the European Parliament under the co-decision procedure (Hill, 1993). Accordingly, the European Union's R&D policy resources will nearly double during the 1990s. This vast increase in the size of the Framework programme, despite tenacious negotiations on its budget and content, begs careful investigation.

Explaining the Politics of European Union R&D Policy

The initial resistance of large member states to the Commission's proposal for Framework IV reflects a fundamental clash of interests between large and small states in European Union R&D policy. The behaviour of Germany, France and the United Kingdom on the Research Council is largely a reflection of the way in which the Framework programme acts to redistribute technological resources from the richest to poorest European Union member states. *Juste retour* is an important governing principle of negotiations on the Framework programme. Its application to European Union R&D policies leads large Member States to complain that too much of the Framework programme funds projects based on political criteria, as opposed to the most sophisticated and promising projects.

At the same time, large European Union member states have found that they lack the resources needed to fund large, strategic projects in IT and other sectors by themselves. The large tranche of European Union funding for IT and communications research reflects the power of an IT policy community, centred around the Big 12 Roundtable, which effectively lobbied national governments for integrated Community actions in the mid-1980s. No less than ten of the original 'Big 12' were domiciled in the United Kingdom (ICL, GEC and Plessey), France (Thomson, Bull and CGE) or Germany (Siemens and Nixdorf).

Moreover, both Germany and the United Kingdom have begun to look to the European Union as a lever for encouraging their domestic firms to become more innovative. Fiscal austerity in Germany following unification and widespread concern about a national 'innovation crisis' (see Eisenhammer, 1993) have weakened the premise that the most promising R&D projects should be funded and conducted in a purely German context. The recession and large defence cuts in the early 1990s led to sharp falls in R&D spending in the United Kingdom (HMSO, 1993; *Financial Times*, 8 September 1993). The United Kingdom – like France – is a net beneficiary of the Framework programme, which is increasingly viewed as a way to compensate for reduced domestic public spending on R&D.

Decisions to approve large increases in the Framework programme's budget are clearly 'history-making' decisions: they determine what levels of European Union resources are to be devoted to R&D for long periods (5 years) at a time. The referral of a decision on Framework IV 'upwards' to the European Council shows that such decisions must be taken at the highest political level.

Crucially, the budgetary proposal for Framework IV considered at the Brussels summit of late 1993 was linked to the Delors Commission's 'growth initiative', designed to stimulate European Union economies at a time of global recession. The European Council's need to be seen to be taking tangible measures to cope with high European Union unemployment and declining competitiveness clearly encouraged agreement on Framework IV's budget. The decisive variable in explaining this decision was the sharp decline in European competitiveness, particularly *vis-a-vis* Asian competition, in an increasingly globalised economy. Neorealists would explain the decision to increase funds for Framework IV as a case of European Union countries seeking to increase their economic power through ad hoc collective action in the face of a common external threat. For their part, neofunctionalists would assume that the growth of the Framework programme is indicative of the trend towards the gradual integration of national R&D policies as an European Union industrial policy is constructed.

The Council of Ministers occupies a 'middle layer' of decision-making on the Framework programme, in that it sets broad priorities for European Union-funded R&D. Here, the new institutionalism provides explanations for negotiated outcomes. European Union R&D policy is 'path dependent' in significant respects. Disputes surrounding the 'large firm bias' of the early Framework programmes have been largely settled by earmarking funding for small, inexpensive, 'type B' projects in which the national firms of smaller states have a chance to participate (see Sandholtz, 1992, p.177), thus institutionalising the redistributive element of the Framework programme. The substantial European Union commitment to developing the biotechnology industry in the 1980s has precluded any meaningful debate about the potential social and environmental costs of biotechnology in the eyes of many critics (see Wheale & McNally, 1993). Despite widespread doubts about its viability, about half of the European Union's budget for energy R&D continues to be spent on nuclear fusion (Ford & Lake, 1991).

Scharpf's (1988, p.257) description of the dynamics of policy-setting decisions, which encourage 'path-dependency', seem particularly relevant to European Union R&D policy:

'(N)on-agreement is likely to assure the continuation of exist-

ing common policies, rather than a reversion to the "zero base"
of individual action ... when circumstances change, existing policies are likely to become sub-optimal even by their own original
criteria. Under the unanimity rule, however, they cannot be
abolished or changed as long as they are still preferred by even
a single member' (emphasis in original).

Yet, the argument that the two most powerful institutional features of European Union politics are intergovernmentalism and unanimous decision-
making (Scharpf, 1988, p.267) neglects the power of other European Union
institutions – particularly the Commission and European Parliament – to
influence policy-setting decisions on the Council. The Commission seeks
increased funds for the Framework programme largely as a means to expand its own industrial policy role. The new 'co-decision' procedure gives
the European Parliament substantial leverage over R&D policy-setting decisions. The European Council's acceptance of the Commission's proposed
budget of 13.1 BECU for Framework IV, with only marginal alterations,
was motivated in part by the stated willingness of the European Parliament
to hold out for more than was being suggested by larger European Union
member states as a compromise figure.

Political agreement on large increases in the Framework programme's
budget seem incongruous with the frequently-voiced suspicions of many
member states – particularly large ones - about the true value of the European Union's programmes. German negotiators remain highly critical
of their 'centralist, bureaucratic decision-making processes' (interview, 11
November 1993). British negotiators complain that 'Framework gets waved
around in front of people as a big EC success, but we're never sure whether
this is money well-spent' (interview, 11 November 1993). A wide swathe of
member states agree that the Commission does not do enough to evaluate
the European Union's R&D programmes.

The laboriousness of political negotiations on the Framework programme
is a product of the perceived inability of Member States to exert much control over European Union R&D policy once it has been 'set'. After political
negotiations on the Framework programme's budget and general content
are complete, many distributional and technical decisions about European
Union R&D policy are subject to relatively weak political controls. In short,
the management and implementation – as well as the design and formulation – of European Union R&D policy are largely the domain of relatively
autonomous sectoral policy networks.

Policy Networks and European Union R&D

Close examination of European Union R&D policy process suggests that
three different but overlapping policy networks exist: one to formulate proposals for the Framework programme, another to shape their content, and a
third to actually manage EC-funded programmes once they are approved at
a political level (see Table 4). Proposals are formulated by the Commission
with the close cooperation of industry and research élites. The Commis-

sion seeks the advice of representatives of COREPER and national research ministries at this stage, but its emphasis is on designing proposals which are widely supported by the recipients of European Union funding. For their part, European research organisations have become increasingly dependent on European Union funding as national R&D budgets have stagnated or shrunk (that is, in Germany and the United Kingdom). Thus, policy networks have emerged, corresponding to specific technological sectors which receive European Union support, in which resource dependencies are strong.

The key actors in the 'policy-shaping' network are the Commission, COREPER, and Council Working Groups. This network is activated after the Commission formulates and then submits its initial proposals. Council Working Groups then scrutinse the details of Commission proposals for individual subprogrammes, such as BRITE or ESPRIT.

Table 4
Policy Networks in Union R&D Policy

Network	*Key Actors*
policy formulation	Commission; industry and research élites
policy shaping	Commission; COREPER; Council Working Groups
policy management	Commission; 'task forces'; regulatory committees

What is most striking about the R&D policy process is that most of what eventually is sanctioned by the Research Council is agreed before the formal negotiating process begins. A British COREPER official suggests that:

'About 90 percent of what eventually becomes the Framework programme is determined by the Commission in its proposal. When they submit a proposal, about 80 percent of it is non-controversial. The other 20 percent may be rather controversial for some member states, so agreement is worked out in Council working groups. Ministers do get involved in the most important stuff: the overall budget and how it is broken down between sectors. But these are really alterations at the margins, representing about 1 to 2 percent of a total proposal.' (interview, 11 November 1993)

Increasingly, the Commission has 'ready-made' coalitions to support its proposals once they are submitted to member states. For example, throughout 1993 the R&D Commissioner, Antonio Ruberti, along with the heads of all relevant Commission directorates, organised seminars to bring together industrialists and researchers concerned with R&D into energy, biotechnology and other sectors targeted for European Union activity in the Framework IV proposal (see *European Report*, 27 November 1993, VI, pp.5-6). Meanwhile, a wide array of European industries issued collective calls for increased funding for Framework IV as negotiations reached an endgame in late 1993. Examples included a proposal for more money for manufacturing R&D by the umbrella organisation of European machine tool manufacturers (Cecimo), a plan for new collaborative programmes in the multi-media sector by Philips and SGS-Thomson, and the launch of a 'European Charter for Industry' by the European Round Table along with Commission President Jacques Delors.[3]

Once an overall budget for Framework is agreed, negotiations then turn to actually setting general priorities and guidelines for individual subprogrammes. Most responsibility for such decisions is delegated by the Council to working groups of national experts. Here, the Commission's proposals are often amended considerably to suit national interests. Although most members of Council working groups are researchers or scientists and essentially 'non-political' actors, they often carry the weight of being the final line of defence of national interests.

After they are approved by Council working groups, the management of individual R&D subprogrammes is delegated to the Commission and 'task forces' of experts. For example the Information Technology (IT) Task Force responsible for Esprit develops an annual 'work programme' which designates which types of research receive priority when funding decisions are made. The Commission's subsequent calls for tender are usually highly detailed and specific. ESPRIT, as all other Framework subprogrammes, is overseen by a committee of national experts, which includes representatives from all member states. The type of committee chosen to oversee large R&D programmes - particularly those with relatively large budgets – is usually a regulatory committee. Regulatory committees have the potential to constrain the autonomy of the Commission, by referring specific proposed actions back to the Council, more than do advisory or management committees (see Dogan, 1992). Committees which oversee Framework subprogrammes must approve lists of projects chosen for funding by the Commission. However, task force recommendations usually are altered by committees only marginally (Peterson, 1991, p.276).

In short, after highly politicised decisions are taken to commit funding to a specific programme, when detailed distributional and management decisions are made 'as such, sovereignty is not an issue' (Watkins, 1989, p.8). Skoie (1993, p.20) reckons that 'on the whole decisions are taken by the Commission's administrative staff – there lies the real decision-making power'. In the language of the literature on policy networks, many individual EC initiatives appear to be highly integrated *policy communities* in which membership is constant, outside influences are resisted and actors are highly dependent on each other for resources (see Peterson, 1992; Skoie, 1993). ESPRIT is the most obvious example: a large share of its funds continue to go to projects involving Europe's largest electronics firms, who are well-represented on the IT task force. Other initiatives, such as those

---

[3] See *Financial Times*, 16 October, 12 November and 4-5 December 1993.

for environmental technologies or biotechnology, offer far less funding to far more research organisations. Negotiations on these programmes take place within *fora* which resemble *issue networks*. But political controls over management and the distribution of funds are generally weak after programmes are approved on the Council.

The autonomy of many European Union R&D policy networks is largely a product of the central position of the Commission across a range of networks for policy formulation, shaping and management. In many respects, the Commission has played its cards skillfully in seeking to expand the Union's *acquis* in R&D policy. It has linked the long recession of the early 1990s with the European Union's lagging competitiveness in technology-intensive industries in its arguments that:

> 'The need for a European industrial policy has reappeared. In the 1970s, industrial policy was characterized by a *dirigiste* and sectoral approach. Today, it is recognized that public interventions in this area must take the form of horizontal activities to achieve the right climate and balance for maximizing the productivity and competitiveness of European industry.' (CEC, 1992, p.22)

In this context, the Commission's proposal for Framework IV put strong emphasis on the development of generic or 'critical technologies'. In future, European Union funding will be more targeted on projects which promise to yield innovations with applications across a broad range of production systems. The Commission also has begun to insist that European Union R&D should fund more downstream, 'near market' projects. In theory, the Framework programme since its origins has been restricted to funding only upstream or 'pre-competitive' R&D so as to avoid charges that the European Union is violating its own rules on distortion of competition. Industry has long complained that such restrictions prevent the use of European Union funds for projects which will deliver enhanced competitiveness quickly (see Peterson, 1993, pp.122-6). Successive commissioners for research – first Fillipo Pandolfi from 1988-92 and now Ruberti – have echoed industry calls to apply European Union competition rules to its R&D programmes less strictly. One way out of this dilemma is for the European Union to fund more 'targeted projects', or those designed to develop 'critical technologies' with multiple applications off the drawing board and into the marketplace.

Moreover, in October 1993 the Commission helped broker a declaration on closer relations between Eureka and the Framework programme. The declaration was a product of political pressures, particularly from France and Germany, to ensure that European Union funds may be used to support projects of national importance which are funded through Eureka (and thus national coffers). Yet, closer European Union-Eureka relations also reflect a convergence of national and European Union policy networks in specific technological sectors. Over time, Eureka has spawned a broad range of 'umbrella projects' to catalyse R&D in sectors such as robotics, environmental technologies etc, as well as large strategic projects such Prometheus, to develop the 'clever car', and COSINE, to federate computer network standards. Since the role of governments in Eureka is essentially confined to straightforward funding decisions, sectoral policy networks within Eureka tend to 'stand alone' and operate autonomously of political controls (Peterson, 1993a, pp.208-14). Industry usually plays a dominant role in these networks, with substantial logistical support from cross-national alliances of civil servants drawn from domestic research ministries. Embracing closer links to Eureka represents the logic of *engrenage* for the Commission, or the interlocking of national élites into networks which promote common strategic actions (see Peterson, 1991).

The Commission's Framework IV proposals also reflects its increasing concern to make the best use of its limited administrative resources in the face of vast increases in European Union R&D activities and funding. The Commission now insists that it should concentrate more specifically on general policy development, as opposed to detailed project management. It has received substantial support from Germany, with its world-class coterie of research organisations, for proposals to decentralise the management of European Union-funded projects to 'networks of excellence' or 'concertation networks' of research organisations. Smaller and southern member states tend to equate decentralisation with the renationalisation of R&D policies, and German officials admit that their position on decentralisation of project management is 'a pretty isolated one' (interview, 11 November 1993). But the Commission can be expected to continue to lobby member states to decentralise project management. This element in the Commission's strategy reflects both its desire to concentrate on broad policy questions as the federative agent for a common European Union industrial policy and its contention that policy networks in specific areas of technology are now self-sustaining and capable of self-management.

Conclusion

This paper has argued that policy networks are a useful theoretical tool for assessing both how European Union R&D policies are formulated at early stages of decision-making and then managed after receiving political approval. However, policy networks provide their most powerful explanations when applied to interactions between private and public élites at relatively early and late stages of the European Union's policy process: when policies are initially formulated and shaped, and then ultimately implemented. The 'middle' stages of the European Union policy process, when policies are 'set' by the Council, are best analysed through the prism of the new institutionalism which provides unique insights into bargaining between the Council and other European Union institutions. Yet, the European Union ultimately remains a collection of sovereign nation-states. The politics of European integration remain intergovernmental in many respects and the European Union's internal politics continue to be profoundly conditioned by broad changes in international economics and politics. 'Macro-theories' such as neorealism and neofunctionalism remain important guides for understanding the European Union's 'history-making' decisions.

A theoretical framework which accounts for the different dynamics of European Union decision-making at different levels of analysis is needed to explain European Union R&D policy outcomes, as well as outcomes across the full range of European Union activities. Policy networks can generate powerful explanations for outcomes in the R&D sector, where a high premium is placed on technical expertise and the power of private actors to deliver on policy goals. But policy networks must be supplemented by compatible models as part of a broader framework which acknowledges that there can be no single 'theory' of EC decision-making.

Whilst a number of studies have deployed policy networks to explain European Union policy outcomes (see Peterson, 1991; Grant et al, 1988; Schneider & Werle, 1992, Smith, 1993; Mazey & Richardson, 1993), the model remains largely untested at the European Union level. The European Union, as a relatively insular and technocratic system of governance, can be understood as a 'hot house' for policy networks. A central lesson of the existing literature on policy networks is that they often arise to make difficult policy tasks manageable (see Marsh & Rhodes, 1992). Policy networks are rife in EC governance because they help minimise the uncertainties which are endemic to a political system that features so many different levels of decision-making and such a diverse collection of actors with influence and resources.

The European Union's policy process remains highly unpredictable, but policy outcomes often can be foretold through careful study of past patterns of policy formulation and implementation. A profitable research agenda for European Union scholars would be to test the policy networks typology across a range of sectors to identify such patterns where they exist and to specify the determinants of European Union policy outcomes and dominant actors in different sectors. If we can identify what types of policy networks operate in which areas of policy, we can learn much about who gets what and why from the operation of the Union as a system of governance.

Bibliography

Bulmer, Simon, & Kenneth Armstrong (1994), *Rule-Making in the Single European Market* (forthcoming).

Burley, Anne-Marie & W.Mattli (1993), 'Europe Before the Court: A Political Theory of Legal Integration', *International Organization*, 47(1) :41-76.

Cameron, David R (1992), 'The 1992 Initiative: Causes and Consequences', in *Euro-Politics: Institutions and Policy-making in the 'New' European Community*, edited by A.M.Sbragia, 23-74. Washington, DC: Brookings Institution.

CEC (1992), *Research After Maastricht: An Assessment. A Strategy.* Brussels: Commission of the European Communities.

Dogan, Rhys (1992), *Comitology – Bankers' Veto or Secured Loan: National Influence on the Powers of Implementation of the Commission of the European Communities*, Milan: Instituto Per Gli Studi Di Politica Internazionale.

Dunleavy, Patrick & Brendan O'Leary (1987), *Theories of the State: The Politics of Liberal Democracy* London: Macmillan.

Eisenhammer, John (1993), 'Germans Need to Translate Angst Into Action', *The Independent*, 6 December, 24.

Ford, Glyn & Gordon Lake (1991), 'Evolution of European Science and Technology Policy', *Science and Public Policy*, 18 (February):38-50.

Garrett, G (1992), 'International Cooperation and Institutional Choice: The European Community's Internal Market', *International Organization*, 46 (Spring):533-60.

George, Stephen (1991), *Politics and Policy in the European Community*, 2nd edition, Comparative European Politics series. Oxford: Oxford University Press.

Grant, Wyn (1993), 'Pressure Groups and the European Community: An Overview', in *Lobbying in the European Community*, eds Sonia Mazey & Jeremy Richardson, 27-46. Oxford and New York: Oxford University Press.

Grant, Wyn, William Paterson & Colin Whitson (1988), *Government and the Chemical Industry: A Comparative Study of Britain and West Germany*, Government-Industry Relations series. Oxford: Clarendon Press.

Green Cowles, Maria (1993) 'The Politics of Big Business in the Single Market Programme', Paper Presented to the European Community Studies Association Conference. Washington, DC.

Greenwood, Justin, Jurgen R.Grote & Karsten Ronit (eds) (1992), *Organized Interests and the European Community*, London: Sage.

Hill, Andrew (1993), 'Deadlock Broken Over R&D Spending', *Financial Times*, 13 December, 3.

HMSO (1993), *Annual Review of Government Funding Research and Development, 1993*, London.

Krasner, Stephen (1984), 'Approaches to the State: Alternative Conceptions and Historical Dynamics', *Comparative Politics*, 16:223-46.

March, James G & Johan P.Olsen (1989), *Rediscovering Institutions: The Organizational Basis of Politics*, New York and Oxford: The Free Press.

Marsh, David & R.A.W.Rhodes (eds) (1992), *Policy Networks in British Government*, Oxford: Oxford University Press.

Mazey, Sonia & Jeremy Richardson (eds) (1993), *Lobbying in the European Community*, Oxford and New York: Oxford University Press.

Peterson, John (1991), 'Technology Policy in Europe: Explaining the Framework Programme and Eureka in Theory and Practice', *Journal of Common Market Studies*, 29 (March): 269-90.

—— (1992), 'The European Technology Community policy networks in a supranational setting', in *Policy Networks in British Government*, edited by David Marsh & R.A.W.Rhodes, 226-48, Oxford: Oxford University Press.

—— (1993b), *Europe and America in the 1990s: The Prospects for Partnership*, Aldershot and Brookfield, VT: Edward Elgar.

—— (1993a), *High Technology and the Competition State: An Analysis of the Eureka Paradox*, London & New York: Routledge.

—— (1994), 'Understanding Decision-making in the European Union: Towards a Framework for Analysis', York Working Papers in Politics 4. York.

Peterson, John & Elizabeth Bomberg (1995), *Decision-Making in the European Union: Who Gets What From Europe?*, forthcoming, London: Macmillan.

Rhodes, R. A. W (1988), *Beyond Westminster and Whitehall*, London: Unwin Hyman.

Rhodes, R.A.W (1990), 'Policy Networks: A British Perspective', *Journal of Theoretical Politics*, 2(3):293-317.

Sandholtz, Wayne (1992), *High-Tech Europe: The Politics of International Cooperation*, Berkeley and Oxford: University of California Press.

Sbragia, A (ed) (1992), *Euro-Politics: Institutions and Policy-making in the 'new' European Community*, Washington, DC: Brookings Institution.

Scharpf, Fritz (1988), 'The Joint-decision Trap: Lessons from German Federalism and European Integration', *Public Administration*, 66 (Autumn): 239-78.

Schneider, Volker & Raymund Werle (1992), 'Networks and Concertation in European Policy Making: The Cases of Chemicals Control and Telecommunications', Paper Presented at the European Consortium for Political Research Joint Sessions. Limerick.

Shackleton, Michael (1993), 'Keynote Article: The Delors II Budget Package', in *The European Community 1992: Annual Review of Activities*, Special Issue of the *Journal of Common Market Studies*, edited by Neill Nugent, 11-25.

Skoie, Hans (1993), 'EC Research and Technology Policies: Some Characteristics of Developments and Future Perspectives', Institute for Studies in Research and Higher Education. Oslo.

Spence, David (1993), 'The Role of the National Civil Service in European Lobbying: The British Case' in *Lobbying in the European Community*, edited by Sonia Mazey & Jeremy Richardson, 47-73, mOxford and New York: Oxford University Press.

Taylor, Paul (1989), 'The New Dynamics of EC Integration in the 1980s', in *The European Community and the Challenge of the Future*, ed. Juliet Lodge, 3-25.

Wallace, Helen (1983), 'Negotiation, Conflict and Compromise: The Elusive Pursuit of Common Policies', in *Policy Making in the European Community*, 2nd Edition, edited by Helen Wallace, William Wallace & Carole Webb, 43-80, Chichester and New York: John Wiley & Sons.

Watkins, Todd. 1989. 'Research Collaboration in the European Community: Innovation, Technology Diffusion and Political Support', Paper Presented to the Inaugural Conference of the European Community Studies Association. Fairfax, Virginia.

Weaver, R.Kent & Bert A.Rockman (eds) (1993), *Do Institutions Matter? Government Capabilities in the United States and Abroad*, Washington: Brookings Institution.

Wheale, Peter & Ruth McNally (1993), 'Biotechnology Policy in Europe: A Critical Evaluation', *Science and Public Policy*, 20 (August):261-79.

Wilks, Stephen & Maurice Wright (eds) (1987), *Comparative Government-Industry Relations*, Oxford: Clarendon Press.

The Intelligence Services

Peter Gill

Liverpool John Moores University

'Information Control and Changes in United Kingdom
Security Intelligence Agencies under Major'

Introduction

On the face of it there has been something of a revolution in the presentation
of security intelligence structures in the United Kingdom since the downfall
of Margaret Thatcher. In November 1991 the name of the new Director
General of the Security Service (aka MI5) was, for the first time, officially
announced, though the media remained dependent for a picture of Stella
Rimington on a fuzzy photograph begged, borrowed or stolen from the *New
Statesman and Society*.[1] Then after his re-election in 1992 John Major referred officially for the first time to the Secret Intelligence Service (SIS aka
MI6), promising legislation to provide it and its sister service, Government
Communications Headquarters (GCHQ), with both a legislative mandate
and some form of oversight.[2] Before this legislation appeared in November
1993, however, further information was made available. First, in July 1993,
Stella Rimington appeared at a photocall accompanying the launch of a
glossy pamphlet on the organisation and functions of the Security Service[3]
and, second, in October William Waldegrave appeared at a press conference
to launch another booklet on the Central Intelligence Machinery which described the role of the Joint Intelligence Committee in co-ordinating the
work of the intelligence agencies.[4] Finally, in November the Government
published its *Intelligence Services Bill*, which was read for a second time in
the House of Lords on December 9th, and in the first unified budget and
public expenditure statement, the Government published the estimates for
the security intelligence services: £900 million, of which MI6 takes £150m,
MI5 £200 m. and GCHQ the rest.[5]

Taken alongside the government's more general proclamation of 'Open
Government' in their July 1993 white paper of that name, this begins to
look like a unilateral reduction of that secrecy which has for so long been
characterised as the 'cement' of the British constitution.[6] However, it is the
contention of this paper that what we are seeing is not so much a march
along a single dimension from secrecy to openness but, rather, is better
characterised as variations in *information control*. This has been defined
this as 'the processes used to make sure that certain people will or will not

---

[1] This had first appeared in the then *New Statesman* during the 1984-5 miners' strike.

[2] *The Guardian*, May 7, 1992, p.4.

[3] *The Security Service*, HMSO, 1993, Foreword by Michael Howard, the Home
Secretary.

[4] HMSO, 1993, with a Foreword by the Prime Minister.

[5] *The Guardian*, December 1, 1993, p.15.

[6] C. Ponting, *The Right to Know*, Sphere Books, London, 1985, p.39.

have access to certain information at certain times'.[7] As such, control over access to information or knowledge is a necessary, if not sufficient condition for the exercise of governmental power. The contemporary analysis of power frequently rests on its symbiotic relationship with knowledge. In general terms this has been most strongly argued by Foucault:

> '... there is no power relation without the correlative consti-
> tution of a field of knowledge, nor any knowledge that does not
> presuppose and constitute at the same time power relations.'[8]

Similarly, in the specific context of this paper, the American scholar Harry Howe Ransom has pointed to the need for students of intelligence to study 'knowledge and power, information and action'.[9]

Four main processes of information control may be identified: surveillance, secrecy, persuasion and evaluation. The first is the process by which information is gathered and stored. There are overt ways in which this may be done, for example, information on individuals may be gathered voluntarily as when they respond to a survey, or as part of an exchange relationship, as with social security or on pain of punishment as with tax and census information. Additionally, information may be gathered covertly, what might be called espionage: 'the process of obtaining information from people who do not want you to have that information'.[10] State espionage includes the normal array of covert techniques, the use of informers and technical devices, but includes also the transfer of information between different agencies. Espionage is not only available to the state, however, 'outsiders' such as investigators working for oversight bodies or journalists who may be seeking information regarding the government's (ab)use of power are using what we might call 'democratic espionage'.

Secrecy is the process of keeping other people from obtaining information you do not want them to have.[11] When the dominant analogy of the polity was that of an organism the rationale for secrecy was its need for self-protection and a 'measure of sacredness' was linked to both state and individual privacy.[12] Later on, as traditional modes of authority became replaced by more bureaucratic/rationalist modes there was an explosion of information and the public scrutiny of private life which simultaneously produced a heightened concern with secrecy. The 'new police' and, later in the nineteenth century, the development of detective branches, may have improved the surveillance of the 'dangerous classes' but they also provided the potential for the invasion of the privacy of the respectable bourgeoisie. Meanwhile the increasing bureaucratisation and size of the state in the

---

[7] Richard W.Wilsnack, 'Information Control: a conceptual framework for sociological analysis', *Urban Life*, 8(4), January 1980, 468. The following is drawn from and adapts Wilsnack's framework.

[8] Quoted in G. Turkel, 'Michel Foucault: Law, Power and Knowledge', *Journal of Law and Society*, 17, 1990, p.179.

[9] H.H.Ransom, 'Being Intelligent About Secret Intelligence Agencies', *American Political Science Review*, 74(1), March 1980, p.148.

[10] Wilsnack, *op cit*, p.470.

[11] *Ibid*, p.471.

[12] S.Bok, *Secrets: on the ethics of concealment and revelation*, Oxford University Press, 1986, p.172.

United Kingdom produced a fresh concern with the security of the state's information, as evidenced by the passage of the first *Official Secrets Act* in 1889.[13]

There are some entirely legitimate reasons for secrecy, for example, when *state* secrecy is necessary to protect the privacy of information gathered about *individuals*, or, as recently in the Middle East and Northern Ireland, when a state seeks to negotiate an end to violence in circumstances where openness would guarantee failure because of the public positions of contending groups. Similarly, for individuals some degree of secrecy/privacy is essential in order to maintain self-integrity and identity.

Within groups measures to safeguard secrecy involve a secondary process of procedures to achieve security of communications. In state agencies these will become elaborate procedures for the classification of documents by which, according to Max Weber, official knowledge is transposed into secret knowledge. This becomes the most decisive means of power for officials by which they secure themselves against external control,[14] quite possibly for less legitimate reasons. Barriers of secrecy are erected to protect one's power/autonomy by resisting the espionage attempts of others.

The strength of a model of information control, however, lies in the fact that it gives as much prominence to what might be described as 'information policy' as it does to secrecy. 'Persuasion' is defined as the process of making sure that other people obtain and believe information you want them to have. Wilsnack points out that it is important to distinguish between 'education' (if the communicator herself believes the information to be true) from 'deception' (if she does not).[15] However, this distinction barely does justice to the complexity of information policies: in addition to these two possibilities one might add 'economy' when, as often, information presented is only a partial representation of what is known to be true and consequently can be misleading. 'Burying' is a technique whereby agencies might attempt to overload outside enquiries, giving them large amounts of information much of which is only marginally relevant. Even 'education' can be damaging; for example, information released by state officials about individuals may be true but can be immensely damaging to that individual. While the temptations of deception, in one form or another, are clear, the damage that it can do to political discourse, never mind individual victims, may be considerable.

The counterbalance to information policy is evaluation – the process of making sure that you learn more from the information you have obtained than just what other people want you to know.[16] 'Facts', in other words, rarely speak for themselves. All information gathering systems, whether organised formally by the state or at the level of the individual, may fall

---

[13] W.Wiener, *Reconstructing the Criminal: culture, law and policy in England 1830-1914*, Cambridge University Press, 1990, pp.246-7. For an account of the origins of Official Secrecy legislation see D.Hooper, *Official Secrets: the use and abuse of the Act*, Secker & Warburg, 1987, ch 1.

[14] D.Beetham, *Max Weber and the Theory of Modern Politics*, George Allen & Unwin, 1974, p.74.

[15] Wilsnack, *op cit*, p.473.

[16] *Ibid*, p.475.

prey to the 'empirical fallacy' that more information will lead to becoming better *informed*. Analysis is a crucial, though often under-rated component of intelligence processes.

Two of these processes – surveillance and persuasion – might be characterised broadly as 'offensive' and the other two – secrecy and evaluation – as 'defensive'. Secrecy is employed as a defence against the efforts of others at surveillance, and evaluation is employed as a defence against others' persuasion. Thus there is a dialectical relationship between these processes of information control which is directly analogous to the relationship between power and resistance:

> 'There is always a dialectic to power, always another agency, another set of standing conditions pertinent to the realization of that agency's causal powers against the resistance of another.'[17]

Consequently information control processes have a potential to intensify. Difficulties in evaluating the meaning of information produced by contending (or, sometimes, allied) groups stimulates attempts at espionage. These will be met by protective security measures which in turn stimulate further espionage, and so on. In the state sector, periods such as Watergate and the Northern Ireland intelligence wars of the 1970s indicate the potential instability when these processes threaten to escalate out of control. In the private sector the rapid growth of private security firms and consultancies also reflect this potential as corporations seek to stay one step ahead of the game like small kingdoms engaged in an arms race.

Evalutating the *Glasnost* of the Major Regime

As recipients of government information policies, how are we to evaluate changes in policy? Three questions might be asked. Why have changes to traditional practices been introduced, what is the apparent intention of the changes and how do they affect the ability of the government to control the process of 'persuasion'?

First, exercises of power and information control breed resistance. Government attempts to maintain total control of 'persuasion' in security intelligence matters have been thwarted by a series of events which have exposed official policies as deceptive and state actions as improper if not illegal. Since 1980 we have seen the unmasking of Anthony Blunt, the exposure of poor security procedures within the intelligence agencies – see the cases of Michael Bettaney and Geoffrey Prime, the use by the government of security intelligence information in order to discredit CND prior to the 1983 general election, criticism of the extent of executive discretion in the United Kingdom by the European Court of Human Rights, the *Spycatcher* fiasco, the poor intelligence upon which some Iraqis were detained at the time of the Gulf War and the McCarthyite tone of some of the questioning when those detentions were challenged before the 'Three Wise Men'. Most spectacular of all, however, was the collapse of the prosecution in November 1992 of

---

[17] S.Clegg, *Frameworks of Power*, Sage, London, 1989, p.208.

three men alleged to have illegally exported machinery to Iraq. Whatever the final conclusions of Lord Justice Scott's consequent judicial inquiry, the product of his public hearings has already produced rare insights into the nature of information control processes.

Government or legislative reaction in other liberal democratic regimes to similar security intelligence embarrassments has been to institute wide-ranging judicial or legislative inquiries.[18] In the United Kingdom, however, the centralisation of state authority has, prior to Scott, enabled governments to make use of those information processes which give least space for the development of resistance. In Thatcher's heyday this would take the form of a simple denial that there was a problem, or, at the most, an assertion that any problem that had existed in the past had now been dealt with. For example, minimal changes in procedures were announced as a consequence of the Security Commission's inquiry into the Bettaney case. Occasionally this strategy has been derailed by a powerful intervention from elsewhere, such as the European Court of Human Rights (ECHR) decision finding United Kingdom procedures regarding the issuing of warrants for interception of communications in breach of the European Convention.[19] Consequently the *Interception of Communications Act, 1985* (ICA) was passed, aimed at ensuring minimal compliance with the ECHR decision.[20]

In the later Thatcher years and under Major, a somewhat more sophisticated strategy has been developed which might be characterised as 'getting your retaliation in first'. Whereas the ICA was introduced as a *reaction* to an adverse ECHR decision, the *Security Service Act, 1989* (SSA) was introduced in *anticipation* of another one. Harriet Harman and Patricia Hewitt were challenging at the ECHR the case of their surveillance by the Security Service while employed by the National Council for Civil Liberties (now, Liberty). In the Swedish case of *Leander* in 1987 the ECHR had established the precedent that citizens must have some redress against domestic security services, which was patently not the case in the United Kingdom. Harman and Hewitt would clearly have won at least part of their case even without the context of government disarray over *Spycatcher* at this time.

However, the *Security Service Act* still came as a surprise when announced in the Queen's Speech in November 1988. It provided for the first time a legal basis for the Security Service, and an extremely broad mandate for its operations in defence of 'national security' and 'economic well-being'.[21] The Act also established a complex structure involving a judicial commissioner and a tribunal to receive and investigate complaints from the public and to apply judicial review standards to the issue of warrants by ministers. This imitated precisely the structure in the ICA, 1985 and, for the purposes of the present argument, is noteworthy because on two

---

[18] In Canada under Justice McDonald 1976-81; in Australia under Justice R.M. Hope 1975-77 and 1983-85; and the US Senate and House inquiries of 1975-76.

[19] Malone Case, ECHR (4/1983/60/94), August 2, 1984.

[20] For details of background to this Act see P. Fitzgerald & M. Leopold, *Stranger on the Line: the secret history of phone tapping*, The Bodley Head, 1987, especially Chapter 6.

[21] For a full discussion of the Act see P.Gill, *Policing Politics: security intelligence and the liberal democratic state*, Frank Cass, 1994, pp.290-96; I.Leigh & L.Lustgarten, 'The Security Service Act, 1989', *Modern Law Review*, 52(6), 1989, pp.801-36.

separate occasions in his speech introducing the Bill, then Home Secretary Douglas Hurd contrasted the proposal with others 'who have argued for a system of oversight and review'.[22] Rather, the system provides for the judicial examination of warrant-issuing and not much else. The Annual Reports of the Commissioner are the only published product of the Act, but hitherto they have provided only limited 'education'. The first three recorded the Commissioner's satisfaction with ministerial behaviour, that the Tribunal investigated 99 complaints and upheld none and the three reports totalled 12 pages in length.[23]

The argument that the intention of this Bill was to maintain rather than loosen in any way central control of information processes is supplemented by the contemporaneous passage of the *Official Secrets Act, 1989*, which replaced section two of the 1911 Act and aimed at more effectively preventing the disclosure of official information in six areas, one of which is security intelligence. The Act shifted the control mechanism for the wrongful disclosure by state servants of other information from criminal to disciplinary rules, but the disclosure of security intelligence information is defined as 'damaging' *per se* and is, in effect, an offence of strict liability.[24]

After the 1992 General Election, as we have seen, John Major indicated his intention to do for the SIS and GCHQ what the 1989 Act had done for the Security Service. However, before that bill emerged, two pamphlets relating respectively to the Security Service and the Central Intelligence Machinery were published. The first is better value in terms of the quality and quantity of information it contains, including some which has previously not been made public, for example, the proportions of Service resources allocated to its three main mandates – espionage, subversion and terrorism.[25] Even by current HMSO prices, the second pamphlet is poor value at £4.95: ten of its 28 pages are blank and four others contain just a heading. At the launch press conference William Waldegrave conceded that the booklet contained nothing that had not already appeared in print.[26]

Therefore the booklet is highly 'economical', apparently wishing to do no more than confirm part of the information already put together over the years by enterprising journalists. As such, it does not indicate any serious willingness to loosen the reins of traditional information control, and there are major omissions in this review of 'the central mechanisms, based in the Cabinet Office, for the tasking, co-ordination and resourcing of the United Kingdom's intelligence Agencies and for overseeing and reporting on the intelligence they produce'.[27]

---

[22] House of Commons Debates, December 15, 1988, cols 1117, 1119.

[23] Commissioner under the Security Service Act, *Reports*, for 1990, 1991, 1992, HMSO.

[24] S.Palmer, 'Tightening Secrecy Law: the Official Secrets Act 1989', *Public Law*, Summer 1990, pp.243-56. In fact much discretion has been exercised in the implementation (or not) of the new law. Robin Robison resigned from the JIC staff on ethical grounds and has since spoken publicly and on TV about aspects of his former work. Though clearly in breach of s.1 of the new Act, he has not been prosecuted because, in part, he says, the Major/Butler team are more relaxed than the Thatcher/Armstrong one was. (Personal communication)

[25] 25, 5, and 70% respectively. 1993, p.12.

[26] *The Guardian*, October 2, 1993, p.6.

[27] *Central Intelligence Machinery*, *op cit*, p.7.

For example, there are various references to 'economic intelligence', which is to be expected given the speed with which all western intelligence agencies have sought to colonise this area of intelligence since the collapse of the Cold War. But there is no reference at all to the separate Overseas Economic Intelligence Committee which produces and disseminates economic assessments to parallel those of the Joint Intelligence Committee (JIC) in the political and military area. 'National security' has in the past been less associated with economic matters and, some would argue, so it should remain,[28] but ministers now emphasise economic intelligence, as did the Lord Chancellor when he introduced the *Intelligence Services Bill* in the House of Lords.[29] The efficacy and propriety of intelligence agencies remain central issues even if core intelligence mandates do shift to economic targets. There is already enough evidence that the problems that occur where 'economic wellbeing' is concerned may be no less fraught than they ever were with military security. In 1992 Lord Justice Bingham published his report into the BCCI including an unpublished appendix detailing the intelligence services' knowledge and, some say, use of BCCI for money-laundering operations.[30] GCHQ intercepts of Robert Maxwell's conversations while on his yacht are said by Robin Robison, a former JIC official, to have been passed during 1989 to the Bank of England.[31] Lord Justice Scott's hearings are showing how the government's desire to maximise arms sales and the intelligence agencies' wish to safeguard sources combined to result in Parliament being misled, resulted in wrongful convictions in the Ordtech case and almost did so in the Matrix Churchill case.

These booklets are economical also in another way. That entitled *Central Intelligence Machinery* concentrates on the JIC and its support structures in establishing intelligence requirements and making assessments. SIS and GCHQ are the 'principal' collection agencies for the JIC, but the Director General of the Security Service is also a member of the JIC and its terms of reference include keeping 'under review threats to security at home and overseas'.[32] Therefore, although distinctions are often drawn between 'foreign' or 'political' *intelligence* and 'domestic' or 'protective' *security*, the omission of the separate committee structure regarding security leaves an incomplete picture of the central machinery. In fact, there is also an Official Committee on Security, chaired by the Cabinet Secretary and serviced by subcommittees dealing with the protective security of property, documents and computerised information networks and the positive vetting system.

This incomplete picture of the central security intelligence machinery results largely from the continuing relative autonomy of the Security Service compared with the other intelligence agencies. This is reflected in a number of ways. First, the JIC provides the main intelligence targets for both the SIS and GCHQ but the Security Service remains largely aloof from this effort at co-ordination. There is no evidence that there is any government

---

[28] For example, B.Buzan, *People, States and Fear*, Harvester Wheatsheaf, Hemel Hempstead, 2nd edition, 1991, p.131.

[29] *The Guardian*, December 10, 1993, p.6.

[30] *The Guardian*, October 23, 1992, p.15. See also July 22, 1991, p.9.

[31] *Financial Times*, June 15, 1992, p.1.

[32] *Central Intelligence Machinery, op cit*, p.23.

structure independent of the Security Service through which the government assesses its needs for domestic security intelligence. Second, the JIC circulates its weekly survey of current intelligence – the Red Book – while the Security Service circulates its own security survey. Also, there is the question of the ministerial relationship. Security intelligence agencies in general have enjoyed high degrees of autonomy from ministerial direction and control,[33] although the revelations of abuse by agencies elsewhere have led to concerted efforts to reduce this, for example, the re-integration of the FBI into the US Justice Department after 1975 and the tighter regime of ministerial direction imposed upon the civilian Canadian Security Intelligence Service compared with its predecessor within the Royal Canadian Mounted Police. Therefore it is significant that while the Chief of the SIS and Director of GCHQ are respectively seen as 'responsible to the Foreign and Commonwealth Secretary'[34] for the work of their agencies, the same is not said for the Director General of the Security Service.

The *Intelligence Services Bill* provides for the continuation of the SIS and GCHQ, gives them a statutory mandate defined in terms of 'national security', 'economic wellbeing' and the prevention and detection of serious crime (clauses 1 and 3) and gives ministers powers to issue warrants legalising the agencies' 'interference' with property and wireless telegraphy (clauses 5 and 6). A minister may also indemnify a member of the SIS for actions taken outside the British Islands which would be illegal under United Kingdom law (clause 7). For the receipt and investigation of complaints from the public the Bill sets up the same elaborate but restricted Commissioner and Tribunal structure as contained in the ICA 1985 and the SSA 1989 (clauses 8 and 9).

The main innovation in the Bill, and one which provides perhaps a potential challenge to central information control, is the proposal for an Intelligence and Security Committee (ISC) that can examine the expenditure, administration and policy of the Security Service, SIS and GCHQ. It will have six members from either Lords and Commons, who will be appointed by the PM after consultation with the Leader of the Opposition. The committee will report annually to the PM, and at other times if it wishes, and a copy of the annual report will be laid before each House, subject to any exclusions of 'prejudicial' material made by the PM[35].

How effectively is this committee likely to be able to 'examine' the security intelligence agencies? In general, one might suggest that any parliamentary or extra-parliamentary review or oversight body needs three main types of 'resource' to be effective. First, it needs adequately broad terms of reference and sufficient staff support; second, unrestricted access to agency information and personnel; and, third, the political will to make use of the first two.[36] Since all three of these are necessary conditions for effectiveness, the absence of just one will be enough to render the review body ineffective.

---

[33] For general discussion see Gill, *op cit*, 1994, pp.217-26.

[34] *Central Intelligence Machinery, op cit*, pp.20-1.

[35] clause 10

[36] P. Gill, 'Symbolic or Real? The impact of the Canadian Security Intelligence Review Committee, 1984-88', *Intelligence and National Security*, 4(3), 1989, pp.550-75, is an example of applying these propositions.

Looking at the Bill, the ISC's terms of reference appear sufficiently broad, although much will depend on the extent of staff and political support for the committee. It is clearly too early to be able to make judgements about the political will of the members since they have not been appointed. However, the legislative intelligence committees established in North America since 1976 were all established in the wake of major inquiries into the agencies which gave them not only a ready-made agenda but also a great deal of information as to the agencies' *modus operandi*. None of this will be available to the ISC.

But the crucial problem for the new Committee concerns its access to information. This issue is covered in Schedule 3 of the Bill. Although carried out in the different context of congressional-executive relations in the US, the Senate Select Committee investigations of the CIA and FBI during 1975-6 represent the most thorough legislative inquiry into security intelligence agencies and, as such, contain useful lessons. As to the process of investigating, the Final Report concluded:

> 'The most important lesson to be derived from our experience is that effective oversight is impossible without regular access to the underlying working documents of the intelligence community. Top level briefings do not adequately describe the realities. For that the documents are a necessary supplement and at times the only source.'[37]

In the case of the various commissioners and tribunals a legal duty has been placed upon members of the security intelligence agencies to provide them with such documents and information as they require (for example, *Intelligence Services Bill*, clause 84) which measures up to what is required for effective oversight.

Whether or not the Intelligence and Security Committee obtains access, however, will be determined by the *minister*. If the Committee ask for information, the agency head can take one of three decisions. First, she can make the information available 'in accordance with arrangements approved by the Secretary of State' (Schedule 3, §3(1)(a)). Second, she can tell the committee that the information cannot be disclosed because the Secretary of State has said it should not be. The minister should not determine this solely on the criteria that the information concerns 'national security', but should apply the test of whether she would produce the information for a Commons select committee (Schedule 3, §3(1)(b)(ii) and §3(4)).

Third, the agency head can tell the Committee that the information cannot be disclosed because it is 'sensitive'. She may disclose the information if she believes it to be safe to do so, or the minister may if she considers release to be 'desirable in the public interest' (Schedule 3, §3(1)(b)(i), (2) and (3)). 'Sensitive' information is subsequently defined as including that which might lead to the identification of or give details of sources or 'operational methods' available to the agencies, that regarding particular

---

[37] Select Committee to Study Governmental Operations with respect to Intelligence Activities, *Final Report*, Book II, *Intelligence Activities and the Rights of Americans*, USGPO, Washington DC., 1976, p.ix, fn7.

operations, past, present or future, and information given by third parties that the donor does not consent to disclose (Schedule 3, §4). These restrictions raise some very specific doubts as to the ability of the Committee to obtain the information necessary for it to assess the effectiveness and propriety of agency policies, for example, examining past operations is a necessary means of developing a picture of agencies' operating procedures, without which it will be impossible to assess the implementation of policies.

But, for present purposes, the crucial point here is that in each of these three different avenues by which the Committee might either receive or be denied information, the final 'gatekeeper' is the minister. Therefore, while the ISC's terms of reference fulfil one condition for effective oversight, the second condition is absent because of the failure to provide the Committee with independent power to obtain access to information. By comparison, as we have seen, the commissioner and tribunal enjoy such access but their ability to conduct effective review is limited by their essentially procedural terms of reference. Thus centralised information control is maintained by this Bill and the prognosis for the new Committee is not good.

Conclusion

Some examples of 'resistance' to treaditional state secrecy in the United Kingdom during the last twenty years have succeeded to the extent that the state has shifted its ground from traditional assertions of an absolute right of secrecy in any matter that can be labelled 'national security' to a more subtle strategy mixing secrecy and persuasion. Recent government presentations of the existence, mandates and heads of security intelligence agencies have amounted to an acknowledgement that sole reliance on secrecy is likely to lead to even greater resistance from alternative sources, for example, from international rights agreements and, possibly, that a tactical retreat might enable the central state better to retain overall control of information processes in the face of more radical proposals for change.

This is the context within which the *Intelligence Services Bill* needs to be considered. The Bill modifies the traditional assertion of complete secrecy but clearly sets out to retain central control by inserting the minister as the gatekeeper of what information the new parliamentary committee may receive. However, the Bill does provide greater political space within which resistance to this continuation of central control can be organised. Security intelligence agencies have guarded most carefully their autonomy from outside review and there is no recorded example in which such an agency has simply volunteered access to its files. Therefore, if no battles take place over access then one might suggest that this would be an early indicator of a lack of will on the part of the Committee to take on the traditionally most secret elements of the central state and to leave untested the process of information control.

If the members of the new committee have the will to conduct genuine examinations of the security intelligence agencies then one would predict a series of struggles between them, the agency heads and the ministers as to what information is made available. In the short term the Committee may well lose those battles but they will still be worth conducting as a form of democratic espionage in order to expose the shortcomings of the Bill's structures and rules.

The Intelligence Services

Philip H.J.Davies
University of Reading

'Institutionalizing Intelligence:
The Development of MI6 Internal Organization
and the Whitehall Village Market for Espionage'

Acknowledgements

I should like to express my thanks and appreciation to my supervisor, Dr.Ken Robertson and the Sociology Department at the University of Reading for all the assistance which they have provided for this project, in terms of supervision as well as the allocation of a Teaching Studentship and other financial support for this research. Thanks are also due to the Committee of Vice-Chancellors and Principles for their allocation of an Overseas Research Scholarship in support of this project.

A Note on Sources

The preceding discussion represents partial results from research which is still on-going. A significant part of this research includes a campaign of interviews with former United Kingdom officials, also still in medias reis. References to 'private information' or 'anonymous intelligence sources' are irritating and make assessment of sources difficult, hence this piece has been written to employ entirely published sources, except where published sources are ambiguous or contradictory.

Introduction

The relationship between the Secret Intelligence Service (also known as MI6) and its governmental masters, both the Cabinet and Whitehall, has been directly and indirectly the main factor in the evolution of the SIS' internal organization. A recent Cabinet Office publication, *Central Intelligence Machinery*, has stressed the importance of requirements in determining the operations of what it calls, in almost American style, intelligence 'Agencies'.[1] SIS and GCHQ, both responsible to Cabinet through the Foreign and Commonwealth Office, conduct operations overseas according to requirements for information set by their consumers primarily through the Joint Intelligence Committee (JIC). The JIC also interprets and analyzes the raw information produced by these Agencies. SIS' operational methods include human intelligence from agents ('HUMINT') and technical methods, for example listening devices and wiretaps. Neither Agency has a brief to analyze the information they produce (apart from evaluating reliability, or

---

[1] Cabinet Office, (HMSO, London, 1993).

placing raw reports 'in context' vis a vis previous reports). In this sense, the SIS differs in role quite profoundly from, for example, the American Central Intelligence Agency, which was originally created to conduct analysis and which acquired espionage in the traditional sense initially only on an *ad-hoc* basis.[2] Because of this, the SIS also differs from the CIA in one other very important respect: the SIS does not set its own operational targets, but has them set for it by its consumers. However, the operational *method* is up to the Agency.

The same document also stresses that 'the strength of the British system' is precisely the centralization of the British intelligence system on the JIC. However, the JIC has only held its current, central position since 1957 when 'as a reflection of the broadened scope and role of intelligence' it was subordinated directly to the Cabinet Office.[3] Prior to this the JIC was the Joint Intelligence Sub-Committee of the Chiefs of Staff[4]; its interests, therefore, were more limited and defence-oriented. In the absence of any central tasking and circulating mechanism from the greater part of its existence, the SIS developed an internal infrastructure for tasking by and circulating reports to its consumers. It retained this infrastructure during the Cold War, potentially by-passing the central tasking and requirements apparatus which developed during the 1950s. Similarly, its operational organization has also developed very much on the basis of demands made on the Agency by its consumers.

The following discussion will trace the development of SIS' internal structure and attempt to examine the relationship between that structure and demands placed upon the Agency by its political and governmental masters. Current literature makes it possible to trace SIS' internal development up to the late 1950s, although the structure which developed during this period characterized the Agency, with superficial changes, at least until the 1970s. Most of the discussion will concern the gross structure of the organizations; SIS, like most organizations, experienced a constant ebb and flow of minor, short-lived *ad-hoc* bodies within it. Its requirements and operational infrastructures have always constituted the core of the Agency, and the following discussion will concentrate upon the internal operational and tasking infrastructure.

1919-1939: *Ad-Hoc* Development

At the end of the First World War the SIS occupied an ambiguous and generally difficult situation within Whitehall. It was officially designated MI 1(c) which placed it within the Military Intelligence Secretariat (MI 1) in the War Office. In practice, however, it was funded from the Foreign Office secret vote, a situation intelligence historian Christopher Andrew describes

---

[2] See, for example, Breckenridge, *The CIA and the American Intelligence Community* (Westview Press, London, 1986) pp.28-33, 144-52; Jeffrey T. Richelson, *The US Intelligence Community* (Cambridge, Massachussetts, 1988) pp.11-21; Walter Laqueur, *A World of Secrets* (Basic Books, New York, 1985) pp.32-37.

[3] *Central Intelligence Machinery*, p.11.

[4] Sir F.H. Hinsley et al, *British Intelligence in the Second World War* (HMSO, Volume I, 1979; Volume II, 1981; Volume III, 1984; Volume IV, 1990) Volume I, pp.4, 36-43.

with understatement as 'anomalous'.[5] In addition, there existed an odd assortment of other espionage networks being run by the War Office (from London), GHQ (from Folkestone), the Admiralty (in the Iberian peninsula) and the Foreign Office. The official history maintains that this was, to some degree, a result of Whitehall dissatisfaction with SIS product. Andrew has, however, countered this claim with the assertion that SIS' assets were directed towards 'strategic' intelligence while the War Office networks were geared towards 'tactical' intelligence, and the Admiralty activities in Iberia were justified by a traditional Naval Intelligence strength in that area. The distinctions between 'strategic' and 'tactical' intelligence are not always entirely clear, and Andrew does acknowledge that the MI 1(c) and War Office tactical networks did 'collide' in Holland and Switzerland.[6] On the strength of these difficulties the Cabinet saw fit to create the first of a succession of Secret Service Committees in 1919, charged in this case with a comprehensive review of British post-war intelligence both foreign and domestic, with a particular eye towards counter-subversion.

The outcome of the 1919 Secret Service Committee, chaired by the Foreign Secretary, was that while the SIS was to be solely responsible for all espionage in the traditional sense (not, that is, communications intelligence such as cryptanalysis) the Service departments' interests and requirements were to be protected by two measures. In the first place they would take turns providing the head of the Agency. In the second place, each Service intelligence directorate would post one of its sections to SIS headquarters to convey their respective departments' requirements, and to relay back SIS intelligence product.[7] These 'liaison sections', originally posted by the War Office and Admiralty [8], were the nascent version of the Requirements Sections which would make up the Cold War Requirements Directorate.

Out of the 1919 Secret Service Committee came two changes in SIS' relationship with the Foreign Office. In the first place, after considerable haggling, SIS' Heads of Station abroad acquired diplomatic cover as Passport Control Officers. The post of PCO was originally directed towards preventing subversive elements such as anarchists and communists from entering the United Kingdom. It was, therefore, jointly administered by SIS, MI5, the Home Office Aliens Branch and another product of the 1919 Secret Service Committee, Basil Thompson's Directorate of Intelligence. Although operationally controlled by the SIS, the PCOs were viewed initially as liaison officers dealing with the security authorities in the host country, even originally forbidden contact with SIS agents. However, when the 1921 Secret Service Committee abolished Thompson's Directorate SIS gained complete control of the PCO system for its own purposes. The resulting system of SIS stations acted mainly as 'post-boxes' collecting reports from sources through cut-outs or 'dead' and 'live' letter drops, while the recruitment and running of agents remained in the hands of 'private individuals paid out

---

[5] Andrew, *Secret Service* (Heineman, London, 1987) p.211.

[6] Hinsley et al, *British Intelligence*, Volume I, p.16; Andrew, *Secret Service*, p.211.

[7] Hinsley et al, *British Intelligence*, Volume I, p.17.

[8] The official history claims that all three Service departments posted liaison sections in 1919, however, as will be apparent below, the Air Ministry did not post a liaison section at SIS HQ until 1929.

of Secret Service Funds' and full-time officers operating from commercial cover.[9] In general the stations were forbidden to operate against their host country.[10]

The post of PCO for cover proved a mixed blessing. On the one hand, the SIS officer had to actually perform the additional duties of passport control, in addition to intelligence work, either of which was potentially a full-time occupation. The Berlin station was virtually incapacitated from 1933, not because of the German countermeasures but because of the pressure on the office from Jews applying 'to proceed to Palestine, to England, to anywhere in the British Empire'.[11] After the Anschluss the Vienna station suffered similar difficulties. Moreover, SIS officers were required to perform this double-duty on a very limited salary. As a result the Passport Control Organization suffered a succession of financial scandals.[12] On the other hand, however, the PCO system was wholly self-financing on the strength of visa fees, and most of those from the United States of America, an important consideration in view of the wholesale reductions in SIS' budget by the financial beleaguered governments of the 1920s and 1930s.[13]

The second change was SIS' receipt of a mandate to collect political intelligence, albeit subject to rigid provisions. The Foreign Office viewed the collection of information abroad as its own preserve, and if SIS was to collect political intelligence it would do so only on behalf of the Foreign Office, and under the explicit direction of the Foreign Office. Furthermore, 'the espionage system was to be kept operationally separate from the Foreign Office's own information system'.[14] Towards this end the Foreign Office attached a liaison section of its own to the SIS in 1921.[15]

The resulting core structure of the SIS during this period was three liaison sections, the Political Section, Military Section and Naval Section, the Passport Control Organization, (subordinate to the Foreign Office on paper but directed in practice by a senior SIS officer) and a small staff of 'G Officers' who coordinated operations and serviced the stations abroad.[16] Around 1924 the SIS also began opening foreign diplomatic bags and photographing their contents at the behest of the Foreign Office. This work was performed by a specialist unit entitled Section N.[17]

---

[9] Hinsley et al, *British Intelligence*, Volume I, p.17; regarding the use of commercial cover see, for example, *John Whitwell (Leslie Nicholson) British Agent* (William Kimber, London, 1966).

[10] Andrew, *Secret Service*, pp.408, 495.

[11] Berlin PCO Capt. Frank Foley, quoted in Andrew, *Secret Service*, p.535.

[12] Andrew, *Secret Service*, p.495.

[13] Andrew, *Secret Service*, p.348; Eunan O'Halpen, 'Financing British Intelligence: The Evidence up to 1945', in K.G.Robertson (ed), *British and American Approaches to Intelligence* (Macmillan, London, 1987) pp.205-6.

[14] Hinsley et al, *British Intelligence*, Volume I, p.17.

[15] Andrew, *Secret Service*, p.408.

[16] Andrew, *Secret Service*, p.408;.

[17] Brown, *'C': The Secret Life of Sir Stewart Graham Menzies Spymaster to Winston Churchill* (Macmillan, New York, 1987), pp.141, 144, 210; Section N's head, David Boyle and his operations against diplomatic bags appear very briefly at the end of West's *MI6*, p.402. H.A.R. 'Kim' Philby also recounts the amusing case of a Polish seal which changed colour under Section N's ministrations and had to be reported 'lost' to the Polish foreign office, Philby, *My Silent War* (Ballantine, New York, 1983) p.63. Dating Section N is not possible from available materials, but the earliest reference to its long term head, David

In 1923 the original 'C', Admiral Sir Mansfield Smith-Cumming (termed C because of his final initial, a title SIS Chiefs have retained since) died and was replaced by the then-Director of Naval Intelligence (DNI), Admiral Sir Hugh 'Quex' Sinclair. Sinclair was to prove an innovative Chief whose vision of the Agency ranged further afield than Cumming's, and in many respects laid the foundations for the Cold War Agency. During the 1919 Secret Service Committee deliberations the War Office's Director of Military Intelligence (DMI) suggested that MI 1(c) absorb the War Office's counter-intelligence organization MI5. Cumming rejected this opportunity on the grounds that, in the words of the official history, 'there was no real connection between counter-espionage and the work of SIS', and, moreover, the main requirements in the interwar period would, he anticipated, be for political and economic intelligence. The net costs of amalgamation in terms of weakened security and increased overall expenditure would outweigh any possible benefits.[18] This was not a view shared by Sinclair who had a reputation as a 'terrific anti-Bolshevik'[19], sharing the 1919 Secret Service Committee's concerns about subversion operations conducted by Soviet agents in conjunction with domestic Communists. As a result, the new C began lobbying for SIS to absorb MI5. This prompted another Secret Service Committee in 1925 which concluded that the costs and benefits of amalgamation were probably indifferent and elected to steer the conservative path not fixing that which is not detectably broken.[20] Not about to be thwarted, Sinclair created his own Counter-Espionage (CE) Section staffed originally by a single officer, former Indian Policeman Valentine Vivian.[21] Evidence indicates that their concerns were not unfounded as Andrew reports that there was, indeed, a constant 'stream' of 'Russian and other Comintern couriers bringing funds, propaganda and exhortation to Bolshevik sympathizers in Britain'.[22] Later, their suspicions would be further reinforced by the ARCOS and Woolwich Arsenal affairs.

A fourth liaison section was created in late 1929 with the establishment of the Royal Air Force as a Service department in its own right. The Air Ministry Intelligence Branch elected to post its own liaison unit with the SIS. This unit was set up by Group Captain Fred Winterbotham (author of *The Ultra Secret*[23]). Winterbotham quickly discovered that his Section was going to have to do rather more than simply relay requirements and circulate reports. The technological expertise required by Air Intelligence was hard to come by (one of his junior officers in the Air Section, R.V. Jones, would later describe the 'average' SIS agent as 'a scientific analphabet'[24]). As a result it fell to the Air Section to train SIS officers in the field to

---

Boyle, running the Section is 1924, Brown, p.210.

[18] Hinsley et al, *British Intelligence*, Volume I, p.18.

[19] Andrew, *Secret Service*, p.478.

[20] Hinsley et al, *British Intelligence*, Volume I, p.19; Volume IV, p.7.

[21] Andrew, *Secret Service*, p.490; Hinsley et al, Volume IV, p.10.

[22] *Secret Service*, p.341.

[23] (Dell, New York, 1974).

[24] Jones, *Most Secret War* (Hodder & Stoughton, London, 1979) pp.63-64. Note also Whitwell's naive account of pickles, a confidence scheme foisted upon SIS purporting to be a nuclear bomb in *British Agent*, pp.37-50; also Andrew's account of this, *Secret Service*, p.493.

recognize the information sought by the Air Ministry.[25] For Winterbotham it went even further than simple training; he also concluded that he would have to recruit appropriate agents himself.[26] The Air Section was to prove a source of considerable innovation within the Service, even undertaking the first systematic campaign of aerial photo-reconnaissance of Germany and the mediterranean during the late 1930s (although the Air Ministry was quick to appropriate this development as its own in 1940).[27]

In 1935, possibly on the strength of intelligence about *German Abwehr*[28] observation of the Hague station[29] Sinclair set up a parallel, independent operational organization run by a notionally disgraced long-standing SIS officer, Colonel (later Sir) Claude Dansey. This so-called Z Organization was to recruit its own agents, mainly on the basis of Dansey's personal network of British business contacts on the Continent, and run them completely independently of the PCO system (albeit operating on SIS funds). This was intended to serve as a fall-back in case the main SIS system was compromised.[30]

Despite the interwar additions of Section N, the CE Section and the Air Section, SIS' operational budget continued to dwindle. By the turn of the 1930s its operations against Italy had been almost completely discontinued for lack of funds. During the 1935 costing-round Sinclair made the now-famous complaint that his Agency's budget was now less than the cost of maintaining a Royal Navy destroyer in home waters.[31] The only variation in this downward trend of resources, linked with an upward trend in demand from Whitehall and the Cabinet, was a brief increase in the SIS budget in the wake of the 1937 Anschluss. However 'financial stringency' returned the following year after the Munich Crisis.[32] Sinclair took the opportunity of increased funds to expand the CE Section headquarters staff, and to set up CE stations in Holland and Belgium to cooperate with Dutch, Belgian and French security intelligence authorities against the Germans.[33] He also made another innovation in SIS organization which would have far reaching consequences. In 1938 Section D was set up to investigate methods of sabotage and similar 'irregular' warfare in peacetime and to implement them in wartime.[34]

Thus at the outbreak of war, the SIS consisted mainly in: four liaison, by

---

[25] Winterbotham, *The Ultra Spy (Macmillan, London, 1989) p.115.*

[26] His field work led him into close contact with many senior members of the NAZI and German military hierarchies, even leading to a brief meeting with Adolph Hitler. This work is recounted in his *The Nazi Connection* (Weidenfeld & Nicolson, London, 1978).

[27] Winterbotham, *The Ultra Spy*, pp.185-194; Andrew, *Secret Service*, pp.653-658; Hinsley et al, *British Intelligence*, Volume I, pp.26-30.

[28] German military intelligence.

[29] Anthony Read & David Fisher, *Colonel Z* (Hodder & Stoughton, London, 1984) p.171.

[30] Read & Fisher, *Colonel Z*, pp.171-173; Andrew, *Secret Service*, pp.537-8.

[31] Hinsley et al, *British Intelligence*, Volume I, p.51. Early warning of the Italian invasion of Albania had to come from an MI5 source inside the German Embassy in London, *op.cit*, p.84; Christopher Andrew, *Secret Service*, p.590.

[32] Hinsley et al, *British Intelligence*, Volume I p.51.

[33] Hinsley et al, *British Intelligence*, Volume IV p.11.

[34] Andrew, *Secret Service*, pp.658-659; M.R.D. Foot, *SOE: 1940-1946* (BBC, London, 1985) pp.11,15.

then called 'Circulating' Sections – Political, Military, Naval and Air; a small staff of G Officers overseeing and coordinating operations on a regional basis; the Passport Control Office (on paper answerable directly to the Foreign Office but quartered at the SIS and staffed by it); and three specialist operational sections, Section N, Section D and the CE Section. Of these sections, the Circulating Sections and Section N were the direct result of the demands of Whitehall consumers. The small staff of G Officers had originally been set up by Cumming to assist him in managing the field stations. Only the CE Section and Section D had been developed on the basis of SIS internal initiative.

1939-1945: Expansion and Refinement

For SIS the war actually began a year early. In 1938 the Vienna PCO was arrested by Austrian NAZI authorities, prompting the withdrawal of the Berlin and Prague chiefs of station.[35] For motives that remain so unfathomable as to seem irrational, in late 1939 and before the actual outbreak of war, the PCO and Z Organizations were merged completely negating any benefits the Z Organization might have afforded the Agency, especially because the Hague station had indeed been penetrated by the German secret services since 1935.[36] As a result of its penetration, the Hague station was the target of a particularly elegant deception operation in which NAZI party *Sicherheitdienst* (SD) officers masqueraded as representatives of an anti-NAZI faction within Germany. This deception resulted in the kidnapping of both the PCO and the Z officer at Venlo on the Dutch-German border. It has occasionally been suggested that the Venlo incident was a result of the SIS slipping the reigns of ministerial control, but according to the official history, documents available to Hinsley an his team clearly indicated explicit Foreign Office, Prime Ministerial and eventually War Cabinet authorization of these clandestine negotiations.[37] In the spring of 1939 the fall of Prague wiped out the SIS system there, and despite a scramble to create 'stay-behind' networks, when Paris fell the Agency was virtually without assets on the continent.[38]

Even as war was declared in September, 1939, Sir Henry Tizzard's Committee for the Scientific Survey of Air Defense posted a scientific officer to Winterbotham's Air Section to investigate the state of German defence sciences. In early 1940 the famous Oslo report found its way onto this officer's desk. The officer in question was R.V.Jones. Like Winterbotham, Jones found SIS' field officers disastrously scientifically ill-informed, often wasting efforts pursuing fantastic accounts of weapons such as 'death rays', ranging from error to outright fraud.[39] Until 1941 Jones worked virtually alone,

---

[35] Andrew, *Secret Service*, p.557-8.

[36] Hinsley et al, *British Intelligence*, Volume I, p.56-57.

[37] Hinsley et al, *British Intelligence*, Volume I, p.57; Andrew, *Secret Service*, pp.609-16; the SD paper on the SIS resulting from the interrogation, 'Der Britischer Nachrichtendienst', has been published as the Appendix to Nigel West's *MI6: Secret Intelligence Service Operations 1909-1945* (Collins, London, 1988).

[38] Hinsley et al, *British Intelligence*, Volume I. pp.51,57.

[39] Jones, *Most Secret War*, 63-64.

receiving only a single assistant in 1940.[40] Jones was not the only officer handling scientific intelligence; the Naval Section officer also collated intelligence relating to chemical warfare. The main difference was that the head of Naval Section was passing raw information back to scientists at Porton; Jones' sub- section was to be staffed by career scientists.[41]

On the fourth of November 1939, in the middle of the pre-Venlo negotiations at the Hague station, Sinclair died, and after a round of dire Whitehall negotiations, his unofficial deputy and head of the Military Section, Stewart Menzies, was confirmed as the new C on the twenty ninth. Menzies appointed Dansey, the former head of the Z Organization, as his Assistant Chief (ACSS). However, reportedly in an attempt to balance Dansey's domineering personality within the Agency he then appointed Valentine Vivian as Deputy Chief (DCSS) during a reorganization in January, 1940. Dansey's biographers assert that Dansey had been placed in charge of the G Sections and Circulating Sections [42], although former Personal Assistant to C, Robert Cecil, has argued that the two posts did not have clearly defined jurisdictions within the Agency.[43] Certainly Vivian's powers and responsibilities were undefined, as is evidenced in a minute from Vivian to Menzies published by Cecil.[44] As a result, the two men spent almost as much of the war campaigning against each other as they did against the Axis.

The January 1940 reorganization also attempted to impose some order on the haphazard assortment of *ad-hoc* Sections making up the SIS. On the one hand the liaison 'Circulating Sections' were grouped according to Roman numerals, and the G Officers Arabic ones in a weak attempt at divisional structure. The Circulating Sections were now: Section I, political; Section II military (War Office); Section III, naval; Section IV, air; the CE Section was rendered Section V. At the outbreak of war the Ministry of Economic Warfare (MEW) was set up, and this included its own Intelligence Branch. As a result, a new Commercial Circulating Section was created to handled economic intelligence.[45] It has not been possible to establish the exact number and jurisdictions of the G Officers at SIS. Vivian's memo to C refers to a G6. Around 1942 the individual G Officers were replaced by staffs of officers in Production or 'P' Sections. By 1944 there were at least eight P Sections, of which P8 dealt with the Low Countries.[46]

---

[40] Jones, *Most Secret War*, p.144.

[41] R.V.Jones, *Reflections on Intelligence* (Jonathan Cape, London, 1989) p.255.

[42] Read & Fisher, *Colonel Z*, p.230.

[43] Robert Cecil, 'C's War', *Intelligence and National Security*, Volume 1, Number 2, pp.177-178.

[44] Cecil, 'C's War', appendix.

[45] Regarding Section VI, Johns, *Within Two Cloaks*, (William Kimber, London, 1979) p.40; Nigel West, *MI6*, p.147. West asserts that Section VI dealt with both Desmond Morton's Industrial Intelligence Centre and the MEW, but Morton's IIC was, in fact, absorbed by the MEW as the 'nucleus' of its Intelligence Branch, Wesley Wark, *The Ultimate Enemy* (Oxford University Press, Oxford, 1986) p.162; Hinsley et al, *British Intelligence*, Volume I, p.100. The overall Section I – VI structure is the widely published version of the wartime SIS organization. See, for example, Philip Johns, *loc.cit*; Andrew, *Secret Service*, pp.488-491; with reservations (see discussion below) West, *MI6*, pp.20-23, 45-148, although West's formulation includes a number of errors concerning the Circulating Sections above VI.

[46] See Robert Cecil, appendix to 'C's War'; George Blake, *No Other Choice* (Jonathan

Late 1939 resulted in other significant changes. With the loss of its field stations and the closure of belligerents' borders the SIS was forced to opt for clandestine radio for communications with its agents abroad. Therefore a small group of officers experimenting with radio were organized under the leadership of Philco sales manager Richard Gambier-Parry into a Radio Section. Later in the war, Radio Section would provide transmitters and technicians for the Political Warfare Executive as well as SIS.[47] Second, the SIS organized and staffed a quasi-autonomous intelligence organization in the Middle East staffed by SIS and serviced by its G Officers/P Sections but under the day-to-day direction of the Middle East Command (GHQ ME). Operating under the cover name of the Interservice Liaison Department (ISLD), this unit also directed SIS' very limited operations in the far east.[48] A similar unit was set up in the United States as an expansion of the SIS New York office. This evolved into the famous British Security Coordination (BSC). BSC's independence has generally been overestimated by its chroniclers; it was, in fact closely coordinated with the main SIS system, frequently providing support for the SIS stations in the Caribbean and South America which generally answered directly to London.[49]

Also during 1940 the SIS suffered a major political defeat within Whitehall. The War Cabinet elected to create a single, central organization for unconventional warfare out of three disparate units: Section D, a similar organization in the War Office MI(R), and a Foreign Office unit planning for psychological and political operations at Electra House on the Embankment. Menzies had been consulted and agreed in principle with the idea of a consolidated special operations organization which would be formally independent of his SIS, but the actual War Cabinet meetings implementing the policy and the new body's separation from SIS were conducted in Menzies' absence. Menzies himself was not informed until September of this action taken in August. This remained a sore point between SIS and the new organization, the Special Operations Executive (SOE) throughout the war.[50]

With the loss of its continental stations SIS' P Sections adopted a new mode of operation, infiltrating agents into enemy territory from the United Kingdom, that is operating *domesticly* against *foreign* targets.[51] This was to prove a significant development; the SIS had been officially forbidden to

Cape, London, 1990) p.86.

[47] Ellic Howe, *The Black Game* (Michael Joseph, London, 1982) pp.86-92; Nigel West, *MI6*, pp.292-293.

[48] Hinsley et al, *British Intelligence*, Volume IV, p.152; Nigel West, *MI6*, p.210; Charles Cruickshank, *SOE in the Far East* (Oxford University Press, Oxford, 1986) pp.21,88.

[49] Hinsley et al, *British Intelligence Volume IV*, p.145; Johns, *Within Two Cloaks*, p.119.

[50] M.R.D. Foot, *SOE: 1940-1946*, pp.18-21. M.R.D. Foot presents the process in such a way as to suggest the absence of any machiavellian considerations underlying the exclusion of Menzies from the War Cabinet negotiations creating SOE. He does, however, point out political motives which made it a good idea for the SOE to be subordinated to a Labour member of the War Cabinet since the SIS and MI5 were both subordinate to established and powerful Tory members of Cabinet, pp.19-20.

[51] The domestic activities of the G/PSections appears in a number of sources in passing; detailed first hand discussions of their work appear in Johns, *Within Two Cloaks*, pp.41-44, and Blake, *No Other Choice*, pp.86-97.

operate domestically by a 1931 convening of the Secret Service Committee,[52] and operating at least from if not within home territories proved a power SIS was unwilling to abandon after the war. SIS was technically only permitted to operate outside British and colonial territories, and outside the three mile coastal limit.[53] The new pattern of operations had its own difficulties, however. Poor performance, mainly because of the paucity of continental assets, weakened the SIS' credibility with the Service Departments (a 1940 enquiry by Lord Hankey found the Foreign Office and MEW on the whole happier with SIS performance than the Services) which in turn weakened its bargaining position when requesting transport for infiltrating agents onto the continent by sea or air. As a result, the SIS created a temporary, *ad-hoc* transport section which acquired a flotilla of Norwegian fishing boats which evolved into the now famous 'Shetland Bus'.[54]

While SIS status in Whitehall reached its lowest ebb in 1941-1942, at least as far as operational intelligence gathering was concerned, its counter-espionage section shared in the successes of Double Cross and Ultra. At that time, C was officially also the Director of the Government Code and Cypher School (GC&CS), renamed GCHQ early in the war. SIS had also absorbed the Radio Security Service in spring of 1941, and therefore held overall control of cryptanalysis and domestic signal intercepts. As a result of GC&CS' ability from 1940 to break both the *Abwehr*'s hand cypher and its Enigma traffic (given the acronym ISOS[55]) Section V found a new role as collator and distributor of espionage communications intelligence. There was also considerable pressure from MI5 to expand Section V in view of MI5's need for ISOS and overseas counterespionage HUMINT in the prosecution of the Double Cross programme.[56] Abroad, Section V was heavily involved in developing and running its own double-agent operations against the German intelligence service, most of which were possible because of ISOS.[57]

By the autumn of 1942 Section V had expanded to twelve officers at Headquarters and another twelve abroad, but even this modest expansion drew criticism (presumably from the Service departments) that the Service was pursuing counter-espionage 'at the expense of ... operational intelligence for the Services'. Nonetheless the Section expanded rapidly and by 1944 numbered 60 HQ staff and the same number overseas. The Section was subdivided into ten sections until the end of 1943. Until then it consisted in six geographical sub-sections and sub-sections for: the use of double cross agents for deception; enemy espionage communications; Soviet espionage

---

[52] Hinsley et al, *British Intelligence*, Volume IV p.7.

[53] Hinsley et al, *British Intelligence*, Volume IV, p.9.

[54] Hinsley et al, *British Intelligence*, Volume I pp.91-92, 276.

[55] Standing for Intelligence Service Oliver Strachey, after the officer in charge of breaking the hand-cypher; work against *Abwehr Enigma* was directed by Dilwyn Knox and distributed under the acronym ISK, Intelligence Service Knox. Both operations were generally referred to as ISOS for short.

[56] Hinsley et al, *British Intelligence*, Volume IV p. 132.

[57] Hinsley et al, *British Intelligence*, Volume IV, *passim*; the official history addresses the SIS end at a vague and institutional level; for a first hand account of double cross abroad, see Desmond14 43, Sunday 9/1/941 Bristow A Game of Moles (Little, Brown and Co., London, 1993).

and Communism; a security section for 'protection of SIS itself against penetration'. At the end of 1943 a sub-section was set up in conjunction with British Security Coordination concerned with German trans-Atlantic smuggling of war materials.[58] A short-lived sub-section was Section V(W). Prior to its subsumption under SIS, the Radio Security Service maintained an analysis and interpretation group called the RSS Analysis Bureau. When RSS was taken over by SIS in May 1941 the Analysis Bureau became Section V(W). This was not a successful change in organization because Section V's passion for need-to-know conflicted with Section V(W)'s need to correspond with GC&CS, MI5 and the Service departments in order to interpret the arcane language of the decrypts. The official history remarks tactfully that this 'running battle' was 'sustained by personal animosities', resolved only when the sub-section was carved out of Section V and promoted to full Section status as the Radio Intelligence Section in the summer of 1943.[59] The increasing importance of counter-espionage is also illustrated by the fact that progressively Section V's officers took over the PCO positions while the mainstream SIS residents were integrated into the general system of consular posts and titles.[60]

SIS had spent the interwar period operating against the Soviet Union and its personnel had few illusions about the impending state of affairs after the war. In March of 1944 the Soviet counter-espionage and international Communism sub-section was excised from Section V and promoted to full Section status as Section IX. Although it was established in 1944, Section IX did not actually become operational until 1945.[61]

One of the puzzles of the history of SIS organization is why the new anti-Soviet Section was Section IX if there were, presumably, only six Circulating Sections at SIS HQ. In the post-war Requirements Directorate R7 was the scientific intelligence section, and R8 the GCHQ liaison.[62] As a result of the 'battle of the beams', the search for Hitler's secret weapons, and the developing 'Tube Alloys' scramble for atomic intelligence, Jones' sub-Section had grown steadily, he himself being promoted to Assistant Director of Air Intelligence (a position potentially outranking the head of Section IV within the Air Ministry) in April 1941.[63] Jones has remarked that by spring 1941 'Scientific Intelligence was now established as a branch having its place alongside and interlocked with the more traditional divisions of Naval, Military and Air Intelligence'.[64] The Scientific Section staff exceeded even the Air Section's wide brief by engaging in analysis of the raw

---

[58] Hinsley et al, *British Intelligence Volume IV p.180.*

[59] Hinsley et al, *British Intelligence. Volume IV p. 183.*

[60] Robert Cecil, 'The Cambridge Comintern' in Christopher Andrew & David Dilks (eds), *The Missing Dimension: Governments and Intelligence Communities in the Twentieth Century* (Macmillan, London, 1985) p.179; this pattern existed in the Lisbon station by early 1942 when Johns was posted there as Head of Station, Within Two Cloaks pp.67-68.

[61] Hinsley et al, Volume IV p.180 Philby, *My Silent War*, pp.101, 109-117; Robert Cecil 'The Cambridge Comintern', pp.178-180; Richard Aldrich 'Secret Intelligence for a Post-War World', in Aldrich (ed), *British Intelligence, Strategy and the Cold War* (Routledge, London, 1992) p.44 endnote 44.

[62] Anthony Cavendish, *Inside Intelligence* (Collins, London, 1990) p.40.

[63] Jones, *Most Secret War*, pp.243-44; Hinsley et al, *British Intelligence*, Volume I p.284.

[64] Jones, *Most Secret War*, p.240.

intelligence as it came in from Ultra, and from slowly, painfully developing HUMINT networks on the Continent. Thus it is probable that at some point between Jones' promotion in mid-1941 and March 1944 the scientific staff were established as their own Section VII. The Radio Intelligence Section may have been the origins of Section VIII/R8, but none of the sources available establish this with certainty.[65]

The Service departments did not, however, benefit directly from these counter-espionage and scientific intelligence successes and during 1942 the Service directors of intelligence once again began to agitate for SIS reform. SIS' inability to produce was still taken to be a failure on the part of the Agency to understand Service requirements and SIS was forced to accept three new Deputy Directors who would 'ensure' that Service requirements 'were better understood'.[66] Menzies exploited the situation by attempting to solve the Agency's serious problems of managerial overload at the top. As C, Menzies continued the pre-war tradition of making himself available to every member of the service, however humble, a practice inapplicable to the expanded wartime organization. While his VCSS and DCSS feuded they did not manage, and Menzies therefore had to do their job as well as his own, already overloaded of his double duty as Director of GC&CS as well as his Whitehall responsibilities. Menzies exploited the posting of these new, senior officers by giving them each the rank of Deputy Director, and along with a senior SIS officer given the same rank, formed a board to oversee SIS operations around the globe with each Deputy Director overseeing a different theatre.[67]

Just as Menzies failed to formally elaborate powers and responsibilities for his feuding deputies, so he seems to have failed to properly integrate the Deputy Directors and their board into the actual SIS chain of command. Most discussions of the Deputy Directors (or 'Service Commissars' as they were nicknamed by SIS staff) regard them as ill equipped in terms of training, experience or aptitude to achieve much at SIS.[68] In late 1943 it was finally admitted that the operational board was not achieving its desired ends and the Deputy Directors were replaced with four SIS officers with the post of Controller overseeing their theatres.[69]

Unlike the Services, the Foreign Office, as the SIS' parent department, had been conscious of Menzies' administrative problems. They addressed the problem differently, and also in 1942 posted to C a Personal Assistant whose main task was to facilitate the administration of the Agency.[70] This

---

[65] Nigel West in his MI6 has asserted that Sykes' Financial Section was labelled Section VII which is relatively improbable. The function of Circulating Sections was intelligence liaison (arguably Section V liaised with MI5), which the Financial Section did not do. However, West's other assertion that a small section responsible for creating cryptosystems for SIS' own operations formed the basis of Section VIII is more plausible. See Nigel West, *op.cit. p.386.*

[66] Hinsley et al, *British Intelligence. Volume II p.18.*

[67] Hinsley et al, *British Intelligence*, Volume II p.18, Volume III pt.1 p.462.

[68] See, for example, Robert Cecil 'C's War, p.180, and Philby, *My Silent War*, pp.118-119.

[69] Hinsley et al, *British Intelligence*, Volume II p.18; Volume III/pt.1 p.462.

[70] Robert Cecil, *'C's War' p.180*, *'The Cambridge Comintern' p.179*; Andrew, *Secret Service*, p.658; Nigel West MI6 pp.233-4, West adds that the PA/CSS' main task was

post was left unoccupied in 1945 when its incumbent was assigned to duties elsewhere.

After 1942 criticism of the SIS abated, mainly because the infiltration work by the United Kingdom P Sections and ISLD had developed systems of agent networks producing larger volumes of increasingly reliable operational intelligence for the Service departments.[71]

1945 and after: The Cold War

Towards the end of the war the conflict between Vivian and Dansey was resolved by reassigning Vivian the specialist post of Chief Advisor on Security, in charge of an Inspectorate of Security while Dansey achieved his goal as undisputed second in command as Vice Chief of Service.[72] In the last months of the war, Menzies, probably under pressure from a sizeable faction of his career SIS staff convened a committee of SIS reorganization to put the Agency on a professional footing for the post-war period.[73] The outcome of the committee was that the assortment of ad hoc administrative posts were consolidated into a Directorate of Finance and Administration. The P Sections were gathered together under a Director of Production, grouped at a theatre level under four Chief Controllers. The BSC was dismantled, but ISLD was replaced with a new cover organization in the middle east, the 'Combined Research and Planning Organization' (CRPO). ISLD's far east work was turned over to a new regional controlling station in Singapore.[74] The Circulating Sections, renamed Requirements Section were assigned to a Directorate of Requirements, while new training and technical development sections were grouped into their own directorate. A short-lived War Planning Directorate was created to set up stay-behind networks in light of Soviet expansion into Eastern Europe in the immediate post-war years.[75]

The Requirements Sections retained the same cardinal order as before. R1 was Political, R2 Military, R3 Naval, R4 Air, R5 Counter-Espionage, R6 Economic, R7 Scientific, and R8 remained the link with GCHQ. Philby was, of course, being highly disingenuous when he implied that SIS had abandoned counter-espionage as a field when he remarked about the committee of reorganization that 'One of the minor decisions of the committee was the abolition of Section V.'[76] In fact Section V and Section IX were consolidated into a single, sizeable R5, consisting in two sub-divisions, one concerned with Soviet front organizations and propaganda, the other with

that of 'peacemaker between the Foreign Office and the SIS'.

[71] Hinsley et al, *British Intelligence*, Volume I p.275, Volume II p.18;.

[72] Philby, *My Secret War*, p.119; Anthony Cave Brown C, extract from interview with Air Commodore Jack Easton, p.693.

[73] Philby, *My Silent War*, pp.121-4; Anthony Verrier, *Through the Looking Glass* (Jonathan Cape, London, 1983) pp.62-3; Richard Aldrich 'Secret Intelligence..' p.25; Aldrich seems, however, to have crossed the wartime Circulating Section titles with the post-war cryptonyms for the various director.

[74] Aldrich, 'Secret Intelligence ...' pp.25-26.

[75] Philby, *My Silent War*, p.124; C.M. Woodhouse Something Ventured (Granada, London, 1983) p.106.

[76] Philby, *My Secret War*, p.124.

operations against hostile intelligence services.[77] The rest of Section V's infrastructure had really been custom fitted to the campaign against the Axis intelligence service. The sections for handling ISOS and deception would simply have outlived their usefulness after the war's end, and the security section had, of course, become Vivian's Inspectorate of Security. R6 survived the dismantling of its original recipient, the MEW, and provided economic intelligence to Whitehall departments requiring such. Although no publications explicitly identify the Treasury as the MEW's successor, it should be noted that after the war, presumably with the relocation of the JIC from the CID to the Cabinet Office, the Treasury became a member of the JIC. R7 was a less ambitious body than Section VII, confined after the war to receiving requirements and circulating product to the Directorate of Scientific Intelligence in the Ministry of Defense and JIC's subcommittees on science and technology.[78]

With post-war demobilization the SOE was dismantled, although many of its staff were absorbed by the SIS and individual cells and networks were absorbed into the SIS production organization.[79] The Atlee government's first Foreign Secretary, Ernest Bevin, took an aggressive stance towards Stalin's expansionist interests in Eastern Europe. Under his supervision the Foreign Office created a new propaganda organization to replace the wartime PWE, the Information Research Department (IRD) and Menzies, with the support of the Chief of the Imperial General Staff an the Chairman of the JIC assembled a Special Operations Branch staffed by former SOE officers to plan and coordinate covert operations along SOE lines. Directed by the Special Operations Branch, former SOE units in the Baltic states and the Ukraine attempted to mount a campaign of resistance against Stalin's Russia comparable to that against Hitler's Germany.[80] Unfortunately, these operations and those against Hoxha's Albania were uniformly unsuccessful, and by the 1951 the Special Operations Branch faded from the scene. In 1951, however, Bevin's successor at the Foreign Office, Herbert Morrison, had his department initiate a scheme to quietly overthrow Iranian president Mohammed Mossadeq who had had the temerity to nationalize the Anglo-Iranian Oil Company's assets in that country. With Eden's return to the Foreign Office after the 1951 election the Foreign Office passed this project instead to the SIS. The Agency which implemented the coup using the resources of its Teheran station and the Middle East regional controlling station (formerly CRPO, now relocated to Cyprus) under the codename BOOT.[81] Bolstered

---

[77] Cavendish, *Inside Intelligence p.41.*

[78] Jones, *Most Secret War*, pp.659, 661, Reflections on Intelligence pp.8-16; Aldrich 'Secret Intelligence ...', pp.29-30.

[79] Central Intelligence Machinery, p.20; Anthony Verrier, *Through the Looking Glass*, p.53; Nigel West The Friends (Weidenfeld and Nicholson, London, 1988) p.10; Woodhouse Something Ventured pp.104-105.

[80] Aldrich 'Secret Intelligence ...' p.26; Verrier, *Through the Looking Glass*, pp.52, 63; this unit is variously known as the Special Operations Branch, the Special Operations Branch and Political Action Group and the Special Political Action Group and Operations Branch depending on source; control of the new Section was originally offered to future Conservative MP, C.M. Woodhouse, *Something Ventured*, 104-105.

[81] Verrier, *Through the Looking Glass*, pp.93-129; C.M. Woodhouse Something Ventured, pp.106-135 – Woodhouse is a particularly good source because he was the Teheran

by the success of BOOT, and in a Whitehall setting evidently favourable to clandestine political action, the SIS created a new Special Political Action Section during the mid-1950s. SPA's brief was less precipitate and more fundamentally political than the Special Operations Branch's. SPA's task was not blowing up trains or cutting telephone lines, but rather 'organizing coups, secret radio stations and propaganda campaigns, wrecking international conferences and influencing elections'[82]

After the war, and after Dansey's retirement, Menzies came under pressure to appoint a successor. He therefore recreated the joint posts of VCSS and ACSS assigning former Director of Military Intelligence, General John Sinclair, as VCSS, and another outsider, Air Commodore James 'Jack' Easton as ACSS.[83] The two posts were no more clearly defined in the late 1940s than they were during the war, beyond the basic idea that VCSS was senior to ACSS. As a result, the posts of DP (Director of Production) and DR (Director of Requirements) became somewhat notional as VCSS doubled as DP and ACSS doubled as DR.[84] The four wartime Controller positions had survived in the form of Chief Controllers for Europe (CCE), the Mediterranean (CCM), the Pacific (CCP) and domestic operations Controller Production Research (CPR). The three former posts were entitled Chief Controllers because each had at least two Controllers beneath him overseeing regions within the theatre; the P Sections were subordinate to the Controllers.

CPR has been described by George Blake as a major change in operational policy, contravening the 3-mile limit agreement. In fact it was designed to preserve the wartime techniques of agent infiltration from within United Kingdom territory. CPR was responsible for SIS' relations with the private sector, for example for arranging cover for SIS officer abroad, and for the United Kingdom Station which would ran the United Kingdom-based agents who operated abroad. CPR also had some overseas responsibilities, originally because it had inherited BSC's jurisdiction over the Americas. Later, because of the difficulties of operating behind the Iron Curtain, the SIS to rely on agents which it deployed from United Kingdom territory as it had done during the war. As a result Soviet bloc P Sections were under CPR.[85]

The SIS chain of command for production placed the Controllers in effect on a footing equal the three supporting Directorates, and the ACSS, and in the late 1950s the Chief Controllers and CPR were given full Directorships as DP1, Western Europe, DP2 Middle East and Africa, DP3, Far East and

---

head of station responsible for developing and coordinating BOOT; Cavendish *Inside Intelligence* pp.139-141, Cavendish' account is second hand, but was based on discussions with the Middle East Controller overseeing Woodhouse' activities, George Kennedy Young, who also wrote the preface to Cavendish' volume; West *The Friends* pp.87-96.

[82] J. Bloch & P. Fitzgerald, *British Intelligence and Covert Action* (Junction, London, 1983) p.39, cited by Bloch and Fitzgerald to an interview with Philby by Isvestia 2 October, 1971. Recently this type of operation made up a large part of a BBC documentary on the SIS, Panorama 22 November 1993.

[83] Brown C, pp.684-5; Philby, *My Silent War*, p.119.

[84] Cavendish, *Inside Intelligence* pp.39-41.

[85] CCE, CCM, CCP are all identified by Anthony Cavendish, *Inside Intelligence*, p.40, he refers to the fourth vaguely as 'an officer of similar rank in charge of the Americas', although George Blake, *No Other Choice*, p.184 identifies the post as Controller Production Research.

Americas, and DP4 United Kingdom and Soviet Bloc. Meanwhile the post of ACSS became simply Director of Requirements.[86] Section N continued to operate after the war, and in 1952, during the tunnelling operations in Vienna and Berlin, a new section was created to translate and interpret the product of those wiretaps, Section Y.[87] At approximately the same time, the COCOM agreement limiting technological exports to the Soviet bloc prompted R6 to create a Strategic Trade Section to coordinate SIS operations monitoring the movements of controlled goods to the USSR.[88]

From 1952 the Foreign Office elected to resume posting a senior, supervisory officer at SIS HQ. The new Foreign Office Advisor (FOA) had a rather more central role than his wartime predecessors. Under the new arrangement the Controller for a region had to clear any new operation with the FOA, thus giving the Foreign Office a veto over any operations which it felt might prove unduly prejudicial to normal diplomatic relations.[89]

Intelligence Demand, Supply and Organization

The preceding sketch of the evolution of the SIS is necessarily incomplete. However, as pointed out in the introduction, the critical features of the SIS have been its operational and tasking features. Administration, technical resources and so forth have tended to follow on in the wake of major developments in the core areas. Most of the developments in the core areas have tended to follow on from developments in the government's demands upon the Agency.

It can be seen from the above that of the two main features of SIS organization one, Requirements Directorate, was entirely the direct product of consumer demand. Most of the specialist operational sections arose out of the demands of SIS' consumers also. Section N was very much a matter of Foreign Office interest, the Special Operations section also, with additional participation by the Imperial General Staff and the Committee of Imperial Defense. Section Y was chiefly a product of Service department pressure, so much so that it continued to operate at Service department pressure, translating intercepts, well after the Berlin tunnel 'blew' in 1956.[90] Much the same can be said about the Strategic Trade Section. The G Officers/P Sections were originally simply a matter of delegating regional responsibilities. On the other hand, their weakness and strength in their respective jurisdic-

---

[86] This development is traced specifically for CPR/DP4 in Blake, *No Other Choice*, pp.182-184; the four Production Directorships also appear in Nigel West, *The Friends*, pp.13-15, and in Richard Norton-Taylor, *In Defense of the Realm?* (Civil Liberties Trust, London, 1990) p.50, although West's text does not conform to his organization chart, and he is evidently confused about how the post of DP relates to the assorted DP1-4, assuming that they are identical to the Chief Controllers but without resolving the issue. Similarly, Norton-Taylor confuses the Director of Requirements post with the Requirement Section heads. Private information.

[87] George Blake, *No Other Choice*, pp.7,10-11.

[88] Bristow, *A Game of Moles p.234-244*; *Private information.*

[89] Nigel West, *The Friends*, p.83; Private information.

[90] Peter Wright, *Spycatcher* (Stoddart, Toronto, 1987) p.47.

tions generally resulted from the willingness, of lack thereof, of the Cabinet to fund SIS operations. The adoption of four theatre-level Controllers, later Directors, was a hybrid phenomenon; the pressure to post additional staff in a supervisory capacity came from the Service departments, although the form of that supervision was evidently an attempt to resolve internal management problems in a rapidly expanding Agency during wartime. Indeed, Menzies' implementation of the Service departments' Deputy Directors met with strenuous protests from the Director of Naval Intelligence, although he found no support from his colleagues.[91]

Thus the SIS has always been very much the government's servant, and its internal structure has developed to reflect that fact. Far from being a rogue elephant the Agency has spent most of its existence caged and malnourished. The demands made upon it by the Cabinet and Whitehall have rarely kept pace with the resources they have typically been willing to convince the Treasury to allocate to it. Thus, in 1980, the Government instructed the intelligence Agencies to direct additional attention to Argentina while simultaneously refusing to allocate additional funds.[92] With the end of the Cold War the international arena has become less certain, less predictable, and the government's need for information can be expected to increase in direct proportion. In this new arena the British government will get only the volume and reliability clandestine services, intelligence and political, for which it is willing to pay, and for which it can establish clear and comprehensive criteria. The SIS is not equipped to do more.

---

[91] Hinsley et al, *British Intelligence. Volume II p.18.*
[92] Lord Franks, *The Falklands Islands Review* (HMSO, London, 1983) p.84.

Women and Democratisation

Georgina Waylen
University of Salford

'Gender and Simultaneous Political and Economic Liberalization'

Introduction

Simultaneous political and economic liberalization is now occurring through-out Latin America, Africa and East/Central Europe. The earliest, and in some cases most through-going, attempts have occurred in Latin America. Since the 1980s political liberalization in Argentina, Chile, Peru and Brazil has also been accompanied by economic liberalization. While there is a growing literature on both gender & democratization, and gender & economic liberalization, particularly in the form of structural adjustment, there is, as yet, no work which looks at gender and simultaneous economic and political liberalization. I intend to undertake a gendered analysis of simultaneous economic and political liberalization in Latin America through the comparative study of four selected case-studies: Chile, Brazil, Argentina and Peru. These countries have been chosen because they demonstrate very different experiences of political and economic liberalization and also have different types of women's movements and women's political and economic activity.

This research therefore aims to fill major gaps in our knowledge about democratization and economic liberalization. There is a need, I would argue, for three things to be done initially.

> First, to improve both the conventional analyses of simulta-neous political and economic liberalization by 'gendering' it;
>
> secondly, to bring together the already existing, but largely separate, bodies of knowledge on gender and democratization and gender and economic liberalization, and
>
> thirdly, to provide new empirical information on gender and simultaneous economic and political liberalization which is currently lacking.

I also believe that it will prove possible to analyse any patterns in the relationship between political and economic liberalization emerging from the Latin American case studies and use them to develop a framework which can be utilised in the gendered analysis of other regions. What I intend to do in this paper is to outline why I believe this to be the case by highlighting some of the gaps in the existing literature and I will then to go on to sketch out some of the issues I believe any study of this kind should focus on. By definition, this work is at an early stage and therefore both very preliminary and speculative.

The Background to this Research

There is now a huge literature on many aspects of democratization and economic liberalization. During the 1980s much of it focused on the questions of why democratization takes place and the conditions necessary to achieve it, whether these were structural or seen as being achieved through purposive action, particularly by the élites, who often formed pacts with the military to bring about negotiated transitions (O'Donnell, Schmitter & Whitehead, 1986; Diamond, Linz & Lipset, 1989). These analyses frequently did not consider economic factors in any great depth. In contrast, much of the literature specifically on economic liberalization (often focussing on structural adjustment) looked at the economic to the exclusion of, particularly, the domestic political sphere and its impact on the political arena. Partly in response to widespread criticism of the literature, the focus of much new work has altered in ways relevant to this paper (Remmer, 1991). I will outline some of the changes which should be considered in a study of this kind.

First, analyses of democratization and political liberalization are becoming more complex and sophisticated. Indeed, some analysts now draw a distinction between political liberalization, which it is argued can take place without democratization also occurring, and democratization itself. According to Qadir, Clapham & Gills 'political liberalisation implies a process of political change controlled from the top-down, as a means of preserving the status quo', while democratization involves 'genuine reform' (Qadar, Clapham & Gills, 1993). However, I think that the distinction made by these scholars is not very useful as they seem to be in danger of setting up an 'ideal type' of 'real democratization', in comparison to which the majority of states generally acknowledged as having democratized would be found wanting. It is better, I think, to acknowledge that the process of democratization and political liberalization is often flawed, and that the return to competitive party politics does not generally involve the emergence of 'real democracy' defined in much wider social, economic and political terms.

Second, while earlier studies also often focussed just on regime breakdown, now the study of democratization is being split up into stages, for example, the process of breakdown of the old authoritarian regime forms the first stage, and is followed by the phases of the transition to and consolidation of the new democratic politics and it is possible to analyses these different phases separately (Nelson 1993). Increasingly attention is being directed towards these later stages of transition and consolidation, rather than simply looking at the conditions which can lead to the collapse of authoritarian regimes. Analysts are now focusing on the differing circumstances which can affect the consolidation of competitive party politics.

Third, as part of this, many more recent studies have become interested in the simultaneity of political and economic reforms, occurring not just in East/Central Europe but also in much of Latin America and Africa. The (re)establishment of competitive party systems has frequently been accompanied in the late 1980s by economic liberalization all over the world (Remmer, 1990, Haggard & Kaufman, 1992). This has led to renewed interest in the question of the links between capitalism and democracy both analytically and empirically (Philip, 1993).

Fourth, the collapse of communism in Eastern Europe and the spread of democratization in the Third World from Latin America, particularly to Africa, has led to a characterization of this as a 'third wave of democratization' beginning in Southern Europe in the mid 1970s (Huntington, 1991). Links are now being made between the different cases and it is accepted that comparison between them is possible for two reasons. First, because of impact that different cases have on one another, described variously as 'snowballing', 'contagion' and 'demonstration effects' and second, because of the underlying similarity of the processes of liberalization involved (Schmitter, 1992; Karl, 1992). Przeworski, in particular, argues this with regard to the economic liberalization taking place in Eastern Europe and Latin America and he concludes with the claim that Eastern Europe 'will confront the all too normal problems of the economics, the politics, and the culture of poor capitalism. The East has become the South' (Przeworski, 1991, p.191).

As a consequence, it has been argued that the experience of the Third World and particularly Latin America has lessons to offer the countries of East/Central Europe (Nelson, 1993). To help further this line of analysis, Nelson makes the distinction between two subsets of third world nations: 'vigorous reformers', which introduced economic changes without political changes such as Chile under Pinochet and the 'Chicago Boys' between 1973 and 1989; and those who attempted both political and economic reforms at the same time, for example, Argentina and Brazil since the late 1980s. Nelson suggests that these broad categories are also useful when examining East/Central Europe and argues that, in the short and medium term, these dual processes both complement and conflict with each other in important ways.

While it is clear that much of this literature is becoming increasingly more sophisticated and raises some interesting questions, one characteristic that, so far, all of it has shared is gender blindness. In contrast to this conventional work, there is another body of literature in which scholars have argued that, without a focus which can include gender, any analysis of political and economic liberalization will be partial and incomplete, and ignores not only the important role played by women and women's movements in the process of democratization but also the impact of both democratization and economic liberalization on gender relations (Elson, 1991). There are now a number of studies of gender and democratization in Latin America, both general overviews and country case studies in the form of edited collections and single authored volumes. These have demonstrated the important role played by a variety of heterogeneous women's movements, particularly in bringing about the initial opening and the 'end of fear' signalling the breakdown of authoritarian rule (Jaquette, 1989, Alvarez, 1990, Waylen, 1993). The activities of the Madres of the Plaza de Mayo in Argentina are often singled out here, as their human rights protests formed the first open and public opposition to a very repressive military junta. This work which concentrates specifically on democratization has been accompanied by the publication of a number of studies which examine the growth of women's popular political protest in Latin America more generally in the 1980s (Waylen, 1992b; Radcliffe & Westwood, 1993: Fisher, 1993).

However, many of these gendered studies have replicated some of the characteristics of the more conventional literature. A number of the analyses of gender and democratization have focused on the political sphere without any detailed consideration of the economic, concentrating particularly on the role of women's movements in bringing about the transition to democratic rule and of women in the resumed conventional party politics (Alvarez, 1990). While, at the same time, studies of economic liberalization in general, and structural adjustment in particular, have highlighted the particular ways in which different groups of women are affected by these policies, almost entirely in economic terms. Poorer women, for example, have been particularly hit in their roles as household managers by the reduction of welfare services and state subsidies while middle class professional women have been hit through the reduction of employment opportunities in the state sector, for example, as teachers, social workers and nurses. These analyses have, however, tended to focus on the economic to the exclusion of a discussion of the political context in which economic liberalization has taken place (Afshar & Dennis, 1992). There has been some preliminary work linking the often contradictory and complex interaction of the economic and the political, but this has been carried out in the context of Chile under the Pinochet regime, which, while a vigorous economic reformer, was not at the time a democratizer (Waylen, 1992c). The literature on Eastern Europe, while at a much earlier stage of its development, has often been forced to unite the analysis of the political and the economic more comprehensively, in part because of the ways in which these processes have often been linked from their very inception (Watson 1993, Einhorn, 1993).

Echoing the emphasis of the conventional literature on the similarity of the processes involved and the links between the different cases, preliminary work comparing gender and democratization in Eastern Europe and Latin America has shown that comparison between different cases is both possible and useful, but that a gendered dimension will highlight some very different aspects to that emphasised by the more orthodox literature (Berkeley Conference, 1992). Some of the similarities and very important differences between the Latin American and the Eastern European cases can be seen through a comparison of: the differing amounts of 'political space' available to facilitate autonomous organising prior to the transition, as far more space for organisation existed under authoritarian governments in Latin America than did under state socialist regimes in Eastern Europe; the impact of different women's movements on state policy; the impact of state policy, particularly economic policy, on gender relations; and the often contradictory role played by differing gender ideologies in complementing and counteracting the processes of simultaneous liberalization, for example, the return to the so-called traditional values of god, family and nation in much of East/Central Europe serve in part to complement economic liberalization, helping to push the increased burden of welfare provision on to women in the family (Waylen, 1994). In contrast, in Chile, the impact of economic liberalization in creating new jobs for women in non-traditional export sectors, for example, commercial agriculture, went against the 'traditional' gender ideology promulgated by Pinochet's military regime (Waylen, 1992c).

I believe that, while there has not been any systematic study of gender, economic and political liberalization undertaken up to now, it is possible to utilise this already existing literature in several ways: firstly building on the conventional literature on democratization and economic liberalization, by utilising a) the recent focus on simultaneity and b) extending the trends towards comparative analyses to develop a general framework; and secondly by bringing together the gendered analyses of democratization on the one hand and economic liberalization on the other. I believe that the best way to do this at the moment is to disaggregate the experience of Latin American case-studies, looking at the specificities of each country and comparing these rather than looking at them together.

The Way Forward?

This research is therefore based on three major hypotheses. First, that a gendered analysis of simultaneous political and economic liberalization will provide useful insights into the role of women in an important political and economic process. Second, a gendered approach will improve existing conventional analyses; both by highlighting new themes which need to be integrated into the main body of the literature, and by providing evidence which can be used to verify existing hypotheses. Third, that it is possible to use the evidence from the Latin American case-studies to derive a framework utilizable in the gendered analysis of simultaneous political and economic liberalization elsewhere in the world.

These hypotheses will be tested in four Latin American case studies: Brazil, Argentina, Chile and Peru, chosen because of their different experiences of political and economic liberalization. Some of their differing characteristics are as follows:

> Brazil experienced a long drawn-out transition, as a result of the negotiation of pacts between élites and the military. The failure of heterodox programmes has been followed by rather unsuccessful attempts at more thorough going economic liberalization.

> Argentina underwent a quick transition to civilian rule catalysed by military defeat but also exacerbated by economic crisis. After the failure of heterodox programmes, the economic liberalization programme implemented by a peronist president, has been deemed a success.

> Chile experienced a long drawn out and negotiated transition, somewhat later than the other case studies. The military regime pursued an eventually successful programme of economic liberalization. The civilian government has continued these policies but also increased social spending.

> Peru went through a relatively quick transition followed by
> several different civilian administrations, the last of which has
> carried out a sort of 'autogolpe' in conjunction with a more
> thoroughgoing attempt at economic liberalization.

The case studies also exhibit differences in terms of the nature of women's movements and women's economic and political activity. The relationship between all these variables will be explored in several ways, informed by Nelson's thesis that the processes of political and economic liberalization both conflict with and complement each other (Nelson, 1993).

First, the relationship between economic and political liberalization and the emergence and subsequent activity of women's movements will be considered. The question of the relationship of the political system and women's movements has already been fairly widely researched. Studies have shown that authoritarianism gave different women's movements space to emerge, as the suspension of conventional party politics, typically male-dominated, often shifted the emphasis of organised activity which could take place from an institutional basis to a community-based one, where women have often predominated (Jaquette, 1989). The women's movements which emerged were not homogeneous. Most studies have identified the emergence of several types of organisations. Two of these – human rights and popular organisations – had women as the majority of their members, and pressed social and economic demands. The urban popular movements were largely made up of poor and working class women. A third type of organization re-emerged, comprising women, organising as women, pressing gender-based demands, that is, groups which were specifically feminist, often made up of middle class professional women have become prominent. Popular or grassroots feminisms, which do not identify themselves with what is seen as middle-class feminism have also emerged (Fisher, 1993). Women's movements therefore differ particularly in their class composition and these difference have to be taken into account in any analysis.

Alvarez has claimed that the greatest space for women's movements to emerge occurred when authoritarian regimes pursued state-led development, for example, Brazil and Peru in the late 1960s and early 1970s. This led to an increase in professional and technical employment for the newly educated middle class women particularly in the state sector, spurring the re-emergence of feminist movements. Conversely it is argued that the least space existed where authoritarian regimes implemented economic policies inspired by the new right where the role of the state in development was reduced, for example, Chile and to some extent Argentina under military regimes (Alvarez, 1990). However, the evidence here is mixed and needs to be explored further. Argentina, for example, did see the emergence of relatively weak feminist movements and urban popular women's movements right at the end of the dictatorship. Relatively strong women's movements, both feminist and popular, emerged in Chile, particularly after political liberalization had begun. Authoritarianism combined with high levels of repression also led to the creation of influential human rights groups in Chile and Argentina, primarily made up of women demanding the return of their missing children.

It is generally understood that the economic hardship, caused, for example, by falling real wages, inflation and the reduction of subsidies, which is often a consequence of structural adjustment packages, has catalysed the emergence of urban popular women's movements. These have been active around consumption issues, at the extreme economic survival, for example, in the form of soup kitchens providing one meal a day for families in the community, service provision, for example, health services, and income generation such as artisanal workshops, for example, bakeries (Safa, 1990). But here again the evidence is mixed and needs further exploration. It appears that in Brazil, whereas the creation of urban popular organisations was an important response to the economic crisis of the late 1970s and early 1980s, the economic liberalization in the late 1980s which has brought renewed economic hardship, has been accompanied by a decline in the activity of the urban women's movements which were previously so important (Caldeira, 1992). It is, as yet, unclear why this should be the case and needs further investigation.

Second, some of the women's movements appear to have been more successful than others in achieving their goals and having an impact on the political system as the processes of transition and consolidation continue. A key task is therefore to ascertain how and why this occurs. In order to understand how and why the complex interaction of political and economic factors favoured some movements over others, it is now clear that these processes have to be disaggregated further. The impact that different women and women's movements have on the political system and policymaking has to be examined, particularly why it is that different women's movements have differing amounts of influence in the subsequent political phases of transition and consolidation. The longer drawn out transitions, for example, Brazil and Chile appear to offer some women's movements greater opportunities in the political arena than the quicker ones, for example, Argentina. However, these are also the transitions based primarily on negotiated pacts between élite groups. Significantly, it also appears that strong predominantly middle-class feminist movements can have a greater impact on state policy-making. This happens, both because some women enter the political élite and because governments profess support for 'women's' issues by establishing women's committees and councils, for example, in Chile and Brazil. But at the same time, popular women's movements often become increasingly marginal in political terms, particularly in the largely middle class negotiated transitions.

The impact of economic and political liberalization on different groups of women forms a third area of investigation. Civilian governments, for example, in Brazil, Peru and Argentina, have often implemented harsher economic policies than military governments, after the failure of more heterodox policies. Thoroughgoing economic liberalization limits the ability of policymakers to improve the position of women through increased welfare provision, despite the commitment of some civilian governments to 'women's issues'. However, there is evidence of a new commitment to increased levels of social justice on the part of some civilian governments. In Chile, the civilian government is now moderating some of the impact of economic liberalization through higher social spending. Economic liberalization therefore needs to be examined in terms of its effect on women's paid and unpaid labour, for example, through the reduction of welfare provision and subsidies, privatisation and the restructuring of the economy and changes in employment. In some cases, economic liberalization, for example, because it increases many women's labour time, affects the capacity, in terms of time and energy that many women have to influence the processes of political liberalization. This phenomenon also needs to be examined. At the same time it may be that political liberalization makes governments more vulnerable to popular pressure to moderate the impact of economic liberalization. The greater concern expressed by some civilian governments about poverty and the question of social justice may be relevant here.

Conclusions

As I have demonstrated, gender and simultaneous economic and political liberalization is an important area of research and needs thorough investigation. I have outlined what I believe to be one appropriate way of doing this is through an examination of four selected Latin American case studies in terms of:

> a) women's representation in conventional politics that is, representation in political parties in terms of numbers elected, presence of women's organisations, and number of women in cabinet positions;
> b) Women's political activity outside of conventional politics, particularly feminist movements and popular movements;
> c) the impact of state policy in terms of
> – 1: the impact of policies on gender issues, both in terms of nature of policies themselves and any bodies set up with special responsibility for women, and
> – 2: the impact of more general policies of economic liberalization on different women.

Research of this kind will therefore fill important gaps in our knowledge and improve both the conventional and gendered literature on democratization and economic liberalization already in existence.

References

H.Afshar & C.Dennis (eds) 1992, *Women and Adjustment Policies in the Third World* (Macmillan, Basingstoke).

S.Alvarez, 1990, *Engendering Democracy in Brazil: Women's Movements in Transition Politics* (Princeton University Press, Princeton).

Berkeley, 1992, Conference on Women and the Transition from Authoritarian Rule in Latin America and Eastern Europe.

T.Caldeira, 1992, 'Justice and Individual Rights: Challenges for Women's Movements and Democratization in Brazil', paper presented to Conference on Women and the Transition from Authoritarian Rule, Berkeley.

L.Diamond, J.Linz & S.Lipset (eds) 1989, *Democracy in Developing Countries*, 4 volumes (Lynne Rienner, Boulder).

B.Einhorn, 1993, *Cinderella Goes to Market: Gender, Citizenship and the Women's Movement in Eastern Europe* (Verso, London).

D.Elson (ed) 1991, *Male Bias in the Development Process* (Manchester University Press, Manchester).

J.Fisher, 1993, *Out of the Shadows: Women, Resistance and Politics in South America* (Latin American Bureau, London)

S.Haggard & R.Kaufman, 1991, 'Economic Adjustment and the Prospects for Democracy', Paper presented to XVth IPSA Congress, Buenos Aires.

S.Huntington, 1991, *The Third Wave: Democratization in the Late Twentieth Century* (University of Oklahoma Press, Nelson).

J.Jaquette (ed) 1989, *The Women's Movement in Latin America: Feminism and the Transition to Democracy in Latin America* (Unwin Hyman, London).

T.Karl, 1992, Paper given at Conference on Women and the Transition from Authoritarian Rule in Latin America and Eastern Europe, Berkeley.

J.Nelson, 1993, 'The Politics of Economic Transformation: Is Eastern European Experience Relevant to Eastern Europe', *World Politics*, 45, April.

G.O'Donnell, P.Schmitter & L.Whitehead (eds) 1986, *Transitions from Authoritarian Rule: Prospects for Democracy* (John Hopkins University Press, Baltimore).

G.Philip, 1993, 'The new economic liberalism and democracy in Latin America: friends or enemies?', *Third World Quarterly*, 14, 3.

A.Przeworski, 1991, *Democracy and the Market: Political and Economic Reforms in Eastern Europe and Latin America* (Cambridge University Press, Cambridge).

S.Qadar, C.Clapham & B.Gills, 1993, 'Sustainable Democracy: formalism vs substance', *Third World Quarterly*, 14, 3.

S.Radcliffe & S.Westwood (eds) 1993, *Viva: Women and Popular Protest in Latin America* (Routledge, London).

K.Remmer, 1991, 'New Wine or Old Bottlenecks', *Comparative Politics*, 23, July.

H.Safa, 1990, 'Women's Social Movements in Latin America', *Gender and Society*, 4, 3.

P.Schmitter, 1992, Paper presented to Conference on Women and the Transition from Authoritarian Rule in Latin America and Eastern Europe, Berkeley.

P.Watson, 1993, 'The Rise of Masculinism in Eastern Europe', *New Left Review*, 198, March/April.

G.Waylen, 1992a, 'Women's Movements and Democratization in Chile', Occasional Paper in Politics and Contemporary History, University of Salford, no 31.

G.Waylen, 1992b, 'Rethinking Women's Political Participation and Protest: Chile 1970-90', *Political Studies*, 40, June.

G.Waylen, 1992c, 'Women, Authoritarianism and Market Liberalisation in Chile 1973-89' in Afshar & Dennis (eds).

G.Waylen, 1993, 'Women's Movements and Democratization in Latin America', *Third World Quarterly*, 14, 3.

G.Waylen, 1994, 'Women and Democratization: Conceptualising Gender Relations in Transition Politics', *World Politics*, April, forthcoming.

Green Politics and International Politics

Peter Doran
University of Kent

'States of Insecurity:
Ecology, Modernity and the Globalisation of Risk'

Introduction

Since the publication of the Brundtland Report (1987)[1] increasing numbers
of environmental policy makers, academics and campaigners have applied
their minds to the notion of environmental security and its implications.
(Myers 1989, Renner 1989, Brown 1990, Deudney 1990) Like that other
conceptual key to 'Our Common Future', 'sustainable development', environmental security must be considered an essentially contested idea which
is wide open to anti-ecological interpretations and co-optation by those for
whom the order of power/knowledge flows from knowing power.

This paper will draw on some of the recent discussions by the poststructuralists and ecofeminists which explore the states' system ideology
(Alger 1984-1985) of security – an ideology which, associated with the institutions and aspirations of modernity as Westernisation, has helped to
conceal the systematic creation of multiple insecurities. The environmental crisis has begun to reveal how the industrial and science-led model of
modernity has generated a 'risk society' which is likely to lead to a radical
re-defining of modernity itself. (Beck 1993) It will be shown that critical
readings of security reveal a profound anti-ecological bias – one that must
be addressed before the term can be meaningfully coupled with environmental values. The paper will also point to the critical social movements
(Walker 1988) in the international system as agents of transformation of
our understanding of security insofar as they have articulated a concept of
security based on a radical reversal of the existing metaphysics of denial
which currently underpin the impossible search for invulnerability in the
politics of modernity, of which the state system ideology is an expression.

Environmental Security

Daniel Deudney (1990) has observed that a striking feature of the growing
discussion of environmental issues in the United States is an attempt by
many liberals, progressives and environmentalists to employ language traditionally associated with violence and war to understand environmental
problems and motivate action. There have been attempts to redefine security and extend it to embrace a recognition of environmental threats. Deudney correctly links the genesis of these efforts to the advancement of this
linkage during renewed Cold War tensions in the late 1970s and early 1980s

---

[1] World Commission on Environment and Development, (1987), *Our Common Future*,
Oxford University Press: Oxford.

'to prevent an excessive focus on military threats' (1990: 462) Similarly, Matthias Finger (1992) has argued that the Brundtland Commission inherited its 'security analogy' from the Cold War, an analogy which has proved useful in the 'transformation of the global ecological crisis into global environmental management' (1992: 3). If, as Deudney suggests, security from violence and security from environmental threats have little in common, and the linkage is 'largely useless for analytical and conceptual purposes' (1990: 463) we must proceed with caution and, with Finger, conclude that the linkage may be useful for actors and purposes associated with system maintenance and management rather than transformation. As Deudney concludes, environmental degradation is not a threat to national security. Rather, environmentalism is a threat to 'national security' mindsets and institutions. This is a rather hopeful statement, of course. For the incorporation of environmentalism into the rhetoric of 'national security' and 'security' discourse is a political project and no mere question of semantics. For language, inhabited always by power, is also legislation, as Roland Barthes has reminded us (Sontag 1982: 460). And is not the establishment of truth always linked to a technology of dissemination and control? (Smith 1992: 252) Nevertheless Deudney has glimpsed the dangers:

> 'For environmentalists to dress their programmes in the blood soaked garments of the war system betrays their core values and creates confusion about the real tasks ahead.' (Deudney 1990: 475)

Shiv Visvanathan read 'Our Common Future' and discovered 'Mrs Brundtland's Disenchanted Cosmos' (1991: 377-378). In the report he discerned a language in the service of a 'new style of control and surveillance' and ultimately, violence 'through concepts; through coding, by creating grammars that decide which sentence can be spoken and which cannot. It is from such a perspective that the Brundtland Report ... must be seen not as a statement of intention, but in terms of the logic of the world it seeks to create'. Brundtland had a decisive influence on the move to expand notions of national sovereignty and security to embrace environmental stress:

> 'The whole notion of security as traditionally understood – in terms of political and military threats to national sovereignty – must be expanded to include the growing impacts of environmental stress – locally, nationally, regionally, and globally.' (1987: 19)

Confirming Marshall McLuhan's observation that politicians have a talent for applying yesterday's solutions to today's problems Brundtland recommended international co-operative management, early warning systems and disarmament, each borrowing heavily from aspirations created by insecurities created by the Cold War logic. To demonstrate just how leading policy makers can transfer traditional security imperatives to the new environmental discourse there is the example of one leading Brundtland author[2], Jim

---

[2] The author in question, Mr Jim MacNeill, was the Canadian Secretary General of the World Commission on Environment and Development who played a leading role in drafting the Brundtland Report.

MacNeill. Joyce Nelson (1993) has described how former Brundtland Commissioner (ex-officio), and the principal author of 'Our Common Future', led a 1988 Trilateral Commission Task Force[3] on environment and development and was principal author of the subsequent report to the 1990 meeting of Trilateral members.[4] Essentially MacNeill indicated that threats to environmental security could be interpreted as those occasions when Third World countries had the audacity to threaten to exert control over their own resources. He wrote:

> 'Today ... the major urban/developing centres of the world are locked into complex international networks for trade in goods and services of all kinds, including primary and processed energy, food materials and other resources. The major cities of the economically powerful Western nations constitute the nodes of these networks, enabling these nations to draw upon the ecological capital of all other nations to provide food for their populations, energy and material for their economies, and even land, air and water to assimilate their waste byproducts.
>
> This ecological capital, which may be found thousands of miles from the regions in which it may be used, forms the 'shadow ecology' of an economy. The oceans, the atmosphere (climate), and the other 'commons' also form part of this shadow ecology. In essence, the ecological shadow of a country is the environmental resources it draws from other countries and the global commons. If a nation without much geographical resilience had to do without its shadow ecology, even for a short period, its people and economy would suffocate ... Western nations heavily engaged in global sourcing should be aware of their shadow ecologies and the need to pursue policies that will sustain them.'
> (MacNeill, 1991: 58-59)

Understandings of environmental threats to security as little more than threats to the 'shadow ecology' of industrialized regions – the availability of mines and toxic sinks in distant lands – translate easily into the 'Planetary Geopolitics' (1990) of Neville Brown, a Professor of International Security Affairs, whose contribution to the debate on environmental security is the suggestion that the model for global co-operation which should be applied is the one provided by the international response to the Persian Gulf crisis in August of 1990, with five permanent members of the United Nations in the vanguard:

---

[3] Founded in 1973 the Trilateral Commission has been described by Joyce Nelson as 'the most powerful and élite organization for world planning' (1993: 2) with a membership of over 300 leaders of global corporations, bankers, politicians and academics drawn exclusively from North America, Europe and Japan. For her analyis of the role of Commission members, including Maurice Strong, in the preparation of the United Nations Conference on Environment and Development in Rio de Janeiro, June 1992, see Nelson's article, 'Great Global Greenwash, or The Sustainable Development Scam', in *Covert Action Quarterly*, Number 44, Spring 1993.

[4] The Trilateral publication, *Beyond Interdependence: The Meshing of the World's Economy and the Earth's Ecology* was co-authored by MacNeill (principal author) along with Pieter Winsemius and Taizo Yakushiji.

'In exactly the same way, a concert of powers may be needed, and on a more enduring basis, if the international community as a whole is to cope with climatic change and other environment and resource problems. By "a concert of powers" one presumably would mean a regular pattern of dialogue and collaboration among the superpowers, the European Community, China and Japan.' (1990: 458)

history of security/insecurity

Security has always been a volatile concept. R.B.J. Walker (1989) has noted that for all its aura of tough-minded clarity the dominant understanding of security is exceptionally flimsy and vague. As a central term of contemporary political discourse 'security' seems to have been abandoned to the propagandists and ideologues and become a concept of mystifying rhetoric (1989: 119). Appeals to the need for security have been used to justify blatant abuses and encourage the resort to escalating levels of violence. Such appeals legitimize vast arsenals and the curtailment of democratic rights and procedures. The concept of security, he concludes, is now more a symptom of the problem than a guide to the possibilities of peace and justice. (1989: 118) The reason for this is clear. The most important use of the concept of security is linked explicitly to state power. The idea of 'national security' arises from the supposed demands of the 'security dilemma' in the states system – one which supposedly legitimizes the resort to war when national security is threatened. He explains:

'The classic European account of the problem occurs in Thomas Hobbes' seventeenth-century depiction of the insecurities arising from competition between more or less equal individuals seeking to preserve themselves in a proto-capitalist society and making each other insecure in the process ... The legitimacy of state power is then claimed to derive in large measure from the state's capacity to bring order to the conflict that results inevitably from the insecurities of competitive self-interested behavior.' (1989: 118)

Walker points out that the states system ideology of security refers to the security of people as citizens, not people as people. This implies exclusion and differentiation. This concept of security reinforces the distinction between friend and foe, self and other ... distinctions upon which the modern concept of the state rests. Another related assumption hidden within the ideology is the possibility of making a distinction between war and peace:

'Within states, it is assumed that communities can develop in peace. Between states war is inevitable. National security - the presumption that security is a matter of the defence of the citizens of sovereign territory – becomes the crucial demarcation, the boundary between chaos and order, conflict and community, violence and justice.' (1989: 119)

Chadwick Alger (1985) has suggested that the ideology of the states system
rests on two assumptions:

(a) States are the most important actors in the world system;
(b) International and domestic politics are held to be qualitatively different and to be subject to different concepts and
modes of analyses.

Among other things, he has observed that the ideology deprives local actors of knowledge about the intricate historical and political relationships
between their local communities and actions and the world system. One of
the post-structuralist theorists who takes this ideology seriously is David
Campbell. In his critique of U.S. foreign policy (1990) he begins with the
argument that seemingly intransigent structures of history are effects (albeit
very powerful ones) of a variety of uncoordinated practices of differentiation
that serve to constitute meaning and identity through a series of exclusions.
The imposition of an interpretation of the ambiguity and contingency of
social life always results in another person being marginalized. Meaning
and identity, in his view, are always the consequence of a relationship between the self and the other that emerges through the imposition of an
interpretation rather than being the product of uncovering an exclusive domain with its own pre-established identity. The implication here is that
the domestic and the external, the state and the international system, and
the sovereign and the anarchic are not domains that exist in essence prior
to a relationship with each other. Identity in global politics can be understood as the outcome of exclusionary practices in which resistant elements
to a secure identity on the inside are linked through a discourse of danger with threats identified and located on the outside. This demarcation is
achieved through an inscription of danger on ambiguity in such a way that
the differences within are transformed into differences between (Campbell
1990: 266). Community therefore comes to exist within the state while
the threat of anarchy is, for the most part, located without. Boundaries
are constructed, spaces demarcated, standards of legitimacy incorporated,
interpretations of history privileged, and alternatives marginalised in the
process. In American foreign policy discourse – a discourse engaged the
establishment of boundaries that help to constitute the state and the international system – serves to enframe, limit, and domesticate a particular
meaning of humanity, incorporating not only national identity but also the
form of domestic order, the social relations of production and the various
subjectivities to which they give rise.

Walker believes there is a complex interplay between economies and military deployments and the role of the state in fostering this interplay between domestic and international spaces. Militarization participates in the
creation of new principles of inclusion and exclusion. In the end, national security as a concept remains locked into an anachronistic account of the logic
of the state system. Walker suggests that any serious critical rethinking of
security must address three fundamental transformations:

(1) There must be a broadening of the understanding of
sources of insecurity. Questions of war and peace cannot be sep-

arated from questions of development, ecological degradation, abuse of human rights, and loss of cultural identity. The enemy is not only 'out there' but ourselves and the structures we, as human beings, have helped to build together.

(2) There must be a broadening of the subject of security to embrace people in general and life on earth, rather than just the citizens of states. Under modern conditions the pursuit of the security of citizens has rendered everyone one more and more insecure as people. The emergence of new structures of inclusion and exclusion that is, the complex social, cultural, economic and political divisions between peoples who can and cannot participate effectively in contemporary global processes – renders one-third of humanity radically unable to secure the minimum conditions for survival.

(3) The modern state must be recognized as a primary source of contemporary insecurity. This is true of the processes connected with the pursuit of national security and true insofar as states threaten the lives of their own 'dissident' citizens. (1989: 121)

Drawing from the projects of critical social movements Walker proceeds to offer a number of clues about the possible directions of a radical reconceptualization of security, notably the need to recognize that an understanding of security as the exclusion of insecurity demands an unrealistic denial. A critical account of this exclusive emphasis and the deeply rooted denial which informs the ideology of state system security is an essential aspect of the debate which must take place before traditional notions of security are hitched up to environmental values. Walker's proposals include:

(a) The development of a more political and democratic understanding of security, and an appreciation of the dialectical interplay between security and insecurity;
(b) An appreciation that there is no absolute physical or psychic invulnerability in human life.

Security and insecurity are complementary and vulnerability can be interpreted positively, creating the opportunities for communication, exchange, learning and commitment.

Securing Modernity

In his introduction to *Biosphere Politics* (1991) Jeremy Rifkin makes the far reaching claim that 'it is the notion of security upon which our entire modern world-view is based that has led us to the verge of ecocide. A thorough understanding of the current ecological crisis will require a vigorous examination of the social forces and philosophical currents that underlie our contemporary views of economic, political and military security.' (1991: 2) He traces the origins of the modern drive for security, leading to the paradoxical creation of multiple insecurities, to the privatization and commodification of nature and man in the wake of the Enlightenment and the philosophical currents which sanctioned both. It was with the Enlightenment that there began a radicalized detachment and isolation from the natural world and a near pathological obsession with creating a secure existence which became identified with autonomy and independence from the forces of nature. Rifkin explains:

> 'Modern man and woman's actions in the world flow inextricably from these Enlightenment ideas about nature and human security. These powerful intellectual constructs make up the rules of engagement in the contemporary war against nature. This being the case, it is naïve to believe it is possible to extricate ourselves from the global environmental and economic crises facing the planet lest we are prepared to confront the set of ideas about security that gave rise to our current predicament.' (1991: 36-37)

Modern assumptions about the nature of security have had a profound effect on shaping a wholesale change in human economic and social relationships. No change was at once more poignant and more devastating than that brought about by the European enclosure movement which had far reaching consequences for human/nature relations. While the Enlightenment provided the philosophical sanction for humanity's separation from nature, the enclosure movement of privatization and commodification which continues in ever new forms today across the earth, constituted the actual set of social and economic practices. This in turn paved the way for the emergence of the industrial and urban revolutions and created the conditions for the construction of integrated national-economies in nation-states:

> 'The Western world constructed a new base for security, which was firmly entrenched along a horizontal plane. Security was to be found in walls and fences, guns, and great masted sailing ships, mechanisms and machines. Security came to be measured more in technological prowess and earthly possessions and less in faith and good works. In return for the great loss ... the new man and woman were offered a form of security that was secular in nature, tangible, and accumulative. Henceforth, money and machines were to be the new guarantors.' (Rifkin 1991: 48)

The nation-state and the business corporation, he concludes, are by their very nature designed to enclose ecosystems, commodify and privatize nature, optimize the expropriation of scarce resources, expand production and consumption, and advance utilitarian self-interest. Hand in hand with the military these institutions of modernity have been chiefly responsible for implementing the knowledge/power order which has flowed from the shadow side of Enlightenment thought. For the industrial journey has been blazed with incendiaries and enclosure secured with firepower. The rise of the nation-state is mirrored in a radical transformation which has been documented by Ivan Illich (1991), a transformation from a subsistence-based understanding of peace to *pax economica*, peace understood as a balance between formally 'economic' powers. For Illich the latter represents the engineered counterfeit of the popular peace which once protected the poor and their means of subsistence against war. He writes:

> 'Peace protected the peasant and the monk ... the oxen and the grain on the stem ... the "peace of the land" shielded the utilization values of the common environment from violent interference. It ensured access to water and pasture, to woods and livestock, for those who had nothing else from which to draw their subsistence. The "peace of the land" was thus distinct from the truce between warring parties.' (1991: 94)

With the Renaissance and the rise of the new world of the nation-state subsistence lost out to an unprecedented peace and unprecedented forms of violence as 'subsistence itself became the victim of an aggression ... the prey of expanding markets in services and goods' (1991: 94) and the understanding of peace was cut to the measure of *homo economicus* who would live on the consumption of commodities produced elsewhere by others. While the *pax populi* had protected vernacular autonomy, the environment in which this could thrive and the variety of patterns for its reproduction, the new *pax economica* protected and privileged production. *Pax economica*, according to Illich, cloaks the assumption that people have become incapable of providing for themselves, empowering an élite to make all people's survival dependent on their access to education, health care, police protection and supermarkets. It exalts the producer and degrades the consumer, labelling subsistence 'un-productive', and tradition 'under-developed'. In addition *pax economica* promotes violence against the environment by translating it into resources and the space for their circulation, encouraging the destruction of the commons. It defines the environment as a scarce resource which it reserves for optimal use in the production of goods and the provision of professional care.

If Wolfgang Sachs (1992) is correct to read the modern language of environmental security and management as little more than a call for the survival of the industrial system and the extension of capital-, bureaucracy- and science-intensive solutions to environmental degradation then it is clear that the concept of security remains embedded within the history and practices of modern economic and political institutions. There has always been an environmental component hidden within the meaning of the state system's ideology of security – a shadow ecological etymology tainted by the bias which has contributed to the degradation of the global commons. As Simon Dalby (1990) has observed, the military understanding of security is one of force and imposed solutions, power and surveillance. Conventional security discourse is trapped within the metaphysics of Western philosophy and the will to dominate and control. Dalby believes that international ecological security will not be feasible without dramatic changes in how industrial structures are organized and economic activities understood.

As Dalby has argued, the dynamics of the state system ideology of security and the dynamics which have given rise to the ecological crises have common origins. The military understanding of security is one of force and imposed solutions, power and surveillance ... in the faithful service of the West's 'romance of decisive mastery'. (Smith 1988: 46). The metaphysics of domination is linked in environmentalist discourse to the domination of nature. Technology and industry exploit nature and remake it according to their demands. Ecology, adds Dalby, is reduced to matters of natural resources management, the administration of nature by a technologically sophisticated state system.

The shared origins of military based notions of modern security and attitudes to nature are also explored by Paul Virilio in his *Popular Defense and Ecological Struggles* (1986). He observes that the elimination of chanceand contingency has been a central preoccupation of military strategists 'from the beginning'. When the possibility of pastoral flight disappeared with the advent of agricultural settlement and the accumulation of non-transportable goods, it was no longer sufficient to know and use one's surroundings to gain the upper hand in conflict. One had also to begin educating the surroundings, 'whence the construction, around the hillock, of protected enclaves, enclosures, and fences intended to slow the aggressor down' (1986: 15). Chance remained the major drawback so the progress of military strategy led to an increasingly geometric preparation of the theatre of war and its infrastructures, on which the operations' speed and scope would depend. As the ability to conduct war became central to the history of European states its conductibility became the trial of the scientific theory of History,[5] the technical limits of the enterprise's progress, its energy and uncertainty factors. The exercise of power by the state – the state system representing the modern geometric preparation of the theatre of war and its infrastructures – is a 'permanent conspiracy', according to Virilio. It marks the stage in the history of civilization/militarization[6] where the fragmentary and unsophisticated production of war passed over to its technological, industrial and scientific development. He sums up the historical effort of the West as the distribution and management of independent, increasingly numerous human groups by the state war enterprise.

For the Western state survival, according to Virilio, depends entirely on the growth of 'pure power' (Sun-Tzu), the capacity to force submission without the need for combat. And in this reading of European history Virilio discovers in the military demands for the 'suppression or replacement of the human factor in the machine's overall workings' (the elimination of chance/absolute security) the true origin of the whole mythology of comfort, 'of a whole "technical sensibility" which claims to do away with effort, born of the necessity to transgress the limits of human energy' (1990: 28-29). This transgression – spurred by the 'Army-State's search for pure power'

---

[5] And the more scientific a history, the more oppressive it tends to be in the experimental laboratory called the third world for it is this idea which has allowed the idea of social intervention to be cannibalized by the ideal of social engineering at the peripheries of the world (Nandy 1992).

[6] William Irwin Thompson (1987) has described President Ronald Reagan's SDI initiative as the open consummation of a process that began in the urban revolution of ancient Sumeria. 'Civilization', he suggests, is a misnomer for this transformation; the word should be 'militarization' because walls and standing armies are the novel institutions that arose in the shift from neolithic village to literate city.

– would later inform the entire ethic of the industrial world. He cites the 'latter-day metaphysician', Marcuse who summarizes the celebration of this transgression/transcendence with the words: 'This economy, adapted as it is to military needs, furthers man's mastery over Nature' (1990: 30-31). For Latouche (1993) the double law of 'maximine' that is, maximum results and enjoyment, minimum costs and effort in attaining them, is none other than the law of progress: the perfecting of all nature, in all its domains, is continuous and cumulative, an infinite and indefinite march. The social contract on which the nation-state is founded is a voluntary association of individuals which, drawing on the law of maximine, ensures maximum rights (peace, security, civil rights) to the parties involved while minimizing their obligations (fiscal, juridical). In this way the state facilitates and expresses modernity's project of constructing a society on the basis of utilitarian reason. For this reason modern political, economic and military organizations break with tradition in every way and can perpetuate themselves by producing a series of 'social traps' in which individual short-term interests (for example economic security) with negative effects for the larger group or distant populations, and 'temporal traps' in which individual short- and long-term interests conflict. Studies in American nuclear weapons factory towns have suggested that the tolerance for associated risks seems to increase with the degree of dependency (Summers 1990). In the words of B.F.Skinner, 'Where thousands of millions of people in other parts of the world cannot do many of the things they want to, hundreds of millions in the West do not want to do many of the things they can do. In winning the struggle for freedom and the pursuit of happiness, the West has lost its inclination to act' (Skinner 1986).

Virilio reflects on the Western celebration of human mastery over Nature – linked to the accomplishment of military technology – and concludes that 'the enemy is not only on the Eastern or Western front; it is in us and among us. It is our own nature exchanging with all of Nature. "Everything being exchanged for fire, and fire for everything; the same as merchandise for gold and gold for all kinds of merchandise" ' (Glucksmann)' (1990: 30). War, he observes, has completely absorbed its dialectic (defence and attack) in an absolute defense which is simultaneously the administration of an absolute attack. This 'two-in-one' development was realized by the doctrine of nuclear deterrence, along with the metaphysical thrust to 'get out of Nature' which, Virilio believes, was always the foundation of colonial strategy which hitched the degree of 'civilization' to the degree of military aptitude:

> 'The 'civilized' countries, in short, are those which, facing the multiplicity and unpredictability of violent attacks, mutually agreed to band together against risk ... from the sixteenth century on in Europe, when historical idealism is reborn, a new colonial adventure begins. Differences are drawn between those populations capable of providing war with the infrastructures of its conductivity; and the subjected, underdeveloped others, chosen for their inaptitude at maintaining this level of violent exchange. Placed 'outside the laws of war', they are considered all the more inapt at every other form of exchange (economic,

cultural, political etc.)'[7] (Virilio 1990: 32)

The limit of historical analysis, then, is the state, final and ideal because it is autonomous; while the *cosmopolis* is that which appropriates and consumes. Lester Ruiz (1988) has recalled that the modern individual born in the minds of Descartes, Hobbes and the rest, was never an innocent 'I'. The European 'I' was from the beginning an 'I conquer'. The emergence of the autonomous and heroic liberal bourgeois political subject led to a deformation of community into contractual relationships. It was accompanied by the triumph of instrumental rationality, modern science, and the domination of nature. For Ruiz the liberal tradition institutionalized this 'possessive individual' where self-interest is the constitutive foundation of political life and politics the 'war of each against all'. Ruiz continues:

> 'When this was coupled with the "fear of death" and "desire for glory", instead of justice as the impelling dunamis of human life, the result was the political theory and practice of the authoritarian state. Institutionalizing the primacy of order, centralism, and positive law – as mechanisms of "order" – was the only way, so the logic of liberalism proclaimed, to prevent anarchy, defend absolute state sovereignty, and assure the continuance of life. Democracy, participation, and solidarity, understood in their global dimensions, were subsumed under this modernist and statist paradigm.' (1988: 159)

The important insight poststructuralists bring to our understanding of domination is its predisposition to logocentricity, the tendency to regard all thought, feeling and action as grounded in some fundamental identity, principle of interpretation or necessary thinking substance which is itself regarded as unproblematic and ahistorical (Ruiz 1988) or, in Roland Barthes' language, rendered natural by a process of mythologizing. This logocentric disposition is manifest in the modernist practices which privilege the state as the primary locus of politics, insist on the subordination of women to men, reject ecological and spiritual insight in the name of economic rationality, and privilege instrumental and technological rationality over the gentler passions of life. Richard Ashley explains that the critical dimension of logocentricity is the projection of an appearance that the principle of interpretation and practice is conceived as existing in itself, as a foundation or origin of history's making, not a contingent effect of political practice within history. The rituals of power surrounding and maintaining the state system are bound up with those modernist practices, including

---

[7] The West's encounter with and construction of the 'inaptitudes' or needs of the 'other' is the history of progress and development. Illich (1981) has shown how the view of the alien as burden has been constitutive for Western society ... without the adopted universal mission to the world outside, inherited from the Christian church of late antiquity, what we call the West would not have come about. From the un-baptized pagan through to the un-colonized native of the colony, the series of constructed identities of the 'other' justified new forms of incorporation (from colonialism to development). And each time the West put a new mask on the alien, the old was discarded and recognized as a caricature of an abandoned self-image.

science and development, associated with 'the ideologies of progress, normality and hyper-masculinity' and growth. Each is but a means of giving legitimacy to ancient forces of greed and violence (Nandy 1983: x). Nandy has demonstrated how the modernist project – resting on the assumption that there exists a legitimate centre or a unique and superior position from which to establish control and determine hierarchies established around a set of polarities including the modern/primitive, secular/nonsecular, scientific/unscientific, expert/layman, and the vanguard/led.

Geneology of Security

When the post-structuralist, James Der Derrian, (1992) attempted a brief critical evaluation of the modernist practice of security he discovered a history of contradiction, denial and a 'talismanic sign ... that seeks to provide what the property of security cannot'. At the heart of the 'onto-theology' of the security concept in the states system ideology is a paradox. Conventional meanings refer to a condition of being protected, free from danger, and safety in the great power diplomacy of the modern states system. Alongside this understanding there has been another connotation. This alternative view or meaning understood security as a condition of false or misplaced confidence in one's position. Der Derrian writes:

> 'Clearly the unproblematical essence that is often attached to the term [security] today does not stand up to even a cursory investigation. From its origins "security" has had contested meanings, indeed, even contradictory ones.' (1992: 74-75)

Der Derrian discerns an interesting and revealing tension of definition inherent in the elusiveness of the phenomenon the term 'security' seeks to describe. At a discursive level security reveals both an aspiration for an impossible invulnerability and an acknowledgement of *hubris* and misplaced confidence. The paradox is to be found in the revelation that in security humans find insecurity, 'originating in the contingency of life and the certainty of mortality, the history of security reads as a denial, a resentment, and finally a transcendence of this paradox' (1992: 75) in an understanding of security as surety or pledge in the face of danger. For Der Derrian the history of security is one of individuals seeking an impossible security from the most radical 'other' of life, the terror of death, which, once generalized and nationalized, triggers a futile cycle of collective identities seeking security from alien others – who are seeking similarly impossible guarantees.

Der Derrian's exploration recalls the eco-feminist (Pietila 1988, Radford Ruether 1983) discernment of a schizophrenia at the heart of patriarchal dualism's construction of human identity. The implication that maleness should be associated with the domination of the body, nature and women developed, in its extreme form, into a flight from the body, nature and woman. Male consciousness focused its energy primarily on a world-fleeing agenda for centuries, adopting ascetics and hermits as heroes by virtue of their attempts to rid themselves of the flesh, and sever the connections between mind and body. Radford Ruether has described how this kind of thinking led to a total overturn of the facts of life when it was connected with the fear of mortality as an obsession of Late-Antiquity. She has parallelled the techno-scientific progress-belief with the theological body-mind dualism, because they both aim to transcend the man (male) above nature and the material. At the heart of this belief-system is a denial of mortality and a desire to escape the necessity of the coming-to-be-and-passing-away cycles of nature.

In her recent contribution to the ecofeminist literature (1993) Val Plumwood shows how the Western model of human/nature relations has the properties of dualism resulting from denied dependency on a subordinated other(nature, woman). By tracing the origins of these relations to Platonic thought she links the subordination of nature to a failure to integrate death into a life-affirming system of thought in the West. She explains:

> 'The key exclusions and denials of dependency for dominant conceptions of reason in western culture include not only the feminine and nature, but all those human orders treated as nature and subject to denied dependency. Thus it is the identity of the master (rather than a masculine identity pure and simple) defined by these multiple exclusions which lies at the heart of Western culture. This identity is expressed most strongly in the dominant conception of reason, and gives rise to a dualised structure of otherness and negation ...' (Plumwood 1993: 42)

Plumwood goes on to suggest that dualism can also be seen as an alienated form of differentiation, in which power construes and constructs difference in terms of an inferior and alien realm. In systematized forms of power, power is normally institutionalized and 'naturalized' by latching on to existing forms of difference. This would appear to be the case with the ideology of the nation-state system, with its built-in dualisms of citizen/alien, internal order/external anarchy etc. As Plumwood adds: 'Dualisms are not just free-floating systems of ideas; they are closely associated with domination and accumulation, and are their major cultural expressions and justifications.' (Plumwood 1993: 42) The interrelated and mutually reinforcing dualisms which permeate Western culture form a fault-line which runs through its entire conceptual system.

Plumwood sets out the key elements in the dualistic structure in western thought in the table on the next page in terms of sets of contrasting pairs. These dualisms, which form a system or interlocking structure, are the key ones for Western thought reflecting the major forms of oppression in that culture: 'In particular the dualisms of male/female, mental/manual (mind/body), civilized/primitive, human/nature correspond directly to and naturalize gender, class, race and nature oppressions respectively ...' (Plumwood 1993: 43). While dualisms such as reason/nature are ancient, others like human/nature and subject/object are associated with modern, post-enlightenment consciousness. Old oppressions stored as dualisms facilitate and break the path for new ones and, since they are formed by power and correspond to stages of accumulation, any account of their development would also be an account of the development of institutionalized power, of which the formation of the state is but one late moment in the story.

culture	:	nature	mind, spirit	:	nature
reason	:	nature	freedom	:	necessity (nature)
male	:	female	universal	:	particular
mind	:	body (nature)	human	:	nature (non-human)
master	:	slave	civilized	:	primitive (nature)
reason	:	matter (physicality)	production	:	reproduction (")
rationality	:	animality (nature)	public	:	private
reason	:	emotion (nature)	subject	:	object

self   :   other

A dualism is more than a relation of dichotomy, difference or non-identity, and more than a simple hierarchical relation. In dualistic construction the qualities, the culture, the values and the areas of life associated with the dualised other are systematically and pervasively constructed and depicted as inferior. Once this process of domination forms culture and constructs identity, the inferiorised group must internalize this inferiorisation in its identity and collude in this low valuation, honouring the values of the centre, which form the dominant social values. Colonization creates the colonized and the colonizer (Memmi 1965: 91). A dualism, then, is an intense, established and developed cultural expression of such a hierarchical relationship, constructing central cultural concepts and identities so as to make equality and mutuality literally unthinkable (Plumwood 1993: 47). It is a relation of separation and domination inscribed and naturalized in culture and characterized by radical exclusion, distancing and opposition between orders constructed as systematically higher and lower, closed to change. The subsequent processes include:

> Backgrounding (denial);
> Radical Exclusion (hyperseparation);
> Incorporation (relational definition);
> Instrumentalism (objectification);
> Homogenization or stereotyping.

It is the denials and backgrounding dynamics of dualism in Western culture which return us to the theme raised by the present exploration of the genealogy of security – the denial of death or mortality associated with the flight from nature.

philosophy of death

For Plumwood the denials inherent in dualism have defined the meaning of the human/nature relationship in the Western tradition. The environment, for example, has been instrumentalised and rendered the status of background noise to 'civilized' human life. She adds: 'Nature in most of its senses and contrasts is subject to radical exclusion, and is conceptually constituted by it, as well as by the other features of dualism' (Plumwood 1993: 70). This radical exclusion is exhibited in the accounts of the mind/body and reason/nature associated with the Platonic, Aristotelian, Christian rationalist and Cartesian rationalist traditions. Plumwood continues:

> 'The polarizing effect of radical exclusion facilitates the conclusion that there are two quite different sorts of substances or orders of being in the world; for example, mind and body, humans and nature. There is a total break or discontinuity between humans and nature, such that humans are completely different from everything else in nature.' (Plumwood 1993: 70)

Plumwood finds in the Platonic world-view an important source of the reason/nature dualism. It is her reading of the 'Timaeus' in which Plato deals explicitly with nature which convinces Plumwood of the importance of Platonic thought ... providing 'the first developed and enduring statement in western history of the otherworldly principles which have dominated so much of the history of western thought' (1993: 89). Plato offers an immensely influential account of human identity, the significance of death and the relation of the soul to the body ... a philosophy of death. His views on the nature of the human self and human identity and virtue are found to illustrate many features of dualism, notably radical exclusion and hyperseparation between the real self and the body, the senses and emotions. The soul is aligned with the immaterial and divine order and the body with the inferior order of nature. In a key passage she explains her reading of Plato's interpretation of the divided self:

> 'Plato's account structures this self dynamically not only in terms which create inevitable conflict, but as a hierarchy of reason over nature, and one which reproduces in the interior sphere of the self the relations of hierarchy and domination which his theory presupposes and supports in the exterior political sphere. A harmony within the self is the Platonic objective for the just and ethical life, but because of the necessarily irresoluble character of the conflict as a denied relationship of dependency, it is one which can only ever be achieved temporarily and only then through the internal analogues of conquest and colonization, namely repression and denial. The right relation between the elements, or health, is defined in terms of colonization, control and subordination of this element – nature within – by reason and its allies within the self (*Republic*, 444D). In the same way, the right order in the universe is the colonization of the world of material nature by logos, as represented in the "world-soul".' (Plumwood 1993: 91)

Foreshadowing Descartes, Plato's early dialogues deny dependency on the body which is dismissed as useless in the attainment of wisdom and knowledge. This gives rise to what Plumwood describes as an 'ape/angel' dualism in which human continuity with the animal and earthly order is denied, and the 'lower appetites which clog and thwart the soul are no part of man at all. She believes that the environmental implications of the doctrine of 'man as a celestial and not a terrestrial plant' are profound ... as it has provided a doctrine and account of the meaning and real location of human life as beyond the earth:

> 'Here is the definitive account of the otherworldly identity, the basis of the millennial "existential homelessness" in which the earth is not a home to be cherished but a trial, a place of temporary passage and little significance compared with the world beyond.' (Plumwood 1993: 92)

The account of human nature also defines a human *telos*, a task to rise above and distance oneself from both nature within and nature without while here on earth. The greatest distance is attained with death, the goal of the philosopher because it is the final and most complete attainment of the goals of separation and denial of dependency. While faith in the forthcoming attractions of life after death has diminished in the modern world the 'distanced' identity remains and is expressed today in the instrumentalisation of the world and an attitude to the sphere of animality and nature without and within which is one of control and domination.

For Plato the journey out of the Cave is the 'great task' of separation, the oedipal journey of the establishment of masculinity; the journey to the vision of *logos*, to true selfhood which leaves 'nature within' behind. It is a reaching out to the sphere of the eternal, unchanging forms, assuring 'freedom from the cave, the womb, the unending cycle of birth and death, the realm of necessity and of women (mother)' (Flax 1983). Plumwood continues:

> 'What is to be left behind in the journey up from and out of the Cave is both the feminine and those aspects of nature associated with it – materiality, the body, the senses, "primitive" stages of human and individual existence. The image of escape from the Cave unifies in a single brilliant metaphor these multiple exclusions, the transcendence (in the sense both of inferiorisation and of denial of dependency) of all these aspects of nature as the primary matrix of being, of the woman and the mother, of the body and the senses, of the whole lower order of physicality and changeability, and finally of the earth itself.' (Plumwood 1993: 93)

Plumwood argues that Western consciousness retains the elements of identity 'outside' nature and largely continues to treat the connection, the dependency on nature, in terms of denial and often with a strong element of vengeance. Plato's explicit instrumentalism laid the foundations for the life-denying tradition of contempt for the earth for 'worldly' affairs which flourished in the Christian tradition. Fallen nature is redeemed first by the *logos* as God, and later by science as god. Colonized nature is 'good', uncolonized nature is 'bad'.

For Plato philosophy centred on the study of death. His hostility to life, expressed in his establishment of an other-worldly identity beyond the earth which is the real source of meaning, is linked in part to the influence of war, militarism and the values of militarism on Plato's thought. His life as master, his ability to lead a life above slavish necessity, depended on war. War became a central organizing principle in his thinking and is closely associated with reason. Plumwood asserts that the City of Reason is structured so as to maximize two inseparable variables – reason and the ability to wage war. In his ideal society, for example, war is viewed as essential. The educational and other arrangements in the *Republic* are designed to facilitate war and the development of the warrior, as well as to serve intellectual goals. The *Republic* consequently advocates praising death and forbidding any representations of it as a tragedy. The Platonic system, argues Plumwood, involves the systematic valorization of death over life. Plato's great accomplishment and the key to the enormous influence of his system was the creation of an intellectual framework for an otherworldly identity which claimed to cancel death. His achievement answered the demands of a number of cultural forces and social groups in Plato's period and later, most obviously those of the warrior. Citing Nancy Hartsock (1985) Plumwood continues:

> '... many of the features of Plato's treatment of the lower order of nature can be seen to flow from the choices of the warrior-hero in a system which confers honour and status in terms of preparedness to risk life in combat. The choice of the warrior-hero is the choice of the spirit, honour and reputation over life, of culture over nature. In the win-lose game of the warrior-hero (Hartsock 1985: 177) those who survive defeat lose both freedom and honour. Such men now deserve their fate as part of the lower order of nature (necessity) as slaves. The warrior in risking death demonstrates his control over and disregard for the body and the emotions, and scorn for mere self-preservation and life.' (1993 98-99)

The warrior-hero experiences nature in the form of death as a hostile force severing continuity, and he experiences culture and 'reputation' as a positive force which provides a form of continuity. In a central explanatory passage Plumwood adds:

> 'The situation of the warrior-hero leads to a demand for a system of thought which provides a way to cancel death and provide continuity, but which does so in a way which is consonant with the rest of the political context of the warrior-hero's life. The Platonic otherworldly identity is a solution to this problem. It provides a strong form of continuity and a locus of meaning in a way which is consistent with the need to promote death over life, to promote control by an élite identified with the logos and devaluation of the lower social orders as lacking logos, and to model the whole in terms of the social relations of the master to inferior orders. Hence the other-worldly identity is not only the choice which comforts the slave (as Nietzsche assumed) but also the choice of the master, the outcome of the system of domination which sustains both identities. This structures the broad outlines of the Platonic system of the primacy of logos, as the

value system not only of the warrior-hero but of what the successful warrior is in interludes of peace, the master of slaves and
women, the citizen who relegates to others the work of necessity,
but who is able to participate in the "free" government of the
polis and to develop his intellectual skills as weapons in friendly
contests of reason with fellow masters and citizens.' (Plumwood
1993: 99)

The modern escape from the other-worldly identity is not yet complete.
Modernity may have dispensed with the other world as the basis for human
identity but the disconnection, opposition, itself has become the basis of
human identity. Human identity has not yet been relocated or reconciled
with Plato's opposing, excluded order of living things and of the earth.
Different solutions to the problem of identity are on offer from science,
progress, technological conquest, and economics, each usually as hostile to
the natural world as the old identity based in denial of human connectedness
to nature. Plumwood concludes:

'Modernity, despite its pride in throwing off the illusions of
the past, has not provided an earthian identity which gives a
life-affirming account of death, or comes to terms with death
as part of the human condition and with the denials and exclusions inherited from the otherworldly tradition ... Death in the
modern western context thus has the overall meaning of alienation, of separation of the individual from any larger order of
significance. Death is a nothing, a void, a terrifying and sinister
terminus, whose only meaning is that there is no meaning. The
meaninglessness of death in modern western culture has much
to do with the meaninglessness of life.' (Plumwood 1993: 102)

The feminist economist, Hazel Henderson, has argued that industrial *machi-
somo* or the need to compete and the fearful need to control, dominate and
appropriate are rooted in the same fear of death and a sense of alienation
from the natural world. Radford Reuther concludes that these drives lead
to the suppression of Nature and those associated with it that is, women.
Paradoxically the fear of death also transforms itself into an ideology which
unavoidably leads to destruction and death. This theme is also explored
by the psychiatrist Robert J.Lifton (1983) who has written that 'central
to the historical process ... is the continuous change of imagery related
to immortality' (1983: 285). History, he insists, must be approached with
a sense of man's eternally inadequate, yet impressively imaginative efforts
to absorb the idea of death and create lasting images of the continuity of
life. Much of human history can be understood – to some degree – as a
struggle to achieve, maintain, and reaffirm a collective sense of immortality
under constantly changing psychic and material conditions. Some of these
historical struggles with death imagery have contributed to expressions of
physical and spiritual destruction resulting from break-downs in man's sense
of symbolic unity and impairment of his sense of immortality. A four-step
sequence has been observed in the process: from dislocation to totalism
to victimization to violence. In a passage which suggests that echoes and

influences from this death-defying aspiration have filtered through to the construction of the (nation) state system ideology, Lifton suggests that the stage of victimization might be explained by the dependence of the collective relationship to immortality upon its collective denial of immortality to others:

> 'Mircia Eliade, for instance, stresses the distinction made in early cultures between what he calls the "sacred space" of their inhabited territory and the "unknown and indeterminant space" surrounding it. There is "our world, the cosmos" and the "other world", a foreign, chaotic space, peopled by ghosts, demons, [and] "foreigners". In the virtually universal process of what Eliade calls "making the world sacred" , there tends to develop a spatial polarization between "life area" and "death area", between those who were within or beyond the pale. We would associate this sacralization of space with early expressions of biological and religious symbolizations of immortality; and its regular accompaniment by a designated and peopled "death space.' (1983: 304)

Modernity has certainly enjoyed notable success in the project of 'putting death to death' according to Latouche (1993). Underpinning the 'myth of the grand society' and modernity, he believes, is the elevation of life as a supreme value. Through all its vicissitudes and despite its rough edges, the West has managed to make life – in the sense of biological survival – (or in the sense of an immune system, in the words of Ivan Illich) – into a universal value. The programmes has had some success on three fronts that is, the eradication of miserable death, violent death and natural death – the latter counting as the most striking achievement as evidenced by the number of people on the planet by virtue of modern medicine and hygiene. Latouche observes that the utilitarian programme has succeeded remarkably well in the goal of producing the greatest number – its second goal. If life is the greatest of goods then utilitarianism has fully succeeded, if happiness is located in abundance. The 'fetishisation of health care demonstrates well this obsession with hunting down death everywhere and at any price' he adds. Hence an important dimension of the threat posed by Aids as Marc Auge has commented:

> 'We have shown up to now a sort of vanity from the fact that we have mastered (or pretend to have mastered) all of the epidemic or endemic diseases. It is indeed on the basis of this capability that the West has brought its civilizing message to the peoples it colonized. Consequently, the inability to master a sudden assault by death would have a very great significance for Western civilization, since if we were no longer capable of stopping death, the very kernel of our power would be placed in doubt, and our whole secure universe (shored up by vaccinations, the prolongation of lifespan etc) would be at risk of collapse.' (*Le Monde*, 1988)

Frederique Apffel Marglin (1990) has questioned 'the entire project of modernization' as development in an exploration of the history and politics of the eradication of smallpox in India. Drawing on Derrida's deconstructive method and the binary oppositions which structure the dominating Western knowledge systems that is, logocentrism or phallogocentrism, she explores the discursive and subsequent practical consequences of the West's health/disease binary opposition (and the associated life/death opposition), comparing it to the non-logocentric view of disease inherent in some local knowledge systems in India. Apffel Marglin argues that the logocentric view leads to a logic of eradication because it is understood that there is a single necessary and sufficient cause for each disease. This is the view in certain strands of biomedicine. In medical ecology, however, which is closer to the Indian approach, there is a recognition that no clear boundary between health and disease, no exclusive dichotomy exists. In the non-logocentric view disease is a process of interaction and adaption between host and environment. The health/illness binary opposition parallels a life/death opposition ... the logic of the logocentric position on disease makes death the enemy to be destroyed. It is this view of death as an absolute negative which, Lifton (1983) holds, can lead to a displacement of fear, pain, and anger.

Observing an Indian ritual she observes that the individual is not viewed – as in the modern West – as pitted against nature in an effort to conquer and dominate it, nor in opposition to society. In this system of thought, the person's very being is understood to derive from his or her integration into nature, society and the cosmos. The relations between agriculture, body and polity are viewed as continuous. Healing and politics form two aspects of the one discourse or system of knowledge and practice. This cultural construction demands and sustains a social and political order in which everyone is interdependent, and each function is necessary to maintain the chain of life. She describes the order as an 'ecological-social-political system' (1990: 137). The pyramidal hierarchy of rational modern bureaucratic political systems, in contrast to the non-logocentric structure observed in India, maintains and legitimizes a chain of authority which is unidirectional from the top to bottom. Apffel Margin argues that the ethos in such modern arrangements is not ecological, the intent not regeneration. Rather it is one of control and domination – of nature, of disease, and of people. She concludes that development understood as greater control by man of his environment rests on a logocentric mode of thought. It is a definition of development embedded in an opposition between man and culture on the one hand, and between man and the environment on the other.

Simon Dalby (1992) echoes and contextualizes these observations on the dysfunctional logocentric discourse of state systems security:

> 'A politics and the related technology, that asserts ever greater power over things, tends to undermine the basis of that power by generating indirect responses, usually in terms of single states attempting to maximize security by increasing power, and so triggering arms race phenomena – the so called security dilemma phenomenon. A similar dynamic works in ecological

matters.

This suggests that the masculine and Western metaphysical understandings of power in terms of domination of nature, which environmental discourse criticizes, and control over territorial states, which anti-geopolitical thinking challenges, are not the appropriate ones for rethinking security. Much more needed are approaches that focus on caring and co-operation, recognition of mutual vulnerabilities, and the necessity to forge consensus and agreement in the face of mutual insecurity' (Dalby 1992; 118).

Modernity: The Globalisation of Risk and Security

Two events in 1992 bring together the themes of ecology and colonialism. They were the United Nations Conference on Environment and Development at Rio de Janeiro (UNCED) and the commemoration of the five hundredth anniversary of Christobal Colon's landing off the shores of the Bahamas – the 'Columbian Encounter'. The 'Earth Summit' attested to our recognition that people have transformed and continue to transform the earth with serious implications for the physical well-being of the planet and its inhabitants. The scale and pace of environmental change associated with the so called Columbian encounter foreshadowed similar transformations associated with the colonization of other countries by Europeans during the sixteenth and seventeenth centuries and with the further escalation of human impacts following the Industrial Revolution. As Rifkin has put it:

> 'The transition to the nation-state took place over five hundred years, the path of development paralleling the worldwide enclosure of the global commons ... Nature was enclosed and commodified and native people subdued and colonized. The great merchant trading companies also brought the Enlightenment worldview with them wherever they established a beachhead and regime ... Efficiency and material progress became the secular watchwords of the age.' (Rifkin 1991: 95-100)

The year 1492 can be viewed as a watermark for both the beginning of the global change which UNCED. addressed and the emergence of the modern world. Modernization and global environmental degradation have historically coincided (Saurin 1993).

Anthony Giddens (1990) has identified the nation-state system as one of the four dimensions of the globalization process which has accompanied the rise of modernity. The others are the world capitalist economy, the world military order, and the international division of labour. Other important institutions are industrialism, the unprecedented surveillance capacities deployed by nation-states to develop coordinated control over delimited territories, and the state's privileged control of the means of violence, enhanced by the sophisticated industrialization of war. Thomas Hobbes, according to Visvanathan (1988) must be counted along with Francis Bacon and Rene

Descartes as a major figure in the genealogy of modern science, with his conception of a society based on the scientific method. For Hobbes modernity demanded a movement from the 'state of nature' to civil society, a rational society constructed so that the sovereign or the state has the monopoly of terror and of man-made instruments of death:

> 'Modernity as society is inaugurated not merely through a contract; but as a theorem, a Euclidian list of propositions which makes society possible. Science, thus, colonizes society at the very moment of inauguration, by conceptualizing it and by policing it. Both the scientist and the sovereign are prior to the Hobbesian polis. Society is based on the violence of the sovereign, but repeated violence makes society uneconomical. To the fear of death is added the structure of quietude, of monolithic order, and that is the role of science. The state as the source of ultimate power does not antedate science; it is coterminal with science ... The violence of modernity arises not merely from the violence of the state, but from the violence of science seeking to impose its order on society. In fact, through a strange twist, the modern state exists more and more as a big machine guaranteeing the production and reproduction of science. In fact it is the grammar of science that provides for the everyday fascism of modernity-as-technocracy.' (Visvanathan 1988: 260-261)

Similarly the Czech philosopher, Vaclav Belohradsky (Havel 1991), has written that the rationalistic spirit of modern science, founded on abstract reason and on the presumption of impersonal objectivity, has, beside its father in the natural sciences, Galileo, also a father in politics – Machiavelli 'who first formulated, albeit with an undertone of malicious irony, a theory of politics as a rational technology of power' (Havel 1991: 6). Václav Havel concludes that 'for all the complex historical contours, the origin of the modern state and of modern political power may be sought precisely here, that is, once again in a moment when human reason begins to 'free' itself from the human being as such, from his personal experience, personal conscience and personal responsibility and so also from that to which, within the framework of the natural world, all responsibility is uniquely related, his absolute horizon' (Havel 1991: 6). The European West provided and frequently forced on the world all that has become the basis of a depersonalized power, governing human conscience and speech: natural science, rationalism, scientism, the industrial revolution, and also revolution as such, as a fanatical abstraction. Visvanathan argues that the contemporary rituals of the laboratory state are most evident in the development project. There are four features:

    1. The Hobbesian project which provides the conception of society based on scientific method.
    2. The imperatives of progress which legitimize the use of social engineering on all those objects defined as backward or retarded.

3. The vivisectional mandate, where the other becomes the object of experimentation which in essence is violence and in which pain is inflicted in the name of science.

4. The idea of triage, combining the concepts of rational experiment, the concept of obsolescence, and of vivisection – whereby a society, a subculture or a species is labelled as obsolete and condemned to death because rational judgement has deemed it incurable. (Visvanathan 1988: 259)

Since the Second World War development and science have joined national security as reasons of state (Nandy 1988: 1). For Visvanathan, therefore, the modern environmental movements are responding to the totalitarian structure of the development project, recognizing that its agent – the modern state has become a prime anti-ecological force. Modernization and global environmental degradation have historically coincided (Saurin 1993). As one of the institutions and instruments of modernity the state is embedded within particular modes of knowledge associated with globalized modernity which displace, marginalise and destroy other knowledge systems.[8] From its ordinary and standard practices large scale and systematic environmental degradation occurs as a result of the mundane operation of a bureaucratized and highly rationalized order (Saurin 1993). Julian Saurin has recently argued:

'It is in the question of administrative form and organizational order, (and the type of knowledge generated therein) that modernity and environmental degradation are most closely bound, alongside what Anthony Giddens terms time-space distanciation and disembedding. Principally through technological change, industrialization and commodification, including the massive diffusion of symbolic tokens such as money, space and place and time become ruptured and distanced.' (Saurin 1993: 3-4)

The globalizing processes accomplished through the institutions of modernity have given rise to a particular sense of the 'global', as the eco-feminist, Vandana Shiva has pointed out. The 'global' in the dominant political discourse 'is the political space in which a particular dominant local seeks global control, and frees itself of local, national and international restraints. The global does not represent the universal human interest, it represents a particular local and parochial interest which has been globalized through the scope of its reach. The seven most powerful countries, the G-7, dictate global affairs, but the interests that guide them remain narrow, local and parochial' (Shiva 1993: 150) She adds:

---

[8] Ashis Nandy has written that modernity is neither the end-state of all cultures nor the final word in institutional creativity. Post-modern societies and a post-modern consciousness may choose to build not so much upon modernity as on the traditions of the non-modern or pre-modern. The flip-side of any cultural self-exploration outside the West has to be an archaeology of knowledge which excavates and fights for a lost or repressed West (Nandy 1992: XVIII).

' "Global environmental problems" have been so constructed as to conceal the fact that globalization of the local is responsible for destroying the environment which supports the subjugated local peoples. The construction becomes a political tool not only to free the dominant destructive forces operating worldwide from all responsibility but also to shift the blame and responsibility for all destruction on to the communities that have no global reach.'[9]

The construction provides cover for a series of logical reversals and denials. While the role of the globalized local in local environmental destruction worldwide is concealed, the multiple facets of destruction are treated as local causes of problems which have a global impact. False causality is applied to explain false connections, according to Shiva. Some UNCED documents, for example, attributed the explosive growth in toxic chemicals in the Third World to population growth; while the 1991 cyclone in Bangladesh was similarly linked causally to the number of babies in Bangladesh (Shiva 1993: 153). Shiva believes that the planet's security has been invoked by the rapacious institutions of the 'North' to destroy and kill the very cultures which employ a planetary consciousness to guide their concrete daily actions. The ordinary Indian woman who worships the tulsi plant and the peasant who treats seeds as sacred are employing reflexive categories which ensure that their actions are informed by an awareness of the links between the great and the small, from planets to plants and people. This kind of knowledge ensures that limits, restraints and responsibilities are always transparent and cannot be externalized. Recognition that the great exists in the small and that every act therefore has not only global but cosmic implications fosters a consciousness in which demands are made on the self, not on others. Shiva argues that the moral framework of the global reach is quite the opposite. There are no reflexive relationships.

Conclusion

Insofar as Shiva is addressing the dominant global environmental discourse she is probably correct in her observation that reflexivity leading to self-limitation has yet to find a place on the agenda. As Wolfgang Sachs (1988) has observed, it is raining reports about the state of the planet ... the curtain of silence has finally been pulled away from the global survival crisis and the evidence is undeniable – up to a point.[10] The proposed policies of resource-

---

[9] A good example of this is illustrated in Anil Agarwal & Sunita Narain's *Global Warming in an Unequal World: a Case of Environmental Colonialism* (CSE 1991). This is a document forwarded by the Delhi-based Centre for Science and Environment to the United Nations Environment and Development programmes and the US World Resources Institute, challenging their findings about the Third World's contributions to global warming emissions – source: *ifda dossier*, 81, April/June 1991, p.79.

[10] In his *Traditions, Tyranny and Utopias* (1992), Ashis Nandy points to a powerful mechanism which suggests that no easy assumptions about confronting denial in the North can be made. Nandy observes an isomorphism in the internal structures of knowledge, persons and cultures and the use of power as a modern means of denial by powerful industrialised countries.

management, however, ignore the option of intelligent self-limitation. The language of the reports continues to promote development as the West's latest cultural mission to the world. Paradoxically, however, it is the unprecedented production of risks[11], hazards and modern insecurities which has opened up the possibility of a radicalized reflexive modernity. Giddens (1990) has characterized the dynamism of modern institutions and its practices as a careering juggernaut. He describes the reflexive appropriation of knowledge as both energising and necessarily unstable. New levels of trust in an expanding environment of risk and insecurity are called for. For Ulrich Beck, another theorist of modernity, the dangerous consequences of scientific and industrial development can no longer be limited in time, as the lives of future generations are affected, and spatial consequences are equally unamenable to limitation. Beck's claim is that the 'effets pervers' of modernization can potentially be dealt with, not through the negation, but through the radicalization of such rationalization. In order for societies really to evolve modernization must become reflexive.

This process of reflexive modernization is already under way, manifest in the critique of science developing in the environmental movement and among the lay masses. These post-modern agents/dissidents are breaking free from the new culturally imposed constraints of scientism which has demanded their identification with particular social institutions and their ideologies, notably in constructions of risk. In the words of Visvanathan:

> 'This insurrection of the local knowledges which demands a return to the sacred is providing the crystal seed around which the challenge to the laboratory states of modernity has begun.' (Visvanathan 1988: 286)

Beck's work refers to a three-stage periodization of social change:

1. Pre-modernity –
2. Simple Modernity – co-extensive with industrial society
3. Reflexive Modernity – co-extensive with risk society

The axial principle of industrial society is the distribution of goods, while that of the risk society is the distribution of 'bads'. Industrial society is structured through social classes while the risk society is individualized. Industrial society survives today alongside the risk society because it is mainly industry together with science that is involved in the creation of risk. Sociologists and anthropologists have made three important observations about risk:

1. Physical risks are always created and effected in social systems, for example by the organizations and institutions which are supposed to manage and control the risky activity.

2. The magnitude of the physical risks is therefore a direct function of the quality of social relations and processes, for example, transparency, accountability, democratization.

---

[11] The concept of risk, according to Beck (1992), is directly bound to the concept of reflexive modernization. Risk may be defined as a systematic way of dealing with hazards and insecurities induced and introduced by modernization itself.

3. The primary risk is therefore that of social dependency upon institutions and actors who may well be alien, obscure and inaccessible to most people affected by the risks in question.

Echoing some of the critiques waged by environmentalists in the wake of the emergent discourse of global environmental management[12] Beck argues that the most common response by those who have been responsible for generating and managing risks has been an attempt to 'adapt procedures and self-presentation in order to secure or repair credibility, without fundamentally questioning the forms of power or social control involved' (1993: 4). Reflexivity is excluded from the social and political interactions between experts and social groups over modern risks because of the systematic assumption of realism in science. In contrast reflexive learning processes would recognize the conditions underpinning scientific conclusion[13], draw out questions of social situation, and examine these with an openness to different forms of knowledge. There would be a negotiation between different epistemologies and subcultural forms, amongst different discourses and must entail the development of the social or moral identities of the actors involved (1993: 5). Beck draws a parallel between the nineteenth century – when modernization demystified privileges of rank and religious world views – and today, as reflexive modernity launches another process of demystification directed at received understandings of science and technology in classical industrial society. Modernization within the paths of industrial society is being replaced by modernization of industrial society. An antagonism has opened up between industrial society and modernity – no longer should we seek to conceive of modernity within the categories of industrial society ... 'we are witnessing not the end but the beginning of modernity – that is, of a modernity beyond its classical industrial design' (1992: 10).

The perspective of reflexive modernity implies that the counter-modernistic protests of social movements and criticisms of science, technology and progress do not stand in contradiction of modernity but represent an expression of modernization beyond the outlines of industrial society. The new modernity is still dimly perceived because 'the classical theoreticians of industrial society or industrial capitalism ... transformed their historical experience into necessities, into hidden *a priorities*' (1992: 12),]. In the words of Cristovam Buarque, 'Economists became the proprietors of progress, but they also became prisoners of their perception of it' (1993: 39).

Beck's thesis is that whereas in classical industrial society the 'logic' of wealth production and the distribution of goods dominated the 'logic' of risk

---

[12]Matthias Finger has argued that nation-states – along with the industrial development and individualistic life-styles they promote – have become a major problem for the biosphere. He describes them as 'industrial development agencies' striving for material wealth and independence from environmental constraints. Putting nation-states in charge of the environmental crisis, as the UNCED process has done, leads only to attempts to sustain this industrial development system in an age of ecologically imposed limitations and constraints (Finger, *Eco-Currents* 1991, Volume 1, Number 4, September).

[13]Scientists' exclusive focus on laboratory bound knowledge can contain both questionable physical assumptions about a risk system and a naïve model of society (Beck 1993).

production, today this relationship is being reversed. Productive forces have lost their innocence in the reflexivity of modernization processes. The gain in power from techno-economic 'progress' is being increasingly overshadowed by the production of risks which can no longer be dismissed as 'latent side effects'. As these risks have become globalized and subject to growing public criticism and scientific investigation they achieve a central importance in social and political debates. These risks constitute irreversible threats to the life of plants, animals and human beings, dangers no longer limited to certain localities or groups but exhibiting a tendency to globalization ... 'and in this sense bring into being supra-national and non-class specific global hazards with a new type of social and political dynamism.' Environmental insecurities are taking centre stage and threaten to force a crisis of legitimation upon modern institutions, including the state, locked as they are in modernistic delusions:

> 'The promise of security grows with the risks and destruction
> and must be reaffirmed over and over again to an alert and crit-
> ical public through cosmetic or real interventions in the techno-
> economic development.' (Beck 1992: 19-20)

For Beck the key to the establishment of a modernity which might free itself from the interest in mastery in favour of 'self control' and 'self limitation', is modernity's encounter with itself. What he seeks is a pedagogy of scientific rationality which will conceive of that rationality as changeable by discussion of self-produced threats. This means transferring the substantive abilities for criticism and learning to the foundations of knowledge and the application of it. This would mean the elevation of the actually latent reflexivity of the modernization process into scientific consciousness. He continues:

> 'But where modernization encounters modernization, this
> word also changes its meaning. In the social and political appli-
> cation of modernization to itself, the interest in mastery that is
> spread in this way loses its technical grip and assumed the form
> of "self control" and 'self limitation".' (Beck 1992: 181)

The accumulation of risks and insecurities throughout the course of modernity has, belatedly perhaps, generated sufficient critical reflection both within the West and within critical social movements in the peripheries, to generate a new understanding and development of modernity itself. In the process our understanding of security rooted in the institutions of modernity – including the state system – will be subject to a critical revision along with the cultural, economic and philosophical prejudices which have given rise to and sustained them by a series of denials guaranteed by power and interest. Central to the struggle to re-define security will be Nandy's observation of an isomorphism in the internal structures of knowledge, persons, and cultures – the view that what we do to others we do not only to ourselves but also to our cognitive ventures, and that power has been and remains the 'legitimate' modern means of denying this isomorphism to ourselves while forcing it upon others. For this reason the environmental politics of international relations must place at its centre the politics of knowledge – and the violence the West has done to its cognitive ventures, its habitat, and the minds it has colonized in the name of progress and realism. This is not to deny progress but to embrace ambivalence and insecurity as intrinsic to the cognition of human/nature.

[*Editor's Note*: The bibliography was unfortunately lost in the ASCII process and when this was discovered it was too late in the very tight publication schedule to remedy it. (JS)]

Contemporary State Theory

Colin Hay
Lancaster University

'Crisis and the Discursive Unification of the State'

Abstract

If, as many recent authors have suggested, Marxist state theory is in crisis then this is largely due to the concept of crisis prevalent within Marxist state theory. The persistence of capitalist state forms in the face of their inherent contradictions and crisis tendencies has left many Marxist theorists rather perplexed and shame-faced at the failure of the crisis of capitalism, apparently always just-around the corner, to materialise. Recent Marxist scholarship has certainly attempted to come to terms with this apparent immortality of capitalism, most notably the reg- ulation approach, but this has merely given rise to a greater reluctance to predict the terminal crisis rather than a systematic attempt to understand the mechanisms linking state crisis and the structural transformation of the (capitalist) state. In recent years Marxist state theory has also been exposed to an external theoretical challenge from Foucauldian and 'post-Marxist' discourse analytical perspectives which have tended to reject the problematic of the state altogether, either viewing the 'state' as a mere discursive resource mobilised in the interlocking disciplining discourses which pervade and constitute the social (Miller & Rose 1990; Rose & Miller 1992; Rose 1993: 286, 289) or concluding, 'la société n'existe pas', 'l'état, ce n'est rien' (Zizek 1985; Rovirosa 1988; Pringle & Watson 1992; cf. Jessop 1990: 292; Abrams 1988: 77).

The relationship between the crisis and structural transformation of the state and the very nature of the state itself, thus represent crucial questions for contem- porary Marxist theory. In this article I hope to make a contribution to a particular resolution of these enduring dilemmas by proposing two related hypotheses:

> *(i) that the concept of crisis should be reconceptualised as a dis- cursively constructed moment of decisive intervention;*
> *(ii) that the state is discursively unified in crisis through the dis- cursive construction of crisis.*

In defending these claims I hope to provide something of a corrective to the subject-less conception of state crisis prevalent within existing Marxist state the- ory which sees crisis as an objective condition, a measurable dysfunctional prop- erty of a system (in this case the state). The problem with such an understanding of crisis is that it gives rise to the apparently intractable problem of distinguishing between a mere contradiction and a fully-fledged crisis – either crisis is everywhere or it is nowhere. In place of this formulation I wish to suggest a conception of crisis much more closely tied to structural transformation and based on the etymology of the term. Crisis (Κρίσις, Κρίνο – 'to decide') is not merely a moment of rupture, but also a moment of decisive intervention. If this is so, then we must consider the conditions of recognising that such a decisive intervention can, and perhaps must be made. This leads to the suggestion that crisis is a discursively constructed political narration of the lived experiences of policy failure, and that it is through crisis (as process) that the state is discursively unified in the formulation of a new state project.

The State as an Inertial System

In considering processes of structural transformation and institutional change we can readily identify two types of social, political or economic systems:

(i) dynamic, *proactive* systems which have an institutionally inscribed preference for change and evolve through processes of reflexive self-transformation;

(ii) inertial, *reactive* systems which tend to be more mono-lithic in nature with well-institutionalised operational practices and procedures and which tend to evolve through processes of response to crisis.

The state is an inertial system. As such it is inherently, and perhaps, inces-santly crisis-prone. For the structural unity inscribed upon it in previous periods of crisis and structural transformation defines a set of sedimented institutionalised state practices which prove increasingly dysfunctional and outmoded in the flux of social and economic dynamics. Periods of state restructuring enable a series of new complementarities between a national accumulation strategy and global economic dynamics. However, the in-stitutional inertia of the state that follows translates these initial assets into fetters on continued capital accumulation. For the practices, struc-tures and modes of social and economic intervention thus established prove increasingly dysfunctional in a global capitalist economy in constant flux. The structural transformation of the state is thus predominantly mediated through moments and 'narratives' of *crisis*.

By contrast, the firm in a capitalist market place is the archetypal dy-namic system. If it is to survive, it must prove itself both reflexive and capable of self-transformation to maintain competitiveness. The success-ful firm thus tends to be proactive and modernising, constantly seeking the knowledge required to re-position itself within a dynamic market. The evolution of the firm is thus predominantly the product of adaptation and reflexive self-transformation.

The inertia of the state derives, in large part from the structure of the state as an apparatus, or rather, as a series of apparatuses. For the state comprises a multitude of specific, though nonetheless interdependent, agen-cies, apparatuses and institutions. *It has, at best, only a tendential (and potential) unity.* The multitude of disaggregated decisions, operations and procedures which take place 'within the state' are only unified inasmuch as they are all enabled/constrained (albeit in different ways) by the legacy of previous attempts to impose a trajectory on the state through its transfor-mation (through the process of post-war reconstruction or the imposition of the Thatcherite state project for example). They remain un-unified in their conception and execution. Thus, the state's unity resides in the legacy of former projects of structural transformation, not in any daily practice, nor even in the interdependence or 'structural coupling' (Jessop 1990: 327-31; Luhmann 1977) of the systems which together comprise it. The internal structure of the state reflects a series of organisational disjunctia (Offe 1984: 51-7), a functional separation of tasks which defines a number of overlap-ping and interdependent policy communities. Such a system, which lacks an obvious and enduring substantive and discursive unity has no innate propensity to self-transformation.

Table 1
**The Structural Transformation
of Inertial and Dynamic Systems**

SYSTEM	INERTIAL	DYNAMIC
Predominant Mode of Operation	*reactive, conservative*	**pro***active, modernising*
Nature of System	*institutionally-fragmented, lacking clear substantive unity*	*clear substantive and structural unity*
Predominant Mode of Structural Transformation	*structural transformation through crisis*	*structural transformation through adaptation and reflexive self-transformation*
Example	*the state*	*the firm in a capitalist economy*

If this is indeed the case, and the state is an inertial system whose evolution is crisis-dependent, then it becomes crucial that we develop a theory of state crisis. Furthermore, if the inertia of the state derives in part from the difficulty of maintaining its substantive and discursive unity, then it becomes clear that we must consider the unification and evolution of the state as related, *and as related in and through crisis*. In reformulating this classic Marxist problematic, I propose a more *diachronic* and processual conception of both state crisis and state unity to that prevalent within the existing literature. In place of the *synchronic* questions 'how is the unity of the capitalist state achieved?' (Poulantzas 1968) or 'how is the tendential/contradictory unity of the capitalist state achieved?' (Poulantzas 1978, 1979), both of which assume a static and invariant degree of unity which provides the *explanandum*, I propose a different series of questions:

- → what are the conditions of any unity/unification of the state?
- → are such conditions satisfied? when? to what extent? and in what context?

Similarly, in place of the orthodox position which takes the 'objective' existence of crisis for granted, conflates contradiction and crisis, and asks, 'what is the nature of the current crisis ? – is it a crisis of overload, ungovernability, overaccumulation, etc.' I propose an alternative conception which interrogates the 'objectivity' of crisis, views crisis as a (discursive) construction and asks:

- → what are the conditions of existence of crisis?
- → how is crisis constituted and constructed? and
- → what is it about the context or moment of crisis that allows it to find purchase?

Crisis (Kpísis) as A Moment of Decisive Intervention

'Language ... provides a mechanism for rendering reality amenable to certain kinds of action.' (Miller & Rose 1990: 7)

In rejecting the dominant and purely objectivist view of crisis, which *conflates*, and in certain cases actually *equates* contradiction and crisis,[1] it is useful to return to the etymology of the term. For, etymologically, 'crisis' (Kpísis, Kpíno – 'to decide') is a moment of decisive intervention, a moment of rupture and a moment of transformation. This conception of crisis as not merely a condition of uncertainty, risk, threat and rupture but *also* as a moment of decisive intervention has become almost completely erased from the existing literature on crisis (though cf. Debray 1973; t' Hart 1993; Keane 1984: 10-13). Yet if we reconceptualise crisis in this way, a clear distinction between contradiction and crisis can be drawn. Furthermore, once we conceive of crisis as a moment in which a decisive intervention is made this immediately raises the question of *subjectivity*, the question of the political and ideological mediation of contradictions and their 'narration' as crisis.

For a conjuncture to provide the opportunity for decisive intervention it must be perceived as so doing – it must be seen as a moment in which a decisive intervention *can* (and perhaps *must*) be made. Furthermore, it must be perceived as such by agents capable of making a response (or decisive intervention) at the level at which the crisis occurs (or is perceived to exist). Thus crisis is not merely a property of a system, it is a lived experience, it is a politically mediated moment of decisive intervention and structural transformation. Moreover, it involves the active display of agency by actors or bodies that have some autonomy *at the level at which crisis exists* (or

---

[1] Poulantzas identifies this tendency in the work of the post-Leninist Communist International (Poulantzas 1976: 24-5; translated 1979: 361).

rather is identified). As a consequence, it makes no sense to speak of a crisis (as distinct from, say, a failure, catastrophe or series of contradictions) of capitalism *per se*, of Fordism, of patriarchy or of modernity since these are all 'subject-less' systems in the sense that they lack an *agency* capable of making a decisive intervention at the level at which their internal failures exist.

Crisis, then, is a *process*, a process of destruction *and* construction, an inherently dialectical moment of transformation. Crisis is *Dämmerung* – dusk and dawn (Keane 1984: 11-12).

Towards a Crisis Terminology

The return to the etymology of crisis facilitates the long overdue task of the formulation of a more precise crisis terminology, based around the distinction between *failure* (a condensation of contradictions) and *crisis* (a moment of decisive intervention).

By failure I refer to the non-reproductive properties or contradictions of a system and the dysfunctional symptoms they generate – whether perceived or not. Failure thus provides the structural preconditions for perceived crisis – the necessary but insufficient conditions for the mobilisation of perceptions of, and hence the construction of the moment of crisis as a moment of crisis.[2] By crisis I refer to *failure perceived*, and hence failure *politically*-mediated. There is no simple correspondence between crisis (and hence the response to crisis) on the one hand and the nature of the contradictions and symptoms of failure that give rise to crisis on the other hand. Failure and crisis are thus relatively autonomous of one another – a set of failures can support a multitude of conceptions (and misconceptions) of crisis.

The distinction between failure and crisis, as Benhabib demonstrates, has its origins in Marx's implicit distinction between system and lived crisis. This is taken up by the Frankfurt School and ultimately mirrored in Habermas' distinction between rationality and legitimation crisis (Habermas 1975: 46-8, 61-75). Nonetheless, as Benhabib clearly demonstrates, the relationship between failure ('system crisis') and crisis ('lived crisis') is never adequately considered. Whereas Marx conveniently overlooks the connection between system and lived crisis, Habermas merely assumes a simple

---

[2] At this point it might be protested that, in redefining crisis as decisive intervention, and failure as the accumulation of contradictions within a given social formation, I have merely displaced the problem of distinguishing between crisis and contradiction which now reappears as the problem of distinguishing between failure and contradiction. However, this is not the case. To posit material or substantive contradictions and failures as distinct from their representation and 'narration' as crisis is not to claim that we can objectively observe and describe such contradictions and failures. All social formations are contradictory, all produce failures. Yet, if we are to understand the evolution of state structures we must recognise that state projects are responses not to 'objective' contradictions and 'real' failures, but rather, to the discourses of crisis which narrate such contradictions. In drawing the distinction between (state) failure and (state) crisis, I am merely suggesting that we distinguish analytically between the contradictions narrated within a crisis discourse, and the discourse itself. An accumulation strategy which produces mass unemployment, high inflation and a decline in manufacturing output can be seen as a sign of state and economic failure whether it gives rise to the mobilisation of perceptions of crisis or not.

correspondence between a rationality deficit and a withdrawal of societal legitimation. In both cases the dualistic separation of system and social integration, system and lifeworld is reproduced. As Benhabib perceptively observes, Marxism as a social theory

> 'seems to vacillate between economistic objectivism on the one hand – emphasizing the moment of functional crisis – and culturalist or psychological perspectives of alienation on the other – corresponding to the moment of lived crisis. The theoretical problem left unresolved by Marx's analysis is the relationship between action contexts out of which lived crises emerge and objective-functional interconnections among action consequences that lead to systemic malfunctioning.' (1986: 127-8)

In developing the distinction between failure and crisis, my aim is to transcend this artificial dualism of structure and agency, subjectivity and objectivity by arguing that failure be seen as a condensation of contradictions, and crisis as a narration of failure. Crisis, then, is a *subjectively experienced, yet structurally overdetermined moment of rupture and transformation.*

This typology of contradictions and the responses they entail can be further extended by distinguishing between *crises* – which involve *intentional* decisive intervention in response to perceived failure and *'tipping points'* (cf. Block 1987: 89-91) in which *decisive* interventions are made *unintentionally* – setting into play what chaos theorists refer to as 'butterfly effects' (Gleick 1988: 23, 306; Kamminga 1990: 55-8). A tipping-point is thus a moment in which a relatively minor intervention is made which ultimately proves to be decisive (whether by unintentionally enhancing the stability of a system, or exacerbating its latent contradictions). In identifying tipping-points analytically, I make use of Miller and Rose's important observation that

> 'lasting interventions have often arisen in surprising and aleatory fashion and in relation to apparently marginal or obscure differences in social or economic existence, which for particular reasons have come to assume particular salience for a brief period.' (1990: 3)

In the evolution of the structures of the British state during the twentieth century, candidates for tipping-points include: i) the decision to go to war in 1939; ii) the decision to rearm during the Korean War; and iii) the signing of the Social Contract between the Wilson Government and the unions in 1974.

1. The decision to go to war in 1939, though clearly of monumental social and political significance at the time, had unintended and decisive implications for the subsequent evolution of the structures of the state in the post-war period (Hay 1994a; cf. Barnett 1986). Thus, with respect to the transformation of the state, the decision to go to war was a tipping-point in the sense that it was to prove a decisive intervention whose impact on the structures of the state was neither fully appreciated nor intended.

2. The decision to rearm in the wake of the outbreak of the Korean War is a more contentious example of a tipping-point. Those who argue that the

origins of Britain's post-war economic decline can be traced to the decision to rearm, when the heart of British manufacturing industry and engineering was effectively withdrawn from production, do indeed interpret this as a tipping-point (Aaronovitch 1981: 70; Boyle 1979; Smith 1981: 77). However, as Burnham has convincingly demonstrated, this thesis is somewhat exaggerated and the impact of rearmament was considerably more ambiguous (Burnham 1990: 15-76; 1993). Were the thesis correct, however, the decision to rearm would represent an archetypal example of a tipping-point.

3. The signing of the Social Contract in 1974 is another, albeit rather different, example of a tipping-point. Initiated as a means of temporarily postponing the inevitable onset of state crisis, it had the unintended effect of channelling the contradictions of the state in such a way that the crisis, when it came, would involve the withdrawal of rank-and-file union support for corporatist conciliation. This set the context in which the crisis became narrated as the crisis of an 'overextended' state 'held to ransom' by the trade unions, paving the way for the Thatcherite state project. The Social Contract thus proved an unintentional decisive intervention in the structural transformation of the British state.

Finally, we can refer to *'catastrophic equilibria'* in which the symptoms of failure are readily apparent yet no decisive intervention is made. Gramsci's notion of a catastrophic equilibrium, in which 'the old is dying yet the new cannot be born' and in which 'a great variety of morbid symptoms appear' (1971: 276) provides a particularly apt description of the current British context. This can be characterised as a period of protracted state and economic failure, yet one not (yet) conceived of in terms of a crisis of the British state. Indeed, this is a context in which the Labour Party, following the *Policy Review* of 1987, has increasingly accommodated itself to the terms of a *post*-Thatcher yet Thatcher*ite* settlement. Yet, ironically, this Thatcherite revisionism has come at a time in which the contradictions of the Thatcherite project are becoming ever more apparent. The Labour Party is thus in danger of accommodating itself to the very neo-liberal orthodoxies that have seemingly trapped the British economy in apparently permanent recession at precisely the moment when this is becoming widely acknowledged.

The above analysis, however, does suggest an alternative, based on an attempt to account for Britain's enduring economic malaise in terms of a *crisis of the state* (as deep, if not deeper than that of the mid to late 1970s) resulting from the contradictions of the Thatcherite project. If the crisis of the 1970s was constructed, and lived in Thatcherism's terms as a crisis of ungovernibility and overload, a crisis of an over-extended state, then the opportunity exists to narrate the current crisis as a crisis of an underextended, retrenched and debilitated state stripped of strategic capacities for economic intervention.

Having returned to the etymology of crisis in order to reconceptualise it as a moment of decisive intervention, and having contextualised this new concept within a broader glossary of crisis terminology, we are now in a position to consider the implications of this theoretical clarification for an understanding the tendential unity of the state.

Table 2
Contradictions and Decisive Interventions

	Moment of decisive intervention	Moment of indecisive or non-intervention
Subjectively perceived contradictions	CRISIS	'Catastrophic equilibrium'
Un-perceived contradictions	'Tipping Point'	FAILURE

Crisis and the Discursive Unification of the State

'The state does not exist as a fully constituted, internally coherent, organisationally pure, and operationally closed system but is an emergent, contradictory, hybrid and relatively open system.' (Jessop 1990: 316)

'The modern state is ... an amorphous complex of agencies with ill-defined boundaries, performing a great variety of not very distinctive functions.' (Schmitter 1985: 33)

'The state comprises a plurality of institutions (or apparatuses) and their unity, if any, far from being pregiven, must be constituted politically.' (Jessop 1982: 222)

Crisis is the moment in which the unity of the state is discursively re-achieved. During crises, and the resulting periods of strategic restructuring (as opposed to piecemeal adaptation) the state is discursively re-constructed as an object (a single object) *in crisis* and hence in need of decisive intervention and restructuring. Such restructuring effectively redefines the responsibilities and boundaries of the state, setting in place the new parameters of conjunctural politics (the day-to-day, managerial politics and political practices associated with a given institutional setting *within* the state apparatus).[3]

In times of relative stability, by contrast, political decision-making on a day-to-day basis takes place at a more micro, procedural level *within* specific

---

[3] Here I draw on Offe's distinction between the structural and the conjunctural. Structural change refers to the profound transformation of the institutions comprising the state form, conjunctural change refers to the minor 'tinkering' and piecemeal adaptation of the apparatuses of the state within the broad constraints imposed by a previous state project (Offe 1985: 223-6; Hay 1993: 3).

institutional contexts or policy communities. The routine politics within the
apparatuses seen to constitute the state, therefore, takes place not at the
level of the state as a unified system, but at the lower level of specific institutional structures and processes. Thus, the unity of the state in periods of
relative structural continuity is not obviously apparent, becoming manifest
only in as much as it imposes constraints (and conditions opportunities)
for procedural or conjunctural politics, and limits (or facilitates) processes
of adaptation to changing social, cultural and economic contexts. If the
broader structures of the state (the structural coupling of the systems and
institutions seen to comprise the state) fail to allow for the degree of institutional reflexivity, reform and operational flexibility necessary to maintain
system stability at the level of specific policy communities,[4] then a series of
contradictions and policy failures arise. In such a context we can refer to
the structures of the state as contradictory and prone to (policy) failure in
as much as they represent fetters on the adaptability of policy communities
to the broader environment within which they are located and over which
they can exercise minimum control. Such contradictions provide the structural context within which discourses of crisis may be constructed and find
resonance with the lived experiences of individuals, narrating and recruiting
such experiences as 'symptoms' of a more fundamental crisis of the state.

In periods of articulated and broadly perceived crisis, a discursive unity
is re-imposed upon the disaggregated structures and institutions of the state
which are thereby (discursively) constructed as an object to be re-regulated,
in much the same way as an economy (local, regional or national) is (discursively) constructed as an object of regulation in the formulation of an
accumulation strategy (cf. Miller & Rose 1990: 5; Mitchell 1991: 78, 90).
In both cases, a project is imposed upon the structures of an object unified
and (re-)constituted through discourse. As Rose perceptively observes, the
vocabulary of the state and political discourse more generally, is

> 'a kind of intellectual machinery or apparatus for rendering
> reality thinkable in such a way that it is amenable to political
> deliberations.' (1990: 289)

Policy failures arising within specific 'policy communities' are narrated as
collectively comprising, and as individually *symptom*-atic of, a crisis of the
state regime itself. *The state is thus discursively unified in crisis, through
the discursive construction of crisis.* This discursive unification of the state

---

[4] The distinction between social and system stability (Lockwood 1964) is in fact somewhat misleading, since what constitutes stability for a specific system or policy community is in part discursively constructed (cf. Benhabib 1986: 373-7; Mouzelis 1974: 396,
402ff.). However in this context, system stability can be said to have been exhausted
when the operational practice of a particular system (in this case policy community)
continues to produce policy outcomes that it was designed to eliminate, that is, when
policy outcomes fall outside of the legitimate expectations sanctioned by the state in a
prior restructuring. For instance, we may identify policy failure or system instability
within the post-war British structures of corporatist intermediation when the representatives of the trade unions could no longer continue to placate rank-and-file members
whilst agreeing to the terms of the increasingly harsh statutory incomes policies and
wage restraint necessarily to prevent fiscal overload elsewhere in the structures of the
state.

through crisis is a condition of its *structural* transformation, the condition of the formulation of a new state project.

This is not to say that the state is merely a discursive construct, or that it has no unity outside of discourse. For the discursive construction of crisis (which, we must remember is ultimately constrained by the 'symptoms' is must narrate) and the project of transformation thus mobilised have substantive material effects. Material practices are shaped and re-shaped; institutions are restructured, reformed, created and destroyed; and the discursive boundaries of the state and hence its perceived responsibilities are redrawn as the state itself is effectively recreated.

the discursive construction of crisis: narration

The process of narration operates through the discursive 'recruiting' of policy failures and the material lived experiences to which they give rise as symptoms of, and as bearing witness to, a broader sickness, a more virulent disease – the crisis of the state. Such policy failures and experiences arise out of the contradictory modes of operation of various policy communities under the constraints imposed by a previous state project. The discursive construction of crisis can thus be seen as a process of abstraction and narration (more accurately, meta-narration) in which the disparate effects of a great variety of independent policy failures and contradictions are brought together in a unified, and deeply politicised crisis discourse. The crisis becomes a point of 'connotive resonance' (Hall 1980b: 174) conjured up in each contradiction, each failure, each symptom. The specificity and complexity of each contradiction is thus denied as an abstracted and simplified meta-narrative, capable of accounting for every 'symptom', and capable of unambiguously attributing responsibility is offered in its place. The mobilisation of perceived crisis is thus about the formulation and triumph of a simplistic ideology which must find and construct points of resonance with the disaggregated and individuated experiences of state and economic failure. This process is described in Figure 1.

'Newsworthy' or 'crisis-worthy' statistics, contradictions and events (industrial disputes, unemployment statistics, political scandals, food shortages, etc.) are selectively sampled and encoded with specific meaning. Notions of direct responsibility are attributed ('greedy labour', 'stubborn bosses', 'incompetent government', etc.) and a narrative structure is inscribed upon, and used a mechanism for ordering, the events. This is a process of primary narration, resulting in the construction of a series of independent narratives which still reflect (albeit to varying degrees) the specificity of each 'story'. The discursive construction of crisis, however, is the product of a process of *secondary* mediation, *abstraction* and *meta*-narration. Here, the products of primary narration (the mediated events themselves) become the subject matter for a further narration. Notions of direct responsibility, causality and agency (action A leads to consequence B) are deleted, as, for instance, a strike is accounted for not in terms of the direct actions of union members, shop stewards, or managers, but in terms of the crisis of an 'overextended' state; or a juvenile crime is accounted for in terms of a breakdown of traditional morality. By importing such simplified and simplifying abstractions, a multitude of disparate events can be recruited as 'symptoms' within the discourse of crisis. The crisis diagnosis is confirmed in each new 'symptom' which can be assimilated within this meta-narrative.[5] It is this politically-mediated and ideologically-filtered construction of crisis, and not to the 'reality' of the failures and contradictions which it narrates that competing state projects must themselves address.

Figure 1
Crisis as Meta-Narrative

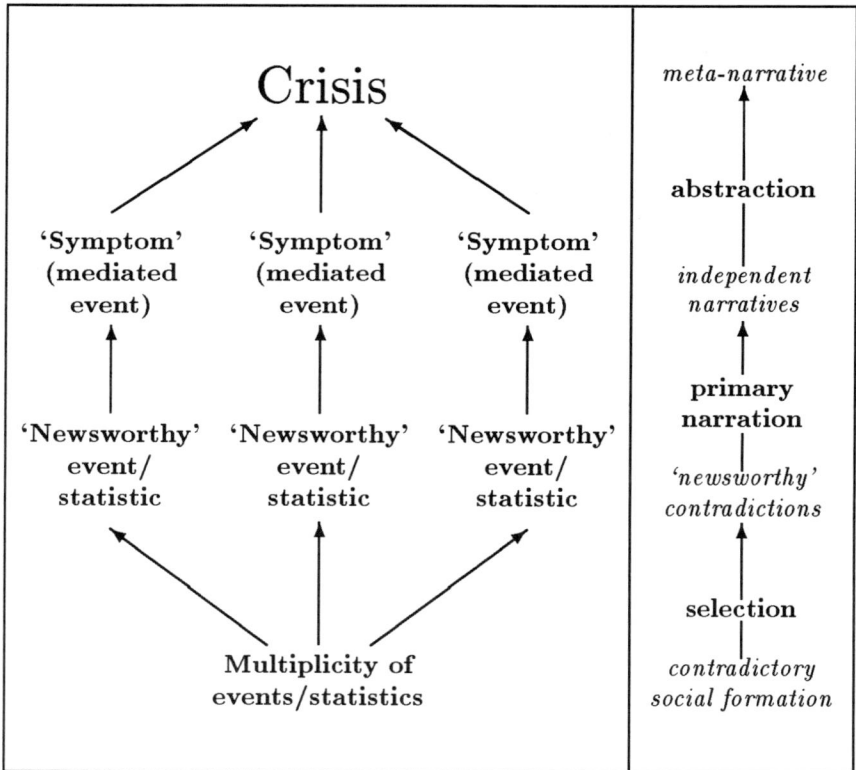

The process of (meta)-narration can be further illustrated by considering the mobilisation of the moral panic surrounding the murder of James Bulger in 1993 (see Hay 1994b). Though a moral panic is not a crisis (in the sense of a ruptural moment of decisive intervention), and may in fact have the effect of displacing 'symptoms' which might otherwise be narrated as crisis

---

[5] The metaphor of crisis as diagnosis is particularly appropriate since, in the writings of Hippocrates and Thucydides, 'crisis' refers to 'the phase of an illness in which it is decided whether or not the organism's self-healing powers are sufficient for recovery' (Habermas 1975: 1; cf. Keane 1984: 10-13; Koselleck 1988: 103-4).

(Hay 1994b; cf. Hall et al 1978), it is an abstraction and a meta-narration. In the construction of the moral panic surrounding the James Bulger incident, a multitude of 'newsworthy' or 'panic-worthy' primary narratives (the abduction and murder of James Bulger, the murder of Edna Phillips by two teenage girls, the Cwmbran child rape case, etc.) were selectively drawn together and unified around the twin themes of the threat posed by juvenile criminality and the subversion of otherwise 'innocent youth' arising out of a breakdown of the traditional 'moral' family unit. Once again, in such panic discourses, direct attribution of agency (Maria Rossi and Christina Molloy killed Edna Phillips) is deleted and replaced by abstract generalisations linking disparate crimes ('it's the broken homes which break the children', *Daily Express*; 'broken homes with mums who could not cope and dads who could not care', *The Sun*).

What such an account demonstrates is the importance of the mediated constructions placed upon events. Given the inertial nature of the state and hence its crisis-dependent evolution, *and* the inherently mediated nature of all moments of crisis, this is a particularly significant observation. Since constructions of crisis (as meta-narratives) often bear very little relationship to the failures and contradictions they purport to narrate, it is crucial that we consider the political and ideological mediation of state and economic failure. State projects and the discourses of crisis on which they are premised do not compete in terms of the sophistication of their understanding of the crisis context. Indeed, their 'success' as narratives relies not on their ability to accurately reflect the complex webs of causation that interact in an aleatory fashion to produce disparate effects, but in their ability to provide a simplified account sufficiently flexible to 'narrate' a great variety of morbid symptoms whilst unambiguously attributing causality (to union bosses, to broken homes, etc.).

For Gramsci, the crisis frames the context within which the ideological struggle to impose a transformatory unity on the structures of the state through restructuring takes place. Out of this struggle a state and hegemonic project is forged (1971: 181-3, 237-9). As Jessop suggests, '... state projects are needed to give a given state some measure of internal unity and to guide its actions' (1990: 315). Yet, the Gramscian conception of crisis on which this observation is made is not unproblematic. In the implicit suggestion that during periods of crisis (whose 'objectivity' is thus taken for granted) competing hegemonic and state projects jostle for position, Gramsci fails to consider the constitution of the moment of crisis *as a moment of crisis* itself. The above analysis would suggest that, *contra* Gramsci, the struggle to impose a new trajectory on the structures of the state is lost and won not in the wake of the crisis moment but in the very process in which the crisis is constituted. Gramsci's 'war of position' is in fact a war of competing narratives, competing constructions of crisis, increasingly fought out in the media between conflicting political élites. As Debray observes with characteristic insight,

'the 'moment of crisis' is not something that can be isolated or neutralised, recognised as a definite milestone of any kind, *it is part of the new process that is growing out of it.*' (1973: 148, emphasis added)

Once the crisis of the British state in the late 1970s had been narrated as a crisis of an overextended and ungovernable state in which the trade unions were 'holding the country to ransom', the success of the New Right was already achieved. As Hall perceptively suggested at the time:

> 'the crisis has begun to be lived in *its* [Thatcherism's] terms ... Its success and effectivity does not lie in its capacity to dupe unsuspecting folk but in the way in which it expresses real problems, real and lived experiences, real contradictions – and yet is able to represent them within a logic of discourse which pulls them systematically into line with policies and class strategies of the right.' (Hall 1979/83: 30, 39, original emphasis)

The crisis is indeed part of the new process growing out of it. The 'Winter of Discontent' as an abstraction, as a meta-narrative of crisis, was an integral part of the Thatcherite state and hegemonic project growing out of it.

Figure 2
Moral Panic as Meta-Narrative

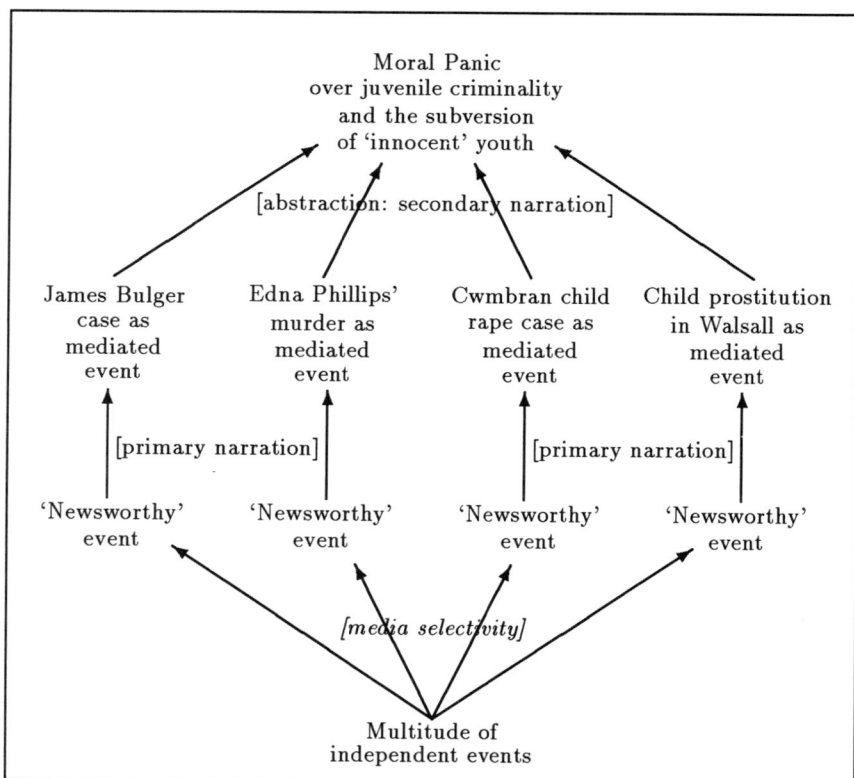

The struggle to narrate the crisis of the state and thereby impose a transformatory unity upon its structures also takes place within a strategically-
selective context, favouring the strategies of certain interests over others.
There is no 'level playing field' on which such wars of position are played
out. The ability to find and construct resonance with the real and lived
experiences of state and economic failure is differentiated according to access to the means of dissemination; the nature of the contradictions and
failures themselves; information and knowledge of such contradictions and
the experiences they give rise to; and the association of those presenting
themselves as the organic intellectuals of a new hegemonic project with the
'symptoms' of the crisis themselves.

making a decisive intervention

> 'Language does not mirror an objective 'reality', but rather
> creates it by organizing meaningful perceptions abstracted from
> a complex world.' (Edelman 1971: 66)

Crisis, as we have seen, is not merely a moment of rupture, but, more
significantly a moment of decisive intervention. But what constitutes a
decisive intervention? The structural transformation of the state through
the forging of a new state project *in and through crisis*, as we have seen,
is dependent on the politically-mediated and ideologically-filtered narration
of contradiction as crisis. As Debray again notes:

> 'the moment of break-up is what we may call crisis, the
> confrontation between contraries, the point of articulation be-
> tween two unities, two periods of history, two political or social
> regimes, two relationships between stable forces.' (1973: 100)

In this sense, what constitutes a decisive intervention is conditional upon
the narration of crisis itself. Hence, we might argue, a decisive intervention is merely that which alters the conditions, whether material or merely
discursive, which sustain the narrative of crisis. The conditions for understanding specific mediated instances (a strike, a lock-in, the rate of inflation,
the balance of payments deficit) as 'symptomatic' of a broader abstraction
and meta-narrative of crisis are both material and discursive. A purely
discursive strategy to dissolve the narrative of crisis can, therefore, be considered no less decisive than a direct attempt to address the contradictions
sustaining such a narrative. For if, as we have suggested, perceptions of
crisis are ultimately more significant (at least with respect to system dynamics) than the contradictions (real or imagined) that they narrate, then
the same can also be said of decisive intervention. *What is important is
being seen to make a decisive intervention, not necessarily the direct impact
of such an intervention on the system 'in crisis'.* Nonetheless, a strategy
for the preservation of the *status quo ante* is unlikely to prove capable of
maintaining societal legitimation for long, regardless of its discursive presentation. The discourse of decisive intervention must be associated with
real policy initiatives, whether symbolic or otherwise.

responses to crisis

This allows us to posit a variety of crisis responses, some, as we shall see purely hypothetical. Given that crisis is discursively constituted (a discursively mediated narration of contradictions and failures), it is important that we distinguish (at least theoretically) between responses that address underlying failures and contradictions *directly* and those which respond to the *construction* of crisis placed upon such 'symptoms'.[6] Though, hypothetically, these may coincide, this is in fact extremely unlikely and it is difficult to think of such a case. Potential strategic responses can be differentiated according to their mode of addressing the 'symptoms' of crisis:

> (1) responses which directly address and resolve the contradictions and failures of a particular social formation in their totality;
> (2) responses which directly address and resolve selective contradictions and failures;
> (3) responses which directly address the crisis as discursively constituted and mediated, resolving the 'crisis' (as narrative) without necessarily resolving the contradictions and failures that sustain such a narrative;
> (4) purely discursive responses, which address the discursive conditions in which the narrative of crisis is constituted.

Though hypothetically possible, the first type of response, in which all the contradictions and failures of a particular social formation are resolved through profound structural transformation, is on closer scrutiny inconceivable. Given that all capitalist social formations are inherently contradictory, such a response would at minimum require the installation of a new mode of production. However, in the absence on the spontaneous global disintegration of capitalist accumulation it is inconceivable that such a social formation could prove sustainable within an international capitalist economy. Furthermore, if as Althusser suggests, all social formations are complicated by the residues and legacies of former modes of production, then it is inconceivable that even the installation of a new mode of production could alleviate all the contradictions of the capitalist epoch (Althusser & Balibar 1970: 307-8; Rey 1969).

At the other end of the scale, a purely discursive response to the crisis of the space, though hypothetically possible, is once again inconceivable. As argued above, though the appearance of making a decisive intervention is ultimately more important than substantive institutional reorganisation and structural change, we do not yet live in a virtual (hyper)-reality where we cannot tell the difference between continuity and change. To sustain its basis of legitimacy a state project must have some impact on the real and lived experiences and contradictions unified through the narrative of

---

[6] In empirical terms it may be extremely difficult to operationalise such a distinction, however analytically it allows us to differentiate between state projects which respond to the contradictions, failures and structural weaknesses of the state and economy, and those which merely manage such contradictions in new ways, thereby exacerbating pre-existing structural tensions.

crisis, even if this impact only manages to confirm the impression that if 'it's hurting, but it might not be working'.

This leaves us with the important distinction between those state projects which directly address failures and structural contradictions (however selectively), and those which address the 'symptoms' of crisis as discursively constituted (as a crisis of an overextended state, as a crisis in which the state is 'held to ransom by the trade unions', etc). Most state projects in fact involve aspects of both – selectively addressing specific failures and contradictions whilst also engaging in the symbolically-significant politics of responding to the crisis as discursively constituted. That the crisis of the British state in the 1970s was narrated as a 'Winter of Discontent' in which the trade unions had 'held the Government hostage' is clearly not unrelated to the subsequent Thatcherite crusade against the organised labour movement. That the crisis was also narrated as a that of an overextended, cloying, and interventionist state stifling the market and creating debilitating relations of dependency is similarly not unrelated to the Thatcherite privatisation programme, the marketisation of the welfare state and the (selective) withdrawal of state intervention from the economy. Yet, an interventionist and developmental role for the state to address the persistent structural weaknesses of the British economy, though clearly incompatible with the dominant construction of the 'crisis', might well have proved more successful in addressing the contradictions and failures out of which it arose.

Conclusion: Crisis as Process, State as Process

Crisis can thus be seen as a *process*, a process in which the tendential unity of the state is discursively renegotiated and (re)-achieved as a developmental trajectory is imposed upon the apparatuses and institutions which together comprise it. Crisis is a process in which the site of political decision making shifts from the disaggregated institutions, policy communities, networks and practices of the state apparatus to the state as a centralised and dynamic agent. The state is constituted anew through crisis (see figure 3).

In the *process* of crisis, therefore, the state is discursively unified within a state project which redefines the material and discursive boundaries of the state, economy and civil society, imposing a structural re-coupling of its institutions and apparatuses. The state becomes not only the object of change, but also the mechanism for its delivery as it is reconstituted as an object in crisis, in need of decisive intervention and with the agency to make that decisive intervention.

The tendential unification of the state through crisis is reversed in periods of relative political and institutional stability (periods of conjunctural or managerial politics). During such 'slower moving political time when the contradictions are ripening' (Debray 1973: 102) there is a tendential dis-unification manifest as a structural un-coupling of apparatuses that had previously been unified through the translation of a state project into substantive institutional change. Individual apparatuses now evolve their own modes of operation and adaptation to their new context. Modes of practice emerge and become entrenched and a new functional separation of tasks between apparatuses is consolidated. Such apparatuses find for themselves discrete areas of autonomy as the former unified and centralised *agency* of the state dissolves into a multitude of interdependent yet nonetheless relatively autonomous *agencies*. This tendential fragmentation of a state apparatus discursively unified through crisis becomes reflected in a variety of contradictions as interdependent apparatuses evolve apart, compete for resources, replicate tasks, and pursue incompatible policy objectives.

Figure 3
Crisis as Process, State and Process

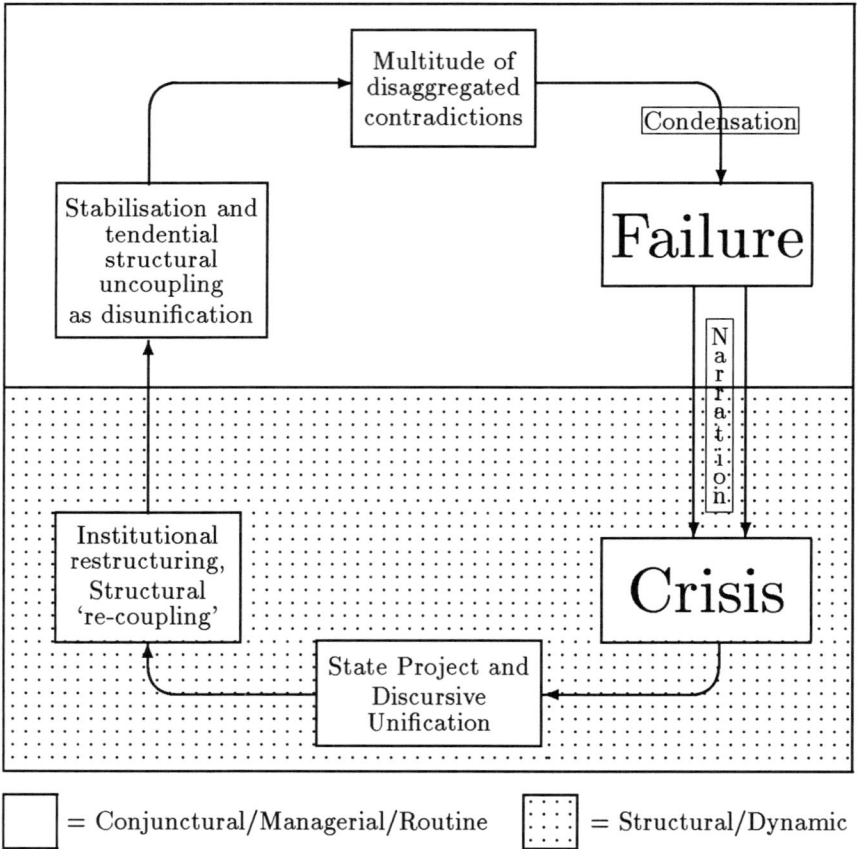

□ = Conjunctural/Managerial/Routine   ⬚ = Structural/Dynamic

The accumulation of policy failures arising out of such tensions and organisational disjunctia eventually gives rise to a ruptural fusion of contradictions, setting the context in which narratives of crisis may find and construct resonance.

Thus, in periods of relative political and institutional stability the unity of the state is latent. The state exists only as a context, as a structure within which the agencies of its relatively independent, yet interdependent apparatuses are realised. The state itself possesses a multitude of fragmented agencies yet no single agency. It becomes a subjectless residue of its former self. In crisis, however, the state is reconstituted as agent, as actor, as process. The state is discursively unified *in* crisis through the discursive construction *of* crisis

Bibliography

S.Aaronovitch (1981), 'The Relative Decline of the United Kingdom', in *idem* (ed), *The Political Economy of British Capitalism*, London: McGraw-Hill.

P.Abrams (1988), 'Notes on the Difficulty of Studying the State', *Journal of Historical Sociology*, 1 (1) 58-89.

M.Aglietta (1979), *A Theory of Capitalist Regulation*, London: New Left Books.

L.Althusser (1969), *For Marx*, London: Allen Lane.

L.Althusser & E.Balibar (1970), *Reading Capital*, London: New Left Books.

C.Barnett (1986), *The Audit of War: The Illusion and Reality of Britain as a Great Nation*, London: Macmillan.

S.Benhabib (1986), *Critique, Norm and Utopia: A Study of the Foundations of Critical Theory*, New York: Columbia University Press.

R.Bertramsen et al (1991), *State, Economy and Society*, London: Unwin Hyman.

F.Block (1987), *Revising State Theory: Essays in Politics and Postindustrialism*, Philadelphia: Temple University Press.

A.Boyer (1988), *The Regulation School: A Critical Introduction*, Chicago: Chicago University Press.

E.Boyle (1979), 'The economist in government', in J.Bowers (ed), *Inflation, Development and Integration*, Leeds.

W.Brown (1992), 'Finding the Man in the State', *Feminist Studies*, 18 (1), 7-34.

P.Burnham (1990), *The Political Economy of Postwar Reconstruction*, London: Macmillan.

P.Burnham (1993), 'The impact of the Korean rearmament programme on the British economy: the value of the vehicle industry', Paper presented at ECPR workshop, Leiden, Holland, Aptil 1993.

M.Carnoy (1984), *The State and Political Theory*, Princeton: Princeton University Press.

R.Debray (1973), 'Time and Politics' in *idem*, *Prison Writings*, London: Allen Lane.

M.Edelman (1971), *Politics as Symbolic Action*, New York: Academic Press.

J.Gleick (1988), *Chaos: Making a New Science*, New York: Viking.

A.Gramsci (1971), *Selections From Prison Notebooks*, London: Lawrence & Wishart.

J.Habermas (1975), *Legitimation Crisis*, London: Heinemann.

S.Hall (1979/1983), 'The Great Moving Right Show', reprinted in S.Hall & M.Jacques (eds), *The Politics of Thatcherism*, London: Lawrence & Wishart.

S.Hall (1980a), 'Encoding/Decoding', in S.Hall et al (eds), *Culture, Media, Language*, London: Hutchinson.

S.Hall (1980b), 'Popular-Democratic vs. Authoritarian Populism: Two Ways of Taking Democracy Seriously', in A.Hunt(ed), *Marxism and Democracy*, London: Lawrence & Wishart.

S.Hall et al (1978), *Policing the Crisis*, Macmillan.

P.t' Hart (1993), 'Symbols, Rituals and Power: The Lost Dimensions of Crisis Management', *Journal of Contingencies and Crisis Management*, 1 (1), 36-50.

C.Hay (1993), 'The Political Economy of State Failure in Britain's State Failure', Paper presented at ECPR, Leiden, Holland, April 1993.

C.Hay (1994a), 'The Structural and Ideological Contradictions of Britain's Post-War Reconstruction', *Capital & Class*, forthcoming.

C.Hay (1994b), 'Mobilisation through Interpellation: James Bulger, Juvenile Crime and the Construction of a Moral Panic', Lancaster University, mimeo.

C.Hay (1994c), 'Environmental Security and State Legitimacy', *Capitalism, Nature, Socialism*, 5 (1).

C.Hay (1994d), 'Tom Nairn's Sole Survivor Thesis: New Exceptionalisms for Old?', *New Left Review*, forthcoming.

C.Hay & B.Jessop (1995), *Beyond the State? New Perspectives in State Theory*, London: Macmillan (forthcoming).

M.Jänicke (1990), *State Failure: The Impotence of Politics in Industrial Societies*, Polity.

B.Jessop (1982), *The Capitalist State*, Martin Robertson.

B.Jessop (1990), *State Theory: Putting the Capitalist State in its Place*, Polity.

B.Jessop (1994), 'Recent Developments in State Theory: Approaches, Issues and Agendas', Lancaster University, mimeo.

H.Kamminga (1990), 'What is this thing called chaos?', *New Left Review*, 181.

J.Keane (1984), *Public Life and Late Capitalism*, Cambridge: Cambridge University Press.

R.Koselleck (1988), *Critique and Crisis: Enlightenment and the Pathogenesis of Modern Society*, Oxford: Berg.

D.Lockwood (1964), 'Social and System Integration', in G.K.Zollschan & W.Hirsch (eds), *Explorations of Social Change*, London: Routledge.

N.Luhmann (1977), *The Differentiation of Society*, New York: Columbia University Press.

L.Marin (1988), *The Portrait of the King*, Minneapolis, MN: Minnesota University Press.

P.Miller & N.Rose (1990), 'Governing Economic Life', *Economy & Society*, 19 (1), 1-31.

T.Mitchell (1991), 'The Limits of the State: Beyond Statist Approaches and their Critics', *American Political Science Review*, 85 (1), 77-96.

N.Mouzelis (1974), 'System and Social Integration: A Reconsideration of a Fundamental Distinction', *British Journal of Sociology*, Number 4.

N.Mouzelis (1990), *Post-Marxist Alternatives: The Construction of Social Orders*, London: Macmillan.

N.Mouzelis (1991), *Back to Sociological Theory: The Construction of Social Orders*, London: Macmillan.

D.K.Mumby (1993), *Narrative and Social Control: Critical Perspectives*, Newbury Pary, CA: Sage.

C.Offe (1984), *Contradictions of the Welfare State*, London: Hutchinson.

C.Offe (1985), *Disorganized Capitalism*, Cambridge: Polity.

L.Panitch (1986), *Working Class Politics in Crisis: Essays on Labour and the State*, London: Verso.

N.Poulantzas (1976), 'Les transformations actuelles de l'Etat, la crise politique et la crise de l'Etat', in *idem* (ed), *La Crise de l'Etat*, Paris: PUF.

N.Poulantzas (1978), *State, Power, Socialism*, London: New Left Books.

N.Poulantzas (1979), 'The Political Crisis and the Crisis of the State', in J.W.Frieburg (ed), *Critical Sociology*, New York: Irvington.

R.Pringle & S.Watson (1992) ' "Women's Interests" and the Post-Structuralist State', in M.Barrett & A.Phillips (eds), *Destabilizing Theory: Contemporary Feminist Debates*, Cambridge: Polity.

P.R.Rey (1969), 'Sur l'articulation des modes de production', in *Les Alliances de Classes*, Paris: Maspero.

N.Rose & P.Miller (1992), 'Political Power Beyond the State: Problematics of Government', *British Journal of Sociology*, 43 (2), 172-205.

N.Rose (1993), 'Government, Authority and Expertise in Advanced Liberalism', *Economy & Society*, 22 (3), 283-99.

M.Rovirosa (1988), *Towards the Impossibility of the State: a Deconstructive Reading*, University of Essex: MA Thesis.

R.Smith (1981), 'The Historical Decline of the United Kingdom', in Aaronovitch (ed), *op.cit.*

S.Zizek (1985), 'La Société n'existe pas', *L'Ame*, October-December, 36-7.

Aspects of National Health Service Reforms

Stephen Peckham
University of Southampton

'The Public Government of Private Sex:
Teenagers, Contraception and the Health of the Nation'

Introduction

This paper provides a preliminary discussion of government intervention
in relation to teenage pregnancy. It explores a number of dichotomies in
government policy and political debate which impinge on the ability to effect
a key part of the *Health of the Nation* strategy.

This White Paper was published in 1992 and contained targets for achieving health gain. One of the areas focused upon is sexual health within which
there is an explicit target set for reducing pregnancies to young women under the age of 16. This requires direct involvement by statutory agencies in
the sexual behaviour of young people. It is clear that without some change
to existing behaviour the target will not be reached. Thus here is a government statement about how young people should conduct their sexual
activity. This can be seen in three ways.

> First as a concern for the health and well being of young
> people themselves to avoid unwanted consequences of sexual in-
> tercourse, a sentiment that has been espoused by groups such
> as the Brook Advisory Service and Family Planning Association
> for many years.
>
> Second, it could, as in the USA, be driven by a financial
> desire to cut public health and social care costs.
>
> Lastly, there is a moral context which relates to the age of
> responsibility of young people and the interaction of parental
> and child rights. This was clearly an important factor in the
> case bought by Victoria Gillick in the 1980s[1] and can be seen in
> much of the recent political debate about sex education.

This last approach has been very visible in the last year or so with the moral
pronouncements made by several government ministers about single parents
in particular (Brindle 1993b). But such moralistic views about teenage sexual activity and teenage mothers have been debated for many years although
they have not been central in any government policy (Durham 1991).

The question arises, therefore, of why this is a current issue and what
has led the government to adopt a target on teenage pregnancy? It is also
important to explore the current political interest in teenage sex and teenage
mothers.

This paper examines the context of the *Health of the Nation* targets and
explores the background to current political views on teenage sexuality. In

[1] *Gillick v W. Norfolk & Wisbech HA* [1985] 3 All England Law Reports 402.

particular it will address the policy frameworks for these suggesting both a pragmatic approach in developing and achieving policy objectives and how this now operates within, at least publicly, a belief system about the rights and responsibilities of children, parents and society.

In order to do this it is first necessary to explore the nature of the 'problem', for while clearly now seen as a major social problem, teenage pregnancy is by no means a recent phenomenon. In discussing the public policy responses in the USA Rhode (1993) has set the question as 'What choices should adolescents make in sexual relationships, what role should the state play in shaping the choices available, and who should decide those questions?' (p.301).

The debate about these issues occurs at a time when the government is pursuing a 'Back to Basics' campaign as a major plank of its philosophy, much of which is concerned about reinstating parental rights and responsibilities. Yet, as Hugo Young has questioned, what is the meaning of 'back', and to what should we go back to? (Young 1993). There are tensions in the government about the role of the state and what the state can afford. These need to be examined to discern the true nature of policies on teenage sex and motherhood.

> 'A large component of the [back to basics] slogan refers to the behaviour of the poor, and the basic presumption that they should do more to help themselves. Self-reliance, and the moral decline that follows from dependency, is the message pouring forth from Cabinet ministers.' (*Ibid*)

Teenage Pregnancy as a 'Social Problem'

In order to determine why there should be particular concern about teenage pregnancy at this time it is worth examining the level of teenage pregnancy in the United Kingdom historically, comparatively with other countries and examine the context and consequences of such pregnancies.

While the conception rate[2] for women under 20 years old in England and Wales rose from 61.9 per 1000 to 69.0 per 1000 between 1979 and 1990 the rate is still lower than in the 1970s. However, conceptions to under 16 year olds are now higher than in the 1970s.

The under 20s birth rate has though, remained fairly constant but the abortion rate rose from 18.8 to 24.6 per 1000. This may suggest that the number of unintended pregnancies has increased. A view supported by the most recent of a series of studies by the Institute for Social Studies in Medical Care, which showed an overall increase of unplanned pregnancies for all mothers from 26.7% in 1984 to 31.3% in 1989 with the major increase being for younger women (Fleissig 1992). In 1991 there was a small decrease in conception rates but figures for later years are not yet available so it is not possible to see if this is the start of a downward trend.

---

[2] Conception rates are the total of all pregnancies leading to maternities or abortions expressed as a rate per 1000 women in age group.

Research in Britain and the U.S.A. has shown that teenage mothers are more likely to have low weight babies, be dependent on state benefits, have poor knowledge of child development, a higher prevalence of fetal distress and premature/postmature babies. In their first 5 years of life children of teenage mothers are twice as likely to be admitted to hospital as a result of an accident or gastroenteritis and score less well on verbal and non verbal ability tests (Peckham 1993).

It is questionable though, whether 'teenage pregnancy' is a problem by definition. In reality it is merely a descriptive term, as there are substantial differences in pregnancy, abortion and birth rates between younger and older teenage women. Neither is it clear whether age is the determining factor giving rise to these negative consequences of pregnancy. Research has clearly shown that certain social factors are associated with increasing the likelihood of teenage pregnancy. These include incomplete education, lower educational attainment and fewer qualifications, lower socio-economic class background, coming from larger families and coming from families where the parents had separated (Hudson & Ineichen 1991, Estaigh & Wheatley 1990). However, it has been suggested that by controlling for the various factors known to be correlated with social class the differences between younger and older mothers are greatly reduced (Phoenix 1991).

While it may be inappropriate to define teenage pregnancy as a problem, clearly there are health and social problems associated with it, and it these, together with more moralistic views, which are inherent in the pronouncements of many politicians. Also while *The Health of the Nation* takes a fairly non-contentious view by targeting under 16 year olds, the high rate of terminations for pregnant teenagers may suggest a failure of family planning and sex education services.

International comparisons show substantial variations between teenage pregnancy rates in different countries. The study by Jones et al (1985) of six industrialised countries in the 1980s showed that there was little difference in teenage sexual activity rates. Generally though, more young people are sexually active at an earlier age than before. In the United Kingdom estimates vary between 25% and 55% of under 16 year olds being sexually active.

However, in the mid 1980s there was a variation in median age at first intercourse of nearly two years. Sweden had the lowest at about 17 years old with about 33% of Swedish girls having had intercourse by the age of 16. By contrast, in Canada the median age was nearly 19 and only 20% of girls were sexually active by the ages of 16-17. In Great Britain, the USA, the Netherlands and France the median was just under 18 years old. It is likely that in all these countries the median age has fallen.

Comparisons of pregnancy and fertility rates[3] show significant variations between countries which appear to be unrelated to sexual activity rates. For example in the mid 1980s the pregnancy rate in the USA was 96 per 1000, in England and Wales it was 45 per 1000 and in the Netherlands it was 14 per 1000. Also whilst abortion rates vary considerably in these countries they do not account for the significant changes in fertility rates.

---

[3] Fertility rates are for live births only.

For example, in Denmark and the Netherlands there has been little variance in the abortion rate since 1980 yet in these countries, between 1980 and 1987 the fertility rates have reduced from 15.2 to 9.4 per 1000 and 6.8 to 5.2 per 1000 respectively.

Thus within the United Kingdom, teenage conception rates have been increasing over the last decade but are not as high as they were in the mid 1970s and birth rates are lower than in the 1960s and early 1970s. International comparisons show that the United Kingdom's teenage pregnancy rates are slightly higher than most European countries but are substantially lower than in the USA. However, compared to the Netherlands the United Kingdom rate is some three times as high. But such international comparisons have shown discrepancies for many years without the same political and governmental interest being shown.

While there does not seem to have been an enormous increase in births to teenagers the fact that over a third of all teenage pregnancies are aborted is a key concern. In addition 90% of conceptions to teenagers were to single women. This fact was emphasised by Charles Murray in *The Emerging British Underclass* where he defined illegitimacy as a key social problem, an issue taken up by Dennis & Erdos (1992). It was these publications, beyond all others, which have provided the intellectual backdrop to comments made by government ministers over the last 18 months. Clearly increasing single parenthood represents a challenge to commentators such as Murray, in terms of ensuring on the one hand that all the children are wanted, and on the other the concept of the two parent family.

It is interesting that the focus is on never-married mothers rather than single parents *per se*, who represent about one third of all lone parents, of which only about 5% are teenagers although 25% started as teenagers.

Given the political and media interest it could be construed that the current interest in teenage sex is a moral panic (Cohen 1972), but with a focus on single teenage mothers. It is difficult though, to follow Cohen's mechanism completely, although many of the reinforcing factors do seem at play. It can be seen that the level of teenage pregnancy is not high by historical standards so we need to seek other reasons for both the moral criticism of teenage parenthood and sexual activity and for the Health of the Nation.

To do this we need to explore the historical perspective of the government's involvement in regulating sex, sexual activity and services for sexually active young people. What is clear though, is that in terms of choices young people are more sexually active today than 20 or 30 years ago.

Policing Sex, Government Intervention and Sexual Activity

Weeks (1981) has argued that:

> 'Victorian morality was premised on a series of ideological separations: between family and society, between the restraint of the domestic circle and the temptations of promiscuity ... This

> was the basis of the dichotomy of "the private" and "the public"
> upon which much sexual regulation rested.'

The legacy of the 1800s was a clear delineation between the control and regulation of public vice and the non-intervention in private heterosexual relations. The late 1800s and early 1900s saw some statutory regulation on the age of consent (raised from 12 to 16), making homosexuality illegal, and regulating sexually transmitted diseases – which acted more as controls on the poor and armed forces (Weeks 1991). On the whole this remained the legal framework until the 1950s when the *Sexual Offences Act, 1956*, came into force. The effect of this was to necessarily make pregnancy in young women under the age of sixteen the result of criminal activity. The main offence is unlawful sexual intercourse[4]. This is committed by a boy or man who has sex with a girl under sixteen, the girl herself is not guilty of the offence.

Even consensual sexual activity between fifteen year olds will be criminal in the eyes of the law. For those advising and supporting young people the implications of the fact that there is unlawful activity where under sixteen year olds are sexually active raises both moral and legal questions as the Act specifically creates an offence of encouraging unlawful sexual activity (s.28).

There is a wide ranging moral debate about young people and sex, influencing the way individuals act and how organisations draw up guidance (Durham 1991). This has added to the confusion over the legal position of those people who are giving advice and contraception to young people under the age of 16. The key two issues where concern arises are in relation to advising about and providing contraception, and maintaining confidentiality. These concerns most clearly arose with the Gillick case in the mid 1980s which although making such services and advice legal for under 16 year olds, left many people unclear about the status of young people's right to confidentiality, ability to obtain contraception and whether advice can be given about contraception and sexual matters because of need to establish the individual's maturity.

In 1991 the Royal College of Obstetricians and Gynaecologists report on unplanned pregnancy highlighted the ambiguities in advice between the General Medical Council and the British Medical Association (RCOG 1991). The result of this ambiguity was found in a recent study for the Family Planning Association and Health Education Authority which suggested that some GPs are unclear about what they can say and provide to young people under 16 and suggest that there is '...a need for more information for general practices on the rights and confidentiality aspects of providing contraception to people less than 16 years old' (Institute for Population Studies 1993). However, the evidence suggests that it is not only GPs who are unsure of the law but also Family Planning clinic staff, practice and community nurses, teachers and youth workers (Allen 1991).

The question of the legality of providing advice and information on contraception to under 16 year olds is currently a key issue within education

---

[4] *Sexual Offences Act, 1956*, s.6.

following the draft guidance issued by the Department for Education following the 'Stallard Amendment'. The draft guidance warns teachers of the possibility of breaking the law by providing advice and information on contraceptive advice and has left many teachers and educational policy makers unsure of the law.

The current state of the law means that a morally contentious issue has a range of legal interpretations and it is possible to draw both a narrow and broad view of the obligations implicit in the *Sexual Offences Act* and the general United Kingdom tradition of the law relating to advice to, and medical intervention with young people. Essentially it is one of parental versus children's rights, again illustrated by the Gillick case.

The legal tide in the United Kingdom is towards children's rights and the idea that maturity is a developing process and that there can be no fixed age of maturity. Neither has the law been amended to fit the growing sexual activity of under 16s, although there have been calls for lowering the age of consent. On the whole the law is there to protect young women from the exploitation of older men, a clear link with the role of government in the late 1800s.

There is, however, another side to government and sex relating to the growth of family planning services. These were first supported by the government in the 1930s (Cabinet Memorandum 153/MCW) with an acknowledgement that married women could obtain contraceptive advice from welfare clinics. However there had been a long battle to gain government recognition by both local authorities and voluntary groups, with both civil and criminal legal action throughout the 1920s. After the Second World War the Family Planning Association rapidly expanded it's clinics but only for married women.

By the late 1950s the FPA clinics were beginning to provide a service to older single women, but it was not until the creation of the Brook Advisory Service in the 1960s that young single women could obtain contraception. In 1974 the NHS took over the responsibility for family planning with free provision of contraceptives. However, services for young people have not been developed uniformly across the country despite government guidance. In addition because of the *Sexual Offences Act, 1956*, and the ambiguity about provision of advice and contraceptives to under 16 year olds, there is still confusion about the legality, as well as the morality of services for this age group. Thus the inclusion of a target in The Health of the Nation is of great interest in terms of focusing attention on this group of young people from a health perspective, where there is clearly a major moral debate which has been developing over the last 20 or 30 years.

More recently the government has taken an interventionist approach in relation to public health issues of HIV/AIDS and in stimulating preventive measures. Young people are seen as a key at risk group and have been specifically targeted in preventive work. There has been a public emphasis on safe sexual practices which has caused outrage for many moral campaigners who wanted to portray HIV/AIDS as relating to deviant behaviour only (homosexuality and drug use) and campaigned for sexual abstinence outside of marriage (Durham 1991).

More than any thing though it was the concern over HIV and AIDS that led to the sexual health targets in the Health of the Nation.

The Health of the Nation

The *Health of the Nation* was an attempt to focus attention and resources on strategies which would improve health. In this sense it can be seen as a rational policy approach. However, there has been much contentious debate about the targets included within the document both in terms of whether they can be achieved, and whether the correct topics had been addressed[5]. It is not my intention here to examine the *Health of the Nation* in its entirety in any detail but rather focus on the inclusion of the reduction in teenage pregnancies as one of main six targets.

In the *Health of the Nation* Green Paper, published in 1991, there was no mention of a possible target relating to teenage pregnancy. However, there is a section on the health of pregnant women, infants and children which raises the issue of effective family planning services and identifies a number of health problems which have been associated with unplanned pregnancies (RCOG 1991), although this link is not made in the Green Paper.

Interestingly there was no national campaign, before or after the publication of the Green Paper, to ensure that the issue of teenage pregnancy was addressed. While groups such as the Brook advisory Centres and the Family Planning Association have been campaigning for improved services for young teenagers they had not specifically pressed the government for action within the *Health of the Nation*.

The key driving force for including the teenage pregnancy target came from the comparison with achievements in the Netherlands where there had been a substantial reduction in teenage pregnancies and abortions. The Department of Health's view was that all pregnancies to under 16 year olds were both unintended and unwanted, and had serious social and health care implications for the teenager and any children. This was viewed alongside the increasing incidence of sexually transmitted diseases among young people and abortions for young women under the age of 20. It was therefore felt important to act positively to reduce the consequences of sexual activity for young people.

Within the *Health of the Nation* there is a specific target to reduce the rate of conceptions amongst the under 16s by at least 50% by the year 2000 (from 9.5 per 1,000 girls aged 13-15 in 1989 to no more than 4.8).

However, while most attention has been focused on this key aim it is important not overlook the general objectives of this target which are:

- To reduce the number of unwanted pregnancies;
- to ensure the provision of effective family planning services for those people who want them.

These broader objectives are extremely important, particularly as achieving the key target of a 50% reduction in the under 16 conception rate will

---

[5] See *Health Service Journal* 1992

be very difficult, if at all possible in some areas. This is partly due to the complexities surrounding teenage conception but also relates to problems in reducing conceptions where the numbers of young women under 16 becoming pregnant is already very small.

There is, however, a broader agenda which can be seen in the philosophy behind the target and the objectives. In the *Key Area Handbook:HIV/AIDS and Sexual Health* the government sets out it's philosophy and how they see this as being achieved.

> 'Planned parenthood provides benefits for the health of individuals, families and communities. Family planning services aim to promote this by providing access to contraception, sterilisation and advice on unplanned pregnancy. Additionally, education, counselling and health promotion can enable prospective parents to choose healthy lifestyles and increase the chances that their children will be wanted and healthy. Delaying and spacing pregnancies and limiting family size contributes to the physical and mental health of mothers and children and general family well-being. The effective use of condoms or other barrier methods of contraception also promotes sexual health by giving protection against sexually transmitted diseases.' (Para. 5.1.3)

While the thinking behind the *Health of the Nation* is one of concern for health and social wellbeing it is easy to see that the aims could be achieved in a number of ways. For the moralists the solution would lie in less sexual freedom, more parental control, deterrence and abstinence. This contrasts sharply with the approach adopted within the Health of the Nation where there has been focus on the provision of advice, information and contraception.

The Battlefields – Sex Education and contraception

While the public attention has focused on the circumstances of single mothers, particularly teenagers, there has been a substantial political debate, and pressure group activity around sex education and the provision of advice and contraception for young people. In the early 1980s an amendment was introduced to the then *Education Bill* allowing parents to inspect sex education teaching materials and to withdraw their child from sex education lessons, an aspiration that may finally be achieved this year. In fact throughout the 1980s there were sustained campaigns on the content of sex education materials (Durham 1991).

Interestingly the views of such moral campaigners for less explicit material and a focus on abstinence is at odds with the sexual practice and views of young people. Surveys of young people in this country consistently show that the current level of sex education is inadequate. Common complaints are that too much is missed out, especially relating to the value of relationships, that the lessons are too late or too early, it is too biological in nature, and that there is a need for single sex, as well as mixed sessions. In addition most surveys show that the majority of parents want schools to provide sex education.

Many others have expressed similar concerns about the quality of sex education and both the Royal College of Obstetricians and Gynaecologists and the House of Commons Health Committee amongst many others have recommended that the syllabus should be broadened to include a greater emphasis on the importance of responsible and caring relationships. Many senior members of the government have also talked about the moral framework of sex education, notably the Secretary of State for Education who has recently spoke about the need for more emphasis on moral values and relationships.

Such an approach has been accepted by the Department for Education and some secondary schools already incorporate this in their sex education curriculum, however, many do not and it is even more unusual in primary schools.

Until recently, despite central guidelines on sex education, the ultimate responsibility lay with individual schools. Thus the provision of sex education varies considerably. The RCOG argued that this was not sufficient and that there should be a nationally developed curriculum providing a comprehensive and co-ordinate sex education programme involving the support of health education and other appropriate medical staff.

As part of the new *Education Act* sex education will become compulsory. This follows the Stallard amendment. This amendment could create substantial confusion within schools as it will allow parents to withdraw children from sex education lessons. More interestingly the draft guidance from the Department for Education takes a very strict or narrow view of the law, perhaps reflecting the current moral overtones of the government, although the second draft avoids the moralistic overtones of the original. Whether this is the correct interpretation is of course debatable but a strict reading of the law may deter teaching staff from giving information and advice on contraception and sexual issues to young people for fear of breaking the law.

The tone of the debates in the House of Lords provide an interesting insight into parliamentary discussion on sex education as they were not about health issues but morality, fear, innocence etc, and the emphasis on the rights of parents to be able to ensure that there children are not exposed to sex education. The amendment which has been take up by the government, but for which only draft guidance is still available, raises a number of concerns about the rights of children and parents over sex education and the role and duty of schools and society in general. Do we want to go down the same road as the projects referred to by Lord Stallard? He quoted the following American correspondence:

> '... American children are learning the A to V of a new kind of sex education – A for abstinence and V for virginity ... students are told to "just say no" in an estimated 5000 of the country's 16000 districts ... In California, teenagers following a course called Sex Respect chant a "chastity pledge" – "Do

the right thing! Wait for the ring", while in New York the city school board... has just demanded that health educators going into schools to teach about AIDS must sign a commitment to emphasise abstinence over safe sex in their classroom presentation.'

Yet what we do know is that in the USA pregnancy rates continue to rise.

The situation regarding contraceptive advice and provision is however very different. The *Health of the Nation* has provided a catalyst for the development of health authority and other services for young people and most areas now have some provision specifically for teenagers. But for moral campaigners, such as Victoria Gillick, the state is removing parental rights and

> '... usurping their role and the innocence of the young is being destroyed ... a movement that held it was taking power away from doctors and from young men and restoring it to its "rightful place" – the mother and father – came up against the opposition of the medical establishment and those who favoured young women's sexual autonomy.' (Durham 1991, p.56)

In some areas of the country local services have been picketed by protesters from LIFE, SPUC, and other campaigning groups, although this is not widespread. This may have more to do with advice on abortion than contraception although these and other groups have campaigned against contraceptive services because they are thought to encourage under age sex. This view is not, however, supported by research (Peckham 1992).

Interestingly the provision of advice and contraception services seems to have remained absent from comments on teenage sexual activity. It is not clear why this should be so. In the USA there is some evidence to suggest that anti-abortionists have been backing contraception services as a way of reducing abortion. In the United Kingdom though such evidence is not forthcoming and neither is known whether those government ministers who have attacked single parenthood and sexual promiscuity in young people are anti-abortion or pro-contraception.

The battlefield here is essentially that identified by Gillick and the House of Lords debate on the Stallard amendment, is the issue of parental rights. Here, the state does seem to have made a statement of pursuing intervention to maintain the rights and choices of young people to engage in sexual activity while at the same time politicians are making moral statements about the role of the family and parental responsibility and rights over their children. What these areas clearly demonstrate is the inherent dichotomy between these two views.

Morals or Money?

Last September Michael Portillo, the Chief Secretary to the Treasury, stated that:

'Teenage pregnancy often leads to a whole life of state dependence, with few luxuries. The teenage mother is rarely able to gain a full education or develop a career.'

The previous year at the Conservative Party Conference Peter Lilley, Social Security Secretary, read out his 'little list' which included 'Young ladies who get pregnant just to jump the housing list'.

Other government ministers have also commented on the financial burden of single mothers. Even Tim Yeo defended his part in fathering an 'illegitimate' child by saying in an interview on the *Today* programme that it was alright because he would ensure that he took financial responsibility. Presumably it is not alright if the child and mother would need to rely on state benefits!

What is clear is that the issue of single teenage motherhood is bound up with the cost of social benefits and general welfare provision such as housing. Yet a young single mother is unlikely to be better off with a child than as a single person drawing benefit so this cannot be seen as an incentive. Evidence also suggests that it is not the promise of public housing which encourages young women to have a baby. The view of welfare dependency argued by Murray (1990) and supported by many government ministers has been refuted by Joan Brown (1990) who has shown that never-married mothers were less likely to be on long term benefit than divorced mothers.

Broader economic criteria may also conspire to cut across moral and health care issues. Recently there has been debate within medical and government circles about the possibility of making contraceptives only available on prescription as a way of reducing NHS costs. If this was to happen there are serious issues about whether young people (mainly women) could afford to continue using contraceptives and for under 16 year olds the question of the parental counter-signature on prescriptions would endanger confidentiality.

The Public and the Private

There is then a series of dichotomies which permeate discussions of teenage sexuality. These relate to the question of rights, health care *versus* moral views of control and how far sexual relationships are private or public. These can be seen as coming from the question set by Rhode in the introduction 'What choices should adolescents make in sexual relationships, what role should the state play in shaping the choices available, and who should decide those questions?'

The history of the government views on regulating sexual activity in this country has been somewhat ambivalent. However, the government is also interventionist in terms of providing a framework of services for young people to make choices about their own sexual activity, except of course for gay men (lesbians have never been subject to legal controls), although the age of consent is to be debated in the current session of Parliament. It is also clear that young people are sexually active in their teens and that in a sense they make choices about sexual involvement. The role of government through the Health of the Nation has been seen to be one of minimising the harm to young people while accepting that they can make choices about contraception and conception.

With the rise of single parenthood though this is now beginning to change. The perceived unwelcome affects of single parenthood, or more precisely motherhood, are seen to be too great to bear. Is this consistent with the *Health of the Nation*? It would seem that given the philosophy behind the target that these are not incompatible. However, it would be wrong to conclude that the *Health of the Nation* grew from a concern about single parenthood. Rather it developed from a concern about the adverse circumstances of unwanted children, it is about improving the ability of young people to make choices about sex and conception without moralising about whether the choice to conceive is wrong.

In discussion with civil servants there is a wish to keep these issues separate but given the moralistic overtones of the 'Back to Basics policy' this may become increasingly difficult. It is unlikely, given recent discussions within the Conservative Party and the media, that the Prime Minister's denial that the 'policy' is not about individual morality will have much impact on how it is viewed. In reality the right to withdraw children from sex education is unlikely to be exercised to any great extent. However, it is possible that a concerted focus on moral issues and parental rights and responsibilities could work against the Health of the Nation.

This could mean a controlling of choices made by young people about sexual relationships which removes the access to services which can support individual choices and replaces them with an emphasis on abstinence which is unlikely to change actual behaviour. The state would move from an advisory and supportive role to one of trying to set the moral framework, somewhat in the face of reality. For parents the results of responsibility could be the forcing of young mothers to live with them where housing is unobtainable or benefits are withdrawn. This is likely to lead to more poverty and an increase in young mothers, and therefore frustrate the government's attempt to achieve the *Health of the Nation* sexual health targets, including that for teenage pregnancy.

References

Allen, I. (1991), *Family Planning And Pregnancy Counselling Projects for Young People*, London: Policy Studies Institute.

Bell, N. J. & Bell, R. W. (eds) (1993), *Adolescent Risk Taking*, Newbury Park: Sage.

Brindle, D. (1993a), 'Lone mothers face benefits cut onslaught', *The Guardian*, 9 November.

Brindle, D. (1993b), 'Curb falls foul of facts', *The Guardian*, 9 November.

Cohen, S. (1972), *Folk Devils and Moral Panics*, London: MacGibbon & Kee.

Coleman, J. & Hendry, L. (1990), *The Nature of Adolescence*, London: Routledge.

Coleman, J & Warren-Adamson, C. (1992), *Youth Policy in the 1990s: The Way Forward*, London: Routledge.

DoH (1991), *Health of the Nation*, CM 1523, London: HMSO

DOH (1992), *Health of the Nation*, CM (), London: HMSO.

DOH (1993), *Health of the Nation Key Area Handbook: HIV/AIDS and Sexual Health*.

Dennis, N & Erdos, G. *(1992), Families without Fatherhood*, IEA Health and Welfare Unit, Choice in Welfare, Number 12.

Doyal, L. (1983), *The Political Economy of Health*, London: Pluto Press

Durham, M. (1991), *Sex and Politics*, Basingstoke: Macmillan

Durham, M. (1993), 'Benefits of Tory morality', *The Observer, 14 November*.

Estaigh, V. & Wheatley, J. *(1990), Teenage Pregnancy, in Family Planning and Family Well-Being*, Occasional Paper Number 12, London: Family Policy Studies Centre.

Family Policy Studies Centre (1991), *The Family Today Fact Sheet 1*.

Fleissig, A. (1991), 'Unintended pregnancies and the use of contraception', *British Medical Journal*, 302, 147.

Garmanikow, E. et al (eds) (1983), *The Public and the Private*, London: Heinemann.

Hudson, F. & Ineichen, B. (1991), *Taking it Lying Down*, Basingstoke: Macmillan

Ingham, R. (1993), *Can we have a policy on sex? Setting targets for teenage pregnancies*, Institute for Health Policy Studies, University of Southampton.

Ingham, R., Woodcock, A. & Stenner, K. (1991), 'Getting to know you ... young people's knowledge of their partners at first intercourse', *Journal of Community and Applied Social Psychology*, 1 (2), 117-132.

Institute of Population Studies (1993), *Sexual health and Family Planning Services in General Practice*, Family Planning Association.

Jardine, C. (1993), 'What future for single mothers?', *Daily Telegraph*, 7 October.

Jones, E. F. et al (1985), 'Teenage pregnancy in developed countries: determinants and policy implications', *Family Planning Perspectives*, 17 (2), 53-63.

Lawson, A. & Rhode, D. L. (eds) (1993), *The Politics of Pregnancy: Adolescent Sexuality and Public Policy*, New Haven: Yale University Press.

Leathard, A. (1980), *The Fight for Family Planning*, Basingstoke: Macmillan.

McLaren, A. (1992), *A History of Contraception: From antiquity to the present day*, Oxford: Blackwell.

McRobbie, A. (1991), *Feminism and Youth Culture*, Basingstoke: Macmillan.

Murray, C. (1990), *The Emerging British Underclass*, IEA Health and Welfare Unit, Choice in Welfare series, Number 2.

Peckham, S. (1992), *Unplanned and Teenage Pregnancy: A Review*, Institute for Health Policy Studies, University of Southampton.

Peckham, S. (1993), 'Preventing unintended teenage pregnancies', *Public Health*, 107, 125-133.

Phoenix, A. (1991), *Young Mothers?*, Cambridge: Polity Press.

Popay, J, Rimmer, L. & Rossiter, C. (1983), *One Parent Families, Parents, Children & Public Policy*, Study Commission on the Family.

Royal College of Obstetricians and Gynaecologists (1991), *Report of the RCOG Working Party on Unplanned Pregnancy*, London: RCOG.

Rhode, D. L. (1993), 'Adolescent pregnancy and public policy', in Lawson & Rhode (eds), *The Politics of Pregnancy*.

Roberts, H. (1981), *'Male hegemony in family planning'*, in Roberts, H. (ed), *Women, Health and Reproduction*, London: Routledge & Kegan Paul.

Smith, T. (1993), 'Influence of socioeconomic factors on attaining targets for reducing teenage pregnancies', *British Medical Journal*, 306, 1232-5.

Tilford, S. (1992), 'Health Matters', in Coleman & Warren-Adamson (eds), *Youth Policy in the 1990s, The Way Forward*.

Weeks, J. (1981), *Sex, Politics and Society*, Harlow: Longman.

Weeks, J. (1985), *Sexuality and its Discontents*, London: Routledge & Kegan Paul.

Young, H. (1993), 'For back to basics read perverting them', *The Guardian*, 9 November.

The Current Problems of the Conservative Party

Andrew Denham
University of Exeter
&
Mark Garnett
University of Exeter

' "Conflicts of Loyalty": Cohesion and Division in Conservatism, 1975-1990'

Introduction

In his speech to the House of Commons on 13 November 1990, Sir Geoffrey Howe declared that his resignation had finally resolved a 'tragic' personal 'conflict of loyalties', to which his Conservative colleagues should now 'consider their own response'. This conflict – between loyalty to the Prime Minister, Margaret Thatcher, on one hand and loyalty to the national interest (as he saw it) on the other – was one with which Sir Geoffrey, by his own admission, had 'wrestled for perhaps too long'[1]. To us, the phrase 'conflicts of loyalty' highlights an important truth about Mrs.Thatcher's leadership of the Conservative Party from the outset. The following paper is a brief exploration of these conflicts. We believe that the most intriguing question is not so much why Mrs Thatcher fell from office (although this will form an important part of our discussion), as how it was that the unstable coalition of forces which sustained her as leader of the Conservative Party were able to do so for so long.

The Conservative Coalition

In a recent paper, Robert Faulkner has discussed the Presidency of Ronald Reagan in similar terms[2]. At the level of ideology, the Reaganite coalition was an unlikely combination of free-marketeers, traditionalist Catholic and traditionalist aristocratic intellectuals, neo-conservatives and the populist New Right of fundamentalist preachers and pro-family moralists[3]. According to Faulkner, the conservative movement in America now has a settled presence and power in its politicians, publishers and writers. But it has been a coalition of diverse views – diverging particularly as to which part of the American tradition ought to be conserved – and, following the collapse of communism and the disappearance of the Soviet military threat, the coalition is now cracked[4]. Since there was an undoubted affinity between

---

[1] Rt.Hon. Sir Geoffrey Howe, Personal Statement of November 13, 1990: *Hansard*, Sixth Series – Volume 180, pp.461-5.

[2] Robert K.Faulkner, 'The United States: Liberals, Conservatives and the Challenge of Liberation', *Political Studies*, XLV (1993), pp.107-32.

[3] *Ibid*, pp.130-1.

[4] *Ibid*, p.112.

the American and British conservative movements during the 1980s, we believe that Faulkner's article suggests some useful insights into the Thatcher project.

The view that the Conservative Party under Mrs Thatcher was a coalition of diverse forces has been common among both critics and admirers of her governments[5]. In the introduction to his re-issued essay *Mill and Liberalism*, Maurice Cowling claimed that her New Right supporters 'had five faces', distinguishable through their beliefs and their roles[6]. His list comprises free-market economists, parliamentarians, educationalists associated with the Black Papers, academics from Peterhouse, the L.S.E and elsewhere, and a 'Fleet Street Right' of journalists.

The overlap between these groups – sometimes even in their personnel – should not be under-estimated. However, their divisions were significant enough to justify Cowling's classification. Even where conflicting priorities were absent, there would often be functional differences; for example, the academics of Peterhouse did not have an electorate to consider, and the need to appease editors or to entertain a mass-readership was not so pressing for members of the 'élite-oriented' Centre for Policy Studies as it was for a journalist like Paul Johnson. One does not need to be a follower of Rousseau to detect in Cowling's analysis the tendency of such sub-groups to generate their own loyalties and factional disputes. The Institute of Economic Affairs, for example, always claimed to be above narrow party considerations, while in Parliament the followers of Enoch Powell would always be suspect to senior Conservatives because of their hero's ambivalent relationship with the Party.

Cowling's account suggests a further source of potential instability among his groups. He discusses the large number of important figures who had changed their political allegiances at least once before, and thus might be expected to do so again. Valuable converts to the New Right included Sir Rhodes Boyson, Dr A.E.Dyson, Lord Beloff, Kingsley Amis, Paul Johnson, Lord Thomas, Alfred Sherman, Lord Young, Lord Wyatt, Sir Alan Walters and even Rupert Murdoch. To complicate matters, these people had been recruited from varying sources – some had been Liberals, some lukewarm Labour voters, and even ex-communists could be found in the New Right coalition. Most of these people were individualistic by disposition; they were easily moved to rebellion. Many of them retained a deep hostility to 'the establishment' – a sentiment which made them unlikely recruits for the Conservative Party, and awkward collaborators in any sustained political movement. Since their beliefs were shaped more by antipathies than by a common positive vision; the need for a constant unifying enemy was particularly urgent for them.

The instability of the New Right, then, was always a potential threat to Mrs.Thatcher's continuation in office. After all, the New Right provided her with her ideas, and the zeal of its diverse factions lent momentum to her crusading projects. However, her success would not have been assured without other important elements in the broader Conservative coalition. The vocif-

---

[5] See especially John Gray's retrospective *Beyond the New Right*, London, 1993.
[6] Maurice Cowling, *Mill and Liberalism*, Second Edition, Cambridge, 1990, ix-xlv.

erous support of constituency parties was undoubtedly a useful factor in the winning of elections, although that continuing support was insufficient to prevent her eventual fall. Of more immediate importance was the attitude of ideologically- uncommitted back-benchers. After the defeat of the Conservative Party in the October 1974 election, Mrs.Thatcher was quoted as a 50-1 outsider to wrest the leadership from Mr. Heath; *The Times* reported that she was a far too divisive figure to stand much chance[7]. Her victory in the ensuing contest has often been attributed to the skilful tactics of her campaign team, led by Airey Neave. Whatever the means used to secure her triumph in 1975, she managed to retain the support of many constituency M.Ps who swallowed their instinctive mistrust of her visionary ideological politics. Although the composition of the Parliamentary Party obviously changed over the years, the number of 'true believers' was always heavily outweighed by those who were reluctant followers of a proven electoral winner; their support depended upon persistent evidence that Thatcher would be able to deliver success at the polls.[8]

An essential reason for the continued adherence of pragmatic backbenchers was the role of William Whitelaw. However much Mrs.Thatcher was associated with an iconoclastic hatred of the old establishment, the enthusiastic co-operation of Whitelaw was sufficient to allay many back-bench fears. Whitelaw's presence at Thatcher's elbow is evidence of another important factor in the success of her coalition. As a leading 'Heathite', Whitelaw had been regarded as an ideological opponent of New Right policies, and the natural leader of the so-called 'Wet' advocates of consensus. In the face of Whitelaw's desertion, the wets were unable to mount an effective challenge. Whatever their private convictions, this group acted as if their primary loyalty lay with the well-being of the Party; there were many rumours of plots, and some voted against the government on particularly contentious issues. But overall the wets' contribution during Mrs.Thatcher's term of office was helpful to her. Every Prime Minister has enemies, and only the most fortunate ones are opposed by people who dislike the notion of faction-fighting. The other bonus for Mrs.Thatcher was that the wets continued to be associated with Edward Heath, who was now generally regarded as an embittered failure. The wets, in short, regularly voted for Mrs.Thatcher, and rallied to her side those who wanted to turn their backs on the Heath years.

This, then, was the Conservative coalition. Superficially, it was a very unpromising collection. One group was totally opposed to Thatcherism in its style and content; another was, at best, tepid in its ideological support. Those who were most vocal in their loyalty were themselves divided in terms of priorities. A more familiar element of instability must be recorded. Of those parliamentarians who were ideologically attuned to Thatcherite doctrines, several were vulnerable to the usual pressures which affect senior politicians. Among those who were seen as potential heirs to her legacy, jealousies and impatience to reach the top were bound to arise. The career of John Moore is a useful example of the tension which this created; an additional problem in his case was the normal problem which arises

---

[7] *Times* editorial, Tuesday, October 15, 1974.
[8] Andrew Gamble, *The Free Economy and the Strong State*, London, 1988, p.120.

between spending and Treasury ministers in even ideologically-unified cabinets. Finally, one can see Geoffrey Howe's resignation as partly the result of departmentally-generated tensions; we regard the European issue as a field in which one Thatcherite principle (the free market) collided violently with another (patriotism). In the Foreign Office, Howe was always more likely to believe that the British economy would benefit from closer union with Europe; although she was very active in foreign affairs, Mrs.Thatcher had never favoured the Foreign Office and part of her antipathy to 'abroad' can be explained in terms of this institutional factor.

Up to this point our analysis has suggested that the coalition backing Margaret Thatcher was unusually divided from the outset. We have briefly indicated some of the reasons why the logical result of such divisions – the end of Mrs.Thatcher's leadership – was so long delayed. Opposition to a perceived enemy, however, was probably the most important factor common to all the groups, and we shall return to this question. For ideological opponents of Mrs.Thatcher, and the uncommitted backbenchers, additional factors were required. Party loyalty, the presence of Lord Whitelaw, and their own disunity were the most significant reasons for the wet attitude of unarmed hostility. The backbenchers were kept happy by electoral successes and the evident enthusiasm of their constituency parties.

The importance of these factors is signalled by what happened when circumstances changed. The departure of Whitelaw in late 1987 had a doubly damaging effect; his reassuring moderation was taken away, and it was apparently replaced by the fervour of close associates such as Charles Powell, Bernard Ingham and Alan Walters, who had no source of independent authority in the Party. The run of poor election results, culminating with the disastrous defeat at Eastbourne in Autumn 1990, indicated to backbenchers that Mrs.Thatcher's coat-tails were unlikely to haul them to another victory. Eastbourne was particularly cheering for the wets; the suggestion that Mrs.Thatcher had become a liability could allow them to square their instinctive loyalty to the Party with opposition to her.

Important as they were, these developments occurred late in Thatcher's premiership. In the closing section of this paper we will contend that the break-up of the Conservative coalition began much earlier. Precision in these cases is impossible, but some time in 1985 can be suggested as a likely date. This was the time when Mrs.Thatcher lost her most important asset in the fight for Conservative cohesion; the existence of unifying enemies. Without this loss, we contend that the events noted above might not have occurred; even if they had, their impact would not have been decisive.

The Need for Unifying Enemies

When a political movement depends crucially upon common enemies for its continuation, it is in a particularly hazardous situation. One might even say that there is only one thing worse than defeat at the hands of these enemies, and that is complete victory over them. Whether Mrs.Thatcher should be credited with personally defeating the foes of the Conservative Party during the 1980s is not at issue here. The essential point is that one by one the enemies either dwindled or disappeared entirely. The Prime Minister might not have been conscious of the importance of enemies, yet it can be argued that her continuing search for new battles to fight was the most significant reason for her fall.

As an opposition leader after 1975, Mrs.Thatcher's most important enemy was the Labour Party. The political situation during these years was particularly conducive to Tory unity; Labour's vulnerability in Parliament provided the Party with an opportunity which could not be squandered through internal bickering, and allies outside parliament had the same reason for throwing their weight behind the leader[9]. After the 1979 election Labour moved significantly to the left, which made the prospect of their return to office unpalatable for all members of the coalition. However, defeat in 1983, and the attempts by Neil Kinnock to 'modernise' his Party, meant that the reality of the Labour threat gradually receded – although, of course, it was still possible to exaggerate it for the public at election-time.

Another vital enemy in 1975 was the Soviet Union. Mrs Thatcher quickly exploited this opportunity, earning herself the soubriquet of 'The Iron Lady' from the Soviet press. Her cold-war rhetoric helped to gain a victory over CND, and the existence of a fully state-controlled economy which was so palpably inefficient enabled her supporters to paint the virtues of the free market in more vivid colours. In December 1984, however, Mrs.Thatcher treated the rising Mikhail Gorbachev as a trustworthy statesman; Gorbachev's attempts at economic reform after he had succeeded to office further reduced the potency of the communist threat. The fall of the Berlin Wall might have helped to produce a feeling that Mrs.Thatcher's confrontational approach to foreign policy was no longer appropriate, but this should not obscure the fact that the Soviet Union had become an unprofitable enemy for her some time earlier.

The most frequently-cited of Mrs.Thatcher's convenient enemies are General Galtieri and Arthur Scargill. The Falklands War certainly distracted public attention away from another threat, the newly-formed SDP – the defeat of this Party in 1983 was so conclusive that they were never able to fulfil their promise as a unifying enemy for the Tories. With the end of the miners' strike in March 1985, a more traditional Tory foe was eradicated. All elements of the coalition could unite on this issue; it is significant that the leading role in the campaign was played by the Heathite Peter Walker. However, the outcome could also be read as a humiliation for Heath, who had been driven from office by Scargill and the miners. Most of Heath's prominent supporters had been sacked, or otherwise neutralised, thus depriving Mrs.Thatcher of a group whose reputed penchant for U-turns could always be used to frighten her hard-line adherents into conformity.

Although the capitulation of the miners might have been regarded at the time as a crowning triumph which rendered Mrs.Thatcher invulnerable, it is our contention that the opposite occured. She had been in trouble before, most recently during the Grenada crisis of the previous year when supposed loyalists including Paul Johnson and Rupert Murdoch had wavered. From this time onwards, however, the problems which she faced could not be de-

---

[9] See R.Blake & J.Patten (eds), *The Conservative Opportunity*, London, 1976.

fused by an appeal to a credible over-riding threat. Later in 1985, Thatcher
was confronted with the growing controversy over Westland helicopters, an
internal Cabinet dispute which showed that a senior cabinet minister was
unafraid to challenge her authority – at least indirectly. Perhaps even more
important was the meeting of 13 November in that year, at which a request
was made by Geoffrey Howe, Nigel Lawson and Robin Leigh-Pemberton for
sterling to join the European Monetary System (EMS). January of 1986 saw
the resignation of Mr.Heseltine; in the following month Mrs.Thatcher signed
the *Single European Act*. In May of that year John Biffen publicly called for
a more 'balanced' Conservative team; at the same time Douglas Hurd delivered a coded warning about the direction of Mrs.Thatcher's government.
In short, the series of victories in the years up to 1985 had clearly failed
to stamp Mrs. Thatcher's authority over the coalition which backed her –
yet this was a time when the economy was picking up, and unemployment
finally beginning to fall.

By February 1987, Nigel Lawson had begun to act as if Britain was a
member of the Exchange Rate Mechanism of the EMS, despite his leader's
earlier veto. In the election of that year Norman Tebbit allegedly provoked
Mrs.Thatcher's wrath by keeping her away from the cameras; Tebbit's an-
gry dispute with Lord Young, who knew relatively little about either the
Party or electioneering, is an astonishing symptom of increasing disunity
even between ideological allies. Mrs.Thatcher's evident support for Young
indicates that the lack of convincing enemies was leading her to seek them
even within the ranks of her closest adherents.

We believe that it is in this context that the Bruges speech of September
1988 should be read. There were, of course, many reasons for Mrs.Thatcher's
outburst; it might be said that Geoffrey Howe arrived at his decision to resign rather tardily, given that the Prime Minister's views must have been
well known to him for many years. However, the most important passages
of the speech strongly suggest that Mrs.Thatcher was hoping to use the
European bogey as a new enemy to rally the Party behind her. The best-
known sentence certainly strikes this note – she claimed that the threat of an
over-mighty state had been defeated in Britain, but a new battle against the
encroachments of a 'European super-state' might be in the offing. Less often
noticed is the fact that the preceding sentence mentions the reforms which
had made the Soviet Union increasingly redundant as a cohesive threat[10].

As John Peterson has shown, polling evidence from early 1988 revealed
a noticable dip in support for the European Community[11]. Unfortunately
for Mrs.Thatcher, this trend was temporary, and approval soon resumed
its earlier rise. Geoffrey Howe reputedly thought that the speech was an
electoral gambit, as did Nigel Lawson[12]. If they were right, then their leader
had made an unfortunate mistake. According to Philip Norton, around
20% of Tory M.P's were firmly committed to Europe by 1990, and a further

---

[10] Rt.Hon Mrs Margaret Thatcher, 'Britain and Europe', speech delivered in Bruges on
20th September 1988, Conservative Political Centre, 1988, p.4.

[11] John Peterson, 'The European Community', in D. Marsh & R.A.W Rhodes (eds),
Implementing Thatcherite Policies: Audit of an Era, Oxford, 1992, p.156.

[12] Hugo Young, *One of Us*, London, 1993, p.550; Nigel Lawson, *The View From Number
11*, London, 1993, p.900.

significant number had a constructive approach to the European question[13]. It is possible that Mrs.Thatcher was aware of this, and felt so strongly on the issue that she decided to appeal over the heads of the Party to a public which might be swayed. Whatever her motives, this was an issue which was likely to pull her coalition apart instead of uniting it. It provoked the leadership challenge of Sir Anthony Meyer, whose defeat was most notable for the fact that sixty M.Ps withheld their votes from Mrs.Thatcher. Even more significantly, Lord Thomas, who headed the Centre for Policy Studies, chose to resign over Europe. As we noted earlier, a belief in the free market is perfectly compatible with pro-European sympathies. If our reading of events is correct, the most ironic aspect of Mrs.Thatcher's fall is the fact that when a truly unifying enemy arrived in the shape of Saddam Hussein, she had committed herself so whole-heartedly to the European battle that she was unable to exploit this opportunity to re-assemble the coalition.

Although there is insufficient space to address this question in detail, it can be argued that in essentials the Poll Tax controversy arose from a broadly similar origin. The long-running campaign against high-spending local authorities had often included a strong suggestion that such bodies constituted an enemy, and the fact that such different characters as Norman Tebbit and Michael Heseltine could join forces against the ILEA indicates the unifying potential of this issue. Yet while attacks on London authorities had the virtue of hitting mainly Labour targets, an assault on local government as a whole carried the risk of alienating important Tory interests. More importantly, while the Poll Tax had the eventual goal of attracting local voters to low-spending councils, in the short- term the benefits seemed to be outweighed by the disadvantages caused by non-payment and demonstrations. Thus it can be seen that local government turned out to be another divisive enemy for Mrs.Thatcher. When one considers Mrs.Thatcher's long-standing promise to reform the rates, it is interesting that the Poll Tax originated in 1985 – the time when more suitable enemies were no longer available. The conclusion which can be drawn from the Poll Tax is that after 1985 Mrs.Thatcher could no longer delay giving some positive satisfaction to her supporters; her attempt to do so by radical reform of local government finance merely demonstrated the impossibility of pleasing more than a fragment of her coalition.

Conclusion

Our focus on the factors which promoted unity in the Thatcher coalition does not challenge the widely accepted *direct* reasons for her fall. Clearly Europe and the Poll Tax, combined with the perceived decline in electoral support, were the immediate causes of the leadership crisis. We contend, however, that the context from which these issues emerged can only be understood by examining the divisions which Mrs.Thatcher inherited (and provoked) in 1975. The existence of enemies, whether external or internal, was necessary to keep the Conservative coalition alive; after 1985, however,

---

[13] Cited by John Peterson, *op.cit.*

Mrs.Thatcher was unable to find anyone to oppose with the united support of the movement. By contrast, Europe and local government were issues which accentuated the existing divisions, rather than obscuring them. Despite the election victory of 1987, Mrs.Thatcher's authority was steadily eroded from 1985 onwards, even among her closest supporters. As Lord Lawson wrote in his memoirs, '1985 was in many respects a watershed year. It was then that all the elements which brought about the downfall of Margaret Thatcher five years later originally emerged'[14]. At the time of publication this seemed an idiosyncratic judgement, but our claim that the most important elements which sustained Mrs.Thatcher had disappeared by March 1985 lends it indirect support.

A brief closing glance at events since 1990 shows that Mr. Major has simply inherited Thatcher's insoluble dilemma. For a while the unifying figure of Saddam Hussein boosted his popularity, but as soon as the Gulf campaign was over the sense of drift began in the absence of suitable enemies. Despite his apparently pragmatic instincts, Major has been unable to resist the more clamorous voices in his coalition. While Mrs.Thatcher often made clear her hatred of the 'dependency culture', her feelings were mostly exercised at the level of rhetoric; even when her need for enemies was at its greatest, she realised that the perception of danger to the welfare state would have unfortunate electoral consequences (however much it would have pleased certain members of her coalition). It is a measure of Major's desperation that he has allowed the more extreme New Right to dictate his policy agenda. However, this might be in the medium-term interests of the Party, since at present it seems sure to cause another period of non-Conservative government which will give the disparate Tory forces a viable new enemy to confront.

---

[14] Lawson, *op.cit*, p.888.

The Current Problems of the Conservative Party

David Baker
Nottingham Trent University
Andrew Gamble
University of Sheffield
&
Steve Ludlam
University of Sheffield

'Mapping Conservative Fault Lines:
Problems of Typology'[1]

Abstract

The most damaging internal divisions within the Conservative Party today are over European integration. Of these divisions the most disruptive of all has been within the Thatcherite wing. Existing typologies of Conservatism do little to help identify or make sense of these divisions. This paper considers such typologies, discusses their characteristics, and suggests an alternative two-dimensional typology aimed at characterising divisions over Europe as a basis for further empirical research.

Introduction

'Political Conservatism ... is not monolithic. ... The messiness of an operational ideology can never approximate to the pristine orderliness of fundemental ideological principles. Yet the stress placed upon loyalty and unity within the Conservative political tradition is an instinct as old as politics itself, all the more potent because Conservatism defends the privileges of a minority. Divisions within ruling strata are potentially more subversive and destructive than manifest divisions between those strata and the majority of the less privileged. ... The Conservative stress on pragmatism, compromise and the tempering of policy disagreements has its roots in the fear that confrontation between factions within the privileged groups could of itself undermine the whole structure of the political organisation of society.' (Norton & Aughey 1981, 50/51)

---

[1] Why use typology rather than taxonomy? The latter carries more overtones of natural science procedure 'especially the systematic classification of living organisms' (OED), the former is defined explicitly in terms of classification of 'especially human products, behaviour, characteristics, etc, according to type' (OED).

Types of Typology

Political scientists have always had difficulty classifying ideological groupings in the Conservative Party. This is a party which officially denies that
it possesses an ideology. Conservatives have tended to regard ideology as a
foreign import, and as part of an approach to politics which gives a higher
priority to doctrine rather than to experience. In rejecting ideology Conservatives are rejecting rationalism and affirming the limits of politics and
political agency. Sir Ian Gilmour could imagine no greater insult to pin
on the Thatcherites than that they had imported an ideological dogma into
the Conservative Party and wrenched the Party from its traditions (Gilmour
1992). Although Thatcher herself is reported to have said 'the other side
have an ideology; we must have one as well' many of her intellectual supporters have insisted that Thatcherism seeks to restore a style of Conservative
politics that is non-ideological and breaks from the rationalist, interventionist Conservatism of the Macmillan/Heath era (Letwin 1992; Gamble
1993). The fierceness of recent internal debate suggests a party suffering
a surfeit of ideology. The recent period may be regarded as exceptional,
but political scientists and historians have never accepted the protestations
of Conservatives that they alone were somehow immune from ideological
contagion. Only a very restricted definition of the term ideology, such as
Letwin's (1992), would support such a contention.

All those who have studied it have however concluded that British Conservatism has particular characteristics making classification of its ideological groupings difficult. British Conservatism evolved as a tradition of
statecraft in which abstract doctrines were subordinated to combining the
realities of governing (the politics of power) with the realities of winning
votes (the politics of support); the European tradition of authoritarian
Conservatism following the French Revolution was much weaker in Britain,
and therefore the distinction between Conservatism and Liberalism was less
sharp; and the emphasis on loyalty and unity within the Party was very
strong, and normally sufficient to inhibit the formation of permanent ideological groupings.

General attempts to analyse Conservatism followed two distinct paths.
The first exemplified by Greenleaf discerns broad sets of ideas or principles, which find expression in specific disputes over policies and leaders.
(Greenleaf 1973, 19). Greenleaf argues that the British political tradition
is constituted by a set of discourses which have two poles – libertarianism
and collectivism. The ideological debates which these occasion do not exist
only between parties but within parties. Greenleaf's formulation of this basic divide restates a tradition of thinking about British politics which has
many antecedents including Dicey and Oakeshott, and remains perhaps the
single most influential distinction, which constantly resurfaces. It suggests
that the key issue in twentieth politics is the scope and role of the state in
the economy.

Greenleaf's method is an idealist one, founded on the belief that ideas are
the basic constituents of political reality. A very different approach is that
of Richard Rose who was much less interested in ideas than in behaviour. In

his classification of organisational forms within British parties into factions, tendencies and non-aligned partisans, Richard Rose offered a left-right ideological typology applicable to Conservatives and to Labour, and offered a basis for making comparisons between them (Rose 1964). Rose offered the following definitions (Rose 1985, 301):

> 'Factions are self-consciously organised groups that persistently advance a programme for government and a leader to govern ... A tendency is a stable set of attitudes rather than a stable collection of politicians. The names and numbers of MPs adhering to right-wing or left-wing tendencies within a party can vary from issue to issue. Non-aligned MPs ignore intraparty differences in order to emphasize differences between parties.'

When Rose first advanced this analysis it was designed to distinguish Labour (a party of factions) from the Conservatives (a party of tendencies). Interestingly, since 1979 these chararcteristics have become reversed. Rose's classification indicates nothing directly about the content of ideological groupings but focuses attention instead on the institutional mechanisms by which ideological differences can be sustained. It pointed political scientists towards the need for a much more detailed exploration of the beliefs and values which politicians hold. Rose directs attention to the political contexts in which ideas are held and shaped, but Greenleaf's emphasis on the grand narratives of the British politics tradition produced a left/right ideological axis that has informed most typologies of Conservatism.

Noting the tendency of academic maps of Tory ideology to have only one wet/dry, right/left dimension, Patrick Dunleavy (1993) recently offered the alternative two-dimensional map discussed below. He conceded that 'the pro- and anti-European feeling does not match up neatly with the basic ideological map of Toryism'. This is a significant qualification, as division over European integration is hardly an ideological sideshow. It has brought the Tories to the brink of catastrophe, hastening seven Cabinet resignations/sackings since 1986, producing the most sustained and perilous backbench revolt for generations, and on July 22nd resulting in the worst parliamentary defeat suffered by the Tories this century, followed by Major's humiliating 'fly me to Maastricht or I kill us all' confidence vote. The most striking feature of these disputes is division within the 1980s Thatcherite wing of the Parliamentary Party, a feature impossible to identify using most of the available maps of Tory ideology.

Figure 1 charts some of the main and most recent typologies of Conservatism. A major distinction between the typologies represented here is their subject matter. Some characterise ideology, others behaviour, and others policy divisions. In methodological terms, a simple distinction exists between those offered as the conclusion of research, and those devised as the basis for research activity. A more fundamental distinction separates those derived by purely quantitative empirical research from those contructed by qualitative analysis of texts and other historical evidence (combined with quantitative research in Norton 1990).

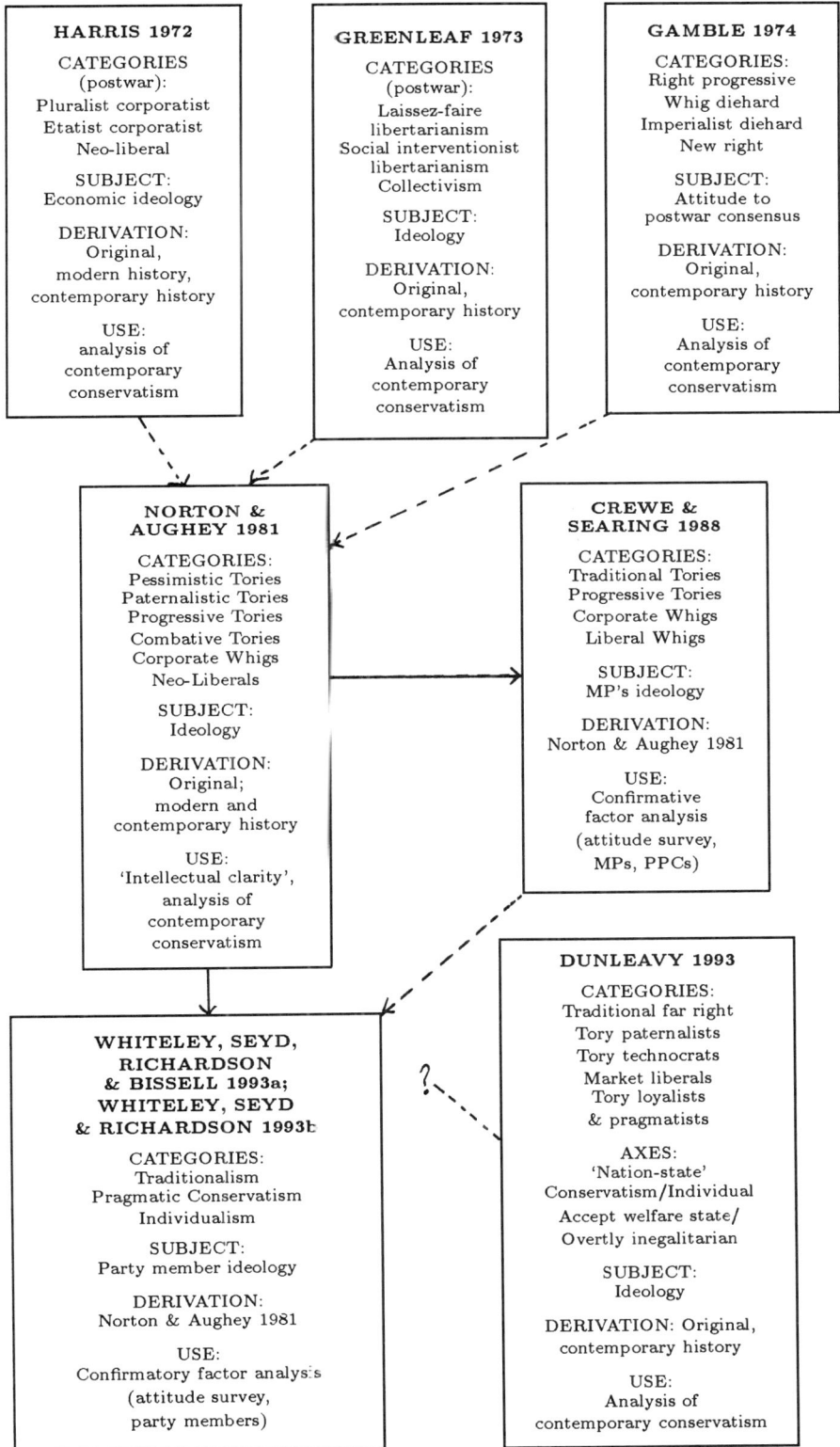

HARRIS 1972

CATEGORIES
(postwar):
Pluralist corporatist
Etatist corporatist
Neo-liberal

SUBJECT:
Economic ideology

DERIVATION:
Original,
modern history,
contemporary history

USE:
analysis of
contemporary
conservatism

GREENLEAF 1973

CATEGORIES
(postwar):
Laissez-faire
libertarianism
Social interventionist
libertarianism
Collectivism

SUBJECT:
Ideology

DERIVATION:
Original,
contemporary history

USE:
Analysis of
contemporary
conservatism

GAMBLE 1974

CATEGORIES:
Right progressive
Whig diehard
Imperialist diehard
New right

SUBJECT:
Attitude to
postwar consensus

DERIVATION:
Original,
contemporary history

USE:
Analysis of
contemporary
conservatism

**NORTON &
AUGHEY 1981**

CATEGORIES:
Pessimistic Tories
Paternalistic Tories
Progressive Tories
Combative Tories
Corporate Whigs
Neo-Liberals

SUBJECT:
Ideology

DERIVATION:
Original;
modern and
contemporary history

USE:
'Intellectual clarity',
analysis of
contemporary
conservatism

**CREWE &
SEARING 1988**

CATEGORIES:
Traditional Tories
Progressive Tories
Corporate Whigs
Liberal Whigs

SUBJECT:
MP's ideology

DERIVATION:
Norton & Aughey 1981

USE:
Confirmative
factor analysis
(attitude survey,
MPs, PPCs)

**WHITELEY, SEYD,
RICHARDSON
& BISSELL 1993a;
WHITELEY, SEYD
& RICHARDSON 1993b**

CATEGORIES:
Traditionalism
Pragmatic Conservatism
Individualism

SUBJECT:
Party member ideology

DERIVATION:
Norton & Aughey 1981

USE:
Confirmatory factor analysis
(attitude survey,
party members)

DUNLEAVY 1993

CATEGORIES:
Traditional far right
Tory paternalists
Tory technocrats
Market liberals
Tory loyalists
& pragmatists

AXES:
'Nation-state'
Conservatism/Individual
Accept welfare state/
Overtly inegalitarian

SUBJECT:
Ideology

DERIVATION: Original,
contemporary history

USE:
Analysis of
contemporary conservatism

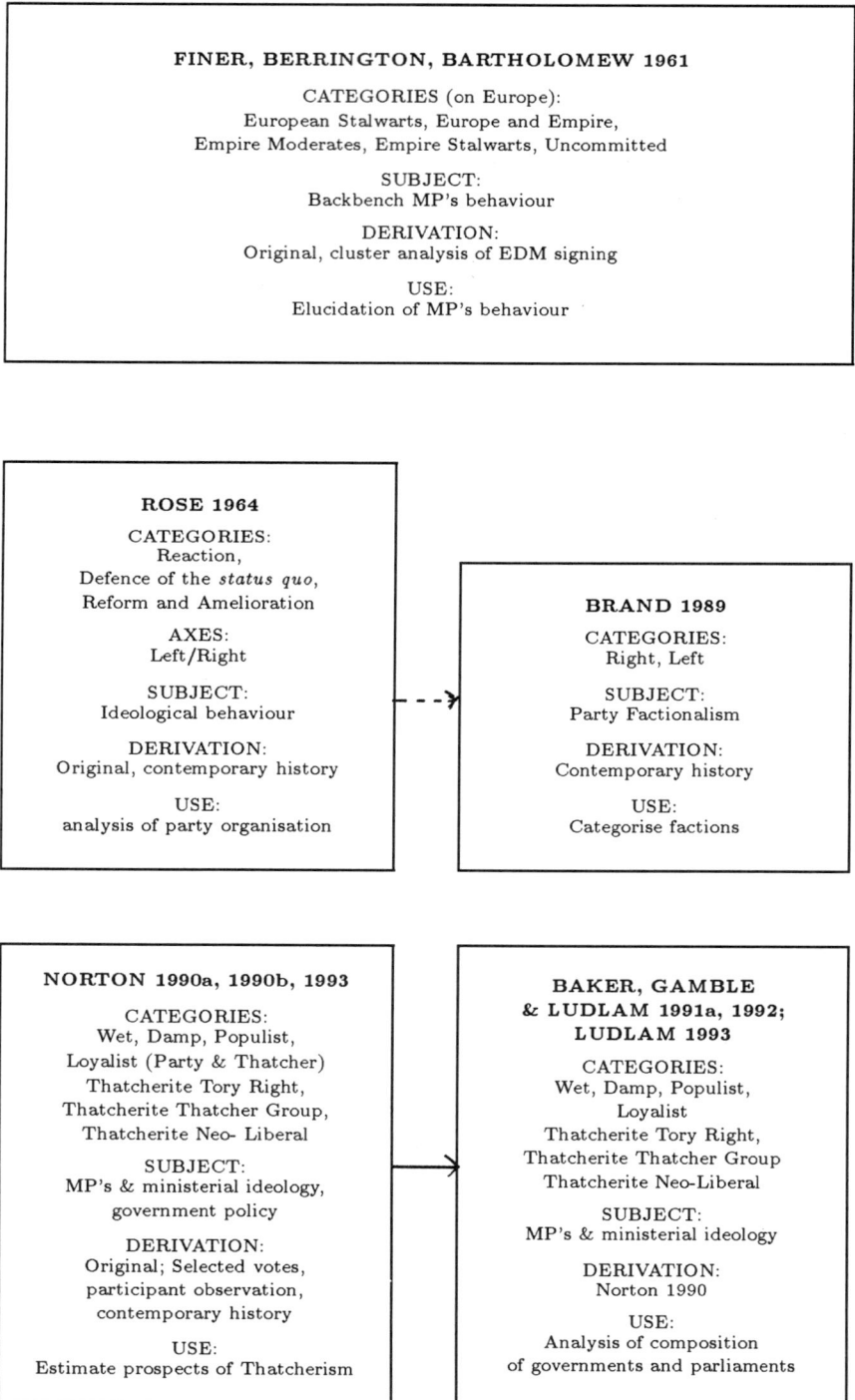

FINER, BERRINGTON, BARTHOLOMEW 1961

CATEGORIES (on Europe):
European Stalwarts, Europe and Empire,
Empire Moderates, Empire Stalwarts, Uncommitted

SUBJECT:
Backbench MP's behaviour

DERIVATION:
Original, cluster analysis of EDM signing

USE:
Elucidation of MP's behaviour

ROSE 1964

CATEGORIES:
Reaction,
Defence of the *status quo*,
Reform and Amelioration

AXES:
Left/Right

SUBJECT:
Ideological behaviour

DERIVATION:
Original, contemporary history

USE:
analysis of party organisation

- - - ➤

BRAND 1989

CATEGORIES:
Right, Left

SUBJECT:
Party Factionalism

DERIVATION:
Contemporary history

USE:
Categorise factions

NORTON 1990a, 1990b, 1993

CATEGORIES:
Wet, Damp, Populist,
Loyalist (Party & Thatcher)
Thatcherite Tory Right,
Thatcherite Thatcher Group,
Thatcherite Neo- Liberal

SUBJECT:
MP's & ministerial ideology,
government policy

DERIVATION:
Original; Selected votes,
participant observation,
contemporary history

USE:
Estimate prospects of Thatcherism

───➤

**BAKER, GAMBLE
& LUDLAM 1991a, 1992;
LUDLAM 1993**

CATEGORIES:
Wet, Damp, Populist,
Loyalist
Thatcherite Tory Right,
Thatcherite Thatcher Group
Thatcherite Neo-Liberal

SUBJECT:
MP's & ministerial ideology

DERIVATION:
Norton 1990

USE:
Analysis of composition
of governments and parliaments

Figure 1C
Typologies of Conservatism
Policy

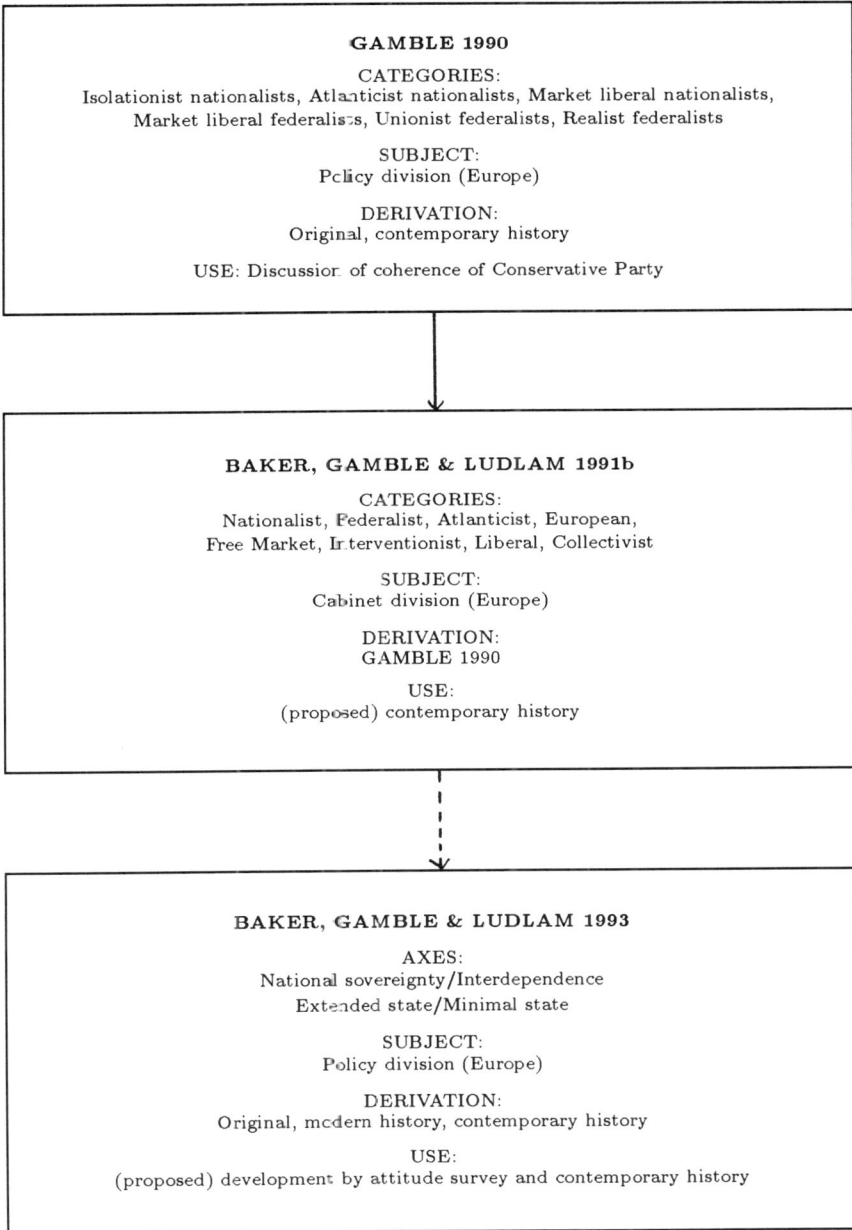

GAMBLE 1990

CATEGORIES:
Isolationist nationalists, Atlanticist nationalists, Market liberal nationalists,
Market liberal federalists, Unionist federalists, Realist federalists

SUBJECT:
Policy division (Europe)

DERIVATION:
Original, contemporary history

USE: Discussion of coherence of Conservative Party

BAKER, GAMBLE & LUDLAM 1991b

CATEGORIES:
Nationalist, Federalist, Atlanticist, European,
Free Market, Interventionist, Liberal, Collectivist

SUBJECT:
Cabinet division (Europe)

DERIVATION:
GAMBLE 1990

USE:
(proposed) contemporary history

BAKER, GAMBLE & LUDLAM 1993

AXES:
National sovereignty/Interdependence
Extended state/Minimal state

SUBJECT:
Policy division (Europe)

DERIVATION:
Original, modern history, contemporary history

USE:
(proposed) development by attitude survey and contemporary history

---

Of the typologies we are aware of, the only one that has actually been constructed on the basis solely of quantitative social scientific research is that of Finer, Berrington, & Bartholomew[2], in which the categories derive

---

[2] Berrington's later (1973) study, *Backbench Opinion in the House of Commons 1945-*

from statistical analysis of measurable political behaviour of MPs (signing early day motions). Their typology is the outcome of original quantitative research, rather than the application of an already existing framework for new empirical research. Other typologies have been borrowed to test further research questions by complex quantitative methods (Crewe & Searing 1988; Whiteley *et al* 1993 – from Norton & Aughey 1981) or simple quantitative methods (Baker *et al* 1991, 1992; Ludlam 1993 – from Norton 1990). The borrowed typologies were constructed qualitatively on the basis of historical and political analysis, mainly of texts (Norton & Aughey 1981), as are, to a greater or lesser extent, all the other original typologies on the chart (bar Finer *et al*). The partial exception is Norton's (1990) work, which is based on a combination of methods that help overcome the narrow range of measureable behavioural indicators, above all in the case of ministers. Unfortunately for our purposes the Finer *et al* typology of positions on European integration predates the first application to join the EEC, in a period when the imperial alternative was still regarded as viable by many Tories, before the resurgence in the 1970s of economic liberalism, entry into the EEC, and the impact of Thatcherism on debate over Europe.

The most widely-cited and deployed typologies have categorized ideology. Norton has been particularly influential. His work with Aughey (1981) produced six categories that synthesized their research and other important qualitative work on postwar conservatism. The main weakness for our purpose is that it too predates the divisions over Europe from the mid-1980s and the full impact of Thatcherism. As they are at pains to point out, 'Attitudes can only be studied contextually to be fruitful' (1981, 55). Insofar as Thatcherites (Thatcher, Joseph, Boyson) appear in person in the 1981 account, it is as 'combative Tories' whose main feature is popularisation of middle class values and 'prejudices'. Paradoxically, the two typologies (Crewe & Searing, Whiteley *et al*) derived from Norton & Aughey to consider the strength of Thatcherism drop the 'combative Tory' category from their refined versions.

Crewe & Searing (1988) refined Norton & Aughey (1981) to use four categories – traditional and progressive Tories, corporate and liberal Whigs – to test a spatial theory of ideological change, in particular whether Thatcherism responded to prior changes in public or Conservative opinion. In the latter case the results of a 1972/3 value ranking survey of MPs and PPCs were used to carry out a confirmatory factor analysis whose purpose was explicitly not to reconstruct a typology ('uncover dimensions beneath a wide field of values') but to test the authors' views of the main values structuring Tory and Whig thinking and of the ranking of such values (1988, 366-370). There is no intention or attempt, naturally, to use survey material predating Thatcher's leadership to construct one new typology of Thatcher's party based on another (Norton & Aughey 1981) that only partially incorporates the Thatcher phenomenon. Nor is the original value ranking survey easily applicable to analysis of divisions over Europe whose protagonists frequently claim to uphold the same general values being ranked, like statecraft, free enterprise, patriotism, efficiency, rationalism, capitalism.

55, covers an earlier period that predates United Kingdom applications to join the EEC.

Whiteley *et al* (1993a, 1993b) also explicitly adapt Norton & Aughey (1981), which they criticize for confounding ideas and styles, and for significant overlap between categories. They adopt the archaeological approach (Maude 1963) of identifying traditions that appear throughout the Party's modern existence at various depths in its ideological history, specifying three: traditionalism, progressive conservatism, individualism. These are then also used to mount a confirmatory factor analysis (and to criticise spatial theory) on the basis of the results of an unprecedented survey of Conservative Party members. The crucial difference from the Crewe & Searing exercise is the analysis of Conservative ideology in terms of contemporary political issues. These issues include several specifically aimed at divisions over European integration. The results suggest that attitudes to the EC, 'an index of traditionalism' were the 'strongest predictor of attitudes to Mrs. Thatcher' (1993a, 18). For our purposes, this typology is nevertheless too general to capture the complexity of divisions among MPs and ministers (as distinct from members) over European integration. There is a particular problem in that a group of leading Thatcherites, including Thatcher, have sought to make Europe an 'index of individualism' in terms of the Whiteley *et al* typology.

Typologies aimed at elucidating the behaviour of MPs generally produce more detailed categories. In our view Norton's has been the most effective recent original typology oriented on behaviour and policy rather than general ideology (1990). A combination of methods (division votes, published opinions, participant observation by a leading Conservative academic) was used that overcame an important limitation of the Finer *et al* research: namely that the 80 or so most important MPs in the governing party, serving ministers, do not sign EDMs, and therefore present no measurable behaviour. None of the votes used by Norton, however, was on Europe, and Europe was a general test of position (pro- or anti-Europe) in only four of his seven categories, four which contained only a minority of MPs and ministers. Norton 1990 is thus not a particularly helpful basis on which to analyse divisions over Europe that have in any case intensified dramatically in the years since his work. His combined methods have nevertheless provided a sound (and unique) basis for commentary on subsequent changes of personnel (Baker *et al* 1991, 1992), even if the gap between ministers' classifications and the policies they now espouse suggests a revised Norton typology would be welcome (Ludlam 1993). Two specific recent Conservative controversies, occurring three years after Norton published, illustrate the general strength of his approach. When commentators first nominated their candidates following Major's remark that his Cabinet contained three euro-rebellious 'bastards', the threesome most mentioned comprised Portillo, Lilley, and Howard. Only occasionally was Redwood mentioned. A glance at Norton's categories, however, identified Portillo, Lilley and Redwood as Thatcherites, with Howard categorised as a more pliable Loyalist. The accuracy of this designation was soon validated as commentators replaced Howard with Redwood on the strength of insider accounts. Later in 1993 when Sir George Gardiner, leader of the Thatcherite Conservative Way Forward group, was ousted from the 1922 Committee Executive for his

Maastricht rebellion, he was replaced by David Evans. Many reported this as a politically neutral or paradoxical event, since Evans was also regarded as a rightwinger, rendering the whole maneouvre inexplicable. Others noted that, although an outspoken rightwing moralist and PPS to Redwood, on Europe Evans was a loyalist. In 1990 Norton had categorised him a Loyalist, rather than a Thatcherite.

Dunleavy (1993) criticises the tendency for academic accounts to give only a more refined one-dimensional version of popular left/right, wet/dry typologies, singling out Norton 1990 and its derivative, Baker *et al* 1992. Given the variety of issues in the seventeen Commons votes used as one source for Norton's typology this is perhaps harsh. And though Norton's categories can be lined up along a broad wet/dry axis, they do include important distinctions within wet and dry camps, and include the large and important 'marais' of loyalists of indeterminate ideological persuasion also featured in the centre of Dunleavy's map. Dunleavy's four other categories – Tory paternalists, Tory technocrats, traditional far right and market liberals – are hard to distinguish from other longstanding academic categories, as the chart suggests. Apart from the admission that it cannot map the crucial divisions over Europe, what is most perplexing, given the stress on the need to provide two dimensions, is the extent to which one of Dunleavy's dimensions (accept welfare state/overtly inegalitarian) appears to be just a kaleidoscopic policy-specific reflection of the other, more general one (nation-state conservatism/individual).

A Typology of a New Type

Our purpose in seeking a workable typology has been to use it to help shed light on the nature and depth of Conservative divisions over European integration, and to help assess whether the Party can contain such divisions. 'Policy' typologies are complicated, because ideology and behaviour that are relatively straightforward to identify or quantify deviate most unpredictably from traditional core positions in response to political and external factors and events. We are attempting to build our typology in the light of the most successful past methods, that have involved both qualitative and quantitative research. We are drawing our axes on the basis of both historical and current policy contexts, 'through time' and 'in time' in terms of Bulpitt's prescriptions for researching the Party (1991, 14-16). The study of the political context of Conservative ideology was also the origin of the analyses of Harris (1972), Gamble (1974) and Bulpitt (1985). All three argued in different ways that in order to understand Conservative ideologies they had to be related to the context in which they arose; Harris emphasised the economic structure, distinguishing between étatiste and pluralist corporatism as the two dominant strands of postwar Conservatism; Gamble emphasised political strategy, conceived as the interplay between the politics of power and the politics of support; while Bulpitt stressed statecraft and the operational code of the political élite. Having identified our main axes on the basis of modern and contemporary historical analysis, we intend to develop the empirical foundations of the typology using a combination of both quantitative and further qualitative analysis. We plan to conduct a survey of Conservative parliamentarians designed to locate them on our map in terms of policy issues related to EC integration. And we intend to conduct an extensive analysis of the 'ideological event' of the EP election using party and printed and broadcast media sources.

Our historical analysis of major Conservative splits and divisions suggested that strategic political economy choices involving different conceptions of state intervention were often central, as over Corn Law Reform and Tariff Reform (Baker *et al* 1993a, 1993b). Both major splits came from a strategic choice of Britain's future role in the world political economy. In 1846 and 1903 legislative sovereignty was not at stake, but in the most recent phase of British decline it has been, first through the transfer of supremacy to the United States, and from 1973 through EC membership. The severity of the divisions over sovereignty suggests a dimension that deserves more attention in discussion of Conservative ideology. We have suggested that the key axes for understanding these crucial disputes are national sovereignty/interdependence and extended government/limited government (Baker *et al* 1993a, 1993b).[3]

Locating the different tendencies of the Party in terms of both the sovereignty/interdependence axis and the extended government/limited government axis emphasises how the struggle for ideological dominance in the Party has concerned not just collectivism in domestic policy, but also interdependence in external policy. Thatcherism can be seen as a return to a limited government tradition but also to the mainstream national sovereignty tradition. If the former consolidated her leadership, the latter helped isolate Thatcher in her Cabinet. As Lawson observed:

> 'It was always clear to me that the Conservative Party could be successfully led only by someone who took their stand in the centre of the spectrum on this issue [Europe], where the silent majority dwelt. Margaret's evident determination to lead the Party from one of the two extremes of that spectrum spelled nothing but trouble.' (Lawson 1992, 923)

The Maastricht rebellion is hitherto the most protracted form that such trouble has taken. The extension of qualified majority voting (QMV), the continuation of the EMU programme, and the prospect of a Maastricht II and EMU Stage 3 emerging from the 1996 IGC, threaten instability for the Conservatives along the sovereignty/interdependence axis for the rest of this Parliament. The European Parliament election will raise all these issues, and is regarded as a critical test of the Major's leadership: it deserves to be closely studied as a major 'ideological event'. Certainly the Party recognises the risk and will attempt to fight the European election along the extended/limited state line, as Major made clear at the 1993 Party Conference (where his ill-fated 'back to basics' push was designed primarily

---

[3] Jim Bulpitt's dismissal, in his 1992 polemic, of national sovereignty and interdependence as 'zombie concepts' is an argument about their usefulness in describing reality, deplorable to him precisely because of their purchase on Conservative ideology (Bulpitt 1992, 263).

to avoid the Conference fracturing over Europe). Douglas Hurd, who chairs
the Party committee attempting trying to concoct a manifesto to unite the
Party, put the point explicitly recently in response to questions about their
objectives (Hurd 1993):

> 'Secondly, to show that the arguments inside Europe are not
> just about integration or decentralisation; there are also some
> old-fashioned left/right arguments. The next summit in Brussels
> next week will be mainly a left/right discussion between those
> governments who on the whole believe that you get recovery by
> encouraging enterprise and those who believe basically you get
> recovery by spending taxpayers' money and that is a left/right
> argument in all our countries and that will be the argument in
> Brussels next week and in that it is very important from my
> point of view that the European Parliament should not have a
> socialist majority.'

In this paper we do not illustrate the extended/limited dimension in any
detail, though in the arguments over the European Union's social dimension we have a fascinating policy area where both our axes can be discerned,
but with very few Conservative parliamentarians (at least in Westminster)
willing to expound both an extended state and interdependence position
with the openness of Edward Heath, who told an interviewer, 'By refusing
to accept the social chapter, and therefore going for sweated labour, we're
cheating' (Guardian 11/06/93). In general, what is striking is how far even
bitter enemies over European integration concur over labour market deregulation. Try working out which of the following two extracts was made by
leading europhile and European Parliamentary candidate Edwina Currie,
and which by diehard rebel Teresa Gorman, both of whom can legitimately
be regarded as star Thatcherites of the 1980s:

> 'The United Kingdom also has low manufacturing costs –
> and we want to keep them that way. ... That is why we have no
> involvement in the social chapter.'
> '... [it] is essentially socialist in nature, designed to create
> a centralized structure for Europe controlling every nuance of
> labour relations, industrial and commercial life, with lots of in-
> terventionist policies and, of course, subsidies.'

Other European policy issues on the extended/limited state axis that should
offer similar cross-cutting include the environment, transport, and education.

Our main concern in this paper is with the sovereignty/interdependence
axis, along which there are important policy areas that illustrate the point
that are not considered here, notably subsidiarity, judicial authority, immigration, and citizenship. Here we consider and offer illustrations of the
positions on currency control, independent central banking, and qualified
majority voting, that might be used to construct a framework for analysis.

The general lines of argument about sovereignty take two forms over Europe. In one form it is a general argument about the wisdom of pooling

sovereignty to maximise British influence, prosperity and security that are seen as the real purpose of possessing sovereignty. The 'pooling' case was argued at length by Geoffrey Howe in his LSE lecture (Howe 1990a, cf. Gilmour 1992, 323/5) and put by him succinctly in the Lords in the Maastricht debates (07/06/93), 'The real question is, does sovereignty depend on our capacity to make rules in this national parliament or upon our ability to maximise our influence as a nation in the world?'. This is a flexible position sometimes based on fine judgements. The opposing rebel point of view was put simply by Michael Spicer, 'I do not understand the concept of pooling sovereignty. One either has or does not have sovereignty' (Commons Hansard 24/03/93 Col 1174).

There are also disputes about what aspects of sovereignty can be legitimately pooled. This second form of the sovereignty argument surfaces over QMV. A key differentiation is sharply presented by Maastricht rebels (Thatcher, Cash) who defend QMV as practised under the *Single European Act* for the purpose of accelerating the creation of single market by curtailing national sovereignty in the higher name of economic liberalism, in pursuit of the limited state, but attack QMV as enhanced by the Maastricht Treaty as a device to undermine the political independence of national legislatures across a wide range of policy issues and strengthen the extended superstate. Others previously regarded as Thatcherites find the distinction harder to make, 'The internal market programme following from the Single European Act of 1986 moves on from classic free trade to what might be called 'deep' free trade. ... It is a massive erosion of the traditional prerogatives of the nation-state' (Willetts 1992, 172). The minimalist position is most bluntly put by Teresa Gorman:

> 'I wish with all my heart we could be an offshore island like Hong Kong, a free trade area with the minimum of government intervention and the maximum of business activity. That's what we need to get our economy going.' (Gorman 1993, 190)

The appended illustrations of positions on sovereignty/interdependence issues demonstrate the significance of this axis in the widely conflicting opinions offered. In all three sets of quotations general positions vary from enthusiastic interdependence (Heath on single currency, Devlin on ECB, Dykes on QMV), through pragmatic interdependence (Howe, Willetts, Lawson on currency management, Lawson on independent banking, Taylor on QMV), to fervent national sovereignty (Thatcher, Cash, Tapsell, Howarth, Spicer, Ridley, Tebbit, *passim*). But the positions illustrated also demonstrate how our second axis, extended/limited state, does help to unravel some of the complexities and tensions of positions adopted, especially on the right.

On currency control and independent banking older divisions along the extended/limited state axis are criss-crossed by new disputes within the 'monetarist' camp of the early 1980s over whether discretion in monetary (including exchange rate) policy should be retained by the British government (Spicer, Cash, Thatcher) or whether it should be 'privatized'/'limited' either to the Bundesbank through the ERM (Lawson, Howe), or to an independent Bank of England (Lawson, Lamont, Renton). Elsewhere on the

Norton (1990) map, some non-Thatcherites prefer an independent European
Central Bank managing a single European currency ('loyalists' Devlin, Butterell), while others (including 'damp' Clarke and 'wets' Dorrell and Tapsell)
are opposed on grounds of national-democratic sovereignty.

A contrasting characteristic of the argument about monetary sovereignty
is the Thatcherite stress on the sovereignty of private actors in the marketplace, not the sovereignty of electorates. This ambiguity is apparent in the
case of QMV discussed above. Similarly, on currency management Thatcher
opposes transferring economic control to 'unaccountable supranational institutions' (ECB), unless, apparently, those institutions are 'the realities of
the market and capital movements' that make fixed exchange rates unwork-
able. 'Fixers v Floaters' is the title of a chapter in the Thatcher memoirs
reflecting a *laissez-faire* antagonism to all fixed exchange rate mechanisms
that unites Thatcher and her adviser Alan Walters (1989) with those, like
Ridley (1991, 194 *et passim*) and Spicer (1992, 96, 100) who are even willing to invoke Keynes's opposition to the return to the Gold Standard in
1925 in their support! This antagonism, combined with a view of exchange
rate management as a treacherous denial of money supply-targetted monetarism, provides a 'limited state' free marketeering foundation for their
anti-interdependence positions on ERM and EMU.

The 'national-populist spillover' that alarmed European political élites
during the Maastricht ratification process has added a 'legitimacy' dimension to the thinking of many pragmatic technocrats that seems to move
them along the sovereignty axis towards their right-wing colleagues (though
current pressure to unite the Party may be relevant here). Kenneth Clarke's
views on independent banking are one example. During the paving motion
debate, Douglas Hurd presented the 'pooling' argument on sovereignty, albeit very defensively:

> 'But one does not stop the debate by refusing to ratify the
> treaty. If we did that we would merely ensure that in the debate
> the voice of Britain was muted and that the opinions of Britain
> carried less weight. We would increase the possibility of combi-
> nations forming on the continent which would deeply affect the
> prosperity and security of these islands but in whose policies we
> would have no say.' (Hurd Commons Hansard 4/11/93 Col 376)

A year later he presented a markedly more defensive view:

> 'The governments of Europe received a warning ... from the
> authors of their authority, the people, and our definition of Eu-
> rope has to take account of that warning. That warning did
> not say: "Stop!" or "Go backwards!" It said: "Be careful!".
> 'The sharing of sovereignty, the centralising tendency has for
> the time being, I believe, run its course and we have to a look
> at an alternative ...' (Hurd 1993)

This last point emphasises that what we need is more regular revisions of
typologies to pay due attention to the constraints that make the 'ideological' politician an 'ideal-type' of fantasy. In their primary role as frameworks

for research conducted to elucidate the nature of a party's ideological, behavioural or policy divisions, they will always become redundant. As Harris noted a long time ago of Conservative ideology, 'Verbal continuities allow the Party to change in practice without acknowledging that it is changing. But the cumulative practical changes then come to contradict the Party's rhetorical appeal' (Harris 1972, 260) Frequent empirical validation in relation to the changing contexts of party politics is essential if typologies of Conservatism are to unravel the cumulative changes from the verbal continuities. The Party leadership's struggle to make interdependence/extended state 'politics of euro-power' practice compatible with nationalist and 'limited state' 'politics of support' rhetoric is an excellent focus for such empirical research.

Appendix

currency management

'We have to face this fact. Either we are going to be out on our own, or we are going to play a full part. I will go still further, because the British government says it's very strongly in favour of the single market. You will not be able to maintain a single market unless you have a single currency, because people will cheat.' (Heath 1993)

'... none of us wants the imposition of a single currency. ... The risk is not imposition but isolation. The real threat is that of leaving ourselves with no say in the monetary arrangements that the real of Europe chooses for itself, with Britain once again scrambling to join the club later and after the power has been distributed by others to our disadvantage. That would be the worst possible outcome.' (Howe 1990b)

'What sort of Europe do I want to emerge from Maastricht ...? I want us not to lose the prospect of a single currency ... I want the security of that prospect – for myself, my children, and my country.' (P.Temple-Morris, Commons *Hansard*, 24/11/92 Col 790)

'I still believe that our period in the ERM was very beneficial and it enabled us to get interest rates down more rapidly than we conceivably otherwise could. I don't believe that Black Wednesday caused the recovery from the recession.' (Clarke 1993, 8)

'... there are many people who believe that a single currency has something to contribute to the development of eceonomic management and an efficient economy within the member states of the Community.' (S Dorrell, Commons *Hansard*, 13/01/93 Col 1142)

'By the summer of 1981, I had become persuaded of the case for making the discipline of the ERM, rather than targets for domestic monetary aggregates, the prime determinant of monetary policy and hence of the conduct of thebattle against inflation.' (Lawson 1992, 111)

'... those who favoured free floating tended to be fired with purist zeal, whereas those who favoured ERM membership on economic grounds did so (as I did) for pragmatic reasons, as probably the least bad alternative in a wicked and imperfect world. The only pro-ERM zealots were those who wanted it on political ('European') grounds.' (Lawson 1992, 652)

'Like him [Lawson], I concluded at least five years ago that the conduct of our policy against inflation could no longer rest solely on attempts to measure and control the domestic money supply. We had no doubt that we should be helped in that battle, and, indeed, in other respects, by joining the exchange rate mechanism of the Euorpean monetary system. ... For a quarter of a century after the second world war, we found that the very similar Bretton Woods regime did serve as a useful discipline.' (Howe 1990b)

'... any serious monetary policy involves the government in relinquishing its sovereign power to debase its own currency. But equally, any rule – be it domestic or external – is voluntarily chosen by the government and could in principle be abandoned however unpalatable that might be. In this respect the ERM is just like the old Bretton Woods system. ... Sovereignty which has been voluntarily renounced and can be regained has never been truly lost.' (Willetts 1992, 175/177)

'In a world of huge capital flows, floating may be the only way of the future, but no one should think that floating is an easy option or that management of the economy through monetary aggregates is straightforward or simple. ... talk of accelerating monetary union is just pious, unrealisable Euro-vision. Far better to abandon the goal of monetary union.' (Lamont 1993b)

'We need more of the peoples of Europe to recognise that European monetary union, a single currency, would not only be impoverishing but must mean the destruction of essential national self-determination.' (A.Howarth, Commons *Hansard*, 04/11/93 Col 352)

'... they want to have fixed exchange rates, not only to get a greater degree of control over the currencies but also to create a single country.' (Cash, Commons *Hansard*, 01/12/92 Col 231.)

'It is as logical as night follows day that the establishment of a single currency should involve the establishment of a single taxation authority and a single economic authority. If that is not the foundation, the makings and the essence of a new sovereign state, I do not know what is.' (Spicer, Commons *Hansard*, 13/01/93 Cols 983/4)

'... if the exchange rate becomes an objective in itself, as opposed to one indicator among others for monetary policy, 'monetarism' itself has been abandoned. ... But EMU itself – which involves the loss of the power to issue your own currency and acceptance of one European currency, one central bank and one set of interest rates – means the end of a country's economic independence and thus the increasing irrelevance of its parliamentary democracy. Control of its economy is transferred from the elected government, answerable to Parliament and the electorate, to unaccountable supra-national institutions.' (Thatcher 1993, 690/1)

'... no fixed exchange rate – be it the gold standard or Bretton Woods – has been sustainable. Unless there is some adjustment to the realities of the market and capital movements, the devil will always take the hindmost.' (Thatcher 1992)

'With a single currency and economic management confined to Brussels, there are no economic weapons left in the hands of national governments if their economies become uncompetitive. Devaluation is no longer possible and interest rates are decided centrally. Even budget policy would have to be controlled from the centre. ... As John Maynard Keynes once said, "Whoever controls the currency, controls the economy." ' (Ridley 1992, 147/149)

'If there is to be drawn a line in the sand over which the United Kingdom could not pass without setting out along the path to the status of a province, not a nation, it is the creatiion of a single currency!' (Tebbitt 1991, 69)

independent central banking

'The point about the European market is its fundamental interdependence ... We have a choice at this point and crossroads in our history of having a deutschmark-dominated continent where all European currencies are at the whim of the deutschmark, or a truly independent currency with a truly independent central bank operating in the interests of all the European economies.' (T.Devlin, Commons *Hansard*, 18/01/93 Col 127)

'... we have nothing to fear from a system that brings a single interest rate, combined with a single currency, throughout the European Community.' (Butterell, Commons *Hansard*, 24/03/93 Col 993)

'One conclusion must be that bankers, not politicians, are better at deciding monetary growth and consequential interest rates. It is not necessarily that they have better brains than we have, but that they do not have to operate within the same electoral cycles as we do.' (Tim Renton, Commons *Hansard*, 20/05/93 Col 413)

'An independent Bank would not, of course, have had the merit of ERM membership of replacing discretion by rules. ... In particular, it would do something to "depoliticize interest rate changes". I also sought to persuade Margaret that an incidental advantage of creating an independent national central bank ... would be to demonstrate that we did not envisage the absorption of the Bank of England into a European central bank.' (Lawson 1992, 868)

'It is my greatest regret that after two-and-a-half years of trying, I have failed to persuade the Prime Minister of this essential reform. ... Britain is one of the few countries where monetary policy remains firmly in political hands and the pressures on politicians to take policy decisions for political reasons can be quite irresistible. With an independent bank we could have lower interest rates for a given exchange rate. Policy would be more credible and it would give us the necessary discipline for keeping inflation down on a permanent basis.' (Lamont 1993a)

'The purists are really saying that key decisions on interest rates, and indeed the whole of monetary policy, should be placed utterly beyond the reach of democratically elected politicians ... I think people would get fed up with me telling Parliament that the most important features of economic policy were practically beyond my control.' (Clarke 1993, 9)

'National parliaments would become like county councils – a comparison which Norman Tebbit later took over. There would have to be a genuinely elected European government to balance a European Central Bank.' (Lawson 1992, 925)

'... I invite him to design a workable system for a European central bank that is politically accountable to a European political process. I do not believe that it would be easy to do and I certainly do not think that it would learn the lessons that are available from other central banks that are divorced from the tax and management authority.' (S.Dorrell, Commons *Hansard*, 13/01/93 Col 1142)

'The creation of that single insititutional framework is also part of the legal union, so we have central banking arrangements, which are about as centralising as anything can be because decisions on economic and monetary affairs are taken by unelected bankers.' (Cash, Commons *Hansard*, 01/12/92 Col 207)

'Independence for the Bank of England in interest-rate policy would remove one of the most vital weapons from a chancellor's armory – just as joining the European Single Currency would do. ... This is the area where sovereignty matters, and where parting with it is the parting of the roads – one going towards a federal Europe and the other towards a Europe of member states.' (Ridley 1992, 152)

'Control over monetary poolicy is central to the function of government. Just as the transfer of power of Crown to Parliament in England was born essentially out of parliamentary control of economic policy, so is the transfer of monetary policy from national governments to a European body intended to herald a fundamental shift in political power.' (Spicer 1992, 51/52)

'European and Monetary Union will remove all the characteristics of sovereignty ... Effectively the European central bank will become the most powerful economic, and therefore political institution in the Community – indeed in the whole free world ... If we lose control over our currency the House will lose the rock on which our democracy is founded – control over the money supply. Our constituents will effectively be disenfranchised.' (P.Tapsell, Commons *Hansard*, 24/03/93 Cols 970/78)

qualified majority votir.g

'The enhancement of intrinsic sovereign power for all member states comes from their collective, reciprocal sharing of that power, based increasingly on majority voting ...' (H.Dykes, Commons *Hansard*, 02/12/92 Col 347)

'It is the provision for majority voting across large areas that enables action to be taken.' (Heath, Commons *Hansard*, 20/05/93 Col 42)

'... one of the reasons why I and so many of my Hon. Friends supported the Single European Act was that it introduced into the Community the greatest measure of qualified majority voting that has ever been introduced in one single dollop.' (Garel-Jones, Commons *Hansard*, 18/01/93 Col 64)

'I pay tribute to the former Prime MInister, Lady Thatcher, who understood only too well that, if Britain was to open up the Community and remove restrictions, hidden and overt, to the free movement of people, goods and services, we needed a strong Commission to initiatte legislation. It also meant we needed qualified majority voting in the Council of Ministers ...' (Ian Taylor, Commons *Hansard*, 24/11/92 Col 796)

'There would, I granted, be a need for improved methods of decision-taking if these ends were to be met. I proposed that we agree now to a greater use of the existing majority voting articles of the Rome Treaty ... The price we would have to pay to achieve a Single Market with all its economic benefits, though, was more majority voting in the Community ... I knew I would have to fight a strong rear-guard action against attempts to weaken Britain's own control over areas of vital national interest.' (Thatcher 1993, 550/553)

'By extending EC majority voting, it [the Maastricht Treaty] will undermine our parliamentary and legal institutions, both far older than those in the Community.' (Thatcher, Lords 07/06/93.)

'I have said repeatedly that I am in favour of the notion of an increase in majority voting for specific purposes relating to co-operation in the commercial field which will enable free trade to develop within Europe ... There is no logical reason for turning over Britain's government and democracy to majority voting. That is political union. The Single European Act was a move towards greater economic union.' (Cash, Commons *Hansard*, 13/01/93 Col 939)

'The most significant trend in the development of the Council is the continuing extension of majority voting and the consequent erosion of the power by veto by a nation state.' (Spicer 1992, 44)

'At what point would movement towards monetary, economic and political union rob the citizens of member states of the ability to determine their own affairs? To a considerable extent that right has been fretted away by the extension of the Community competence and by majority voting in the Council of Ministers.' (Tebbit, 1991, 66/7)

References

Baker, D, Gamble, A. & Ludlam, S. (1991a), 'Conservative MPs: a Research Agenda', Political Studies Association, Elections, Parties and Public Opinion Specialist Group Annual Conference, September 1991 (Oxford).

Baker, D, Gamble, A. & Ludlam, S. (1991b), 'Conservative Cabinet Ministers and European Integration 1979-1990', Unpublished research paper – ESRC application.

Baker, D, Gamble, A. & Ludlam, S. (1992), 'More Classless and Less Thatcherite? Conservative Ministers and new MPs after the 1992 election', *Parliamentary Affairs*, Volume 45, Number 4, October 1992.

Baker, D, Gamble, A. & Ludlam, S. (1993a), '1846, 1906 ... 1996? Could European Integration Lead the Conservative Party into the Wilderness again?', Paper presented to the Political Studies Association Annual Conference April 1993 (Leicester).

Baker, D, Gamble, A. & Ludlam, S. (1993b), '1846 ... 1906 ... 1996? Conservative Splits and European Integration', *Political Quarterly*, Volume 64, Number 4, October 1993.

Baker, D, Gamble, A. & Ludlam, S. (1994), 'The Siege of Maastricht 1993: Conservative Divisions and British Ratification', *Parliamentary Affairs*, Volume 47, Number 1, January 1994.

Baker, K, *The Turbulent Years: My Life in Politics*, London, Faber & Faber.

Brand, J. (1989), 'Faction as its Own Reward: Groups in the British Parliament 1945-1986', *Parliamentary Affairs*, 1989.

Bulpitt, J. (1985), 'The Discipline of the New Democracy', *Political Studies*, 34/1.

Bulpitt, J. (1991), 'The Conservative Party in Britain: a Preliminary Portrait', paper delivered to the Annual Conference of the Political Studies Association, Lancaster, April 1991.

Bulpitt, J. (1992), 'Conservative Leaders and the "Euro-Ratchet": Five Doses of Scepticism', *Political Quarterly*, 63/3.

Cash, B. (1993), 'Eurosceptics and Eurorealists', *European Journal 1993*, Volume 1/1.

Clarke, K. (1993a), 'The lovable pooch at Number 11. Kenneth Clarke interviewed by Andrew Hicks', *Crossbow*, October 1993.

Clarke (1993b), Swiss Bank Corporation Lecture, 14/09/93

Crewe, I & Searing, D. (1988), 'Ideological Change in the British Conservative Party', *American Political Science Review*, Volume 82, Number 2, June 1988.

Dunleavy, P. (1993), 'The Political Parties', in Dunleavy, P. et al (eds) (1993), *Developments in British Politics*, 4, Macmillan.

Finer, S, Berrington, H.B. & D.J. Bartholomew, D.J. (1961) *Backbench Opinion in the House of Commons, 1955-59*, Oxford, Pergamon.

Gamble, A. (1974), *The Conservative Nation*, London, Routledge & Kegan Paul.

Gamble, A. (1990), 'The Great Divide', *Marxism Today*, October 1990.

Gamble, A. (1993), 'The Entrails of Thatcherism', *New Left Review*, 198.

Garel-Jones, T, 'Tories must set agenda for tomorrow's Europe', *The Times*, 21/06/93.

Gilmour, I. (1992), *Dancing with Dogma: Britain under Thatcherism*, London, Pocket Books.

Gorman, T. (1993), *The Bastards: Dirty Tricks and the Challenge to Europe*, London, Pan Books.

Greenleaf, W.H. (1973), 'The Character of Modern British Conservatism', in Benewick, R. et al (eds), *Knowledge and Belief in Politics*, London, George Allen & Unwin.

Harris, N. (1972), *Competition and the Corporate Society: British Conservatives, the State and Industry*, London, Methuen.

Heath, Sir E, 'Interview', *The Guardian*, 11/06/93.

Howe, G. (1990a), 'Sovereignty and Interdependence: Britain's Place in the World', *International Affairs*, Volume 66, Number 4.

Howe, G. (1990b), Resignation speech, 13/11/90.

Hurd, D. (1993), *The Fifth Gerold von Braunmuhl Memorial Lecture*, Bologna 29th November 1993, London, Foreign and Commonwealth Office.

Lamont, N. (1993a), Resignation speech, 09/06/93.

Lamont, N. (1993b), 'The Day I almost Quit', *The Times*, 16/09/93.

Lawson, N. (1992), *The View from Number 11: Memoirs of a Tory Radical*, London, Bantam.

Letwin, S.R. (1992), *The Anatomy of Thatcherism*, London, Fontana.

Ludlam, S. (1993), 'Majorism – Shuffling to the Left?', *Politics Review*, November 1993.

Major, J. (1993), 'Raise Your Eyes, There is a Land Beyond', *The Economist*, 25/09/93.

Maude, F. (1963), 'Party Palaeontology', *The Spectator*, 15/03/63.

Norton, P. (1990a), ' "The Lady's Not for Turning", But What About the Rest? Margaret Thatcher and the Conservative Party 1979-89', *Parliamentary Affairs*, 43/1, January 1990.

Norton, P. (1990b), 'Choosing a Leader: Margaret Thatcher and the Parliamentary Conservative Party', *Parliamentary Affairs*, 43/3, July 1990.

Norton, P. (1993), 'The Conservative Party from Thatcher to Major', in King, A. (ed), *Britain at the Polls*, Chatham House.

Norton, P. & Aughey, A. (1981), *Conservatives and Conservatism*, London, Temple Smith.

Ranelagh, J. (1992), *Thatcher's People*, London, Harper Collins.

Ridley, N. (1992), 'My Style of Government': the Thatcher Years, London, Fontana.

Rose, R (1964), 'Parties, Factions and Tendencies in Britain', *Political Studies*, Volume XII, Number 1.

Rose, R. (1985), *Politics in England*, London, Faber.

Spicer, M. (1992), *A Treaty too Far: a New Policy for Europe*, London, Fourth Estate.

Tebbit, N. (1991), *Unfinished Business*, London, Wiedenfeld.

Thatcher, M. (1992), article, *The European*, 08/10/92.

Thatcher, M. (1993), *The Downing Street Years*, London, Harper Collins.

Walters, A, 'My Deviant Economics', *The Independent*, 26/10/89.

Whiteley, P, Seyd, P, Richardson, J. & Bissell, P. (1993a), 'Party Strategy and Thatcherism in the British Conservative Party', Paper presented to the American Political Science Association, Chicago, September 1993.

Whiteley, P, Seyd, P. & Richardson, J. (1993b), 'Thatcherism and the Conservative Party', Paper presented to the Elections, Parties and Public Opinion specialist group of the Political Studies Association, Lancaster, September 1993.

Willetts, D. (1992), *Modern Conservatism*, Harmondsworth, Penguin.

The Politics of Small States in Europe
Case-studies in Domestic Politics

David Arter

Leeds Metropolitan University

'Estonia: the Case of an Anti-Party System'

Quotation

'100,000 dollars and I could wipe out this government.'
(Jüri Toomepuu, Leader of the Estonian Citizens).

Introduction

In a seminal article in 1990, Richard Katz asked: 'How have parties, their strategies, their roles in elections in particular and European democracy in general changed in response to the challenges of the last quarter of the twentieth century'?[1]

Katz's question regarding the adaptive nature and role of parties, whilst timely, referred only to their evolving modus operandi in Western Europe. The primary focus of the present paper, however, is the role of political parties in one of the new democracies and, indeed, one of the smallest 'successor states' of the New Europe of post-1989 – that is, Estonia.

Placing the investigation into a wider comparative framework, there is evidence to suggest a growing convergence between the party systems of the 'Two Europes'. In Western Europe, the evolution has been from multi-party towards anti-party systems. The classic anti-system parties (of the communist and fascist variety), first identified in the mid-1960s by Giovanni Sartori, have virtually disappeared, but it may not be far-fetched to describe Western Europe as inclining towards a bloc of anti-party systems. The shift has been from anti-system parties to anti-party systems. In Eastern Europe the progression has been from one-party to anti-party systems. A multiplicity of parties and proto-parties have sprung up, to be sure, but they operate in the context of strongly anti-party cultures. Before pursuing this theme in more depth, a brief note on Estonia is in order.

Estonia as a Small European State

On August 20 1991, the Estonian Supreme Soviet adopted a resolution on national independence which re-affirmed the *de jure* continuity of the Estonian state founded in 1918. The declaration appealed to the international community not for the usual recognition of a new state, but the restoration of diplomatic relations with the legally-existing republic of Estonia.

---

[1] Richard S. Katz, 'Party as Linkage: A Vestigial Function?', *European Journal of Political Research*, 18, 1, 1990, pp.143-163.

Against the background of the struggle for power in Moscow following the (abortive) anti-Gorbachev coup on August 19, a previously divided Estonian political élite united to restore national independence. Estonian territorial sovereignty had been flagrantly violated in 1940 when the country was illegally annexed by the Soviet Union in accordance with the secret articles of the Molotov-Ribbentrop Pact of August 23, 1939. Two days after the restoration of independence, Iceland became the first country to 'recognise' Estonia, followed four days later by Boris Yeltsin's Russian Federation and on September 2, 1991, the United States.

The inter-war Estonian republic was a successor state of the Czarist Romanov empire. It became an active member of the League of Nations; enacted a liberal law on Cultural Autonomy in 1925; and possessed in the 1922 constitution one of the most democratic documents in contemporary Europe.[2] Perhaps it was too democratic since, in allowing the outcomes of referenda initiated by the people to override – where they clashed with the decisions of – the national assembly, the *Riigikogu*, it provided a mechanism which extremists could (and did) use to discredit and undermine the structures of representative democracy. In any event, when the impact of recession was superimposed on a new state experiencing the familiar teething troubles of building durable cabinets, the 'strain' became too much and in 1934 pluralist democracy gave way to an authoritarian regime under the presidency of Konstantin Päts.

After its incorporation by the Red Army in April 1940, Estonia became a member republic of the Union of Soviet Socialist Republics and suffered systematic 'ethnic cleansing' at the hands of Stalin. Estonia lost one-third of its population which was in turn replaced by hundreds of thousands of colonial settlers. The indigenous nation (Estonia) was subordinated to the imperialist Soviet state. The Estonian economy was destroyed and rendered completely dependent on the USSR and the Estonian people, together with their language and culture, were rigorously repressed. Only the Finnish television offered the population of northern Estonia a window on the wealth of Western Europe (it is quite possible to speak Finnish in Tallinn, much less so in Tartu, for example).

The restoration of independence in 1991 meant that Estonia became one of the smallest states in the New Europe with a population which, at one and a half million, was broadly similar to that of Slovenia. Approximately 900,000 are Estonians and 600,000 non-Estonians, mainly Russians. Economically, Estonia has made giant strides forward. It became the first country in the former Soviet Union to break out of the rouble zone and on June 20, 1992, introduced its own currency, the *kroon*, which has been strictly linked to the *deutschmark*. Consequently, whereas in 1991 95% of Estonia's overall trade was with Russia, by 1994 this had dropped to 20%. Finland has become Estonia's leading trading partner and free trade agreements have been reached with Finland, Sweden and Norway and there is

---

[2] On the inter-war Estonian republic, see *inter alia* Toivo U.Raun, *Estonia and the Estonians*, Second Edition (Hoover Institution: Stanford, California, 1991); Kärt Jänes (ed), *Tundmatu Eesti Vabariik* (Jaan Tõnissoni Instituut, 1993); Georg von Rauch, *The Baltic States: Estonia, Latvia, Lithuania: The Years of Independence 1917-1940* (Hurst: London, 1974).

another with the European Union (EU) which grants Estonia GSP treatment. Partly on the back of a well-educated but cheap labour force, Estonia has attracted as much foreign investment as Latvia, Lithuania and Belarus put together.

Yet as a small state dedicated to free trade, it has been haunted by the spectre of the parochialism and protectionism that dogged the inter-war European economy. As the prime minister, Mart Laar (a historian who has plainly learnt the lessons of history) noted in a speech in summer 1993:

> 'As Europeans, we cannot allow protectionist sentiments to build obstacles to the economic development of the Central and East European countries – to which the Baltic states undoubtedly belong – because, in the end, such obstacles will become a hindrance to the economic growth of Western Europe as well.'[3]

His words could almost have been those of Milan Hodža between the wars.[4]

On the international political stage, Estonia has succeeded in re-integrating herself to good effect. She was admitted to the Conference on Security and Co-operation in Europe (CSCE) on September 10, 1991 and became a member of the Council of Europe on May 14, 1993. Meetings of the Baltic heads of state and prime ministers, moreover, have become routine and a modicum of regional policy harmonisation has been achieved. Thus, at its third session in Tallinn in October 1993, the Baltic Assembly, a sixty-strong body of parliamentarians, vested a newly-created Baltic Council, working under its auspices, with the task of co-ordinating arrangements in the fields of justice, the environment, communications, culture, education, science and foreign and security policy.

Russian actions continue to be viewed with suspicion and a Russian threat is still acutely felt – it was heightened by the success of Zhirinovsky's *irredentism* at the Duma elections of December 12 last year. Russian troops are still stationed in Estonia (as also in Latvia) and agreement has not yet been reached on a deadline for their withdrawal; the Russian naval base at Paldiski, which was completely closed to Estonians, remains derelict and the town, lacking a register of citizens, was unable to participate in the local government elections of October 1993; and, not surprisingly, there was strong Estonian opposition at the CSCE foreign ministers' meeting in Rome in November 1993 to Russian pressure for financial support for its proposed 'peacekeeping activities' in the former Soviet states.[5] Exactly one week after Lithuania's formal application for NATO membership on January 4, 1994 the Estonian *Riigikogu* voted decisively in favour of preparing a draft law on an application for NATO membership. In the longer term, Estonia aspires to European Union membership, although at the Estonian Greens' annual

---

[3] Speech at a Colloquium of the German Foreign Policy Association, Bonn, 28.6.1993.

[4] David Arter, *The Politics of European Integration in the Twentieth Century* (Dartmouth: Aldershot, 1993), pp.68-70, 271-2.

[5] 'CSCE cautious over Russian 'peacekeeping', *The Baltic Independent*, 3-9.12.1993. Ironically, a newly-conceived Baltic peacekeeping battalion is scheduled to begin training exercises early this year. It is largely the brainchild of the Commander of the Estonian Defence Forces, Major General Aleksander Einseln (a retired American army colonel with battle experience in North Korea and Vietnam).

congress in January this year it was argued, very much as former Finnish president Mauno Koivisto had argued, that poor relations with Russia are a poor recommendation for seeking to join the European Union.[6] Despite the economic promise, several problems remain on the domestic front. Production structures remain generally weak and purchasing power low; the delapidated transport infrastructure is in urgent need of capital investment; the domestic real-estate market is a legal jungle; the issue of the restitution of land to its pre-1940 owners is proving immensely complicated; the newly-privatised farmers, who receive no subsidies, are finding it difficult to compete in an Estonian market flooded with subsidised Western and Russian products; and, although private enterprises account for 30-40% of the turnover of the Estonian economy, according to a recent study by the Small Business Association (EVEA), take-up loans under the European Union's PHARE programme have been limited by the problems of SMEs putting together suitable business plans. Unemployment is high in the countryside, especially in southern Estonia, and there is real poverty in many areas.[7] Although private clinics are mushrooming, the state health care system is in need of fundamental overhaul. Above all, Estonia faces tough competition from Finland and a number of CIS states in its battle for 'gateway' (transit) trade.

The question of the future of over half a million non-Estonians (mainly Russians) remains unresolved and there is a CSCE monitoring mission in the Russian-dominated town of Narva where unemployment currently stands at 50% and where many residents have sought work across the river in Ivangorod. None the less, the Swedish prime minister Carl Bildt's article in the *International Herald Tribune* in which he referred to Russia's policy of 'ethnic cleansing' in Narva was unhelpful and, following the October local elections, the town's hardline communist leadership was replaced by moderates from the Russian Democratic Movement. The much-disputed citizenship law was itself submitted to the Council of Europe for inspection and was subsequently modified.[8]

Estonia has the highest crime rate in Europe: the increase in mafia-related murders (often in broad daylight) is alarming and so, too, is the incidence of Perm and Chechenya-related smuggling.[9] Ironically, it was a measure of the success of the *kroon* and the increased sums deposited (often by foreigners) that there was a sharp rise in the number of bank robberies in 1993. In 1992 there were none at all! Policing is a problem. The average age

---

[6] See David Arter, 'Finland's 'European Policy': Unioinist "Quickstep" or Nationalist "Tango"?' (in Finnish) *Ulkopolitiikka*, 2/1994.

[7] According to the Minister of Agriculture, Jaan Leetsar, reform has left about eighty-thousand people without work in the Estonian countryside. Under Soviet rule there were 360 collective farms each employing hundreds of persons. These have been replaced by 4,300 private farms, more than 1,200 stock companies and 1,300 shareholding companies. 'Property reform leaves rural jobless', *The Baltic Independent*, 14-20.1.1994. Official figures put the unemployment level in southern Estonia at 7% though, according to the National Labour Market Board, actual figures are about three times as high.

[8] Commission on Security and Co-operation in Europe, *Russians in Estonia: Problems and Prospects* (Washington: September 1992): 'Report on the application of the Republic of Estonia for membership of the Council of Europe', Council of Europe 14.4.1993.

[9] There are presently five thousand prisoners in Estonian prisons in conditions which are poor and where tuberculosis is common. Figures quoted on Finnish TV 9.1.1994.

of policemen is 25-27 years and their average experience only two and a half years (earlier the police force was Russian-dominated). Moreover, relations between the police and the Defence League (a voluntary force revived in 1990) are strained and several criminal elements joined the Defence League after independence largely in order to gain possession of firearms.[10]

Yet despite these social and economic problems, the transition to democracy has proceeded without undue incident – at least until very recently. A new constitution was approved at a referendum in June 1992; a general election the following September constituted the first post-Soviet *Riigikogu*; and a right-wing coalition dominated by the *Isamaa* (Fatherland) party has been in power ever since. True, there has been a series of political scandals, ministerial resignations and indeed outright sackings. But it was not until January 1994 that Estonia experienced a fully-blown constitutional crisis. The president, Lennart Meri, initially refused to confirm four new ministerial appointments which formed part of a cabinet re-shuffle. Although he did, ultimately, ratify the posts, Meri's venomous attack on Laar in the *Riigikogu* did nothing to enhance the office of either president or prime minister. Incidentally Estonia is a young nation-state (in its revived form) which is dominated by a younger generation of politicians and officials. The ages of the new cabinet ministers range from 27 to 36!

The transition to democracy was accompanied by a proliferation of political parties – or, more accurately, proto-parties – which emerged from cracks in the 'movement society'. It was the mass popular movements – the Greens, Popular Front and citizens committees of the Estonian Congress movement – which provided the initial motor of change (or, in the case of the Russian-speaking Interfront, resistance to it). It is with the challenges of these nascent parties in a predominantly anti-party culture that the rest of this paper will concentrate.

The Shift from One-Party to Anti-Party Systems

There is a widespread assumption in the West of a connection between parties and democratization in post-communist Europe. Thus, as early as 1990, Geoffrey Pridham observed that:

> 'In Eastern Europe it is already clear that political parties are crucial actors in the transitions to liberal democracy from Communist state systems and act as a guarantee of the new political pluralism.'[11]

---

[10] The restoration of the Defence League (Kaitse liit) possessed a symbolic as well as military importance, since it was originally founded in 1918 to maintain law and order during the two-year War of Independence. The Defence League resumed its activities after the abortive Communist coup in 1924 and eight years later had over 32,000 members. During the 1940s and 1950s, many of its former members were 'Siberianized'. Revived on February 17, 1990, its remit, according to Tarto, was to protect the citizens of Estonia.

[11] Geoffrey Pridham, 'Political Actors, Linkages and Interactions: Democratic Consolidation in Southern Europe', *West European Politics*, 13, 4, 1990, p.105. Also Geoffrey Pridham (ed), *Transitions to Democracy: Comparative Perspectives from Southern Eu-*

He added that the stage of democratic transitions was complete not simply when a new constitution was enacted, but when the system operated with a popularly-elected government. The emergence of embryonic parties has, indeed, been part of a response to strong Western pressure to democratize. It has represented a statement of good intent, so to speak. Equally, the main West European party families have adopted their fraternal fledglings in Eastern Europe and sought to sponsor their development with funding and other forms of 'technical assistance' For example, there were moves early in 1993 in the European Democratic Union (EDU) to promote the creation of a Conservative Party in Russia – still essentially a nation of clans – but despite lip-service to the idea from President Yeltsin, nothing came of it.

Clearly, a primary function of parties in post-authoritarian systems is the recruitment of an accountable and, by extension renewable political élite as an alternative to rule by non-responsible groupings such as the army, church or, indeed, organised criminal associations. The emphasis here is on the *role of parties in state-building.* In other words, the focus is on their participation in constructing the legal framework of the new state by prescribing the basic rules and regulations (constitution-making); the recruitment of officials to replace the old *nomenklatura* (élite renewal); and the contribution of the parties to the effective management of the affairs of state in terms of élite co-operation in *inter alia* government-formation and policy-making. It cannot be in question that the responsible and effective use of power can serve to legitimize democracy.

Equally, parties perform a crucial task in organising, mobilising and so-cialising citizens and, in this way, in internalizing democracy at the grass-roots. The focus here is on the politics of linkage and *the role of parties in society-building.* Society-building involves developing forms of collective participation in multiple public organisations. A strong civil society is pro-active; there is a popular engagement in decision-making and/or the belief in the possibility of exerting influence through participation, that is, a high level of subjective competence among citizens. A weak civil society displays passivity and cynicism among ordinary people who eschew involvement in politics and political bodies.

Eastern Europe before 1989 comprised a bloc of one-party states in which the monopolistic or hegemonic communist or socialist party controlled the apparatus of the state – both through its stranglehold on the means of coercion and, more routinely, its vast nomenklatura network – and domi-nated, if it did not entirely emasculate political society. Elections, though widespread, were 'non-competitive', being designed essentially to legitimize Communist Party control. Against this backdrop, it was not perhaps sur-prising that when the 1989 autumn revolutions facilitated competitive elec-tions and the advent of liberal democracy, Eastern Europe was made up of a series of 'anti-party systems'.

As a generic type, *an anti-party system* may be defined by reference to three key conditions:

> 1. that partisan allegiance provides the basis of candidate choice for only a minority of active voters at general elections.

rope, Latin America and Eastern Europe (Dartmouth: forthcoming).

There is a tendency in short to reject the whole concept of 'party'.

2. that non-voting (abstentionism) describes the electoral 'behaviour' of a significant section (say over one-quarter) of the electorate.

3. that there exists an 'anti-party' or anti-parties, diametrically opposed not only to the agenda, but also the style of the other political groupings.

Plainly, what constitutes an anti-party is ultimately a matter of informed judgement. Whilst an anti-party is a protest party, not all protest parties are anti-parties. The difference lies in the latter's excessively irreverent and/or iconoclastic attitude to the rules of the political game which the other parties seek conscientiously to observe. In any event, the challenge of the mainstream parties in an anti-party system is clear: namely, to work to create a political culture in which parties are accepted as legitimate instruments of representation and interest articulation.

A Sketch of the Estonian Party System[12]

De facto multipartism in Estonia pre-dated the Estonian Supreme Soviet's amendment on February 23, 1990, of article six of the constitution enshrining the Estonian Communist Party (ECP)'s leading role. No less than thirty-one parties or 'proto-parties' contested the Supreme Soviet elections on March 18, 1990, and they included three women's parties. Moreover, at the first post-Soviet general election on September 20, 1992, seventeen parties or electoral alliances contested the 101 seats in the unicameral *Riigikogu*. Nine were ultimately successful in gaining parliamentary representation, although the Greens and Entrepreneurs returned only a single member each. The distribution of parliamentary votes and seats by party/electoral alliance is set out in table one. The turn-out of 67.8% was virtually the same as at the referendum held to approve the new constitution on June 28, 1992. In contrast to Lithuania, not a single candidate from the ECP (re-named the Party of Democratic Labour) was elected.

In proceeding to give a very rudimentary sketch of the parliamentary parties, it is convenient to distinguish the three groupings, the Estonian National Independence Party (ENIP), Isamaa and Moderates – which formed a majority coalition after the 1992 election – from the opposition parties.

The Estonian National Independence Party – Eesti Rahvusliku Sõltumatuse Partei – was officially (and illegally) formed on August 20, 1988 and became the first party openly to oppose the Communist Party not only in Estonia, but throughout the Soviet Union.[13] Its active founding figures were virtually all former dissidents, several of them with a long history of

---

[12] Table 1 at the end of this section summarises the 1992 election results.

[13] All the material on the parties (considerably simplified and abbreviated) is based on extensive field-work and élite interviews conducted by the author. See also Marjut Kuokkanen, 'Puolueiden muodostaminen Virossa' *Ulkopolitiikka*, 4/91, pp.47-56. On the fluctuation in support for the embryonic parties, see Erik Andersen, 'Estland: Påvej mod selvstændighed?, *Nordisk Ost: Forum*, 3, 1989, pp.35-40.

dissidence. Prior to the 1992 election it was the one party in Estonia to have a significant mass membership (1100 persons) and network of local organisations. It may be, however, that with its primary goal, the restoration of independence realised, the ENIP has been overtaken by events and run its natural course. Whilst some independence parties can survive – the Icelandic is a case in point – the ENIP has displayed signs of fragmentation and indeed disintegration in recent months.

Although the Isamaa electoral alliance was formed essentially to fight the 1992 general election, the five parties operating beneath its umbrella were considerably older than that and, curiously, they included two christian parties. The one, the Estonian Christian Democratic Party (*Eesti Kristlik Demokraatlik Erakond*) was, in fact, the first of the re-emergent parties stemming back to the Singing Revolution of summer 1988 – its creation on July 23 pre-dating the ENIP by a month. The second, the Estonian Christian Democratic Union (*Eesti Kristlik Demokraatlik Liit*), founded on December 17, 1988, claimed to be the ideological heir of the Christian People's Party between the wars. The other three member-groups were all founded in 1990. The Conservative People's Party (*Eesti Konservatiivne Rahvaerakond*) was set up in January by activists close to the National Heritage Society with Enn Tarto, a former political prisoner, as the leading figure; and the Estonian Liberal Democratic Party (*Eesti LIberaaldemokraatlik Partei*), formed on March 9, 1990, was the product of the merger of two liberal groups. Finally, the Republican Coalition Party (*Eesti Vabariiklaste Koonderakond*), which emerged in September 1990, brought together three groups: the Respublica group of young intellectuals; the Union of Work Collectives, consisting in the main of the managing directors of those large firms that remained independent of Moscow; and a group known as the Independent Right. The Isamaa bloc (minus the Liberals) united into a single party under the same name in January 1993. The ENIP declined an offer to join in the merger.

The third arm of the governing coalition has been made up of the Moderates, an electoral alliance in September 1992 which brought together the Social Democrats and Rural Centre Party. The Social Democratic Party (*Eesti Sotsiaaldemokraatlik Partei*) was formed from a merger of three groups on September 19, 1990. The largest was the Estonian Social Democratic Independence Party which was based in Tartu and formed in January 1990 under the leadership of Marju Lauristin, a prominent figure in the Popular Front.[14] The second group was the Estonian Democratic Workers' Party, based in Tallinn under Vello Saatpalu, and the third, the Estonian Russian Social Democratic Party under Josif Jurovski, which had its strength in the north-east towns of Narva and Sillamäe. The Rural Centre Party (*Eesti Maa-Keskerakond*) was founded on April 7, 1990, in Türi in central Estonia by forty activists led by Ivar Raig, again a prominent leader in the Popular Front. The aim was to represent the class of newly-privatised farmers.

The leading opposition parties following the 1992 general election were

---

[14] For Lauristin's first-hand (albeit rather discursive) account of the foundation and activities of the Popular Front, see Marju Lauristin, Peeter Vihalemm & Rein Ruutsoo, *Viron vapauden tuulet* (Gummerus: Jyväskylä-Helsinki, 1989).

grouped into two electoral alliances – the Popular Front (*Rahvarinne*) and Secure Home (*Kindel Kodu*). In the first half of 1991, the core of the Popular Front – following the emergence of the Social Democratic and Rural Centre parties – formed a distinct faction in the Supreme Soviet and talks about converting the previously mass-mobilising social movement into a separate party made little headway. This was not least because its founder and prime minister, Edgar Savisaar, was concerned about losing support from allied parties if he created his own.[15] However, the achievement of independence twisted the Popular Front's arm and the People's Centre Party was founded by a number of its leading figures on September 4, 1991. It adopted the name Centre Party (*Keskerakond*) in 1993 when plans to wind up the Popular Front were completed. Like the ENIP, the Centre Party faces an uncertain future. By 1994 three of its *Riigikogu* faction, including the Popular Front activist, Mati Hint, complaining about the very strict discipline in the party, left to found a group of Independents.

The Secure Home alliance embraced three groupings. The Estonian Rural Union (*Eesti maaliit*) was registered on October 24, 1991 although it went back to 1989 when it was created by kolkhoz and sovkhoz bosses as the rural ally of the 'nationalist' wing of the ECP. The Estonian Democratic Justice Union (*Eesti Demokraatlik Õigusliit*) was founded in December 1991 to act like a pressure group to protect and promote the interests of marginal groups such as pensioners and invalids. The Estonian Coalition Party (*Eesti Koonderakond*) – named after the right-wing *Kokoomus* party in Finland – was also founded in December, 1991, and was based on two core groups: those former managers of small and larger state enterprises who sought to retain their privileged position in the new market system and the reformist communists in the so-called Free Estonia (*Vaba Eesti*) group who lost their manifest rationale after the achievement of independence. Under Tiit Vähi, a former prime minister and currently chairman of the Tallinn City Council, the Coalition Party is the most popular party with over 20% in the opinion polls.

Two other opposition groups in the *Riigikogu* are virtually indistinguishable from the personalities at their helm. The Estonian Citizens (*Eesti Kodanik*) are dominated by the demagogic Jüri Toomepuu, a US army veteran, whilst the single-member Entrepreneurs' Party (*Eesti Ettevõtjate Erakond*) is the work of the populist Tiit Made, one of the architects of the 1987 economic self-management programme for Estonia (IME) and a former Green. The Independent Royalists (*Kuningriiklane*), founded in September 1989, started as something of a joke on a satirical television programme. Finally, the Greens were initially the only movement to attract support equally from Estonians and non-Estonians. By summer 1989, however, the movement had become debilitated by internal power struggles and the following year two separate Green parties were founded. In September 1992, one Green, Rein Järlik, was elected to the *Riigikogu*.

---

[15] Rein Taagepera, *Estonia's Return to Independence* (Westview: Boulder-San Francisco-Oxford, 1993), p.196.

Table 1
The Distribution of Votes and Seats
by Party/Electoral Alliance
at the Riigikogu election
of September 1992

Party/Alliance	Votes	%	Seats
Isamaa	100,828	22.0	29
Secure Home	62,329	13.6	17
Popular Front	56,124	12.2	15
Moderates	44,577	9.7	12
ENIP	40,260	8.7	10
Independent Royalists	32,638	7.1.	8
Estonian Citizens	31,553	6.8	8
Greens	12,009	2.6	1
Entrepreneurs	10,946	2.3	1
Others		14.3	0

Estonia as an Anti-Party System

Significantly, relatively few of the groupings vying for *Riigikogu* seats in September 1992 called themselves political parties in the sense of using the international loan word *partei*. Rather, the somewhat dated term *erakond* was preferred – especially by right-wing groups – to denote a break with the past and a new beginning. The mass political culture was none the less antipathetic to the new parties. Survey data revealed that before the 1992 election only one in ten Estonians and one in twenty non-Estonians 'believed in' parties. The only institution Estonians trusted less than parties was in fact the Russian army stationed in Estonia! The police, courts and trade unions all rated more highly than the political parties.[16] The transitionto pluralist democracy, in short, saw Estonia display all three primary features of an anti-party system.

First, the significance of the partisanship of candidates in determining Estonian voter choice at the polls in September 1992 was relatively low when compared with the role of their personality and past history. In a survey of one-thousand citizens conducted in October 1992, only 31% regarded the party orientation of candidates as important, compared with over half who viewed their personality and/or 'pedigree' (past record etc) as the decisive factor. A week after the election, moreover, one-quarter of voters could not even remember the party/alliance their candidate represented.[17] The importance attached to a 'clean' past and the absence of a history of (close) association with the previous regime – viz for 'new blood appointments' – was illustrated by the case of an expatriate, working as an Attorney at

---

[16] Rain Rosimannus, 'Parteistunud Eesti on vaid kujutelm V', *Hommikuleht*, 30.7.1993.

[17] Juhan Kivirahk, Rain Rosimannus & Indrek Pajumaa, 'The premises for democracy; a study of political values in post-independent Estonia', *Journal of Baltic Studies*, XX1V,2,1993, pp.149-160.

Law in the United States, who travelled back to Estonia only a week before polling, ran a vigorous media campaign – which hammered home his candidate number with a variety of jingles – and was duly elected for the ENIP in the Tartu district.

A second feature of the Estonian anti-party system has been the extent of electoral abstentionism. The contrast between the mass mobilisation of the revolutionary period and the demobilisation which followed the achievement of independence was striking. 67% of eligible voters turned out at the 1992 election – the same proportion as took part in the constitutional referendum in June that year – and this represented a lower electoral participation rate than in any West European state except Switzerland in recent years. Turn-out was particularly low among young persons below the age of twenty-four. A generally poor response among young voters also characterised the first post-communist local elections in October 1993. In the university town of Tartu it appeared that the greater the degree of economic marginality the higher the level of voter activity. Pensioners (who also campaigned on behalf of low-income groups in general) secured nineteen of the forty-nine town council seats, prompting *The Baltic Independent* to lead with the story 'Pensioners to govern the city of youth'.[18]

In the wider post-communist perspective, it might be argued that the level of electoral participation in Estonia since regaining independence has been comparatively good. At the Polish general election in September 1993 turn-out was only 53%, broadly the same level as voted to approve Yeltsin's constitution in Russia on December 12 the same year. In Lithuania, moreover, the November 2 1993 by-election in the Kaišindorys region had to be staged again because only 36% of the electorate turned out to vote.[19] None the less, the contrast between the present downward electoral trend and the popular activism of the Singing Revolution is sharp. In Tartu in October 1993, only 34.2% voted.

A third characteristic of the Estonian anti-party system has been the existence of numerically significant anti-parties, diametrically opposed to the agenda and style of the other political groups. In the 'hardline' category there has been the Estonian Citizens; the Independent Royalists, in contrast, have been more 'softline'.

When a US Information Agency poll, conducted shortly before the September 1992 general election, revealed only 14% support for the political parties, the sixty-two year old American Estonian, Jüri Toomepuu, a systems analyst by training, drew the obvious conclusion that in order to be successful it was imperative not to set up a political party! Accordingly, a month before polling, he pulled a group of Independent candidates 'off the streets' and set up the Estonian Citizens as an anti-party umbrella organisation. In the space of a mere four weeks, a vigorous campaign transformed Toomepuu into the best-supported politician in Estonia.

In addition to inveighing against the Old Guard (politicians with a KGB past) and seeking radically to revise the basic constitutional ground rules, Toomepuu, fearful of ultimate Russian control of Estonia ('they are breeding

---

[18] 'Pensioners to govern the city of youth', *The Baltic Independent*, 28.10.-4.11.1993.
[19] 'Low turn-out voids Lithuanian election' *The Baltic Independent*, 26.11.-2.12.1993.

faster'!) has argued the need for a well-financed programme of repatriation and decolonisation carried out under the auspices of the United Nations. Lacking the '100,000 dollars that could wipe out the government', the Estonian Citizens' propaganda for the October 1993 local elections simply juxtaposed a list of the Isamaa-dominated government's promises at the polls in 1992 with their track-record of failing to keep any of them.

The distinctive feature of the Independent Royalists has been their highly irreverent style. In the 1992 election campaign their leaders appeared in public wearing everything from shamanistic head-dresses to dustbin liners.[20] The Royalists have indeed systematically ridiculed both the old and new class of Estonian politicians and the rules they have sought assiduously to apply. According to their leader, the self-styled Territorial Marshall (*maamarssal*) Kalle Kulbok, the Independent Royalists believe in absolute monarchy not democracy and, whilst they have no particular heir or pretender to the throne in mind, they have indicated that the Swedish Crown Prince, Karl Philip, is the type of person who would be well-suited to become King of Estonia. In September 1992 the Independent Royalists offered voters nothing but fairy-stories and Kulbok subsequently compared their iconoclastic style to Wachtmeister and Karlsson's New Democracy in Sweden. Yet the fact that, according to the opinion polls, they have comfortably maintained the 7% support they gained in September 1992, suggests that the Independent Royalists are still able to trade off widespread disillusion with the party system.

The Bases of Anti-Partism

The grounds for the existence of an anti-party culture are not difficult to divine. Above all, the concept of 'party' has been tarred with the brush of the party – the ruling Communist Party – and, accordingly, associated in the minds of citizens with an authoritarian and repressive past they prefer to put behind them. The ECP effectively crushed civil society, leaving prospective party members to ponder an inhuman and unethical choice. As portrayed by Marju Lauristin at the Popular Front's inaugural congress in 1988, this choice lay between 'party membership and integrity; party membership and compassion; party membership and the freedom of the Estonian nation'.[21] First and foremost, then, popular anti-partism constituted a powerful statement of anti-communism.

For many electors, moreover, the sheer multiplicity of parties was confusing and disorienting and the presence of so many competing groups appeared to symbolise the destruction of the unity and fraternity of the revolutionary period. The Singing Revolution was a cathartic experience – a collective

---

[20] Anatol Lieven, *The Baltic Revolution* (Yale University: New Haven & London, 1993), p.286. In this context, *The Times* correspondent Anatol Lieven has related how in September 1992 he asked a Royalist voter if she really wanted a King. 'Oh, no', she replied. 'I am a very moderate Royalist'! He added that few Royalists seemed to have heard the widespread rumours that they were not a joke at all, but a group deliberately and secretly created by former Popular Front leader, Edgar Savisaar, to split the right-wing vote. *Ibid*, p.284. There is no evidence to confirm this rumour.

[21] Lauristin et el (1989), *op.cit*, p.98.

purging of the lies and fears of the past and the generation of a new solidarity, conviction and set of aspirations for the future. On September 11, 1988, no less than 300,000 people – one-third of the entire Estonian population – gathered in the Song Stadium in Tallinn. Mass mobilisation on this scale betokened the incipient collapse of the hierarchical Soviet system and the re-creation of civil society. Only four years later, however, the emergence of a plethora of parties substituted a picture of conflict for the previous show of unity.[22]

The emergence of the embryonic parties also coincided with an economic downturn and the inevitable hardships – especially in the rise in the cost of living – involved in the shift to a market economy. The parties could offer no panaceas for the teething-troubles of privatisation and also suffered to a degree from the perceived inability of democracy to deliver the economic goods.

Interestingly, the media have both reflected and reinforced the prevalent anti-party attitudes. Leading politicians are in practice unable to publish newspaper pieces which present party policy; rather, the contribution must appear as a personal view signed by the author him/herself. Equally, if an article attempts to be too political and didactic in content it will be self-defeating (that is, skipped by the ordinary public) and in order to gain a readership the content must be suitably diluted and 'livened up'. In practice, only information from the Riigikogu parliamentary factions (groups) escapes the tight editing (self-imposed or otherwise) which is the fate of other political contributions.

Before rounding off this present paper, a postscript on the low level of partisanship in Estonia is in order, since the new electoral law, although incorporating a Finnish-style individual preference vote, was expressly designed to consolidate the position of the parties. The single transferable voting system (STV), used for the December 1989 local government elections and the Supreme Soviet elections in March 1990, was abandoned and PR list voting adopted, precisely because, it was claimed, STV was suited to 'multi-candidate elections' but not to a multi-party poll. Thus, after the initial allocation of seats on the basis of personal votes, the second stage of counting involves the allocation of seats on the basis of the total party list, that is, the total party list vote divided by the electoral quota. If seats still remain to be filled (there were sixty altogether in September 1992) they are transferred to a national pool for allocation in proportion to the national votes of those parties exceeding a 5% threshold of the total vote. A modified d'Hondt divisor is then deployed in respect of the national lists of party candidates.

Yet the engrained culture and tradition of voting for individuals may prove difficult to eradicate, especially in a country where the Estonian population numbers little more than Greater Manchester. In its assessment of the 1992 election, undertaken by the International Foundation for Electoral

---

[22] Ironically, at an election meeting in September 1992, an elderly lady, bemoaning the state of things, inquired why it was not possible to have just one party. On being politely advised by the candidate that this was exactly the situation Estonians had sung out in protest against, she relented somewhat and declared: 'Alright then, three or four parties, but not more!' Interview with ENIP MP K.Jaak Roosaare.

Systems, it was concluded that in the future, 'those candidates who adopt
a more personalised campaign should have an advantage ... The framers of
the electoral law who hoped it would consolidate "parties" over "personalities" may well be disappointed to find that their intentions are somewhat
frustrated by the combined actions of the candidates and voters'.[23]

Conclusions: Parties and Democracy in Estonia

There are only three passing references to political parties in the new Estonian form of government. However, despite the paucity of the constitutional recognition afforded them, Estonia may already be considered a party
democracy in the sense that the infant parties control the state. Parties do
not yet control or dominate political society and the mobilisation, socialisation and organisation (input) functions are but imperfectly performed.[24]
Moreover, with two anti-parties, the 'hardline' Estonian Citizens and 'softline' Independent Royalists claiming a combined 14% of the vote in September 1992, Estonia could perhaps be considered a case of an anti-party system. Certainly the primary challenge for the parties in the middle term is
to legitimise their position and work towards moulding a political culture
in which parties are perceived as legitimate channels of representation.

Anti-parties are by no means peculiar to the former communist systems.
In Western Europe anti-parties have claimed support in large part as a reaction against the élitist and cartellised character of the established parties
and the 'democratic deficit' which has developed between their leaders and
rank-and-file members. West European parties have to varying degrees atro-
phied as voluntary membership organisations. Richard Katz has suggested
two principal reasons for this. One, television has become the pre-eminent
source of political information and the dominant channel of communication for élites. Two, state support to parties has allowed these élites to
insulate themselves financially from members. As Katz concludes: 'Party
becomes a label by which a group of leaders is known and an organisation
for co-ordinating élite activity'.[25] Indeed, the irony would appear to be
(put crudely) that whereas in Western Europe party is a label which gives
identity to élites and legitimizes and co-ordinates their activity, in Eastern
Europe élites give (at least some) identity to parties and the label in turn
is designed to authorise and legitimize the actions of their founding-figures.
The challenge in Estonia is now to depersonalize the embryonic parties and
to seek to develop them towards the very type of mass party – linking state
and society – whose future in Western Europe looks so problematical.

The extent of the organisational challenge facing the political parties can
be guaged from the situation on the eve of the October 1993 local elections.

---

[23] International Foundation for Electoral Systems, 'Republic of Estonia. An Assessment
of the Election to the Riigikogu and the Presidency', 16-24.9.1992.

[24] On the popular indifference to, and ignorance of reprersentative structures and processes in Estonia today, see Mare Kukk, 'Estnisk publik åser maktkupp och lokalval',
Nordisk Kontakt, 10/1993, pp.11-12.

[25] Katz (1990), *op.cit*, p.

Many small towns reported that they had not boasted a single branch of any political party since the ECP was disbanded in 1991, whilst in Rahva Hääl Tiit Kubri from Nõo wrote: 'As a rule people in the countryside do not wish to join any party and leave this hobby to townsfolk'.[26] Ironically, a draft law on political parties – setting their minimum membership at two-hundred – went before the Riigikogu in November 1993. If the figure was two-hundred active members, none of the existing parties would qualify!

Although political parties are only weakly internalised, democracy in Estonia hardly appears at serious risk since it is broadly synonymous in the popular mind with liberation from the Occupation state. The main question is not perhaps whether democracy will work, but how it will work and in particular what will be the impact of economic reform on social stratification and, by extension, the stabilisation of the parties. According to Rein Ruutsoo, 'political parties have collapsed and the movement society is reproducing itself'.[27] This seems highly exaggerated. There is, though, the interesting question of interest-group formation and the prospect of corporatist decision-making. It is just possible that Estonia will not chart the 'party democracy' course to the twenty-first century.

---

[26] Cited in *The Baltic Independent*, 15-21.10.1993.

[27] Conversation with Rein Ruutsoo, a Popular Front activist and presently a researcher in the Estonian Academy. See Rein Ruutsoo, 'Transitional Society and Social Movements in Estonia', *Estonian Academy of Sciences, Humanities and Social Sciences*, 42,2,1993. Also, Enn Põldroos, 'Oh seda vaesk demokraatiat ehk legend rahvussühtsusest', *Päevaleht*, 28.5 1993.

The Politics of Small States
Case Studies in Domestic Politics

Liesbet Hooghe
Nuffield College, Oxford

'The Dynamics of Constitution Building in Belgium'

Introduction

Here is a paradox. Belgian politics displays a great capacity for flexible constitutional settlements, despite the fact that the rules of the game try to discourage reformers; but it also reveals an incapacity to settle down afterwards, again, despite the fact that tough rules try to guarantee stability. The dynamic process of constitutional change has become a fast track for separatism, much to the dismay of many Belgians.

Belgium is probably the most paradoxical case around, but it is also a crucial case study for constitutional reformers throughout the world: Canada, Northern Ireland, East and Central Europe, the European Union, South Africa. How could one have peaceful, negotiated, flexible and effective constitutional adjustments (the bright side of the Belgian coin) without falling into the trap of eternal constitutional modifications–constitutional tinkering (the dark side).

How can we make sense of the paradox? Students of Belgian politics usually tap from two strands of literature: there are the explanations based on consociationalism, both the traditional kind and a very stimulating rational choice variant, and the literature of particracy, or to use the original word *partitocrazia*. My argument is going to evolve from the same two concepts: consociational regime and political parties, structure and agency. I will argue that consociational regime characteristics have increased the capacity for flexible settlements, but that consociational devices are at the same time prone to exacerbate nationalist challenges. Political parties as the core agents in constitution building have played an ambivalent role, enhancing effectiveness and facilitating constitutional tinkering.

That will be my Belgian explanation. What can we learn from this particular case for constitution building in general? We need to lay bare the structure and the logic of such a regime, and understand how particular mechanisms and devices for conflict management may produce this puzzle. Similarly, we need to reach beyond the parties, and identify when and how certain actors become core agents in constitution building.

A Crash Course in Belgian Politics

As Belgian politics is usually not headline news, let me remind you of some basic characteristics.

The ten million inhabitants are distributed over three regions: Flanders in the north (58%), Wallonia in the south (32%), and Brussels (10%). The three official languages are Dutch or Flemish (55%), French (44%), and German (1%). Flanders and Wallonia can be considered unilingual.

Like in Canada, the unity of the country has been challenged by nationalism/separatism. Or actually, there are two nationalist movements in Belgium, each of which is rooted in a distinct set of grievances. Flemish nationalism is rooted in nineteenth and early twentieth century linguistic discrimination, and it has led to demands for group autonomy. Walloon nationalism is rooted in mid-twentieth century socio-economic grievances, a reaction against the typical industrial decline of an early industrialized area [north-England]. That led to demands for regional autonomy. The transformation of grievances in separatist challenges was a long historical process, which cannot be detailed here. The two nationalisms became formidable challenges by the 1960s. The federal state structure, with its duality of communities and regions, reflects these two strands. The close match between challenge and response gives an indication of the nature of the political regime in Belgium. However, in practice the three regions Flanders, Wallonia and Brussels have become the main actors.

Turn now to the political parties. Belgium has a multiparty system, but for our purposes it is sufficient to know that two parties dominate, each being the largest one in its region. The christian-democrats are number one in Flanders, the socialists in Wallonia. Of the two, the christian democrats are most central to the system. Important to note: there are no nation-wide parties – not a single one; each party caters for one language group only. That is why one gets a schizophrenic federal parliament, with two christian democratic parties, two socialist parties etc.

Finally, two regime characteristics, which are the core elements of my argument. I organize them around two questions.

The first is who runs the political system? The answer in Britain or Canada would be: the executive backed by a parliamentary majority. That's why we call it parliamentary government. The answer in Belgium, like in Italy, like in Japan, has been: the political parties. In a particracy, political parties systematically command more power than other public actors like the cabinet, president, legislature, courts ... It means for example. that party leaders conduct coalition formation negotiations, that they chose the ministers (not the prime minister), and follow the cabinet activities closely and comment on it (and especially of their own ministers). Remember that there are no nation-wide parties in Belgium. Hence the party headquarters monitor the regional governments as well as the federal government.

On the question of how is the system run? the answer is through consociationalism. You are all familiar with the concept, so that allows me to go straight to what is relevant to my argument. As you know, the leaderships of the groups occupy a pivotal position in a consociational regime. They go to the central state to extract resources for their groups, but they have also an interest in preserving the centre, because they want to make sure that they return to get more resources. Hence they essentially believe that cooperation pays off better than defection. The strategic game is a game of 'chicken'. This encourages élites to strike odd package deals which often contain unrelated concessions. *Package deals*, because they strike a delicate multidimensional balance – among one another, but also between group interests and national interests. *Odd* package deals, because they need to be flexible, pragmatic and attentive to accommodate potential challengers, for example, ecotax in return for a federalization package in July 1993.

In Belgium, as in most genuine consociational regimes actually, the party leaders have taken up this role. Hence, particracy has been embedded in consociationalism. Moreover, electoral system and party system have conspired to make a christian democratic-socialist coalition the most natural option. It is no coincidence that the four major packages of constitutional reform (1970, 1980, 1988, 1993) were negotiated under christian democratic-socialist governments (enlarged with variable other parties).

Constitution Building and the Logic of a Consociational Regime

Let us take now some distance of the Belgian reality, and try to understand the logic of such a regime. We are trying to find out regime and agent characteristics which produce effectiveness and flexibility on the one hand, and a self-perpetuating process of change, a centrifugal process, on the other hand.

Structure of the regime can be summed up in three basic features: there is no formal hierarchy, partners around the table have in principle equal status no matter how large or how small they are, and the centre has no autonomous power base (not even autonomous interests) and is instead run by the partners. That means that the actors need to sit around the table and work out a deal to govern the centre.

There are two relevant *structural features* of the agents. Agents are the critical gatekeepers between the national arena and their own arena, and they are the dominant managers of the national arena. Agents, in this case political parties, wear multiple hats, and they work in multiple arenas simultaneously. That enables them to play off one issue against another, jump from one arena to another.

Take a Flemish christian democratic party leader. He/she is the spokesperson for his group (catholic pillar), but he is also the guardian of the national interest. Federalization has added two other arenas: the community arena for Flemish cultural and group interests, and the regional arena for Flemish territorial interests. That burdens him with many responsibilities towards his constituencies, but it also enables him to negotiate more freely as he can offer and ask as a christian democrat (or catholic), a Belgian citizen, a Flemish-speaker, and a citizen of the Flemish region, and in a way he/she is free to choose the constituency he/she decides to please most. This form of personal fusion is widespread in a consociational regime.

It all sounds very benign, cooperative. That is usually what is emphasized in the literature on consociationalism. Have a second, more critical look. These features, how benign they might sound, may also generate a centrifugal spiral in this regime. Groups may want to keep what they once gained. Suppose they do; who is going to stop them. They have the mileage to play this tough: their equal status gives them *de facto* veto power, there is no autonomous centre to fight them off, there is no hierarchical structure to force them to give in, and their double gatekeeper role gives them free access to the centre. Hence the trade-off and compromise may become a one-way street: from centre to periphery, and only a trickle from periphery to centre. I am not claiming that this is always and in every circumstance the case. However, the potential for a centrifugal course is embedded in the structure.

Now one could think of several strategies to diminish this risk. One would be to cheat with the 'equal status' principle, by giving certain actors more weight than others, and perhaps accept one (informal) leader – a *primus inter pares* [Germany in the European Union; USA in NAFTA; soft hegemony in one-party dominance]. Actually, you introduce some hierarchy through the backdoor. In Belgium, the Flemish christian democratic party has effectively been the voice for Flanders, and the Walloon socialist party for Wallonia. The two dominant parties set the parameters for an agreement, and then seek for ways to coopt potential opponents. *Cooption* of potential opponents, rather than *consensus-seeking* between potential allies, is the crucial mechanism in a regime like that in Belgium. That can happen in various ways: incorporating new issues and new vocal individuals or groupings, bribing or handing out support, even accepting them in a coalition government. They would use mainly positive incentives rather than negative incentives. The style of decision making is accommodating, not confrontational, flexible, not rigidly rule-bound. However, notwithstanding the amiable face, the hegemons set the rules. It sounds less positive than the purely consociational consensus-seeking, but it is much more efficient. In Belgium, particracy enhances the effect. However, the Belgian case is a partial success at best. Hegemony is shared between two parties which alternate between competition and cooperation. That is why this strategy sometimes breaks down in Belgium.

If you can't adjust the structural features of the regime, then you must work more efficiently within them. As long as the parties believe there is more to gain by cooperation than by going it alone, the centre is safe. The classical consociational devices and mechanisms perform exactly that function: they specialize in maximizing benefit to the actors while minimizing loss from the centre.

The Politics of Constitution Building: Flexibility in Return for Eternal Change

Let us have a closer look at these devices in the Belgian context, and scrutinize the two sides of the coin: *flexible adjustment* and a *centrifugal spiral* in Belgium.

flexible adjustment

There are many ways to bring order in the diverse set of consociational devices, I would distinguish between four types. The first set are about reshuffling power at the centre – they are the most economic devices for the centre. The next two cost the centre a bit more; they are about manipulating power between centre and group. Rather than citing the whole list, I will concentrate on the most economical tool in Belgian conflict management: 'carving up the centre'.

Carving up the Centre

Parties are usually not interested in controlling every single issue, every single policy area. Now a conflict manager can work creatively with that piece of knowledge. He simply carves up the centre, and assigns control over different bits to different actors according to their preferences.

For example, this technique has traditionally been applied to allocation of ministerial portfolios in Belgian federal governments. Big spending departments like defence, public works, housing etc. tended to go to Walloon socialist ministers; agriculture and culture, on the contrary, tended to go to Flemish christian democrats. It allowed the parties to keep their constituencies happy.

This is only one example, but it gives a sense of what is going on: élite actors in a consociational system have a wide variety of devices, which allows them to react flexibly on challenges.

Interestingly, scholars don't often make explicit the philosophy behind consociationalism. First of all, process is more important than outcome. How a deal is negotiated matters more than what is actually negotiated. Form before substance. Parties want a fair deal: it must contain something for all partners, and it is not made on the terms of one partner only. Now in that frame of mind, many, many things could be used as bargaining chips. Perhaps more importantly, consociationalism accepts that deep conflict is a fact of life; it cannot always be sorted out. Consociational rules are as much about reducing the negative consequences of disagreement, as they are about conducing compromise. Putting brakes on the centrifugal process is as important as reverting the centrifugal process.

Containing a Separatist Challenge?

I think I have illustrated the flexibility of this battery of consociational devices. Have these consociational devices proved to be useful in containing the separatist challenge in Belgium? To put it another way, has conflict management been able to make the indivisible good of nationalism divisible? So, what has the record been in Belgium?

Consociational devices allowed the peaceful, gradual but controlled incorporation of nationalist claims in politics and institutions. In the same vain, these devices have managed the transformation of a Belgian élite into regional élites, a process which in itself was triggered off by social change. In other words, they have been quite useful in protecting the continuity of the political and social system. But there are down sides.

Constitutional dev.ces have been expensive. It is no coincidence that Belgium has the highest public debt per head in the European Union (about 135 if 100 would be the annual GDP per head). Public finance ran out of control in the late 1970s, a period of chronic nationalist conflict and social friction, paralysed governments, and expensive deals between the parties in power.

But overspending is not the main fault of the consociational logic. The fault is that it makes conflict pay off. And perhaps we needed game theory and George Tsebelis to bring this message home to the field of study. Flexible adjustments have made it more likely that demands are going to be met. Under those circumstances, even a non-nationalist party may find it useful to raise the nationalist banner to get what it wants. Tsebelis, for example, modelled the conditions under which nationalist conflict could be initiated by the élite. Similarly, the devices make it less disastrous to disagree. Hence the parties are less eager to compromise, which in turn induces them to stick to their demands. It may erode the pragmatic and consensual style of decision making.

I may still have to call on your imagination to jump from these features to the never-ending spiral of constitution building, but not much. Because nationalist conflict pays off so well, nationalist demands have become part of the standard competitive game between the parties. They are tackled by standard consociational devices: reshuffling goods, devolving goods, the redesign of policy procedures and practices, reshuffling powers, devolving powers, the redesign of polity structures and practices. When you take all this together, it adds up to constitution building, or actually constitutional tinkering.

And at this stage, the particular features of the political regime are working out their less benign, uncooperative potential: the regional political parties in their privileged gatekeeper position, and reinforced by particracy and shared hegemony, are well-placed to turn a non-nationalist issue into a nationalist conflict. They are a fast transmission belt to constitutional tinkering.

For example, the Fourons issue in 1987 as a substitute for the concerted defence by christian democrats and socialists of the welfare state – this triggered off the major constitutional reform of 1988-89.

Hence the reform of the state, constitution building, has become part of general party politics. Belgium is a stark case, but not an exception; the same is happening in Russia, be it in a totally different context. On a smaller scale, the electoral system in France has become a pawn in the partisan competition between left (proportional representation) and right (absolute majority system), switching between PR to AMS as the government coalition changes colour. In Belgium, Flemish christian democrats and Walloon socialists are in a way in an analogous position to France's Right and Left.

I have finally arrived at the last stretch of this long journey. Particracy and christian democratic-socialist hegemony, embedded in a consociational regime, seem responsible for an ambivalent outcome. Is there no way out? Is there no way to separate flexible change from uncontrollable change?

Imagine that particracy and shared hegemony would wither away. Would this create an opportunity to recast the politics of constitution building in Belgium, that is, preferably to retain the flexibility but to lift constitutional change out of the game of standard party competition? The experiment might become true.

Recasting the Politics of Constitution Building? the Demise of Particracy

The power of the political parties in Belgian political life has eroded significantly since 1980, and the once hegemonic position of Christian Democrats in Flanders and Socialists in Wallonia has been weakened seriously. In the political arena, the parties have lost much power to the executives. The shrinking of the two regional hegemons is followed by the fragmentation of the political landscape, not by the emergence of a new hegemon. Politics will probably become more competitive.

This change is influenced by general processes of social and political change in advanced industrial societies, although one could also point at special Belgian factors. Rather than dwelling on the causes and documenting the demise of the old order, I would like to conclude with a sketch of the new opportunity structure in Belgian politics. Is there a chance to get the process of constitution building back under control? We start with the old devices (within the confines of the regime), and then move on to more innovative thinking (bringing in structural regime changes). I will end on a moderately hopeful note. Just a quick taste of new times.

the devices for conflict containment

Diminishing Resources

What do Belgian actors still have in their closet to appease separatist challengers in the 1990s? Can they buy off challengers, or are they able to postpone conflict?

Expensive goodies are out. The treasury is broke. What is left?

One could still use competences as bargaining chips, and the Belgian actors have done so since the early 1980s. However, that is a one-way process with a predictable ending: an empty Belgian state centre. The last reform devolved some aspects on agriculture for example and more importantly external competences. The next round of constitutional reform will almost certainly take substantial slices of social welfare, probably the health sector. There is not much left at the centre: foreign policy (high politics), defence, justice and the home office (law and order, but not local government), regulatory powers in certain areas, social security ... and the public debt (62% of the federal budget of 1993 was for interest payments on public debt. There is one positive side: the extensive federalization has decreased the decision load of the centre; hence, there are fewer contentious issues left.

Creative Deals

Creative deals, like the one in 1993? However, my hunch is that this could well have been the last deal of this magnitude. Such comprehensive deals have become very costly: the effort for the hegemons to forge the necessary coalition, the consequences for the centre (further depletion), and the difficulty for the challengers to convince their constituency that compromise is better than principled opposition (tension within the green party; split in the Flemish nationalist party). So in this more competitive political system, the tough constitutional reform procedure might finally start to deter reformers, but at the expense of the capacity to respond flexibly to challenges. I would therefore expect an increasing number of deadlocks in Belgian politics around constitutional and non-constitutional issues alike.

Summing up: the spiral of constitutional reform is likely to slow down, but there is a price tag attached to that. Flexible adjustment becomes increasingly difficult because there are fewer bargaining chips, and deadlocks become increasingly likely, which could be very destabilizing. Hence there are few signals thus far that the actual process of constitution building has been brought better under control.

Innovative Alternatives? Structural Changes

Thus far not very bright news, but then, we have only taken a brief superficial glance. Let us look more systematically at the structure of the political regime. Which structural changes has this post-particracy context brought with it? Have these changes increased the chances to disconnect the politics of constitution building from the standard game of party competition?

new gatekeepers

The most dramatic change: core actors are now the executives. This is partly the result of federalization, as the new regional institutions started to flex their muscles. Territorial politics has grown steadily. The shift to executives was also partly the result of a conscious decision by the party leaders and senior politicians themselves in the early 1980s.

The emergence of executives as core actors in the constitution building has changed the character of the political game profoundly, although the effects are still not clear-cut.

First a few words on the new structure in which the executives play their game. The federal reform of 1989 set up an elaborate machinery for intergovernmental collaboration and conflict resolution. At the top of the hierarchy sits a *comité de concertation*, which consists of an equal number of federal and regional/community ministers (including the prime ministers of the governments). It deliberates on general policy guide-lines and to solve conflicts of interests between the arenas (competence conflicts are dealt with by the Constitutional Court). Why is this set-up unlikely to be as effective as the partisan set-up has been, with respect to solving conflict as well as with respect to containing a centrifugal process?

– The shift from parties as gatekeepers to governments is a shift away from personal interlocking to a sort of negotiated cooperation. These forms of cooperation are very fragile if they are not embedded in a hierarchical system.

– The context is less integrative than with parties as gatekeepers. The rules compel actors even less to cooperate. For example. if the parties fail to negotiate a settlement, the rules permit them explicitly to go it alone.

– The actors are unequal. Among the three actors, the federal government is the only one which structurally speaks for a multiple set of interests. It speaks for federal interests, naturally, but at decisive moments the ministers tend to line up against one another along regional or linguistic lines. Hence in a sense, the federal government is the true successor of the regional political parties, the gatekeeper with interests in multiple arenas. But contrary to the political parties, it sits around the table with regional governments which speak unambiguously for regional interests. The odds are against the federal level – or if you wish the centre. Structure seems to predict more autonomies challenges.

– Political practice gives one counter-indication though. The executives have developed a tendency to refer deadlocked conflicts (and there have been quite a few) to the Constitutional Court, even for conflicts which are not strictly competence conflicts. Hence they seem to be looking for an internal hierarchical discipline.

Conclusion: Executives have replaced political parties as gatekeepers between centre and regions. They are less well-equipped to steer constitution building away from a centrifugal course. The causes are structural: lack of an overarching hierarchical structure which could compel the actors to work out a compromise, and unequal status of the actors (one with multiple hats, the others with one hat). In this context, old habits may still prove powerful: new solutions are likely to be cast in the old mould of constitutional adjustments. Intergovernmental competition seems to have replaced party competition in the politics of constitution building, but it has not yet changed how problems and solutions are defined.

more autonomous centre

The subsequent reorganizations have gradually disentangled federal and regional levels. The reform of 1993 rounds this process off. The dynamics of territorial politics may further strengthen the autonomy of the federal government. However, until now, the federal government has nearly always split along linguistic or regional lines, when conflict pitted one region against the other. The new logic must fight against old habits.

a new arena and an external discipline: Europe

And then, perhaps, the *deus ex machina*. The European arena opens up possibilities for federal and regional levels to find common ground. It would give the regional governments an extra hat. In other words, they would be compelled to find compromises between narrow regional interests and broader European interests (and indirectly Belgian interests, and the interests of the other regions), to act more consensual. There is one condition: regional governments need direct access to the European arena, which has recently become possible. At the European level, the Maastricht Treaty allows regional ministers to represent a member state in the Council. At the Belgian level, the latest constitutional reform has given the regions international competence within the range of their powers.

Europe may also help in a different way, by providing the hierarchical structure which is lacking in Belgium. European regulations limit the range of policy choices at either domestic level. European politics may also compel all the Belgian actors to work out a common stand-point to be presented at the European level.

Hence, Europe may help to contain the separatist challenge. It should not come as a surprise that the Belgian federal government in particular is the most ardent supporter of a more tightly knit European Union.

Conclusion

It is difficult to retain the capacity for flexible adjustment to new challenges, while at the same time avoiding that the process gets out of control. The Belgian example shows that it is very hard to break a set pattern of political interaction. Once constitution building has been internalized in ordinary politics, it tends to be used over and again as a frame for understanding new problems, mobilizing resources to deal with them, and choosing solutions. However, the Belgian example shows that change is possible. The political leaders themselves have taken several conscious steps to regain control over a constitutional dynamics gone out of control; they have seized the opportunity created for them by wider changes in politics and society. The most effective brake on separatism, though, may well come from outside: the European Union. It would be misguided to see the European Union as simply the traditional hierarchical superior; it is best described as a regime where communication, exchange and commitment is facilitated rather than imposed. How this regime makes its trade-off between flexible response, effectiveness, and controllable process management, is a topic for another talk. What matters here, is its constraining impact on the Belgian separatist challenge.

Bibliography

Anderson, Benny (1991), *Imagined Communities*, Verso.

Covell, Maureen (1981), 'Ethnic Conflict and Elite Bargaining: The Case of Belgium', *West European Politics*, 4 (3): 197-218.

Dewachter, Wilfried (1987), 'Changes in Particracy: The Belgian Party System from 1944 to 1986', in H.Daalder (ed) (1986), *Party Systems in Denmark, Austria, Switzerland, the Netherlands and Belgium*, Frances Pinter.

Dewachter, Wilfried (1992), *Besluitvorming in Politiek België*, Acco.

Elazar, Daniel (1985), 'Federalism and Consociational Regimes', *Publius*, 15 (2): 17-33.

Hooghe, Liesbet (1991), *A Leap in the Dark: Nationalist Conflict and Federal Reform in Belgium*, Cornell University Press (Western Societies Program, Number 27).

Hooghe, Liesbet (1993), 'Belgium: From Regionalism to Federalism', in J.Coakley (ed), *Territorial Management of Ethnic Conflict*, Frank Cass.

Hooghe, Liesbet (1994), 'Belgian Federalism and the European Community', in M.Keating & B.Jones (eds), *Regions in the European Community*, Oxford University Press.

Lijphart, Arend (1977), *Democracy in Plural Societies*, Yale University Press.

Lijphart, Arend (1989), 'Democratic political systems: types, cases, causes, and consequences', *Journal of Theoretical Politics*, 1 (1): 33-48.

Lijpart, Arend (1984), *Democracies: patterns of majoritarian and consensus government in twenty-one countries*, New Haven: Yale.

McRae, Kenneth D. (1986), *Conflict and Compromise in Multilingual Societies: Belgium*, Wilfried Laurier Press.

Obler, Jeffrey, Steiner, Jürg & Dierickx, Guido (1977), *Decision-Making in Smaller Democracies: The Consociational Burden*, Sage.

Scharpf, Fritz (1994), 'Games real actors could play. Positive and negative coordination in embedded negotiations', *Journal of Theoretical Politics*, 6 (4): 27-53.

Scharpf, Fritz (1988), 'The Joint Decision Trap: Lessons from German Federalism and European Integration, *Public Administration*, 66, 239-278.

Tsebelis, George (1990), 'Elite Interaction and Constitution Building in Consociational Democracies', *Journal of Theoretical Politics*, 2 (1), 5-29.

Round Table
Political Science and the PSA

Fred Nash
University of Southampton

'Editorial Gate-keeping'

Acknowledgements

For helpful comments cn a draft of this paper, the author is grateful to Liam O'Sullivan, University of Southampton.

Summary

The close of 1993, marking a change in the editorship both of *Political Studies* and *Politics* affords an opportunity to reflect upon some wider issues. After preliminary thoughts about the PSA, a sketch account of *Political Studies* and *Politics* will be followed by some thoughts on the gate-keeping function of editors in learned journals.

The Political Studies Association of the United Kingdom (the PSA)

Oddly, the PSA has never been the subject of analysis. While we have experts in our midst on just about every aspect of politics anywhere, yet, as a body of political scientists, we appear to have neglected the way our Association is governed. There are no accounts of it, and an appeal to the Charities Commission, where one would expect to find basic documentary evidence of its past and mode of governance, proved a huge disappointment: except for a recent set of accounts, the file, all of six pages, has not been updated since 1976.[1]

The PSA was established as an educational charity in 1950 to '... encourage education and advancement of learning', and, subsequent to the *Charities Act, 1960*, and the *Education Act, 1973*, it was registered in March 1973. We must not make too much of this, for it is, after all, only a supervisory scheme offering exemption from taxation, in the process imposing certain restrictions. Importantly, this means that the charity must be within the jurisdiction of the High Court; its government must be acceptable to the Charities Commissioners, who must be informed of any changes; the aims and objectives of the charity cannot change without the approval of the Commissioners; they must receive a copy of its annual accounts; the constitution of a charity and its accounts are public documents, available for

---

[1] Charities Commission, registration number 313863. Wilfrid Harrison in his editorial introduction to Volume 1, Number 1, gives a glimpse of the conditions and the background to the establishment of the Political Studies Association.

inspection upon demand, and are not protected by copyright. Furthermore, under the terms of *Charities Act, 1992*, certain people are automatically disqualified from acting as charity trustees. Moreover, the Commissioners, since the *Charities Act, 1960*, extended by *Charities Act, 1992*, can, under certain circumstances, cause a trustee to be suspended or removed. Finally, and if necessary and relevant, they can appeal to the High Court for specific alterations (cy-prés powers).[2]

The implications of all this for the governance of the PSA are, altogether, rather limited, for the duties expected from trustees are only the minimum that may be expected of any director. Any incorporation is guided by its articles and stated aims, which is precisely the case with a charity such as the PSA, except that these aims and objectives are incapable of change without destroying its charitable status.[3] In this, but only this, sense is our constitution fixed and inflexible.

The 1989 document is not our current constitution; a change to Article 6 (Durham Conference) allows for the time and place of Annual Conference two years hence to be decided. On the other hand, an amendment to Article 5.2, proposed for decision at Belfast Conference, seeking to impose a maximum number of terms for members of the Executive Committee and its Chair proved contentious and was referred back to the Committee: this item did not appear on the agenda at our Leicester Conference; presumably it is still under consideration. There are oft denied rumours of at least one 'revolutionary' change at the top, the story of which beckons further study.

To be sure, the constitution, as amended in 1974 to insert Article 8(vi) was, in effect, no more than a minimal instrument necessary to obtain registration as a charity. *Inter alia*, amendments have since expanded Article 5, added Article 9, and rearranged Articles 2 to 4. But these changes and additions do not significantly alter its bare-bones nature. Thus, the PSA is governed not by a full-fledged working constitution, but by an instrument the primary purpose of which was to satisfy legal requirements rather than to ensure its good and orderly governance.

Now, as a profession, we are quick off the mark and good at categorising all manner of forms of government. And the basic values which we tend to apply – and ask questions about later are precisely those that enable us to determine the extent to which a system may be said to be 'democratic'. Yet, apparently, we are content with a system of government for our own Association which can hardly be said to be so. While it is difficult to precisely pigeon-hole its system, *Elective Guardianship* seems the most appropriate way of describing it. If it is true that Plato meant to ridicule guardianship as a meaningful form of government, then the joke is on us!

One feature of the PSA constitution is its brevity and paucity of rules. There are four groups of articles in the constitution as of 1989:

---

[2] A doctrine that enables gifts to a charity that would otherwise fail, to be diverted to a related purpose, and to remove possible obstacles on the achievement of the objects of the charity. See *Tudor on Charities*, 7th edition, Blackwell, 1984. For a simpler account see P. McLoughlin & C. Rendell, *Law of Trusts*, Macmillan, 1992, chapter 14, section 9.

[3] Constitution of the PSA, Article 8 (vi).

Purpose	Articles	Remarks
Objectives	1 [& 8(vi)]	1: 'advancement of education'. 8 (vi): constitutional guarantee of its Charitable status.
Membership appointment	2, 3, 4, 7, & 9	2: eligibility or membership: in political studies and allied subjects at an institution of higher education; special category, and rates, for retired members. 3: graduate membership, for a maximum of five years; not eligible for office 4: others, whose participation is deemed to be advantageous to political studies may be admitted at the discretion of the Executive Committee. 7: Subscriptions; different for ordinary and graduate members. 9: Corporate membership; special rates; no voting rights.
Executive body	5.1 to 5.7, & 6	5.1, 5.2 and 5.3: ten elected members, Hon. Sec, Hon. Treasurer; for three years, but staggered: yr. 0; Hon. offices, yr. 1; five members; yr. 2; five members; yr. 3; Hon. offices... 5.4: Single Transferable Vote, and postal ballot, 5.5: co-opting powers for the Executive Committee 'as it deems appropriate', e.g. editors of journals, convenor of conferences, etc. 5.6: casual vacancies to Hon. Offices are filled by the Executive Committee from its members until the next annual round of elections, followed by election(s) or byelection(s), 5.7: casual vacancies in the Committee: filled by co-opting from members, otherwise as 5.6. 6: Chairperson, President and vice presidents; appointed by the Executive Committee. Committee is responsible for organising the Annual Conference, during which an Annual General Meeting is held, *inter alia* to decide, or to remit to the Committee, the date and the place of the next Conference..
Constitutional amendments	8, i to vi	i-iv: rules and procedures for amendments v: Amendments require a qualified majority of votes cast.

And there are a number of significant omissions:

- 1. timetable and the procedure for nominations to elected offices;
- 2. the co-opting powers of the Executive Committee under Article 5.5 are not specified; some co-options are clear: for example, the editors of its publications and the convenors of the Annual Conference,
- 3. eligibility requirements for Chairperson, the President and vice-presidents (other than former Chairs) are not specified;
- 4. Powers of the Chair and the President;
- 5. the extent and the nature of the 'advisory' role of the President's Panel;
- 6. Accountability? Recall?

Political Studies

According to Wilfrid Harrison[4], *Political Studies* (1953) was meant to fill a gap, for, as he put it, while there were specialised and academic journals, none was devoted to the general study of government and politics. Precisely what is meant by this is not clear. At the time five journals were being published in this country: *Public Administration*, since 1923; *International Affairs*, 1924; *The Political Quarterly*, 1930; *Parliamentary Affairs*, 1947, and *Soviet Studies*, 1949; there is no obvious gap, perhaps the idea of a 'gap' ought to be examined from another perspective, namely the (academic or other) fissures that from time to time appear to have bedevilled the history of the profession. Whether there was a gap to fill, or this journal filled it, *Political Studies* was published as the 'organ' of the PSA, which explains the appearance of the phrase '... to develop and promote the study of politics' in every issue of the journal since.

The journal was intended to exemplify British and foreign research, and to offer '... contributions that will be of first importance to all who are concerned ... with contemporary developments in the study of politics'. This, it was thought, would necessarily emphasise concept and method, but all contributions would be judged on the basis of their 'qualities of precision and criticism', and every articles would be vetted by anonymous external referees, selected from an unpublished 'list', which, according to the Editor's Report for 1992 (Annual Conference, Belfast), has some 1100 names on it. Whether this is the list of book reviewers only, or is the list from which referee are selected is not clear. One would expect, however, that there are two lists; Oh, but to be on the other list!

Wilfrid Harrison was the first editor of the journal, and, as he so modestly declared, came to the job without a clue as to what it involved. But, nevertheless, he felt in duty bound to declare his position: the interests of the journal would be historical, current, and individual, with no recognition of any fixed demarcation lines between fields and disciplines. He was to be assisted by an editorial board of some thirteen members, most of whom

---

[4] *Political Studies*, Volume 1, Number 1, Editorial Introduction.

came to dominate the field in one way or another for a generation or so, to be succeeded by their protégés for a further generation. This is not said by way of criticism; after all the association in 1950 was only 130 strong, mostly drawn from a few centres. The development of 'redbricks', the expansion of the tertiary sector, and the increasing number of polytechnics offering courses in politics and cognate subjects multiplied the 'profession' and with it the membership of the PSA, but even now the numbers are not all that many. Indeed, the 'profession' does not coincide with the membership of the PSA: out of a possible United Kingdom total of 1182 (1991 Staff Directory, PSA) only 507[5] are members; happily non-members attend the conferences and workshops, thus, wider contact is not, for that reason, lost. There are no published statistics: however, gleaning the few niggardly crumbs of information the annual accounts can yield, total membership can hardly exceed 650 (which raises questions about the 1100 names on the reviewers' list).

We have had seven editors for *Political Studies*[6] : each is appointed on the basis of a submission, so to say, their 'mission' statement, setting out their hopes and aspirations. But if ever was the road to hell paved with good intentions, that litter must include most, if not all, the 'mission' statements of editors. One's hopes and desires for the content and the direction of a journal do not necessarily determine its final shape; in a seriously important sense, the final shape is a function of submissions for publication. Yet, if seen simply as an end-result, as outcome, even a cursory comparison of the few first issues with the latest volumes will reveal, apart from minor matters (for example, abstracts), three important differences: firstly, whereas both sets will show a cosmopolitan spread of subject matter, the first was exclusively by British academics, while the two most recent volumes include a high percentage of non-British contributors: in volumes 40 and 41 (10 issues) there are 54 British and 35 non-British contributors, and in 5 issues the balance is with the non-British group. Secondly, whereas in the early 1950 the external fixation was with France and continental matters (still?), in the 1990s this has become much enlarged and influenced by American 'Political Science'. These differences are, indeed, a summary indicator of the story of the post-war period.

The 'general' character of the journal has been preserved, but between 1989 and 1991 one issue per volume was devoted to a set theme. In 1992 the number of issues was increased to 5 per volume in order to accommodate a special issue. These contain commissioned papers discussed at private gatherings of the authors and invited guests, at meetings held in the rarefied atmosphere of Oxford. One assumes that these papers are not vetted by external referees. This is the third difference, indicating a clear departure from tradition.

---

[5] This tally is subject to correction as it excludes members under Articles 3 and 4. The tally of postal votes in 1993 Executive Election was 378. *PSA News*, Summer 1993, p.24.

[6] Editors of *Political Studies*: Wilfrid Harrison, volumes 1-10; Wilfrid Harrison and Peter Campbell, Volume 11; Peter Campbell, volumes 11-17; F.F.Ridley, volumes 18-23; L.J.Sharpe, volumes 24-29; Jack Lively, volumes 30-35; Jack Hayward, volumes 36 to 41, and currently Michael Moran, Volume 42 continuing.

Politics

By every account, Patrick Dunleavy was instrumental in the creation of *Politics*; he also served as its first general editor, and defined its original mission in terms of improving the flow of professional information in the form of short articles in any area of the discipline, offering a fast response to both empirical and theoretical developments, thus helping to replace lost channels of debate.[7] Moreover, in 'assessing' submissions, level of complexity or viewpoints expressed were to be disregarded, but the final decision was with the editorial board. Broadly, the objectives as defined remain in force.

Submissions are assessed ('normal reviewing procedures') in terms of academic importance and clarity of presentation. *Politics*, intended to bridge the breach between *Political Studies* and *PSA Newsletter*, was intended to afford an opportunity to the newly inducted to make a first attempt to publish, perhaps based on a recent thesis. There is now more (renewed?) emphasis on postgraduate contributions, as indicated by the new joint editors, but the tally has been in favour of the members of the professions, while the balance between the two elements has hardly changed.

The occasion of the recent change of editors[8] was seized as an opportunity for a re-launch. In the process Andrew Taylor raised a number of questions[9] and defined the challenge of the future, emphasising the need for 'developmental editing' in order to make the submission 'publishable'; to include surveys and debates, and generally to enhance its role. The proof, to coin a phrase, is in the print. However, while the preliminary indications are that the new joint editors have taken a sound 'steady as it goes' attitude, they, nevertheless, seek to enhance its profile through a 'post-graduate friendly' approach, and make *Politics* contribute to reflections on the discipline through a 'State of the Art' feature – bibliographical ('literature') guides to recent developments by specialists. More interesting, and potentially more valuable – depending on how it pans out – is a new 'Blind Alleys' feature, devoted to 'critiques' of contemporary political science. Anyhow, normal reviewing procedures apply, but, so it appears, the new editors, while retaining the final decision, will make use of the reviewers list for *Political Studies*.

Editors and 'Learned Journals'

'When editorial work is done properly, it leaves no sign that it has been done.' This truism is profound, yet utterly misleading: its profundity is simply obvious, but its implications are veiled and complex.

The available literature on the subject tends to concentrate upon journalism. However, despite obvious differences between journalism and learned

---

[7] Editorial, *Politics*, Volume 1, Number 1, back page.
[8] General Editors of *Politics*; Patrick Dunleavy, Volume 1; Joan Woodall, volumes 2-4; Ursula Vogel, volumes 5-6; Vicky Randall, volumes 7-10; Andrew Taylor, volumes 11-13; Gary Browning and Ben Rosamond, Volume 14 continuing.
[9] *PSA News*, Summer 1993, p.25.

journals, arguments about the one are, *mutatis mutandis*, applicable to the other.

The job of an editor is to assess and choose items to be published. Hodgson[10] offers a threefold category of editors: the 'writing editor' which he calls the scourge of the reporters. for he/she will interfere much; the 'production editor', usually promoted from the ranks, who is preoccupied with technicalities; and the 'political figure', often also a public personality, who will politicise everything, and is over-concerned with the image of the paper. Moreover, the activity of being a newspaper editor has to be contextualised within the world of news gathering and its dissemination. Indeed, there is the further constraint that newspapers must inform and entertain on a daily basis in a world of rapid succession of events, else they will not retain their readership, therefore 'their' share of the market, and, consequently, their revenue from advertising, without which their financial viability, and with it the independence of the paper, will be in jeopardy.[11]

A newspaper editor will apply criteria such as proximity of events, personal/personality factor, and special interest. There is also the question of competing interests and news items vying for prominence. Martin Walker[12] offers a fascinating glimpse into this side of the business in his compilation of the manner in which a number of prominent/leading newspapers reported the events culminating in a revolution. It underlines the extent to which the judgement of the different papers about the location of the events, their significance, and indeed the mix of items on the subject, differed between newspapers mostly on the basis of political considerations, ranging from their perception of 'national interest' and the political colour of the paper in the 'free world', to the requirements, indeed orders, of regimes elsewhere. There simply is no 'objectivity' in the final selection of items, as there is no unbiased account of a news item: editors bring to the job the full impact of their personality and temperament.

Now, learned journals are not in the business of entertaining their readers: we do not expect specialist crosswords, juicy gossip, or 'other' diversions; we are conditioned not to expect them, for a learned journal is a serious matter – although there is nothing to stop readers making their own entertainment on the margins of the pages! However, this is not all that may be understood by 'entertaining', for, in an important sense, by taking a less 'intense' view of what we do and what we are, we will not only better understand what we do, but also help remind ourselves that we are, after all, primarily concerned with 'talk about talk', although, in the nature of things, we are also intensely concerned with 'talk', perhaps even recognise that, lamentably, we have too much of the latter and not enough of the former. One would – with Feyerabend – wish to say that if we take our discipline and ourselves as practitioners too seriously, we are liable to lose

---

[10] F.W.Hodgson, *Modern Newspaper Practice*, second edition, Heinemann, Oxford, 1989, p.63.

[11] For a succinct history of the British press see Francis Williams, *Dangerous Estate: The Anatomy of Newspapers*, Longmans, Green & Co, 1957.

[12] Martin Walker, *Powers of the Press: The World's Great Newspapers*, Quartlet Books, London, 1982, chapter 14: 'Each Newspaper's coverage of Iran from 1971 to the fall of the Shah'.

sight of some mundane but all too important facts, such as our place in the universe, the meaning of our worth as human beings, and the finite, indeed all too obvious, limits of our abilities to shape the world and our universe of discourse. Equally, when we deal with 'momentous' contingent or philosophical issues, and passionately debate the right and the wrong of each point, we are talking about precious and unique, simply irreplaceable, moments in human life, and are not engaged in some 'modern' version of disputes about how many angels can be found on the tip of a needle, nor are we able to change the world to suit as we go. Evidently, this function of 'reducing ourselves to size' does not appear to be part of the expected role of a learned journal, and, therefore, has no place in the reckoning when our editors choose. Of course, they are concerned to ensure that the articles are readable, which is not the same as 'publishable', although, without putting too fine a point on it, one is not sure that they always succeed to achieve either objective!

Learned journals are not conveyors of news, but they are in the business of informing their learned readership about the discipline, subject, field – whatever euphemism may currently be in vogue. Evidently, indeed crucially, it is here that our editors come into their own. To be sure, an editor must choose, and the more equal considerations may be: the frequency of publication; the size of each issue; costs of production; the balance between articles, debates, reviews and book notes, each of which perform a different function. These are important determining factors, and we must not remove them from the ambit of our consideration. Furthermore, editors are faced with these problems in and for each and every issue. To repeat, we are apt not to see the work of an editor when his/her work is done properly; and when we open the pages of an issue, we see, but hardly perceive, a job well done. We are equally apt to forget that this job was done as an additional chore by the editor and his/her team; among other sacrifices, their weekends, free evenings, and, inevitably, a number of family rows are invested in each issue. All this is true, and the ultimate reward of recognition from colleagues does not even begin to balance the scales. We remain indebted.

Yet, this is where the simple description of the role of the editor is also utterly misleading. For when we successfully describe all that they must do, we fail to describe the 'reality', that is to say the essential meaning, of what they have done. The contingent reality of the work of an editor is merely the surface signs of a whole array of other 'occurrences' which can have no contingency as their visible mark.

Political Studies, as the organ, that is, tool, of an educational charity is, by definition, committed to the purpose of 'advancement of knowledge', for the Association is legally required to pursue 'advancement' of education in all its activities. There are two, though related, aspects to the legal meaning. While the law of trusts goes back a long way, and the notion of 'charitable' finds its origins in the preamble to the *Poor Law Act, 1601*, the 'modern' understanding, and indeed the change of emphasis from 'learning'[13] to 'ed-

---

[13] 'For the benefit, advancement and propagation of education and learning ...', Whicker v. Hume [1858], 7 H.L.C. 124.

ucation' was, in effect definitively, stated by Lord MacNaghten.[14] This situation has not changed, while a number of subsequent cases have clarified its meaning. In a celebrated case, Vaisey J affirmed that education can include 'not only teaching, but also the promotion or encouragement of those arts and graces of life which are, perhaps, the finest and best part of human character'.[15]

It is clear that by advancement is meant the *spread* of education, widely construed, in the sense of making 'it' available to more people. This advancement is, so to say, horizontal in its effect. And it is precisely this that defines its second aspect, namely that it can only be for public benefit, else it can not be a charity.[16]

Wilfrid Harrison thought the journal ought to contain contributions which will be of 'first importance to all who are concerned ... with contemporary developments in the study of politics' which contributions are judged on their 'qualities of precision and criticism'.[17] Years later, reflecting upon his editorship he revealed two interesting points. Firstly, that in 1953 he had the task of editing a new journal without any clear paradigms to enable the necessary selections to be made. Consequently, he considered it prudent to keep 'as many doors as possible open'. But, more than that, he felt that even in 1975 he could not detect any paradigms for the discipline.[18] We have, thus, a situation in which 'advancement of knowledge' is the avowed objective, while there are no clear signs as to what this 'knowledge' is, nor, for that matter, how it may be advanced. Yet, Harrison pursued this goal of nonhorizontal advancement with no evident difficulty, and, as he pointed out, since there was no shortage of material, selection 'became possible'.

To be sure, Wilfrid Harrison was mindful of his position, and took care to 'understand' what he was doing: the editor of a learned journal is responsible (what a much abused word!) for the development of the subject, but this was conditioned by his responsibility to authors, readers and the publishers. Clearly the 'development of the subject' is of primary importance, and indeed Harrison went on to say that, in discharging this aspect of the demands of the job (just to avoid saying responsibility!), one had to be guided by one's own conception of what that development would involve, and pay heed to the views of other 'qualified' people.[19] Indeed he agonised over this: an 'organ' must be representative (another much abused word), avoid being eccentric, respond to developments elsewhere, and be mindful of the requirements of the subject, the readers and the authors. These contradictory demands create tension, and it is up to the editor to resolve it. Harrison deals with this rather enigmatically:

---

[14] He enumerated four types; relief of poverty etc, advancement of education, advancement of religion, and others. Commissioners for Special Purposes of Income Tax v. Pemsel, [1891] A.C. 531, and 583.

[15] D.G. Cracknell, *Law Relating to Charities*, 2nd edition, Oyez Longman, 1883, p.9.

[16] See L.A.Sheridan & G.W.Keeton, *The Modern Law of Charities*, 3rd edition, University College of Cardiff Press, 1983, chapter 4; and D.G. Cracknell, *Law Relating to Charities*, Chapter 1. A school for prostitutes or pickpockets, or a library devoted to pornography have been ruled out! See Cracknell, *Ibid*, p.8.

[17] *Political Studies*, Volume 1, Number 1, pp.3 and 5.

[18] *Political Studies*, Volume 23, Number 2, p.186.

[19] *Political Studies*, Volume 23, Number 2, p.189.

> '... the editor is likely to conceive that he has a special obli-
> gation towards the members of his association as contributors,
> although it could scarcely be expected that he should regard
> himself as no more than their agent, obliged to ensure publica-
> tion for whatever they wanted to have published.'[20]

What is important in this formulation is precisely that which Harrison only
hints at. Jack Hayward formulated this notion in his usually modest way
when he said that each editor leaves an '... indistinct imprint upon what is
published'[21] and went on to declare his policy to be one of opening up of
the agenda, more foreign members and contributors, but without foregoing
the requirement of 'quality' in the articles. On 'listening to other qualified' people, L.J.Sharpe, in his inaugural editorial, commented that while
secrecy enables, perhaps encourages, unnecessary comment and indulgence,
nevertheless such comments are useful in all cases (that is, papers accepted
or rejected), articles are improved, and, amazingly, that the assessors also
learn in the process![22]

Our problem is yet not solved: true that the three former editors here
quoted have all been concerned with how it is that they do that part of the
their job which leaves only an indistinct mark, yet what they have said does
not amount to an account that remains unproblematic, for it still leaves the
question unanswered: what is *it* that they do, in terms of which concept(s)
can we understand such actions, and what are the implications of it for all
concerned?

Clearly, the views quoted above all have the imprint of editorial paternalism, even though their authors may not feel that this is what they do,
nor harbour any desire to act in this manner. In a sense, the editor of a
learned journal cannot but act paternalistically, it is part of the territory;
yet, this is precisely what has to be examined.

The notion of 'advancement' has, since Bacon, dominated the history of
science. It is an epistemological notion, which, despite all else, is incapable
of being presented as an eternal truth, except as an assumption. As such
it has a whole baggage of ideas that, increasingly, we find more difficult
to accept. Is theoretical simplicity or complexity a mark of advance? Is
'explaining' 'more' a mark of advance? Without prolonging an unnecessary,
if not irrelevant, argument, the notion of advance as a move in the right
direction is fatuous except when we know the destination, in which case,
one would have thought, we are already there! On the other hand, if we
do not know where we are going, then we have already arrived! The logical
impossibility of the notion of advance renders it meaningless, except in
relativistic terms, in which case an advance is no longer a move towards an
end, but a hop from one idea to another, each hop being validated in its
own terms.

Our evident difficulty would be less of a problem were we in a position
to give a coherent meaning to 'learned'. Again, we feel the heavy hand of

---

[20] *Political Studies*, Volume 23, Number 2, p.192. Ghost of 'Guardianship' stalk these
words!

[21] *Political Studies*, Volume 36, Number 1, editorial note.

[22] sl Political Studies, Volume 25, Number 1, pp.1-2.

the dead upon the meaning of this notion: historically this was of course a description intended to mean 'versed in the law', which sense itself derived from the idea of profound knowledge gained by study. Surely, this is clear enough; what then is the problem? Well, none other than the fact that it is simply a tautology: we have given content to the meaning of 'learned' by the meaning of 'knowledge', but the content of 'knowledge' remains a problem, while the two terms are intrinsically related. We must ask: what is 'knowledge' *in the study of politics*? Do we have an unproblematic body of knowledge which is imparted to the novice, as is done, for instance, in medicine, engineering, or, indeed, the law? Do our novices, when they have 'learned' that body of knowledge and have become conversant with it up to an *objectively* required level, also become learned? Do we have an *episteme* capable of generating *techne*? Wilfrid Harrison thought we did not have such paradigms in 1953, nor in 1975; we still do not. This might appear less than generous as well as controversial. Certainly we are constrained by 'human' history and 'human' ideas, knowing about which is the initial starting point of any approach to the study of politics. But, so it seems, this is all that we have, and from that point on we tend to differ even on the meaning of our historical categories, the use we might make of them, indeed even *how* to understand them. That which unites the study of politics is not politics, classics of political thought, history, nor, for that matter, empirical analysis of the currently contested issues, but a timeless dialogue in time about how it is that we arrive at any understanding of 'human' action and society. Indeed, should we become 'learned' in this, we shall know it by the selfconsciousness of our *doubts* about what we say, and not by the certainty of what we know.

Moreover, there is an inevitably incestuous relationship between 'learned' journal/society, 'development of education/knowledge', and the policing of its progress; in effect the real role of the editors of learned journals is no more than that of 'gate-keeper': they perform one function, and one function only, to determine whether to 'keep in' or 'keep out'. Now, in each individual case the determination has a total effect, and the multiplicity of these effects over the years has a definite impact upon the shape and the contents, indeed the overall colour of the discipline. As much as one hates to disagree with Jack Hayward, but, alas, he is wrong when he says the effect is 'indistinct': it may appear to be so, but only because the gate-keeping function is itself constitutive of, and a determining force in 'creating' the present. And because there is no reality that is truly an alternative to this 'present', it is not possible, except in the form of an irrelevant 'might have been', to argue about where the discipline would be today had a different course of action been taken. So far as the public face of the discipline is concerned, editors of learned journals make 'our' history but not in conditions of our own choosing. But this argument is not intended to become a fanciful dream about alternative realities; rather the question must be: How do we understand the impact that inevitably editors have? To achieve that we must examine the situation theoretically – it would, surely, be too pompous to say philosophically.

Now, our learned journals present a *vision* of the discipline. Since there are always more submissions than any one issue can contain, editors are in the happy position of being able to choose. It is through this function that an editor creates an issue containing articles which have passed the 'unofficial sensors', and therefore are, to that measure, 'approved'. Admittedly, except for commissioned papers, this act of creation is conditioned by constraints already mentioned, including the fact that he/she can only choose from what has been submitted

But the 'gate' at which our editor performs his/her gate-keeping does not exist, not even as a metaphor, except as a point of entry into the 'unofficially' sanctioned world of the discipline. This raises some difficult questions – happily not ontological questions, for truly our editors and 'sensors' exist. Now, accepting that the activity of being an editor requires the regular performance of apparently non-controversial functions, how are we to understand their gate-keeping function?

The obvious starting point is to say that an editor is, as Harrison emphasised, also a practitioner, and has his own judgement about the discipline. He/she is there because he/she was selected and appointed, which, in terms of the hugely problematical theory of the Mandate, means his/her 'mission' is accepted: *hic Rhodus, hic salta*! But Harrison was also keen to say that he would not act alone, and that the judgement of other *qualified* people would matter. Qualified? Of course; but only to the extent that the editor is so qualified, and not necessarily any more so than most other members of the profession. In other words, while it is certainly possible to distinguish between the novice and the experienced, one must, rather in line with J.S.Mill[23] also imagine and adhere to it as a point of cessation of that demarcation, that is to say a point beyond which 'society' ought not to claim tutelage over the individual. Moreover, to claim that the necessary hierarchy of the 'learned/novice' (the red-letter L-Driver) in fact extends into that of 'more learned/not novice' (the green-letter L-Driver) is no longer to adumbrate a theory of induction into a body of knowledge about the study of politics, but to offer a highly conservative view of the structure of the discipline. Such a view is, however, simply belied by the rather obvious fact that (repetitive) experience is not a necessary requirement for having good ideas. Indeed, although he does not have a good press, one must again think of Feyerabend. If that is too painful, then think of the recent example of some sixth form pupils being given a chance to conduct experiments in chemistry; their evident lack of 'knowledge' is their greatest intellectual asset, for they dare and do, and obtain results which established theory, propounded by established academics, is seemingly incapable of locating.[24]

The picture is further complicated by the fact that there are, so to say, many rooms in this mansion, and that we – our editors included – are in one way or another 'specialists' in the dimensions of one, at most a few, rooms, and know only the broad contours of the rest, if at all. If this was not bad enough, *how* we know the dimensions of a room determines how

[23] ,J.S.Mill, *On Liberty*, in *Utilitarianism, Liberty and Representative Government*, pp.138-140, Everyman edition, London 1971.

[24] 'School for budding scientists', in *The Times Higher Educational Supplement*, 12 November, 1993, p.7.

we perceive changes to it: new ideas, especially when they are not our own, are unlikely to hit us except as challenges to established ideas. Usually, of course, difficulties such an account may create are lost in the fog of obfuscation rising from allegorical notions such as that of the liberal open-market view of the world of scientific thought, or the unstated implications of the idea of the 'global village of learning', where each 'scientific community' decides the canons of its own discipline. Such a view is often supplemented – in line with the historical notion of 'advancement of knowledge' – by the claim that growth in science is incremental, and that innovations only add a little to an existing literature. This is the language of the conservative, and it is the language of 'authority' – which is now recognised for what it has always been, a defunct notion in the history of science. Yet the 'theory' of incremental advance is suspended, but always retrospectively, when the innovator happens to be an Einstein, a Galilei, a Newton, defended and then succeeded by a new priesthood who, enthused by the superpatriotism of the convert, proceed to police the boundaries of the new orthodoxy. Importantly, though, this kind of belated revolutionary change is a feature of 'sciences' in which some concrete demonstration is possible; for us the whole enterprise is about the morality of human action, propounded in attempts to convince others of the force of our arguments.

Sitting in a room – to go on with the simile for a little longer our editor must also act in respect of other rooms, so he/she enlists the help of a multiplicity of a 'qualified another'; but whereas we know the identity of the editor, normally, that of the 'qualified another' remains a mystery. Within an intellectual fraternity, this is an obnoxious exercise, and one hopes that it will cease; private judgement in a specific public space is an oddity the meaning of which defies sensible explanation. That said, however, we are still in some difficulty, for the actions of one, or a secret select, does not, as such, surmount the problem of the fact that they are not the guardians of an unproblematic orthodoxy, but that they are part of a tradition of thought which they cannot but defend. They are, whether they know it or not, secret judges who also have a stake in the judgement. Again, it must be said, we have no parameters on how an alternative system might work, for we have denied ourselves the experience of open assessment of contributions to the field.

What this amounts to is that the gate-keeping function, as assisted, works, but in a paternalistic sense. Now, *paternalism*[25] is fairly simple, and its only meaningful application is to a 'natural' relationship in which a number of conditions obtain: a definite need for protection of the child; the child is, by definition, incapable of independent action; the parent, through the bond of paternal/maternal love has the best interest of the child at heart; and, crucially, has the knowledge of what to do, and when to do it. And, importantly, when parents teach their children, they are concerned with education (strictly horizontal), not its (non-horizontal) advancement. Moreover, there is also a natural limit to this relationship: at some age the child will no longer be a child, and the parent can no longer exercise any

---

[25] See F.Nash, *Meta-Imperialism: A Study in Political Science*, Avebury Series in Philosophy, April 1994, Chapter 8, 'Power and Morality: Paternalism'.

kind of paternalistic authority. Now, truly, inducting the novice (creating the next generation of practitioners) is also education, and this part of the activity is hardly relevant to the idea of its advancement. On the other hand, research work, the very essence of learned articles, is the vehicle of advancement. Of course our editors, as assisted, are inevitably involved in horizontal 'advancement' as they prepare another issue for publication. But the choice they make is not simple. And whatever may be 'selected' as the parameters for the choosing, in applying them they act paternalistically. But, so the argument runs, to do so, it is necessary to have a *given* body of knowledge, one that is shared by its scientific community (and is not contested), which they must apply ... But at this point it becomes apparent that social paternalism is not on a par with *paternalism*, and teaching what we know is not the same as directing how that 'knowledge' is to be constructed and changed, nor determining which ideas are presented as the fruits of successful research.

Oh, Dear, ... we are back at the problem of knowledge with all its uncertainties in respect of the study of politics. Editorial gate-keeping cannot be defended as the innocent application of the rules of some universally held body of ideas. The gate-keeping function thus performed is, therefore, far more esoteric than one might have hoped, while the decision as to *what* to keep in or out has far-reaching implications the consequences of which cannot, in the nature of things, be isolated and examined. Yet, importantly, as *organs* of our association, our learned journals are the public face of our profession; they collectively present (thereby further the cause of horizontal advancement) 'accepted' fruits of our learned research (reports of non-horizontal advancement), and because they include only 'vetted' articles, they present the authors with valuable (though authoritarian, indeed conservative) kudos. The implications of this too are incapable of simple isolation and examination.

The 'Blind Alleys' feature of *Politics* will perhaps provide a greatly needed new venue, though much will depend on the rigour of its 'vetting' procedures. More importantly, though, the decision to publish PSA Annual Conference papers stands out as one significant move in remedying this state of affairs; this little competition will, dare one hope, go a long way.

The Core Executive
Analytic Approaches to Developments under Major

Oliver James
University of Warwick

'Explaining the Next Steps Reorganisation
In the Department of Social Security:
An Application of the Bureau-Shaping Model'

Acknowledgements

*I would like to thank Patrick Dunleavy and Peter Law for their
helpful comments on sections of earlier versions of this paper.*

Introduction

This paper develops the bureau-shaping model which explains the reorganisation of bureaux as the result of the behaviour of rational bureaucrats. Reorganisations are explained as bureau-shaping strategies by bureaucrats who seek to alter their bureaux to suit their self-interests (Dunleavy 1991: 200-09). The model is applied to the Next Steps reform in the Department of Social Security (DSS) and explains why the change took the form of establishing separate executive agencies, some of which are now candidates for privatisation, rather than management reform within an integrated department.

The bureau-shaping model is part of a wider research project evaluating theoretical approaches to explaining change in the organisation of the British central state. Theoretical approaches are required to advance our understanding of change beyond the existing unsystematic official explanations and descriptive pluralist accounts of reform. The official explanation of Next Steps by the civil service portrays the reorganisation as part of a coherent reform strategy which includes the Financial Management Initiative and the Citizens' Charter and is intended to improve the efficiency and quality of public services (OPSS 1993: 7-8). In practice these reforms have at times conflicted with each other, indicating that official explanations are unsatisfactory. Alternative descriptive pluralist explanations tend to contain weak, informal theorising which stresses the political environment in which the Conservative Government, strengthened by a long continuous period in office, was able to impose private sector business methods on the civil service; for examples see Chapman (1991: 1) and Metcalfe (1993: 352).

In contrast the bureau-shaping model is an attempt to explain the Next Steps reorganisation in the DSS using an explicit theoretical approach. The first section of this paper develops the bureau-shaping model. The second section places the DSS reform in the context of the wider Next Steps reform in the British central state and uses an analytical typology to represent the reorganisation of the DSS. In the third section the bureau-shaping model is applied and evaluated as an explanation of the change in the DSS.

The Bureau-Shaping Model

The model seeks to explain the size of a public bureau's executive activity and policy work responsibility and to explain why these may be changed by a reorganisation such as Next Steps. Executive activity involves the implementation of public policy through administrative structures and procedures. This activity can be distinguished from policy work which entails setting the aims of executive activity, evaluating implementation structures and proposing new structures.

Public sector bureaux are defined as organisations whose resources are owned publicly (Lane 1993: 15) and which are under the stewardship of elected politicians. The organisation of a bureau is determined by the interaction of politicians and senior bureaucrats who pursue careers organising and running bureaux on politicians' behalf. Senior bureaucrats are assumed to be the most significant bureaucrat actors in a reorganisation. They use bureau-shaping strategies to change the level of executive activity and policy work in an attempt to maximise their personal career related utilities. The use of individual actors who behave as if they maximise their own interests gives the model the characteristics of the rational choice or public choice approach to political science (Lane 1993: 155). However the bureau-shaping model contrasts with traditional rational choice models, such as Niskanen's model (1971), which concentrate on static bureaux rather than reorganisation and explain the size of a bureau's output without distinguishing between policy work and executive activity which constitute different types of output.

The potential of bureau-shaping strategies as an explanation of reorganisation has been noted by Dunleavy (1985: 320-24; 1991: 225-27). However Dunleavy's explanation is incomplete because he does not model individual bureaucrats' decision to contribute to bureau-shaping strategies. The bureau-shaping model developed here constructs a model of individual bureaucrats' motives in contributing to bureau-shaping strategies and identifies factors which trigger bureau-shaping behaviour and cause reorganisations to occur. The bureau-shaping model is developed by discussing firstly senior bureaucrats' preferences for the organisation of bureaux, secondly the constraint on bureaucrats imposed by politicians and thirdly bureau-shaping strategies pursued by bureaucrats.

senior bureaucrats' preferences for the organisation of bureaux

Senior officials have preferences about alternative forms of organisation of their bureaux because different forms affect the level of their career-related utility. The bureau-shaping model assumes that the level of a bureau's executive activity is positively related to the level of the bureau's core budget and that policy work is positively related to the proportion of policy work time in the total work time of officials in the bureau. Bureaucrats derive utility from several sources which are grouped into utility derived from the core budget and utility derived from the proportion of policy work time.

utility derived from the core budget

The core budget is the part of a bureau's budget which is spent on the running costs of the bureau, which includes the cost of administrative structures such as offices, machinery and staff costs (Dunleavy 1989a: 253). The core budget gives bureaucrats utility through both pecuniary and non-pecuniary job benefits. Direct pecuniary benefits accrue because core budget includes bureaucrats' pay. Restrictions on officials' ability to set their own pay levels often reduces the importance of this benefit. However the size of core budget may be one of the factors used to assess the pay level of senior bureaucrats and officials supervising larger core budgets are likely to be rewarded with higher pay. Non-pecuniary benefits from the core budget come from expenditure on pleasant offices and other perks which yield utility for officials.

A bureau's core budget *per* senior bureaucrat indicates the utility received by an individual senior official. The adjusted level of core budget gives a better indication of benefits which go to the individual than the total core budget because the number of senior officials determines the size of the section of core budget which individual officials manage and consequently influences the benefits they receive. Small core budgets *per* senior bureaucrat may result in lower pay for officials than large core budgets and are more likely to make a perk of a given value stand out as an unreasonable extravagance, making perks more difficult to obtain.

The core budget is more strongly associated with bureaucrats' utility than alternative definitions of the budget, such as that used by Niskanen's model (1971). The Niskanen model does not distinguish between different components of a bureau's budget, the budget includes both core budget and money which is passed on by the bureau to be spent by other bodies, which is less likely to benefit officials in the first bureau because they cannot use it to obtain perks for themselves.

utility derived from proportion of policy work time

The model assumes that bureaucrats gain utility from undertaking favourably valued work tasks as well as from core budget. The significance of utility derived from work tasks has been noted by Dunleavy (1985: 320-22; 1991: 200-02). In the model officials' total work time is assumed to be fixed and composed only of policy work time and management work time. Bureaucrats value policy work time favourably and desire the highest possible proportion of policy work time in total work time and by implication the lowest possible proportion of management work time.

Policy work is liked because it involves innovation, often entails working in small staff units and requires officials to have a close proximity to political power sources such as ministers. In contrast management work, involving the routine implementation of procedures and the monitoring and direction of junior staff, is disliked. Management work often involves working in a large extended hierarchy rather than small staff units and tends to consist of work at the point of delivery, remote from political power sources.

The preferences of a senior bureaucrat for possible combinations of pro-

portion of policy work time and levels of core budget *per* senior bureaucrat
are shown on the indifference curve map in Figure 1. The model does not
assume that bureaucrats are identical, which would not adequately reflect
the diversity of bureaucrat actors. The model only requires that bureaucrats
have similar preferences concerning the core budget *per* senior bureaucrat
and proportion of policy work time relating to their bureau. Avoiding this
assumption by modelling individual bureaucrats with heterogeneous preferences is problematic because there are difficulties in deriving aggregate
preferences of bureaucrats from individual preferences. The more complex
alternative approach is in any case unnecessary if simple models can be
shown to adequately explain bureaucrats' behaviour.

Figure 1
Individual Bureaucrat's Preferences

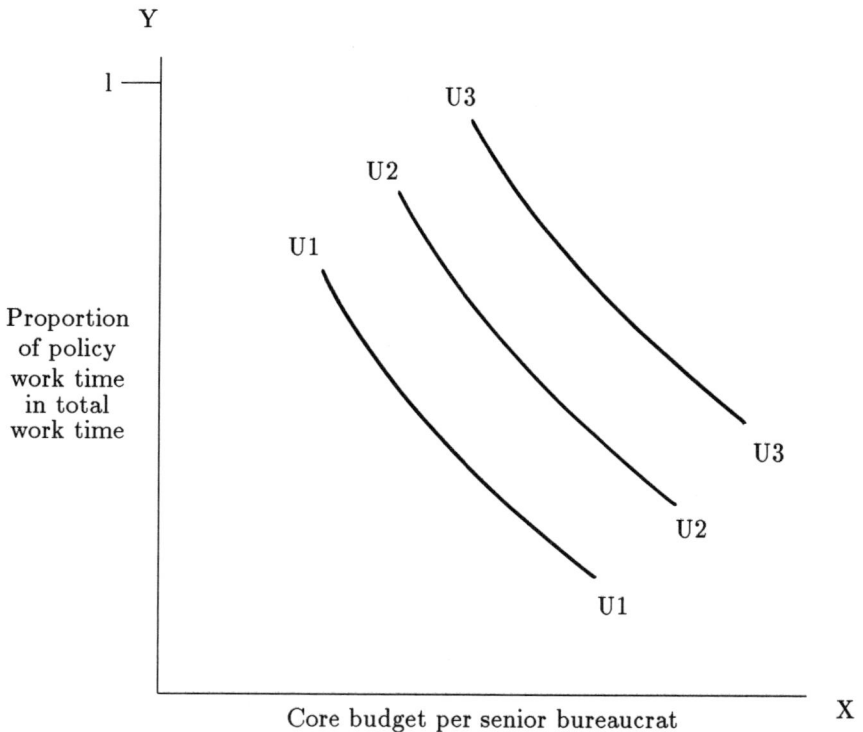

Each indifference curve in Figure 1 links points of equal total utility, the
slope of each curve representing the rate of substitution required between
levels of core budget *per* senior bureaucrat (X) and proportion of policy
work time in total work time (Y) to maintain a particular level of total
utility (U). The curves are ranked ordinally with curves furthest from the
origin representing higher levels of total utility (U3 > U2 > U1 in Figure
1). The curves are convex to the origin because a diminishing marginal rate

of substitution between X and Y is assumed, implying that to maintain a constant level of total utility at high levels of core budget bureaucrats require more additional core budget to compensate for the loss of a unit of policy work time than at low levels of core budget. The shape of the curves also reflects the assumption that the contributions of core budget *per* senior bureaucrat and proportion of policy work time to total utility are independent of each other. Independence implies that policy work time and core budget levels affect utility only by the sum of their separate contributions and not by forming particularly desirable or undesirable combinations.

the constraint on bureaucrats imposed by politicians

Because bureaucrats attempt to maximise their total career related utilities they prefer to have the utility level represented by the highest possible indifference curve. However bureaucrats are not free to choose any combination of proportion of policy work time and level of core budget *per* senior bureaucrat because they are constrained by the actions of politicians.

Figure 2
Equilibrium of a Constrained
Utility Maximising Bureaucrat

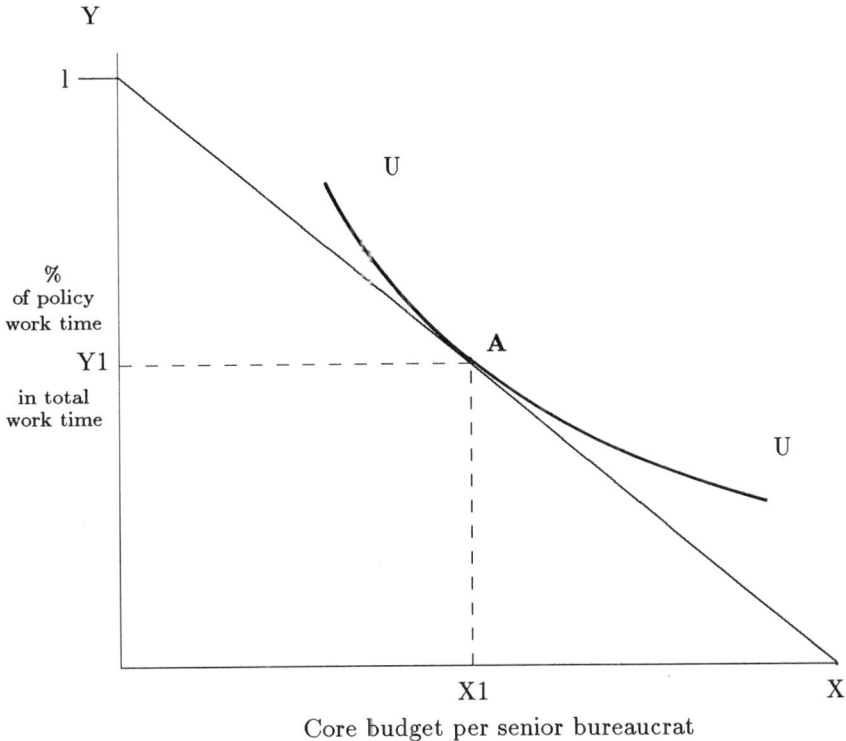

In the model politicians are viewed as principals who employ bureaucrats as their agents to organise and run public services on their behalf. Politi-

cians are assumed to have the goal of achieving the highest possible level
of public services within the limited resources at their disposal in order to
maximise their political support among the consumers of services. Consequently politicians value efficiency in the production of public services,
that is, that desired outcomes are produced using the least possible level of
input.

The politicians' interest in efficiency conflicts with the self-interest of bureaucrats who desire higher proportions of policy work time and larger core
budgets regardless of the effect on efficiency. It is difficult for politicians to
directly observe the level of efficiency which results from a bureau's organisation. However politicians can observe the mix of policy work time and
management work time in a bureaucrat's total work time. Politicians are
assumed to have the reasonable belief that to avoid detrimental effects on
efficiency bureaucrats must spend higher proportions of management work
time in total work time to manage larger core budgets *per* senior bureaucrat.
Consequently politicians attempt to protect their interests by setting and
enforcing a certain proportion of management work time which bureaucrats
must spend supervising each unit of core budget *per* senior bureaucrat.

Politicians can ensure that bureaucrats comply with their instructions
because their position as principal enables them to remove bureaucratic
agents for non-compliance. The threat of removal is credible to bureaucrats
because the model does not assume that bureaucrats have an informational
advantage over politicians which might prevent politicians from detecting
undesirable behaviour. Because the model has a conflict of interest between
principal and agent but the agent does not have an informational advantage
the model does not use the full principal/agent framework (Moe 1984: 756-
57).

The politicians' insistence that bureaucrats spend a proportion of work
time on management which is positively related to the size of the core budget
constrains bureaucrats' ability to maximise their utilities. In Figure 2 the
individual bureaucrat maximises utility subject to the constraint at the
optimum point A. The maximisation problem is analogous to the simple
economic model of a consumer seeking to maximise utility subject to a
budget constraint.[1]

---

[1] The model of the constrained utility maximising bureaucrat can be expressed formally:

The bureaucrat's utility function is:

$$U = X^{1/2} + Y^{1/2}.$$

Where U is total utility, X is core budget *per* senior bureaucrat and Y is proportion of
policy work time in total work time.

The bureaucrat's constraint imposed by politicians is:

$$Y = 1 - aX.$$

Where 1 is the limited work time available to the bureaucrat, (a) is the proportion of
management time in total work time which politicians insist a bureaucrat must spend
supervising each unit of core budget *per* senior bureaucrat and $0 < a < 1$.

The slope of each indifference curve is given by the marginal utility of Y divided by X:

$$dY/dX = -(1/2X^{-1/2})/(1/2Y^{-1/2}) = -Y^{1/2}/X^{1/2}.$$

The slope of the constraint is given by:

The intuition behind the result is that at point A in Figure 2 the constraint is tangential to the indifference curve, indicating that the bureaucrat is on the highest indifference curve possible within the constraint; total utility cannot be increased by substituting units of X for units of Y or *vice versa*.

Bureau-Shaping Strategies

Senior officials act together to pursue bureau-shaping strategies in a reorganisation to achieve their ideal levels of core budget and proportion of policy work time corresponding to point A in Figure 2. Bureaucrats shape their bureau by adding or shedding executive activity to alter core budget *per* senior bureaucrat and by adding or shedding policy work to alter the proportion of policy work time.[2] The level of policy work is largely independent of the level of core budget *per* senior bureaucrat. A negligible level of core budget *per* senior bureaucrat is required to undertake policy work compared to that involved in executive activity because policy work is labour intensive in terms of senior officials and tends to be less resource intensive than executive activity.

Executive activity can be shed from a bureau in several ways. Shedding can involve termination of the activity, privatisation to a privately owned firm in a free market or privatisation to a privately owned firm in a regulated market. Alternatively shedding can occur by contracting out provision of an activity to a private firm or by passing on the responsibility for management to a lower tier of government such as local authorities or to the same tier in the form of a semi-autonomous executive agency.

Senior bureaucrats will prefer forms of shedding executive activity which do not threaten the survival of their bureau or the position of individual officials in the bureau, which threaten bureaucrats' continued consumption of career related utility. Shedding by terminating the executive activity or by privatisation to free market provision involve a drastic reduction of policy work; there is less need for public policy concerning an activity provided in an unregulated market than one provided by a publicly owned bureau.

$$dY/dX = -(1/2X^{-1/2})/(1/2Y^{-1/2}) = -Y^{1/2}/X^{1/2}.$$

The slope of the constraint is given by:

$$dY/dX = -a.$$

At the interior optimum, the slopes of the constraint and indifference curve are equal:

$$Y^{1/2}/X^{1/2} = a.$$

The equations for the optimum values of X and Y are:

$$Y^* = 1/1 + (1/a)$$
$$X^* = 1/a(1+a)$$

[2] The bureau shaping model assumes a stable relationship between changes in executive activity and core budget *per* senior bureaucrat and between changes in the level of policy work and proportion of policy work time. Stability requires that the number of senior officials is constant and that efficiency in the use of core budgets and policy work time is constant. Without these assumptions core budget, for example, could be reduced by increased efficiency leaving the level of executive activity unchanged.

The reduction in policy work may threaten the survival of the bureau; these forms of shedding are likely to be viewed unfavourably. However contracting out, privatisation to regulated market provision or passing on the activity to an executive agency with arms length policy control or to a subordinate tier of government are tolerated. These forms of shedding allow the bureau to maintain or increase policy work related to the executive activity.

The organisation of executive activity which has been shed is of little direct concern to senior officials beyond their interest in the different types of shedding. Because senior officials are uninterested, it is likely that the organisation of executive activity will be partly determined by the preferences of officials working in the activity. For example, the number of separate units formed by shedding executive activity may be determined by the number of different groups of officials with common interests in forming separate units, such as the existence of groups of officials who are specialists involved in a particular part of a shed executive activity.

Bureau-shaping strategies for altering the levels of executive activity and policy work require individual senior bureaucrats to act together to bring about the necessary alterations. The bureau-shaping strategies discussed by Dunleavy imply that individual bureaucrats incur costs and benefits from pursuing strategies (Dunleavy 1991: 205). The model developed here assumes that strategies are near costless for senior officials to pursue. This assumption is reasonable because politicians set the range of possible combinations of core budget *per* senior bureaucrat and proportion of policy work time and are indifferent between these points. Consequently bureaucrats do not incur the costs of persuading politicians to sanction a change involving a move between these combinations.

The lack of costs incurred in bureau-shaping strategies avoids potential collective action problems for bureaucrats. The strategies are pure public good for bureaucrats because they involve jointness of supply, several bureaucrats must participate, and it is difficult to exclude those who do not contribute from consuming the benefits (Mueller 1989: 11-12). Public goods tend to lead to free riders who seek to benefit without contributing to costs, which may result in the good not being provided at all. However because shaping strategies are near costless to bureaucrats it is only necessary that bureaucrats perceive their common interest in order for them to occur. Because bureaucrats are normally in close communication with each other they are likely to satisfy this criterion.

The Next Steps reorganisation and the Department of Social Security

The Next Steps reorganisation gained its name from the report to the Prime Minister by the Efficiency Unit, *Improving Management in Government: The Next Steps*, which was published in 1988 (Efficiency Unit 1988). The report's main recommendation was that agencies should be established to carry out the executive activities of government within a policy and resources framework set by departments (Efficiency Unit 1988: 9). The creation of agencies as part of Next Steps has occurred quickly. At the end of 1993 there were 92 agencies which together with units in HM Customs and Excise and the Inland Revenue operating on agency lines employed 60% of the civil service; around 20 per cent more staff worked in agency candidates (OPSS 1993).

The Next Steps reform is now moving into a new phase of privatisation of agencies. Although candidates for agency status have been examined for possible privatisation since the start of the reform the case for privatisation is now being pursued more strongly. The 1993 Government Review of agencies proposed that the status of existing agencies as part of the public sector should be kept under periodic review and that privatisation should be an option considered (Willman 1993).

Despite the common theme of the creation of agencies the Next Steps reform is not a uniform change. As Hogwood (1993) points out there is considerable variety in the origin of the activities which now form agencies. Some agencies were separate non-ministerial departments, for example the Intervention Board, or were non-departmental bodies such as the Training and Employment Agency (Northern Ireland) (Hogwood 1993: 6-7). In some cases the agency status which Next Steps brought was not a very significant change. The Queen Elizabeth II Conference Centre Agency, supervised by the Department of Environment, is an extreme example of this type. Although the centre was established as an executive agency in July 1989 it had been run at a distance from the Department since its opening in 1986.

Many agencies did, however, come from previously integrated departments. It was in these cases where the reform has created agencies handling executive activity separate from core departments involved in policy work, that Next Steps has brought about the most dramatic changes. The changes in the Department of Social Security are an example of the Next Steps reform in an integrated department.

the Department of Social Security (DSS) in 1989 and 1993

The Next Steps reform in the Department is represented using Dunleavy's typology of bureaux (Dunleavy 1989a: 253). The typology represents the change in terms of the effect on the number of bureaux, the composition of bureaux' budgets and the types of bureaux. The analytical approach to representing the reform is preferable to using the official description of the changes which does not distinguish between nominal changes and reforms of real significance.

According to the typology a bureau can be classified according to the relative sizes of the components of its program budget (Dunleavy 1989a: 253; 1989b: 391-402). The components are the core budget, bureau element, program element and portfolio element which when combined form the program budget. The core budget is the budget spent directly on the bureau's running costs and the bureau element contains money paid out to the private sector in the form of grants, contracts with private firms and transfer payments. The program element contains money supervised by the bureau but passed on to sub-central government bodies for use in implementation and the portfolio element consists of money supervised by the bureau but passed on to other bodies in central government for use in implementation (Dunleavy et al 1994: Chapter 3).

Delivery, regulatory, taxing, trading and servicing types of bureau have core budgets which form a large part of program budget because they spend most of their budgets on running costs. Delivery bureaux directly produce goods or services, regulatory bureaux limit or control the behaviour of individuals or other bodies, taxing bureaux raise government finances, trading bureaux operate in economic markets in a quasi-commercial mode and servicing bureaux provide services for other public sector bureaux.

Transfer and contracts bureau types have bureau elements which dominate program budgets because most money is passed on to be used by the private sector. Transfer bureaux pay subsidies or entitlements to individuals or firms and contracts bureaux place and monitor contracts with private sector firms. In control bureaux the program element and/or portfolio element dominate the program budget because the bureaux supervise money passed on to other public sector bodies (Dunleavy et al 1994: Chapter 3).

Table 1
Components of the DSS Program Budget in 1989

PROGRAM BUDGET £49,324 m, comprising, a) core budget, b) bureau element, c) program element and d) portfolio element.

a) CORE BUDGET £1,702 m, comprising,
– Salaries of staff.
– Capital and other running costs.

b) BUREAU ELEMENT £41,192 m, comprising,
– Benefit payments to clients.

c) PROGRAM ELEMENT £4,958 m, comprising,
– Grants to local authorities for administrative and benefit costs of housing benefit and rent rebates.

d) PORTFOLIO ELEMENT £1,472 m, comprising,
– Payments to Department of Employment for administrative and payment costs of delivering some benefits to unemployed clients.
– Payments to Department of Health and Social Services, Northern Ireland for administering benefits.

Sources

House of Commons, Paper 242 -XIV (1990), *Department of Social Security Supply Estimates 1990-91, Session 1989-90*, London, HMSO.
Department of Social Security (1992), *Departmental Report: The Government's Expenditure Plans, 1993-94 to 1995-96*, Cm 2213, London, HMSO.

In 1989, before the Next Steps changes occurred, the DSS was responsible for the development and implementation of the government's social security policy. The DSS's core budget included spending on the executive activities of administering social security payments to clients, collection of contribution payments and maintenance of records for the National Insurance scheme, running internal information technology services and managing resettlement units consisting of hostels and other facilities for homeless people. The executive activity of paying social security benefits resulted in the bureau element forming the bulk of the DSS program budget. The dominance of the bureau element in the program budget made the DSS a transfer bureau, with the size of the core budget indicating that the transfer function required a large administrative structure. The DSS also had a less significant role as a control bureau conducting policy work and supervising money passed on to other government organisations, illustrated by the size of the program and portfolio elements. The components of DSS total program budget are summarised in Table 1.

Much of the control activity was conducted in sections of the DSS which were separate from the parts involved in administering benefit payments, the latter parts included the Regional Directorate, Regional Offices and DSS local offices. The sections involved in policy work tended to contain a higher proportion of senior officials than those carrying out executive activity. A tendency for senior officials to concentrate their time on policy work rather than executive activity was therefore apparent before Next Steps.

By 1993, as part of the Next Steps reform, the DSS had shed most of its executive activity to four agencies and had a much smaller core budget. The DSS had changed bureau type from a transfer to a control bureau. A core Headquarters department now forms the rump of the old DSS and is mainly involved in policy development and strategic management planning for the executive agencies (DSS 1993: 2). The program budget, summarised in Table 2, is dominated by a large portfolio element containing agencies which are primarily concerned with executive activity. The agencies are-

Benefits Agency: This agency has the largest core budget of the four agencies. Its staff are involved in the running of the benefits payment system which consists of a network of local offices, benefit centres and directorates providing central services (Benefits Agency 1993: 5). The program budget is dominated by the bureau element consisting of benefit payments to clients, which makes the Agency a transfer bureau. In the financial year 1992-93, which was the most recent set of budget figures available for this study, the Child Support Unit was located in the core budget of the Agency. The Unit became the Child Support Agency in April 1993.

Contributions Agency: The Agency's core budget dominates the program budget and its main task is collecting payments and maintaining payment records for the National Insurance scheme (Contributions Agency 1993: 1), making the Agency a taxing bureau.

Information Technology Services Agency (ITSA): ITSA provides the DSS Headquarters and agencies with information technology services, a role which is reflected in the core budget forming a large part of program budget. The Agency has a bureau element, derived from the task of purchasing of information technology goods and services for other parts of the DSS

(ITSA 1993: 4). ITSA is consequently classified as a servicing bureau with a smaller contracts bureau role.

Resettlement Agency: The Agency is responsible for running resettlement units and the core budget forms over half the program budget as a result, making the Agency a delivery bureau. However the Agency also administers grants to local authorities and private sector voluntary organisations (Resettlement Agency 1992: 10-11). This function results in bureau and program elements forming the rest of the program budget, indicating additional contracts and control bureau roles.

These agencies were initially established as part of the public sector. However as part of the new phase of Next Steps involving the proposed privatisation of some existing agencies the Contributions Agency and ITSA have been identified as possible candidates for privatisation (Willman 1993). In the typology privatising an agency moves it from the DSS Headquarters' portfolio element to the bureau element, which contains contracts with private firms. An increase in the significance of the bureau element would cause the Headquarters to be reclassified as a contracts instead of a control bureau.

Table 2
Components of the DSS program budget in 1993

PROGRAM BUDGET £73,859 m, comprising,

a) CORE BUDGET £161 m, comprising,
– Running costs of Headquarters

b) BUREAU ELEMENT,
– Insignificant.

c) PROGRAM ELEMENT £5,113 m, comprising,
– Grants to local authorities for administrative and payment costs of housing benefit and tax rebates.

d) PORTFOLIO ELEMENT, £68,585 m, comprising,
– *Benefits Agency* £65,481 m, comprising, core budget (£1,976 m) of administrative and other costs, bureau element (£63,493 m) mainly composed of benefit payments to clients, portfolio element (£12 m) mostly consisting of payments Department Health and Social Services, N. Ireland, insignificant program element.
– *Contributions Agency* £155 m, comprising, core budget (£155 m) consisting of administrative and other costs, other budget components are insignificant.
– *Information Technology Services Agency* £436 m, comprising, core budget (£299 m) of administrative and other costs, bureau element (£137 m) mainly consisting of contracts with private sector computer firms, other budget components are not significant.
– *Resettlement Agency* £27 m, comprising, core budget (£15 m) of administrative and other costs, bureau element (£6 m) containing grants to private

charities, program element (£6 m) consisting of grants to local authorities, insignificant portfolio element.
– Payments to Department of Employment for administrative and payment costs of delivering some benefits to unemployed people.

Source: HC Paper 495 - XIII (1993), *Department of Social Security Supply Estimates 1993-94, Session 1992-93*, London, HMSO.

Applying the Bureau-Shaping Model to the Next Steps Reorganisation in the DSS

The first part of this section explains how a shift in politicians' constraint on bureaucrats triggered bureau-shaping strategies by senior officials in the DSS. The second and third parts explain the behaviour of senior civil servants outside the DSS who were involved in the reform. In the fourth part the Next Steps reform is discussed as a rational strategy by bureaucrats to protect their position as consumers of career related utility.

the shift in politicans' constraint on bureaucrats

The bureau-shaping model explains the Next Steps reorganisation in terms of a shift in the optimum point of bureaucrats which triggered bureau-shaping strategies to achieve their new optimum levels of core budget *per* senior bureaucrat and proportion of policy work time. In the model the optimum point shifts because of exogenous changes in either the preferences of the bureaucrat or in politicians' assessment of management time required for supervising core budget and the adjustment these changes cause within the model.

The preferences of senior officials in the DSS, defined as those civil servants of Grade 7 (Principal grade) and above, did not radically alter during the time period covered by the Next Steps reform. Senior officials exhibited a preference for policy work time rather than management work time. Sir Robert Armstrong, a former Cabinet Secretary and Head of the Civil Service, commented on senior officials' continued preference for policy work despite the attempts of reforms to increase the profile of management tasks (Hennessy 1990: 737-8). A study which examined civil servants' attitudes to the Financial Management Initiative supports this view. Zifcak quotes a Deputy Secretary who said, 'Management is a tiresome business, nobody goes into it unless they have to' (Zifcak 1992: 45).

In the period prior to Next Steps politicians' changed their attitudes concerning the amount of time officials should spend on management. Government ministers perceived that in order to improve efficiency civil servants should spend more time managing the services for which they were responsible. The change in attitudes in the 1980s has been called the rise of neo-Taylorism by Pollitt (1993: 53). Neo-Taylorism is the view that efficiency is improved by increasing the monitoring of the use of resources, especially the achievement of individual employees who are rewarded in accordance with their performance. A senior minister, Michael Heseltine, expressed the monitored and costed, when information is conveyed in columns instead of screeds, then objectives become clear and progress towards them becomes measurable and far more likely' (Pollitt 1993: 58). Politicians' changed attitudes are represented in the model as an increase in the proportion of management work time for each unit of core budget *per* senior bureaucrat which politicians' required of bureaucrats. This change is shown as a shift in the constraint curve from 1 to 2 in Figure 3.

Figure 3
The Effect of Political Changes

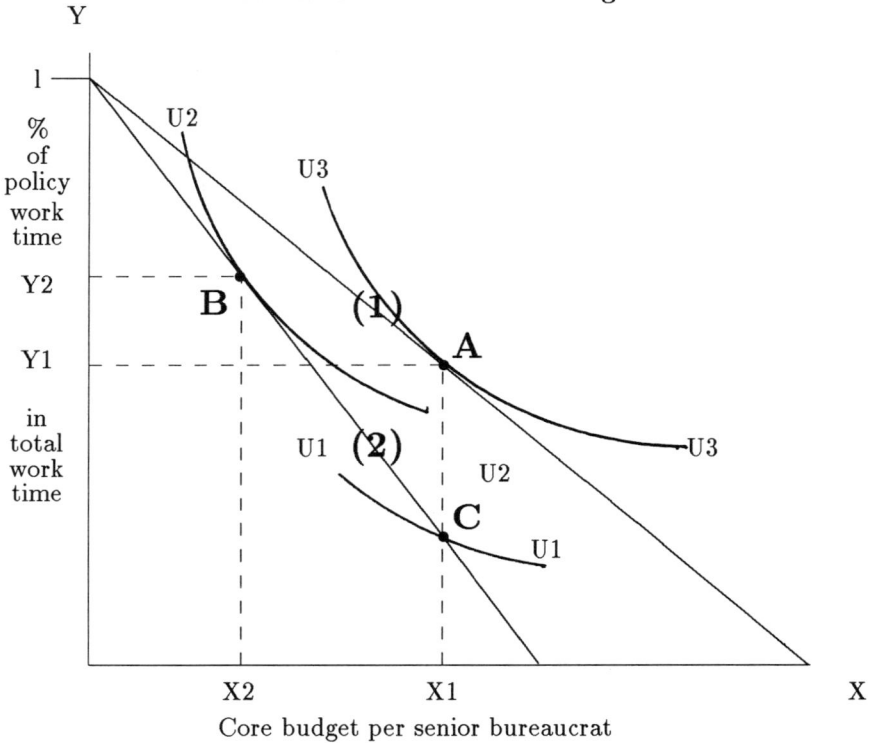

Core budget per senior bureaucrat

note:
This figure maps the changes to the core budget per senior bureaucrat & proportion of policy work time which are caused by a shift in politicians' constraints on the bureaucrat.

Senior officials in the DSS attempted to maximise total utility under the new constraint in which the time cost of pursuing core budget *per* senior bureaucrat had increased, shown by constraint 2 having a steeper slope than constraint 1 in Figure 3. The increased cost caused senior civil servants to substitute proportion of policy work time (Y) to replace core budget *per* senior bureaucrat (X). The increased cost of X also reduced the time available to pursue both X and Y. The optimum moved from A to B and X fell from nior bureaucrat (X). The increased cost of X also reduced the time available to pursue both X and Y. The optimum moved from A to B and X fell from X1 to X2 and Y increased from Y1 to Y2, with a corresponding reduction in the level of total utility[3]. However total utility at point B is higher than that at point C which would have been achieved by a reform which increased the proportion of management work time with an unchanged level of core budget *per* senior bureaucrat. The lower total utility corresponding with point C explains why the alternative management reform of maintaining the DSS as an integrated department with senior officials increasing their proportion of management work time was rejected.

The reduction in core budget *per* senior bureaucrat and rise in proportion of policy work time were achieved by the bureau-shaping strategy of shedding executive activity and concentrating on policy work instead. The creation of agencies relieved senior officials of responsibility for managing executive activity by changing the DSS bureau type from a transfer bureau with a large core budget to a Headquarters control bureau with a smaller core budget. This change enabled officials to increase the proportion of policy work time. DSS officials stated in a memorandum to the Treasury and Civil Service Committee that one of the main effects of agency working had been on 'clarifying the identity of the core department and thus highlighting the need to focus its management effort on strategy and planning rather than on routine issues' (HC 481, 1990, 107). Strategic management and planning amounts to policy work and the use of the term 'management' to describe the activities of the Headquarters demonstrates how senior officials have adopted the rhetoric of management reform. The use of rhetoric by officials illustrates the danger of taking official descriptions of the change at face value.

A complete division of policy work from executive activity did not occur and agencies conduct some policy work. The Benefits Agency has a Planning Unit which conducts policy research work to assist management in their assessment of the costs of the benefit delivery system (Interview, Paver 1993). However the main responsibility of the agencies is managing executive activity.

Some senior officials ended up working in agencies rather than the Headquarters department. However the reform does not prevent them from moving to the DSS Headquarters or the equivalent policy making core of other departments later in their careers. Senior officials are unlikely to object to spending some time involved in management work in the expectation of achieving policy work positions later in their careers.

---

[3] The tightening of politicians' constraint on bureaucrats is expressed formally by a rise in (a). The equations for optimum X and Y imply that a rise in (a) will cause a fall in X and a rise in Y. The utility function used in the formal representation of the model is chosen for simplicity and is an example of the general utility function of $U = Xg + Yh$, where $0 < g < 1$ and $0 < h < 1$, which is compatible with the model. The model assumes that both X and Y have the properties of normal goods, that is, the bureaucrat would desire to increase them if the constraint was made less severe by politicians. The model also assumes that the marginal utilities of both X and Y are positive, diminish with increases in the levels of X and Y and are independent of each other. A further assumption is that for Y the substitution effect of a rise in (a) outweighs the income effect such that a rise in (a) causes a rise in Y.

The creation of agencies was broadly in line with the wishes of DSS officials as is shown by an internal departmental report recommending reforms similar to those suggested in the Efficiency Unit report. The internal report suggested setting up separate structures to handle the implementation of social security policy which resembles the idea of executive agencies (Moodie et al 1988). Senior officials' favourable opinion of the Next Steps reform was further demonstrated by the speed with which the change occurred. The DSS was responsible for choosing agency candidates and setting them up, which could have facilitated delaying tactics if senior officials opposed the reform. Instead the Resettlement Agency was established in May 1989, ITSA in April 1990, the Contributions Agency and Benefits Agency in April 1991 and the Child Support Agency in April 1993. The order in which agencies were established was most significantly influenced by the administrative complexity involved. The Resettlement Agency was set up first because it was a smaller and more self contained unit than later agencies such as the Contributions Agency and Benefits Agency.

Not all the officials of Grade 7 and above involved in Next Steps were located in the DSS. Some officials worked in different institutional environments which influenced their desire and ability to embark on bureau-shaping strategies. The variation produced groups of civil servants who had different motivations and behaviour in the reform process.

civil servants in the Efficiency Unit and Next Steps Project Team

The Next Steps reform was not proposed by officials in the DSS, instead the recommendation came from officials in the Efficiency Unit. Officials in the Unit had less interest in bureau-shaping strategies than those in the DSS. The Unit was supervised by the Adviser to the Prime Minister on Efficiency, Sir Robin Ibbs, who had spent much of his career in private industry at ICI and was not a career civil servant (Hennessy 1990: 612). Although the unit was staffed by civil servants these officials were located outside mainstream departments and so their utility was less dependent on the organisation of departments such as the DSS. Whilst officials in the Unit might have expected to move to a department later on in their careers their promotion and career prospects depended on the success of their reform as perceived by politicians.

Officials in the Efficiency Unit recognised that the cooperation of senior career civil servants in the departments was required to successfully implement the reform. This requirement led the staff in the unit to anticipate the reaction of departmental civil servants to the proposed reform. Efficiency Unit officials saw that a reform involving shifting executive activity to agencies was more likely to be accepted than one forcing senior civil servants increase their proportion of management work time.

The Next Steps Project Team, located in the Cabinet Office, monitored progress in Next Steps reform and provided assistance to departments in their task of implementing the changes. The team was initially headed by Sir Peter Kemp who came from the Treasury and was a career civil servant. In a similar way to the Efficiency Unit the promotion of members of the team depended on the successful implementation of the reform which reduced their interest in bureau-shaping strategies. However the Project Team had to anticipate the reaction of career civil servants in the departments to ensure successful implementation.

civil servants in the Treasury

A significant group of civil servants involved in the establishment of agencies in the DSS was located in the Treasury. The Treasury examined agency candidates, considering if privatisation, contracting out or abolition of the activity were more suitable alternatives (Middleton HC 494-II 1988). Most senior officials in the Treasury are career civil servants, however the Treasury is a significantly different environment from that which exists in other departments. The Treasury's main function is as a central coordinating body with responsibility for controlling government expenditure. Treasury officials further their careers by fulfilling the functions of expenditure control and coordination which reduces their interest in bureau-shaping strategies.

The attitude of Treasury officials towards the reform was conditioned by their perception of its effect on their ability to control public expenditure. At the start of the reform they feared that autonomous agencies might weaken their control. The initial doubts of Treasury officials were reported by the Cabinet Secretary, Sir Robin Butler (Butler HC 494-II 1988: 57). However their opposition waned when it became clear that the Treasury could maintain controls to prevent unwelcome calls on the public purse. Treasury officials are likely to be especially keen on the privatisation of agencies because this tends to remove an agency's claim for public subsidy.

Next Steps and the structure of the senior civil service

The Next Steps reform had an additional benefit to rational senior officials, as well as being a bureau-shaping strategy. The reform enabled senior civil servants to protect their position as consumers of career related utility by deflecting demands for change to the pattern of recruitment and promotion to senior posts. If the jobs of senior officials were put up for open competition the future career related utility of existing officials would be at risk because they might be forced to leave the service. In 1993 only 10% of the top 620 officials in the civil service had been recruited to their posts through open competition. The appointment of people who are not career civil servants tend to be high profile exceptions, such as Sir Terry Burns, Permanent Secretary to the Treasury (Blitz 1993).

Senior officials did not intend Next Steps to be a stage on the way to a radical reform of the senior service. Their intentions were demonstrated by the unusually early retirement of Sir Peter Kemp. He was an increasingly radical critic of what he called the 'old attitudes and the old guard' in the senior civil service and was in disagreement with other senior officials before his early departure (Blitz 1993). A recent Efficiency Unit report which investigated the recruitment and career paths of senior officials has proposed that more appointments should be made from outside the service.

However the radical implications of the report are severely restricted by its assertion that the existing system of internal appointments to senior positions should not be dismantled because of the incentives it gives to officials already in the service (Efficiency Unit 1993). It is possible that radical change to the career structure of senior officials will eventually take place. Such a change should not be taken as evidence that senior officials have miscalculated or that they have lost out because of their short term outlook. There is little reason why today's rational senior officials should be concerned about the career related utility of future generations of senior civil servants.

Conclusion

The bureau-shaping model advances our understanding of reorganisation beyond existing unsystematic official and descriptive pluralist explanations because it uses an explicitly theoretical approach. The model is also an improvement on these explanations because they are incomplete accounts of why Next Steps occurred. The official explanation claims that Next Steps builds on the achievements of the Financial Management Initiative. This explanation fails to explain why responsibility for the-day-to-day management of executive activity was passed on to agencies with senior officials concentrating on policy work in core departments instead of senior officials increasing the proportion of their work time spent on management. Similarly descriptive pluralist explanations are incomplete because they do not explain why politicians' concern with business management lead them to establish executive agencies separate from policy making core departments.

In contrast the bureau-shaping model can explain the seemingly counter intuitive result that senior civil servants have concentrated more time on policy work and decreased the proportion of their time spent managing in response to politicians' demands that officials should spend more time managing executive activity for which they are responsible. The model explains that rational senior officials reacted to politicians' demands by shaping their bureaux, shedding responsibility for managing executive activity to agencies in order to protect favourably valued policy work time. The creation of agencies responsible for managing executive activity was preferred by officials to the alternative reform of maintaining integrated departments with senior civil servants increasing their proportion of management work time.

The importance of bureau-shaping strategies in bringing about the reform is demonstrated by the application of the model to the reorganisation of the Department of Social Security, which is part of a continuing empirical investigation of the model by the author. The change in the DSS is represented using Dunleavy's analytical typology of bureau. The Department changed from a transfer bureau with a large core budget to the DSS core Headquarters which is a control bureau with a smaller core budget. The Headquarters has the highest concentration of senior officials and it makes policy for several agencies which are responsible for managing executive activity. Although some of the complex processes in the reform are not fully explained by the bureau-shaping model, such as the behaviour of

Treasury officials, the model does explain the main features of the creation of executive agencies in the DSS.

References

Benefits Agency (1993), *Benefits Agency Annual Report*, 1992-93.

Blitz, J (1993), 'Civil Service Urged to Draw from Private Sector', *Financial Times*, 20th-21st November 1993.

Chapman, R A (1991), 'Concepts and Issues in Public Sector Reform: the Experience of the United Kingdom in the 1980's', *Public Policy and Administration*, 6 (2): 1-19.

Child Support Agency (1993), *Child Support Agency Business Plan*.

Contributions Agency (1993), *Contributory Agency Annual Report and Accounts 1992-1993*.

Department of Social Security (1993), *Department Report: The Government's Expenditure Plans 1993-94 to 1995-96*, Cm 2213, London, HMSO.

Dunleavy, P (1985), 'Bureaucrats, Budgets and the Growth of the State: Reconstructing an Instrumental Model', *British Journal of Political Science*, 15 (3): 299-328.

Dunleavy, P (1989a), 'The Architecture of the British Central State, Part I: Framework for Analysis', *Public Administration*, 67 (3): 249-275.

Dunleavy, P (1989b), 'The Architecture of the British Central State, Part II: Empirical Findings', *Public Administration*, 67 (4): 391-417.

Dunleavy, P (1991), *Democracy, Bureaucracy and Public Choice*, Hemel Hempstead, Harvester Wheatsheaf.

Dunleavy, P, King, D & Margetts, H (1994), *Leviathan Bound: Bureaucrats and Budgeting in the American Federal State*, unpublished book manuscript, London School of Economics.

Efficiency Unit (1988), *Improving Management in Government: The Next Steps*, London, HMSO.

Efficiency Unit (1993) *Career Management and Succession Planning Study*, London, HMSO

Hennessy, P (1990), *Whitehall*, London, Fontana Press.

House of Commons, Paper 494 (1988), *Treasury and Civil Service Committee, Eight Report, Civil Service Management Reform: The Next Steps, Volumes I-II, Session 1987-88*, London, HMSO.

House of Commons, Paper 242 - XIV (1990), *Department of Social Security Supply Estimates 1989-90, Session 1989-90*, London, HMSO.

House of Commons, Paper 481 (1990), *Treasury and Civil Service Committee Progress in the Next Steps Initiative Session, 1989-90*, London, HMSO.

House of Commons, Paper 550 (1991), *Minutes of Evidence Taken Before the Social Security Committee: 25th June 1991, Volume I Session 1990-91*, London, HMSO.

House of Commons, Paper 495 - XIII (1993), *Department of Social Security Estimates 1993-94, Session 1992-93*, London, HMSO.

Hogwood, B W (1993), 'The Uneven Staircase: Measuring up to Next Steps', Strathclyde Papers on Government and Politics Number 92, University of Strathclyde.

Information Technology Service Agency (1993), *Annual Report and Accounts 1992-93*.

Lane, J-E (1993), *The Public Sector*, London, Sage.

Metcalfe, L (1993), 'Conviction Politics and Dynamic Conservatism: Mrs Thatcher's Managerial Revolution', *International Political Science Review*, 14 (4): 351-71.

Moe, T M (1984), 'The Economics of Organization', *American Journal of Political Science*, 28: 739-77.

Moodie, M, Mizan, N, Heron, R & Mackay, B (1988), *The Business of Service: Report of the Regional Organisation Survey*, Department of Health and Social Security.

Mueller, D C (1989), *Public Choice II*, Cambridge, Cambridge University Press.

Niskanen, W A (1971), *Bureaucracy and Representative Government*, Chicago, Aldine-Atherton.

Office of Public Service and Science (OPSS),(1993), *Next Steps: Agencies in Government: Review 1993*, Cm 2430, London, HMSO.

Paver, M (1993), *Interview*, Benefits Agency, Planning Unit, Quarry House, Leeds, 9th August 1993.

Pollitt, C (1993), *Managerialism and the Public Services*, Cambridge, Massachusetts, Blackwell Business.

Resettlement Agency (1992), *Annual Report and Financial Statement 1991-1992*.

Willman, J (1993), 'Civil service open to bidding', *Financial Times*, 10th December 1993.

Zifcak, S M (1992), *Administrative Reform in Whitehall and Canberra in the 1980's: The FMI and FMIP Compared*, PhD Thesis, London School of Economics and Political Science.

The Core Executive
Analytic Approaches to Developments Under Major

Patrick Dunleavy
London School of Economics & Political Science

'Estimating the Distribution of Influence
in Cabinet Committees under Major'

Acknowledgements

I would like to thank Helen Margetts, Keith Dowding, George Jones, John Barnes and Alan Beattie at LSE, Peter Hennessy from Queen Mary Westfield, and Rod Rhodes from the University of York, all of whom commented on an earlier draft. So many valuable criticisms and suggestions are incorporated here that identifying them all would take several pages: I hope this inadequate global acknowledgement may suffice.

The data reviewed are computed from three Cabinet Office mimeoed listing documents, two versions of 'Ministerial Committees of the Cabinet: Membership and Terms of Reference', dated 19 May 1992 and 29 January 1993 respectively; and 'Government in Partnership: Factsheet No.3 – Cabinet Committee' (no date, but issued November 1993), dealing with the Ministerial Committee for Regeneration. All Tables refer to the May 1992 situation.

Introduction

In February 1978 the Labour Prime Minister James Callaghan signed a solemn memo explaining why he proposed to continue the long-standing practice of refusing to disclose any details at all of the Cabinet committee system. After dismissively noting 'some Press allegations about Whitehall obscurantism', he argued:

'The method adopted by Ministers for discussing policy questions is however *essentially a domestic matter*, and a decision by a Cabinet Committee, unless referred to the Cabinet, engages the collective responsibility of all Ministers and has exactly the same authority as a decision by Cabinet itself. Disclosure that a particular Committee had dealt with a matter might lead to argument about the status of the decision or demands that it should be endorsed by the whole Cabinet.' (Hennessy, 1986, p.89: emphasis added)

By 'a domestic matter' Callaghan meant that how ministers came to take a decision was not a matter of legitimate public interest, but rather a purely private internal decision of the government members themselves, fundamentally a house-keeping issue.

His defence of total secrecy went on to cite the usual repertoire of White-hall memos down the ages. He claimed that committees existed solely to ease the decision-making burden on Cabinet itself; that any disclosure of committee details (even the existence of committees) would be misleading, since some of them could not be revealed on security grounds and others were ephemeral; and that disclosing anything at all would lead to Parliamentary select committees asking committee chairs to explain the reasons for decisions, instead of (or as well as) the departmentally responsible ministers (who might have been outvoted). His conclusion was that the existing policy of saying nothing at all about committees, not even to confirm the names of the main committees, was the only defensible one: anything else would open up a crack through which would slip progressively more details of the government's operations.

As a testimony to the self-serving (almost paranoid) suspicion which prevailed for well over half a century in core executive 'reasoning' about these issues, Callaghan's memo could hardly be bettered. As Hennessy (1986, p.88) notes he was 'an arch traditionalist' in his attitudes. In the whole far-rago of nonsense justifying blanket official secrecy, by far the most bizarre claim was that Cabinet committee arrangements were 'essentially domestic' in character. The logic of committee decision is a push towards creating more 'partial' governments, in the twin sense of vesting the power to decide issues in more restricted sets of people, who are also (potentially) more biased − more selective in what they take into account, and less broadly representative of the government as a whole in their values or experiences. Probably in no other governing system in the Western world would senior elected officials so blandly attempt to deny that the forums used to make decisions can affect the quality of consideration accorded them or the nature of the outcomes reached. Notice too that British official doctrine says nothing about Cabinet committees improving the quality of decisions, for example, by bringing to bear more concentrated expertise in more specialized settings. Implicitly the justification of committees as a simple load-shedding device to relieve full Cabinet seems to admit that committee decisions are inherently less collegial and hence less legitimate than full Cabinet consideration.

In May 1992 John Major consigned the more farcical Whitehall defences of secrecy to the junkheap of history by publishing a full listing of the names and membership of the Cabinet's standing ministerial committees and sub-committees. No details were given of the more temporary committees (those labelled as GEN committees under one Prime Minister, and as MISC committees under the next), nor of the official committee network which parallels the ministerial committees and pre-processes issues which they consider. However details of ministerial committee memberships and chairs were provided, together with brief terms of reference and a few lines on how sub-committees report to the full committees. This official disclosure for the first time makes feasible an attempt to assess the distribution of influence within the permanent structures of the Cabinet committee system, and the extent to which different ministers share in committee decision-making.

The remainder of this paper first discusses methods for ranking ministers in terms of their committee influence and measuring their linkages with Cabinet colleagues. Committee influence is considerably segmented between domestic policy ministers, Cabinet members involved in overseas and defence policy committees, and non-departmental ministers chairing committees – each of whom acquire influence in different ways, with the Prime Minister as an additional special case. The second section analyses the extent to which committee influence can be seen as concentrated or fragmented, and how easy or difficult it is for different 'coalitions' of Cabinet ministers to control the overall committee system. Finally the conclusions explore some implications of these findings for public discussion and understanding of core executive operations, and for future core executive studies.

Measuring the Distribution of Influence in the Cabinet Committee System

Table 1 gives the salient details of committees and sub-committees as at May 1992 – including names and abbreviations, the committee's chair, its size, number of non-Cabinet ministers and a weighting score (explained below). The Prime Minister chairs all of the full committees in the Overseas Policy and Defence (OPD) fields, which generally have a smaller membership. In addition, the Prime Minister chairs two committees in very cognate fields, dealing with the Intelligence Services and with Northern Ireland. Five of these committees have either four or five members only. In addition the Prime Minister chairs two larger domestic policy committees, EDP the premier committee dealing with strategic economic policy-making, and EDS handling technology issues. These additions bring the average size of all nine of the Prime Minister's committees up slightly to seven members. Only one minister from outside the Cabinet sits on any of the committees chaired by the Prime Minister.

All but one of the remaining domestic full committees have over 12 members, and in July 1992 were chaired either by the Lord Privy Seal (then Lord Wakeham) or the Lord President of the Council (Tony Newton). The five committees prefixed ED ... generally include two or three area ministers (for Scotland, Wales and Northern Ireland), plus one or two non-departmental ministers, the Chancellor and one or more heads of economic departments (such as the Board of Trade, Employment, or the Chief Secretary) and the heads of major spending departments in domestic policy. One of the full committees deals with Civil Service Pay (defined as public sector employees directly controlled by ministers). Two domestic committees deal with Legislation and Future Legislation: they have more of a technical character and include several junior ministers from outside the Cabinet dealing with legal matters and Parliamentary timetabling and discipline.

There seem to be three kinds of ministerial sub-committee. The three OPD sub-committees form a distinct group with significant responsibilities and memberships composed of Cabinet ministers. The sub-committee on European Questions is larger because its European Community role involves domestic departments whereas the other two (covering Terrorism and Eastern Europe) are closer to the OPD norm with eight members each.

Table 1
The Cabinet Committee structure in May 1992

Committee Name & Abbreviation	Chair	Size	A	B
Overseas Policy and cognate committees				
Overseas Policy and Defence OPD	PM	6	0	100
Nuclear Defence Policy OPDN	PM	4	0	100
MC on the Gulf OPDG	PM	4	0	100
European Security OPDSE	PM	4	0	100
Hong Kong OPDK	PM	8	1	88
Intelligence Services IS	PM	5	0	100
Northern Ireland NI	PM	7	0	100
Domestic policy committees				
Economic and Domestic Policy EDP	PM	13	0	100
Science and Technology EDS	PM	12	0	100
Home and Social Affairs EDH	LPS	18	1	94
Industrial, Commercial and				
Consumer Affairs EDI	LPS	13	0	100
Environment EDE	LPS	13	0	100
Local Government EDL	LPS	15	1	93
Civil Service Pay EDC	LPC	12	1	92
The Queens Speech and Future				
Legislation FLG	LPC	9	4	56
Legislation LG	LPC	12	6	50
Overseas Policy sub-committees				
Eastern Europe OPD(AE)	FS	9	1	44
European Questions OPD(E)	FS	15	1	47
Terrorism OPD(T)	HS	8	0	50
Domestic sub-committees				
Public Sector Pay EDI(P)	LPS	12	0	50
Health Strategy EDH(H)	LPC	13	3	35
Drug Misuse EDH(D)	LPC	10	9	5
Alcohol Misuse EDH(A)	CDL	12	11	4
Women's Issues EDH(W)	EMP	13	12	4
Co-ordination of Urban				
Policy EDH(U)	ENV	14	13	4
London EDL(L)	ENV	12	11	4

Notes:

Column A = *Non-Cabinet Members; Column B = Weighted Influence Score.*

The first three letters of the abbreviation for a sub-committee indicate the full committee to which it reports.

The Chair column uses the following abbreviations: PM Prime Minister; LPS Lord Privy Seal; LPC Lord President of the Council; FS Foreign Secretary; HS Home Secretary; CDL Chanellor of the Duchy of Lancaster; EMP Secretary of State for Employment; ENV Secretary of State for the Environment.

A second group includes two domestic sub-committees with multiple Cabinet members. One covers Public Sector Pay, paralleling the full committee on Civil Service Pay. Its lower status seems to stem chiefly from the fact that it meets only episodically, before the annual pay round starts: but its membership is virtually the same as that of a full Cabinet committee. The other covers the government's health strategy, and includes nine Cabinet members and four junior ministers. By contrast with these important OPD and domestic sub-committees, the remaining six domestic sub-committees(covering alcohol abuse, drug abuse, women's issues, coordination of the government's urban policy, and London issues) have a different character. Their membership is almost entirely composed of junior ministers, with only a single Cabinet member acting as chair in each case. These sub-committees have very low salience in political terms. They are often set up more for 'window-dressing' or symbolic purposes, to serve as a visible governmental response to social problems, or as a reaction to the need to accommodate relatively minor issues, rather than to transact key quantities of government business.

In summary, the official two-level distinction between committees and sub-committees masks an underlying structure of four different levels of committee. In the first rank are the small full committees with the OPD prefix and the IS committee. The second rank includes the domestic policy full committees. The third rank includes the OPD sub-committees and the two domestic sub-committees with multiple Cabinet members. And the fourth rank consists of the remaining 'symbolic' domestic sub-committees.

To make full use of this new information we need to develop some generally accepted indices of the extent to which ministers are advantaged or disadvantaged by their placings within the Cabinet committee system. A first step is to measure the relative importance of committees described above. I suggest the following formula:

$$\text{Committee weighting} = 100 * S * (C/N)$$

Here S means the official status of the committee, and can be scored by counting a full ministerial committee as one, and a sub-committee as 0.5.[1] C means the number of Cabinet members who sit on the committee, and N denotes the total number of ministers who are members. Thus a committee's weighting depends on its formal status and its salience (as measured by the proportion of its members who are Cabinet ministers). Table 1 above gives these weightings for all 26 committees. Full committees with exclusively Cabinet members score 100, while those with one junior minister drift downwards into the 90s. The two legislation committees are unusual as full domestic committees because they are fairly small and have several non-Cabinet ministers as members: their scores accordingly dip down to around 50. Ministerial sub-committees with exclusively Cabinet members score 50, while those with one or two junior ministers score in the 40s. The 'symbolic' domestic sub-committees score just 4 or 5 on this index. In

---

[1] I offer no detailed rationale for the choice of these weightings at this point, since it is a complex issue of fairly specialized interest: readers interested in technicalities should turn to the Appendix, which briefly discusses other possible assumptions, and shows how they would affect the estimations of committee influence.

the Cabinet committee system as a whole there are a total of 1719 score points. So a committee with 100 points absorbs 5.8 per cent of the total, a sub-committee with 50 points counts for 2.9 per cent, and a 'symbolic' sub-committee for 0.3 per cent.

The next step is to partition out the weighting of each committee among its members. Since we have no information about ministers' behaviour on committees, the simplest rule would be to divide the weighting score for each committee by the number of members, regarding each as equal to all others in influence. But an obvious difficulty here has been raised by earlier authors who suggested that committee chairs enjoy considerable influence, by virtue of their central role in agenda-setting and controlling discussion:

> 'The job of chairing Cabinet committees is of very high political status. In effect, the chairman [sic] is over other ministers. The chairman's task is to resolve differences between ministers in ways acceptable to the disputants, while also promoting the general interest of the government, that is, the Prime Minister's interest.' (Rose, 1989, p.88)

To cope with this widely recognized importance, we can simply consider the chair as an additional role to be assigned influence. So in attributing shares of the committee's weighting score we divide the total by N + 1, and assign a double share to the chair (one share in virtue of their membership, and another for chairing). Thus for a normal committee member, their personal weighted score is:

$$(100 * S * (C/N))/(N + 1)$$

The score for committee chairs will be twice this amount.

Table 2 shows the results of this calculation for all members of the Cabinet and some of the most important junior ministers involved in Cabinet committees in 1992, together with counts of their committee and sub-committee memberships and chairs. This analysis assumes that the weighted scores for committee influence will produce an overall increment or decrement to the other sources of influence accorded to Cabinet members, such as departmental ministers' control of large-scale resources, and the Prime Minister's influence as party leader and 'team manager' of the Cabinet. Aggregate patterns of committee influence will show up across a range of issues and a long period of time, but need not be discernible in the outcomes of any particular round of a single issue.

Non-Cabinet ministers are indicated by an asterisk *. The Ministers of State at the Foreign Office and Home Office are the deputies to the Foreign Secretary and Home Secretary, and the Financial Secretary is third-in-line at the Treasury. The Lord Advocate is a Law Officer for Scotland. The Chief Whip's formal title is Parliamentary Secretary to the Treasury, and that of the government Whip in the Lords is the Captain of the Gentlemen at Arms.

Table 2

Committee Influence Scores for Senior Ministers, 1992

Minister	Committee influence		Committee	Chairs
	Weighted score	% of total	places	
Prime Minister	256	14.9	9 + 0	9 + 0
Foreign Secretary	155	9.0	10 + 3	0 + 2
SS for Defence	138	8.0	9 + 2	0 + 0
Chanc Exchequer	110	6.4	9 + 3	0 + 0
Home Secretary	82	4.8	7 + 3	0 + 1
Ld Pres of Council	76	4.4	8 + 3	3 + 2
Chanc Duchy Lanc	76	4.4	9 + 3	0 + 1
Presi Bd of Trade	75	4.4	7 + 4	0 + 0
Lord Privy Seal	74	4.3	7 + 1	4 + 1
SS for Scotland	66	3.8	8 + 4	0 + 0
Attorney General	65	3.8	5 + 2	0 + 0
SS for Environment	62	3.6	7 + 6	0 + 2
SS for Nthn Ireland	57	3.3	6 + 3	0 + 0
Chief Secty, Treasury	56	3.3	7 + 1	0 + 0
SS for Transport	45	2.6	5 + 3	0 + 0
SS for Wales	41	2.4	6 + 2	0 + 0
SS Employment	38	2.2	4 + 4	0 + 1
Min Agriculture	32	1.9	3 + 3	0 + 0
SS Health	25	1.4	3 + 2	0 + 0
SS for Education	22	1.3	3 + 1	0 + 0
FCO Min of State*	21	1.2	2 + 2	0 + 0
SS Social Security	20	1.2	3 + 1	0 + 0
SS Natl Heritage	18	1.0	3 + 0	0 + 0
Chief Whip*	17	1.0	2 + 1	0 + 0
Finan Sec, Treasury*	16	1.0	3 + 0	0 + 0
Lord Chancellor	14	0.8	3 + 0	0 + 0
Lord Advocate*	9	0.5	2 + 0	0 + 0
Govt Whip, Lords*	9	0.5	2 + 0	0 + 0
Environment Min State	6	0.3	1 + 1	0 + 0
Home Off Min State	4	0.2	1 + 3	0 + 0
All others	17	1.0	0 +58	0 + 0
Total	1719	100	154 +119	16 +10

[The Notes to this table are on the next page.]

Notes to Table 2

In the third column, the first figure shows committee memberships, and the second figure sub-committee memberships. The fourth column follows a similar format for chairs of committees or sub-committees.

In the list of ministerial titles SS means 'Secretary of State' (the basic Cabinet rank). The titles Lord President of the Council, Lord Privy Seal and Chancellor of the Duchy of Lancaster are traditional titles for equivalently ranked non-departmental posts. The Chancellor of the Exchequer, President of the Board of Trade and the Minister for Agriculture, Fisheries and Food are departmental heads of the Treasury, the DTI and MAFF respectively. The Attorney General and Lord Chancellor are Law Officers. The Chief Secretary to the Treasury is the second-in-command at the Treasury but a Cabinet member.

One striking feature of Table 2 is the prominence of the Prime Minister's score, more than a hundred points above a group of three major rivals, the Foreign Secretary, Defence Secretary and Chancellor of the Exchequer. Together these four roles clearly constitute a 'first division' in the ranking. The Defence Secretary's relatively high ranking compared with the Chancellor is surprising. It may reflect a greater tendency for overseas and defence issues to be formally handled by the Cabinet committee system (dating back to the long history of earlier committee organization on defence issues than on domestic policy). By contrast, a great deal of Treasury influence may be exercised in department-Treasury bilaterals without formally running through the committee system. In addition, unlike any other department the Treasury's committee places are split between the Chancellor and the Chief Secretary. Their combined score (166) surpasses that for any other department's Cabinet representative.

A second-ranked group of ministers includes two prominent departmental ministers, the Home Secretary and President of the Board of Trade. Since the Home Secretary's role is conventionally described as one of the 'four great offices of state' its lower position here is noteworthy. Also in this second division are three non-departmental ministers (sometimes deprecatingly called 'floaters' by departmental colleagues), two of whom are the Lord President and Lord Privy Seal: between them they chair all the domestic committees and non-symbolic sub-committees which the Prime Minister does not attend. Traditionally one or both these people are the fixers and business managers of the system, lubricants, swing-voters in finely balanced committees, and guardians of electoral and party interests. The third minister without portfolio is the Chancellor of the Duchy of Lancaster, who in 1992 was William Waldegrave, head of the relatively small Office for Public Service and Science in the Cabinet Office (OPSS), with responsibility for science policy and Major's Citizen's Charter initiative.

In the somewhat larger third-ranked group there are several types of ministers. The heads of the three area ministries (Scotland, Wales and Northern Ireland) sit on considerably more committees because of the multi-functional interests of their departments (see Parry, 1989; Thomas, 1989; Bell, 1989). The Attorney General (the government's chief law officer) and the Chief

Secretary (the Treasury's second Cabinet member, with responsibility for controlling public spending) have specialised roles which bring them assignments to influential committees. The Environment Secretary and the Transport Secretary are the most prominent of the departmental spending ministers, the Environment brief including responsibility for local government. And two lower-ranked 'economic' departments, Employment and the Ministry for Agriculture, sit on relatively fewer committees.

The 'fourth division' of ministers in Table 2 is composed of five Cabinet members and three others from outside its ranks. The low-ranked Secretaries of State include the heads of the three biggest spending welfare state departments, Social Security (whose budget alone accounts for over a third of public spending), Health (with responsibility for the NHS) and Education. Also in this group is the newest and smallest Whitehall spending department, National Heritage (set up only in 1992 to provide a role for a Major ally, David Mellor, and supervising broadcasting and conservation). The lowest ranked of all Cabinet members in committee influence is the Lord Chancellor, whose highly untypical and rather separate department administers the operations of the courts and selects the judiciary. One interpretation of these results is that single-track ministries sit more on the fringes of the committee system, because their work is more self-contained, while less important but conglomerate departments (such as the three area ministries) play a more prominent role. Another view sees significance in the marginalization of 'welfare state' departments (Social Security, Health and Education) from the committee process, despite their huge budgetary size and social importance, while relatively low-spending 'economic' ministries (DTI, Employment and MAFF) play more central roles.

Three non-Cabinet ministers have comparable committee influence rankings with the bottom rungs of the Cabinet: the Foreign Office Minister of State (the deputy for the Foreign Secretary, in 1992 the influential Tristan Garel-Jones); the Chief Whip, in charge of all parliamentary discipline; and the Financial Secretary, the third Treasury minister in the rankings.

Finally for comparative purposes Table 2 includes individual scores for a number of other junior ministers who serve not on the 'symbolic' subcommittees but on one of the more salient committees with a preponderance of Cabinet members. Junior ministers serving only on the symbolic subcommittees are classed as 'others', and account for less than 1 per cent of the overall weighting score in the Cabinet committee system.

The approach in Table 2 focuses on aggregating ministers' influence across all the committees on which they sit, to reach an estimate of their influence across the Cabinet committee system as a whole. It might be objected that what matters to ministers is instead only their degree of influence within the committees on which they do sit. Table 3 accordingly presents data for all Cabinet ministers, showing their top, bottom and median influence scores, and their mean influence score across all their committees.

Table 3
**The Influence Scores of Cabinet Members
on Cabinet Committees and Sub-committees
on which they sit**

Minister	Weighted scores on committees where they sit				N of cmtee and sub-cmte scores
	Mean	Top	Median	Low	
Prime Minister	28.4	40	25	14	9
Defence Secretary	12.5	20	13	4	11
Foreign Secretary	12.0	20	9	6	13
Lord Privy Seal	9.3	14	9	4	8
Home Secretary	9.1	17	7	3	10
Chanc Exchequer	8.4	20	7	3	12
Attorney General	8.1	20	6	3	7
Lord President	7.0	14	7	1	11
Presi Bd of Trade	6.8	14	7	3	11
Chanc Duchy Lanc	6.3	17	7	1	12
SS for Nthn Ireland	6.3	13	7	2	9
Chief Sec, Treasury	6.3	13	7	4	8
SS Natl Heritage	6.0	7	6	5	3
SS for Transport	5.6	8	6	3	8
SS for Education	5.6	8	5	4	4
SS for Scotland	5.5	8	6	2	12
Min Agriculture	5.3	8	6	2	6
SS for Wales	5.2	7	5	2	8
SS Social Security	5.1	7	5	2	4
SS Health	5.0	8	4	2	5
SS for Environment	4.8	8	5	1	13
SS Employment	4.8	7	4	1	8
Lord Chancellor	2.9	6	5	4	3

Notes:

The first column shows the minister's mean weighted score across all the committees and sub-committees on which she sits. The second column shows the top value for each minister's weighted scores across all her committees, and the third and fourth columns show the median and lowest value. The last column shows the total number of committees and sub-committees on which the minister sits.

On this basis Cabinet ministers seem to fall into three groups. At the top of the table, the Prime Minister, Defence Secretary and Foreign Secretary all sit mainly on small and powerful committees. The Prime Minister's average influence score is 25-28 points (compared with the base level score of 100 for committees composed exclusively of Cabinet ministers), while the other two have scores half this level. The Prime Minister's chairing role largely accounts for this difference. A second group of ministers in Table 3 sit on a mixture of some small and other large committees, giving them mean scores of between 6 and 9, but with top scores in double figures. This group includes the three non-departmental ministers, the Chancellor and Chief Secretary, the Attorney General, the Home Secretary, President of Board of Trade, and Northern Ireland Secretary. The remaining Cabinet ministers are the third group. They sit solely on larger committees, almost entirely handling domestic policy, and their mean influence scores are virtually identical between 5 and 6, with only minor variations across committees.[2]

Hence the picture offered by Table 3 is of a less differentiated (perhaps more 'equal') Cabinet where the median minister has a mean score of 6.3 across the committees where they sit. Ministers' influence is fairly standardized: 15 out of 23 Cabinet members have mean scores within plus or minus 1.5 points of this median. The Prime Minister has a mean score four and a half times greater than the average minister, and the Foreign and Defence Secretaries' mean scores are both roughly twice as great. Five other ministers stand out from the crowd to a lesser extent: the Lord Privy Seal, Home Secretary, Chancellor of the Exchequer and Attorney General are more influential than the norm, while the Lord Chancellor is less involved.

There is a third way in which to assess the information on Cabinet ministers' allocations, this time looking simply at who comes into contact with whom in the committee system, rather than trying to uncover measures of relative influence. This exercise covers all full committees and all the sub-committees which included two or more Cabinet members (thereby excluding only the 'symbolic' domestic sub-committees). For each minister an interaction table was computed, showing the number of colleagues with whom their committee work brings them into contact (Appendix: Table B). With 23 ministers this table is too complex to be easily analysed. And a simple numerical comparison of contacts (as in a network analysis) would anyway be distorted, since some ministers sit on larger committees than others. Instead Table 4 abstracts the most salient details from Appendix Table B.

Whereas Tables 2 and 3 suggested basically consistent rankings of ministers, the ordering in Table 4 is quite different. Heading the list of ministers with committee links to colleagues are the Scottish Secretary (who is almost omni-present in the committee system) and the Environment Secretary (who sits on all the large domestic committees). The Chancellor of the Exchequer, Chancellor of the Duchy of Lancaster and President of the Board of Trade are also prominent. Some of the top-ranked ministers in Table 2, such as the Prime Minister, Defence Secretary and the Attorney General come well down the list on Table 4, reflecting their role on the smaller OPD committees. Other ministers at the bottom of Table 4 are the same as on Table 2, however, such as the Education, Social Security, Health and National Heritage Secretaries, and the Lord Chancellor. Their low influence

---

[2] The Lord Chancellor is the only slight exception, with a mean score below 3.

scores derive from their restricted committee places, which also reduces the
extent of their contacts with colleagues.

Table 4

**The Linkages between Cabinet Members
created by Joint Membership of
Committees and Sub-Committees**

Minister	Average linkages	Number of Colleagues with links:	
		4 or over	*1 or 0*
SS Scotland	5.7	17	0
SS Environment	5.4	17	2
Chanc Duchy Lancaster	5.0	17	1
Chancellor of Exchequer	5.0	16	1
President Bd of Trade	4.9	16	2
Lord President of Council	4.5	12	0
SS Northern Ireland	4.3	13	2
SS Transport	4.2	16	2
Home Secretary	4.0	14	2
SS Wales	4.0	13	2
Foreign Secretary	3.9	11	7
Lord Privy Seal	3.8	12	3
SS Employment	3.5	11	4
Chief Secretary	2.9	7	4
SS Defence	2.8	6	8
Minister Agriculture	2.7	9	7
SS Health	2.6	5	5
Prime Minister	2.3	5	11
SS Education	2.3	5	7
SS Social Security	2.1	4	7
Attorney General	1.9	2	9
SS National Heritage	1.9	0	7
Lord Chancellor	1.1	0	17
Average Cabinet members	3.5	9.7	3.7

Notes:

Coverage includes the 16 ministerial committees and the
five sub-committees which include multiple members of the Cabinet.

The second and third columns in Table 4 show the number of colleagues with whom each minister has more than the average of 3.5 committee link-ages, or on the other hand has colleagues with whom their committee places produce little overlap. At the top of the table, the Scottish Secretary will see over four fifths of his or her Cabinet colleagues in four or more committees, whereas the Prime Minister overlaps to this extent with only a fifth of the Cabinet (primarily those who sit on the OPD network of committees). The last column shows that the Lord Chancellor and the Prime Minister have the largest number of Cabinet colleagues with whom they barely overlap in committees, the Lord Chancellor because she or he sits on so few commit-tees, and the Prime Minister because she or he is primarily involved in the OPD network.

An interesting question is to estimate how these various dimensions of Cabinet members' committee roles feed through into the overall index of their committee influence. An appropriate method for trying to parti-tion the various factors involved is multiple regression, with each minister's weighted committee influence score acting as the dependent variable, and denoted by I. After considerable investigation three explanatory variables were entered:

- $\rightarrow$ the minister's average number of committee links to Cabinet colleagues, denoted by L;
- $\rightarrow$ the number of chairs of Cabinet committees or sub-committees held by the minister, denoted by C; and
- $\rightarrow$ a dummy variable denoted by D indicating whether the minister is involved in two or more OPD committees (scored 1) or not (scored 0): the ministers scored 1 are the Prime Min-ister, Chancellor of the Exchequer, Foreign Secretary, Defence Secretary and Attorney General.

A final dummy variable (denoted P) was included to estimate the extra influence attaching to the Prime Minister's role (score 1 for the Prime Min-ister and 0 for everyone else): this is equivalent to running the equation on the data set excluding the Prime Minister. The final equation is then:

$$I = 11.0L + 12.6C + 80.6D + 103.8P - 3.4$$

In other words, the basic expected influence score of most Cabinet mem-bers is simply 11 times their average number of committee links, minus a constant of 3.4. If they are also a committee chair then 12.6 times their number of chairs is added to their expected score. If they are a core member of the smaller OPD committees an increment of 80.6 is added to their basic score. And if they are the Prime Minister, a further increment of 103.8 is added. This model has an R^2 of 92 per cent, outperforming all the other models tested.

Yet the result needs to be interpreted very cautiously, since the number of chairs a Cabinet member has is directly built into the calculation of the overall influence score. In addition the number of committee linkages is related to the number of committee placements a minister has, and place-ments are also built into the calculation of overall influence scores. So the purpose of the regression is not to *explain* the influence scores, whose con-struction is completely artefactual. But the model does allow us to estimate numerically the relative importance of the various components of the scores as constructed. In particular it clearly demonstrates that most Cabinet ministers' committee influence depends primarily on cumulating committee positions on the larger domestic committees. By contrast, those ministers on the mainly separate OPD network gain influence from its exclusivity, while the non-departmental ministers accumulate influence by chairing committees. Finally the Prime Minister has a substantial increment of influence simply in virtue of her or his office, accounting for around two fifths of their overall committee influence score. These results can be regarded as a first ranging shot at estimating the importance of the different factors underlying committee influence.

Coalitions and the Fragmentation of Influence in the Cabinet Committee System

Despite the prominence of the Prime Minister's large lead over other ministers, his or her committee influence is by no means dominant. The Prime Minister absorbs almost 15 per cent of the total scores available, equivalent to the influence of more than three high-salience Cabinet committees. On the other hand, any two of the other 'first division' ministers can wield rather more committee influence, in addition to controlling their own important departments. If we can assume that senior and junior ministers in departments take the same positions then the combined Treasury score in Table 2 (for the Chancellor, Chief Secretary and Financial Secretary) rises to 182 points (or 10.6 per cent), while that for the Foreign Secretary and FCO Minister of State to 176 (10.2 per cent). A coalition of both departments would then push past the Prime Minister in committee influence, as would a coalition of either with the Defence Secretary. However, by the same logic a careful Prime Minister would ensure that the non-departmental ministers in the 'second division' group (the Lord President, Lord Privy Seal and Chancellor of the Duchy of Lancaster) were particularly loyal colleagues. If these three ministers always acted cohesively with the Prime Minister, the bloc would control 28 per cent of committee influence, including chairing all full Cabinet committees.

There are a number of different ways of assessing the degree of fragmentation of influence in the Cabinet committee system. One measure (the Hirschman-Hirfindahl index) derives from work on industrial concentration ratios, and has been applied to assessing the number of effective parties contesting elections (Taagepera & Shugart, 1989, pp.77-91). It entails dividing one by the sum of the squares of each ministers' share of the overall committee influence (expressed as a fraction rather than a percentage). On this basis the fragmentation of the Cabinet committee system is very high, with the number of effective actors in the system being 18. However, if we could assume that the non-departmental ministers act with the Prime Minister in one bloc, and that the Treasury, Foreign Office and Home Office ministers act cohesively in departmental mini-blocs, the number of effective actors would be rated much lower, at just over 9 (out of a Cabinet of 23).

A second approach is to ask how many ministers would be required to act together so as to control the overall operations of the Cabinet committee system. We have no definite information about what would be needed here, but it is feasible to proceed on the assumption that a winning coalition of ministers would need to assemble just over half the overall total of influence scores in the Cabinet committee system (that is more than 860 out of the 1719 points). In practice, the threshold involved is likely to be considerably lower than this, since many Cabinet ministers will choose not to become involved in issues which do not affect their departments. However, if we assume a 50.1 per cent threshold, the lessons drawn will apply to lower thresholds *pro rata*.

To assess the viability of different coalitions we assume that a set of central actors who have concerted their stance must seek the support of extra actors. If they are being rational, the central actors will seek additional support by working down the list of other ministers in the order of their influence scores ranking. In this way they will be able to construct a 'minimum winning coalition' (one commanding 50.1 per cent influence) which has the fewest number of actors in it: the smaller the number of actors in a coalition the easier it will be to construct and to maintain its cohesion.

A basic finding of considerable significance from Table 2 is that almost any winning coalition constructed in this manner (and hence including the Prime Minister and other first division ministers in it) will have seven actors. Another important criterion for assessing an individual minister's influence is how easy it is for other ministers to organize a winning coalition excluding her or him, that is, construct a *hostile* coalition. Forming a hostile coalition excluding the Prime Minister or another of the first division ministers involves recruiting a larger number of members. For example, keeping out the Prime Minister (influence score 256 points) may entail recruiting four ministers with influence scores of 70–80 points, a net increase of three people in the minimum coalition size. Similarly, excluding the Defence Secretary (influence score 138 points) may entail recruiting two ministers with influence scores of 70 points, increasing the minimum coalition size by one member. By contrast, excluding ministers lower down the rankings will rarely trigger an increase in the size of the minimum winning coalition. The difference between the sizes of a coalition involving the actor and that of a hostile coalition can be taken as indicating that minister's *advantage* in coalition forming.

Table 5 presents the salient data for coalitions where the central actors are either individual ministers or groups of ministers. The first row shows the data for the Home Secretary, the top scoring 'second division' minister in Table 2, with 4.8 per cent of total influence scores. If she recruits other ministers in the sequence in Table 2 (that is including the Prime Minister and first division ministers) then she will need six extra actors to succeed, making seven members in all. But a hostile coalition excluding the Home Secretary could also be constructed with seven actors, so her advantage is zero. If the central actor is the Foreign Secretary (or the Chancellor or Defence Secretary), because they control more of the total influence score a hostile coalition would have to be slightly larger than a friendly coalition, giving an advantage of one. And for the Prime Minister alone the advantage rises to three. Combinations of the Prime Minister and one or two other first division ministers will enjoy proportionately larger advantages.

Table 5

The Coalitional Prospects for Cabinet Ministers

Central actors	% of total scores	Extra actors needed	Size of hostile coalition	Advant-age
HS or other minister	4-5	6	7	0
FS/CE/DS	6-9	6	8	1
PM	15	6	10	3
PM + 1[FS/DS/CE]	24	5	11	4
PM + NDMs	28	3	10	3
PM + NDMs + 1[FS/DS/CE]	37	2	12	5
PM + 2[FS/DS/CE]	33	4	13	6
PM + NDMs + 2[FS/DS/CE]	45	1	–	max

Notes:

The following abbreviations are used; PM Prime Minister; FS Foreign Secretary; DS Defence Secretary; CE Chancellor of the Exchequer; NDMs the three non-departmental ministers, Lord President, Lord Privy Seal and Chancellor of the Duchy of Lancaster.

The sign / means 'or'; and + 1[...] means 'and one of'. Hence PM + 1[FS/DS/CE] means the Prime Minister and one of the Foreign Secretary or the Defence Secretary or the Chancellor of the Exchequer.

The Prime Minister may select the three leading non-departmental ministers carefully so that they act as a cohesive bloc with her or him. But although this bloc would need to recruit only three more actors to succeed, hostile coalitions could form more easily against it than against a coalition involving the Prime Minister and one of the first division ministers – because the non-departmental ministers carry less influence than the Foreign Secretary or Defence Secretary of Chancellor of the Exchequer. If the Prime Minister plus bloc can also involve at least one of first division ministers then opponents must recruit more than half of the Cabinet to outvote them. Similarly the Prime Minister plus two first division ministers requires a hostile coalition to recruit 13 Cabinet members to outweigh them. If the Prime Minister plus the non-departmental ministers can recruit any two of the Foreign Secretary or the Defence Secretary or the Chancellor of the Exchequer then no hostile coalition is feasible. The six central actors here would need to recruit only one additional voice to control the committee system, and they would already be a 'blocking coalition' in their own right, since there is insufficient weighted influence among the remaining Cabinet members to reach over 50 per cent of the total. We could strengthen these results somewhat if we assume that all the Treasury ministers (inside and outside the Cabinet) act cohesively together, as do the Foreign Office ministers.

These results throw a new light upon the experience of the 1980s, when the Prime Minister Margaret Thatcher had two rather different coalitional experiences. In the early 1980s, in coalition with her Chancellor of the Exchequer and Defence Secretary plus the non-departmental ministers, she easily pushed through her monetarist economic policies against probably a majority of her Cabinet, including two sceptical Foreign Secretaries. But from the mid 1980s until 1990, she failed to secure her own way against a coalition in favour of entering the European Exchange Rate Mechanism which included two successive Foreign Secretaries and two Chancellors of the Exchequer. As a detailed decisional study by Thompson (1994) makes clear, Thatcher could manage only a blocking rearguard action against ERM entry, and eventually conceded defeat in October 1990. There seems to be a close fit between the empirical evidence here and the conclusions suggested by Table 5.

That the Prime Minister is in a powerful coalitional position despite commanding only 15 per cent of the total influence scores in the committee system might suggest that she or he is in a position akin to that of a shareholder who manages to control a publicly quoted company despite holding much less than 51 per cent of the shares. A minority shareholder can have a controlling stake because many of the other shareholders are inactive, often because they are so fragmented that the costs of organizing prevent them exercising their formally assigned influence over the company. Something analogous often goes on in the Cabinet committee system, where ministers tend to stay out of other people's battles and look after their own department's interests first, perhaps extending a lower level of support to colleagues pushing issues which are important to that minister's particular faction within the governing party.

Many features of core executive operations in Britain reinforce this basic separatism – including the importance of departmentalism in Whitehall's 'federal' structure; the fragmentation of the committee system; and the predominance of bi-lateral deals between the Treasury and individual spending ministers in the budget process. In addition, Cabinet government conventions frown on any overt log-rolling between spending ministers and stress large-majority or 'consensus' decisions (which are virtually impossible to achieve without the consent of the Prime Minister and the other 'first division' ministers). The only ministers who have the freedom to roam more broadly over the issues that Cabinet committees consider are the Prime Minister, the non-departmental ministers, and the Chancellor of the Exchequer/Chief Secretary – who are highly likely to operate as a coalition on issues such as determining overall public expenditure levels or holding spending ministers to compliance with budget targets.

Conclusions: Committee Influence and Research on the Core Executive

Given that information on Cabinet committees has only recently become available, this study has necessarily been exploratory. The Appendix setting out alternative ways of computing committee influence scores emphasizes the need to be cautious in interpreting the numerical estimates included above. These scores should not be fetishized, nor any fine or precise significance attached to them. Their value is primarily heuristic, in providing pegs which help us to think further about the ways that Cabinet committees and ministerial influence over decision-making may be patterned. If in future some alternative construct can better perform this role – for example, if we can develop improved data about ministers' actual committee behaviour – then the indices used here will be obsolescent.

However, for the moment even the modest advances made here open up some substantial research opportunities. An obvious question is whether the 1992 pattern of committees is different from other governments or not. In recent years some good quality work on comparing across Cabinet systems has begun to be carried out.[3] There is an obvious scope for this trend to be developed further, especially since most of this work seems to lack the necessary analytic concept of the 'core executive' to guide it, and hence largely neglects to discuss committees.[4]

In Britain previous work on Cabinet committee structures has established only a basic listing of which committees existed, even in the period for which full Public Records Office files are available. Hennessy & Arends (1983) provide a full listing of 'Mr Attlee's Engine Room', the committee structure of the post-war Labour government. Even the 'standing groups' here are virtually unrecognizable in 1992 terms, with only the Defence Committee, Future Legislation, Kings Speech and Legislation Committees having any close contemporary counterparts. Even here, however, no systematic information is available about the Attlee committees' memberships, or even most of the chairs, although the number of meetings is recorded. A full listing is also given of 244 *ad-hoc* groups, only 11 of which met more than ten times.

The next available comparison point seems to be 1984, where again Hennessy (1984) provides an unofficial but broadly reliable listing of 27 Cabinet standing committees and sub-committees (excluding the 'symbolic' sub-committees which barely involve Cabinet members).[5] Comparing 1984 and 1992 shows some commonalities, notably in the Prime Minister's committees, and those of the Foreign Secretary (apart from an extra OPD sub-committee coping with the post-1989 changes in Eastern Europe) and the Home Secretary. But it also shows some differences:

---

[3] See especially, Burch, 1993.

[4] Blondel & Muller-Rommel, 1993; but Andeweg, 1993, p.34, does mention the British case as an example of 'dominated Cabinet committee arrangements'.

[5] This data is reused in Rose, 1989.

Table 6
Committee/Main Sub-Committee Chairs

Minister	1984	1992
Prime Minister	10	9
Lord President	7	4
Chanc Exchequer	6	0
Lord Privy Seal	1	5
Foreign Secretary	1	2
Home Secretary	1	1
Total	27	21

In 1984 the Lord President chaired far more of the domestic committees than the Lord Privy Seal, whereas in 1992 they split the roles more evenly. In 1984 the Chancellor of the Exchequer chaired six forums, but by 1992 none – an apparently substantial change.

However, Major's change in policy towards openness about Cabinet committees was a permanent one, and in 1993 a new listing was produced. In preparation for the winter 1993 budget a new Cabinet standing committee (EDX) was set up to decide on public expenditure cutbacks, given the prospect of a £50 billion public sector borrowing requirement: and this key committee was chaired by the Chancellor of the Exchequer. Later in 1993 a new Cabinet committee (EDR) was set up to co-ordinate the economic regeneration of the regions, further illustrating the fairly constant change in the committee structure.

The next agenda for research should be to establish comparable data about Cabinet committee memberships for the whole of the post-war period not covered by the thirty year rule. However, the Callaghan/Whitehall doctrine that committee structures were 'domestic' matters continues to exert a baneful influence. It apparently means that no revelations about committee structures inside the thirty year rule period can take place without the permission of the premier involved – which is unlikely to be forthcoming, certainly for the Thatcher and Wilson years. But as the 'open government' period stretches into the future, and as the thirty year rule progressively unrolls, so the closed gap will reduce in significance, and comparable data for the period before 1965 and after 1992 will increasingly dominate our thinking about committee government.

By maintaining complete secrecy about Cabinet committees previous British governments in the twentieth century continued the Bagehot tradition of urging citizens 'to venerate what they cannot presently comprehend'. Now that the official stance has cracked a little, the onus is on political science research to widen the gap further.

Appendix

Alternative Methods of Weighting
Committees and Members' Scores

There are potentially many other ways of assigning influence to committees and partitioning these scores amongst individual committee members. I review three sets of options:

(i) <u>Relative weighting of committees and sub-committees</u>

One obvious possibility is to weight sub-committees differently relative to full committees. Appendix Table A shows what happens to the scores of Cabinet members under various options. If sub-committees were weighted at 0.25 of the full committee score then the Prime Minister's lead over other prominent ministers would lengthen slightly, whereas if sub-committees were weighted at 0.75 or at parity with full committees then the Prime Minister's prominence would be reduced.

Only if sub-committees were weighted *above* full committees (at say, 1.25) would the Prime Minister's score be significantly pulled down towards those of other 'first division' ministers. It is possible to think of a logic for such a weighting. For example, in many administrative systems a Chinese box syndrome is created where power lies with the innermost body. Here sub-committees might pre-process and shape issues to such an extent that the full committee's decision becomes a *fait accompli*. But the only part of the Cabinet business where sub-committees carry out this role extensively is over Europe. And here assigning a weighting of 1.25 to large sub-committees reporting to the small OPD full committee seems implausible.

(ii) <u>Relative weighting of Chairs and Members</u>

A second possible area where the weightings could be changed is in the handling of the chair's influence. Treating the chair as akin to doubling that committee member's score might be a conservative estimation, and Appendix Table A shows the effects of assigning double or triple increments to committee chairs (so that the holder gets a triple or quadruple influence share respectively, and committee weightings are divided by either $N + 2$ or $N + 3$).

Predictably enough the effect is to make more pronounced the Prime Minister's lead over other high-scoring ministers, and to promote the non-departmental chairs of the domestic committees into the first division, especially the Lord Privy Seal. However, any such higher weighting for the chair seems decidedly arbitrary. In the current state of knowledge, once we move away from the intuitively plausible stance of treating the chair as simply an extra committee role, we have no basis at all for selecting an appropriate alternative.

Table A

The Committee Influence Scores of Cabinet Ministers
with different weightings for sub-committee status
and for the additional influence of chairs

	Sub Cmttees count as:				Chair's increment is:	
	0.25	0.75	1.00	1.25	2x member	3x member
PM	256	256	256	256	331	389
FS	145	165	176	186	142	133
DS	133	143	148	153	119	105
CE	104	115	121	126	97	87
HS	73	91	100	109	79	77
LPC	72	81	85	90	89	99
CDL	73	80	83	86	70	65
PBOT	66	83	92	100	68	63
LPS	71	78	82	86	97	116
Scot	58	73	80	88	61	57
AttGen	60	69	73	77	57	50
Env	54	69	73	77	58	55
NI	51	62	68	73	52	49
ChSec	54	58	60	62	52	48
Tran	39	51	57	64	42	39
Wales	39	44	47	50	39	37
Empl	32	44	50	56	36	34
MAFF	27	37	42	47	30	28
Health	22	28	31	34	23	22
Ed	20	24	26	28	21	20
SocSec	19	22	23	24	19	18
NatHer	18	18	18	18	17	16
LdChan	14	14	14	14	13	12

Notes:

All scores show the effect of making each variation within an otherwise unchanged weighting formula used in Table 2. However, when increments for chairs are increased the 'effective' actors per committee also go up from N+1 to N+2 or N+3 respectively. Variations in scores for lower-ranked ministers than those shown are minor.

(iii) Iterating the calculation of committee scores

In the main body of the paper I have presented calculations based on assuming that all full committees composed only of Cabinet members start off with the same amount of influence. It is possible to variegate the influence scores of Cabinet committees by iterating (redoing the calculations a second, third, or fourth time). Here the committee's second round influence would be varied to reflect the sum of its individual members' scores from the first round. Hence the committees with more influential ministers as members would be rated higher, and those with less influential ministers lower. The new committee scores could then be partitioned out again, and a new estimate made of ministers' influence.

Using this procedure across all committees (and a complicated formula which is too lengthy to set out here) produces rather unattractive results. Basically the OPD committees suck in influence points but at the expense of the domestic committees. The Prime Minister's score increases rapidly to start with on the second round of the iteration, but by the fifth round of the iteration it stabilizes at around 25 per cent of all influence in the Cabinet committee system. This change might seem plausible, but it also results in the Defence Secretary and Foreign Secretary each being accorded 12-13 per cent of total influence. The Chancellor's rating goes down (because she or he sits on many domestic committees), as does the influence of non-departmental ministers. In fact every domestic minister's rating is squeezed down by this across-the-board iteration.

An alternative way of iterating is to partition out the OPD and cognate committees and sub-committees and iterate only within that grouping, and similarly to iterate only within the domestic committees. This procedure prevents the OPD committees' influence from appreciating. But it also leaves ministers' rankings virtually unchanged from those shown in Table 2. The Prime Minister's score appreciates most, but by only just over one per cent. The shifts involved seems insufficient to justify adopting this much more complicated method of computing influence.

There are some important methodological issues to be considered here, which may have considerable relevance for substantive issues such as the 'segmented decision' model of how the Cabinet and core executive operate (Dunleavy & Rhodes, 1990, pp.13-15). But at present it seems that iterating the calculation of committee rankings does not produce intuitively improved results from the simpler procedures used above.

References

Andeweg, R. (1993), 'A model of the Cabinet system', in Blondel & Muller-Rommel (eds) (1993), pp.23-42.

Bell, P.N. (1989), 'Direct rule in Northern Ireland', in Rose (1989), pp.189-226.

Blondel, J. & Muller-Rommel, F. (eds) (1993), *Governing Together: The Extent and Limits of Joint Decision-making in West European Cabinets* (London: Macmillan).

Burch, M. (1993), 'Organizing the flow of business in West European Cabinets', in Blondel & Muller-Rommel (eds) (1993), pp.99-130.

Dunleavy, P. & Rhodes, R.A.W. (1990), 'Core executive studies in Britain', *Public Administration*, Volume 68 Number 1, pp.3-28.

Hennessy, P. (1984), 'Whitehall's real power house', *The Times*, 30 April.

Hennessy, P. (1986), *Cabinet* (Oxford: Blackwell, 1986).

Hennessy, P. & Arends, A. (1983), 'Mr Attlee's Engine Room: Cabinet Committee Structure and the Labour Governments, 1945-51' (Glasgow: Department of Politics, University of Strathclyde), Strathclyde Papers on Government and Politics, Number 26.

Parry, R. (1989), 'The centralization of the Scottish Office', in Rose (1989), pp.97-141.

Thomas, I.C. (1989), 'Giving direction to the Welsh Office', in Rose (1989), pp.142-88.

Rose, R. (1989) *Ministers and Ministries: A Functional Analysis* (Oxford: Clarendon Press).

Taagepera, R. & Shugart, M. (1989), *Seats and Votes* (New Haven: Yale University Press).

Thompson, H. (1994) *Joining the Exchange Rate Mechanism: Core Executive Decision-making and Macro-economic Policy, 1979-90* (London: London School of Economics and Political Science, PhD Thesis).

Table B
Linkages between Cabinet Ministers
via overlapping committee memberships

	1	2	3	4	5	6	7	8	9	10	11	12	13	14	15	16	17	18	19	20	21	22
(2) FS	8																					
(3) DS	8	–																				
(4) CE	5	9	–																			
(5) HS	4	5	7	–																		
(6) LPC	2	3	4	5	–																	
(7) CDL	3	4	2	6	5	–																
(8) PBOT	4	7	5	9	6	7	–															
(9) LPS	1	1	0	5	4	5	6	–														
(10) Scot	2	5	3	8	6	8	7	5	–													
(11) AttGen	3	5	4	8	6	8	9	8	7	–												
(12) Env	2	5	3	2	6	7	1	3	6	3	–											
(13) NI	2	5	3	6	5	6	3	2	6	10	1	–										
(14) ChSec	1	4	0	4	3	6	8	4	5	5	3	1	–									
(15) Tran	1	2	2	6	4	7	6	5	4	8	0	5	7	–								
(16) Wales	1	3	2	5	4	7	6	5	6	8	2	7	6	4	–							
(17) Empl	1	4	4	6	5	6	6	5	4	6	2	7	7	3	4	–						
(18) MAFF	1	1	2	4	5	4	5	2	4	6	1	4	5	4	4	4	–					
(19) Health	1	1	2	3	3	3	5	3	3	5	0	5	4	3	4	3	3	–				
(20) Ed	1	1	2	3	2	3	5	3	3	4	0	4	3	2	4	2	2	2	–			
(21) SocSec	1	1	2	4	3	4	5	4	4	4	0	5	2	3	2	4	1	1	4	–		
(22) NatHer	0	0	1	2	2	2	2	2	3	3	0	3	3	3	3	3	1	1	2	2	–	
(23) LdChan	0	0	0	2	1	3	2	1	3	2	2	1	1	1	1	1	1	0	1	1	1	1

Note

The cell entries show the number of committees and sub-committees where both the column and the row Cabinet ministers are members.

Hegel and Hegelianism

David Sullivan
Coleg Harlech

'Fukuyama and the Idea of Progress'

The belief in progress is a powerful motif in modern Western culture. The very idea of modernity itself incorporates a conviction that what is most recent – most modern – is in some important senses an improvement on what preceded it. Yet despite the abiding power of the belief in progress, it seems almost impossible in the last decade of the twentieth century to recapture the optimism that was so prevalent in Western Europe and the United States in the closing decade of the nineteenth century. Much that has happened in the intervening years has forced us to rethink our belief that we have progressed. And a great deal is happening at the present time which prompts us to consider whether we might yet regress further. From the Holocaust and the Gulag to the ominous resurgence of nationalism and anti-Semitism in Eastern Europe and the Balkans, Europe's hope in its own future, let alone that of the rest of the world, has been savagely tested. If belief in progress is still an option it must be buttressed with some very powerful arguments.

Many writers have claimed that no such arguments are available, and some have been driven towards a much more pessimistic view of events. Paul Kennedy's two most recent books, *The Rise and Fall of the Great Powers* and *Preparing for the Twenty-First Century*[1] are symptomatic of this pessimism – the very title of the earlier book implies a view of historical change which is far from an optimistic belief in linear progression. The enormous interest which his thesis provoked on first publication was due in no small part to the manner in which it struck a chord in the Chancelleries of Europe and the think tanks of North America.

But the belief that human society is progressing still has important and influential advocates. Most notable among its recent defenders has been Francis Fukuyama who has argued forcefully in his article 'The End of History?' and his book *The End of History and the Last Man*[2] that the idea of progress is central to our understanding of the modern world. To reject the idea of progress is, he claims, to jettison any realistic hope of understanding our present situation. Fukuyama does not believe that his arguments are particularly new, rather the opposite, he regards himself as a faithful disciple of Hegel who is doing little more than applying the master's teaching to the late twentieth century. That contention is, to say the least, controversial[3], but there are certainly genuinely Hegelian elements

---

[1] *The Rise and Fall of the Great Powers*, London: Fontana Press, 1988; *Preparing for the Twenty-First Century*, London: Harper Collins, 1993.

[2] 'The End of History?' in *The National Interest*, Number 16, Summer 1989, pp.3-18; *The End of History and the Last Man*, London: Hamish Hamilton, 1992.

[3] One extremely controversial matter is the extent to which Fukuyama is too heavily reliant on the work of Alexander Kojeve in his reading of Hegel. I shall not pursue this

in Fukuyama's work. I shall argue in this paper that Fukuyama's use of Hegel is instructive in two ways. The first is that he relates some Hegelian themes to the modern world in ways that are illuminating; and here I shall look in particular at his use of the concept of recognition. The second is a more negative comment: there is a large aspect of Hegelian thought missing from Fukuyama's theory. This absence is crucial, and I shall argue that it undermines the credibility of much of Fukuyama's position.

The central thesis of both 'The End of History?' and *The End of History and the Last Man* is that history is not only coming to an end but that the end is a positive one. This is a striking claim, and one that needs to be filled out in detail before we can properly assess its validity. In saying that the end of history is upon us, Fukuyama is arguing that the human race is moving beyond the conflicts and oppression of the past into an era of peace and freedom. He claims that a 'remarkable consensus' has emerged over 'the past few years' that liberal democracy as a system of government has 'conquered rival ideologies like hereditary monarchies, fascism and more recently communism'.[4] But it is not merely a practical political triumph which Fukuyama is arguing for. His argument is deeper, in a way that has important implications for his general perspective. At the heart of the triumph of liberal democracy is an intellectual success. Liberal democracy has emerged as the dominant ideology of the modern world. Even more than that, it has come to be recognised as the final ideology, the one that has ultimately triumphed. Because of this, no further development in political ideology is desirable or even possible. Any new political ideology which emerged as a rival to liberal democracy would inevitably be false. This is not to say that all modern states are, or soon will become, democratic, nor is it to deny that some countries which achieve a liberal democratic form of government might not, as he puts it, temporarily 'lapse back into other, more primitive forms of rule like theocracy or military dictatorship'.[5] What is central to his argument is that 'the ideal of liberal democracy' cannot be improved upon.

As we will see later, Fukuyama is not arguing that the end of history is to be understood solely in terms of the intellectual triumph of liberalism, but the intellectual victory over all possible rivals marks a crucial battle in the war. It also reflects an important Hegelian strand in Fukuyama's thought – that ideas are a dominant force in the world which give order to social and political structures.

This argument about the primacy of ideas in the political order is central to Fukuyama's belief in the inevitability of progress. But there are also other strands in his thinking, one of the most important of which is his view that modern natural science provides a vitally important contribution to human progress.

Fukuyama offers two reasons for stressing the centrality of science. The first is that science, and the technology which it produces, gives decisive

---

issue here but it is well to point out that some of the themes which are most problematic in Fukuyama – his systematic playing down of the metaphysical element in Hegel, for instance, may well be explicable in terms of the influence of Kojeve.

[4] *The End of History and the Last Man*, p.xi.

[5] *The End of History and the Last Man*, p.xi.

military advantage to those states which posses it. It might seem that that is hardly progressive. Indeed, many critics would argue that the development of modern science has been bad for humanity, not least because it has placed such powerful destructive forces in the hands of governments and the military. Fukuyama does not disagree fundamentally with this. He is not defending war but simply arguing that the impetus of modern science is so great that governments cannot afford to ignore it, not least because potential enemy states will embrace the technology. So governments continue to finance scientific research which in turn leads to further scientific progress.

The second reason for emphasising the beneficial and progressive nature of science is more positive. This is that the products of modern science and technology make peoples' lives more comfortable and more secure. Those who live in the scientifically advanced societies of the Western liberal democracies have more than ample food and clothing, good medical care: in essence, all that is needed and more, to secure the basic necessities of life. And they have the added advantage of being able to pursue intellectual and cultural activities. Scientific progress leads to the good life.

In making this claim Fukuyama is clearly assuming that there is a close relationship between scientific development and economic change. Indeed, he makes this point explicitly when he traces a close connection between advanced industrialisation, which he understands to have been created by modern natural science, and capitalism. In other words, scientific progress brings capitalism.

This much is clear and straightforward for Fukuyama. But while that relationship is clear the connection between capitalism and democracy is more problematic.

> '... [T]he relationship between economic development and democracy is far from accidental, but the motives behind the choice of democracy are not fundamentally economic. They have another source and are facilitated, but not made necessary, by industrialization ...'[6]

Fukuyama is so concerned to stress that democracy cannot be explained exclusively in economic terms that he spends time considering and rejecting three arguments which purport to show that the motives behind the choice of democracy are fundamentally economic. It will be helpful to look at these in some detail because they illustrate a good deal about his central thesis.

The first attempt to explain democracy in terms of the rise of capitalism is a functional, or pragmatic, argument. On this view, democracy has emerged because it alone is capable of mediating the complex web of conflicting interests that are created by a modern economy. The examples which are often referred to here are those such as conflicts of interest between the working class and the middle class or the difficulties raised by new groups of people claiming economic and political rights such as women or racial minorities.

Fukuyama rejects this interpretation and argues that while democracy is best at settling disputes when there is already a large measure of consensus

---

[6] *The End of History and the Last Man*, p.109.

present within a society, it is much less successful at resolving disputes where there are deep seated sectional differences within that society. In particular, democracy is poorly equipped to settle disputes between different ethnic or national groups. He points to a number of examples which he thinks illustrate his point, notably the problem of fully integrating blacks into American society.

So he rejects the argument that democracy has arisen simply as a pragmatic means of mediating between competing interest groups. The second argument which he considers and rejects shares important features with the first. This is the argument that the highly complex nature of the capitalist system makes it impossible to control other than by democratic means.

The difficulty with this view, says Fukuyama, is that it does not explain what he takes to be a central feature of history, namely that there is a universal evolution in the desire for liberal democracy.

> 'For by this account, democracy is not the *preferred outcome* of any of the groups struggling for leadership in the country. Democracy becomes instead a kind of truce between warring factions, and is vulnerable to a shift in the balance of power between them that would allow one particular group or elite to reemerge triumphant.'[7]

In other words, this interpretation makes democracy a by-product of economic development and not an end to be desired for its own sake.

The third, and in Fukuyama's view the most powerful, line of argument linking economic development with the progress towards liberal democracy is the claim that successful industrialization produces an educated middle-class whose members demand political participation. Because industrially advanced societies need these skilled and educated workers the views of these workers have to be taken into consideration and as a consequence society gradually liberalises.

This argument assumes that education leads to the inculcation of liberal values. Fukuyama seeks to rebut this by pointing out that there is no necessary connection between education and liberalism. As in the first two arguments, democracy is not something which emerges as a by-product of some other force. However, Fukuyama does not push this counter argument very strongly, partly because he recognises considerable value in the claim that education can be a very important force in helping democracy to emerge. In so far as education is understood as an economic force – workers have to be educated to a high level in order for capitalism to function efficiently – Fukuyama cannot accept that it is an explanation for the emergence of democracy. However, seen as a means of enabling people to use reason more effectively, and to articulate their values and desires more cogently, education is very much a contributory factor in the development of democracy.

Fukuyama's crucial point is that democracy is not explicable as the by-product of economic forces, rather it is sought for its own sake, because it embodies values which men and women aspire to. This explains why

---

[7] *The End of History and the Last Man*, p.136. Italics in the original.

liberal democracy has succeeded, not only as the most successful political system in the modern world but also and, more importantly, as the dominant political ideal. If it were merely the pragmatic by-product of economic forces there would be no guarantee that its success would be anything more than transitory. It would be quite plausible to assume that as economic conditions change democracy would cease to be useful and its place could be taken by some other political system more suited to the needs of the economy. For Fukuyama, democracy has to be desired (and be desirable) for its own sake. More than that, it not only has to embody values which people aspire to, it has to do so better than any other possible political system or theory.

This being the case, the nature of such values becomes a cardinal question. Unless Fukuyama can provide a powerful set of values to bear the weight that his system requires of them his theory will collapse. He is, of course, aware of this, and in his attempt to provide an explanation Fukuyama introduces the Hegelian concept of recognition, which he claims is a key concept in making sense of the contemporary world. We can best approach his account of recognition by seeing how he introduces it in the context of the dialectic.

Fukuyama utilises the concept of dialectic to emphasise that everything contains within itself internal contradictions. As these contradictions work themselves out they give rise to a newer and higher reality, and it is these contradictions which propel history forward. As the internal contradictions in each historical epoch are overcome in a higher phase of social and political life, so a new social structure is inaugurated at a richer and more integrated level. The end of history will be reached when there no longer any significant contradictions in society. Fukuyama claims, of course, that liberal democracy is the society at the end of history, from which all significant contradictions have disappeared. But what does this claim mean? Most importantly, what could count as 'significant contradictions'?

Fukuyama's answer is clear.

> 'We could recognise a contradiction if we saw a source of social discontent sufficiently radical to eventually cause the downfall of liberal democratic societies ... as a whole. It is not sufficient to point to "problems" in contemporary liberal democracies, even if they are serious ones like budget deficits, inflation, crime, or drugs. A "problem" does not become a "contradiction" unless it is so serious that it not only cannot be solved within the system, but corrodes the legitimacy of the system itself such that the latter collapses under its own weight. ... Conversely, we can argue that history has come to an end if the present form of social and political organization is *completely satisfying* to human beings in their most essential characteristics.'[8]

What are we to make of this argument? One problem with it is that Fukuyama seems to play down the reality of at least some of the problems which plague modern liberal democratic societies. Budget deficits may

---

[8] *The End of History and the Last Man*, p.136. Italics in original.

be things that come and go and inflation can be brought under control –
but these are, in the last analysis, technical problems. Crime and drugs
are a different matter – they raise profound moral issues. Are the hor-
rendous problems of crime and drug abuse which exist in America's inner
cities merely technical problems something like the budget deficit or inflation which the right management strategies on the part of government can
solve? Or do they reveal deeper contradictions within that society?

I think that in many cases Fukuyama does play down the importance
of specific social and political problems. This is significant for his overall
position because it reveals a reluctance on his part to take sufficiently seriously many of the darker features of the modern world. This reluctance is
symptomatic of a deeper problem to which I shall return later in the paper.

Despite these reservations about how the seriousness which Fukuyama
accords to some problems, the last sentence of the quotation brings us back
to his contention that that it is a desire to express the correct values that
lies at the heart of progress. It is at this point that Fukuyama introduces
the concept of recognition.

Fukuyama begins his account of recognition by referring to a key passage
in the *Phenomenology*, where Hegel introduces the idea of a primitive first
man at the dawn of history. This first man shares with the animals certain
basic natural desires such as the desire for food, sleep, shelter and, above all,
for the preservation of his own life. But the first man is radically different
from the animals in that he is also a social being who needs to be recognised
by other people. His own sense of self-worth and identity is intimately
connected with the value that other people place upon him, upon their
willingness to recognise his value as a human being. The most fundamental
way in which a man can assert his own value, and be recognised as a man
by others, is through risking his life. Thus his encounter with other men
leads to a violent struggle in which each seeks to make the other recognise
him by risking his own life. This can lead to one of three results.

First, it can lead to the death of both of the combatants, in which case,
obviously neither succeeds in being recognised. Secondly, it can lead to the
death of one of the combatants. This is an undesirable outcome for the
victor because he is still left with no one to recognise him – he is no closer
to having his humanity recognised than he was before the battle. Thirdly,
it can terminate when one of the combatants surrenders to the other and
agrees to submit to a life of servitude rather than face the risk of violent
death. 'The master is then satisfied', Fukuyama argues, 'because he has
risked his life and received recognition for having done so from another
human being'.[9]

Fukuyama does not claim that this violent battle ought to be recreated
in modern society, any more than Hegel does. What he does claim is that
the desire to be recognised as a human being with dignity, worth and value
in one's own right, is one of the major forces at work in human history.
Progress is in large part defined by Fukuyama as the process of developing
social and political organisations which allow men and women to have their
worth recognised. Modern liberal democratic society is the most progressive

---

[9] *The End of History and the Last Man*, p.147.

because it provides this recognition in a better way than any other possible society.

Hegel's use of the concept of recognition in his work is certainly powerful and suggestive, but Fukuyama is not content with using it by itself. Instead he seeks to enhance the concept's usefulness for his purposes by introducing alongside it Plato's concept of *thymos*.

A precise translation of the Greek word 'thymos' is not easy to render. On some occasions it is translated as 'spiritedness' at other times as dignity, courage, self-respect or honour. Fukuyama's use of the term focuses on his view that men and women are motivated not only by economic and material concerns, but also from a sense of their own dignity and worth, and a desire to have that recognised. It is this, he claims, which lies at the heart of the movement towards democracy. 'If human beings were nothing but reason and desire (the other two elements of the soul which Plato identifies), they would be perfectly content to live in a South Korea under military dictatorship, or under the enlightened technocratic administration of a Francoist Spain, or in a Guomindang-led Taiwan, hell-bent on rapid economic growth. And yet, citizens of these countries are something more than desire and reason: they have a thymotic pride and belief in their own dignity, and want that dignity to be recognised, above all by the government of the country they live in.'[10] He makes the same point about civil rights in the United States and apartheid in South Africa.

Fukuyama's concern with *thymos* is important. If there is a thymotic element in human nature then it may indeed help to explain the desire which many people do appear to have to have their inherent worth and dignity recognised by their governments. It also helps to highlight an important aspect of the concept of recognition, which is that people often have to strive actively to achieve a society in which their dignity is recognised. It is not enough to passively wait for such a society to emerge; the spirited activism of people committed to ending injustice is also necessary. Such an argument fits in well with Fukuyama's claim that progress towards liberal democracy does not come about as the by-product of economic fires but as a consequence of being desired for its own sake.

The idea of *thymos* has a powerful, positive role to play in Fukuyama's account of progress. Yet as he recognises, there are also darker sides to the concept. He refers to two problems in particular. The first is that people may not only desire recognition as equals, but may come to desire that they be recognised as superior to others. They may well seek to become masters and to enslave others. The second problem emphasises the opposite danger, that people will become so concerned to prevent others achieving a greater recognition than they have that they will insist on an egalitarianism which is so unnatural that it can only be imposed by an authoritarian state. Fukuyama is so concerned to highlight these dangers that he invents two new terms to describe them, *megalothymia* and *isothymia*.

'The desire to be recognized as superior to other people we will henceforth label with a new word with ancient Greek roots,

---

[10] *The End of History and the Last Man*, p.206.

megalothymia. ... Its opposite is isothymia, the desire to be recognized as the equal of other people.'[11]

This is not a merely intellectual recognition of possible misuses of the thymotic element. Fukuyama sees two major political forces of the modern world as exemplifying these two dangers in virulent form and with catastrophic results.

The first is these is nationalism, which he sees as 'very much a manifestation of the desire for recognition, arising out of thymos'.[12] What the nationalist craves is not primarily economic well being but recognition for his or her own nation as a nation among others. For this the nationalist will be willing to endure all manner of hardships, even the deathly struggle of war. In a powerful passage Fukuyama compares the nationalist with the aristocratic master in Hegel's account of the first man.

> 'In a sense nationalism represents a transmutation of the megalothymia of earlier ages into a more modern and democratic form. Instead of individual princes struggling for personal glory, we now have entire nations demanding recognition of their nationhood. Like the aristocratic master, these nations have shown themselves willing to accept the risk of violent death for the sake of recognition.'[13]

It is necessary to temper Fukuyama's comments with the fact that there are different kinds of nationalism, not all of which are aggressive in the way that he suggests they are.[14] But directed against many forms of nationalism of this century, current as well as past, the comment is perceptive and compelling.

Fukuyama makes an equally important criticism of what he takes to be representative of the other extreme misuse of *thymos*. He refers to this as 'the Marxist project', though in fact his criticisms apply not to all forms of Marxism but most specifically to the Soviet Union and those other countries which became communist in this century. Whereas nationalism is characterised by megalothymia, Marxism is distinguished by *isothymia*. It seeks to promote an extreme form of social equality at the expense of liberty, by eliminating what Fukuyama regards as natural inequalities.

> 'All future efforts to push social equality beyond the point of a "middle class society" must contend with the failure of the Marxist project. For in order to eradicate those seemingly "necessary and ineradicable" differences, it was necessary to create a monstrously powerful state.'[15]

---

[11] *The End of History and the Last Man*, p.182.

[12] *The End of History and the Last Man*, p.201.

[13] *The End of History and the Last Man*, p.201.

[14] One important distinction in the discussion of nationalism is that between the liberally oriented *risorgimento* nationalism of people such as Mazzini and Ghandi and the integral nationalism which lies at the heart of many fascist movements. Fukuyama's arguments are more relevant to the second than to the first. For an influential discussion of this distinction see Peter Alter, *Nationalism*, translated by Stuart Mckinnon-Evans, London: Edward Arnold, 1989.

[15] *The End of History and the Last Man*, p.293.

As with nationalism, Fukuyama's point about a certain variant of Marxism, which was very successful in forcing itself on large parts of the human race for a substantial part of the twentieth century, is an important one – the rulers of the Soviet Union and its ideological acolytes around the world did impose a monstrously oppressive state onto their subjects.

But acknowledging the force of Fukuyama's argument does not mean accepting his optimistic conclusions about the triumph of liberalism. Given the power of these two forces in the twentieth century, and given that in Fukuyama's view they represent the two extremes of *thymos*, what confidence do we have that such extremes will not occur again? Why, in other words, should we assume that liberal democracy has really tamed *thymos*? This brings us to Fukuyama's discussion of the last man who will emerge at the end of history. The thymotic element in man has always lead him in the past to struggle against dangers and problems, and in doing so he gained the self-esteem which came through others' and recognition of him. The person who wished to prove his own humanity, as the first man proved it in the primeval struggle to the death, could do so most emphatically by going to war. Hegel, indeed, thought that wars were essential for the on-going health of societies, when people could not only prove themselves as human beings but also identify all the more closely with their own society. At the end of history wars will, in Fukuyama's view, cease. What will happen to men and women when they no longer have great challenges to stretch them?

One possibility is that the last man will lose an essential aspect of his humanity when he no longer needs to struggle. But there is also a darker possibility – the danger that men who are no longer presented with great challenges – with great deeds to do – will become dissatisfied and restless. If that is so, perhaps liberal democracy will be overthrown by people seeking to prove themselves in something akin to the original battle for recognition.

The single most important defence against this happening and plunging the world back into the chaos of history is, in Fukuyama's view, the mechanism of modern technology and economic development and the enormous benefits which they bring.

In saying that events are progressing towards the end of history Fukuyama does concede that there might be temporary setbacks. But such setbacks can be no more than temporary because they would mean 'a break with this powerful and dynamic economic world, and an attempt to rupture the logic of technological development'.[16] He cites Japan and Germany in the 1930s and early 1940s as countries which for a time were driven by a desire for national recognition to wage wars in the attempt to secure their superiority over other states. But, very significantly, he argues that they were also driven by a desire to secure their economic future, and that 'subsequent experience' demonstrated 'that economic security was much more easily obtained through liberal free trade than through war, and that the path of military conquest was utterly destructive of economic values'.

There are two particular problems with this argument which in turn bring us to a fundamental difficulty with Fukuyama's position.

The first problem is that Fukuyama is giving a confusing (and perhaps

---

[16] *The End of History and the Last Man*, p.336.

a confused) account of the relationship between economic progress and the desire for recognition. As we saw when discussing Fukuyama's account of the relationship between liberal democracy and capitalism, it is the desire for recognition which is most important and, while economic progress may run parallel with the progress towards liberal democracy the former cannot supersede the latter. Usually Fukuyama is clear that economic progress cannot guarantee progress towards liberal democracy, and that to the contrary, it is liberal democracy which ultimately guarantees economic progress. But there are times, as in the above examples of Germany and Japan, where this relationship comes close to being reversed.

This leads to the second problem. If recognition has to be defined and understood separately from economic and scientific matters, what guarantee is there that the urge for recognition may not go off in different directions from those laid out by economic and scientific progress? Fukuyama's claim that they all share the same long term goals is no more than a unjustified claim – what arguments could be used to bolster his position?

This second problem may be approached from a different angle. As we have seen, Fukuyama conflates the Hegelian concept of *recognition* with the Platonic concept of *thymos*. However Plato's account of *thymos* in the *Republic* is by no means unproblematically positive. In his discussion of reason, desire and thymos in *Republic*, Book IV, Plato claims that in the just man thymos will be the servant of reason, as the auxiliaries in the state are the servants of the philosopher rulers. But even here Plato allows that sometimes thymos might become more dominant than reason and lead to unjust actions. More significant, for our present purposes, is the fact that in the discussion of imperfect societies in Book XVIII it is thymos which first leads people away from the just state. The timarchic man is precisely the man who has allowed thymos to predominate in his soul, with the consequence that reason has been dethroned.

So *thymos* properly controlled by reason, the faithful auxiliary of reason as Plato puts it, is an important part of the soul – but it must not be allowed to act independently. When it does so it becomes dangerous. But what is meant by reason? It cannot be scientific knowledge or economic theory, because, as we have seen, Fukuyama regards these as distinct from the thymotic striving for recognition. In fact, Fukuyama has no deeper explanation of what motivates the striving for recognition than simply the observation, on his part, that recognition is a powerful factor in human life.

The depth of Fukuyama's problem becomes more apparent when we contrast his position with Hegel's. Hegel's answer to the question of what motivates the struggle for recognition, and makes of it something positive and creative but also directed towards an ultimate goal, is an answer at the metaphysical level – that Spirit is at work through history, using human endeavours for its greater purposes. In Hegel's system, any idea of a permanent reversal of history is made impossible precisely because the whole process of empirically observable historical change is grounded in the metaphysical doctrine of Spirit. Ultimately, observable historical progress is only the outer appearance of a more profound movement, which Hegel variously describes using such terms as the will of Providence or the rule of

Reason. He makes the point explicitly in the *Introduction to the Philosophy of History* –

> '[t]he only thought which philosophy brings with it, in regard to history, is the simple thought of Reason – the thought that Reason rules the world, and that world history has therefore been rational in its course.'[17]

The importance of this argument becomes apparent when we consider again Fukuyama's claim that we are approaching the end of history, and have been since the latter half of the eighteenth century. From a purely empirical perspective the history of the time between then and now has not been such as to bear this out. Quite to the contrary, human societies have become if anything more barbaric and irrational. Nationalism in its extreme fascist form has brought untold misery to the world, and continues to do so. It is a common place to quote the Holocaust as an example of the barbarity of the Twentieth Century, but Fukuyama's discussion of that appalling event shows the problem it poses for an optimistic view of human history.

Fukuyama argues that the Holocaust does not provide a counter example to the idea of historical progress. Rather, he claims, it as a unique event brought about by the conjunction of specific circumstances in Germany in the 1920s and 1930s. But this is false because the Holocaust is not uniquely evil. Fukuyama himself mentions Pol Pot and Stalinism.[18] We can certainly add others, not least the ethnic cleansing in Bosnia. Why should we see these as atypical, as somehow out of the mainstream of the twentieth century? Such an attitude seems in many ways bizarre, why would anyone want to argue that they are not a central feature of the modern world?

For Hegel, it would be possible to argue that such appalling phenomena do not disprove the claim that history is progressive by appealing to his doctrine of Spirit. Indeed, his account of progress is explicitly presented as a theodicy in which the sometimes apparently inexplicable evils that occur are explained in terms of the inscrutable will of Providence. Set against such a background these evils are seen to be part of a greater overall purpose which includes the ultimate good of the human race – the cunning of reason is at work even though many who are its instruments have no sense of its ultimate goal. This is not to deny that there are difficulties with Hegel's attempt to provide such an account of history, what I am concerned to stress here is that Hegel does not have to ignore the reality of evil in the world. Evils such as the Holocaust can be seen from an Hegelian perspective not as unfortunate aberrations to be ignored in explaining human affairs but as real and constant dangers to be avoided.

Because Fukuyama rejects the metaphysical account of Spirit, which he redefines in a highly reductionist way as 'universal human consciousness'[19], he is left with little with very little to justify his optimism. But more

---

[17] See *Elements of the Philosophy of Right*, translated by E.H.Nisbet and edited by A.W.Wood, Cambridge: Cambridge University Press, 1992, Sections 341-60, and *Introduction to the Philosophy of History*, translated by L.A.Rauch, Hackett, 1988. The quotation is from *Introduction to the Philosophy of History*, p.12.

[18] *The End of History and the Last Man*, p.128.

[19] *The End of History and the Last Man*, p.60.

important then that, his persistence in maintaining such optimism blinds him to much of the horror of the modern world. The crimes and drug abuse which are endemic in America's inner cities are technical problems to be solved by good will and the proper application of reason. Evils such as the Holocaust, which are too great to be categorised in this way, are shunted aside as unrepeatable aberrations which arose through a unique set of circumstances. Such a view is potentially very dangerous. At the least it can lead to a naïve and partial interpretation of events, at the worst it can cause politicians to act unrealistically in situations which are deeply precarious.

Fukuyama's position is full of insights – the centrality of the drive for recognition, the power of *thymos*, the reassertion of the potential that modern science has to be beneficial to humanity – but the lack of an overall core concept linking them together undermines the overall tenability of his argument. It may be, of course, that no one central core concept is available. Hegel doctrine of Spirit is, to say the least, problematic, and his aim to justify the ways of God to a mankind suffering in a dangerous and volatile raises the most acute problem in the philosophy of religion. Perhaps the idea of progress is itself untenable.

The Political Agenda in Eastern Europe and Russia

Neil Robinson
University of York

: "Have Model, Will Travel":
Russian and Western Reform Agendas'

Introduction

In a short book published towards the end of last year, two American economists, Walter Adams & James Brock, explored two approaches to economic reform in the former Eastern bloc through the medium of a fictional dialogue between a 'Prime Minister' and an itinerant American 'advisor'. The 'Prime Minister' is concerned with the social turmoil that might result from too direct an attack on existing economic and social institutions. Although he sees the need for reform, he argues for sensitivity and worries that Western experts are too like 'medieval doctors, who – no matter what the ailment – prescribed the same remedy: apply leeches and bleed the patient'. The 'advisor' on the other hand is a neo-liberal with blind and total faith in the market, Adam Smith and the 'economic' rationality of all people. He sees no need to take account of existing practices or institutions since he believes that the laws of economics, like the laws of physics, apply everywhere (Adams & Brock, 1993: 10, 5).

Adams & Brock's characters successfully give a flavour of two of contrasting positions that can be taken on economic reform. However, we would be hard put to match their fictional 'Prime Minister' and 'advisor' to Russian reality. Instead of fundamental differences over reform, there was an almost complete convergence between the views of foreign advisors, both independents and bureaucrats from international financial institutions (IFIs), and the Russian government. This convergence meant that the Russian government's proposals for economic reform were not, no matter what they claimed, a specific, Russian agenda for change. The government's agenda was worked out with, and reflected, the concerns and prejudices of Western agencies, governments and theories. In the ensuing pages I shall try to analyze why the agendas of the Russian government and the West converged and what effect this has had on Russia's political development. Essentially, I see the failure of the Russian government to develop its own agenda as a result of the Russian leadership's need for strong and legitimate leadership in the wake of the failed August coup of 1991. The agenda proffered by the West legitimised strong government and offered (in theory) a quick fix to economic decline and the destruction of the remaining vestiges of the old regime. But the converged agendas had to prompt opposition to the Yeltsin government because they entailed massive dislocations in existing social, economic and political relations. The net result was the turmoil that marked Russian politics between 1991 and the destruction of the old Russian parliaments in October 1993.

The Path to Convergence: Western Plans and Russian Needs

The Western reform package that the Russian government was eventually to try to implement was worked out for the Soviet government under Gorbachev. The convergence between Russian and Western reform agendas was therefore accidental to a degree: IFIs produced a plan for reform and a set conditions for the receipt of aid that was acceptable to Western governments just as a government was coming to power in Russia which needed an economic policy that would fulfil certain tasks and was legitimated by the international community. The plan that the Russian government was to accept was worked out by the IMF, the World Bank, the European Bank for Reconstruction and Development (EBRD) and the OECD in response to a request from the Houston G-7 summit in July 1990. These IFIs produced two documents, a three volume study of the Soviet economy and a shorter summary of findings and recommendations (IFI, 1991, 1990). These documents represented the first multi-national attempt to draw up a framework for market transition in Russia and have since formed the basis for all the main international plans to reform the Russian economy (cf. IMF, 1992, World Bank, 1993). The joint plan presented by the IFIs found favour with Western governments for two reasons.

First, the IFI proposals did not threaten Western states with too great or too immediate a financial burden. The IFIs' joint plan set out firm economic conditions for the receipt of aid. Their recommendations asserted that only radical economic reform could have an effect and secure the transformation of the Soviet economy, and the receipt of most types of aid was linked to the pursuit of such reform (IFI, 1990: 18-19, 47-48). Since the plan described Gorbachev's reform plans as having a 'relatively gradualist approach' and stated that 'the date on which far-reaching reform will be introduced is not now know', the immediate outlay expected of Western states through IFIs was low (IFI, 1990: 12, 48). This was doubtless welcome to Western states, none of which wanted or could accept responsibility for financing the Russian transition. Although estimated costs for financing the Soviet transition varied, they were high.[1] Accepting the IFIs' proposals shared the cost of assisting the USSR, set the amount of aid required at a lower level than many independent estimates, and many of the types of aid that were suggested were potentially of relatively low cost[2] or were non-governmental.[3]

Second, the IFIs' proposals were attractive to Western states because they were broadly supportive of the political *status quo* in the USSR. Although the proposals recognised the process of national disintegration that was afflicting the USSR and becoming Gorbachev's overriding concern, they were based on the assumption that all-Union markets would be maintained, that policy mechanisms like fiscal regulation would remain in the hands of the central state and that there would be a general clarification of powers *inside* the existing federal system. The IFIs' proposals could therefore

---

[1] See, for example, Collins & Rodrick, 1991.

[2] Such as technical assistance, food aid and project assistance (IFI, 1990: 47-48).

[3] Such as foreign direct investment (IFI, 1990: 47-48).

be presented as a bulwark against the disintegration of the USSR and the dangers of a strategic vacuum that would follow.

The IFIs' proposals therefore legitimated Western inactivity, the West's preoccupation with Gorbachev's political fortunes and his preoccupation with the survival of the Soviet Union as an integral unit. They provided little in the way of substantial support for Gorbachev's efforts, however. There was no way that the types of reform that the IFIs proposed could be implemented. The radical strategy proposed by the IFIs envisaged reform as a two stage sequence. In the first, stage a 'strong macroeconomic stabilization program' would be introduced to cut the budget deficit to 2 to 3% of GDP. Concomitant with this would be price deregulation, the privatisation of small economic concerns the establishment of a legal framework for property ownership, the deregulation of foreign trade, the commercialisation (subjection to market forces) of large enterprises, the de-monopolisation of production and the reorganisation of financial services. In the second stage, prices would be fully deregulated, privatisation and the de-statisation of economic management would be completed (IFI, 1990: 18 *passim*). This was broadly the same sequencing for reform that the Balcerowicz government in Poland was beginning to pursue (Lipton & Sachs, 1990). However, unlike Balcerowicz, Gorbachev did not have the power, the authority or the inclination to force through a reform package of this type. Gorbachev's commitment to radical economic reform was shaky, and his statements on the economy showed a preference for a combination of Soviet socialism and an idealized, politically neutral market, rather than for a full-scale assault on the Soviet economic system (Gorbachev, 1989). Moreover, although the IFIs' proposals were broadly supportive of the maintenance of the USSR as a integral political unit, Gorbachev, ironically, could not hope to accept their proposals and preserve the Union. At the very moment that the IFIs' proposals were issued, he was becoming dependent upon the support of conservatives in his struggle with the republics (the so-called 'turn to the right' of late 1990/early 1991) and the Russian republican government, his main opponent, had accepted a reform programme in September 1990 that was far more in tune with the IFIs' proposals. (Miller, 1993: 169-171, Shatalin et al, 1990, *Pravda*, 12 September 1990). Gorbachev could not therefore accept IFI proposals for reform since to have done so would have meant the loss of the support base he was trying to build and would have conceded too much to the Russian government.

The IFIs' proposals therefore remained just that, proposals. For them to come off the drawing-board and become the basis for actual policies, a government had to come to power that was not only committed to economic reform, but which was also in need of a programme that had and gave a wider legitimacy than it could itself produce. The Russian government that seized full power after the failed hardline coup of August 1991 was such a government. Although, as has already been mentioned, the Russian government had been committed to radical economic reform from September 1990, it needed to move beyond this and accept the IFIs' proposals as the basis of its policies because of its weak legitimacy. In its struggles with the central Soviet state, the Russian government had been able to legitimate its actions by nationalist and anti-communist appeals. These had served to make Yeltsin the most popular politician in Russia by the time of the August coup, but they were no longer sufficient. Although the government, like all other political forces, was to continue to try to appropriate symbols of 'Russianness' to diminish the claims of other groups to a say in the course of Russia's development (Urban, 1993), Yeltsin could not be certain of lasting popularity if there was no transformation of the economic fortunes of the Russian people because of the incompleteness of the anti-communist revolution and the absence of a clearly defined constituency for radical economic reform. The incomplete nature of the anti-communist revolution prevented the government claiming legitimacy (in a Weberian sense) since it could easily be denied that it had the right or power to rule all of the territory of the new Russian nation-state, indeed that there was such a thing as a Russian nation-state. The anti-communist revolution was incomplete because of the natural, uneven effect of Gorbachev's *perestroika*. Political change in reforming communist systems develops an evolutionary momentum from below, but the economic reforms that a communist regime embarks upon do not necessarily lead to marketization and are far more dependent upon party leadership for implementation than political reform (Hasegawa, 1992: 69). Because of this fundamental difference between political and economic reform, parts of the Soviet power structure were able to survive *perestroika* and increase their autonomy. Local political élites moved from ruling through party committees to ruling through local Soviets and their executives (McAuley, 1992). Local economic élites (managers of state enterprises) converted the partial autonomy that they had gained under the 1987 'Law on State Enterprises' into ownership by renegotiating the legal status of enterprises and transferring the 'residual rights of control' from the Soviet state into their own hands (Johnson & Kroll 1991: 283).

There was therefore a powerful constituency opposed to radical economic reform already in place before any reform had taken place or been accepted. This constituency could reject the writ of the new central Russian government with ease and in many ways (Hanson, 1993) and even threaten, as many local authorities were to do, to secede from the Russian Federation. A clearly defined constituency for radical economic reform to counter this opposition could only be created by successful reform empowering the emerging private sector and stopping the immiseration of the population. The situation was made worse by the fact that except for the presidency, the political institutions that emerged from the *perestroika* period were unstable and unsuitable for the task of conducting economic reform. The Russian parliaments, the Congress of People's Deputies (CPD) and the Supreme Soviet, had largely completed their progressive function by the time of the August 1991 coup. In 1990-1991, the parliaments had provided a focus for the diverse and pluralistic opposition to the party-state and provided the legislative means with which to set up barriers to the central Soviet government's exercising of its powers. However, the parliaments were fractious and weak institutions that reflected the frailty of the emerging multi-party system. Democratic Russia, the umbrella group of reformist deputies, was a solidarity organisation which contained a mass of very different politicians and interest groups. When these groups and deputies had a common purpose or a clear objective against the central state, Democratic Russia was successful and the parliaments moved the cause of reform forwards. But after, and in between, its successes, Democratic Russia was subject to internal divisions and splits which effected the movement's ability to organise into a mass party and weakened Yeltsin's control over parliament.[4] These divisions, plus the unwieldy size of the CPD and the presence of a large number of deputies who owed allegiance not to Yeltsin but to the factions that succeeded the Communists of Russia bloc in the parliaments, meant that making economic policy through the parliaments would have been difficult, perhaps even impossible The only existing institution capable of formulating and implementing radical economic reform without prevarication was the Russian presidency that Yeltsin had won in June 1991. But the post of president was no more legitimate a political institution than the parliaments: both were elected by direct franchise and whilst Yeltsin was the most popular politician, the powers of the office that he held it were dependent upon the CPD which had the power to change the Constitution.

Yeltsin, as President, therefore needed to both accumulate power to reform, and to acquire a greater legitimacy for his reformist actions. Securing power was to prove relatively easy in the short-term. In the turmoil after the August 1991 coup, the Russian parliaments were unable to resist granting him additional powers. On 1 November 1991, Yeltsin was assigned the power to rule by decree by the CPD until the end of 1992. On 6 November 1991 he decreed himself prime minister and began to appoint his own cabinet without having to bother with obtaining parliamentary assent. However, this power still had to be used its use viewed as legitimate and opposition overcome.

Accepting the IFIs' proposals would, it was hoped, confer legitimacy because of the international backing for these proposals. As Aleksei Mozhin (1993: 65, 71), the Head of the Council Of Ministers of Russia Department for Interaction with International Financial Institutions, was to admit, the government had 'three main reasons for' entering into negotiations with the IMF: first, it wished 'to gain valuable experience', second it wished 'to gain international support for its economic policy' and, third, it believed that 'on the basis of international support' it would 'gain political support at home for its economic policy'. It would gain this support in two ways. First, international support allowed it to claim competence. If the government's reform plans were broadly the same as those of IFIs, it could refer to them, the international community and to their experience of managing capitalism, to justify its actions.[5] Second, the conditionality of aid reinforced the straight-forward possibility of legitimation by reference to the authority of IFIs and Western governments by making disagreement with the government's reform package more difficult. Any argument or policy proscription advanced against radical economic reform could be condemned as irresponsibly threatening the receipt of foreign funds.

Consenting to the IFIs' proposals for reform therefore gave the Russian

---

[4] See Hosking et al 1992: 88-100, Sakwa, 1993: 156-157.
[5] See Sachs 1993: 159, for a patronising argument along these lines.

government a broad number of arguments with which to justify its actions. These arguments could also be, and were, used to justify the power of the political institutions and agents that sought to implement radical economic reform, Yeltsin the President, and his government under the general direction of Yegor Gaidar. The IFIs' proposals demanded that there be a strong political centre to carry out reform. The sequencing of radical economic reform (first price liberalisation and budgetary stabilisation, then privatisation) required that there be a clear control over economic mechanisms and a dedicated pursuit of reform if it was to have a chance of success.[6] Moreover, this sequencing of reform also seemed to offer the chance to balance quickly the remaining power of old élites too. Launching reform in two stages promised the re-engineering of Russian society and of economic, social and political relationships. The rapid liberalisation of prices and associated monetarist policies would, it was assumed, mop up the excess cash held by Russian citizens, cut the state budget deficit by ending subsidies and stimulate the flow of goods to consumers by providing profit incentives and a knowledge of market prices to producers. These measures and changes would, it was hoped, help bring inflation under control and begin to promote basic forms of market exchange for all economic units by either 'commercialising' them (major economic enterprises) or privatising them (small concerns and retail outlets) and by forcing them to be efficient. This would begin to transform the nature of production and the relationships between state, management and labour. To enable their enterprises to survive the first stage of reform, managers would have to start making harsh economic decisions because the soft-budget subsidies of central planning would be removed. Instead of relying on the state, they would be made dependent on private investment and credit and would have to cut costs by becoming efficient users of capital and labour. The weaknesses and inability to compete of those who refused to reform would be exposed by this and change forced upon industrial management before any sector of society gained extensive (legal) property rights. In some sectors, the power of industrialists would be broken totally since they would be forced out of business or removed by a frustrated labour force that found itself impoverished by managerial inability to cope with the new economic environment. As industries were forced out of business and had to shed the provision of utilities to workers, the relative power of foreign capital (helped by the liberalisation of foreign trade) and of the new entrepreneurs from the nascent private sector would grow. This would consolidate the development of a labour market and balance the power of the old managerial stratum with a new economic class that could act as a social constituency for the government.

Launching economic reform with price liberalisation and currency stabilisation before the de-statisation and privatisation of industry would therefore, it was hoped, both disenfranchise a part of the old economic élite, break up their relationship with workers and unreformed regional political élites, to whom managers would no longer be able to turn for aid, and change the conditions under which those parts of the old élite that managed to survive

---

[6] For details of the strategy see Gaidar & Matyukhin, 1992, Fischer, 1992, Lipton & Sachs, 1992.

the transition to a market exercised their power. The belief that this change in the structure of economic power would be brought about meant that the government would be able to be relatively openhanded about the form of the second stage of economic reform, privatisation. Because managers would have an entirely new relationship to the state and, as the 'survivors' of first stage of reform, would have some vested interest in the continued existence of the government, the government would be able to reward those who adapted to the market. Who ended up finally owning and running industry was not important. What mattered to the reformers was the establishment of market conditions that would force whoever ended up running industry to be 'efficient' capitalists supporting the government and its market policies, rather than as a dependent group of inefficient supplicants for economic aid and state intervention (Chubais & Vishnevskaya, 1993: 90-94, Russian Government, 1992: 77-78).

Acceptance of Western ideas about the sequencing of reform and of the conditions for economic assistance therefore seemed to offer a solution to nearly all the problems that the Russian government faced at the end of 1991. But changes as dramatic as those that the government and IFI plans proposed could not go unopposed. Political conflict of some kind was probably inevitable whatever reformist course was followed. But there was nothing that could prevent it from developing once the IFIs' plans were accepted as the basis of reform, because there was no way in which consensus or political pacts could be developed.

Uncontrollable Political Conflict: Opposition to the Russian Government and the Destruction of Converged Agendas?

The supposed key to success to the government/IFIs strategy was the rigorous and diligent pursuit of reform. This meant that it could not compromise its hold over policy by seeking an active alliance with any interest group. Compromise would have meant that the justification for 'shock therapy', the idea that it was the only way possible to reform, would have been diminished. Presidential autonomy had to be protected and striven for in the face of opposition if the government was to pursue the course that it had chosen in agreement with IFIs. Because of this, the government was unable and unwilling to extend itself and make pacts with powerful forces by buying them off. This had a detrimental effect on the stability of the political system and made the conflicts that racked the Russian polity far worse than they might potentially have been. The government's following of the IFI course for reform precluded the construction of alliances and pacts (social and political) of the type that were important to ensuring political stability in other cases of transition (O'Donnell & Schmitter, 1986: 37-47, Przeworski, 1991: 90-91, 184-185). Because no pacts were made, there was little to bind the various competing forces together and none of them had any incentives to abide by, or even formulate, any common rules to the political game: there was no 'negotiated compromise under which actors agree to forego or underutilize their capacity to harm each other' in Russian politics after 1991 (O'Donnell & Schmitter, 1986: 38). Instead, each side tried to inflict the maximum damage on the other. The only limits to the damage that each side could inflict on the other were those of resource mobilisation. Fortunately, these limits were quite extensive. Neither side could mobilise sufficiently to defeat its rival until Yeltsin used force to disband the main symbol of opposition, the parliaments, in September-October 1993. Prior to this, each side was limited by the popular apathy to politics that prevented any popular revolt, and by the divisions and shifting alliances within the parliaments. These limits to resource mobilisation meant that each side was forced to insincerely compromise at critical moments since neither side could hope to win any final battle. But these insincere compromises – such as the December 1992 deal between Yeltsin and the parliaments on a referendum on the Constitution – did not last long and the political system reeled from crisis to crisis. The December deal on a referendum was reneged on by parliament which tried to impeach Yeltsin; he retaliated by decreeing emergency rule; a deal was struck on a referendum by both sides; this referendum lacked any real legal force so that its results were ineffective.

Acceptance of the IFIs' proposals as the basis of its plans for radical economic reform therefore made the political conflicts of post-communist reconstruction more intense than might otherwise have been the case, and, in a way, meaningless: political conflict became almost an end in itself rather than a means to consensus. The parameters of this conflict was defined by the governments' economic policies, as well as exacerbated by it. The need to rigorously and diligently pursue reform and the emphasis on the power of the government and the rule of the presidency that this led to, had to alienate powerful forces and vested interests. This in turn eroded the government's ability to conduct reform so that the IFI-style reforms that the Russian government followed turned politics into a zero-sum game from which there could be no winners.

Very rapidly after the appointment of the Gaidar and other radical reformers, Ruslan Khasbulatov, the Chair of the Russian Supreme Soviet and Aleksandr Rutskoi, the Vice President, began to criticise the government and to mobilise opposition to its policies in the parliaments. This conflict was to result two years later in the shelling of the Russian White House and the arrest of Khasbulatov and Rutskoi. In between their coming out against the government and the eventual destruction of the parliaments, the opposition organised under the general leadership of Khasbulatov and Rutskoi managed to weaken the government's ability to conduct reform by issuing countermanding laws and decrees, supporting the Central Bank's deficit financing policies and using parliament to try to change the composition of the government. These policies eroded the government's initial success in liberalising prices by stimulating inflation, maintaining a high budget deficit and dividing the government. The continued high rate of inflation and failure to curb spending in turn blocked off access to Western financial assistance since the targets set by conditionality were not met.

The opposition of the parliaments to reform was helped by the resistance to reform of industrial directors. This resistance took two main forms. First,

there was the organised opposition and lobbying of organisations like the
Union of Industrialists and Entrepreneurs (UIE), and its affiliated organisations like Civic Union, which called for a gradualist approach to marketisation, and which had supporters in the parliaments (Peregrudov et al,
1992, Rutland, 1992, Lohr, 1993, Ellman, 1993, Lysyakova, 1993: 28-26,
88-89). Second, there was indirect opposition to the government's reform
plans. This type of resistance consisted either of ignoring the government's
instructions and the demands of the inchoate market and carrying on as
per usual, or of using structural economic power to subvert reform. The
chief effect of the 'carrying on as usual' strategy was a huge build-up of
inter-enterprise debt as industry continued to trade by circulating goods on
credit (Whitlock, 1992). The Russian Central Bank paid of this debt by
issuing credits, but this only solved the problem in the short-term, added to
the inflationary pressures in the economy, allowed enterprises to ignore government attempts to force hard-budget constraints and boosted the state
budget deficit.[7] Industrialists used their structural economic power to subvert reform in two ways. First, monopoly producers used their control
to take advantage of price deregulation and profiteer. This prevented an
increase in the flow of some goods to the market and, again, added to inflationary pressure. Second, managers used their positions to subvert attempts
to diversify ownership through privatisation by buying worker support and
blocking the flow of information necessary to the privatisation process. This
stopped the diversification of ownership from reaching the levels wanted by
the government and acted as a barrier to the fuller emergence of a new
economic class.

Overall, then the Russian government's acceptance of the IFIs' proposals
for reform was therefore a double-edged sword. Although it conferred a
measure of international legitimacy, it precluded political peace between
Russia's élites and established resistance to reform that held up the flow of
foreign assistance. The end result of the conflict between the government
and the parliamentary and economic élites was the political impasse between
Yeltsin and the parliaments that was solved by military action against the
parliaments in October 1993. The full effect of this event is still unclear.
But, what is clear is that the destruction of the parliaments by the military
and the elections that followed has created the possibility for a realignment
of political forces. In turn, this might mean the end of the converged reform
agendas of Russia and the West, or their renegotiation.

The election campaign that followed the destruction of the old parliaments allowed the divisions that existed within the government over economic reform to come to the fore. The most obvious sign of these divisions
was the split in government support for electoral blocs. Ministers and presidential aides supported the Russia's Choice bloc (Gaidar, Fedorov, Chubais,
Kozyrev, Filatov, Pamfilova), the Yabloko bloc (Adamishin), the Party of
Russian Unity and Accord (Shakrai, Shokhin, Kalmykov, Stankevich, Sliva,

---

[7] *RFE/RL News Brief*, 1993, 2:4, 6: 4, Bush, 1992, *Russian Economic Trends*, 1992, 3:
16, 19, 27, *Russian Economy*, 1992: 27-42, 40-56, 71-73. The government only managed
to overcome this problem by transforming inter-enterprise debt into promissory notes in
1993, in effect making debt a means of forcing privatization and a threat to managerial
control. See *Russian Economic Trends*, 1993, 3:26-27.

Malei, Melikyan), the Agrarian Party of Russia (Shcherbak, Zaverukha) and the Women of Russia bloc (Lakhova) (Rahr, 1993: 2-3). Of these, only the Russia's Choice bloc can be said to be completely in tune with the IFI proposals for reform. The others, to varying degrees, all called for more moderate economic reforms. These divisions amongst the government were compounded by the post-electoral politicking over reform that was stimulated by the relative electoral success of Vladimir Zhirinovsky's ultra-nationalist Liberal Democratic Party (LDP) in the PR list seats to the State Duma. Zhirinovsky's success in capturing the vote of a previously marginal segment of the Russian population has emboldened the criticisms and rein-forced the hand of politicians like Chernomyrdin, the Prime Minister, whose line on reform has always been less than enthusiastic.

The political balance amongst the major players in Russia has therefore become precarious. Where Yeltsin sympathies lie is as yet unclear and it is too soon to say what kind of government will emerge and what its position on future economic reform will be. The only way in which radical economic reform can continue is if Yeltsin uses his powers as President to ignore the results of the elections and push on with reform by reappointing all of the radicals from the government and reining in sceptics like Chernomyrdin. If this happens, the conflict over reform will continue albeit in a new form. The new legislatures lack the powers to oppose the President that their pre-decessors had, but they can keep Russian politics on the verge of perpetual crisis by threatening to make Yeltsin call new elections. Who, after the last elections, would want to see another in the immediate future?

Alternatively, Yeltsin might try to force compromise between the radi-cal reformers and the gradualists who have more fully come out into the open. The first problem with this is that after two years of conflict, who remains for peace to be made between? The forces of the centre have been severely squeezed by the elections. Caught between Russia's Choice and Zhirinovsky's LDP, none of the centrist forces did well in the elections to the State Duma (the industrialist Civic Union was particularly hard hit). If a centre bloc is to emerge as a partner in a moderate reform coalition, it will have to be from an alliance of the centre blocs and the many successful independent candidates (whose qualities are still unknown). The second problem is that the public pronouncements of radicals show only contempt for a compromise solution.

Russia's future therefore seems as uncertain as it was before the shelling of the White House. A basis of political peace has to be found if Russia is to overcome its economic chaos and social destruction. But what the foundations of such a peace might be are still unclear and may not exist. One step forward might be that a new, more moderate reform agenda emerges from the West. However, despite the comments of Al Gore and Strobe Talbott, powerful institutions have vested interests in not seeing such an agenda emerge, as the recent joint declaration by the IMF and the World Bank against anything but further radical economic reform demonstrates. If Yeltsin opts to take their advice once again and force the policies of the last two years through with vigour using his new presidential powers, the future political stability of Russia will be hard to guarantee.

Bibliography

Adams, W & J.W.Brock (1993), *Adam Smith Goes to Moscow*, Princeton: Princeton University Press.

Bush, K (1992), 'The Russian Budget Deficit', in *RFE/RL Research Report*, Volume 1, Number 40.

Chubais, A & M.Vishnevskaya, 1992, 'Main Issues of Privatisation in Russia', in A.Aslund & R.Layard (eds), *Changing the Economic System in Russia*, London, Pinter.

Collins, S & D.Rodrick (1991), *Eastern Europe and the Soviet Union in the World Economy*, Washington: Institute for International Economics.

Ellman, M (1993), 'Russia: the economic program of the Civic Union', *RFE/RL Research Report*, Volume 2, Number 11.

Fischer, S (1992), 'Stabilization and Economic Reform in Russia', *Brookings Papers on Economic Activity*, Number 1.

Gaidar, Ye & G.Matyukhin (1992), 'Memorandum ob ekonomicheskoi politike Rossiiskoi Federatsii', *Ekonomika i zhizn*, Number 10.

Gorbachev, M.S (1989, 'Sotsialisticheskaya ideya i revolutsionnaya perestroika', *Pravda*, 26 November

Hanson, P (1993), 'Local Power and Market Reform in Russia', *Communist Economies and Economic Transformation*, Volume 5, Number 1.

Hasegawa, T (1992), 'The Connection between Political and Economic Reform in Communist Regimes', in G.Rozman, (ed), Dismantling Communism, Baltimore: John Hopkins University Press.

Hosking, G et al (1992), *The Road to Post-Communism*, London: Pinter.

IMF (1992), *Russian Federation*, Washington: IMF.

IFI (1990), *The Economy of the USSR. Summary and Recommendations*, Washington: World Bank.

IFI (1991), *A Study of the Soviet Economy*, 3 volumes, Paris: OECD.

Johnson, S & H. Kroll (1991), 'Managerial Strategies for Spontaneous Privatization', *Soviet Economy*, Volume 7, Number 4.

Lipton, D & J.Sachs (1990), 'Creating a Market Economy in Eastern Europe: the case of Poland', *Brookings Papers on Economic Activity*, Number 1.

Lipton, D & J.Sachs (1992), 'Prospects for Russia's Economic Reforms', *Brookings Papers on Economic Activity*, Number 2.

Lohr, E (1993), 'Arkadii Volumesky's Power Base', *Europe-Asia Studies*, Volume 45, Number 5.

Lysyakova, L.M (1993), *Fraktsii i bloki Rossiiskogo parlamenta*, Moscow: Institut sravnitel'noi politologii.

McAuley, M (1992), 'Politics, Economics and Elite Realignment in Russia: a case study', *Soviet Economy*, Volume 8, Number 1.

Miller, J (1993), *Mikhail Gorbachev and the End of Soviet Power*, Basingstoke: Macmillan.

Mozhin, A.V (1993), 'Russia's Negotiations with the IMF', in A.Aslund & R.Layard (eds), *Changing the Economic System in Russia*, London, Pinter.

O'Donnell, G & P.Schmitter (1986), *Transitions from Authoritarian Rule. Tentative Conclusions about Uncertain Democracies*, Baltimore: John Hopkins University Press.

Peregrudov, S et al (1992), *Business Associations in the USSR – and After*, PAIS Working Paper, Number 110, University of Warwick.

Przeworski, A (1991), *Democracy and the Market. Political and Economic Reform in Eastern Europe and Latin America*, Cambridge: Cambridge University Press.

Rahr, A (1993), 'Preparations for the Parliamentary Elections in Russia', *RFE/RL Research Report*, Volume 2, Number 47.

Russian Economy (1992), *Rossiiskaya ekonomika osen'yu 1992 goda*, Moscow: Institute of Economic Politics.

Russian Government (1992), 'Proekt programmy uglubleniya ekonomicheskikh reform', *Obzor ekonomiki Rossii*, Number 1.

Rutland, P (1992), *Business Elites and Russian Economic Policy*, London: Royal Institute of International Affairs.

Sachs, J (1993), 'Western Financial Assistance and Russia's Reforms', in S.Islam & M.Mandelbaum (eds), *Making Markets*, New York: Council on Foreign Relations Press.

Sakwa, R (1993), *Russian Politics and Society*, London: Routledge.

Shatalin, S. et al (1990), *Perekhod k rynku. Chast' 1. Kontseptsiya i programma*, Moscow: Arkhangel'skoe.

Urban, M (1993), 'The Politics of Identity in Post-Communist Russia', Paper to the Workshop on Global Security and Ethnic Conflict, University of California.

Whitlock, E (1992), 'A Borrower and a Lender be: interenterprise debt in Russia', *RFE/RL Research Report*, Volume 1, Number 40.

World Bank (1993), *Ekonomicheskie reformy v Rossii*, Moscow: Respublika.

The Political Agenda in Eastern Europe and Russia

Karen Henderson
University of Leicester

'Divisive Political Agendas: the Case of Czechoslovakia'

Introduction

The division of Czechoslovakia was an event predicted by few outside or within that country as little as a year before it happened, and it is therefore of interest to seek the reasons behind the 'velvet divorce'. The fact that the separation of the state was effected so peacefully suggests that, if the process were fully understood, it might provide an admirable model for other small peoples with nationality problems. The ability of Czechs and Slovaks successfully to negotiate with each other a political transaction of such acute complexity inevitably raises another question, too: why were these skills not used to negotiate a satisfactory method of continued coexistence within a single state? In the debate on political agendas in the new democracies, it is important to examine whether those of the Czechs and Slovaks really differed so markedly that they could not be adequately addressed other than by the governments of independent countries.

The need for two separate states was usually justified by ruling politicians within the country with reference to the 'national' and 'emancipatory' aspirations of the Slovaks. The 1992 election manifesto of the victorious Movement for a Democratic Slovakia (HZDS) had as its first point 'to complete the emancipatory development of Slovakia in a democratic and legitimate fashion',[1] and very similar language was also used on the Czech side once the decision to divide the country had been taken.[2] Even Václav Havel mentioned the 'emancipatory efforts of the Slovak Republic' when he resigned from the office of Czechoslovak president.[3] However, national aspirations are not formed overnight, and the relative speed and intensity with which this issue came to dominate Czech/Slovak politics clearly suggests that it cannot provide a complete explanation for the events of 1992.[4]

The aim of this paper therefore is to investigate the extent to which the Czechs and Slovaks were divided from one another by their differing attitudes to various aspects of post-communist reform. All formerly communist countries must proceed with their transformation processes within societies which are internally divided on some issues, but Czechoslovakia attempted to mitigate such inevitable conflicts of interest by its legal division into two

---

[1] Volby (1992), *predvolebný bulletin*, HZDS, Bratislava, 1992, p.1. ,

[2] For discussion of this, see, for example Richard Štencl, 'Emancipační smršt', *Prostor*, 24.7.1992, p.3.

[3] *Lidové noviny*, 18.7.1992, p.1.

[4] A counter-argument beyond the scope of this paper is that it was only the communist takeover in 1948 that prevented the separation of country in the wake of the Second World War.

separate polities. What, then, were these conflicts of interest? Investigating the post-communist agenda is a far from simple task, since even isolating the actual divergences of public opinion between Czechs and Slovaks involves making assumptions which are themselves contentious because they have an inherent tendency to apportion blame. Nor are the most prominent items on the agenda always clearly distinguishable, since formation of opinion results from an intricate interlinking of many issues. Nevertheless, there are three areas which appear worth highlighting in order to provide a framework for discussion.

Firstly, there is the fact that Czechs and Slovaks appear to have had different views on the desirability of economic reform and the optimal *tempo* of change. In this, the Slovaks are normally held to have been leftist in their views while the Czechs were more right-wing. Secondly, there is the issue of the actual prioritisation of economic reform on the political agenda. Here, the normal assumption is that the Slovaks were primarily concerned with national issues and problems of constitutionally rearranging the Czechoslovak federation, while for Czechs economic questions were paramount. Finally, it remains to question whether there was an undisputed coincidence between the agendas of the emergent political élites who negotiated the division of Czechoslovakia and the peoples which they represented. The reasons for country's demise may lie less in irreconcilable differences between its two main peoples and more with the underdeveloped political structures of a state which had so recently suffered from forty years of communist rule.

The Economic Agenda

The first assumption – that Czechs and Slovaks had incompatible views on the desirability of rapid economic transformation – is underpinned by a number of public opinion surveys conducted in the first three years after November 1989. It has been observed that the differentiation of attitudes between Czechs and Slovaks first emerged about five months after the Velvet Revolution, in the spring of 1990.[5] An example is provided by surveys conducted by the Prague-based Association for Independent Social Analysis (AISA) in January and May 1990, which showed that a difference of about 10% between views of Czechs and those of Slovaks emerged during the period between the two surveys. While in the January, 43% of Czechs and 41% of Slovaks favoured fast and radical reform with quick improvement over softer reform with slower and longer improvement, these percentages had changed to 61% and 51% by May. In the same period, fear of losing one's job had also increased more markedly among Slovaks than among Czechs.[6] Such discrepancies in the views of the two nations were regularly repeated in virtually all other public opinion polls conducted prior to the division of the state, and when questions were asked which can be directly linked to western definitions of 'right' and 'left', Slovaks normally emerged

---

[5] See for example Jan Hartl, 'Jací jsme a kam směřujeme', *Respekt*, 6-12.9.1993, p.6; Marián Timoracký, 'Verejná mienka o česko-slovenských vztahoch', Fedor Gál a kol., *Dnešní krize česko-slovenských vztah*, Prague, 1992.

[6] AISA, *Czechoslovakia – May 1990: Survey Report*, Prague, 1990, appendix p.1.

to be more left-oriented than Czechs. A 1991 survey, for example, found margins varying from 4% and 21% between Czech and Slovak responses on whether incomes should be made more equal, whether individuals or the state should take responsibility for providing for every family, and whether state ownership or private entrepreneurship was the better way to run an enterprise.[7]

Explanations for the differing emphases in the views on economic reform in both parts of Czechoslovakia can be sought at the most simple level in the differing rates of unemployment in each: while unemployment was a minimal 3% in the Czech Republic, it rose to over 10% in the Slovak Republic. Such bald statistics interacted, however, with more subtly differentiated perceptions about the morality and fairness of economic change. Slovaks were more inclined than Czechs to assign negative characteristics to those who made money from the liberalisation of the market, such as 'lucky', 'use political connections, nomenklatura', 'take advantage of other people', while Czechs were more likely to believe that it was qualities such as hard work and intelligence that counted.[8] However, caution must be exercised in assuming that the Slovak agenda incorporated an intrinsic distrust of the free market economy and scepticism towards the establishment of a meritocracy. A more complex analysis of the perceptions of successful life strategies in comparison to general satisfaction with the situation in Czechoslovakia concluded that interrelationships between the two in the Czech and Slovak Republics may have diverged on another level. It has been suggested that 'different things have occurred in each republic' – namely, that in the Slovak Republic, reforms were progressing more slowly, so that the loss of social security was more evident to many than the beneficial effects of a developing market economy.[9] In the Czech Republic, the advantages of economic change were more visible.

All these arguments can, however, be accommodated by the notion that the division of Czechoslovakia occurred because no such thing as 'Czechoslovak society' had ever developed. Czechs and Slovaks lived in separate societies, and because these were objectively different, it was inherently likely that neither the effects of post-communist transformation nor popular reactions to it would coincide in the two republics. This argument has been presented most cogently by Jiří Musil, who attempts to clarify the differences between the two societies by means of comparative structural analysis.[10] The initial propositions he has tested are that there are economic, social and cultural differences between Czech and Slovak society, and that the processes of modernisation in each have been asynchronous and dissimilar; furthermore, the sovietisation of society had brought different results in the two parts of the country, and the processes by which the political, economic and cultural institutions of communism were rectified were not the same

---

[7] AISA, *Czechs and Slovaks Compared: A Survey of Economic and Political Behaviour*, Studies in Public Policy No. 198. University of Strathclyde, 1992, pp.6-7.

[8] Ibid, p.5.

[9] Jadwiga Šanderová, 'Differences Between Czech and Slovak Perceptions of the Economic Transformation', *Czech Sociological Review*, Vol. 1, No. 1, 1993, p.55.

[10] Jiří Musil, 'Czech and Slovak Society', *Government and Opposition*, Vol. 28, No. 4, 1993, pp.479-495.

either. Particularly significant is the timing of the modernisation processes. Economic data indicate that the transition from an agrarian to an industrial society took place in about 1900 in the Czech Lands and around 1950 in Slovakia, but that neither proceeded to the post-industrial phase where the tertiary (service) sector of the economy is prevalent.[11]

What this means in practical terms is that whereas the Czech Lands constituted a fairly modern society even before Czechoslovakia was founded in 1918, the Slovaks did not reach a similar stage of development until the onset of stalinisation at the beginning of the communist period. Thereafter, however, Slovakia modernised with great speed and rapidly converged with the Czech Republic, at least in terms of macroeconomic indicators. As a consequence, while living standards in the Czech and Slovak Republics appeared remarkably similar in 1989,[12] people's perceptions of what had happened to their society over 40 years of communism would tend to differ. For the Czechs, the socialist economy with its underdeveloped tertiary sector had clearly held them back from enjoying the technological advances of the west, while for Slovaks, the same period had greatly increased their social security and educational opportunities. Even if Slovaks did not consciously attribute such benefits to the communist political system, it nonetheless remained less likely than in the case of Czechs that they would regard the pre-communist First Republic as their image of the desirable society.[13] Additionally, the very speed of the Slovak modernisation process meant that it had created a society which was structurally different from the Czech Republic in other ways too. Family and social links were inevitably affected by the recent urbanisation of Slovakia; and the patterns of communist industrialisation, particularly in the post-1968 period, left it after 1989 with much obsolescent heavy industry and many towns which had grown up dangerously dependent on one large enterprise. The unviability of such industrial works was one of the structural causes of the higher Slovak unemployment rate.

However, even if one accepts that Czech and Slovak society were structurally different and that this caused Czechs and Slovaks to support divergent agendas for post-communist economic reform, it remains to be proved that this discrepancy in views was a major factor leading to the division of the country. Such an assumption can be contested on two grounds. Firstly, it is perfectly normal for any society to be divided on grounds of economic self-interest[14]: this is the basis of the left-right cleavage underlying many western party systems. It is notable that on most economic questions, both Czech and Slovak society were themselves internally divided, and that these internal divisions were more marked than those which differentiated the two

---

[11] Ibid. Note that Musil's argument is more complex than in the brief summary here, and he concludes, among other points, that élite mobilisation theory is necessary to complement modernisation theories.

[12] For data, see: Pavel Machonin, 'Česko- slovenské vztahy ve světle dat sociologického výzkumu', Gál, *Dnešní krize*, pp.97-101.

[13] For divergent attitudes to the First Republic, see Pavol Frič, Zora Bútorová & Tatiana Rosová, 'Česko-slovenské vzt'ahy v zrkadle empirického výskumu', *Sociológia*, vol. 24, no. 1-2, pp.43-74.

[14] For discussion of this point, see: Richard Rose & William T.E.Mishler, *Reacting to Regime Change in Eastern Europe: Polarization or Leaders and Laggards?*, Studies in Public Policy No. 210, University of Strathclyde, 1993, p.14.

societies from each other. Secondly, in a post-communist society the public's political views are particularly prone to fluctuation. Such alteration of opinions may be due less to changes in voters' basic attitudes and value orientation, and more to their increasing awareness of the implications of certain policies with which they had been unfamiliar under communism.

The crucial question, therefore, is not whether there were differences between Czech and Slovak economic attitudes, but whether these differences were insuperable. When viewed in isolation, the most likely answer would appear to be 'no'. Not only were the differences in Czech and Slovak views on aspects of economic transformation no greater than those one would normally have to reconcile within a single society, but long-term trends might well have won Slovaks over to a more market-oriented standpoint. The Strathclyde-based project on 'Social Welfare and Individual Enterprise in Post-Communist Societies' investigated views in a number of East European countries in both 1991 and 1992/93, on the assumption that there is a 'dynamic dimension' in the formation of an attachment to democratic norms. One conclusion was that citizens may be divided between 'leaders' and 'laggards'.

> '*Leaders* are those who favour a pluralistic system before they experience the new regime; this commitment may be a reaction against the old regime or an abstract commitment to democratic norms. An optimistic interpretation of those who have not immediately formed a positive opinion of the new regime is that they are sceptics or don't knows, cautious about making a commitment to an unfamiliar and untested regime until it has shown what it will do. This would make them *laggards* in the progress toward democracy.'[15]

The validity of this proposition for Eastern Europe in general is supported by the data from the survey, and it can be suggested by extension that it also provides some grounds for supposing that, on economic policy at least, the Czechs were 'leaders', and the Slovaks 'laggards', whose opinions, given time, would have tended to converge with those of the Czechs. When respondents were asked to rank, on positive or negative scales of 0 to 100, the previous and current economic and government systems, and also their expectations of them in five years' time, Czechs demonstrated more positive views than the Slovaks about the current systems of both economics and government compared to the situation under the previous regime. Significantly, however, when asked about their economic expectations for five years' time, Slovak views began to converge with those of the Czechs.[16] Generally, therefore, there seems little reason to suggest that either Czech or Slovak society was permanently polarising into 'democrats' and 'reactionaries'.[17]

---

[15] Rose & Mishler, *Reacting to Regime Change*, p.4.

[16] For data see: AISA, *Czechs and Slovaks Compared*, pp.22-28; Richard Rose & Christian Haerpfer, *Adapting to Transformation in Eastern Europe*, Studies in Public Policy No. 212, University of Strathclyde, 1993, Tables 16-18 & 23-25.

[17] For further discussion of this argument see Rose & Mishler, *Reacting to Regime Change*, pp.10-19.

In the light of this data, one might well ask why Czechoslovakia had to divide when time and experience of the new system might have healed the divisions on economic issues. An obvious answer is that these issues were not viewed in isolation, but became entangled with the other questions of post-communist reform. In the elections of June 1992, the Czech and Slovak Republics returned markedly dissimilar results, with a preponderance of Slovak votes for parties labelled 'left-wing', while the Czechs preferred parties that identified themselves as rightist and conservative.[18] Since the disparity in election results was greater than that between Czech and Slovak economic attitudes, further factors must be examined, and nationalism is other area where Czech and Slovak agendas diverged most openly.

The national agenda

Like all states which had nominally been federations under communist rule, democratic Czechoslovakia was faced with the task of converting existing state structures into an authentic federation. Here, the agendas came to diverge on two separate dimensions: firstly, they differed in content, as Slovaks were more likely to support an increase in the competencies of the Republics rather than those of the Federation,[19], and secondly, they differed in the priority accorded to this rearranging of the relationship between Czechs and Slovaks.

In order to understand the argument, it needs to be emphasised that, just as Czech and Slovak societies were separate, so the Czech and Slovak nations were quite distinct. They were not geographically intermingled to a significant extent, in spite of both the general ethnic diversity in East Central Europe and their 70 years' coexistence in a single state, and they had relatively little shared history. They had fought neither world war as a common state, and even the mutual tragedies and triumphs of 1968 had been dulled by the demoralising normalisation process which followed. Accordingly, when Czechs and Slovaks were asked to name their heroes and the most (or least) glorious times in their history, they produced lists with very little in common.[20] Furthermore, the Czechoslovak political system effectively consisted of two different polities: not only was it a federation comprising Czech and Slovak parliaments and governments as well as a Federal Assembly and Federal Government, but under democratic conditions, each Republic quickly developed its own party system, and by 1992 these contained numerous elements without precise equivalents in the other part of the country. This feature distinguished it from the world's democratic federations, but resembled the situation in the other post-communist states (Yugoslavia, Soviet Union) which disintegrated in the process of converting communist pseudo-federations into viable democracies.

While this may not have boded well for the future of Czechoslovakia,

---

[18] For election results see: Jiří Pehe, 'Czechoslovakia's Political Balance Sheet, 1990 to 1992', *RFE/RL Research Report*, vol.1, no.25, p.29.

[19] See, for example: AISA, *Czechoslovakia – November 1990: Survey Report*, Prague, 1990, pp.7-8

[20] Frič, Butorová & Rosová, 'Česko-slovenské vzt'ahy', pp.43-52.

the differences in the Czech and Slovak nationalist agendas after 1989 were not entirely clear-cut: there may have been many political disputes about the redistribution of federal competencies, yet all opinion polls prior to the 1992 elections, and some afterwards, showed that the majority not only of Czechs, but also of Slovaks did not want two independent states. In the 1992 elections themselves, the only substantial party to promote Slovak independence, the Slovak National Party (SNS), gained less than 10% of the Slovak vote. The winning party in Slovakia, Vladimír Mečiar's HZDS, gained some 35% with a programme promoting five steps towards Slovak statehood which amounted to a form of confederation.[21] While many Czechs maintained that the Slovak electorate's support for Mečiar was an expression of its desire for an independent state[22], this interpretation was hardly supported either by the content of the HZDS (or most other) election manifestos, or by opinion polls. From the autumn of 1991 until the election, the proportion of Slovaks who said they wanted an independent state rarely exceeded 15%, which was approximately the same as the percentage who stated a preference for a unitary state with one government. Of the remainder, slightly more were in favour of some kind of federation rather than a confederation of the kind advocated by Mečiar.[23] Two problems remained unsolved, however: one was that it was unclear precisely what was meant by a confederation, and the other was that this option was unacceptable both to Czechs as a whole, and to Václav Klaus, whose Civic Democratic Party (ODS) went on to win the June 1992 elections in the Czech Republic.

It is also significant to note that, according to a survey conducted in April 1992, even 59% of the supporters of Mečiar's party favoured the continuation of a common Czechoslovak state (that is, either a federation or a unitary state), whereas only 22% wanted the creation of a confederation – the party's actual election programme – and a mere 19% supported Slovak state sovereignty, which was the eventual outcome of the party's election victory.[24] Additionally, there were indications that it was economic rather than more traditionally nationalist concerns that influenced Slovaks to vote for Mečiar.[25]

The picture that emerges, therefore, is that neither general attitudes to economic reform nor nationalist desires for independence on their own can account for the discrepancy in voting patterns between Czechs and Slovaks. The basic agendas of Czechs and Slovaks on the desirability of developing a market economy, and on living together in some kind of union of the two peoples, do not account for the wide differences in their party preferences. It appears that at some point the economic and the nationalist agenda interacted in a fashion that divided Czechs from Slovaks.

How the two agendas reinforced each other can be pinpointed from opin-

---

[21] Volby (1992), p.1.

[22] See, for example, Czech Premier Klaus's New Year Speech on the first day of independence: 'Novoroční projev českého premiéra Václava Klausa', *Lidove noviny*, 4.1.1993, p.3.

[23] IVVM figures from: *Lidove noviny*, 1.11.1991, p.2; *ibid.*, 27.5.1992, p.2.

[24] Zora Bútorová, 'A Deliberate "Yes" to the Dissolution of the CSFR?', *Czech Sociological Review*, vol.1, no.1, 1993, p.61.

[25] *Budování státu*, vol.III, no.5, p.10.

ion polls, which show where the widest gulf between Czech and Slovak perceptions lay. As early as 1990, in the surveys conducted by AISA, there was one set of responses where Czech and Slovak views polarised on national lines to such an extent that the divisions between the two nations were far more salient than the divisions within each of the two societies taken on their own. It was found that 'an absolute majority of the Slovak population believe that in the Czech Republic the situation is better in practically all respects'[26] (for example standard of living, cultural possibilities, job opportunities, wages); and also it was the belief of most Slovaks, and also of most Czechs, that 'their' republic was subsidising the other.[27] The latter finding re-emerged constantly in the period up to the 1992 elections[28]: there was a widespread view, held by a good half of the population, that resources were being redistributed in a way that disadvantaged their nation. Put simply, it was felt that the 'system' was unfair. This sense of injustice was no doubt heightened by the general tensions of post-communist societies, where all previous criteria of who is entitled to what and why have been overturned, and all definitions of equity and entitlement are open to renegotiation.

As the relationship between Czechs and Slovaks became an ever more contentious subject of debate between 1990 and 1992, a satisfactory solution to arguments over redistribution of both power and economic resources came no nearer. By 1992, attitudes had crystallised on the Slovak side into what has been referred to as the 'complex of a minor', whereby more than two-thirds of Slovaks felt that they were not treated as adults.[29] It would appear that the clearest cause of discontent among Slovaks related not to their attitudes on the desirability of a market economy, nor to their views on the best way to rearrange the federation, but rather to more nebulous feelings about the way they were treated by Czechs. Their unease was experienced on an emotional rather than a purely rational level: economic and nationalist grievances merged because Slovaks were not convinced the Czechs could be relied upon to protect their economic interests. In these circumstances, the election of a strong character whom the Czechs would find it difficult to ignore (that is, Vladimír Mečiar) was a not illogical response, regardless of whether his specific policies on economics or constitutional arrangements tallied with preferences expressed by Slovak voters to opinion pollsters. The need to assert Slovak desires in the face of Czech indifference assumed more importance than the actual content of these demands. The major cleavage of Czechoslovak politics was thus that between Czechs and Slovaks.

A further conclusion which can be derived from this is that specific policy options are not the only criterion determining how people vote: their trust that a politician will, in general, be capable of defending their interests is also of import. While Mečiar's tendency to make irrational or contradictory statements was often documented by the media both inside Czechoslovakia

---

[26] AISA, *Czechoslovakia – November 1990*, p.11.

[27] Ibid., appendix pp.7-8.

[28] See, for example, Frič, Bútorová & Rosová, 'Česko-slovenské vzt'ahy', pp.68-69; Michael J. Deis, 'A Study of Nationalism in Czechoslovakia', *RFE/RL Research Report*, vol.1, no.4, p.11; *Lidové noviny*, 15.5.1992, p.2.

[29] 'Komplex nedospělého', *Lidové noviny*, 15.5.1992, p.2.

and outside,[30] this appeared a matter of little concern to many Slovak voters: after all, they too had problems of orientation in a new, complex and confusing environment.[31] It was the apparent sincerity of his desire pragmatically to protect Slovak interests which for them counted most. It must also be pointed out, in order not to overgeneralise, that it was less than 40% of Slovak voters who voted for Meciar. It is possible to have a relatively clear electoral mandate within a society which is divided: no politician needs to convince the whole of their nation in order to gain power.

The Elite Agenda

The final proposition which must be investigated is that it was the Czech and Slovak politicians who were most heavily influenced by divisive political agendas. If a politician like Mečiar, or Klaus in the Czech Republic, gained authority among and the trust of a substantial minority of their electorate, they were in a strong position to guide and manipulate the political agendas of voters. In these circumstances, Czechoslovakia could be divided less by the fact that it comprised two separate societies, and more by the fact that it comprised two separate political élites. One was the new Slovak political élite, and the other was the Czech or Czechoslovak élite. In order to avoid debate over the extent to which 'Czech' and 'Czechoslovak' are in some contexts interchangeable terms, it is easier to designate the élites as 'Prague' and 'Bratislava', according to the centre of the political orbit in which they were circulating. The division of the country between a Czech or Czechoslovak élite in Prague and a Slovak élite in Bratislava was promoted by the asymmetry of the federation, whereby the federal capital and parliament were situated in the largest Czech city, together with the Czech capital and parliament, while only the Slovak parliament was located in Bratislava. Unfortunately, power relations were perceived to mirror this arrangement, with federal power lying largely with the Czechs. Slovak politicians who went to Prague to take up federal office soon became regarded by those they left behind as 'federal Slovaks' with a Czechoslovakist orientation, and were suspected of pursuing their own careers with more vigour than Slovak interests,[32] while Slovak concerns were effectively represented only in Bratislava. The new post-communist Slovak élites therefore tended to have professional aspirations that centred on Bratislava and not on the federal capital: in the 1992 election, most Slovak party leaders stood for parliamentary seats in the Slovak National Council, whereas Czech party leaders mostly ran for one of the two chambers of the Federal Assembly rather than the Czech National Council.

The separation of the Czech and Slovak élites was fatally reinforced, however, by the previously-mentioned fact that no real Czechoslovak parties existed once the Communist Party of Czechoslovakia had split in 1990. Ini-

---

[30] See, for example, Marián Leško, *L'udia a ludkovia z politickej elity*, 1993, p.176.

[31] See Vladimír Krivý, 'Slovenská a česká definícia situácie', *Sociologický časopis*, vol.29, no.1, pp.77-8.

[32] For comment on this see Jana Klusáková, *Nadoraz: Petr Pithard*, Prague, 1992, pp.28-29.

tially, this situation had not appeared problematic since the citizens' movements Civic Forum (in Prague) and Public Against Violence (in Bratislava) had been able to cooperate in a coalition government also including Christian Democrats during the 1990-1992 parliament. However, as the next free elections approached, there was no existential need for any politician to modify their policies with deference to the sensibilities of the electorate in the other republic. The five per cent threshold of votes that a party required to gain parliamentary representation was applied separately to each republic. Politicians and parties were thus free to choose to exploit any aspect of the political agenda which would best enable them to mobilise their own voters in their favour.

Václav Klaus, the leader of Civic Forum's most popular successor party, chose economics. This was not merely a campaign strategy, but also accorded with his own personal priorities as an economist by background. Most significant, however, is the fact that it remained precisely economic issues which enabled him to play a dynamic policy role and acquire authority among Czech voters: in this area, he could be proactive, whereas in questions of rearranging the federation, Czech policies were almost invariably a reaction to Slovak initiatives. This only changed when Klaus as Czech Prime Minister began negotiations with Mečiar after the June 1992 elections. At this point, Klaus took the initiative by arguing that Mečiar's conception of confederation – most particularly the creation of two states which were subjects of international law – was tantamount to independence, and that if that, rather than a 'functioning federation', was what the Slovaks wanted, it could be arranged. His main priority was leadership of a state whose economy could be efficiently controlled, and for these purposes an independent Czech Republic was more rational than a confederation, once a 'functioning federation' seemed beyond political reach. He thus appeared publicly to be reacting to Slovak demands, but was in fact initiating a policy of his own.

For a Slovak party, on the other hand, it was hard to profile itself on the Slovak political scene by promoting economic initiatives, since these were largely determined in Prague; a further transfer of competencies to the Republics was an essential precondition for a Slovak politician with domestic support to be pioneering in this field. Able only to react to Czech/Czechoslovak economic policy, in 1991 and 1992 Mečiar therefore courted the Slovak electorate with an agenda for transforming Slovakia's international status and its relationship with the Czech Republic. This was an issue he could effectively exploit to demonstrate political leadership. It is notable that during his first period as Slovak Prime Minister, from June 1990 to March 1991, he had been clearly pro-federalist, and it has been suggested that it was his ire at being ousted from this office by his opponents within the citizens' movement that lay at the root of his transformation to a nationalist.

Both Czech and Slovak leaders appear, therefore, to have promoted political agendas which emphasised either economic or national issues according to their objective possibilities of influencing them from their respective Prague and Bratislava power bases. This they did with little regard for the future of the common state. One further policy area, however, is worth mentioning, and this involves foreign policy. Although there were some assertions that Slovak policy was more eastward-oriented than that of the Czechs, and there was a certain politicisation of the Slovak fear of Hungarian irredentism, foreign affairs were not high on the policy agenda because it was not commonly felt that Czechoslovakia was under any imminent threat from its neighbours. The international arena was generally perceived to be friendly, and future integration into western structures was the main political concern. This made it possible for both the Czech and Slovak élites to adopt political agendas which had an internally polarising effect within Czechoslovakia without risking a loss of power through foreign intervention. The emergent Czechoslovak political system after 1989 could be described as a consociational democracy[33], and analyses of such arrangements for governing divided societies indicate that their success is heavily dependent on élite cooperation, and that the presence of an external threat is instrumental in achieving this.[34] Had the Czech and Slovak Republics been threatened by a common danger, their politicians would have had a far more urgent incentive both to reconcile their differences, and to propagate this policy amongst their citizens. In the situation prevailing in 1992, however, maximisation of the leaders' power was better served by dividing the state.

The proposition that Czech and Slovak politicians exploited nationalist differences to suit their own ends was one discussed within Czechoslovakia. In surveys conducted from 1990 onwards, the majority of both Czechs and Slovaks felt that dividing the republics was a 'game' of the politicians, who were using nationalism for their own purposes.[35] However, to suggest that the state was divided because of the power-oriented agendas of the political élites rather than differing views held by their electorates does not explain the passivity of citizens in the face of the impending split they claimed not to support. Here three other factors may have played a role.

Firstly, Czechoslovakia was divided not merely by the differences of views between Czechs and Slovaks, but also by the perception that they were irreconcilable. No-one was able to advance a credible case that a viable common state could be created. While the citizenry were overwhelmingly in favour of being permitted to express their views on the break-up in a referendum[36], it was true that a referendum was likely to have indicated the option people did *not* want – independent states – without providing any positive constitutional solution acceptable to both Czechs and Slovaks. Crucial to the passive consent to division was the growing sense of its inevitability. Slovaks did not believe that the Czechs were willing to grant them the autonomy, through transfer of powers to the republics, which they would have con-

[33] Lijphart describes it as 'a textbook example of consociational democracy': Arend Lijphart, 'Democratization and Constitutional Choice in Czecho-Slovakia, Hungary and Poland 1989-91', *Journal of Theoretical Politics*, vol.4, no.2, 1992, p.216.

[34] For elaboration of this point see Karen Henderson, *Czechoslovakia: The Failure of Consensus Politics*, University of Leicester Discussion Papers in Politics, No.P93/4, 1993.

[35] AISA, *Czechoslovakia – November 1990*, appendix pp. 7-8; Deis, 'A Study of Nationalism', p.12; Bútorová, 'A Deliberate "Yes" ', p.69.

[36] *Telegraf*, 2.9.1992, p.3; *Práce*. 25.7.1992, p.1.

sidered to constitute an 'authentic federation'. The Czechs, on the other hand, appear consistently to have overestimated the Slovak desire for independence. Opinion polls indicated that Czechs had a more pessimistic view of relations between Czechs and Slovaks than Slovaks did.[37] This may be attributable to the fact that they were simply more distant from Slovak society and hence unable to differentiate extremist minority views from the much lower level of discontent experienced by the majority. It has also been suggested that Czechs underestimated the symbolic nature of many Slovak demands[38], and that early gestures indicating acceptance of the Slovaks as equal partners might have stemmed the tide of discontent. Unfortunately, the political élites did little to counteract these misunderstandings.

The second factor relates to the specifics of post-communist societies. On the one hand, misperceptions of Czechs and Slovaks, while due in part to the existence of 'separate societies', had also been facilitated by the atomisation of communist society which had yet fully to be overcome. While the country had, in 1992, a functioning democratic system with a plurality of political parties, much of the more complex infrastructure which mediates between governments and citizens in democracies had yet to develop. Once the leaders had been elected, there appeared to many citizens to be no way of stopping them from implementing even the most extreme of policies for resolving Czech/Slovak differences. People had little belief in their own political efficacy. Their inexperience of democratic politics and the lengthy processes of debate and negotiation needed to reconcile conflicting interests may also have contributed to the early onset of citizen fatigue with the seemingly endless political wrangling. Nor did the leaders manifest much concern at carrying public opinion with them to the point where they might have felt it was safe to attempt to legitimise their acts by a referendum. In mitigation of the reactions of both the public and the politicians, however, it has to be acknowledged that post-communist societies are faced by an exceptionally heavy decision-making burden;[39] simply eradicating a contentious issue from the political agenda therefore had a certain rationality that would not have existed in more stable democracies.

The third factor is that, in a world of competing political agendas, the creation of a truly Czechoslovak society was not a high priority for either Czechs or Slovaks. Czechs were quick to write off Slovak demands for a truly balanced federation of two equal nations as a mere manifestation of distasteful Slovak nationalism. This was exacerbated by the Slovak tendency to promote their cause by insistence on a separate Slovak identity, rather than encouraging positive steps towards genuine integration of the two nations.[40] Czechs could not perceive that the merging of the Czech and Czechoslovak identities was a problem, and once Slovaks responded by

---

[37] Timoracký, 'Verejná mienka', pp.83-84; J. Mišovič, 'Názory na vzajemné vztahy Cech a Slovak', *sociologické aktuality*, no.7, 1992, p.8.

[38] See Klusáková, *Nadoraz: Petr Pithard*, p.96-97.

[39] This relates to the problems of 'triple transition'; see Claus Offe, 'Capitalism by Democratic Design? Democratic Theory Facing the Triple Transition in East Central Europe', *Social Research*, vol. 58, no. 4, 1991, pp.865-892.

[40] See Ján Bunčák, 'Slovensko – spoločnost v rekonštruckcii', *Sociologia*, vo,.25, no.1-2, pp.6-7.

regarding the notion of 'Czechoslovakism' as offensive, all future efforts to bring the two nations together were doomed in advance.

Conclusion

Conclusions drawn from comparing political agendas in the Czech and Slovak Republics can only be tentative. It appears that while there were distinct differences in the political aspirations of the two nations, it was the way that these were mobilised by the separate Czech and Slovak élites which actually led to the division of the country. The reactions of both voters and leaders were influenced not only the fact that no politically integrated Czechoslovak society existed, but also by inexperience of democratic procedures and the particularly taxing demands of a post-communist society. It is possible that a cautious public, given time, might have progressed to widespread acceptance both of the market economy and of a new form of Czecho-Slovak common state if they had been able to identify with leaders supporting both these policies. Given the lack of such leaders, simplifying the agenda may actually have promoted democracy.

Policy Communities and Urban Governance

Lawrence Pratchett
De Montfort University

'Policy Networks, Information Technologies & Local Government:
Defining a Relationship'[1]

Introduction

Along with many other public and private sector organisations, local authorities are spending increasingly large proportions of their budgets on information and communication technologies (ICTs). In the five years that SOCITM (the Society of Information Technology Managers in Local Government) have been collecting information on IT (Information Technology) trends in local government, the estimated expenditure on IT by local authorities has grown from £480 million in 1987 to £1050 million in 1992 (SOCITM 1992). The growth in IT budgets has greatly exceeded the annual rate of inflation in all but one of these years. In financial terms, therefore, ICTs are growing in their importance. Beyond their financial significance, many commentators now recognise that ICTs have profound implications for the future structure and organisation of public administration in general, and local government in particular (for example, Audit Commission 1990, Taylor & Williams 1991, Hepworth 1992).

Despite the apparent importance of ICTs, few attempts have been made to consider their impact in relation to more substantive theoretical perspectives on contemporary government. This paper addresses this omission by developing an analysis of the relationship between ICTs and the emerging policy networks paradigm. It argues that within local government this is a two-way process: networks are both influenced by ICTs and can themselves influence the value of particular technologies in specific network contexts.

A major criticism of policy network theory is that it fails to provide an adequate account of change, either of networks, or of the policies that emerge from them. Recent attempts to consider elements of change (Marsh & Rhodes 1992, Smith 1993) remain at an embryonic stage. One reason for the inadequacies of network theory in accounting for change is that despite rhetoric to the contrary, most analyses concentrate upon policy processes, and ignore aspects of articulation between networks and their macro-level contexts. A focus upon the role of ICTs provides one means of addressing this articulation, because it has relevance at a number of different levels of analysis. The international expansion of ICTs and the informatisation of public administrations can be explained by a number of competing macro-level theories. Post-Fordist analyses, in particular, identify new technologies as an essential element of their theory, with ICTs facilitating the flexible specialisation essential for the transition to a new regime of accumulation (Hoggett 1987, Stoker 1990). A focus on ICTs transcends the parochial

---

[1] Please do not quote without the permission of the author.

boundaries of individual networks and provides an important means by which macro-level developments can be articulated to networks, and vice versa. By developing an analysis of the relationship between ICTs and policy networks, therefore, this paper also aims to further the comprehension of how networks change.

Before developing an understanding of the relationship between ICTs and policy networks it is important first to provide a brief definition of the technologies that are under analysis. The term 'information and communications technologies' concerns all technologies that collect, store, process or transmit information within or on behalf of local authorities. This includes corporate, departmental and personal computing facilities, the software systems in use on these computers, and the networks and other telecommunications facilities that exist to communicate information within or across local authority boundaries. Consequently, the term ICTs is used to convey the full extent of hardware, software and systems that combine to impact upon local government. As a definition this is not restricted to the physical properties of computer systems or telecommunication links, but encompasses the ways in which the physical components are organised, and the aggregated knowledge of individuals which combine to make the physical parts of use to the organisation (Street 1992). New technologies, therefore, are viewed as a process within local government rather than as simply the combination of machines and systems used by authorities (Scarbrough & Corbett 1992). Consequently, the ways in which ICTs are interpreted by individuals and organisations are more important than the functional abilities of discrete items of hardware or software. These contextual and interpretive elements of ICTs in local government are of particular significance when they are considered in relation to policy networks.

ICTs and the Informationisation of Local Government

In common with many other public and private sector institutions, ICTs first emerged in local government as a means of automating routine clerical tasks (Hackney 1989), but their spread into local government now extends far beyond this automation process. Information and communication technologies are enabling new disaggregated forms of management to be implemented in local government, based around the innovative use of management information systems (Dockery 1992) and the extensive utilization of output measures such as performance indicators (Burningham 1992) which allow local authorities to coordinate and steer the delivery of services at arms length. As compulsory competitive tendering (CCT) in local government has gathered pace it has become unthinkable to consider separating the client and contractor parts of a particular function without implementing a computer system to administer and monitor the relationship. New technologies are also allowing new methods of service delivery to be developed, for example, in the provision of library services (Taylor & Williams 1991). Local authorities are also beginning to use ICTs to pioneer new roles for themselves. Oxfordshire are the first of a number of county councils to experiment with the provision of Community Information Points, giving local residents access to a wide range of public service data held by the council (*Local Government Chronicle*, 19 November 1993). Consequently, ICTs are rapidly becoming an integral part of the very fabric of contemporary local government.

The most important aspect of all of these innovations is that the implementation of function specific systems has provided an emerging role for information as a distinct and unique asset of local government. The proliferation of administrative and functional systems has given rise to a wealth of additional data on local government processes. As well as automating specific functions, therefore, ICTs are involved in a process of 'informating' them (Zuboff 1988), making the events and activities of each function more transparent to both policy makers and service providers. New ICTs enable this data to be analyzed and related to other sets of data. For example, social services information on elderly people can be combined with housing records to ensure that those most vulnerable to bad weather conditions receive priority in the upgrading of heating and insulation of properties. This is in direct contrast to the traditional practices of upgrading such facilities on an estate by estate basis (except where individuals made a strong case on their own behalf). In this instance the integration of functionally differentiated systems provides additional value to the authority beyond that offered by the straight forward automation of tasks. Indeed, such examples go further than contemporary management information systems in providing unique information of value to local authorities. Consequently, along with other public institutions, local authorities are moving beyond the automation of procedures into an era of 'informatisation' (Bellamy & Taylor 1992). This era of informatisation is characterised by the emergence of new information, new uses for existing information, and most significantly, by the emergence of new information flows and the rearrangement of existing information flows (Frissen 1992). Informatisation, therefore, places both information, and the ICTs upon which informatisation is dependent, at the heart of contemporary local government.

The implications of the informatisation of local government for an analysis of policy networks are threefold. Firstly, it suggests that information is becoming increasingly important to local government as a whole, and consequently, must be of importance to actors participating in the various local government networks. It follows that access to appropriate ICTs and the ability to use them will become of critical importance for power/dependence relationships within networks. Secondly, as new information flows emerge through informatisation the relative status and power of individual actors may change. The capacity of ICTs to facilitate the aggregation, analysis and transfer of information may have the effect of marginalising previously important actors and give new emphasis to the role of others. Indeed, a similar argument of marginalisation may be applied to entire networks in some instances. Thirdly, informatisation has led to the ascendancy of a new and increasingly dominant network, centred around the development and implementation of ICTs in local government (Pratchett 1994). This network is composed mainly of computer manufacturers, software houses, information consultants and the technical experts employed within local authorities. It interacts with other policy networks to encourage the rapid implementation of ICTs in all areas of local government. The danger for local government is that by encouraging functions to become increasingly dependent upon particular ICTs, the technical network is imposing a straight-jacket on future policy options. Consequently, the ICT network is hijacking the organisational and policy futures of local government.

The Impact of ICTs on Policy Networks

There are a range of policy network characteristics that are affected by ICTs. As classifications of these characteristics are potentially extensive[2], the objective here is to selectively identify those characteristics of policy networks that are most vulnerable to influence from ICTs and those which can be exploited by particular professional groups or organisations. This section, therefore, will concentrate upon four characteristics of policy networks that are especially relevant in the context of ICTs in local government. Each of these characteristics has the potential to be enhanced or reduced by the introduction or innovative use of new technologies within the network. This does not imply that an enhancement or reduction of any particular characteristic is necessarily good or bad, but highlights the additional tensions which ICTs can introduce into policy networks. It also emphasises the inherent ambiguity of ICT impacts on networks.

informal/voluntary participation

Networks are voluntary groupings of actors and organisations that operate in an informal and unconstitutional environment. Thus, Jordan & Schubert (1992) employ the term 'voluntary social action' to emphasise the non-coercive nature of relations between network participants. Actors are under no legal or constitutional obligation to participate in a policy network, but do so voluntarily in order to achieve some personal benefit. There may, however, be significant political, social or economic pressures which compel actors to become involved. Similarly, relations within a network are not governed by formal, constitutional arrangements, but by a shared ideology (Smith 1993) and agreed 'rules of the game' (Rhodes 1988) which bind actors together and provide for a consensus on policy outcomes based upon mutually acceptable resource exchanges.

The informal and voluntary nature of network relations may be enhanced by the introduction of some ICTs. For example, the extension of integrated voice and data telecommunications networks allows more rapid and timely access to information resources such as databases by various actors. Both data and people can become more available as a result of ICTs, allowing greater levels of informality. From this view, therefore, ICTs enhance the informality of networks by increasing the opportunity for *ad-hoc* participation.

---

[2] For examples , see Rhodes 1988, Marsh & Rhodes 1992, Waarden 1992, Smith 1993.

Alternatively the introduction of ICTs into networks has the potential to greatly reduce the informality of network relations. New technologies introduce a greater degree of formality into network structures and relations by codifying the previously informal rules upon which resource exchanges are based. They also have the tendency to distance actors, encouraging interactions through technology based communications rather than through face-to-face contacts. Information resources are particularly vulnerable to formalisation by ICTs. The methods of data collection and timetables for the exchange of information between actors becomes structured in rule-based computer systems which reduce the capacity for discretion amongst individual actors and enforce greater rigidity in relationships. In the case of highway inspections, the Department of Transport (DTp) introduced a computerised Routine Maintenance Management System in 1989 in order to prescribe to local authorities the precise process by which inspections should be undertaken (Carter 1989). This has brought about a greater degree of formality in policy processes between individual local authorities and the regional offices of the DTp, reducing the capacity of individual authorities to plan inspections to meet local needs, and increasing the formality through which financial claims are made to the DTp. By arguing that ICTs increase the formality of network relations, however, is not to suggest that the overall negotiation processes of the network become structured by these new technologies. The shared values and consensus amongst actors will still dominate the policy making process. It is the individual transactions between actors that become more structured and formalised by ICTs, and this has the underlying effect of reducing the voluntary nature of participation and increasing the formality and rigidity of policy outcomes.

complexity/opacity

The internal processes of networks are a sophisticated and complex arrangement of power/dependence relationships which cannot be decomposed to a simple set of relations. Policy making is not the domain of one single actor, but is the outcome of interactions and negotiations between a 'plurality of interdependent organizations or individuals' (Schneider 1992). Consequently, although relationships between actors are potentially asymmetric (Rhodes 1988) the policy process remains essentially polycentric (Hanf & O'Toole 1992). The complexity of multi-organisational relations renders the processes of the network opaque. Policy outcomes cannot be attributed to the strategies or actions of individual organisations, but must be understood in terms of a complex process of negotiations and resource dependencies between a multiplicity of organisations.

This complexity remains obscure and impenetrable, even to actors within the network, leading to an uncertainty and ambiguity of policy outcomes. This also leads to questions of network accountability and the implications of obscure network processes for open and democratic government (Raab 1992).

The introduction of new technologies into networks clearly has the potential to further obfuscate the policy process. Technical complexities can add to the existing intricacies of internal network processes, making them even more impenetrable and opaque. In addition, ICTs encourage a far greater level of communication between actors across a much wider range of media than conventional relations enabled. The use of 'fax' machines for the transmission of documents, of wide area networks for data transfer and the general promotion of voice and video telecommunications, increases the intensity of network interactions and compounds the complexities of relationships. Finally, the processing and modelling capacities of modern computers introduce a further dimension of complexity by allowing a much greater range of policies to be considered, and indeed implemented.

At the same time ICTs also offer the ability to reduce the complexity and opacity of networks by giving structure to the policy process and increasing the overall transparency of network activity. Firstly, the rule-based logic of computer systems means that as networks become more exposed to ICTs, so more of their processes become subject to clearly stated principles and procedures. Thus, in developing software, systems analysts attempt to define a rigid set of rules that cover the full extent of professional action. Whilst there are serious doubts as to the feasibility of developing systems that can capture the full range of inferences and knowledge of experts (Ravetz 1993), the implication for policy networks is that the opacity of professional knowledge, and hence the opacity of some network relations, is gradually being eroded by the introduction of function specific-computer systems. Secondly, the ability of ICTs to aggregate and transmit large quantities of information across wide areas, and to a potentially wide range of recipients, also suggests an increase in network transparency. The use in local government of management information systems is an attempt in many policy areas to make the activities of the network more transparent to managers and council members. Extending this information to the community, as is being attempted in Oxfordshire, serves to further reduce opacity and enhance transparency.

barriers to membership

This concerns the extent to which networks represent closed and exclusive interests, the ability of the network to insulate itself from outside interference and the exclusion of actors who do not share the common values and ideology of the network. In order to maintain the stability of the network and to preserve their own status and power within it, individual actors will seek to restrict membership and exclude those that are seen as a threat. Membership of a network, therefore, is restricted to those who abide by the 'rules of the game' and who have resources to exchange with other members of the network. Consequently, in any policy area there are likely to be a core group of actors who form the main focus of the network, and a peripheral group who are allowed occasional access but are excluded from continuous influence over policy (Smith 1993).

Information and communication technologies present opportunities both for those attempting to restrict membership and for those attempting to break down the barriers. On the one hand, ICTs can provide a useful technological barrier to external parties seeking access to the network. Until it was deemed anti-competitive behaviour it was common for local authorities to include a technical ICT specification for information systems as part of the CCT process for services such as buildings maintenance. This had the effect of excluding many potential competitors who lacked the technical knowledge to understand the ICT specification element of the tender document, let alone implement it. This form of exclusion can be extended to policy networks, where the primary actors develop sophisticated ICT resources on which policy processes become dependent. For example, by testing IT competency as part of its entry examinations, CIPFA (the Chartered Institute of Public Finance and Accountancy) has indicated the importance of ICTs to the financial networks of local government. New ICTs such as sophisticated spreadsheet models and financial management systems reassert the traditional importance of qualified accountants and exclude other actors from detailed involvement in financial policy processes. The use of ICTs by local authorities acts both to contain the complexities of financial management and to maintain the status and power of CIPFA members relative to other local government professions.

On the other hand, ICTs can also be used by those on the margins of a network to gain access to the core group of policy makers. The advent of relatively low-cost computerised housing management systems has enabled a broad range of housing associations to participate in the provision of social housing without the substantial administrative back-up that local authorities have traditionally needed for the management of house lettings. In the imminent CCT of housing management, housing associations with modern ICT resources are expected to be in a strong position to compete with those authorities whose ICT resources are not fully developed. Some technologies, such as open systems (the intercommunication of computers from different manufacturers and the open interchange of software and data between them) also have the effect of opening networks up to intrusion from other actors. Thus, whilst local authorities are rapidly implementing open systems policies as a means of defending their services through the use of up-to-date technologies, they are also increasing their vulnerability to attack on other dimensions (Pratchett 1993).

interdependence of actors

The main incentive for actors to participate in networks is for the exchange of resources, leading to a mutual dependency between them. The policy process, therefore, is centred around these mutual dependencies, and policy outcomes are the result of resource exchanges between a number of organisations who collectively form the network. Interdependency fosters a consensus on policy amongst actors and prohibits any individual actor from taking unilateral action. Consequently, even though the objectives of two actors may be different, a consensus must be found within the network which meets the needs of both (Hanf & O'Toole 1992). It follows that where a dependency breaks down, actors risk exclusion from the network. Consequently, the ability of ICTs to vary resource exchanges, and hence, interdependencies is of great significance.

ICTs can increase interdependencies within a network by providing a technological dimension to existing relationships in two ways. Firstly, investment in ICTs by actors has the effect of locking them into relationships with other actors which are subsequently difficult to reverse. As well as the financial costs of implementing ICTs the significant opportunity and learning costs associated with new technologies prevents either individuals or organisations from abandoning their investments too readily. Consequently, ICTs can be used to add structure to dependency relations. For example, local education authorities are now being encouraged to exchange statistical monitoring information on schools (known as 'Form 7') with the Department for Education (DFE) using telecommunications networks or magnetic media. Whilst the benefits of such exchanges in terms of improved efficiency and accuracy are clear, once locked into such a policy it will be difficult for local authorities to withdraw from it, at least in the short-term. Secondly, ICTs can significantly reduce the costs of transactions associated with resource exchanges. Again, by providing structure to relationships negotiations can become automated. By using ICTs actors can reduce their transaction costs and strengthen interdependencies.

Whilst ICTs can be used to strengthen interdependencies, they can also be used to change existing power relations within networks, to sever others and to establish new dependencies. In the example of information exchanges in the education policy community cited above, ICTs were used to strengthen, in the short-term at least, the relationships between schools, local authorities and the DFE. The same technology, however, may be part of a longer term shift in power relations which is serving to marginalise the role of local education authorities. As part of the local management of schools, the delegation of finance and responsibilities to individual schools has seen a corresponding rise in computerised administration systems in schools. These systems have the ability to collect and transmit performance information in much the same way as the local education authority. There is no reason, therefore, why 'Form 7' and other information cannot be transmitted directly to the DFE computers without intervention from the local authority. Together with other legislative changes (for example, encouraging grant maintained schools), ICTs may fulfil an important role in radically altering the power relations and dependencies within the education policy community, leading to the eventual peripheralisation of local education authorities.

These four characteristics are not exclusive, and there remain others to be explored that may be equally vulnerable to the influence of ICTs. The value of the foregoing analysis, however, is that it highlights the extent to which the very nature of policy networks can be altered by the introduction of ICTs. It also illustrates the ambiguity of impact which ICTs may have on networks. The impact of ICTs on networks, therefore, must be viewed in relation to the broader strategies and objectives of those introducing or making use of them. Individual actors, or confederations of actors can use ICTs to radically alter the dimensions of the network, for example, by enhancing the transparency of processes to themselves whilst further obfuscating them from others. In addition, it must be assumed that ICTs will have consequences for the network which no actor had anticipated. These unanticipated consequences can further alter the dimensions of the network, especially where they change the 'rules of the game' and expose the network to attack from external actors. Consequently, ICTs can both enhance and reduce particular characteristics, so leading to much broader changes in the processes and relationships of policy networks.

The Impact of Policy Networks on ICTs

Just as ICTs influence policy networks, so it is also clear that policy networks can have a significant effect in mediating and altering the implementation of particular technologies. The same technology implemented in different networks may have different impacts and different levels of success, and may lead to different types of outcome, depending upon the characteristics of the network and the purpose of its actors in utilising ICTs. Although there is a diverse range of factors which can influence the use of ICTs by networks there are two which are of particular significance.

Firstly, the dominant culture and ideology of each network is of central importance. As policy networks in local government have emerged around professional functions, the culture and ethos of these professions will be significant in determining the ways and extent to which ICTs are used in the internal processes of the network. Each profession operates within a different paradigm based upon distinct value systems and ideologies. This paradigm pervades all actors in the network, defining the policy agenda, the alternatives available, and the processes through which policy is determined and implemented (Smith 1993).

The influence of network cultures on ICTs can be illustrated by contrasting two distinct professional networks in local government. Civil engineers operate within a highly structured, systematic and technical environment, in which precision is vital to achieving a final and absolute solution to any problem. This environment gives rise to a dominant culture which emphasises technical solutions over intuitive judgements. It is a culture which readily accepts and encourages ICTs, and which attempts to exploit technical capacity to its limits. Consequently, civil engineering departments take advantage of by far the widest range of ICTs in local government, including CAD (computer aided design) software, geographic information systems and the extensive use of customised personal computing software, as well as functional management systems. Civil engineers use an array of ICTs in their day to day jobs.

By contrast social workers operate within a much different frame of reference. The underlying ideology of the social services network gives much greater emphasis to the intuitive judgements of individual social workers, and rejects the notion of one best solution for every problem. Indeed, it accepts that the underlying problems are often difficult to identify, and that competing theories and answers to problems are all relevant. Consequently, it gives much greater emphasis to processes than it does to final solutions. Introduced into this culture, ICTs are not received with such enthusiasm.

The intuitive and highly personal nature of social work produces an ideology which is indifferent to or suspicious of technologies, and consequently, the use of ICTs is much more restricted. Despite the rapid expansion of new technologies in local government, therefore, ICT innovations in the social services remain limited to department-wide information and management systems for the administration of client records. There is little evidence of social workers using ICTs in their day to day work.

The second factor which influences the role of ICTs in policy networks concerns the degree of integration and interdependency between actors. The extent to which the network facilitates long-term stable relations and inter-dependencies will determine not simply the amount of ICTs used by the network, but also the types of ICTs used and the purpose and meaning of them to network processes. Fragmented and unstable networks will encourage actors to develop protective and isolated applications for ICTs. Hence, individual actors will adopt a defensive and insular approach to ICTs which emphasises the safeguarding of individual information rather than encouraging mutually beneficial information exchanges throughout the network. The introduction of CCT in many areas of local government has had the effect of fragmenting the relationships within policy sectors, and has encouraged actors to use ICTs as a tool with which to protect their own domains. In the area of buildings maintenance, ICT systems were originally developed to provide mutual information for both the client and contractor elements of the process, with some safeguards to protect the integrity of the tender process. Running on shared hardware and encouraging cooperative relations between the relevant parties, the Direct Labour Information Systems (DILIS) developed by ICL in the early 1980s was a classic example of software designed to benefit both the client and the contractor elements of an authority. In contrast, more recent software developments have been designed specifically to encourage greater division between client and contractor, to rely much more upon a separation of hardware facilities, and to foster an ethos of independence rather than cooperation. In fragmented networks, therefore, ICTs can be used to unsettle power relations and shift the balance of power between actors.

Networks that are highly integrated use ICTs to enhance the interdependencies and integration of actors. New technologies are used to reinforce the stability of relations, and to reduce the costs of individual transactions. They reaffirm the commitment of individual actors to the relationships of the network, and protect them from incursions from external parties. The development of ICTs in library services is a good example of new technologies being used to enhance the interdependencies of the network. As well as introducing technologies for the primary benefit of internal services, ICTs are also being used to augment and streamline relationships with other libraries, suppliers, and users of services.

Combining these two factors, it emerges that those networks which have a culture that is more open to technological solutions, and which have a high degree of integration and interdependency amongst actors, are more likely to make extensive and effective use of ICTs as an integral part of network processes. Similarly, fragmented networks with cultures and ideologies that do not lend themselves so easily to ICTs will find it more difficult to achieve successful implementations of ICTs, and to gain real benefits from them. This may appear to be a somewhat unexceptional conclusion, but its significance should not be overlooked. In the rush to informatise local government, it is tempting to assume that because a technology works in one policy area, its benefits can be achieved elsewhere as well. Returning to the definition of ICTs developed in the introduction, it becomes clear that technologies are not confined to the physical entities of a system, but also include the processes and ideologies of the networks in which they operate. If ICTs are to be successfully introduced into a policy area, it is as important to consider the impact which the ideology and interdependencies of the network will have on the technology, as it is to consider the technical factors of implementation. Policy networks have an important bearing upon the efficacy and meaning of ICTs in particular contexts.

Conclusion

The relationship between ICTs and policy networks is a complex and ambiguous one. It is complex because ICTs affect many dimensions of networks at the same time, strengthening some elements whilst weakening others. This complexity is compounded by the fact that networks are not only affected by new technologies, they also affect the technologies themselves. Networks interact with ICTs in a dynamic relationship which constantly alters the meaning of new technologies to the network, and their impact upon the network. The relationship is also ambiguous, because introducing new technologies does not produce predictable policy outcomes or processes. New ICTs can have varying effects upon networks depending upon such factors as the strategies and objectives of individual actors, the degree of integration between them and the disposition of the overall culture and ideology of the network.

The growing informatisation of public administration has profound implications for policy networks and their internal processes. At the normative level, ICTs will lead to changing policies, brought about by changing relationships within and between networks. New technologies have the potential to change the nature of discourse on policy, the extent of network interactions, and to shape and restrain policy options. The concern at this level is that ICTs may be used, as was suggested earlier of the education network, to marginalise the role of local authorities in the policy process. The challenge for local government, therefore, is to find ways of using ICTs that will bring directly elected and accountable local authorities to the centre of policy networks. This means using ICTs to engineer new and unique information roles for local government. Initiatives that aim to give more information on policy to local citizens are one example of this. Of greater importance, however, are more radical initiatives that will use ICTs to involve local citizens in democratic policy processes. This does not simply mean using ICTs for the electronic polling of citizens, but means finding new ways of developing real discourse with citizens and increasing their access to local government. By so doing, local authorities will be able to reassert their claim to unique representation of their localities.

At the theoretical level, ICTs can also be used to explain and analyze articulation between the policy processes of individual networks and broader socio-economic and political developments. As well as being relevant to an analysis of changing power and dependencies within individual networks, ICTs are also relevant to broader, macro-level analyses of structural change. New technologies transcend the levels of analysis and provide an important means of articulation between them. The foregoing analysis of the relationship between ICTs and policy networks provides the nucleus for an analysis of this articulation. As just one element of the articulation between levels of analysis, however, there remains scope for much further development.

The consequences for ICTs in public administration are only beginning to be considered. The relationships that are now developing between ICTs and policy networks could have policy implications that last long after the physical technologies have become redundant. It is important, therefore, to analyze and understand this relationship now.

References

Audit Commission (1990), *Preparing an information technology strategy: Making IT happen*, London: HMSO.

Bellamy, C & J.Taylor (1992), 'Informatisation and new public management: an alternative agenda for public administration', *Public Policy and Administration*, 7, 3, 29-41.

Burningham, D. (1992), 'An overview of the use of performance indicators in local government', in C.Pollitt & S.Harrison (eds), *Handbook of Public Services Management*, Oxford: Blackwell.

Carter, P. (1989), 'Routine maintenance management systems', Paper to Institute of Civil Engineers seminar, February 1989.

Dockery, E. (1992), 'Management and the usefulness of information', in L.Willcocks & J.Harrow (eds), *Rediscovering Public Services Management*, London: McGraw-Hill.

Frissen, P. (1992), 'Informatisation in public administration: research directions', paper to the ESRC/PAC seminar on information and communication technologies in public administration, Regents College, London. March 1992.

Hackney, R. (1989), 'Considerations for prototype advanced information technology applications within United Kingdom local government', *Local Government Studies*, 15, 4, 35-47.

Hanf, K & L.O'Toole (1992), 'Revisiting old friends: networks, implementation structures and the management of inter-organizational relations', *European Journal of Political Research*, 21, 1-2, 163-180.

Hepworth, M. (1992), 'The municipal information economy?', *Local Government Studies*, 18, 3, 148-157.

Hoggett, P. (1987), 'A farewell to mass production? Decentralisation as an emergent private and public sector paradigm', in P.Hoggett & R.Hambleton (eds), *Decentralisation and Democracy: localising public services*, Bristol: SAUS.

Jordan, G & K.Schubert (1992), 'A preliminary ordering of network labels', *European Journal of Political Research*, 21, 1-2, 7-28.

Marsh, D & R.A.W.Rhodes (1992), 'Policy networks in British politics: a critique of existing approaches' in D.Marsh & R.Rhodes (eds), *Policy Networks in British Government*, Oxford: Clarendon.

Pratchett, L. (1993), 'Open Systems and Closed Networks: the role of policy networks in determining local government policies towards ICTs', Leicester Business School – Occasional Paper 9.

—— (1994), 'Open systems and closed networks: policy networks and the emergence of open systems in local government', *Public Administration* (forthcoming).

Raab, C. (1992), 'Taking networks seriously: education policy in Britain', *European Journal of Political Research*, 21, 1-2, 69-90.

Ravetz, J. (1993), 'Modelling support systems in the public sector', paper to the ESRC/PAC seminar on ICTs in public administration, London, June 1993.

Rhodes, R.A.W. (1988), *Beyond Westminster and Whitehall: The sub-central governments of Britain*, London: Unwin Hyman.

Rhodes, R.A.W & D.Marsh (1992), 'Policy communities and issue networks: beyond typology' in D.Marsh & R.Rhodes (eds), *Policy Networks in British Government*, Oxford: Clarendon.

Scarbrough, H & J.Corbett (1992), *Technology and organisation: power, meaning and design*, London: Routledge.

Schneider, V. (1992), 'The structure of policy networks: a comparison of the chemicals control and telecommunications policy domains in Germany', *European Journal of Political Research*, 21, 1-2.

Smith, M. (1993), *Pressure, Power and Politics*, London: Harvester Wheatsheaf.

SOCITM (1992), *IT Trends in Local Government 1992*, Society of Information Technology Managers in Local Government.

Stoker, G. (1990), 'Regulation theory, local government and the transition from Fordism' in D.King & J.Pierre (eds), *Challenges to local government*, London: Sage.

Street, J. (1992), *Politics and Technology*, London: Macmillan.

Taylor, J & H.Williams (1991), 'Public administration and the information polity', *Public Administration*, 69, 171-190.

Waarden, F.Van (1992), 'Dimensions and types of policy networks', *European Journal of Political Research*, 21, 1-2, 29-52.

Zuboff, S. (1988), *In the Age of the Smart Machine: the future of work and power*, Oxford: Heinemann.

Women and Democratisation

Rohini Hensman
Bombay University

'The Role of Women in the Resistance to
Political Authoritarianism in Latin American and South Asia'

Today, thanks to the work of feminist historians who have painstakingly excavated the evidence buried by a male-biased view of history, it would be hard to deny that women have played a significant role in resistance struggles and national liberation movements. What is argued in this paper, however, is a stronger position: namely, that in the countries considered, women have in specific conjunctures played a crucial or leading role in the resistance to political authoritaranism, an autonomous role independent of male leadership.

The autonomous intervention of women in politics in Argentina, Chile and Brazil became significant precisely at a point when political life as a whole was at its lowest ebb. The best-known case is probably that of the Madres of the Plaze de Mayc in Argentina, 'who began meeting in April of 1977 to publicize and resist disappearances of their sons and daughters' (Feijoo, p.74), after the military coup in March 1976. In a situation where state terrcrism had virtually destroyed all forms of organisation within civil society, the Madres succeeded in sustaining a political organisation and agenda through developing 'new forms of mobilization, such as a walk (ronda) around the plaza; giving old symbols a new meaning (for example, the white handkerchiefs); [and] their capacity to resignify a public space (the plaza)' (Feijoo, p.78). While the loss of their children affected both mothers and fathers, it was women who took the courageous decision to organise themselves and give public, political expression to their private anxiety and grief, thus initiating a process of organised political protest against the dictatorship.

In Chile, massive state repression unleashed after the military coup of September, 1973, terrorised the population and immobilised political protest for several years. In 1979, it was women who broke the fear psychosis by

'stepping out of the family, leaving the allegedly protected environment of their homes to invade the streets with their presence and demand a return to participatory democracy. They did so many years before men dared manifest themselves publicly against the regime. The formation of the umbrella organisation Mujeres por la Vida (Women for Life) brought together diverse women's organisations, including the Movement of Shanty-Town Women (Movimiento de Mujeres Pobladoras), The Women's Union Coordinating Committee (La Coordinatora Sindical Femenina) and the Feminist Movement, with the slogan "Democracy in the country and at home". ' (Bunster 211-12)

As this slogan indicates, the experience of political self-organisation led women to question their normal marginalisation in the public, political sphere and relegation to a private sphere where their role was defined purely in terms of their reproductive potential. Their opposition to the dictatorship and participation in the struggle for democracy was the context in which the demands for recognition as equal partners, women's liberation, and the democratisation of private life emerged as important issues (Chuchryk, p.162). Even among the many Chilean feminists who continued to emphasise the centrality of class struggle, machismo and women's oppression came to be seen as being divisive of the working class, and therefore to be opposed even from a purely class perspective (Chuchryk, p.171).

In Brazil, as in Argentinia and Chile, women made their appearance on the political scene at a time when military rule and state terrorism had virtually stamped out all other forms of political life. The survival of women's organisations in such a situation has been explained as follows:

> 'The ingrained belief that women are indifferent to politics may have led the military rulers of Brazil to believe that any-thing women do is intrinsically "apolitical". Thus, even when women began organising campaigns against the rising cost of living or for human rights in Brazil, the military seems to have allowed women's associations greater political leeway than was granted to militant left, student and labor organisations, which were seen as more threatening to "national security". The 1975 celebrations of International Women's Day were thus among the first public assemblies permitted since the mass mobilizations of 1967-1968. The Feminine Amnesty Movement was allowed to organise in the mid-1970s when a conventional movement of that sort might have been actively repressed. In short, the in-stitutionalized separation between the public and private may, in an ironic historical twist, have helped to propel women to the forefront of the opposition in Brazil.' (Alvarez, pp.25-26)

This does not mean that women were immune to repression; many were tortured, some disappeared. Nonetheless, they confronted the military authorities with a dilemma; how could they be repressed simply for trying to be good wives, mothers and howsewives? The state's own gender ideology thus gave women a small space for manoeuvre: they used 'the "social construction" of femininity, by making legitimate their cultural female re-sources – "mother power" – in the political arena. They ... consciously used their nurturing role as a powerful political instrument aimed at destabilizing the military junta' (Bunster, p.211).

The reason why women were able to utilise this minimal space to such striking effect was that they adopted innovative forms of organisation which were unfamiliar to the state authorities and therefore more difficult to han-dle. When the dictatorship banned political parties and trade unions, the traditional male-dominated forms of organisation, men were paralysed, de-prived of their power of organised action. Women, traditionally less organ-ised, were also less bound by the traditional forms of organisation and could use their imagination and skill to organise not merely nationally but also internationally in order to combat authoritarian military regimes.

The situation in Nicaragua was slightly different, in that the Sandinista National Liberation Front (F.S L.N.) was already engaged in struggle when women's groups became active. In 1977, the Association of Nicaraguan Women Confronting the Nation's Problems (AMPRONAC) was formed to publicise atrocities committed by the National Guard and campaign for the release of political prisoners.

> 'Nearly three-quarters of the people who took to the streets in the popular insurrection were under twenty-five, and supporting them in their clandestine activity, coming to their defence when threatened and tortured by the National Guard, seemed a natural extension of motherhood ... AMPRONAC actively recruited women around this aspect of their lives."We women experience this political crisis as citizens, wives and housewives", declared its programme ... The opportunity to take part in politics through development of their normal roles was a significant factor in the extent of women's involvement in the war!' (Harris, pp.193-4)

In 1979 AMPRONAC was renamed the Luisa Amanda Espinoza Association of Nicaraguan Women (AMNLAE) after the first young woman guerilla to be killed by the National Guard, and took on the task of fighting inequality and discrimination against women. Although it continued to emphasise the incorporation of women in the struggle to defend liberated Nicaragua, there was also an attempt to insist on the recognition of women's rights, and they were successful in pressurising the Sandinista Government to take up problems like domestic labour and paternal irresponsibility (Harris, 196-7, 206). In a sense, the politicisation of motherhood in an earlier phase of acute political repression made it easier for women to gain recognition for the social contribution made by their normal day-to-day work in maintaining the home and to question the convention which laid the entire burden of this work on them alone.

A similiar politicisation of motherhood occurred in Sri Lanka, where since the late '70s a civilian dictatorship and civil war have resulted in a thoroughgoing militarisation of society and the development of increasingly authoritarian political forces on both sides of the Sinhala/Tamil ethnic divide. In this situation, women have not contented themselves simply with opposing repression from the 'other' side, but have tackled the difficult task of opposing it within their own ethnic group. For example, in 1986 Tamil women in the Eastern Province armed themselves with rice pounders – a common but potentially lethal domestic implement – to prevent the dominant Liberation Tigers of Tamil Eelam from massacring unarmed members of a rival Tamil group. Perhaps the most spectacular instance and the one most reminiscent of Latin America was the Mother's Front rally, consisting mainly of Sinhalese women, in Southern Sri Lanka in 1991. Counter-insurgency operations by the Sinhalese government against a Sinhalese militant group, carried out through the military as well as unofficial death squads, had resulted in tens of thousands of disappearances and extrajudicial killings, not only of suspected insurgents but also of civilian critics and opponents of the government. The consequence was an almost palpable atmosphere of terror, in which people were afraid even to voice criticisms in private, much less organise in open opposition to the state. The success of the Mothers' Front rally, undertaken in defiance of a government ban, was a crucial element in breaking the terror which had gripped the South and opening the way once again for organised civilian opposition.

The ability to be critical of authoritarianism within their own ethnic group has also enabled Sri Lankan women to oppose the ethnic war as such, seeing it as a power struggle with only negative consequences for most people of all communities. While organised opposition to the war has been confined to a few small groups such as Women for Peace, emotional and verbal oppposition is far more widespread and a potentially powerful force. For example, the remark by a woman refugee – greeted with laughing assent by her friends – that 'Earlier the old men used to talk and waste time; now the young men are fighting and wasting time', expresses a very common scepticism about the antics of male leaders (see Hensman).

In India too, the peace-making role of women has been very evident. After every round of communal violence, women's organisations have been in the forefront of relief work, peace marches and door-to-door canvassing for communal harmony. While so far this activity has tended to follow rather than forestall the actual violence, it has played a significant role in limiting the damage and minimising feelings of rancour which could lead to further violence.

In India, as in Pakistan and Bangladesh, authoritarian politics has taken the form of religious fundamentalism or revivalism. The threat posed by these movements to women's rights is so dire that the emergence of women's organisations as their strongest opponents is hardly surprising. The revivalist threat to women is least obvious in India, where Hindu revivalism has vey cleverly adopted elements of feminist discourse while in practice affirming the subordinate position of women, and has used traditional symbols of female strength to argue that Hindu women do not need liberation because they already have it within traditional Hinduism. Islamic fundamentalism, on the other hand, has been less subtle. Muslim Family Law in all South Asian countries systematically and blatantly discriminates against women, and the growing strength of fundamentalism has deprived Muslim women even of the rights they formerly had. The process has gone furthest in Pakistan, where the *Hudood Ordinance*, enacted in 1979, makes it possible for a rape victim who cannot prove she has been raped to be sentenced to public flogging for adultery (Khawar & Shaheed, pp.100ff) and the *Law of Evidence, 1984*, makes a female witness equivalent to half a male witness in a court of law (Khawar & Shaheed, pp.106ff).

While international organisation among South Asian feminists has not reached anywhere hear the impressive level achieved by Latin American feminists, there have been significant attempts at solidarity and networking, especially important in a region where each country has been in a war or near-war situation with at least one of the others. A draft South Asian Feminist Declaration issued by a joint conference in 1989 remarked that:

'Feminism as a movement in South Asia has asserted the principle of autonomous organisation for women, while linking with broader movements at the same time ... Linking together in concrete actions, formulating and campaigning on a joint charter of women's rights, sharing visions and developing alternatives to existing development models at the South Asian level from a feminist perspective would be an important contribution towards overcoming the tensions, distrust and political, economic, social and cultural crisis affecting our countries today.'

It is notable that all four video films made in Bombay in the wake of the anti-Muslim pogroms of December 1992 – January 1993 as part of a movement of resistance to Hindu religious revivalism were produced by women, while the novel 'Lajja' (Shame) written by Bangaladeshi feminist writer Tasleema Nasreen in protest against retaliatory violence against Hindus in Bangladesh, was banned by the government and the novelist was issued with a 'fatwa' (death sentence) by Islamic fundametalists.

At this point it is important to emphasise that this is not an argument that women are by nature anti-authoritarian, or that they do not play a part in right-wing movements. There are many examples which demonstrate the opposite, Chile and India being two of them. In Chile, while Mujeres por la Vida emerged to coordinate organisations mobilising women to oppose the Pinochet regime, the military regime was also busy mobilising other women to turn them into a base of support for the very same regime. And the effort, begun in 1973 was not unsuccessful. By 1987, pro-regime women's community organisations controlled thousands of women and permeated civilian life.

'The two most important organisations, because of their sophisticated structure and management and their massively articulted impact on women from all social classes (were) Cema-Chile (Chilean Mother's Centres) and the Secretaria National de la Mujer (Women's National Secretariat), or S.N.M ... By 1983 Cema-Chile had 6,000 volunteers responsible for organising and indocrinating 230,000 members in more than 10,000 mothers' centres; the S.N.M. boasted of having 10,000 volunteers in 321 branch officers: and it is estimated that during the ten-year period, 1973 to 1983, its activities had involved more than two million women.' (Bunster, 213-14)

The president of both organisations was Pinochet's wife, Lucia Hirart de Pinochet; in the case of S.N.M. appointed by Pinochet himself. Typically S.N.M. volunteers would be upper-middle and middle-class, middle-aged women whose lives were not in any way threatened by the military regime; most Cema volunteers were wives of officers of the armed forces and police. These organisations offered such women a chance to play a prominent role in public life without challenging power relations at the domestic or national level.

In India the Rashtriya Swayamsevak Sangh (RSS), a right-wing Hindu organisation formed in 1925, 'is virtually unique among modern Indian socio-political organisations in being exclusively male. It did, however, set up a women's branch, the Rashtrasevika Samiti, the first, in fact, of its affiliates, way back in 1936' (Basu et al, p.41). It currently has a membership of around 100,000 mainly middle-class women, typically with male relatives in the RSS. Alhough there are sessions (*shakhas*) providing members with physical and ideological training, there is a greater stress on family work:

> 'Simple daily rituals are prescribed for home use, with even a "correspondence course" of postal instructions for those who, after marriage, are unable to attend the *shakhas*. Members make it a point to visit each other's homes, help out in domestic crises and maintain contact even with those who can no longer find time for Samiti work. Ideology is spread through sustained kinship and neighbourhood contact with non-Rashtrasevika women, and there is a system of informal training for unaffiliated wives of RSS members and sympathizers.' (Basu et al, p.42)

The efficacy of this 'molecular' model of ideological mobilisation is borne out by the participation of 20,000 frenzied women activists (*kar sevikas*) in the demolition of the Babri Mosque in Ayodhya in December 1992, while women activists of the Mahila Aghadi of the Shiv Sena subsequently participated in the gruesome anti-Muslim pogrom in Bombay. As in Chile, these organisations provide an opportunity for mainly middle class, middle-to-upper-caste Hindu women to play a role in public life and assert themselves at the expense of a defenceless minority community.

The role of women as mothers is highlighted in these cases too; but what distinguishes it from the subversive motherhood of resistance organisations is that it is firmly located within a patriarchal structure. In Chile:

> 'The "patriotic mother" drummed up by the Pinochet regime is ... strictly subordinated to the pater familias and particularly to the pater patrias (father of the nation); the "patriotic mother" has a derived secondary identity stemming from her unconditional admiration for the "father of the homeland", Pinochet himself.' (Bunster, p.216)

Similarly in India, the RSS model is one of

> 'faithful motherhood in which the women affiliated to the RSS would confine themselves to the proper training of children and spreading the word through quiet domestic and neighbourhood contacts ... Members pool resources to reduce the burden of dowry, instead of campaigning against it. Sevikas are always told to try persuasion, but never openly revolt against their families, in matters of choice of husband, marital ill-treatment, or even participation in Samiti work ... They disapprove of divorce and offer no legal counselling to women fighting against their families for their rights!' (Basu et al, p.42)

A very different example underlines what these women's organisations have in common. In Sri Lanka, the 'Freedom Birds' are women fighters in the

Liberation Tigers of Tamil Eelam (LTTE), an organisation which has the ostensible aim of winning 'self-determination' for the Tamil minority in Sri Lanka, but has attempted to achieve this aim not only through atrocities committed against civilians of other communities, including children, but also by ruthless suppression of dissidents and critics among Tamils themselves. These women are undoubtedly playing a non-conventional role, and there is no question of motherhood here: indeed it is believed that one of the factors driving young women to take up arms in the war-ravaged North and East of Sri Lanka is the virtual impossibility of their ever having a normal family life. Instead, the object of their unquestioning devotion is the male leader V. Prabhakaran (who might be called the father of the Tamil Nation) for whom they declare themselves unconditionally ready to fight and die.

What these three examples show is that women, in large numbers, can be drawn in to support authoritarian regimes or leaderships; the subservient role played by these women contrasts sharply with the independent, autonomous role of women's resistance groups and organisations. The prominent presence of women on opposite sides in these conflicts emphasises the dangers of treating 'women' as a homogeneous category, ignoring differences of class, community and political orientation; it would obviously be wrong to say that all women are opposed to authoritarian politics. And yet we still have to explain the fact that women have proved themselves capable of active, autonomous, vehement opposition to authoritaran politics in situations where men of the same class, community and political orientation have been much weaker in their opposition if not virtualy silenced.

Two possible reasons come to mind. Firstly, women can be consistent in their opposition to authoritarianism in both public and private life, while for many men there is a contradiction between their resistance to state authoritarianism and their desire to perpetuate some degree of male domination in gender relations. As the Chilean feminist Julieta Kirkwood pointed out after the coup in 1973, 'Now, confronted by (military) authoritarianism, women, in a certain sense, are faced with a phenomenon well known to them: authoritarianism in their daily experiences ...' (Chuchryk, p.162). The gender oppression suffered by women means that they can be more single-minded and principled in their opposition to authoritarianism as such.

This first reason would be more operative amongst conscious feminists, whereas the second would affect a much wider mass. This is the fact that even the conventional gender roles ascribed to women become impossible to carry out in conditions of extreme repression except through acts of organised resistance. When the simple task of ensuring the survival and welfare of their loved ones is frustrated by widespread torture, disappearances and extrajudicial killings, women in their thousands take to the streets, they organise and resist. Where political repression is combined with strructural adjustment programmes, as it has been in most of these countries, the most conventional gender roles of mother, wife and housewife come to involve opposition to the political and economic policies of the state. The emotional intensity of their response, the fearlessness and tenacity with which they confront the most fearsome authoritarian regimes, are engendered by a division of labour which socialises women and girls into being the guardians of life and the repositories of love. Thus the politics of groups like the Madres of the Plaza de Mayo is 'based on the all-out defense of the most basic principles – the defense of life and of the right to love' (Feijoo, p.78).

To recognise the enormous potential for anti-authoritarian political action which large masses of ordinary women in these countries have displayed is not to glorify the gender division of labour which, of course, is also responsible for depriving women of political effectiveness in times of less acute repression. The suggestion, rather, is that a vision of political and economic democratisation in both public and private life backed up by the fervour of an all-out defence of life and the right to love can be the basis of a feminist movement which goes beyond resistance to authoritarian politics and begins to carry out a more profound transformation of society, bringing traditional 'feminine' concerns – affirmation of life, satisfaction of needs, relationships of love and caring – out of the private, domestic sphere and into a public life currently dominated by life-denying, profit-seeking, power-obsessed competitive relationships.

References

Akhter, Farida, 1992, *Depopulating Bangladesh: Essays on the Politics of Fertility*, Narigrantha Prabartana, Bangladesh.

Alvarez, Sonia E, 1989, 'Women's Movements and Gender Politics in the Brazilian Transition', in Jaquette, Jane S (ed) 1989, *The Women's Movement in Latin America, Feminism and the Transition to Democracy*, Unwin Hyman, USA.

Basu, Tapan et al, 1993, *Khaki Shorts, Saffron Flags*, Orient Longman, New Delhi.

Bunster, Ximena, 1988, 'The Mobilization and Demobilization of Women in Militarized Chile', in Isaksson, Eva (ed), 1988, *Women and the Military System*, Harvester, Great Britian.

Chuchryk, Patricia M., 1989, 'Feminist Anti-Authoritarian Politics: The Role of Women's Organisations in the Chilean Transition to Democracy', in Jaquette (ed), *op.cit.*

Feijoo, Maria del Carmen, 1989, 'The Challenge of Constructing Civilian Peace; Women and Democracy in Argentina', in Jaquette (ed), *op.cit.*

Harris, Hermione, 1988, 'Women and War: The Case of Nicaragua', in Isakesson, Eva (ed), *op.cit.*

Hensman, Rohini, 1992, 'Women and Ethnic Nationalism in Sri Lanka', *Journal of Gender Studies*, November 1992, Hull.

Mumtaz, Khawar & Shaheed, Farida (eds) 1987, *Women of Pakistan: Two Steps Forward, One Step Back?*, Zed Books, London.

Women and Democratisation

Delia Davin
University of Leeds

'Chinese Women: Media Concerns and the Politics of Reform'

Introduction

A paper on China is not an obvious candidate for a panel on women and democratisation since the process of democratisation observable over so much of the contemporary world has not yet taken root in China. The point is frequently made that China has implemented economic reform without any profound political reform and by implication without political change or democratisation. Social scientists debate whether the lack of political reform will at some point bloc further economic growth, or alternatively whether economic growth will produce irresistible pressures for political reform.[1] It may be that this discourse defines 'political' in too narrow a way, or sets up too absolute a division between political reform and economic reform in the very broad sense it has been implemented in China. There was minimal democratic reform of the organs of the party and the state in China in the 1980s, but there was an enormous growth in alternative sources of power, influence and information in the form of a freer press and publishing industry, the establishment of private companies, voluntary associations, private schools and other institutions as a result of what are usually referred to in China simply as 'the reforms'. Despite the obvious existence of limits and constraints there is also a much greater tolerance for private or grass-roots debate or dissent. In a new departure for China it is possible for alternative candidates for local People's Congresses to stand against and defeat official party candidates: a development which while not bringing a democratisation of power, has encouraged some limited democratic debate. Some analysts argue that this has produced the beginnings of a civil society in China.[2] I do not wish to push this argument too far, but I hope I have said enough to show that the process of change in China known as 'the reforms' has begun a process of what could be called 'pluralisation' which includes some very basic (and very limited) democratisation.

Women's issues have attracted an enormous amount of attention in post-reform China in all types of publications from the most popular magazines to serious academic journals. What is striking about this writing is its great diversity. Some is complacent about the situation of women in contemporary China; much is quite critical. It is written from many perspectives, some feminist, many which are not and some which are clearly anti-feminist.

The variety of this writing in terms of standpoint, subject-matter and objectives marks it out clearly from most writing on women which appeared

---

[1] See the discussion in Andrew Nathan (1990), *China's Crisis: Dilemmas of Reform and Prospects for Democracy*, Columbia University Press

[2] Gordon White (1993), *Riding the Tiger: the Politics of Economic Reform in Post-Mao China*, Macmillan.

in the first three decades of the People's Republic. After 1949, most writing on women closely reflected current Party policy.[3] Policy on women did undergo changes and development over the years but in most periods writing on women's issues was stereotyped and predicable in its focus, shifting in accordance with changes in broader Party concerns rather than women's specific needs. It informed its audience about policy and contrasted the misery and oppression suffered by women in the old society with the enormous improvements offered under the new. These improvements were to be brought about by a range of measures among which the most important were the reform of the old arranged marriage system through the marriage law, and the drawing of women into paid employment outside the home to give them economic independence and social respect. Accordingly the marriage law and women's employment were given detailed media coverage. If inequalities or injustices to women were reported at all they were explained in terms of remnants from the old society and a lack of thoroughness in implementing communist policy; the possibility that the policy itself was inadequate was not considered.

By contrast, writing on women in contemporary China is not informed by a consistent policy or line. It deals with a wide variety of topics and is produced by a wide variety of people from feminist academics to journalists and officials. It is useful both for what it can tell us about actual problems for women today and for the differing ways in which these problems are viewed. In the rest of this paper I propose some explanations for the widespread concern with women's issues now current in China and discuss some examples of recent writing on women's issues.

Ideology and Women's Issues in Post-Reform China

Since the introduction of the economic reforms at the end of the 1970s, China has experienced extraordinarily rapid social, economic and even political change. GNP has soared, and standards of living have risen with it. The average Chinese is very much better off than 15 years ago. But change has inevitably brought its own stresses and strains. The benefits of growth are unevenly distributed, giving rise to glaring inequalities. Inflation and price reform create great anxieties for those on salaries and pensions. Generation gaps have opened up. The young tend to take for granted and fully participate in the newly-developing acquisitive, consumerist society while older people criticise their greed and extravagance. Corruption is widespread, crime rates are rising and prostitution is obvious in all the big cities. Migrants have left the countryside in their millions in the hope of a better life in the towns. In the general atmosphere of uncertainty, and even anxiety, moral panics are easily generated, and, as elsewhere, often focus on such issues as family life, child-rearing, sexual mores, women's roles and

---

[3] Delia Davin (1978), *Woman-work: women and the party in revolutionary China*, Oxford University Press; Judith Stacey (1983), *Patriarchy and Socialist Revolution in China*, University of California Press.

female comportment. To some extent therefore the concern with gender divisions and women's issues can be read as reflecting a deeper and more pervasive concern about what is happening in Chinese society.

This unease has produced articles urging contradictory courses for women. The official line continues to urge that there should be no discrimination, and that women should be treated equally at work, at home and in education.[4] In 1992 a law protecting the legal rights of women was promulgated although its effects have been limited because no machinery was set up to monitor or promote its implementation.[5] Moreover official literature gives out somewhat mixed messages; since the beginning of the reforms much of it has emphasised the special role of women and their physiological limitations, implying or even arguing that at least a degree of division of labour based on gender is necessary and desirable.[6] An officially-backed campaign for women to be 'virtuous wives and good mothers' (a Confucian concept once condemned in Maoist China) and to create good harmonious families has flourished since the early 1980s.[7] Even more extreme, early in the reform era two economists suggested that women should withdraw from the labour force leaving their jobs to men.[8] The party-led Women's Federation expressed strenuous opposition to this idea but it has been brought up again quite frequently again in the last decade. A later article in the same vein urged that the 'natural division of labour' should be respected with women doing lighter work or part-time work to allow them time for household chores[9] On the other hand, in other articles, the discrimination against women in employment which has become very pronounced in the wake of the reforms is vigorously attacked. Women are urged to overcome it by working and studying harder and building up their self-confidence.[10] Whatever the line taken, articles of this type tend to be didactic and written in a tone of great certainty. The fact that they offer such contradictory views reflects the general lack of consensus on social development in China today.

---

[4] 'Party official says policy on women remains unchanged', *Xinhua News Agency*, 12.1.1988.

[5] For the Chinese text see *Chinese Women*, 10.4.1992.

[6] See 'Men and women are different: cultivate strengths and avoid weaknesses', *Tianjin Daily*, 15.10.1980, translated in Emily Honig & Gail Hershatter (1988), *Personal Voices: Chinese Women in the 1980s*, Stanford University Press

[7] Feng Bian, 'On the concept of good wife and mother in the 1980s', *Women of China*, 7.7.1984.

[8] Letter of August 15 from the secretariat of the All-China Women's Federation to comrades Wan Li and Peng Chong, in All-China Women's Federation (ed), *Selected Women's Movement documents from the period of the Four Great Modernisations 1981-3* (in Chinese), Beijing, Chinese Women's Press, n.d; Wang Shulin, 'The question of urban employment for women', *Management Modernisation*, Number 1, 1983, translated in *Chinese Sociology and Anthropology*, Fall 1987, Volume XX, Number 1.

[9] Ji Zheng, Deviation of women's liberation in China and a tentative plan for instituting a new system of female employment', *Society*, 6.12.1986, translated in *Chinese Sociology and Anthropology*, Spring 1988, Volume 20, no 3.

[10] Anhui Provincial Women's Association (1985), 'How women can become achievers', translated in *Chinese Sociology and Anthropology*, Fall 1987, Volume XX, Number 1.

Political Participation

Women's political participation has been another area of concern in recent years both in the official press and in women's studies publications. It is noted that the reforms appear to have reduced women's political activity at all levels from village committees right up to provincial and central level government.[11] Women were badly under-represented in politics even in the pre-reform era, what is disturbing about contemporary China is that they are losing ground not gaining it. Female membership of the Central Committee peaked in 1973 at 10.3%, by 1992 it was down to 7.5%.[12] While women were 25% of the members of the Standing Committee of the National People's Congress of 1975, they made up only 9% of the Standing Committee in 1993. Data from many sources indicate that this trend is typical at all levels of government. There is a debate about whether this problem is best addressed by quotas which were used formally and informally in the past, especially in the Cultural Revolution era of the early 1970s, but are not applied at present. The introduction of multi-candidate elections in 1987 appears to have disadvantaged women. Where there is a choice, voters prefer men. Analyses of the appointment of rural cadres indicate that women are only appointed as to posts traditionally reserved for females such as women's representative or birth control worker.

The explanation for women's lower participation in all kinds of political activity is again the change in the political climate. There is no longer any real pressure to appoint even token numbers to political office and indeed male political officials may be reluctant to see them in plum jobs. On the other hand women are less willing than in the past to take on the voluntary political responsibilities of a party member or a low level street committee member because it is no longer regarded as praiseworthy for them to take this time away from family responsibilities.

Gender and Employment Issues since the Reforms

There can be no doubt that although women as part of the general population have benefited from China's growing prosperity, the reforms have adversely affected women in certain specific ways. Growing discrimination against women has been noted in many spheres of employment.[13] There have been many reports of companies and government offices demanding to be allocated male rather than female graduates.[14] Investigations of discrimination against women in employment usually come up with the explanation

---

[11] The whole issue of *Chinese Law and Government*, September-October, 1993, Volume 26, Number 5 is devoted to translations of articles on this subject.

[12] *Ibid*, p.4. For more detail see Research Institute of the All-China Women's Federation (1991), *Statistics on Chinese Women 1949-89* (in Chinese), Chinese Statistical Publishing House.

[13] For examples and discussion see Honig & Hershatter, *op.cit*, Chapter 7.

[14] See Yang Xingnan, 'Rejection of female college graduates must be stopped', *Chinese Women*, 27.2.1985.

that women's reproductive functions make them expensive to employ since they will require paid maternity leave and time off to care for sick children. In the era of economic reform when enterprises still usually bear the costs of welfare provision, but are also responsible for their own profit and loss, this is obviously an important consideration. Nevertheless it is not wholly satisfactory as an explanation. Firstly, urban women in present-day China rarely bear more than one child and therefore their time off for maternity leave and childcare is comparatively short. Secondly, in urban China it is normally the man's employers who are expected to provide a newly married couple with rented accommodation, a heavy welfare cost which does not apparently discourage employers from recruiting men. It is difficult not to conclude that once the political pressure not to discriminate was reduced, employers simply felt freer to follow their prejudices.

There are other areas of employment, new since the economic reforms, for which women are actively recruited. These include factory and sweatshop work in the Special Economic Zones and other newly industrialising areas where cheap Chinese labour has attracted foreign and Chinese investors. Working conditions in these enterprises are known to be poor and their safety record is bad as demonstrated in the appalling loss of life in two factory fires at the end of 1992.[15] Complaints in the official press and investigations follow such accidents but they continue to occur. The women employed are often vulnerable migrants from poor inland provinces tempted by earnings higher than they could hope to obtain at home and unlikely to demand safer conditions.

The maidservants who undertake domestic work in the homes of urban families in the big cities are another group of vulnerable migrant workers.[16] These women are much discussed in the media, usually from the employers' point of view. They are therefore characterised as greedy, lazy, ignorant, unskilled and so on. It is rarely pointed out that these girls who are usually young and far from home may be very vulnerable and have little defence against unreasonable demands or ill treatment. The only space they can call their own is often a bed partitioned off from the family living area by a curtain. If employed for childcare they may spend their days alone with a baby, frequently isolated in a high-rise. On the other hand, women who have been in the city long enough to find their way around can take advantage of the fact that there is now a shortage of maids to bargain for shorter hours and better pay. Maids who return to the countryside often take with them enough savings and knowhow to set up small enterprises and become very much more prosperous than their peers who stayed in the countryside.

Gender Issues in Education

At primary and secondary level girls' school enrolment rates are significantly lower than those of boys. Pragmatic peasants see no advantage in paying

---

[15] See John Gittings, 'Sixty die as blaze engulfs Chinese factory', *The Guardian*, 20.12.1993.

[16] See Wan Shanping, *From Country to Capital: A Study of a female migrant group in China*, unpublished PhD thesis, Oxford Brookes University, 1992.

fees to educate girls who will be lost to the family when they marry, and prefer to keep get them to work on the family plot or to earn money in rural industry. The difference in enrolment rates is therefore considerably greater in the higher grades of primary school. For example in 1983, 59.15% of 7 year old girls were in school against 64.9% of boys. For 13 year olds it was 38.0% of the female cohort in school against 51.2% of the male cohort.[17] Eighty per cent of illiterates in China are female.[18] Women are also only in a minority in higher education although their numbers have moved from under one quarter to around a third.[19] This under-representation partly reflects their smaller numbers among those who finish secondary school, but there are other factors. Many colleges admit that they require higher admission grades of female than of male applicants. This is most often justified by the argument that females are disciplined about learning by rote and thus perform better in exams than men whereas the latter with a stronger and more lively intelligence, ultimately have the greater potential.[20] Sometimes employers' preferences are referred to. For example, a school of foreign trade claimed that if it admitted too many women they would end up unemployed however good their grades because employers wished to recruit men.[21] At post-graduate level women's numbers are even smaller. It is widely reported that men are reluctant to marry women more highly qualified than themselves and this is thought to deter women from taking post-graduate courses.

Women and Population policy

Unlike many other gender issues, population policy is discussed in the press only in rather limited ways. This is not an area in which the state would tolerate dissent. Opposition to the policy is not openly expressed although its strictness has occasionally been obliquely questioned in academic journals. In newspapers and magazines read by the general public campaigns are supported, demographic data is reported and news of successes and infringements is printed.

Most Chinese couples are required to limit their families to one child although two or even three are allowed in certain defined circumstances. For example, since the late 1980s, most peasant couples whose first child

---

[17] See Research Institute of the All-China Women's Federation (1991), *Statistics on Chinese Women* (in Chinese), Chinese Statistical Publishing House, p.209. A table on p.219 shows that girls are usually kept away from school because their labour power is needed. See also *10% Sampling of the 1990 Population Census of China* (in Chinese), China Statistical Publishing House, 1991, pp.184-7.

[18] For illiteracy rates see *Census Sampling*, p.180.

[19] *Chinese Statistical Yearbook 1990*, pp 675.

[20] See Suzanne Pepper (1984), *China's Universities: Post-Mao Enrollment Policies and their Impact on the Structure of Secondary Education*, Center for Chinese Studies, University of Michigan, pp.112-4

[21] See Ju Ning, 'My perspective on the discrepancy between the respective scores for admission of men and women for colleges and universities in the Shanghai region', *Shanghai Women*, 10.7.1990, translated in *Chinese Education and Society*, Spring 1993, vol 26, no 2.

is a girl have been permitted a second birth.[22] Faced with the situation that the birth of a daughter will mean that they are not allowed to try again for a son, some couples resort to desperate measures. There were many reports of female infanticide in the early years of the policy. More recently, sex determination tests and selective abortion have been used to assure the birth of a son. Such procedures are forbidden and those carrying them out are subject to considerable penalties, but some experts believe that they are quite commonly resorted to.[23] The 1992 census certainly produced a distorted sex ratio among the youngest age groups although it is impossible to tell which of the possible factors contributed in what proportion to this.[24] It may be that some of the missing girls were simply not registered by parents who wished to have a second child unnoticed by officialdom. Another evil produced by population policy which has been widely reported is the ill-treatment or beating of women who give birth to girls by disappointed husbands or in-laws. Writers of popular science columns insist that women are not responsible for the sex of their babies but apparently this problem persists.[25]

Because it has given rise to such tragic phenomena, the restrictive birth policy has focused attention on the strength of son preference in China and has made it impossible to argue that gender equality has already been achieved. This forced a careful consideration of factors underlying son preference such as patrilocal marriage, an old age support system in which parents depend heavily on their sons, the generally higher earning capacity of males over females and so on. Media coverage of these issues has produced a greater awareness of the structures underlying son preference, though no real solutions have been found.

Women in the Market-Place

In contemporary China as elsewhere in the world everything from clothes to washing machines is now sold by the use of images pretty young women in advertising. The Women's Federation protested against this practice on the grounds that it was demeaning to women when it became commonplace in the early 1980s but commercial interests proved too strong. The issue is still debated in the press, but protests have no effect on practice.[26]

The Communist Party has consistently argued that the custom of giving a brideprice and the exchange of large amounts of money or property at the time of marriage amounted to the sale of women or mercenary marriage.

---

[22] Delia Davin (1990), 'Never mind if it's a girl you can have another try', in J. Delman et al (eds), *Remaking Peasant China*, Aarhus University Press

[23] Zeng Yi et al, 'Causes and implications of the recent increase in the reported sex ratio at birth in China', *Population and Development Review*, 19, Number 2, June 1993.

[24] Terence Hull, 'Recent trends in the sex ratio at birth in China', *Population and Development Review*, 16, Number 1, March 1990.

[25] Delia Davin (1987), 'Gender and Population in the People's Republic of China', in Haleh Afshar (ed) (1987), *Women, State and Ideology*, Macmillan.

[26] See 'Love one's wife = Buy her a washing machine? On male chauvinism in television commercials', and various other articles translated in *Chinese Education and Society*, Summer 1993, Volume 26, Number 3.

Despite repeated campaigns these customs were never wholly eliminated. However, it is widely acknowledged that since the reforms both brideprice and the amounts spent on equipping the new couple's home and on the wedding feast have risen enormously. The rise in brideprice probably reflects the higher value of the girl's labour to her family who have to be compensated for its loss. The huge amounts spent on furnishing and equipping a home for the new couple are to be explained by rising expectations and new consumerist values. Political calls for frugality are still made, but in the new climate they are quite ineffective.[27]

A clearer example of the commoditisation of women is the trafficking in women which has been reported from many places in China.[28] Poor rural women are taken sometimes by coercion, sometimes as volunteers, across hundreds or even thousands of miles to be sold as wives to strangers. The women are recruited in the poorest parts of China and sold in wealthier regions where bride-price for local women is high and imported women offer a cheap alternative for men who would otherwise be unable to afford a wife. The explanation for the traffic is both demographic and economic. Unmarried men of marriageable age outnumber women in everywhere in the Chinese countryside and the working of the market ensures that men in the wealthier areas are able to draw in women from poor regions. Many prosecutions of traffickers have been reported, but the trade basically reflects the magnitude of regional economic inequality in China and it will be difficult to eliminate in the near future. Similar factors have no doubt contributed to the increase in prostitution which has been very widely observed in China.

External Influences

The discussion and treatment of women's issues in China has been very clearly influenced from the outside in various ways. China is part of a global culture to a far greater extent than ever before. Though 'western feminism' is frequently decried as bourgeois in China, or more politely rejected as irrelevant, there can be no doubt that some of its ideas and methods have had an influence both direct and indirect. Many Chinese now travel or study abroad. Some, especially among the women, have been influenced by women's movements in other countries. They are of course a tiny minority in China's vast population, but they are significant among the serious writers on women's issues today. Female academics have set up women's study and discussion groups on many campuses and women's studies centres have been established in various universities, notably at Beijing University, Zhengzhou University and Tianjin Normal University. The women involved in these groups are often familiar with trends in feminist scholarship elsewhere and are influenced by its ideas although some are quick to insist that their task

---

[27] Yang Zhangqiao, 'Mercenary marriages in rural Zhejiang province', *Youth Studies*, February 1987, translated in *Chinese Sociology and Anthropology*, Spring 1989, Volume 21 Number 3.

[28] Zhuang Ping, 'On the social phenomenon of trafficking in women in China', *Sociology Research*, May 1991, translated in *Chinese Education and Society*, Summer 1993, Volume 26, Number 3.

is to develop a new women's studies adapted to Chinese conditions. Their work tends to be more open, scholarly and analytic than earlier writing on women in the People's Republic. Large women's studies conferences were held at Zhengzhou University in 1989 and at Beijing University in 1992 with some international participation.[29]

Another source of outside influence are development and aid agencies. Many of these make it a condition that a certain part of their aid be targeted on women. Thus the growing sensitivity to gender issues among those working in development has its parallel in China.

Even before China was open to the outside world, the Chinese authorities were extremely sensitive to foreign commentaries on and criticisms of China. This remains the case today. Chinese reaction to a Canadian study of the position of women which placed China 132nd in the world illustrates this sensitivity. It was reported in the Chinese press and the Women's Federation was funded to do a large scale survey with the implicit aim of refuting the Canadian study.[30] The indicators chosen for this 1988 study made it inevitable that China's position in the ratings would be low. They were:

(1) attitude towards male and female infants;
(2) rates of school enrolment of boys and girls;
(3) rate of employment of young men and women;
(4) proportion of women among the top leaders in state organs;
(5) position of women in their homes;
(6) percentage of women's personal property in social wealth.

If we look at them one by one, it is obvious that China would do badly on the first as the strength of son preference has been made clear by the introduction of the extremely restrictive birth policy. We have also seen that girls' school enrolment rates compare badly with those of boys. Discrimination against the recruitment of women in employment and the fact that the majority of rural migrants who go to the cities to seek jobs are young males produces a higher employment rate for young men. It is not clear how position in the family was assessed, *de facto* power in the Chinese family varies with individual circumstances, but for formal puposes it is still usual to name the oldest male or the oldest working male as the household head. The only women likely to be identified as household heads are widows, divorcees or women whose husbands have been absent for a long time. Women are poorly represented in political office at the highest levels. Finally, there is little personal wealth in China: the major form of property by tradition is family property. The government has recently tried to introduce the idea of marital and personal property and to reinforce women's property rights

---

[29] Beijing Municipal Women's Federation (1992), *Women's theoretic studies in China from 1981-1990* (in Chinese), Chinese Women's Press.

[30] All my information about both the Canadian study and the Chinese survey is from Stanley Rosen, 'Women and Reform in China', *News Analysis*, 15.1.1993, and from the 'Preliminary Analysis Report in the Survey of the Social Status of China's Women' translated with an introduction by Rosen in *Chinese Education and Society*, Summer 1993, Volume 26, Number 3.

and rights of inheritance but without much success.[31]

It seems only fair to point out that China might have done much better on some other selection of criteria, for example, the proportion of women amongst students studying engineering, the proportion of doctors who are female, women's life expectancy and legal rights, or access to maternal and child health services. Nonetheless the study was taken seriously in China.

The Women's Federation survey commissioned as a response to the Canadian study was based on 42,000 interviews involving almost equal numbers of male and female and urban and rural respondents. It covered employment, education, family status, attitudes and the respondents' own assessment of gender inequality in China.

The findings compared women both to their mothers and to men. For example 87.21% of the female respondents were either working or had retired from a job, 8.9 percentage points lower than for men but 20.7 points higher than for their mothers' generation. Of women under 40, only 5.18% were engaged solely in housework whereas for their mothers' generation the figure had been 27.54%. Employed women in urban areas earned 81.68% of what the males earned. The level to which women had been educated varied with age being much higher among younger people. Of the women surveyed 53.32% were able to name the Party General Secretary, the Premier and the President as against 74.78% of the men.

Differences in attitudes between the sexes towards women's proper place were quite small. For example 48.15% of the males and 51.21% of the females disagreed with or doubted the validity of the saying that a man's place is in society and a woman's place is in the family. Asked whether women should avoid surpassing their husbands in social status, 65.50% of the males and 67.79% of the females expressed disagreement or doubt. Asked where equality had been established, 81.07% thought it greatest in the area of legal rights. Only 40.39% thought it had been established in ideas and concepts. Asked about the sort of inequalities they had observed, the survey respondents came up with a list which corresponds closely with the issues already mentioned in this paper. Women who gave birth to a girl were felt to be looked down on (35.91%), women suffered discrimination in employment (33.09%), it was hard for daughters to inherit property (20.56%), and there was inequality in the score required of males and females to enter schools and colleges (19.74%).

The treatment of timespans in the survey masks the fact that many of the improvements which it found in women's employment and education status and in attitudes towards women probably dated from before the reforms. It has little to tell us about the specific impact of the reforms on women with which the media coverage discussed in this paper is so concerned.

Conclusion

The considerable volume of writing about women and gender issues published in China over the past decade is to be explained by several factors.

---

[31] Delia Davin (1987), 'China: the new inheritance law and the Chinese peasant household', *Journal of Communist Studies*, December, Volume 3, Number 4.

Firstly, in a society undergoing rapid change, the questioning in the writing stands for a more general unease. Although the party line on population is not open to challenge, comparative freedom of discussion is permitted on other gender issues which the state does not seem to regard as threatening. Secondly, the reforms have had a specific and sometimes negative effect on women. The examples looked at in this paper are employment, education, population control, and the commoditisation of women. Among many omissions the most notable one is the position of women in the peasant household which I have discussed elsewhere but have not included here for reasons of space.[32] Thirdly, as the reforms have resulted in a much freer gathering and dissemination of information, the educated élite who do the writing are probably more aware of social problems affecting women than in the past. Finally, Chinese are now far more aware of trends in the world outside China and of foreign commentary on China. This has also contributed to the growing awareness of gender issues. The development of this awareness, and the debates and discussion to which it has given rise, are just one example of the political spin-off from China's primarily economic reforms.

---

[32] Delia Davin (1991), 'Chinese models of development and their implications for women', in Haleh Afshar (ed), *Women, Development and Survival in the Third World*, Longman.

Women and Democratisation

Haleh Afshar
University of York

'Women and the Politics of Fundamentalism in Iran'

Summary

> *This paper is concerned with understanding what Islamic funda-*
> *mentalism means to women who choose to adopt it and how, if at all,*
> *it could be used as a means for political struggles? The intention is*
> *to move away from the usual condemnatory approach to Islamic fun-*
> *damentalism and consider it in the light of the views and activities of*
> *its adherents. Specific examples will be given with reference to Iran*
> *and the women's organisations and their activities in that country.*

What is Fundamentalism?

Fundamentalism has for long been associated with greater or lesser degrees of oppression of women. Given the rise of fundamentalism and the decision of many women to consciously reject feminisms of various kind the adoption of the creed makes it important for some of us to consider what it is and why so many have chosen it? It may be worth while to stand back and consider the reasons that many Muslim women have offered for adopting Islamic fundamentalism and 'returning to the source', both in the United Kingdom and elsewhere.

Part of the problem of understanding fundamentalism has been in terms of definitions and terminology. Muslims themselves do not use the terms fundamentalist at all; the twentieth century Islamists argue that they are revivalists, and are returning to the sources of Islam to regain a purified vision, long since lost in the mire of worldly governments. Shiias, who are a minority school of Islam, but form 98% of the Iranian population have for long seen themselves as the guardians of the poor, the dispossessed and those trampled on by unjust governments.[1] For them revivalism in merely a matter of succeeding in their centuries-long struggle against injustice.

Thus fundamentalism for the Muslims is a return to the roots and a recapturing of both the purity and the vitality of Islam as it was at its inception. In this pursuit of the past, the Muslims, like all those glorifying their histories, are returning to an imaginary golden episode to lighten the difficulties of their current day existence.[2] The golden age for the Shiias is the short term rule of the Prophet about a decade long and the even shorter one of his nephew and son-in-law Ali who ruled for less than five years. The Sunnis who accept the first four caliphs of Islam as being pure and worthy of emulating can lay claim to about 40 years of just rule; from the *hijrat,*

---

[1] See, for example, Momen, M, *An Introduction to Shii Islam*, Yale U.P., 1985.
[2] Chhachhi, A, 'Forced Identities: the State, Communalism, Fundamentalism and Women in India', in Kandiyoti, D. (ed), *Women, Islam and the State*, Macmillan, 1991.

the Prophet's move to Madina in 622 to Ali's death in 661 AD. In addition all Muslims claim to adhere absolutely to the Koranic laws and accept the Koran as representing the very words of God as revealed to his Prophet Mohamad.

> 'The Koran, which is divided into 114 Suras, contains expressly or impliedly, all the divine commands. These commands are contained in about 500 verses and of these about 80 may be regarded by WESTERN lawyers as articles of a code.[3]

Thus in their pursuit of the golden age the Muslims are equipped with fifty years of history and 114 verses of a holy book, perhaps as good a resource as those offered by any other ideology or utopists' vision.

But like all utopias the past and the holy book has difficulties adjusting to the present. It is the domain of interpretation and adjustments to history that Islam is deemed to have become degraded. Yet without such adjustments, it would find it hard to survive as a creed. Thus the notions of return, and revivalism are very much anchored in the processes of interpretations and adjustments. They seek to present new interpretations, puritanical interpretations, interpretations that wipe out the centuries of misdeed and hardship and open the way for the future.

Women and Revivalism

In the twentieth century domain of interpretations, women have been active in their own right. Although the bulk of Islamic theology has been adapted and interpreted by male theologians who have claimed exclusive rights to instituting the Islamic laws, *sharia*, women have always maintained a presence, albeit a small one, in the domains of politics and theology.[4]

They have consistently and convincingly argued that Islam as a religion has always had to accommodate women's specific needs. Since the first convert to Islam was the Prophet's redoubtable and wealthy wife Khadija, no religion which she accepted could discriminate against women. Khadija, who was nearly 20 years older than the Prophet, had first employed him as her trade representative and subsequently commanded him to marry her; overcoming his reserve and reluctance by informing his uncle that she was the very best wife that he could ever have. Their marriage was a happy one and the Prophet did not take another wife till after her death.

Thus some 14 centuries ago Islam recognised women's legal and economic independence as existing and remaining separate from that of their fathers and/or husbands and sons. Islamic marriage was conceived as a matter of contract between consenting partners (*The Koran*, 4:4, 4:24), and one

---

[3] Afchar, H, 'The Muslim Concept of Law', in *The International Encyclopaedia of Comparative Law*, J.C.B.Mohr, Tubingen, The Hague and Paris, p.86.

[4] For detailed discussions see Abbott, Nadia, *Aishah: The Beloved of Mohamad*, University of Chicago Press, Chicago, 1942: Ahmed, Leila, *Women and Gender in Islam*, Yale U.p., New Haven and London, 1992; Keddi, R. & Baron, B. (eds), *Women in Middle Eastern History: shifting boundaries in sex and gender*, Yale U.P., New Haven and London, 1991; Mernissi, Fatima, *Women and Islam: an historical and theological enquiry*, Blackwell, Oxford, 1991.

that stipulated a specific price, *mahre*, payable to the bride before the con-summation of marriage. Women must be maintained in the style to which they have been accustomed (2:238, 4:34) and paid for suckling their babies (2:233).

Besides personal and economic independence, women were also close con-fidants and advisor to the Prophet. Khadija supported him in the early years and undoubtedly her influence protected the Prophet against the var-ious Meccan nobles who wished to quench Islam at its inception. After her death Mohamad's favourite wife Aishah, who married him as a child and grew up in his household became not only his spouse, but also his closest allay and confident. She is known as one of the most reliable interpreters of Islamic laws.

Besides being a renowned source for the interpretation and extension of Islamic laws, Aishah was also an effective politician and a remarkable worrier; like many of the Prophet's wives, she accompanied him on his campaigns. After his death she ensured that her father Abu Bakre and not Mohamad's nephew Ali succeeded to the caliphate, and led the Muslim community. Subsequently when Ali became the Caliph Aishah raised an army and went to battle against him, taking to the field herself. Although she was defeated, Ali treated her with respect, but beseeched her not to interfere in politics.

Thus, if fundamentalism is about returning to the golden age of Islam, Muslim women argue that they have much reason for optimism and much room for manoeuvre. Furthermore, many highly educated and articulate Muslim women regard Western feminism as a poor example and have no wish to follow it. Not only do they dismiss Western feminism for being one of the many instruments of colonialism, but also they despise the kinds of freedoms that is offered to women under the Western patriarchy.[5] Using much of the criticism provided by Western women themselves, the Islamist women argue that by concentrating on labour market analysis and offering the experiences of a minority of white affluent middle class women as a norm, Western feminists have developed an analysis which is all but irrel-evant to the lives of the majority of women the world over.[6] They are of the view that Western style feminist struggles have only liberated women to the extent that they are prepared to become sex objects and market their sexuality as an advertising tool to benefit patriarchal capitalism.[7] They are particularly critical of the failure of Western feminism to carve an ap-propriate, recognised and enumerated space for marriage and motherhood. They argue that by locating the discussion in the domain of production and attempting to gain equality for women, Western feminists have sought and

---

[5] See, for example, al-Gahzali, Zeinab, *Ayam min hayati*, Dar al-shurua, Cairo, n.d, quoted by Hoffman, Valeri J, 'An Islamic Activist: Zeinab al-Ghazali', in Warnok Fer-nea, Elizabeth (ed), *Women and the Family in the Middle East*, University of Texas Press, Austin, 1985; Ahemd, *Women and Gender in Islam; Rhanavard, Z, Toloueh Zaneh Mosalman*, Tehran Mahboubeh Publication, n.d.

[6] For detailed discussions see Afshar, Haleh, 'Fundamentalism and its Female Apolo-gists', in Pendergast, R. & Singer, H.W. (eds), *Development Perspectives for the 1990srm* , Macmillan, 1991, pp.303-318.

[7] See, for example, al-Ghazali, Zeinab, *Ayam min hayati* and Rhanavard, Z, Toloueh Zaneh Mosalman.

failed to make women into quasi-men. They have failed to alter the labour market to accommodate women's needs and at the same time have lost the benefits that women had once obtained in matrimony. Thus Western feminists have made women into permanent second class citizens. Not a model that most women, in the West as elsewhere, choose to follow.

By contrast the Islamist women argue that they can benefit by returning to the sources of Islam. They are of the view that Islamic dictum bestow complementarity on women, as human beings, as partners to men and as mothers and daughters. They argue that Islam demands respect for women and offers them opportunities, to be learned, educated and trained, while at the same time providing an honoured space for them to become mothers, wives and home makers. They argue that unlike capitalism and much of feminist discourse, Islam recognises the importance of women's life cycles, they have been given different roles and responsibilities at different times of their lives and at each and every stage they are honoured and respected for that which they do. They argue that Islam at its inception has provided them with exemplary female role models and has delineated a path that can be honourably followed at each stage. Mohamad's daughter Fatima, for the Shiias in particular, provides an idealised and idolised role model as daughter to the Prophet and wife to the imam, Ali. For all Muslims Khadija represents a powerful representative of independence as well as being a supportive wife. The Sunnis admire Aishah for her powerful intellect as well as her political leadership. Thus, in the revivalist context, Muslim women have no need of Western examples, which are in any case alien and exploitative. They have their own path to liberation which they wish to pursue.

Islamist women are particularly defensive of the veil. The actual imposition of the veil and the form that it has taken is a contested domain.[8] Nevertheless many Muslim women have chosen the veil as the symbol of Islamification and have accepted it as the public face of their revivalist position. For them the veil is a liberating, and not an oppressive force. They maintain that the veil enables them to become the observers and not the observed; that it liberates them from the dictates of the fashion industry and the demands of the beauty myth. In the context of the patriarchal structures that shape women's lives the veil is a means of bypassing sexual harassment and 'gaining respect'.[9]

As post modernism takes hold and feminists deconstruct their views and allow more room for specificities and differing needs, demands and priorities of women of different creeds and colours,[10] it is no longer easy to offer pat denials of the Islamic women s positions.

---

[8] For a detailed analysis see Mernissi, Fatima, *Women and Islam: an historical and theological enquiry*, Blackwell, Oxford, 1991.

[9] As one of many examples this statement was made by a women interviewee in Algeria, for the *Today* programme, 21 September 1993.

[10] See, for example, Afshar, H, The Needs of Muslim Women and the Dominant Legal Order in the United Kingdom", forthcoming; Mirza K, 'The Silent Cry: second generation Bradford women speak', in *Muslims in Europe*, 43 Centre for the Study of Islam and Christian-Muslim Relations, 1989.

Iran and the Practical Politics of Islamist Women

Like all political theories, the Islamist women's has had difficulties in standing the test of the times. Although Islam does provide a space for women, it has been as difficult for Muslim women, as for their Western counterparts, to obtain and maintain their rights. The throng of women who supported the Islamic revolution in Iran were no exception to this rule. On its inception the Islamic Republic embark on a series of misogynist laws, decrees and directives which rapidly curtailed the access of women to much of the public domain. Female judges were sacked, the faculty of law closed its door to female applicants and article 163 of the Islamic constitution states that women cannot become judges.

Subsequently the Islamic laws of retribution (*Qassas* laws) severely eroded women's legal rights. Not only were two women's evidence equated with that of one man, as required by the *Koran* (2:82), but women's evidence, if uncorroborated by men, was no longer accepted by the courts. Women who insisted on giving uncorroborated evidence are judged to be lying and subject to punishment for slander (article 92 of the laws).

Murder is now punished by retribution; but the murderer can opt for the payment of *dayeh*, blood money, to the descendants of the murdered, in lieu of punishment (Article 1 of the Qassas laws). Whereas killing a man is a capital offence, murdering a women is a lesser crime.

Men were also entitled to kill anyone who 'violates their harem', men who murdered their wives, or their sisters, or mothers on the charge of adultery, were not subject to any punishment. But women do not have such rights.

Politically too women were marginalised, article 115 of the Islamic constitution follows Ayatollah Khomeini's instructions in insisting that the leader of the nation, *Valayateh Faqih*, would be a man, and so would the President. Since its inception the Islamic has never had a female member of the cabinet and the numbers of female *Majlis* (Parliamentary) representatives had been less than five in all but the last *Majlis*, where they reached nine.

Thus with the arrival or the Islamic Republic, with the notable exception of the vote, Iranian women lost all they had struggled for over a century. The situation seemed grim indeed.

The Politics of Feminist Fundamentalism

But to despair of the plight of women is to fail to recognise the formidable resilience of Iranian women. They refused to be daunted by this onslaught of patriarchy, as they had been for the past hundred years or more. Although some bowed to the pressures of the Islamic Republic, many remained firm, both as women and as believers in the faith. It was only as devout Muslims that women could counter the demands made of them by the Islamic Republic. Given the Islamic nature of the national political discourse, the defenders of the faiths of women took the Republic to task for failing to deliver its Islamic duties. For Iranian women revivalism has almost literally been a God sent. They have fought against their political, legal and economic marginalisation and although victory is yet to come, they have won considerable grounds and are continuing to do so. Throughout their arguments have been anchored in the teachings of Islam, the Koranic laws and the traditions and practices of the Prophet of Islam.

Using the Koranic instruction that all Muslims must become learned, women have finally succeeded in removing many of the bars placed on their education. Women who gained their training and expertise in the pre-revolutionary days of equality now command high salaries and many run their own successful businesses in the private sector.[11] Private sector schools have simply defied the laws of gender segregation and employed male science and mathematic teachers to teach girls. As a result Iranian girls regularly come top in the University entrance examinations in most subjects!

The Struggle for Equal Employment Opportunity

Islamification has led to a severe cut back in female employment rates. Nevertheless neither the public nor the private sector could operate without female employees, nor for that matter could most households survive without the women's income. Thus despite all attempts women continue to have a presence in the workforce, though in terms of percentage, this presence is much lower than before the revolution.

Elite women such as Azam Taleqani, the redoubtable daughter of the late leading ayatollah Taleqani and member of the first post-revolutionary Parliament, have staged a long hard battle against the marginalisation of women in the labour force. Azam Taleqani who founded the Women's Society of Islamic Revolution, told the press:

> 'Two third of women in this country live and work in the rural areas and carry a major burden of agricultural activity. Nevertheless we do not allow our women to study agricultural sciences at the University.'[12]

Similarly Zahra Rahnavard, a leading Islamic feminist and the wife of the previous Iranian Prime Minister, denounced discrimination against women on religious and political grounds:

> 'Our planners say "we don't have the means to invest equally in men and women and must spend our limited resources on those who provide the highest return for our society. Therefore as women's natural obligations, in giving birth and raising their children, means that they work less, we cannot allocate too great a portion our resources to them."
> We respond that this is wrong since all Muslims are required to pursue knowledge regardless of their gender. It is of

---

[11] For detailed discussion see Afshar H, 'Women and Work: ideology not adjustment at work in Iran'.

[12] 25 December 1990.

the essence, in terms of religious requirement and social well-being, that no barriers be put between women and their quest for knowledge.'[13]

By placing the argument squarely in the Islamic domain, Rahnama Taleqani and others succeeded in gaining the support of some of the leading politicians like Hojatoleslam Nateq Nouri. The long serving, enlightened Minister of Interior declared:

'Islam places no limitation whatever on the participation of women in the public, political and cultural domains.'[14]

In fact legally Iranian women are entitled to equal rights of access to the labour market in Iran and they had been promised a less discriminatory future at the inception of the revolution. Article 43 of the Constitution undertakes to provide employment opportunities for all and states that full employment is a fundamental aim of the revolution. Thus, even after the revolution, the Constitution, Labour Laws and the State Employment Laws make no distinction between men and women. As Azam Taleqani explained:

'Article 28 of our constitution declares that anyone can choose any profession that they wish, provided they do not contravene Islam and public and social interests. The government must provide equal opportunities for every one in every job according to social needs.

The failure to implement this law properly has destroyed the trust of women in Islam and the government.'[15]

Of course in practice women do not benefit from equal pay for equal work provisions. Married women pay higher taxes on their incomes than do married men; and women pay higher child insurance premiums than do men. It is the men who benefit from the married man entitlement whereas it is usually women who end up paying for nursery care of their children. Men get larger bonuses, because it is assumed that they are the head of household, and they are entitled to cheap goods from the civil service cooperatives; their share increases with the numbers of their children. Not so for women who do not even get a share for themselves.[16]

Zahra Rahnavard has repeatedly warned the government that such discriminations eroded much of women's support for the regime. By 1990 she denounced the government for failing to include women in its political agenda:

'We have no strategy for including women in this country's destiny and in this respect we have fallen far short of our political aspiration ... In the five years plan women are only mentioned once ... despite all our protests we have remained invisible. It is essential that women's role in the development process is clearly delineated.'[17]

---

[13] 10 February 1990.

[14] 14 March 1985.

[15] 25 December 1990.

[16] Jaleh Shahriar Afshar, feminist researcher, interviewed on 29 August 1992.

[17] 10 February 1990.

The Politics of Activism, Resistance and Compromise

Activists such as Rahnavard and Taleqani eventually found a foothold in the High Council of Cultural Revolution which determines policies at a national level. There they managed to formulate an Islamic female employment policy. On the 11th of August 1992, 17 months after Zahra Rahnavard had joined the Council, it issued an official document on female employment. Despite President Rafsanjani's directives to the Council 'to educate women about the correct ways of dealing with their husband and children',[18] when the Council chose to educate the rulers about women's liberation it did so by making concessions and focusing on areas where it was possible to make gains.

The High Council accepted that women's first priority was to remain the home and family. But it went on to note that not all women are mothers at all times. It requested that women's life cycles be noted and 'suitable jobs' be provided.

Where the Council's resolution is of interest is in its demand that the familial duties of women be formally recognised. Hence the policy demanded that in addition to equal pay for equal work, in the segment of the labour market allocated to women, the government should also allow women paid time off to enable them to fulfil their 'mothering obligations'. It stated that they should be entitled to shorter working hours and an earlier retirement age; measures which would recognise women's double burden of unpaid domestic work and paid employment.

If, as the Council has suggested, the recognition of 'mothering duties' results in some flexibility in working hours, without cut backs in pay, then women workers would indeed fare much better.

The High Council's declaration further demanded that working women be entitled to job security, unemployment benefits and welfare provisions (article 10). In addition it stated that women who are heads of household should be entitled to special retraining programmes to enable them to return to the labour market (article 11) and the government is urged to provide co-operative type organisations to facilitate home working for women who wish to combine their paid and unpaid jobs (article 12). Thus, in return for accepting women's domestic obligations, the Council's directive sought to extract concessions which would enable women to fulfil both their paid and unpaid duties. Its declaration forms part of the slow, but sanctioned, progress of women in Iran in clawing back the rights that were summarily curtailed by the post-revolutionary state.

Women in Public and Politics

Although they fought shoulder to shoulder with men, women were not given high office by the revolutionary government. It has never appointed

---

[18] 26 December 1991.

a woman to a Ministerial post. A point made by Zahra Rahnavard in 1990 when she complained:

> 'Women have been and continue to be present, at times in larger numbers than men, in our public demonstrations, for the revolution and in its support. But when it comes to public appointments, they are pushed aside ...
>
> Women like myself have continuously campaigned for better conditions. We have made our demands ... in the press and in the public domain. But no one has taken any notice and our voices are not heard.'[19]

But getting elected is only the first step, women members of are severely constrained by the ideological views that designate them as inferior, demands of them to be modest, silent and invisible.[20] Maryam Behrouzi, a veteran representative who had served a prison sentence before the revolution and whose 16 years old son was 'martyred', still found herself firmly discriminated against. She pointed out that women are never elected to high powered committees. Nor did they become chair or officers of other parliamentary committees.[21] Azam Taleqani who gained a seat in the first post-revolutionary *Majlis*, explained that women were expected to be 'naturally modest' and this prevented them from 'saying too much in the *Majlis*'.[22]

Nevertheless the women representatives have not been silent or ineffectual. In April 1991 as the country was preparing for the Parliamentary elections, Maryam Behrouzi demanded that bills allowing an earlier retirement age for women, reforming some of the more draconian divorce laws[23] and provision of national insurance for women and children be put before the next session of the *Majlis*.

In the subsequent *Majlis* nine women were elected. In a remarkable move, they managed to alter the divorce laws to make it more expensive for men to leave their wives at will. In fact except for a brief period, the Post-Revolutionary government had not succeeded in closing down the Family Courts set up before the revolution to curb divorce, or defend the aggrieved party, who was usually the wife, in familial disputes. The Islamic government had restored the male prerogative to easy divorce. By using the marriage contract, and insisting on the Koranic right to fair treatment, many Iranian women had continued going to the Family Courts.[24] Nevertheless on the whole the courts favoured the men and on divorce women were not entitled to any of their husband's property. As Azam Taleqani explained:

---

[19] 10 February 1990.

[20] For a detailed analysis see Milani, Farzaneh, *Veils and Words: the Emerging Voices of Iranian Women Writers*, Tauris, London, 1992.

[21] 30 January 1988.

[22] 20 January 1991.

[23] For a detailed analysis see Mir-Hosseini, Ziba, 'Women, Marriage and the Law in Post-Revolutionary Iran', in Afshar, H (ed), *Women in the Middle East*, Macmillan, 1993, pp.59-84.

[24] For detailed discussion see Mir-Hosseini, Ziba, 'Women, Marriage and the Law in Post-Revolutionary Iran', in Afshar, H (ed), *Women in the Middle East*, Macmillan, 1993, pp.59-84.

'Unfortunately after the revolution ... the government ... and even the clergy have not paid enough attention to women as full human beings. All their efforts has been concentrated on making women stay at home, at all cost; to make them accept self sacrifice, oppression and submissive. Even if they go to court to get their due, I am not saying that the courts are totally patriarchal; but unfortunately there are these tendencies. So the problem is presented in a way that does not illuminate the truth.'[25]

However the 1993 bill sought to curtail men's automatic right of divorce, by demanding that men who 'unjustly' divorce their wives should do their Koranic duty and pay 'wages' for the wife's domestic services during their married years.

Behrouzi also succeeded in pushing through a bill which allowed women to retire after 20 years of active service, while the men still had to serve 25 years. Her success was in part achieved because it permitted women to return to their proper sphere, that of domesticity, all the sooner.

For those who were actively campaigning for women, these bills mark remarkable successes. In 1991 the Women's Cultural-Social Council, despite its conservative membership, still submitted 13 women's projects to the High Council of Cultural Revolution; but only one of these was considered and ratified by the Council. It was a proposal to eliminate the prejudicial treatment of women in higher education and in the selection for degree courses. This was no mean feat since there were discriminatory measures against women in 119 academic subject areas.[26]

Women's Organisations

It was in quango and organisations outside the direct control of the government that women activists were most successful in struggling for better economic and political opportunities. Although in the public domain success depended on espousing an Islamic stance, Islam itself is sufficiently flexible to allow a diversity of interpretation and much leeway for women. Azam Taleqani for example set up the Islamic Republic's Women's Organisation, a non-governmental activist group, whose members have included Zahra Rahnavard, as well as more conservative women such as Monireh Gorgi, a woman representative in the Assembly of Experts, which is responsible for nominating the national leader, and *Majlis* representative Gohar Dastqeib.

Within the civil service it was women in the lower echelons of the governmental organisations who fought effectively for the cause. By 1992 the Minister of Interior had been prevailed upon to set up women's affairs committees to serve the social councils in all the provinces. Women working on these committees were much clearer about their aims than Mrs. Habibi ever could be. Jaleh Shahrian Afshar, a member of Western Azarbaijan's women's committee, explained that first and foremost they wished to be

---

[25] 25 december 1990.
[26] 31 August 1991.

independent, to have better opportunities and facilities and to embark on a wide ranging family planning programme.[27] They had taken their demands directly to the *Majlis*. But the only one of their suggestions to meet with approval was the family planning one.

In this they were helped by the population explosion and tragically by the outburst of self-emulation; more and more women chose to burn themselves rather than tolerate difficult marriages or rivals. Of course in this, as in all other issues concerning women, the demise of Khomeini was in itself of the essence. After his death, and the return of the vanquished warriers after eight years of fruitless war, the demand for 'manpower' to feed the war and labour to work in the war industries, diminished dramatically and gradually the government came to the realisation that it needed to control the population explosion.

The Population Debate

By 1990 the Iranian population reached 59.5 million and was growing at an average annual rate of 3.9% Yet though there was some disquiet, the devout were not panicking. Nevertheless both the high birth rates and temporary marriages came under new scrutiny.

The daily newspaper warned that the country had only 12 million hectares of cultivable land which would feed 30 million people at most.[28] Already in 1988 the Islamic government had introduced a bill for population control and a year later a five year programme was announced to curb the explosion.

By 1990 Ayatollah Yousef Saneyi was advocating birth control. He told the population control seminar in Isfahan that he had come to the conclusion that:

> 'None of the wise and learned people has ever said that it is good and desirable to have lots of children.'[29]

The population crisis posed a severe dilemma for the Islamic government. It had long since outlawed the pre-revolutionary abortion law and dismantled the family planning clinics. Suddenly it found itself with families averaging 5 or more children and no clear policy for halting the momentum. In July 1991 the government decreed that for a fourth birth, working women were not entitled to their 3 months paid maternity leave, nor could a fourth child be allowed any rations or a ration card. Any family that chose to have a fourth child would have to share out its resources and spread it more thinly, with no help from the state. At the same time the Minister of Health, Dr. Reza Malekzadeh, suggested to husbands that they should choose to have a vasectomy. A year later the courts decided to reconsider the abortion laws:

> 'It remains absolutely illegal to have an abortion or to carry out an abortion. Article 91 of the Criminal code imposes the

---

[27] 29 August 1992.
[28] 18 September 1991.
[29] 3 February 1990.

death penalty, according to the Islamic laws, for anyone murdering an unborn child "if that child possesses a soul". But
"before the soul enters the body of a being" if a doctor is of
the opinion that it is dangerous to continue with the pregnancy
and issues a certificate to that effect; then the pregnancy can be
terminated.'[30]

At the same time the newspapers published the list of 50 hospitals in the
country offering free vasectomy and female sterilisation.

By 1993 the Ministry of Health had its own population control bureaux,
with a 20 billion rials budget that was 300% higher than that of the previous
year. Assisted by an additional $300 million loan from the World Bank
the Bureaux was about to launch a massive population control campaign
offering free services at national, provincial and rural levels. The aim was
to reduce population growth to 2.7% per annum.[31]

Azam Taleqani ceased the opportunity to point out the close links between polygamy and increasing birth rates. Before the revolution Iranian
women had managed to curb men's right to polygamy, by making remarriage
subject to the consent of the first wife and ratification by Family courts.
Khomeini had restated men's right to permanent and temporary marriages
and his successor Rafsanjani had endorsed this position during the war.

But women's opposition to polygamy continued. In this they were assisted by the Koranic dictum that no man, other than the Prophet of Islam,
could treat all his wives equally and therefore it was advisable for them to
take only one. As Azam Taleqani stated:

> 'There are 500,000 fewer women than men in our country ...
> Yet we are told that we must accept that our husbands have the
> right to remarry. I even went to some of our religious leaders and
> asked them whether they were backing the family or planning
> to destroy it? Since it is obvious that the moment a second
> wife steps in, effectively the fist wife is discarded and her life is
> ruined ... But they are forcing women in this country to accept
> polygamy, if they don't then they are told that they have to quit
> and divorce the husband ... How can you have such a policy and
> still claim that women are respected and valued? What is there
> left of such a women? How can she become a good mother and
> raise a healthy family? [32]

Although during the war the religious institution had been largely supportive of polygamy, afterwards, with the advent of population explosion,
some of its more enlightened members conceded Taleqani's point. In February 1990 Ayatollah Yousef Saneyi asked:

> 'Who says there are no barriers to polygamy in Islam? You
> should study Islamic law and then see whether you can make

---

[30] 1 August 1992.
[31] 18 April 1993.
[32] 25 December 1990.

such a claim. The only thing that some men know about the *Koran* is the right to polygamy.'[33]

As yet polygamy has not been outlawed. But the prospect of curbing it have improved. What has been a marked success is the decision in the summer 1993 to revise the *Qassas* laws and make honour killings punishable. The newly elected women members of *Majlis*, Azam Taleqani's Women's movement and Zahra Rahnavard, made a concerted effort to outlaw honour killings. They documented the growing numbers of murders and atrocities committed by husbands, fathers and brothers on their unsuspecting womenfolk and demanded that the judiciary defends women. Finally the head of the judiciary Ayatollah Mohamad Yazdi issued a decree revising the laws and making male murders, be they kin or not, subject to state prosecution. He agreed to remove the requirement that made the male 'guardians' responsible for seeking justice in such cases. The decision was a land mark; it demonstrated that the *Qassas* laws, supposedly Islamic and eternal, were, like other aspects of the Islamic rule, responsive to pressure and subject to change.

Conclusion

The rule of Islam in Iran has not been easy on women. They lost much of the ground that they had won over the previous century and the way to recapturing some of those rights has been slow and barred by prejudice and patriarchal power. Undaunted Iranian women have struggled on. For the moment they have had to concede the veil and its imposition in the name of Islam, though they have done so reluctancy and have continued the discussions about its validity, relevance and the extent to which it should be imposed. But the bargain that they have struck[34] has enabled them to negotiate better terms. They have managed to reverse the discriminatory policies on education, they are vociferously attacking the inequalities in the labour market and demanding better care and welfare provisions for working mothers. Although the road to liberty is one that is strewn with difficulties, Iranian women, as ever, have come out fighting and have proved indomitable.

---

[33] 3 February 1990.

[34] For detailed discussions see Kandiyoti, D, 'Bargaining with Patriarchy', *Gender and Society*, Volume 2, Number 3, September, 1988.

Labour's Problems and the Changing Values of the United Kingdom Electorate

Adrian Sackman
University of Manchester
&
Blackburn College Corporation

'The Political Marketing Organisation Model
and the Modernisation of the Labour Party, 1983-87'

Summary

Labour's 1987 General Election is viewed as a landmark in disciplined campaigning. However, to what extent did this represent a significant phase in the modernisation of the Party? The following paper uses a marketing organisation model to suggest that 1983-87 was a period of organisational learning, where Labour had to grapple with the forces of change and the legacies of the past.

Introduction

Organisational change seldom takes place without a period of development and experimentation. While this may be an obvious truism, it is nevertheless an important *caveat* to any account of how a political party adjusts to changing circumstances that are not of its own making. Developments in the Labour Party's approach to general election campaigning since 1983 demonstrate this essential feature of organisational development: that a party must struggle with legacies of the past if it is to respond to the challenges of an uncertain future

This issue of change and the appropriate response from a political party are examined by an ideal-type model which identifies the mechanisms of adaptation developed by the Labour Party during the 1980s, and in so doing points to a number of features shared by all political associations in their evolution. A marketing organisation model is introduced which views Labour's campaigning between 1983 to 1987 as an exercise in environmental monitoring and self-regulation. An essential features of this approach is to emphasise organisational responses to hostile electoral and social forces, and how the Party was obliged to change in the wake of such pressure. One strength of this analysis is to unite the campaign specific studies of Nuffield and others with the long range accounts of the Party's move from a democratic socialist position to its social democratic orientation of 1992 and beyond.

A further objective of this paper is to question some of the conventional accounts of Labour's 1987 election campaign. Much has been written on Neil Kinnock's control of the Party, his commitment to victory and the impact of key individuals from the Leader's Office and Shadow Communications Agency (SCA) in the projection of leader and party. This paper argues that while packaging and marketing of the leader took place, the campaign concealed powerful tensions of identity and mission, where the forces of modernisation met head on the power of history.

Given the distinctive approach adopted in this account, it is necessary to examine the current state of the art in campaign studies, in particular the contribution of the Nuffield authors, and the special role of the marketing organisation model in the analysis of the campaign phenomenon.

The Nuffield Studies and the Marketing Organisation Model

The Nuffield Studies have for a generation been the central account of the election campaign. They provide an important commentary of the troubled history of the Labour Party, and its attempt to meet the threats of a volatile and unpredictable electorate and the new disciplines of media conditioned campaigning. The account of the June 1983 general election is particularly important since it demonstrates the unique approach of political history where evidence is assembled for a unique historical event, the authors documenting the failure of Labour's policy, personnel, and organisation. The Nuffield Studies are justly regarded as classics in the field of modern electoral history.

Despite these qualities, students of campaigning have become dissatisfied at the lack of an approach which bridges the gap between the highly specific Nuffield Studies and the long range accounts of voting behaviour and party systems. Although *Political Communications* edited by Ivor Crewe provides a broader perspective, focusing upon the specific communications dimensions of modern elections, these accounts are just that; case studies which are not integrated into a broader framework of analysis and explanation. A recent contribution is the political marketing approach which views the political party as a 'player' in the political market, exploiting the techniques of audience research and persuasion in a similar way to actions of a commercial firm operating in competitive market. Despite the heuristic value of this form of analysis, a point overlooked by Martin Harrop in 1990, few accounts go beyond a somewhat mechanical rehearsal of marketing concepts applied to a political campaign. Further, with the conspicuous exception of the political journalism of Hughes & Wintour (1990), many students of the campaign fail to contextualise the general election preparations of the Labour Party of the 1980s as part of a more profound process of party modernisation, where specific election preparations are used as a mechanism for long term organisational change and ideological development.

This paper addresses the gap in the literature by viewing Labour's 1987 campaign in the light of a heuristic model first introduced at the PSA Conference of April 1992. It key features may be summarised thus:

> – Socio-economic forces have reshaped the electoral landscape of modern Britain. The composition and expectations of voting electorate have undergone profound change, and led to the weakening of traditional class loyalties, and a segmented

electorate of voter groups very different from the two class model of post war Britain.

– This has created a highly unpredictable electoral system of parties competing for votes in a way not dissimilar to the activities of a commercial organisation operating in the economic market.

– Electors are therefore viewed as voter-clients, but clients whose perceived interests and concerns are powerfully conditioned by the central agencies of mass communications.

– A political party operating within this environment selects voter-clients on the basis of their value in ensuring survival and growth to the organisation.

– The party must therefore take account of the concerns of existing and potential supporters if it is to retain a competitive advantage in electoral market.

– A party will establish a unique 'brand' image to distinguish itself from both ideological rivals and competitors, who will of course be undertaking a similar process of market positioning. Understanding of market conditions is therefore essential and requires systematic market research as an indispensable part of campaign planning.

– This research informs both policy development and the preparation of publicity materials for the legally defined campaign period and the unofficial 'long-campaign'.

The model provides two categories of analysis –

• The Responsive Political Organisation:

a. Party Mission: Agreeing the Party Vision, and Leadership Commitment to Change.

b. Managing the Mass Party: Leaders, bureaucrats and the mass membership.

c. Professionalisation of the Party Machine: Integrating media professionals and political strategists into the campaign organisation.

• Campaign Planning Processes:

a. SWOT Audit of Performance: Analysis of party in terms of its strengths, weaknesses, opportunities and threats.

b. Researching the Market: Identification of target voters and competition for the vote; Understanding the ideological terrain.

c. Developing Strategy: Establishing the long, medium and short term aims of the party in the light of its mission and the political realities of the electoral market. Need to identify a competitive advantage which is consistent with the values and traditions of the party.

d. Policy Development: Based upon tailoring of political 'product' in the light of market research.

e. The Design of Campaign Messages: Developing promotional concepts ('Adcepts') informed by market research. Creative work and its pre-testing.

f. Scheduling and Setting: Devising arrangements for the delivery of the long and short campaigns. Includes questions of controlling campaign messages through the mass media; peaking and pacing, deployment of personnel and feedback methods for the short campaign.

Two implications flow from this model of a campaigning party. Firstly, in addressing the changing concerns of target groups, the party becomes a responsive political organisation qualitatively different from the class based parties of the post-war period. Secondly, in meeting change, the party will itself undergo modification if new or emergent groups are to be attracted. Clearly, the support of traditional supporters will be important, but only in as much as this is combatable with electoral value and the traditions of the party. Thirdly, the market research function is a central mechanism in this process whereby the party seeks intelligence about the concerns of voters as a means of identifying the levers of persuasion which could then be used to present the distinctive offering of the campaigning party. Emphasis is placed upon research as a device to shape and inform, though not determine, what and how the party will appeal to its electorates, a point underlined by Geof Bish in the wake of the 1983 defeat. Indeed, this is a necessary part of any act of political persuasion since the objective of a party is to shift opinion towards its own distinctive vision, embodying as this does the traditions and values which are a necessary part of a party's ideological position. Further, the model suggests that this process is not confined to the legally defined campaign period, but implies a process of long term planning, involving as it does detailed costing and resource deployment of personnel and research operations. Political marketing therefore goes beyond a brief few months work directed at winning an election; it is concerned with the fundamental analysis and reappraisal of a party's mission and the shaping of that mission in such a way as to attract support. This process is ideological in the sense of offering distinctive values through a social and economic programme, but it is also powerfully conditioned by the imperatives of the electoral market. Political marketing has organisational consequences in that an effective campaign involves the efficient distribution of party resources, both financial and human, in an attempt to achieve campaign objectives. Marketing is the organisation writ large, the survival of the political organisation being dependant upon a long term process of campaign planning.

To what extent did Labour reflect these characteristics in the period 1983 to 1987? The following account refers to three characteristics of Labour's campaign planning: Neil Kinnock and corporate management of the Party; marketing processes; and the legacies of the past.

The Corporate Management of the Party

The impact of the 1983 defeat on the Party is now part of established political history; Labour was lucky not to have come third after the Alliance. Academic and journalistic comment record Neil Kinnock's commitment to a programme of reconstruction which was to involve a long term process of steering the Party back to the middle ground of British politics. Many authors record the fact, with the benefit of hindsight, that it required two election defeats before a new image could be constructed, and a number of lost votes regained. However, it is significant for the case presented in this paper that the long haul back to electability had been envisaged by Kinnock and others in October 1983. Thus, 1987 represented not a defeat, rather the securing of a strategic position for a subsequent assault on the Conservatives at the next election. These electoral objectives had political and organisational implications for the leader and the management of the Party. Hughes & Wintour (1990) point out that first Kinnock would gain control of the Party, defeat the Alliance, and then finally win in 1992. While reconstruction was far from complete in 1992, and is continuing under John Smith, significant change had taken place under the Party leader, and it is therefore important to evaluate the role of Neil Kinnock in this respect.

Much has been written on the ideological position of Neil Kinnock and his place in Labour history. This paper's view of leadership is in marked contrast to the accounts offered by the political historian or journalist. The marketing organisation model tends to eschew individualist explanations of the Party leader as a distinctive individual of great vision, or the personification of Party values and traditions. Although these may be significant features of a leadership style, political marketing recasts this figure as a manager of a political organisation, who is in command of a variety of resources, financial, material, human, and ideological; assets which can be exploited for the satisfaction of a desired set of organisational goals. The corporate analogy implied by this term is appropriate in that Neil Kinnock's dilemma is familiar to any chief executive as a head of an organisation: either accept the shrinkage of Labour to a marginal position in the electoral market, appealing to small minorities of opinion, or reverse this process of decline by winning back past voters and seeking to expand its appeal to new groups.

Thus Kinnock became head of an organisation which was failing to compete effectively, due not only to presentational failures, but also to a 'product' which did not address the concerns of valuable voters, the aspirational working class being particularly important in this respect. This is a marketing problem, quite distinct from the presentation of leader, party and policy in the best possible way at election time. Tackling this required more than a leader's political oratory, or vision. Whether Kinnock illustrated these to a greater or less degree compared to previous incumbents, is in one respect beside the point. Modern politics is characterised by the skilful management of audience perceptions which renders the individual act of political genius an anachronism, more suited to the conditions of the Great Reform Act. Parties and politicians are rewarded and penalised by the market place in media messages: a party enjoys privileged access to press and television news reporting, but also suffers from the unforgiving disciplines of television stop watch culture.

Neil Kinnock had mastered such disciplines, an advantage he had over his predecessor Michael Foot. However, his most significant skill was that of a manager of change, achieved through his control of the Party machine, and the professionalisation of campaign planning. Shaw (1988) supports this view of Kinnock as a party manager whose modernisation strategy involved centralisation and ideological closure. This enabled the Leader to import non-elected advisors such as Charles Clarke and Patricia Hewitt into key positions in the Leader's Private Office, as well as ensuring that Peter Mandelson got the job of Director of Communications in October 1985. Indeed, it is possible to argue that by 1987 the leadership of the Party included a team of non-elected political and media advisors, centred in and around the Leader's Office who were responsible for the determination of campaign strategy. It is appropriate to view this group, particularly Charles Clarke, Patricia Hewitt, Peter Mandelson and Philip Gould from the SCA, as a leadership support network whose legitimacy rested upon political acumen, professional expertise and loyalty to Kinnock. The managerial problem was quite considerable in that they did not exist constitutionally, they could not, for example, go to NEC meetings because they were operating outside recognised structures for much of the time. However, despite this, key members of the Leader's Office, in particular Charles Clarke and Peter Mandelson, wielded enormous power by virtue of Kinnock's support for their operations.

This highly centralised structure resembles a traditional top-down model of corporate administration where executive decisions are made by a senior management team and communicated to lower levels of the organisation. There were casualties to this approach, most conspicuously the Campaign Strategy Committee (CSC). Originally established as the official body for campaign decision making in 1983, it represented all sections of the Party and had been closely involved in the detailed aspects of campaign preparation. However, by early 1986 the Committee became marginalised with the development of the Leader's Office and the rise of Peter Mandelson, the Director of Communications, reporting to the CSC only to receive approval for decisions taken elsewhere. This left the CSC as a rubber-stamping body and as a tension release mechanism for those, Tony Benn, for example, who disagreed with Kinnock's style of leadership and his support for campaign professionalism. The corporate approach was taken a stage further with an organisational audit of Walworth Road carried out by the Party's management consultant. As a result Labour's HQ was re-organised into a number of functionally specific directorates under Mandelson, Bish and Joyce Gould. Clear lines of managerial authority were established with a consequent reduction in the power of trade unions. Minkin (1991), points out that the precepts of industrial democracy had given way to the dictates of organisational efficiency and the ethos of corporate administration. Walworth Road had ceased to be the 'pennyfarthing machine' described by Wilson decades earlier, a body for itself and its employees; it had become the handmaiden of the leadership campaign network described above.

Labour's Development of Political Marketing (1983-1987)

Many accounts of the campaign emphasise the work of Peter Mandelson and Philip Gould, and do so quite rightly; they were significant and complementary actors at the heart of campaign development, Mandelson as 'fixer' and campaign manager, and Gould as political strategist and coordinator for the SCA. Gould must also be credited with the far reaching communications audit which he did for the Party in late 1985, a preliminary to the formation of the Shadow Communications Agency.

However, the strength of political marketing as an analytical approach is to direct attention to the functional roles and their relationship to marketing processes, relating the individual actor and performance to the dynamics of change within the party as a whole. This approach supplies a necessary addition to the literature of the period, dominated as it is by references to Mandelson, Hewitt and Gould and the revolution they inaugurated in the presentation of the Party. As a result little is said about innovations which predate the meeting of Mandelson and Gould in October 1985. This is a period often neglected by scholars, but it is an important one, since it marks the start of the learning curve which the Party was to travel towards the modernisation of campaigning.

The fundamental principles of the new approach were established in November 1984, when Robin Cook assembled an informal group of advertising and marketing people to survey and analyze particular segments of voters, using all the elements of the marketing mix, and to do so with the full approval and encouragement of the leadership. Unlike 1983 the Party now saw its escape from oblivion in the expertise of people from the advertising and media industries; the information was invited from the leadership and positively received by it, Robin Cook channelling it directly to his colleague Neil Kinnock. As early as February 1985, Tim Steel (managing director of TVWA) had tabled a paper to Cook's Breakfast group. His thinking echoes the principles outlined by the marketing organisation model, as indeed it is obliged do given the logic of marketing. In particular, he examines Labour's predicament in terms not unfamiliar to a commercial marketing consultant, advising a with-profit client. Entitled 'A Marketing Plan for the Labour Party', Steel offers a prescient analysis of the Party's role in the political market place, the importance of issues and targeting, and the vehicle for the delivery of the strategy. Emphasis is placed upon the role of political marketing in the development of the campaign, the Party needing to understand the needs of the market place, and its capacity as an organisation to operate effectively within it. References are made to the symbolic role of leader, the identification of party mission, research and the full segmentation of Labour's electoralgroups.

While this was a first draft, and there were to be many steps between the breakfast speculations and assembling of the shadow communications agency, it is clear that a new era had begun, some eight months before the arrival of Peter Mandelson. A new realism were to develop as the Party was taught, then practised, and perfected new campaigning skills and applied these in by-elections and the European elections of 1984. Labour's efforts in these respects are significant in that they established a test bed for handling the media and represented a marker for changes already made. By June 1984, the Party had established its Campaign Strategy Committee under the control of Neil Kinnock; this gave him control of PPBs, away from debate within the NEC; the production of political advertising was removed from the free service offered by the BBC, and given to John Gau who now had responsibility for the complete production process; with a gifted public relations expert in the form of Patricia Hewitt as Press Secretary for the Leader. Labour's campaign messages were for the first time professionally marketed in terms of simple messages targeted at a specific audience and repeated by key speakers who were centrally coordinated.

The impact of the rejuvenated relationship between MORI and the Party should also be noted, as relations between the two represent an important dimension for the 1987 campaign. Formally, director Robert Worcester and Brian Gosschalk would present their findings to meetings of the CSC, NEC, PLP and SCA. An equally important reporting relationship was through Worcester's informal contacts with the leadership, a privileged access which date from his association with Wilson in 1970. This relationship, founded upon the company's acknowledged expertise in public opinion polling and the personal interest which its Director took in its work for the Party, led to one of the closest and most intelligent relationships in the history of political market research. Indeed, the quantitative work undertaken by MORI is a classic illustration of the craft of political market analysis and was particularly important in the period before the election where by-elections were analyzed, key voter groups and constituencies targeted, and issues identified. Before June 1987 some twenty surveys were carried out by Mori using a cross cutting battery of questions designed to identify the strengths and weaknesses of all the political parties in terms of issues, leadership rating and party image as viewed by specific voter groups.

Yet, MORI was not to be the only source of market research. The communications audit carried out by Philip Gould in late 1985 had suggested that MORI's expertise in quantitative research should be retained, but that qualitative work should come from another source. This distinction in market research is important. Quantitative work enables a party to view a map of its performance in the electoral market in relation to competitors and ideological rivals whereas the qualitative 'goes behind the numbers' to examine the motivations and feelings of voters, matters which an empirical technique is less able to fully explore. Both techniques are necessary in marketing and advertising, and while the Party had made extensive use of the former thorough Mori, Gould felt that the state of the art qualitative research undertaken by advertising professionals was a necessary addition to the political market research process. An illustration of the unique contribution of this type of work is contained in 'Communications Debrief: Society and Self' presented to the Campaign Strategy Committee on 24 March 1986. Undertaken by Roddy Glenn (Strategic Research Unit), Chris Powell (Boase Massimi Pollit), and Leslie Butterfield (AMDV), the analysis revealed that the Party's 'imagery' was closely associated with history, and political ideas, whereas the Conservatives related more to individual aspiration with the Alliance seen as weak, its imagery diffuse and reflected lack of knowledge about them. These views were the more compelling because they originated from the 'professionals', of the 'persuasion industry'. These people spend their working lives trying to discover the motivational levers of buyer behaviour, using qualitative insight as a basis for the presentation of product in the best possible light.

The bulk of the qualitative research was completed by January of 1987 and was presented to the Party in February. It contained an extensive analysis of voter perceptions and concluded that people were dissatisfied with the poor quality of life, had doubts about the extent of the country's economic strength, yet felt personally better off. However, the conversion of research into strategy had already taken place in 'Society and Self': that a lack of economic knowledge and interest by the electorate, combined with their perceptions of individual prosperity, suggested that money and economic matters were less of an issue than social 'end-results'. The document stresses the view that money should be spent on curing specific social ills rather than on remote economic 'causes', since these are often seen as much longer term or even endemic or permanent. This was to be the basis for the 1987 strategy: the Party should alert voters to their concerns about the declining quality of life, and respond by positioning itself as a party of hope, in contrast with the Conservatives who represented despair. This was to be achieved by exploiting the emotions of people in the social caring areas which represented Labour's competitive advantage: the Conservatives were better for a few, Labour was better for everybody. Underpinning these strategic decisions were detailed scheduling and setting arrangements for 1987. These had taken shape in the Autumn of 1986 when planning groups were established for the mini campaigns on defence and industry. Key members of the SCA allocated creative work, particularly copy writing to the decentralised team of media professionals who had volunteered their services to the Party. Arrangements were also made for a range of campaign delivery functions including: media billing and costing; scheduling of PPB; Tory strategy group; rallies; media events.

It is clear that the Labour's preparations for its 1987 campaign, were in marked contrast to 1983. Neil Kinnock had invested substantial amounts of political capital in the belief that commercial market research and image making could do for Labour what it had accomplished for commercial organisations. The campaign team had been given the authority to engage in the systematic exercise of image development of Party and leader closely tailored to the concerns and predilections of voters. The red rose and sober dark suits were but manifestations of a deeper commitment to image management and the needs of a mass audience. Extensive use had been made of market research in an intelligent and relevant way. This may have been the packaging of Neil Kinnock and the Labour Party, but is this political marketing as defined by the model outlined at the beginning of this paper?

The Legacies of the Past (1985-1987)

A central feature of marketing is the tailoring of the product to meet the concerns of existing and potential consumers. Despite advances in campaigning techniques, powerful legacies of the past remained which cast doubt upon the extent of the Party's commitment to responsiveness. Failures in policy development and dysfunctional relationships in the campaign organisation acted as a brake upon the strategy of developing a response to the electoral market.

mission and policy failure

Despite the fact that few members of the mass electorate ever read a party manifesto, it is clear that such a document functions as an anchor point for the campaign, reference being made to it by supporters and opponents alike as well as key opinion formers in the attentive élite. Under the tight control of Kinnock, substantial modifications had been made to the unsaleable document of 1983 in terms of council house sales, the EEC, individual worker rights, and nationalisation. Style mattered as much as substance in that the drafters of the manifesto had adopted 1980s 'ownership' discourse by referring, not to the 're-nationalisation' of Gas, Telecom and Water, but rather their 'social ownership'.

Yet as a centre-piece for the campaign, the document was fatally flawed, not so much by reference to 'safe' Labour policies on health, and education, but its inability to tackle the key 'competence' issues of defence, economic management and the trade unions. The established literature documents the damage this caused the Party in convincing target groups that it was at last qualified take public office. Even constituency campaigners viewed the manifesto as a liability; in a post-election poll commissioned by the Party, MORI identified that some 34 percent of candidates and agents saw a lack of information on taxation as a gap or omission in materials supplied from Walworth Road. It was clear that the manifesto was not well received by either candidates or agents, only one candidate in three using it, only half of which regarding it as of any use in the election.

Failure occurred in three aspects of policy, each demonstrating the link between substance and presentation in modern election campaigns and the force of history in a party's attempt to respond to change. In terms of defence, the unilateralist position of 1983 had been softened, but only in as much as it had been replaced by an ambiguous position on a conventional strategy, against a US nuclear shield. Further, the attempt to expunge the 'loony left' image of the early 1980s through 'responsibility' and 'trustworthiness' failed to counter the Party's association with the activities of a few Labour authorities. Finally, there was a substantial credibility gap in the Party's economic strategy. Professional advice had been available in abundance, both from the Leader's Office and from work carried out by the SCA which indicated that the Party could exploit Mrs Thatcher's 'there is no alternative'. The resulting anti-poverty and unemployment package agreed by the Shadow Cabinet in January 1987 presented a distinctive Labour economic policy. However, private polling and independent BES work demonstrate the limits of such professionalism; the Party was still failing to communicate its vision and reshape long standing voter-perceptions of a high spending, high taxing party of previous years.

How is this problem of policy weakness consistent with the view that the campaign of 1987 was a revolution in terms of professionalism? Neil Kinnock and the leadership network had established a centralised regime of control over the Party, and assembled a team of professional advisors, using state of the art techniques of audience research in the projection of Party and leader. Despite Hewitt and Mandelson's favourable assessment of the campaign as a landmark in British politics, this paper argues that it was a marketing failure. Labour had not reformed its ideological bedrock. The Party was still unable to appeal to the large number of C2 voters who were now looking for sound economic management of their life styles and reassurance that Labour had adopted an unambiguously orthodox defence policy. These two issues signalled the fact that the Party was offering the same product as it had done in the early 1980s, despite the cosmetic changes introduced by Kinnock and the leadership network. Effective presentation served to illuminate the Party's policy failure, the product being sold was fundamentally identical to that of 1983.

Political marketing then, involves something more than a set of campaign materials distributed by a publicity machine. A party committed to a process of modernisation must address its core values and associated traditions in such a way as to shift the perceptions of voters towards its position. Labour had moved along this path, and had come of age in terms of political advertising, but had failed to redesign its political product. In terms of product, Labour was still attached to a pre-Thatcherite values consensus, and as such had failed to address the realities of the electoral market of the late 1980s. Yet, given the political realities which prevailed in the Party at the time, particularly the need to retain the support of key groups, it is clear that Kinnock was at the limits of this stage of the modernisation process. He accepts that defeating the Alliance was the central objective of the 1987 campaign, and that policy design was to be key objective of the review which took place in 1988.

tensions in the campaign team

This paper has argued that the value of the marketing organisation model is to illuminate certain features of campaign preparation within the context of a systematic framework of analysis. Although Harrop (1989) suggest that political marketing tends to mask conflict, the very stuff of political debate, the framework functions in quite the opposite way; an ideal type which illuminates features of an empirical case. This is desirable quality of any approach, particularly a study of the campaign phenomenon where there are limits to rationality. Rose (1968) pointed out that carefully planned and organised campaign procedures may not necessarily produce rationally executed outcomes.

The marketing organisation model develops this concept of limited rationality, by examining the contingent role of individuals within the campaign staff, and how the management of change is seldom achieved without the weakening of past networks and loyalties, and their replacement by new thinking and new personnel. A process of modernisation will have disruptive affects upon the individuals who work in the organisation, and the model stipulates that management of change implies the resolution or mediation of conflict. This represents a significant strength of the model where the behaviour of individuals can be related to the processes of party modernisation and electoral responsiveness. Internal mechanisms are therefore linked to the external inputs and outputs of the political party. This form of analysis is valuable in terms of Labour's 1987 campaign, where doubts are raised as to the near universal claim that Labour fought a flawlessly organised campaign.

The political organisation model approaches the issue from a different perspective by suggesting that a party must respond to changes in the electoral market by change within itself. This paper has suggested earlier that Kinnock was a manifestation of such change; Mandelson was another in terms of a party leader's delegation of authority to those who can best manage people and resources required to achieve the political objectives set by the leader. It therefore follows that Mandelson was a necessary addition to a party undergoing change and a complement to Kinnock's commitment to modernisation achieved through ideological discipline, organisational efficiency and professional competence. Thus, it can be argued that during a time of organisational change, clear and decisive management techniques are necessary to overcome the forces of tradition and organisational inertia. This much was recognised by Philip Gould's communications audit for the Party. Delivered in December 1985, it recommended that the Director of Communications should be in complete charge of Party communications. Mandelson fulfilled the role of a campaign manager given the corporate model which Kinnock was promoting at the time. Thus, it was inevitable that while he was but one of three Walworth Road Directors, he was to enjoy a degree access to the leadership unrivalled at Walworth Road. His influence permeated to the heart of Party decision making, with direct access to Kinnock, Hewitt and Clarke and close contacts with the SCA through Philip Gould. He was the Party's first campaign manager based on the American model.

However, there is evidence to suggest that in centralising the campaign machine, Mandelson also created tensions in the process of change. This goes beyond the hostility of a number of front bench spokesmen who saw Mandelson as promoting some and marginalising others within the Party. Centralisation disrupted long standing channels of professional advice. The manifestation of this was the decision not to re-appoint MORI for the 1992 campaign, the polling agency having had an unbroken relationship with the Party since the days of Harold Wilson. This had occurred after a long period of tension between Mandelson and Worcester, tension that were to affect the conduct of market research for the 1987 campaign. These tensions illustrate how non-rational or non-marketing factors may contribute to the shape of the campaign, and how the management of change also implies the management of conflict. The tensions between Worcester and Mandelson had a number of origins. Robert Worcester as Director of MORI was more than the senior partner of the firm; he was also a political scientist in his own right, who had direct and uninterrupted access to the leadership of the Party for over a decade. It is clear that a degree of rivalry was inevitable when Mandelson quickly assumed a pivotal role within the campaign organisation. As indicated above he became one of Kinnock's main political counsellors along with others in the Leaders Office. As a result Worcester became marginalised as part of the inner core of campaign decision making.

One conventional explanation for this rivalry is that conflict is inevitable between different generations, particularly so given the rapid rise of Mandelson into the Party hierarchy. The marketing organisation focuses not so much upon these personal factors, or the extent of Mori's expertise with qualitative work. This paper argues that the episode represents the breakdown of a professional relationship between client and pollster. MORI interprets its function as best served through a close client-agency relationship, where the full implications of quantitative research would be discussed with senior members of the Party. A high premium is placed upon direct contacts with key decision makers, that is, the senior politicians, particularly the Leader of the Party. Further, MORI regarded the client as the Party as a whole, including members of the Campaign Strategy Committee and front bench spokesmen. A highly plausible interpretation of the centralisation process of campaigning under Peter Mandelson would suggest that an extra layer of communications had been established between pollster and client. Clearly, within the totality of factors which determine the outcome of elections campaigns, this was one factor amongst many, the Party being deficient in a number of respects as indicated in the previous discussion. It is however, indicative of a failure of conflict management where it is important to introduce change which does least damage to those valuable legacies of the past.

Conclusion

The argument advanced this paper is central to an understanding of the predicament of the British Labour Party. Using the insights provided by the marketing organisation it is clear that significant processes of political marketing had been established between 1983 and 1987. It is also clear that before the arrival of Peter Mandelson, the Party was following what one advisor described as a steep learning curve: within five months of Kinnock's election, professionals were presenting a marketing strategy. There were major innovations in the campaign planning process, mparticularly the use of commercial marketing and advertising expertise, and a tight organisational regime, features unknown in the Party's efforts in 1983.

The Party had succeeded in selling its existing policies in the best possible light, using state of the art audience research and political advertising. However, an impressive publicity campaign does not equal a marketing strategy. Labour was as unreconstructed in ideological terms as it had been in 1983,the Party still clinging to a values consensus of a pre-Thatcherite era. This view suggest that strong elements of traditional labourism existed side by side with image and policy innovations, such that 1987 represents an exercise in political selling, the effective promotion of an existing 'product' rather than the fundamental reshaping of its appeal to the market. The Party would have to wait until the policy review for a more radical exercise in political marketing.

Organisationally, the Party had moved a long way from the chaos of 1983.

Most significantly, Kinnock had seized control of the Party machine, and established a network of professional advisors directly under his authority. As distinct from other accounts, the marketing organisation views Kinnock not as a leader of great vision, but an astute politician, who became master of the Party machine. The enabled him to become a manager of change and return Labour to a position where it could defeat the Alliance in 1987 and challenge the Conservatives in 1992. Change, however does not come without tension and it is clear the centralisation of campaigning under Peter Mandelson was achieved at the some personal cost to Robert Worcester, and it has to be said to the Party as whole in terms of value for money from its pollsters at Queen Anne Street.

Finally, this paper demonstrates that modern campaigning can be most usefully analyzed from a perspective which views the election campaign as vehicle for the reconstruction of a political party. It is clear that the changes introduced between 1983 and 1987 were but the beginning of a process which was to continue for 1992, and beyond.

Bibliography

Benn, T, *The End of an Era* (Hutchinson, 1992).

Butler, D & Kavanagh, D, *The British General Election of 1983* (Macmillan, 1984).

Butler, D & Kavanagh, D, *The British General Election of 1987* (Macmillan,1988).

Butler, D. & Kavanagh, D, *The British General Election of 1992* (Macmillan, 1992).

Cockerell, M, *Live from Number 10* (Faber & Faber, 1989).

Crewe, I & Harrop, M, *Political Communications, The British General Election of 1983* (Cambridge University Press, 1986).

Crewe, I. & Harrop, M, *Political Communications, The British General Election Campaign of 1987* (Cambridge University Press, 1988).

Heffernan, R & Marqusee, M, *Defeat From the Jaws of Victory: Inside Neil Kinnock's Labour Party* (Verso, 1992).

Hughes, C & Wintour, P, *Labour Rebuilt: The New Model Party* (Fourth Estate, 1990).

King, A. et al, *Britain at the Polls 1992* (Chatham House, 1992).

Kotler, P, *Marketing for Non-Profit Organisations* (Prentice Hall, 1975).

Kotler, P, 'Marketing and Public Relations' in *The Journal of Marketing* (October, 1978).

Knokkes, D, *Political Networks: The Structural Perspective* (Cambridge University Press, 1990).

Mauser, G, *Political Marketing: An Approach to Campaign Strategy* (Praeger 1983).

Minkin, L, *The Contentious Alliance: Trade Unions and The Labour Party* (Edinburgh University Press, 1991).

Morgan, K.O, *Labour People: Leaders and Lieutenants* (Oxford University Press, 1987).

O'Shaughnessy, N.J, *The Phenomenon of Political Marketing* (Macmillan, 1990).

Panebianco, A, *Political Parties: Organisation and Power* (Cambridge University Press, 1988).

Pugh, D.S, (ed), *Organisation Theory: Selected Readings*, Third Edition (Penguin Business, 1990).

Richards, G, 'Reflections in the Eye of an Eagle', *Times Higher Education Supplement*, January 1993, p.40.

Rob, B, 'The GLC's "Anti Bill" Campaign: Advancing the Science of Political Issue Advertising', in Channon, *20 Advertising Case Histories* (Cassel, 1989).

Rose, R, *Influencing Voters: A Study of Campaign Strategy* (Faber & Faber, 1967).

Sackman, A.I, 'Bringing the Party to Market', Manchester Papers Series, May 1992.

Shaw, E, *Discipline and Discord in the Labour Party* (Manchester University Press, 1988).

Thompson, G, Francis, J, Levacic, R & Mitchell, *Markets, Hierarchies and Networks: The Coordination of Social Life* (Sage, 1991).

Hillel Steiner on Rights

Hillel Steiner
University of Manchester

'*An Essay on Rights*'

Reference

Hillel Steiner, An Essay on Rights, Oxford: Blackwell; ISBN 0-631-13165-5 hb, 0-631-19027-9 pb.

Overview

There have got to be less daunting tasks in this life than summarising a book which one has taken twenty-five years to write and to which one has only recently given birth. For even though the gestation has been that protracted, I reckon that the author's capacity to discriminate between the essential and the incidental is bound to remain fairly feeble until he and the book have weathered some feedback, or maybe even just weathered. The wood-for-trees danger is, to say the least, not reduced by having spent a long time in the trees.

So I've taken the easy way out. Or, at least, partially. What I've done below is to reproduce the book's table of contents, along with most of its very short introductory chapter. These supply a pretty fair indication of its general orientation and direction as well as the stations along the way. But since the latter part of that chapter contains only the briefest outline of the structure of my argument, I've substituted a number of longer paragraphs amplifying its account of some of the claims advanced in subsequent chapters. And I've indicated below the point at which that substitution begins. Needless to say, there's never an adequate substitute for actually reading the book itself – especially a personally purchased copy of it!

The Table of Contents is listed on the next page.

CONTENTS

Introduction

Two questions. What is justice? And what is it for? A principal theme of
this book is that, insofar as the first question has an answer, the second does
not. Perhaps this will strike you as a somewhat affected way of signifying the
intrinsic and non-derivative value of justice, its existence as an independent
citizen in the republic of values. But it's more than that.

'The whole creation', Francis Edgeworth once observed, 'groans and
yearns, desiderating a principle of arbitration, an end of strifes.'[1] To be
sure, a world free of groaning is no mean aspiration. And any principle
promising to secure it ought therefore to command our respectful attention
on that ground alone. Nonetheless, human nature being what it probably
is, not least in my neighbourhood, we should be unduly sanguine to reckon
on the efficacy of justice (or any other principle) as a sure-fire prophylactic
against groaning.

Nor indeed would a just and even groanless world – a world devoid of
strifes – be a best world, though I think it would be a better one. Not best,
because there are other values whose realisation our best worlds would still
await. Our problem is that these other values are not the same for each of
us, but the world in which we pursue them is.[2]

These several pursuits can and do obstruct one another. We unavoidably
restrict one another's freedom. And justice is about how those restrictions
ought to be arranged. What it's not about are the ends which might be
achieved by that arrangement. Questions of justice arise precisely where
the moral permissibility of one person's restricting another's freedom is
not determined by the comparative merits of the ends to which they are
respectively committed.

Delineating a desirable arrangement of restrictions, without reference to
any purpose which might be advanced by that arrangement, is evidently a
tricky business. And it's thus not surprising that we currently find ourselves
confronted with a plethora of competing theories of justice, some of which
have made quite singular contributions to our understanding of the interpersonal impartiality suggested in the previous paragraph. Yet however much
these theories may be seen as engaged in a common enterprise and even as
sharing many basic premisses, they are different.[3] Societies deemed just by
some of them must be condemned as unjust by the rest. Worse still, in the
apparent view of some critics, there is not one of these theories that allows
all of our cherished intuitions about justice to emerge unscathed. So how
are we to choose?

A sensible strategy, it seems to me, is to begin at the elementary particle
level since all big things are made from small ones. The elementary particles
of justice are rights. Rights are the items which are created and parcelled

---

[1] Edgeworth, p.51. However, he continues, 'the star of justice affords no certain guidance ... unless it reflect the rays of a superior luminary – utilitarianism', p.52.

[2] This interpersonal diversity of values is certainly true of our non-moral ends and may
or may not be true of our moral ends.

[3] Sen, Chapter 1, characterises this common enterprise as one of advancing arguments
for interpersonal equality, with the differences consisting in the choice of space for equality,
that is, of what is to be equalised. Interpersonal differences of values and capacities pretty
much guarantee that equality in one space sustains or produces inequality in others.

out by justice principles. We learn something about justice by examining the formal or characteristic features of rights. These features constrain the possible content of justice principles in much the same sense as architectural precepts must be informed by the properties of the construction materials they orchestrate.

And we learn something more about justice when we discover how there can be two (or more) of these elementary particles. That is, the linch-pin of this essay's argument is that the mutual consistency – or compossibility – of all the rights in a proposed set of rights is at least a necessary condition of that set being a possible one.[4] A set of rights being a possible set is, I take it, itself a necessary condition of the plausibility of whatever principle of justice generates that set. Any justice principle that delivers a set of rights yielding contradictory judgements, about the permissibility of a particular action, either is unrealisable or (what comes to the same thing) must be modified to be realisable. Particular applications of such a principle would too frequently drive us to say 'Leave it to the judge/the legislator/heaven to sort this one out'. And they, after all, seem sufficiently busy already.

Quite a lot of mileage can be got out of this compossibility test, which does exemplary service in filtering out many candidate conceptions of justice. A few more can be dismissed by reference to certain formal features of rights, apart from those bearing on compossibility. Our aspiration, obviously, is to pass through the eye of this needle with at least one theory of justice still intact. But it would be unduly optimistic to imagine that all our intuitions could similarly survive such a journey.

The reason for this, familiar enough, is that our moral intuitions tend to be uncomplex. In particular, they don't respond well to problems where what is wanted is not some missing piece from a best world jigsaw puzzle, but rather some way of distinguishing the pieces of second-best worlds from those of third-best ones. Demarcating this elusive boundary is quintessentially a task of justice theories.

Now for a few disarming apologies. The experience of presenting bits of this argument in articles and papers suggests that many persons deeply exercised by the evils of oppression, exploitation, discrimination and poverty will doubtless find much of it exceedingly intricate and overly preoccupied with abstract niceties so remote from the substance of these problems as to be utterly frivolous. A measured apology is offered to such readers. An apology, because these matters are indeed urgent. Much is morally at stake in discussion of them. And it is, to say the least, unbecoming to fiddle while others burn. But a measured apology, because of the unwelcome fact that these issues cannot be effectively engaged without an armoury of abstract niceties. Unedifying gallops from fragmentary moral convictions to full-

---

[4] The notion of 'compossibility' is due to Leibniz. For him, some things (objects, events, concepts) which are each independently possible may not be jointly possible, that is, elements of one and the same possible world. Mates, pp.43-44, explains: 'Now some things that in themselves are possible are not compossible. There could be a world in which there was no sin, and there can be (indeed, is) a world in which there is forgiveness of sin, but there cannot be a world with both of these features; likewise, there could be a world in which there was no poverty, but such a world would exclude the exercise of charity, which in itself is possible (and also desirable)'.

blown institutional and policy prescriptions, can be avoided only through preliminary conceptual analysis. Only with the distinctions supplied by such analysis can one make informed consumer choices from among the multiplicity of justice theories presently on offer.

For contrary to what some have suggested, it's simply untrue that exploring the meanings of words can furnish little assistance in assessing these competing theories, and that we must perforce consult our moral intuitions and assorted unreflective beliefs about the propriety of various activities, in order to reach any practical conclusion. Indeed, there's a certain oddity in the related claim that analyses of the meanings of moral concepts are, ineluctably, a form of moral advocacy. It's true that moral commitments frequently influence the choice of concepts to be analysed. There is, for instance, an obvious sense in which much philosophical work done over the past five decades on the subject of justice has been haunted by the Holocaust and has participated in the struggle to grasp its significance. But there's simply no necessary connection between the factors motivating the choice of an *analysandum* and the content of its analysis. A misanthrope is perfectly capable of delivering a philosophically respectable account of benevolence, a coward of courage, and so forth. And it's difficult to see why the case of justice should be any different in this respect.

Which brings me to a second and less measured apology. Large parts of this exposition are presented in the form of some pretty limp dialogue, ranging from the slightly stilted to the downright didactic. What this dialogue lacks in animation it more than makes up for in pedantry. The jointly sufficient explanations for this are my own sheer dramaturgical incompetence and my desire to exhibit certain technical points – in moral philosophy, jurisprudence and economic theory – as informally as possible. Theories of justice are inseparable from the concerns of these several disciplines and need, I think, to be worked out in generally accessible terms.

But clarity is an expensive virtue. And the cost of trying to practise it here has been that ideas which are commonplace in one or another of these fields sometimes receive rather laboured elucidation at the hands of my unscintillating protagonists. Chief among the latter are two persons, Blue (female) and Red (male), whose differing genders ought to make for less ambiguous adjectival and pronominal reference. They're assisted by a host of other colourful colleagues, as well as various specialised functionaries, who will be trotted out when the need arises.

****

[What follows is an amplification of some paragraphs near the end of the introductory chapter in An Essay on Rights.*]*

The argument of the book works like this. Getting a grip on what makes two rights incompossible requires an understanding of what makes two actions incompossible: that is, incapable of jointly occurring. In the second chapter, on liberty, I develop an account of unfreedom as action-incompossibility and try to display the conditions under which it makes sense to say that someone is free or unfree to do a particular action. The concept of freedom deployed here is the one some writers have described as 'pure' or 'crude' negative liberty. Its salient features are shown to include the following: that threats against doing certain actions do not render their recipients unfree to do them; that one's freedom to do an action entails one's possession of the physical (spatio-temporal, material) components of that action; and that the socially aggregated amount (whatever it might be) of that freedom is a constant-sum magnitude and is, therefore, not subject to absolute increases or decreases but only to redistribution.

The third chapter supplies an analysis of the concept of 'a right' along the lines of the Will or Choice Theory of rights: a theory which it extends and defends, using Hohfeld's classification of jural relations to criticise the traditional rival account, the Interest or Benefit Theory of rights. Construing rights as normatively assigned domains of personal choice, I proceed to identify the conditions for all the rights in any proposed set of rights to be compossible. And drawing upon the argument of the previous chapter, I argue that one of these conditions is the reducibility of all those rights to discrete property rights, to mutually exclusive entitlements to possess the physical components of those actions which are the duties correlatively entailed by those rights. Rights are thus normative allocations of pure negative liberty. A further condition of their compossibility is seen to be their having mutually consistent pedigrees. That is, for all the titles in a set of rights to be mutually exclusive, those titles must derive from exercises of liberties and powers attached to antecedent titles. Sets of compossible rights thus have a history as well as a topography, and this history consists in their being exhaustively partitionable into mutually exclusive foundational and derivative rights. This conceptual requirement tells in favour of 'historical entitlement' theories of justice, inasmuch as their rights satisfy it whereas those of rival theories don't. It also highlights the significance, for the moral validity of a set of rights, of the ultimately antecedent or foundational or original rights from which all other rights derive.

Rights and liberty are then put temporarily aside in order to inspect some features of consistent moral reasoning, in Chapter 4. Here my aim is to identify the structural properties of those moral codes into which a set of compossible rights can be embedded. I do this by looking at several ways of understanding and dealing with moral dilemmas. Moral codes are classified as either mononomic or polynomic, as embracing either a single primary rule/value or a plurality of them. In the latter case, the conditions of rational and principled decision-making require that (contrary to Intuitionism) these rules/values be prioritised by some form of ordering and/or weighting. Various such forms, including lexicographic ordering, are reviewed.

Chapter 5 tours the axiomatic foundations of economic reasoning. The structure of such reasoning is said to be neutral with respect to the sets of ends people pursue: in identifying a person's optimal option in any choice situation, economic reasoning purportedly takes his/her ends and their prioritization as given. My principal effort in this chapter is devoted to showing how the set of economic axioms – specifically, the Axiom of Continuity – lacks such neutrality inasmuch as it entails that our ends form what decision theorists call a 'compensatory set', that is, one which excludes any lexically ranked elements. I then go on to explore the significance of this fact for our conception of exploitation and for the place of rights in economic theory. The overall aim of this chapter is to illuminate what can be meant by claims that some action/policy, though morally desirable, is economically impossible. And its suggestion is that such claims cannot be true in the case of actions/policies whose moral desirability is due to their sustaining rights.

All of these analyses get fed into the discussion of justice, in Chapter 6. Taking justice as a rule for rights, it isolates the sort of adversarial circumstance in which rights are non-redundantly invoked, and explores the requirements of such closely related ideas as neutrality and impartiality in such conflict situations. Principled resolutions of these conflicts are shown to derive only from a rule allocating sphere of personal freedom. Moreover the content of this rule, as well as its ordered location within moral codes containing it, are seen to be strictly constrained by the requirements of rights-compossibility. To better situate some of these points, the chapter includes a discussion of Kant's conceptions of justice and virtue and their relation the first two formulations of the Categorical Imperative. And the upshot of its argument is that justice is a lexically-prime rule which distributes freedom equally to all persons through a set of foundational and derivative rights.

The seventh chapter, on original rights, explores the general content and incidence of these rights. Foundational rights are shown to consist in each person's entitlement to self-ownership and to an equal portion of initially unowned things (which, as a first approximation, are interpreted as raw natural resources). Exercises of these rights yield derived rights to the fruits of labour. In the course of this argument, I explore a consequent and sometimes noted paradox in the right of self-ownership: namely, that persons themselves are the fruits of other persons' labour. And I propose a solution which denies both that minors are self-owners and that they are entirely the fruits of others' labour. The set of right-holders is also shown to exclude deceased persons, whose belongings thereby join raw natural resources in the category of initially unowned things. And it further excludes members of unborn generations, in whose behalf justice (though not other values) therefore encumbers present persons with no duties to save, conserve the environment, etc. Finally, I argue that inter-societal boundaries place no just restrictions on duties to respect other persons' moral rights. The demands of justice have global scope.

And the last chapter, on just redistribution, interprets the application of just rights and their correlative duties to present persons who are generationally differentiated and who inhabit a limited natural environment: that is, who are real people. Affirming their standard classical liberal (*laisser-faire*) rights, it goes on to consider the broad redistributive implications of their original rights to an equal share of initially unowned things. Designating those persons whose respective shares exceed such parity as 'over-appropriators', and their deficient counterparts as 'under-appropriators', it offers an analysis of what the former owe to the latter and the basis for this assessed liability. The reader is invited to conceive of the owed total as constituting a 'fund' and, moreover, a 'global fund' (following the argument mentioned at the end of the previous paragraph). Each person's entitlement is one to an equal portion of the value of all items counting as initially unowned things. The bulk of the chapter is then taken up with identifying these types of item. Among them are: geographic sites (including supra- and sub-terranean locations); the belongings (including the cadavers) of dead persons; and, for reasons derived from the aforementioned solution to the self-ownership paradox, the germ-line genetic information of parents. In all cases, private or state ownership of these items is justly encumbered by a proportionate levy from the global fund. A plausible conjecture is that the operation of such a fund, along with the rectification of past rights-violations and exploitations, would effect a considerable, lasting and global reduction in economic inequality.

****

What emerges from all this, then, is an historical entitlement conception of justice with some reasonably strong redistributive implications. My hope, of course, is that this will succeed in capturing a fair proportion of your intuitions. But my own chastening experience suggests that, if it captures all of them, something has gone badly wrong.

References

Edgeworth, Francis, *Mathematical Psychics* (London: C.Kegan Paul, 1881).

Mates, Benson, *The Philosophy of Leibniz: Metaphysics and Language* (Oxford: Oxford University Press, 1986).

Sen, Amartya, *Inequality Reexamined* (Oxford: Oxford University Press, 1992).

Race and the Politics of Identity and Difference

Michael Rowe
University of Leicester

'Constructions of British "Race Riots" '

Introduction

The purpose of this paper is to examine the nature of *race* in society and to attempt to develop a theoretically convincing approach to the nebulous construction of the concept. In particular it will challenge the work of a number of writers who have sought to explain the construction of race since the 1970s in terms of a perceived change in the role and nature of the state in response to a crisis in production relations. Authors such as Hall et al, (1978) and the CCCS (1982) have argued that 'race' was deployed during and after the 1970s in an attempt by the new right to re-organise a class-based society into one based around a particular notion of national identity. This paper argues that explanations of *race* based on a supposed link with structural features of society mistakes the actual generation and constitution of the concept in distinct instances. In short it will argue that such attempts to periodise *race* into convenient (usually decennial) categories mistakes the construction of the concept over time and suggests that *race* is a cogent formation deployed for ideological reasons rather than a contradictory and partial concept. Such authors have tended to make fleeting reference to Britain's imperial legacy in order to explain the salience of race during particular periods. This paper argues that this historical legacy is in fact a vital and meaningful constituent of contemporary constructions of race. One advantage of the conceptualisation offered here is that it allows us to recognise the often contradictory and inconsistent nature of *race* . It emphasises the need to examine the specificity of race in localised (both in time and space) contexts and the concomitant danger of attempting to build universal models of the concept which inevitably blur the fragmentary aspects and produce generalised forms of this essentially contestable concept.

The approach of this paper is to examine how *race* has been constructed in relation to four incidents of public disorder that have occurred in Britain this century. It is not claimed that *race* has occurred in the same manner in other policy areas or that the field of public disorder is somehow pre-eminent. Three of the four cases have been selected because they were contemporaneously defined as 'race'; a term which is nothing more than a convenient label employed by the media and politicians. The fourth case study, namely that of the disorders that occurred in the 1936 'Battle of Cable Street' does not appear to have been labelled in this way but it has been chosen because the political reaction to it shares many similar features to the other incidents which demonstrates that notions of *race* and *nation* are relevant to aspects of political reality beyond obvious and apparent *race relations* matters. Namely the case studies are: the 1919 disorders in Liverpool; the 1936 'Battle of Cable Street'; the disorders in Nottingham and Notting Hill in 1958; and the Broadwater Farm disorders of 1985. Each of these events may be considered as specific and discreet at one level and yet they also serve as conceptual benchmarks in the process of race in British politics. Michael Keith (1993) reminds us (in a slightly different context) of the theoretical dangers of reifying distinct occurrences into broad generalisations and this approach is central to the work offered here. The four case studies may be considered as 'a specific conjuncture of issues (providing) the raw material for a more general drift of history' (Keith, 1993, p.237). It is not suggested that other events could not have been validly selected but only that those discussed here can offer some insight into the broader question of the role and constitution of *race* in British society.

Constructing 'Race Riots'

This paper will continue by examining the constructions of *race* particular to the events outlined and will attempt to do this in two complimentary ways: by exploring those reactions which can be understood as part of the processual development of *race* ; and by considering reactions that can be understood only in terms of the specific local context of the events. Table 1 indicates the division of the reaction to each event in terms of the process of racialization and in terms of the specific context of each event. It is to this that the paper now turns.

The paper argues that if in order to understand any of the events outlined above it is necessary to explore both aspects of their construction. In other words, each event has its own specific history which is not (and cannot be) directly transferable to any other event. However there is also a longitudinal aspect to understanding any of them which draws attention to the historical development of the concept of *race* and its explanatory power. Any of these events can be considered as a discrete and specific set of actions, they can also be considered as links in an historical chain. *Race*, then, occurs as both a particular concept with certain meanings in certain circumstances and as a process which both influences subsequent events, and is in turn influenced by them.

One difficulty that becomes apparent when researching incidents of public disorder is caused by the apparent similarities in political responses to events which may appear to the researcher very different and may have occurred decades or even centuries apart. Pearson (1983) offers a prime example of this. In charting the history of reactions to disorders he reminds us that what politicians and police officers claimed to be a new phenomena of the 1980s is actually a very well established part of the political process. One disadvantage of being reminded of the apparent historical pervasiveness of disorder is that is easy to overlook the distinct and particular nature of each event occurring in a unique context. This section of the paper does not intend to suggest that, because of the parallels between each case study, it can be assumed that there is nothing distinct between them. Rather they have each been constructed in the light of events which proceeded them and, in turn, have shaped reaction to events which followed them. They each are affected by the deployment of 'race' and in turn act as an effect on the nature of *race* itself.

Table 1
The Context and Process of 'Riots'

	Racialization	Specific location of events
Liverpool 1919	'Otherness'/Fear of Stranger as cause of tensions.	Repatriation introduced as policy response.
	'Understandable' response by white residents.	Shaped by post-war international situation, for Bolshevism on Clydeside, 'Land fit for Heroes'
East End of London 1936	'Otherness' as cause of tensions.	Free speech for the B.U.F. became an issue.
	Defined as a law and order issue.	Need to avoid descent into extremism (of any sort) & avoid problems of Europe.
Nottingham & Notting Hill 1958	'Otherness'/Fear of Stranger as cause of tensions.	Debate on immigration control accelerated.
	'Understandable' response by white residents.	References to the U.S. experience. Seen as a harbinger.
Broadwater Farm 1985	'Otherness'/culture as cause of disorder.	Creation of 'enemy within'. Police-black conflict, for example, 1981 , disorders as context.
	Defined as a law and order issue.	Unforgivable criminality, that is, NOT understandable.

Otherness as a Cause of Riots

The disorders that occurred in Liverpool during June 1919 (see Fryer, 1984, and Jenkinson, 1993, for further discussion) consisted of attacks on the local African population of migrant seamen by sections of the white community who lived around the docks. These attacks consisted of assaults, arson, looting and, in one case it seems, murder. The extent of these attacks grew so large that many local Africans were kept in the local police station for their own protection and 'an anti-black reign of terror raged in Liverpool'[1].

The public political response to these events was ultimately contradictory, seeking to at once locate the blame for the events at the door of the black community whilst, overtly at least, recognising that this community was also the victim of unwarranted violence. Press reports of events were couched in terms which sought to understand the attitudes of the white attackers who resented what they regarded as the unjustified employment by shipping companies of African crews. The white attackers were seen as unfortunate victims of circumstances beyond their own control which led them to take the unjustifiable (but understandable) actions which occurred. An excellent example of this tone is from the *Daily Herald* in which an article entitled 'RACE RIOTS: THE ROOT CAUSE' commented that 'the racial trouble – an outcome of the importation of coloured men during the war – is spreading with the return of our men to civil life'. The article continued by arguing that such returnees were being overlooked for jobs which were 'rightfully theirs' and concluded that the attackers 'are actuated only by patriotic motives'.[2]

The response of the local police to the disorders seems to have adopted a similarly inconsistent position of blaming the victims of attack for their own predicament. Jenkinson (1993, p.98) argues that 'the police views, when it came to the trials of those arrested in connection with the disturbances, remained the same: the blacks initiated the violence'. As was mentioned above some 700 members of the local black community sought protection from attack in local police stations. It is unclear whether this was at the initiative of the police or the black community itself but it paved the way for the policy response which exemplifies the racialized construction of events: repatriation.

The scheme of voluntary assisted repatriation that was introduced in the aftermath of the riots that occurred in Liverpool and elsewhere in 1919 does not appear to have induced much response from those eligible. The scheme was initiated by an inter-departmental committee established by the Cabinet and administered at a local level by Repatriation Committees established in ports around the country which offered financial inducements to black people who had suffered violence and were willing to be repatriated. From the available information it is not possible to ascertain how many of Liverpool's black community took up this offer but the evidence from other cities suggests that only a small number left (Jenkinson, 1993, pp.103-108).

That such a scheme could be introduced, even without much 'success', demonstrates the construction of these events in terms of the inherent incompatibilities of those of different 'races'. Despite the condemnation of those who indulged in racist attacks and the occasional reminder that 'the negro is almost pathetically loyal to the British Empire and he is always

---

[1] Fryer, 1984, p.301.
[2] *Daily Herald*, 13-06-19.

proud to proclaim himself a Briton'[3] it is clear that the fundamental blame was laid with the black community. Often competition for employment was regarded as reason enough to 'understand' the motives of the racist attackers. In other cases the press suggested that the cultural proclivities of the black population in Liverpool acted as further provocation. *Race* made the events intelligible and allowed the authorities to shelter behind a culture-based explanation which excused their (in)actions.

The influence of World War One on this construction of the events in Liverpool in 1919 was created by the apparent contradiction between the rhetoric of the post-war 'Land Fit For Heroes' and the material reality of unemployment and deprivation that faced many of those demobilised. The role of the Africans living in the docks area during the war became an articulator of the themes of patriotism and *otherness* that have already been mentioned. A trade union official explained the rationale of the rioters: 'all over the country officers – captains, mates, chief engineers – hold that the white men who have done the fighting should be shipped before the blacks'.[4] Despite the press coverage that had accompanied the role of black soldiers and sailors during the war[5] the reactions of the demobilised white workers was to scapegoat the black residents as the supposed cause of their own plight. Such context explains why *race* was such a powerful concept at this time, millions of people had been affected by the experience of the previous four years so it is easy to conceive that such themes of national identity and *otherness* would find resonance with the public.

Another contemporary event that helps to explain the deployment of *race* during this period was the Bolshevik revolution and the subsequent fears that working class revolutionary fervour would develop in Britain. The events in Liverpool in 1919 were not the only public disorders of that year and it is interesting here to point out that Clydeside was the first location for such 'race riots'. The history of 'Red Clydeside' cannot be discussed here but any construction of the material problems facing many working class communities in terms which suggested a *racial* rather than a *class* conflict was at least coincidental to the requirements of the state. This is not to suggest that the state overtly encouraged explanations which referred to the inherent *otherness* of the black communities, but it surely helped to prevent the influence of the Russian Revolution spreading further.

'Un-British weeds in British soil'

Notions of patriotism and national identity that were deployed on occasion in response to the events in Liverpool in 1919 played a central role in responses to the 'Battle of Cable Street' of 1936. The anti-racist movement has developed a romanticised mythology of these disorders by suggesting that they were a clash between Mosley's British Union of Fascists (B.U.F.) and the amassed ranks of the left which eventually ended in the fascists' defeat. In fact the B.U.F. never clashed with anti-fascists on that occasion

---

[3] *The Times*, 13-06-19.
[4] *Daily Herald*, 13-06-19.
[5] see Fryer, 1984, Chapter 9.

and the disorders that occurred were between the police and those gathered to oppose Mosley's attempt to march.

The violence that surrounded the activity of the B.U.F. which culminated in the events in the Cable Street in October 1936 did not lead directly to the introduction of a *Public Order Bill* that November (see Stevenson & Cook, 1977, Chapter 12). However, the subsequent parliamentary debates are littered with references from MPs of all parties to the B.U.F. and the then recent violence. In introducing the Bill the Home Secretary referred to the rise in political extremism across Europe and argued that a common characteristic of these movements was a belief in the use of force. In a remark echoed by the Chief Constable of the Metropolitan Police when he described the urban disorders of 1981 as 'alien to our streets', the Home Secretary warned 'if these foreign doctrines get a footing in this country ... then Parliament must secure that the methods which are employed in support are consistent with our tolerant traditions'[6].

As well as referring to the supposed *alienness* of extremism and violence to British life other similarities can be observed in the reactions to this case study and to the others. Perhaps the most notable of these is the tendency to explain the events of October 1936 in terms of natural conflicts arising from the incompatibility of 'aliens' in British society. This view can be found in the definitions of the disorders offered by the press, politicians and the Commissioner of the Metropolitan Police, Sir Philip Game. *The Times*, for example, spoke of the 'uncrystallized dislike' of Jews common amongst the working class of the East End and to the 'traditional grumbles against Jewish price cutting, clannishness, and their problematical wealth or dirtiness'.[7] In the committee stage of the *Public Order Bill* Commander Bower MP explained the disorder occurred due to the 'large numbers of Oriental races who live in (the East End and) find it necessary to provoke and assault the police'. Similar violence did not occur in the West End, he continued, although 'it is a mistake to think we are not just as much provoked. We are, however, law-abiding citizens'.[8]

Although the Metropolitan Police report for 1936 stated that the disorders were ultimately caused by the adoption of anti-Semitic policies by the B.U.F, Benewick (1972) refers to a meeting between Sir Philip Game and the Board of Deputies in June 1938 to discuss the policing of the B.U.F. Game 'stated that there was "naturally" some resentment on the part of the police at having to give up their free time in order to cope with disturbances to which the Jews had contributed by their presence'[9], again suggesting that the victims of racial violence somehow contributed to their victimisation.

As has been mentioned the inclusion of this event in a discussion of *race* appears at first to be incongruous. It did not involve racist attacks in this specific instance since the B.U F. were not directly involved in the violence. Furthermore they were not labelled as 'race' by press or politicians. The reason why it has been included is that reactions to it demonstrate the pervasiveness of *race* to popular political conceptions of public disorder. This

---

[6] Hansard, *Parliamentary Debates*, Commons, 1936-7, Volume 317, column 1350.

[7] *The Times*, 20-10-36.

[8] Hansard, Parliamentary Debates, Commons, 1936-7, Volume 318, column 67-8.

[9] Benewick, 1972, p.256.

construction was conveyed in this case by reference to notions of traditional English liberalism and sanctity of the legal process in settling disputes. In this sense *otherness* is constructed in terms of a dichotomy between political extremism and liberalism as exemplified by the imputed law-abiding and peaceful character of political dispute in Britain. In other cases discussed here *otherness* has referred to supposedly natural cultural hostility between the *races* and has implied a natural 'fear of the stranger'. Even though race was not a central explanatory factor many of the sentiments expressed echoed those used in the other case studies discussed. This indicates how *race* is informed by other related concepts (for example, *national identity*) and at the same time acts as an influence on them. Not only is *race* constructed and processed it is also parasitic on other political themes.

Black Skins or White Prejudice?

The political reaction to the disorders that occurred in Nottingham and Notting Hill in August and September 1958 allowed previously marginal calls for *immigration* control to accelerate and take a central role in national debate. Often described as a 'watershed' in British race relations, the 1958 disorders and the reaction to them did not mark a distinctive change in the politics of *race* in Britain.[10] A less prescriptive understanding of *race* suggests that the effect of these events on the ideological climate only occurred because of the coincidence of a historically produced concept with a particular context. 'Race' was not simply deployed in an instant in 1958 in response to underlying changes in the requirements of the labour market or demands on the social fabric. Rather *race* offered a convenient means to understand and process events that would otherwise raise profound social or structural questions.

On one level the theme of the response to events in 1919 re-appeared in 1958 in that overt condemnation of the actions of white 'hooligans' was tempered with an underlying assertion that the West Indian community had somehow contributed to their own situation. *The Times*, for example, explained that the disorders in Nottingham were caused by the 'happy-go-lucky' nature of the black community which meant that they behaved in manner 'perfectly natural in their own country, (but) misunderstood over here'.[11] Other political reactions did construct the 'problem' of the black community's presence in a more active manner. In a memorandum to the Cabinet, Lord Hailsham, then Lord President of the Council, suggested that there was no great public concern about immigration but rather tensions were confined to particular areas with relatively large black populations. Problems arose, then, when 'property has been bought up by coloured landlords, who have then made the position of white tenants intolerable, and entire streets have gone over to a coloured population'.[12]

Again, though, contradictory positions were taken. The Chief Constable of Nottingham went so far as to cite the black community as 'an example

---

[10] see Solomos, 1988, pp.34-5.
[11] *The Times*, 27-08-58.
[12] Quoted in the *Sunday Telegraph*, 01-01-89.

to some of our rougher elements'.[13] A local magistrate commented that the black community in Nottingham were no more than 'an excuse for lawless rowdies to create a violent disturbance'.[14]

Despite such views the fundamental construction of the disorders located the problem as the presence of the black community in British cities. This definition is implicit in the deployment of the apparently neutral label 'race riot'. The phrase, in this context at least, removes any obvious blame for the events and converts them into natural 'understandable' phenomena. The only fault lies in the ignorance of the white 'hooligans' who do not share the mainstream British tradition of tolerance. The unstated result of this portrayal is to define the black community as problematic by their very presence: a passive (as well as on occasion an active) threat. The particular response to *1958* reflected that from earlier periods in as much as prevention of future immigration became the axiomatic understanding of what needed to be done, in a similar way to the calls for repatriation in 1919 reflected a particular construction of the event. The constitutive role of white racism in the disorders was marginalised by such explanations and definitions. As Miles & Phizacklea (1984, p.37) argue 'understanding the 1958 disturbances in terms of *race/immigration* implied that they had a natural rather than a social origin'. One effect of this was to disengage politicians from any responsibility other than the possibility of introducing immigration controls.

The specific context of the events of 1958 needs to be examined briefly if a full understanding of the construction and deployment of 'race' is to be gained. Ultimately, *1958* can be regarded as a harbinger of Britain's uncertain future. At this time Britain had only recently begun to emerge from the period of post-war austerity and yet the boom years of the sixties were still only just on the horizon. The Parliamentary debates and press coverage of events are littered with references to the need for the government to avoid the problems of the United States colour-bar by developing strict 'immigration controls'. The logic of the argument may be obscure but a different set of references can be seen from those to the Empire in 1919 (although Commonwealth political reaction was apparent in 1958). The local Nottingham press also asserted grim parallels between the events in Britain and the experience of the United States. One report was accompanied by a photograph of disorders in Arkansas with the byline 'IT MUST NOT HAPPEN HERE!.[15] This creation of a parallel with events in the United States became a central component of the moral panic surrounding 'mugging' in the early 1970s.[16]

'This is not England its just madness'

The press coverage of the disorders at Broadwater Farm, Tottenham, in October 1985 reduced the particular history and context of the events into a

---

[13] quoted in the *Sunday Dispatch*, 31-08-58.

[14] quoted in *The Times*, 02-09-58.

[15] *Nottingham Evening News?*, 31-08-58.

[16] see Hall, et al, 1978.

single all-encompassing variable: *race* . The press coverage referred to those involved as 'mostly black' (*The Times*), 'largely black' (*The Guardian*), or 'hundreds of West Indian youths' (*Daily Telegraph*) and elsewhere described the 'predominantly black Broadwater Farm Estate' (*Daily Mail*)[17] as the scene of 'Britain's most horrific race riot' (*Daily Express*)[18]. Again one outcome of this was to identify the entire black community (regardless of their individual involvement, or otherwise, in the disorders) as a location of conflict in the heart of Britain's cities. It has been mentioned above that a common response to the disorders of 1919 and 1958 was to understand but not condone the activities of white racist youths involved in the disorders. In this way such perpetrators are distanced from the wider 'respectable' community, who can be re-assured that they are not part of the problem. In this instance the process is reversed so that the black youths involved in the disorder are not only presented as mindless criminals but they become identified as representative of the entire black community. This process is seen in the reporting of the Home Secretary's statement that the government would 'get tough' with those responsible for the 'lawlessness which has broken out amongst ethnic communities in inner city areas'[19]. In defending criticisms that community policing had contributed to the disorders at Broadwater Farm, Sir Kenneth Newman, Commissioner of the Metropolitan Police, stated that 'in a volatile ethnic area what you need is policing that is emphatic'[20], re-enforcing the notion that the problem is within the community as a whole rather than any section of it.

This conflation of an entire population with a small minority of its members was further developed in the press reaction to the subsequent (ultimately successful) campaign to establish the innocence of the 'Broadwater Farm Three' who were convicted of killing P.C.Blakelock during the disorders. The Sun newspaper consistently attacked the campaign on the grounds that the feelings of Blakelock's widow and family were being ignored by the 'do-gooders' who were engaged in a politically motivated campaign. When the convictions were finally over-turned in November 1991, the collective culpability of the black community was again cited. The gist of the *Sun's* argument was that if the three convicted men did not commit the murder then the wider community at Broadwater Farm must be shielding the real culprits. Even the action of the police officers in securing the wrongful convictions could be explained in this way:

> 'Understandably, the police were under tremendous pressure
> to make arrests. They were met with a wall of silence so they
> doctored the evidence. If the people of Broadwater Farm had
> offered up the real killers, Winston Silcott would not have been
> wrongly convicted.'[21]

---

[17] In his unofficial inquiry into the disorders Lord Gifford estimated that 42% of the estates population was black and a further 3% from the Indian sub-continent, Gifford, 1986.

[18] All quotes from 07-10-85.

[19] Quoted in *Daily Telegraph*, 08-10-85.

[20] quoted in Daily Telegraph, 07-10-85.

[21] *The Sun*, 28-11-91.

As is shown above the press has already (falsely) established that 'the people' of Broadwater Farm were black. Their (possible) lack of co-operation
with the police was not considered as a potentially understandable reaction
to their day-to-day experience but as further demonstration that they were
outside mainstream values.

In the case of the disorders at Broadwater Farm 'race' became synonymous with the law and order agenda that was asserted as the primary
practical response to the events. Unlike the previous examples the actions
of those involved in the disorder was not a result of particular psychological
or social disadvantage. Rather it was a symptom of the inherent *otherness*
of the black community who were understood as pathologically criminal.
Any potential alternative definition was cast as an attempt to excuse the
criminal actions that occurred and were an offence to the 'common sense'
explanations outlined here.

One difference between the construction of the disorders of 1985 and
those discussed above was the immediate history of conflict between the
police and black people, especially young black men. Not only were the
disorders of 1980 and 1981 recent memories but the debates about policing and police accountability were well established in many urban areas.
A central component of such struggles had been the experience of racist
policing that was common to many parts of London, and elsewhere. This
context gave *race* a potency which made it both a convenient vehicle to
explain what had occurred as well as an image that the public could easily
identify with. In this sense '1985' was a powerful event in the racialization
of politics which was a feature of the new right project. This was not simply
because *race* had arrived on the scene in the 1970s, as I have shown many
of the themes employed had a long and irrespectable pedigree in explaining
disorders. What may have been different in 1985 was the convergence of
this historical process of racialization with a particular and specific set of
circumstances. Nothing of substance that is distinctly new or different can
be identified in the reactions to the disorders at Broadwater Farm, rather
old established themes re-appeared in a particular environment which rendered them powerful. That they were old established themes is not simply
a pedantic observation: it is central to the process. It is because the themes
of *otherness* and the alleged importance of the law to the identity of the
'English nation' are such persistent features of British political discourse
that such a deployment could be effective.

Conclusion

The brief outline of events that is offered above is intended to demonstrate
that *race* can only be fully understood when it is examined in the particular
context in which it is produced. *Race* is a socially constructed concept, but
this does not mean that such construction occurs in a fixed manner that is
applicable to a variety of situations. It does not even mean that *race* can be
considered as a cogent or consistent phenomenon. This paper has examined
only a very narrow range of case studies in a particular field and yet has
shown that, despite certain recurring themes, the construction of *race* is

partial and often self-contradictory. Thus black people can be portrayed as both the victims of ignorant white racists who attack them at the same time as policy responses demand that black people are the 'problem' to be removed or further policed.

The implication for the manner in which *race* is conceptualised may be that it is necessary to avoid searching for a definitive location of *race* . Rather it needs to be considered in the discreet and specific areas in which it is produced. This does not suggest that *race* does not have any independent identity applicable across time and place but rather that this identity is always mediated through specific experiences and contexts.

To claim that 'race' became a feature of British political discourse as part of the new right's position in a 'battle of hegemony' during the early 1970s betrays a simplistic conception of *race* . It is not suggested that *race* did not occupy a crucial place during this era, or even that this was something which had not occurred to the same extent during the 1950s and 1960s. Such notions of *race* , *culture* and *nationhood* were not, however, particular to this era. They were not deployed in any straightforward sense in response to an exterior situation, rather *race* played an important part in the ideological struggles of the period precisely because of its historical resonance. If this is overlooked then our explanatory power is reduced. It can be demonstrated that *race* was an important constituent of politics during this time. It is only possible to understand why and how this was the case by examining *race* both as a process and as a concept employed in particular contexts.

Attempts to extract *race* from its context and to consider it as an analytically distinct concept mistake the reality of the experience of *race* . *Race* is always contingent because it is always constructed in society. The nature of this construction will vary over time (as this paper indicates) but also between places: the meaning of 'race' will be different, for example, in a rural community than in an inner city 'ghetto'.

For this reason the *race-class* debate that has occupied neo-Marxist writers for the last two decades or so involves a misunderstanding of the reality of the concept of *race* . It is unhelpful to reify *race* into a macro-level concept and seek an ultimate meaning for it. Identity is contingent on context. This does not mean that *race* can never exist at a more general level – the construction of black youth as criminal, for example, does influence the criminal justice system and it would be arrogant to suggest that somehow this is not a real experience for many people. Ultimately, however, such general constructions depend on a particular context existing. Essentially *race* exists in (at least) two places at once. In a particular context which may not be transferable to any other, and that specificity exists as part of a process of *race* which has its own momentum and influence.

Reactions to specific *race* (and associated criminality) by academics have concentrated on the ideological construction of 'black youth' as signifier of socio-political crisis. Locating *race* to such specific instances tends to marginalise the momentum of *race* as it unfolds over time. This is a tendency with the approach of Hallet al (1978) and the CCCS (1982) which affirmed a relationship between an organic crisis in production relations and the deployment of a particular construction of *race* . This tends to organise *race* around discreet events instead cf explaining *race* as a process which can only be understood as an evolving social construction. Thus the construction of *race* may be deployed in a particular way relating to particular events (such as those of the 1970s) but such a deployment only makes sense with reference to previous constructions, each of which can be regarded both as isolated and discreet, and as part of a process of racialization.

References

Benewick, R (1972), *The Fascist Movement in Britain*, London: The Penguin Press.

CCCS (1982), *The Empire Strikes Back: race and racism in 70s Britain*, London: Routledge.

Fryer, P (1984), *Staying Power: the history of black people in Britain*, London: Pluto Press.

Gifford, Lord (1986), *The Broadwater Farm Inquiry: report of the independent inquiry into disturbances of October 1985 at the Broadwater Farm Estate, Tottenham*, London: The Broadwater Farm Inquiry.

Hall, S et al (1978), *Policing the Crisis: mugging, the state, and law and order*, London: Macmillan.

Jenkinson, J. (1993), 'The 1919 Riots', in Panayi P (ed), *Racial Violence in Britain 1840-1950*, Leicester: Leicester University Press.

Keith, M (1993), *Race, Riots and Policing: lore and disorder in a multi-racist society*, London: UCL.

Miles, R. & Phizacklea, A (1984), *White Man's Country: racism in British politics*, London: Pluto Press.

Pearson, G (1983), *Hooligan: a history of respectable fears*, London: Macmillan.

Solomos, J (1988), *Black Youth, Racism and the State: the politics of ideology and policy*, Cambridge: Cambridge University Press.

Stevenson, J. & Cook, C (1977), *The Slump*, London: Quartet Books.

Race and the Politics of Identity and Difference

Rose Gann
Swansea University

'Apartheid Reconsidered: Beyond the Race/Class Debate'

Introduction

The aim of this paper is to examine the impact of post-structuralist social and political thought[1] on the debate concerning explanations of the phenomenon of apartheid. Historically, this debate has focused around two distinct groups divided by a commitment to either a liberal or marxist perspective – the former group arguing that apartheid was the 'irrational' archaic political policy of Afrikaner Nationalism contradicting the 'rational' economic forces of capitalism, the latter arguing that apartheid was a cheap labour policy derived to enhance capitalist accumulation. This paper suggests that an approach informed by post-structuralism can move beyond the limitations of the race/class debate. It does so through providing a critique of the underlying assumptions of both the liberal and marxist accounts of apartheid, and an outline of an alternative approach to the phenomenon of apartheid.

For the purposes of this paper I shall outline one of the many liberal accounts of the phenomenon of apartheid. This approach has been referred to as the 'liberal modernisation thesis' (Wolpe 1988, p.7), and was first put forward during the 1960s and 70s in the work of Hutt (1964), Horwitz (1967), Houghton (1960), O'Dowd (1974) and Van Den Berghe (1967). The liberal modernisation thesis asserts that apartheid was a purely political phenomenon imposed by the Nationalist Party government. Its proponents argue that as a political policy of racial discrimination, apartheid contradicted the logic of the economic forces of capitalism. Apartheid restricted the economic sphere, hindering what would otherwise be 'normal' capitalist development. Apartheid was an 'irrational', archaic policy, dysfunctional to the rational logic of capitalism. In *The Political Economy of South Africa* Horwitz argues that 'the polity has always sought its ideal and its ideology – the white man's supremacy. The network of economic development had to follow accordingly' (1967, p.12). The liberal modernisation thesis assumes that the political and ideological processes are distinct from those of the economy. Furthermore it assumes that although apartheid was extraneous to the economic system, it somehow impinged on it.

This analysis of apartheid, as the political policy of Afrikaner Nationalism, is problematic on two counts; firstly, it is based upon the presumption that the category of race is the single most important determining factor in South African society. Race is the determinant category in both the

---

[1] By poststructuralist social and political theory I am referring mainly to the work of Michel Foucault and Jacques Derrida.

political and economic spheres It thus relies upon a form of race reductionism. Secondly, explaining apartheid as the policy of Afrikaner Nationalism
endows it with an *a priori* given essence.

The liberal modernisation thesis goes on to argue that the continued development of the capitalist economy would gradually break down the racial
barriers imposed by the political sphere. Horwitz asserts that 'economic rationality urges the polity forward beyond its (racial) ideology' (1967, p.427).
Horwitz's account is informed by modernisation theories in which the development of a capitalist economy is linked to the emergence of liberal and
democratic political systems. According to Van den Berghe except for the
political deviations 'South African society has behaved typically as an economy in transition from underdevelopment to industrialisation' (1965, p.212-
213). Here the liberal analysis shifts from a form of race reductionism –
in which apartheid and category of race determine all aspects of the South
African society – to a form of economic reductionism in which the economic
forces of capitalism become determinant as they override the outdated policy of racial discrimination.[2]

From the 1970's onwards liberal analysis of the phenomenon of apartheid
came under increasingly fierce criticism. The most significant attack came
from approaches located within the marxist tradition. As with liberal accounts, marxist approaches are diverse and varied and again for the purposes
of this paper I shall outline just one. This approach has been referred to as
the radical thesis and can be found in the work of Johnstone (1970, 1976),
Legassick (1975) and the early work of Wolpe (1970 & 1976). The radical thesis critiques the liberal approach as fundamentally flawed because of
its commitment to neo-classical economics. Contrary to the liberal modernisation thesis, the radical account argues that far from capitalism being
hindered by apartheid – it has, at least initially, benefited from policies of
racial discrimination. Apartheid is understood through its relationship with
the capitalist mode of production. Johnstone argues that 'the relationship
between capitalist development, apartheid policies and the core structure
of white supremacy are essentially collaborative ... ,' (1970, p.139). The
radical approach maintains that capital accumulation, productive relations
and class struggle are the principle analytical categories necessary to explain
apartheid. It asserts that racial discrimination in South Africa serves the
economic interests of white capitalists. As Johnstone argues, the policies
of apartheid provided a cheap labour supply for various capitalist interests, 'the true rationale of apartheid policies is thus to maximise economic
development both for the sake of white prosperity and for the material protection of white supremacy' (1970 p.126). The radical account argues that
Afrikaner Nationalism and apartheid developed as a result of the particular
manner in which capital accumulation occurred in South Africa. Apartheid
is explained through economic categories in which class interests are determinant. However, I would argue that the problem with this approach is
that it reduces the analysis of apartheid to the analysis of class and pro-

---

[2] In relation to this point I would agree with Lipton (1985, p.11 & p.373-376); that there
is a convergence between various liberal and marxist approaches. However, I would argue
that her reformulation of the relationship between class and ethnicity fails to overcome
the limitations of either the conventional liberal or marxist accounts being discussed here.

ductive relations. It is class reductionist in that the productive forces of
capitalism are determinant, whilst race and apartheid are merely epiphe-
nomena – tools through which capitalist accumulation can be reproduced in
the South African context. Racial discrimination is explained as the result
of capitalist accumulation in the particular context of South Africa. [3]

The range of explanations of the phenomenon of apartheid within the
liberal and marxist perspectives is much wider than the two approaches
outlined above. However, despite this variety, they are all derived from
assumptions about the nature of conceptual frameworks that entails some
form of class or race reductionism – that is in one way or another they seek
to explain apartheid either in term of race or in terms of class. These accounts also assume that apartheid has some essence – be it that of Afrikaner
Nationalism or capitalism.

I wish to argue that the problem of reductionism and essentialism within
these accounts operates at the more fundamental level of the assumptions
behind modern social theory itself. The reductionism and essentialism are
a result of the underlying methodological and epistemological claims of the
modern social and political theory upon which these accounts are based.
Difficulties arise as the result of difficulties inherent in the theoretical and
conceptual frameworks that inform them. Post-structuralism provides a critique of these accounts of apartheid at the level of the knowledge claims implicit in them. It offers a critique of the general epistemological assumptions
that underpin the social and political theory concerning race and apartheid.

The liberal and marxist conceptual representations of apartheid rely on
particular assumptions intrinsic to their epistemology that conceives knowledge in terms of a relation between an abstract and autonomous subject
and an independently existing realm of objects. They assert a correlation
between the objects of knowledge and language – which through representing the real world enables the subject to acquire knowledge of these objects.
This representational view of knowledge assumes access to a real world and
an objective standpoint through language. Not only is there a correlation
between the subject and an object of discourse but a further assumption
intrinsic to this epistemology is that certain levels of knowledge are seen as
directly effecting this correlation. These forms of discourse provide a means
of directly designating the independently existing objects and as such rest
on the belief that there can be a privileged basis for cognitive certainty. It is
presumed that the true nature of society can be known and that this objective knowledge can be represented intact through language. Thus the conventional, normative social and political theory underpinning these accounts
presupposes that social reality can be examined and explained through sets
of pre-given principles assumed true beyond 'mere belief'. That is, upon
fixed *a priori* assumptions concerning the nature and the mode of operation of social reality. The aim of this theory is to set out basic premises, and
concepts, providing an overarching conceptual framework for the analysis

---

[3] The problem of the class reductionism inherent in the radical account has been
addressed in various neo-marxist approaches (see Wolpe (1988, p.50-54), Stasiulis (1980,
p.475) and Murray (1984, p.88). Whilst I would agree with Murray that these accounts
have produced some 'scholarly achievements' (1984, p.98), they fail to overcome the
problems of class reductionism and economic determinism.

of society. As such these conceptual frameworks act as a yardstick against which other claims to knowledge may be judged.

There are several difficulties intrinsic to the epistemology of this social and political theory. Firstly, asserting a privileged level of conceptualisation has the effect of generating a totalising theory in which all aspects of social and political life are explained through one particular framework. *A priori* assumptions are considered to have a universal applicability, providing a total view of society. However the very process of asserting one truth presupposes the non-existence of another. The effect of the epistemology of modern political and social theory is that binarisms such as subject/object, rational/irrational are built into the very process through which knowledge is produced. In both marxist and liberal accounts a uniquely privileged level of conceptualisation provides the basis from which claims to knowledge concerning apartheid may be evaluated. For example, marxist explanations of apartheid privilege the concept of the economy as the determinate force, whilst liberals emphasise political and ideological factors. Secondly, conceptual representations of apartheid assume that the concepts used by way of explanation reveal the essence of the real. This results in conceptual definitions always explaining apartheid in terms of something else. For example, within marxist discourse apartheid is a mechanism for capitalist exploitation whilst liberal discourse describes apartheid as the ideology of white nationalists. In both instances apartheid features as the phenomenal expression of some essence, be it capitalism or Afrikaner Nationalism. Thirdly, as the relationships between concepts represent the essential form of the connections between objects, such connections can only be viewed in terms of highly reductive and universalised forms of causality, leading, for example, to explanations of apartheid as always operating in the interests of capitalism or always working against the interests of capitalism.

This critique implies that essentialist and reductionist conceptualisations of race and apartheid are not accidental, but are the result of the limits imposed upon such concepts by the epistemological foundation of the modern political and social discourse upon which they are based. Both liberal and marxist approaches can be seen to share this common epistemological problem. Therefore they are both equally problematic in their attempt to provide an explanation of the phenomenon of apartheid.

I wish to explore the possibilities of an alternative approach informed by post-structuralist theory. This approach rejects the central tenets of the epistemology that informs these representations of apartheid and argues for a non-dogmatic, non-essentialist and therefore non-epistemological approach to the phenomenon. The contention is that knowledge is not acquired through the abstraction of an autonomous subject from a separate world of objects, rather knowledge is constituted through forms of discourse. Knowledge is a discursive construct and objects of knowledge – whether social, political or ideological – are constituted in discourse by means of specific conceptual forms. The connections between these objects can only be conceived as a function of the forms of discourse in which those objects are specified. The notion of subject and object are therefore, discursive constructs and no binary division between them can be sustained. Hence this approach rejects the notion of knowledge as representative of essential single truths because it rejects the dualistic nature of epistemology and the assumption that a true account of an external reality can be obtained. Instead it asserts a plurality of truths whose appearance is contingent on particular discursive arrangements.

This, however, leaves us with the fundamental question of how meaning is deployed? This issue can be addressed through the notion of 'difference'. The notion of difference has been used in a variety of contexts. Sassure's theory of linguistics locates meaning in the context of the difference between signs, rather than the sign as a reflection of objects in the real world. For example, the terms 'white' and 'black' do not refer to real objects in the world, but acquire meaning through a contrast with what they are not, for example yellow, brown, red etc. Thus racial terms are social/discursive conventions, not a reflection of some external reality.

In the work of Jacques Derrida, difference refers to neither 'a concept nor a word' but to what he calls 'an undecidable', it marks the possibility of conceptuality, the possibility of a conceptual process and system in general. 'Differance', states Derrida, 'is a notion which ... by analogy I have called (an) undecidable, (it has) 'false' verbal properties that can no longer be included within philosophical binary opposition, but which, however, inhabit philosophical (binary) opposition, resisting and disorganising it without ever constituting a third term, without ever having room for a solution in the form of speculative dialectics' (1981, p.43). Difference can never be totally resolved, it is not to be confused with a Hegelian form of idealism. According to Derrida, its marks, its effects '... cannot be governed by a referent in the classical sense, that is by a thing or by a transcendental signified that would regulate its movement' (1981, p.44). Difference destroys the opposition between two terms by revealing the confusion of the opposition they supposedly represent. Difference cannot be defined in terms of oppositional predicates – it is neither this nor that but rather this and that (for example, it is the act of differing and of deferring) without being reducible to a dialectical logic. As a non-concept it 'governs nothing, reigns over nothing exercises no authority' (1982, p74). As Derrida states 'Not only is there no kingdom of difference but difference instigates the subversion of every kingdom' (1982, p.74). It operates to uncover the hierarchies and binary oppositions within theoretical discourse. Binary pairs, such as rational/irrational, white/black, male/female, are not just simple alternatives – one side is privileged over the other, one is original the other secondary derivative and worthless. One side is privileged as having an original coherent identity – is a self in its own right, whilst the opposition is seen as 'the other', something non- original and valueless. Difference exposes this implicit privilege within epistemology, showing how all claims to true knowledge inhibit or exclude another. The notion of difference does not seek to overcome or transcend hierarchical dualism, rather it enables the assertion of an identity or the self to be addressed in terms of the other that is always suppressed by the dualistic nature of epistemology. In epistemology the other is not only suppressed but is equated with the absence of value. A non-epistemological approach asserts that the identity of the other is necessary in order to acquire knowledge of the self. Difference, as the regulator of the relationship between the self and the other, overcomes the one-sidedness of epistemological accounts, enabling phenomenon such as particular forms of racism and apartheid to be examined in their own terms.

Timothy Mitchell, in his work *Colonising Egypt*, explains the role of difference in the construction of meaning in the following way:

> 'meaning arises because the word is always a repetition in a double sense. It is a repetition in the sense of something non-original, something that occurs by modifying or differing from another; and a repetition in the sense of same-again. Meaning is an effect of the paradoxical quality of sameness and difference, whereby a word happens to be just the same only different.' (1988, p.145)

Within a non-epistemological account meaning is constituted through the play of differences between words and their different contexts. Difference is central to the construction of political identity. Mitchell states:

> 'the identity of a political group is not fixed as a rigid boundary containing those inside. The inside is contingent upon the designations of an exterior, and exists only in relation to particular exteriors. Political identity, therefore, never exists in the form of an absolute, interior self or community, but always as an already-divided relation of self/other. Political identity, ... is no more singular or absolute than the identity of words in a system of writing.' (1988, p.167)

The relationship between political identity and difference is a complex one. According to Connolly identity

> 'stands in a complex political relationship to the differences it seeks to fix. This complexity is intimated by the variations in the degree to which differences from self identity are treated as complementary identities, contending identities, negative identities or non-identities.' (1991, p.65)

When a powerful identity tries to establish itself as coherent or uniform it necessarily involves the exclusion of any differences from this identity and the transformation of these differences into otherness and evil. 'When these pressures prevail, the maintenance of one identity involves the conversion of some differences into otherness, into evil ... ' (1991, p.64).

In the context of South Africa, I wish to reconsider apartheid as the institutionalisation of absolute difference. This account rests on the following assumptions: firstly, it rejects an epistemological conceptualisation of social relations as pre-given objectivities. There is no totalising general theory through which explanation can be provided – as social relations are neither uniform nor structured. It therefore rejects any *a priori* conceptualisation of what constitutes race or class outside any given context. Secondly, it rejects the historicist-essentialist conceptions of apartheid; that is, the functioning of apartheid cannot be explained with reference to its origins. Apartheid is not a single coherent, unchanging phenomenon. As with the notion of difference, it has no specific content, it is not an unchanging object of knowledge, rather, it can be given different contents and signify different social-cultural and ideological relations. The constituent elements of apartheid have diverse histories that cannot be reduced to a single uniform essence; be it economic, political or ideological.

Apartheid, as the institutionalisation of absolute difference, marks the process through which political identities are constituted. Apartheid operates to delineate the boundaries of inclusion and exclusion of the political identity of the white community and its other, the non-white community. In the words of the National Party's Policy statement, it regulates the '... separation (apartheid) between the white races and the non-white racial groups, and the application of the policy of separation also in the case of the non-white racial groups' (1948 National Party Policy). Political identities constituted through difference are not a reflection of intrinsic or true essences but constructed through a series of differences which are constantly open to change and flux. The political identities of white and non-white communities in South Africa are constructed and defined through what deviates or is different from them. What marks out the specific process of apartheid is its tendency towards the *absolutisation* of these differences. Apartheid can be explained as the process through which difference becomes absolutised, or, to use Connolly's terms, apartheid is an example of the 'dogmatism of identity' (1991, p.159).[4]

Before the election victory of the National Party in 1948, there was little to suggest that any notion of a coherent and uniform political identity of either the white or non-white community existed. Political identities were constructed through a difference in which the boundaries of inclusion and exclusion had a certain amount of fluidity – they were not absolute. The white population did not possess a singular or uniform identity, rather, the composition and political make-up of white identity was highly diverse and heterogeneous. It was divided by a whole range of differences; difference of language, culture, economics and politics. As with the white population, its other, the non-white population was comprised of an equally heterogeneous and diverse set of cultural, linguistic, political and economic differences.

The election of the National Party to government in 1948 and the introduction of apartheid changed the nature of identity construction in South Africa. The white community represented by the National Party government sought to assert a coherent, uniform and exclusive white identity. To present their identity as intrinsically 'true', Afrikaner Nationalists necessarily positioned all those who were not included within this identity (that

---

[4] By dogmatism of identity, Connolly is referring to the tendency for identity to assert itself as true and hence negate any differences that comprise it. Difference is necessary in order for identities to have meaning and yet identities often strive to present themselves as intrinsically true and self contained. To do so requires the very denial of difference and leads to the construction of absolute others. Connolly asserts that the 'multiple drives to stamp truth upon ... identities function to convert differences into otherness and otherness into scapegoats created and maintained to secure the appearance of a true identity' (1991, p.67).

is, non-whites) as not only different but absolutely other. This led to the construction of an absolute difference between white and non-white identities. The identity of the non-white communities was defined in terms of its 'otherness' and fixed as something negative. This process was brought about by the introduction of a whole variety of juridico-political and legal measures and state policies and practices implemented by the Nationalist Party from 1948.

From 1948 official discourse and legislation implemented by the South African government operated to construct different and seemingly monolithic categories of the South African population. In 1953 Prime Minister Malan stated that there was 'a fundamental difference between the two groups, white and black. (He continued to state that) the difference in colour is merely the physical manifestation of the contrast between two irreconcilable ways of life, between barbarism and civilisation, between heathenism and Christianity, and finally between overwhelming numerical odds on the one hand and insignificant numbers on the other ... ..Theoretically the object of the policy of apartheid could be fully achieved by dividing the country into two states, with all the whites in one, all the blacks in the other'.[5] An exclusive white identity could only be presented through the exclusion of those different from or outside of this identity. As the white identity was delineated in terms of colour likewise those excluded were defined solely in terms of colour. The South African government presented the white group as a unified and coherent identity through its contrast with those excluded that is the non-white population. This involved a twofold process; firstly the attempt to unify those within the white community – that is, eliminating the differences within the white community and, secondly, the attempt to establish the differences of those outside as absolutely other.

There is not the space within this paper to provide a detailed account of the processes involved in the South African government's attempts to construct a white and non-white political identity. However, I hope I have demonstrated two main points; firstly, that post-structuralist social and political theory provides a critique of the theoretical assumptions underlying the race/class debate in South Africa. Secondly, that post-structuralist theory provides the possibility of a reconsideration of apartheid as the absolutisation of difference. Furthermore this reconsideration of apartheid can overcome the reductionism and essentialism of the approaches located within the race/class paradigm.

References

Connolly, W. (1991), *Identity/Difference*, Cornell University Press.

Derrida, J. (1982), *Margins of Philosophy*, Brighton, Harvester Press.

Derrida, J. (1981), *Positions*, Chicago University Press.

Foucault, M. (1972), *Archaeology of Knowledge*,

---

[5] Quote by Dr Malan in 1953, from Legassick (1975, p.22).

Foucault, M. (1980), *Power/Knowledge*, edited by C.Gordon, Brighton, Harvester Press.

Hobart Houghton, D. (1964), *The South African Economy*, Oxford University Press.

Horwitz, R. (1967), *The Political Economy of South Africa*, Weidenfeld & Nicholson.

Hutt, W.H. (1964), *The Economics of the Colour Bar*, London: Andre Deutsch.

Johnstone, F. (1970), 'White Prosperity and White Supremacy in South Africa Today', *African Affairs*,

Laclau, E. & Mouffe, C. (1990), *New Reflections on the Revolution of Our Time*, Verso.

Legassick, M. (1974/5), 'Legislation, Ideology and Economy in Post-1948 South Africa', *Journal of South African Studies*, Number 1.

Legassick, M. (1975), 'South Africa: Forced Labour, Industrialisation and Racial Differentiation', *The Political Economy of Africa*, edited by R.Harris, John Wiley.

Lipton, M. (1985), *Capitalism and Apartheid*, Gower/Temple Smith.

Mitchell, T. (1988), *Colonising Egypt*, Cambridge University Press.

Murray, M. (1984), 'The Triumph of Marxist Approaches in South African Social and Labour History', *Journal of Asian and African Studies*,

Nolutshungu, S. (1982), *Changing South Africa*, Manchester University Press.

O'Dowd, M.C. (1978), 'The Stages of Economic Growth and the Future of South Africa', *Change, Reform and Economic Growth in South Africa*, edited by L.Schlemmer & E.Webster, Ravan Press.

Stasiulis, D. (1980), 'Pluralist and Marxist perspectives on racial discrimination', *British Journal of Sociology*, Volume 31, Number .

Van Den Berghe, P. (1967), *South Africa: A Study in Conflict*, University of California Press.

Wolpe, H. (1976), 'Capitalism and cheap labour-power in South Africa: from segregation to apartheid', *Economy and Society*, 1, 4.

Wolpe, H. (1970), 'Industrialism and Race in South Africa', *Race and Racism*, edited by S.Zubiada.

Wolpe, H. (1988), *Race, Class & the Apartheid State*, James Currey.

Race and the Politics of Identity and Difference

Rodney Barker

London School of Economics and Political Science

Abstract

The central role of legitimacy in politics has been given insufficient attention because legitimacy has been indadequately conceptualised. A more variegated and multi-dimensional conception of legitimacy is outlined which employs the concept of political identity and identification, and distinguishes between both the various persons according legitimacy and those to whom legitmacy is accorded.

The Problem of Legitimacy

The problem of legitimacy is strikingly illustrated by the fundamental difference between the assessment made by political scientists and that made by those whom they study. Citizens, rulers, and politicians behave in a way which gives high priority to political authority. They asssert it, deny it, and argue at length about its location.[1] Political scientists have by contrast tended to discount, undervalue, or oversimpifly its contribution.[2] It is striking that in the work on the events of 1989 in Eastern Europe, legitimacy has frequently been either ignored, marginalised, or dismissed.[3]

There are two principal reasons for the failure of political science adequately to take account of legitimacy. The first is the conception of legitimacy as passive and static belief. Legitimacy is treated as a measurable characteristic of public consciousness, instead of as a form of active politics, as fixed and given, rather than as dynamic. It is seen not as the language in

---

[1] 'The most difficult thing for a political society is to have legitimacy – to have people trust the established authority.' Charles Moore, editor of *The Sunday Telegraph*, interviewed by Zoe Heller, 'A Better Class of Person', *The Independent on Sunday*, Sunday Review, 31st January 1993. But whilst journalists may provide neat illustrations, it has to be admitted that the language of politics is not so amenable to simple universalising analysis. But it is possible. In May 1992, during the popular demonstrations in major Thai cities which led to the restoration of a form of representative democratic government after a period of military intervention, the crowds were reported as shouting 'Down with the illegitimate regime'. Saitip Sukatipan, 'Political Legitimacy in Thailand: A Reassessment', Paper presented to second workshop on Political Authority and Legitimacy in Southeast Asia, Chiangmai, February 1993, p.1. Whatever they were shouting, it couldn't have been that.

[2] There is another problem, to which I do not address myself in this paper. Normative political theory has consistently attempted to develop a prescriptive theory of legitimacy, and has in consequence, though not from logical necessity, been hostile to attributing legitimacy in circumstances where the rulers, policies, or constitutions are considered morally unacceptable. This is an important but distinct issue.

[3] See, for example, Adam Przeworksi, *Democracy and the Market: Political and Economic Reforms in Eastern Europe and Latin America* (Cambridge, 1992). By contrast F.M.Barnard takes the arguments emerging in Czechoslovakia before the resurgence of democracy as the basis for a normative theory of democracy. F.M.Barnard, *Pluralism, Socialism and Political Legitimacy. Reflections on 'Opening-Up' Communism* (Cambridge, 1991).

which politics is conducted, but as a set of beliefs which may well be private until liberated by survey investigation, but which can nonetheless act as a kind of *deus ex machina* or additional surprise factor when all other explanations fail. In the work of Margaret Levi, for instance, legitimacy is given the role of an emergency generator, called into play only when other sources of explanatory power have failed.[4] The second reason is the conception of legitimacy as an undifferentiated belief by subjects or citizens about the political regime, rather than as the various forms of authority successfully claimed by a variety of governors, regimes, and forms of political association and accorded to them in different ways by a variety of sections of society. The term 'regime' frequently serves to mask important distinctions, just as does the equally homogeneous categorisation of subjects. One of the consequences of this is that though legitimacy is variously attributed to policy objectives, policy outcomes, rulers, political leaders, constitutions, or even governing parties, this variety is not addressed because it is concealed beneath a concept of legitimacy which does not allow for it.[5]

A theory of legitimacy as active and as differentiated or variegated makes possible by contrast a far fuller understanding of both political stability and political change, fills the lacuna left by existing accounts, and provides a basis on which political science can develop a more comprehenisve understanding of both contemporary uncertainties and past politics. It makes possible, too, a clarification of the enormous but largely unacknowledged and hence confusing variety of persons, institutions, and relationships to which the term 'legitimacy' has been applied: governments, governors, policies, constitutions, economic or social outcomes, or even entire economic systems.[6]

Such an account of legitimacy would have two dimensions which are in general missing from existing accounts. First, it would distinguish between legitimacy accorded to different persons, institutions, or associations. Second, it would distinguish between the various groups, individuals, and classes by whom legitimacy is accorded.[7]

---

[4] Margaret Levi, *Of Rule and Revenue* (London, 1988). This approach is to be found either stated or implied in a number of works, for example, Rosemary H.T.O'Kane, 'Against Legitimacy', *Political Studies*, 41, 3, (1993), pp.471-487. But see also Rodney Barker, 'Legitimacy: The Identity of the Accused', *Political Studies*, 42, 1, March 1994.

[5] The eclectic use of the term 'legitimacy' has been commented on in criticisms of Marxist usages of the term in the work of writers such as Jurgen Habermas; for example, Patrick Dunleavy & Brendan O'Leary, *Theories of the State*, (London, 1987), p.266.

[6] A variegated and multi-dimensional account of legitimacy is not of course without precedent, and there are acknowledgments of the need for something of the sort in existing literature. What is lacking is a pursuit of the implications of such a felt need, and an outline of a consequently fuller and more flexible account of legitimacy. See, therefore, the account of the differing roles of legitimacy for rulers and subjects in Rodney Barker, *Political Legitimacy and the State* (Oxford, 1990); in Ben Kirkvliet, 'Thoughts about How to Talk About Legitimacy', Paper delivered to East-West conference on Legitimacy in South East Asia, Honolulu, 1992. Kirkvliet talks of 'circles or rings of authority within a country's public political system'.

[7] A further distinction, in which types of legitimacy are distinguished by the nature of the authority claimed or ascribed, is not precluded by the revised conception proposed here. It is complementary to it, but has already been discussed at some length both by Weber, its original formulator, and by those who have commented on his categorisation.

Legitimacy and Identity

When legitimacy is claimed or acknowledged, this is in the first place a matter of claiming or acknowledging both a particular character in the person or institutions claiming authority or having its authority acknowledged, and a particular relationship between that character, and the character of those over whom the authority is claimed, or those who acknowledge the authority. The according of legitimacy to a ruler or an institution involves the recognition of both affinity and difference between the possessor of the legitimacy and the person who accords it.

This is most obviously the case when rule which is seen as alien is rejected by those who see themselves as a colonised people. For nationalists in India and Africa in the quarter century after the end of the Second World War, western colonial or imperial rule was illegitimate because it was alien – there was no shared identity between rulers and ruled. Nationalist leaders, by contrast, were legitimised by their combination of ordinariness and exceptionality. They were both essentially of their people, yet marked off from them by an heroic intensification of indigenous virtues.

But the same absence of identification is characteristic of far less spectacular or momentous confrontation. The apocryphal diner who, in the Savoy Grill as the results of the 1945 British General Election came through, exclaimed, 'But this is terrible! They've elected a Labour government. The country will never stand for that', was making the same point.

This does not call into question the primary importance of the character of the persons claiming authority. There is a fundamental sense in which authority arises neither from consent nor from mandate: it is recognised rather than accorded. Nevertheless, what is recognised in one society would be accorded little attention in another. What is charismatic in Tehran would be merely quaint in Tucson.[8]

Identification, or lack of it, is a central feature of our relations with government. The fit, between our conception of ourselves and our conception of government, is a crucial element in our satisfaction and in government's stability. One aspect of identity is, moreover, identification. To see oneself as a Muggletonian or a professional political scientist or an Arsenal supporter is to see oneself as part of a community or class or group of Muggletonians, professional political scientists or Arsenal supporters by virtue of shared characteristics.

an anatomy, not a model

What I suggesting is not a model of either identity or legitimacy, but a taxonomy of the various possible or observable dimensions. The disadvantage of a model is that it cannot take account of the particularities of circum-

---

[8] But there may be very real problems when the person or persons exercising an authoritative function, particularly if that function is seen as lying close to the heart of government, is replaced by some person or organisation with a quite different identity. If that is the case, then the problems which the private commercial organisation Group 4 has had with transporting prisoners may not be simply a matter of unfamiliarity or inefficiency.

stance. The advantage is that, albeit in a mechanical manner, it can be historical and dynamic. What I attempting to provide are the ingredients for particular analyses and accounts, in the manner of Weber's ideal types.

The Creation of Identity

Identity is neither natural, inherent and immutable, nor a matter of unfettered individual or collective freedom. Identities are constructed, but are constructed from socially derived components which both provide opportunities and place constraints. When the identity is political, the socially derived components of legitimacy are shaped in the interplay between citizens and rulers, and in this interplay rulers rather citizens can play the major role.

This recoginition of the role of identity in political thought and conduct is widespread, though not necessarily widely articulated, within political science. It forms the working assumption of some Marxian and most Weberian accounts. Thus, for instance, Richard Bellamy, discussing the origins of liberalism in Europe, writes that 'Liberalism corresponds in large part to the self-image and aspirations of the emergent middle classes'.[9]

subjective and objective identity

There is a tradition within political science of distinguishing between subjective and objective identity, between a class by itself and a class for itself, between interest groups and cause groups, or between endogenous and exogenous identity. What the distinction obscures is the element of both objective reality and of intellectual aspiration in all collective identities. Objective and subjective should be seen not as a line of distinction lying between one set of groups and another, but as aspects or dimensions running through all groups, though in ways which cause great differences in the relative significance of each. Whilst it is possible to conceive of an identity which is wholly objective or wholly subjective, for the vast majority of cases the question to be asked is not whether they are one or the other, but in what particular combination the two elements occur.

So the conservatives are right, that identity is rooted in history; the socialists are right in that it has some of those roots in the system of property; and the liberals are right in that the social fact of collective identity is made by human actions and not received either perfect or static from the past or from anywhere else.

four dimensions of identity

This identification has four aspects: *polity/community, constitution/state, government or personnel* and *policy.*

1. POLITY/COMMUNITY

---

[9] 'Liberalism' in Roger Eatwell & Anthony Wright (eds), *Contemporary Political Ideologies* (London, Pinter, 1993) p.29.

If we see ourselves as Scottish, but the state which governs us as not at all Scottish but as English masquerading as British, then there is a disjuncture of the most fundamental kind in our political identification. On the other hand cultural identity is not necessariy national identity. In Scotland, to feel yourself more Scottish than British may involve a cultural identity but have no implications for the way you think about the political community or nation of which you are a part.

National identity is not the identity of nations, but people's identification <u>with</u> nations. Those nations, if they do not correspond with the actual governed territory in which people live, will necessary be ideal rather than actual. If the desired nation needs to be formed out of part of an existing governed territory or people, then it is clearly ideal rather than existent. If on the other hand the aspirant nationalists wish to join an existing nation, that again is ideal because their hoped-for nation is not the same as an existing one, but an enlarged or extended version of it.

The identity of the polity is not necessarily seen as the identity of a nation, or at least not without stretching the modern usage of that term, or going back to an earlier usage. The community or the polity is not always seen as consisting of all the adults in a particular geographical space, or speaking a particular language, or having some common origin. It may be constructed out of distinctions of class, or race, or gender. So in South Africa there was until the start of the present reforms a disjuncture between the communal identity of the black population and the whiteness of the polity. Similar disjuncture occur in other states on lines of gender, though their consequences for legitimacy are unclear.

The polity may too be seen as extending beyond the conventional or even desired boundaries of nations. Thus even though few might do so, it was possible to think 'of the European Community as an embryonic polity in which a different understanding of citizenship might play a part'.[10]

2. CONSTITUTION

If we see ourselves as supporters of government by aristocracy, then we will not feel at home in a democracy, if as republicans, we will be ill at ease under a monarchy.

The constitutional arrangments are not simply a matter of rules and procedures. They include symbols and rituals. In the United Kingdom the monarchy is one of these symbols, however contentious and unclear its function. Identification with these symbols confers stability, a failure of identification, tension. Thus *The Times*, on the occasion of Princess Margaret's wanting to marry Group Captain Peter Townsend, whose previous marriage had ended in divorce, commented that the monarchy must symbolise our higher selves, recognisable yet at the same time elevated: 'The Queen is a mirror in whom her people see their better selves reflected, and since part of their idea is of family life, the Queen's family has its own part in the reflection'.[11] The obverse of this is dissonance in a multi-cultural

---

[10] Elizabeth Meehan, *Citizenship and the European Community* (London, Sage, 1993), p.ix.

[11] *The Times*, 1955, quoted by David Sinclair, 'Gone with the Windsors', *Scotland on Sunday*, December 13th 1992, p.8.

society.

It is often assumed, and I have argued, that constitutional identity is weaker than national or 'community' identity. That is why it can be argued that democracy will give way to nationalism every time. But constitutional identity can, in certain circumstances, define rm national identity. That is the argument of such champions of civic republicanism in the United States as Liah Greenfeld or Samuel Beer.[12] The identity of the nation is seen to consist in the equal rights and powers of indviduals as citizens; they are a nation because of how they conduct themselves in their government and politics. So Beer describes the Federalists as seeing

> 'the American nation as a body whose basic unit was not kindred, clan, or corporate community but the individual. This nation of individuals, nonetheless, was united by bonds as strong as those constituting the old organic order. In America, as in Europe, nationalism immensely strengthened the modern state, increasing its control at home and its impact abroad.'[13]

In such a nation, there is a clear demarcation of public from other dimensions, and it is the public world of political arrangements which gives the nation its identity: 'Nationality made these individuals "one people", imparting to them the common principles and public affections necessary for self-government'.[14]

3. GOVERNMENT/PERSONNEL

The third dimension consists of the identity of the incumbents of office. As a pure form, without associations with either the nation/polity or the state/constitution, it can only occur within systems of government where the exercise of directive or ministerial power has no necessary associations with the symbols of state authority or the prevailing character of the polity, a situation most readily found where ministerial office circulates as the result of frequent elections. Thus it is possible to feel little common identity with President Regan or President Clinton, without necessarily having any similar feelings about either the constitution or polity of the United States. Hostility towards Margaret Thatcher had many consequences, but constitutional crisis was not one of them. In Malawi or Burma, or Iran, by contrast, alientation from Dr Hastings Banda or from the the military leaders of SLORC or from the Ayatollah Khomeni or his successors would be difficult to disassociate from similar feelings towards the constitutional settlement.

4. POLICY

And if our conception of our financial well-being gives a high place to our mortgage repayment, we will feel threatened by a policy of reducing tax allowances on home-loan interest. This is aspect of relations between

---

[12] Liah Greenfeld, *Nationalism: Five Paths to Modernity* (London, Harvard University Press, 1992); S.H.Beer, *To Make a Nation: The Rediscovery of American Federalism* (London, Harvard University Press, 1993).

[13] Beer, p.382.

[14] Beer, p.382.

government and governed which has received most attention in writing on legitimacy. It is in general the least important, though the prevailing assumption of the spectrum from Marxism to rational choice theory involves giving this overwhelming attention .

Analytical Clarity and Historical/Empirical Complexity

Each of these aspects of identification will of course frequently overlap and intermingle. Though passion can well up when there is a disjuncture in any of the four dimensions, some are of more consequence for the maintenance of legitimate government than others. But it is by examining the tensions which arise when the identity of citizens and government fail to connect that it is possible to see why the European enterprise is so difficult, or why we may not yet have heard an end of nationalisms to the north and west of England.

tensions

The more points of tension, lines along which alienation is perceived, failures of identification, the greater the insecurity, the less legitimacy for the existing arrangements. The essential character of legitimacy is a high level and wide distribution of corresponding identities; the essential character of the erosion or failure of legitimacy is a low level and narrow distribution of correspondence. The advantage of a different sort of separation of powers is here seen. The greater the insulation between one sphere or identification and another, the stronger the bulkheads preventing identification failures in one area becoming identification crises for the whole.

It is ironic that the tendency to lump together all the relations or dimensions of legitimacy as if they were a single undifferentiated whole has been the product of a political science whose own experience of constitutional liberal democracies had demarcated those four areas more firmly than any where else or at any other time.

relative weight of the four dimensions of identity

People's identification with a polity or community is the primary identification, which gives context to the other three. It is, for instance, a prior requirement of identification with a democratic constitution that one identifies with the constituent parts, segments, or parties to that constitution. If some of the players in the democratic game, and more to the point any of the potential winners, are seen as not part of or compatible with the community with which a group identifies, then for that group the democratic constitution is invalidated by being stretched across incompatible parts or impassable divisions. Democracy involves, as Adam Przeworski points out, the acceptance of uncertain outcomes. But only up to a point. It does not involve the acceptance of any outcomes whatever they may be nor, more fundamentally, placing oneself on an equal footing in the democratic enterprise with 'others' or 'aliens'. <u>Some</u> outcomes, in other words, are precluded from the very start.

If identification with the state or governed community is the most powerful form of identification, identification with policies is the least.

relations between the four dimensions of identification in the creation or erosion of legitimacy

Though analytically separate, the relation between the four dimensions is historically organic and reciprocal. Each can sustain the other. Thus the opposition to the poll tax in Scotland between 1989 and 1993, the nationalist sentiment, and hostility to the Conservative government combined to nourish each other and to cultivate non-payment. In Vichy France, alienation from the Pétain regime and support for the maquis greatly increased when the regime contaminated wine in June 1943 as part of their intention of requisitioning wine for fuel alchohol. 'More than any rational arguments, more than any patriotic explanation, these glasses of heating oil adulterating a fine Pouilly-Fusse swung the winegrowers of the Macon hills to the Resistance'.[15]

Three Kinds of Participant: Citizens, Custodians, Cousins

The first dimension of legitimacy is identity: the person, persons, or institutions to whom legitimacy is accorded. The second dimension is accorder: who it is who recognises or claims something as legitimate. This is not the same as the source of legitimacy, and some confusion has in the past arisen from assuming that it was. Democracy can be a means of according legitimacy without the people thereby becoming its source.

It is important to recognise that democracy is a game with more than two players. Much writing on the topic has argued, implied, or assumed, that legitimacy is a matter between a homogeneous 'regime' on the one hand, and a democratically equal and equally homogeneous mass of subjects or citizens on the other. But it is possible to distinguish more divisions than this.

The three kinds of participants can be designated citizens - the ordinary subjects, voters, people; custodians - all those engaged in governing; and cousins - those who stand in a privileged position in relation to the custodians, without themselves actually governing. The legitimacy accorded by custodians is the most important - and it is accorded by them to themselves.[16]

---

[15] Lucie Aubrac, 'Outwitting the Gestapo' , quoted Eugen Weber, *London Review of Books*, 15, 11, 10 June 1993, p.21.

[16] There is a concise identification of this in the historical passages of Adam Przeworski's *Democracy and the Market*, which is oddly not only ignored but denied when in the theoretical passages he writes that what 'is threatening to authoritarian regimes is not the breakdown of legitimacy but the organisation of counterhegemony', p.54. The answer

Although Weber distinguished between legitimacy for ordinary subjects and legtimacy amongst the administrative strata, recent worked has ignored this distinction. Identity tensions become more important the further up the governmental tree you climb. And what has frequently been ignored is that, as Weber points out, legitimacy functions as self-justification for the administrative apparatus of government. It may well be, though he did not see this, that this is the most important function and location of legitimacy.

Conclusion

A variegated and two dimensional concept of legitimacy makes possible an approach to the understanding of politics which both takes proper account of the empirical centrality of legitimacy and permits its variety in terms of both the persons who accord it and the persons or institutions to which it is accorded to be acknowledged.

The theory of legitimacy outlined has little predictive power. But it can suggest both possiblities and improbabilties, and assist in the understanding and categorisation of human government. It is not a model, but can be used to construct many models.

If political activity is to be seen as social activity, and if social contexts and social actions are in any significant degree particular rather than universal, then a theory of identity, or a language in which we may discuss identity, will be essential tools for any enterprise in the post-modern world, whether it be the delineation of legitimacy, the full understanding of rational conduct, or the study of the character of politics as a general human activity. The study of politics in this manner seems to place restraints on the possibilities of a foundationalist liberalism, even if it be of a proceduralist kind. The reality of community or polity overrides the best shaped constitutions.

---

is of course that either or both can be important, but that Przeworski's description of events in Eastern Europe leading up to the democatic revolutions of 1989 are full of examples of the fomer. But the crucial loss of legitimacy was not of that accorded by subjects or citizens, but that accorded by custodians to themselves.

Appendix

Table
Poll Tax Opposition

1. United Kingdom	2. United Kingdom
P/C C	P/C C
Scotland	England
P G	P G

Random Examples

3. United Kingdom	4. United Kingdom
P/C C	P/C C
SNP	BNP
P G	P G
5. United Kingdom	6. Malaysia
P/C C	P/C C
Ponting	Malaysian Chinese
P G	P G
7. United Kingdom	8. European Union
P/C C	P/C C
Spycatcher	⁓ Bruges Group
P G	P C

Examples of the Application
of a Two-Dimensional Variegated Scheme

- 1. Scotland and the poll tax: non-identification with *community, personnel* and *policy*, identification with *constitution*.

- 2. England and the poll tax: identification with *community* and *constitution*, non-identification with *personnel* and *policy*.

- 3. Scottish National Party. non-identification with *community, policy* and *personnel*, identification with *constitution*.

- 4. British National Party: identification with *community*, non-identification with *constitution, personnel* and *policy*.

- 5. Clive Ponting: identification with *community* and *constitution*, non-identification with *personnel* and *policy*.

- 6. Malaysian Chinese: identification with *policy* and *constitution*, non-identification with *community* and *personnel*.

- 7. *Spycatcher*: identification with community, non-identification with *constitution, personnel* or *policy*.

- 8. Bruges Group and European Union: total non-identification.